Lecture Notes in Computer Science 10288

Commenced Publication in 1973
Founding and Former Series Editors:
Gerhard Goos, Juris Hartmanis, and Jan van Leeuwen

More information about this series at http://www.springer.com/series/7409

Aaron Marcus · Wentao Wang (Eds.)

Design, User Experience, and Usability

Theory, Methodology, and Management

6th International Conference, DUXU 2017
Held as Part of HCI International 2017
Vancouver, BC, Canada, July 9–14, 2017
Proceedings, Part I

 Springer

Editors
Aaron Marcus
Aaron Marcus and Associates, Inc.
Berkeley, CA
USA

Wentao Wang
Baidu, Inc.
Beijing
China

ISSN 0302-9743   ISSN 1611-3349 (electronic)
Lecture Notes in Computer Science
ISBN 978-3-319-58633-5   ISBN 978-3-319-58634-2 (eBook)
DOI 10.1007/978-3-319-58634-2

Library of Congress Control Number: 2017939729

LNCS Sublibrary: SL3 – Information Systems and Applications, incl. Internet/Web, and HCI

Printed on acid-free paper

This Springer imprint is published by Springer Nature
The registered company is Springer International Publishing AG
The registered company address is: Gewerbestrasse 11, 6330 Cham, Switzerland

Foreword

The 19th International Conference on Human–Computer Interaction, HCI International 2017, was held in Vancouver, Canada, during July 9–14, 2017. The event incorporated the 15 conferences/thematic areas listed on the following page.

A total of 4,340 individuals from academia, research institutes, industry, and governmental agencies from 70 countries submitted contributions, and 1,228 papers have been included in the proceedings. These papers address the latest research and development efforts and highlight the human aspects of design and use of computing systems. The papers thoroughly cover the entire field of human–computer interaction, addressing major advances in knowledge and effective use of computers in a variety of application areas. The volumes constituting the full set of the conference proceedings are listed on the following pages.

I would like to thank the program board chairs and the members of the program boards of all thematic areas and affiliated conferences for their contribution to the highest scientific quality and the overall success of the HCI International 2017 conference.

This conference would not have been possible without the continuous and unwavering support and advice of the founder, Conference General Chair Emeritus and Conference Scientific Advisor Prof. Gavriel Salvendy. For his outstanding efforts, I would like to express my appreciation to the communications chair and editor of *HCI International News*, Dr. Abbas Moallem.

April 2017   Constantine Stephanidis

HCI International 2017 Thematic Areas and Affiliated Conferences

Thematic areas:

- Human–Computer Interaction (HCI 2017)
- Human Interface and the Management of Information (HIMI 2017)

Affiliated conferences:

- 17th International Conference on Engineering Psychology and Cognitive Ergonomics (EPCE 2017)
- 11th International Conference on Universal Access in Human–Computer Interaction (UAHCI 2017)
- 9th International Conference on Virtual, Augmented and Mixed Reality (VAMR 2017)
- 9th International Conference on Cross-Cultural Design (CCD 2017)
- 9th International Conference on Social Computing and Social Media (SCSM 2017)
- 11th International Conference on Augmented Cognition (AC 2017)
- 8th International Conference on Digital Human Modeling and Applications in Health, Safety, Ergonomics and Risk Management (DHM 2017)
- 6th International Conference on Design, User Experience and Usability (DUXU 2017)
- 5th International Conference on Distributed, Ambient and Pervasive Interactions (DAPI 2017)
- 5th International Conference on Human Aspects of Information Security, Privacy and Trust (HAS 2017)
- 4th International Conference on HCI in Business, Government and Organizations (HCIBGO 2017)
- 4th International Conference on Learning and Collaboration Technologies (LCT 2017)
- Third International Conference on Human Aspects of IT for the Aged Population (ITAP 2017)

Conference Proceedings Volumes Full List

1. LNCS 10271, Human–Computer Interaction: User Interface Design, Development and Multimodality (Part I), edited by Masaaki Kurosu
2. LNCS 10272 Human–Computer Interaction: Interaction Contexts (Part II), edited by Masaaki Kurosu
3. LNCS 10273, Human Interface and the Management of Information: Information, Knowledge and Interaction Design (Part I), edited by Sakae Yamamoto
4. LNCS 10274, Human Interface and the Management of Information: Supporting Learning, Decision-Making and Collaboration (Part II), edited by Sakae Yamamoto
5. LNAI 10275, Engineering Psychology and Cognitive Ergonomics: Performance, Emotion and Situation Awareness (Part I), edited by Don Harris
6. LNAI 10276, Engineering Psychology and Cognitive Ergonomics: Cognition and Design (Part II), edited by Don Harris
7. LNCS 10277, Universal Access in Human–Computer Interaction: Design and Development Approaches and Methods (Part I), edited by Margherita Antona and Constantine Stephanidis
8. LNCS 10278, Universal Access in Human–Computer Interaction: Designing Novel Interactions (Part II), edited by Margherita Antona and Constantine Stephanidis
9. LNCS 10279, Universal Access in Human–Computer Interaction: Human and Technological Environments (Part III), edited by Margherita Antona and Constantine Stephanidis
10. LNCS 10280, Virtual, Augmented and Mixed Reality, edited by Stephanie Lackey and Jessie Y.C. Chen
11. LNCS 10281, Cross-Cultural Design, edited by Pei-Luen Patrick Rau
12. LNCS 10282, Social Computing and Social Media: Human Behavior (Part I), edited by Gabriele Meiselwitz
13. LNCS 10283, Social Computing and Social Media: Applications and Analytics (Part II), edited by Gabriele Meiselwitz
14. LNAI 10284, Augmented Cognition: Neurocognition and Machine Learning (Part I), edited by Dylan D. Schmorrow and Cali M. Fidopiastis
15. LNAI 10285, Augmented Cognition: Enhancing Cognition and Behavior in Complex Human Environments (Part II), edited by Dylan D. Schmorrow and Cali M. Fidopiastis
16. LNCS 10286, Digital Human Modeling and Applications in Health, Safety, Ergonomics and Risk Management: Ergonomics and Design (Part I), edited by Vincent G. Duffy
17. LNCS 10287, Digital Human Modeling and Applications in Health, Safety, Ergonomics and Risk Management: Health and Safety (Part II), edited by Vincent G. Duffy
18. LNCS 10288, Design, User Experience, and Usability: Theory, Methodology and Management (Part I), edited by Aaron Marcus and Wentao Wang

Design, User Experience and Usability

Program Board Chair(s): **Aaron Marcus, USA, and Wentao Wang, P.R. China**

- Sisira Adikari, Australia
- Claire Ancient, UK
- Jan Brejcha, Czech Republic
- Hashim Iqbal Chunpir, Germany
- Silvia de los Rios Perez, Spain
- Marc Fabri, UK
- Patricia Flanagan, Australia
- Nouf Khashman, Qatar
- Tom MacTavish, USA
- Judith A. Moldenhauer, USA
- Francisco Rebelo, Portugal
- Kerem Rizvanoglu, Turkey
- Christine Riedmann-Streitz, Germany
- Patricia Search, USA
- Carla Galvão Spinillo, Brazil
- Marcelo Márcio Soares, Brazil
- Virginia Tiradentes Souto, Brazil

The full list with the Program Board Chairs and the members of the Program Boards of all thematic areas and affiliated conferences is available online at:

http://www.hci.international/board-members-2017.php

HCI International 2018

The 20th International Conference on Human–Computer Interaction, HCI International 2018, will be held jointly with the affiliated conferences in Las Vegas, NV, USA, at Caesars Palace, July 15–20, 2018. It will cover a broad spectrum of themes related to human–computer interaction, including theoretical issues, methods, tools, processes, and case studies in HCI design, as well as novel interaction techniques, interfaces, and applications. The proceedings will be published by Springer. More information is available on the conference website: http://2018.hci.international/.

General Chair
Prof. Constantine Stephanidis
University of Crete and ICS-FORTH
Heraklion, Crete, Greece
E-mail: general_chair@hcii2018.org

http://2018.hci.international/

Contents – Part I

Aesthetics and Perception in Design

User Experience Evaluation Methods and Tools

User Centered Design in the Software Development Lifecycle

DUXU Education and Training

Contents – Part II

Mobile DUXU

Designing the Playing Experience

Designing the Virtual, Augmented and Tangible Experience

Wearables and Fashion Technology

Contents – Part III

DUXU Practice and Case Studies

Design Thinking and Design Philosophy

Towards Establishing Design Principles for Balancing Usability and Maintaining Cognitive Abilities

Gayathri Balasubramanian[1], Hyowon Lee[2(✉)], King Wang Poon[1], Wee-Kiat Lim[3], and Wai Keet Yong[1]

[1] Lee Kuan Yew Centre for Innovative Cities,
Singapore University of Technology and Design, Singapore, Singapore
[2] Singapore University of Technology and Design, Singapore, Singapore
hlee@sutd.edu.sg
[3] Nanyang Business School, Asian Business Case Centre,
Nanyang Technological University, Singapore, Singapore

Abstract. While technology has improved the speed, accuracy, and efficiency of work, its prolonged use also weakens users' cognitive abilities over time. By creating usable, efficient, emotive, and engaging experiences, HCI researchers and practitioners have inadvertently led users to offload their innate capabilities onto their devices. How should technology be (re)designed so as to reduce the negative effects of on users' cognitive abilities when used over time? In this paper, we discuss a set of design principles intended to help designers consider how long-term use of their artefacts could maintain and even improve users' unassisted abilities and reduce negative impacts of over-reliance on technology. We illustrate the design principles by redesigning commonly-used applications, and report the findings from a workshop conducted with digital natives to obtain feedback on these redesigned applications.

Keywords: Design practice · Technology use over time · Persuasive System Design · User interface · Gamification

1 Motivation

While technology has improved the speed, accuracy, and efficiency of work, its prolonged use also weakens users' cognitive skills over time. By automating our cognitive tasks such as problem-solving and decision-making, we reduce our ability to "translate information into knowledge and knowledge into know-how" [1].

Many research efforts conducted among different domains corroborate this. Through a series of experiments van Nimwegen and colleagues observed that computer-game players who received minimal guidance in the game had better conceptual understanding of the game, strategised better and finished the game faster than players who received assistance from the system [2]. Similar observations were made with experiments involving the use of everyday applications

© Springer International Publishing AG 2017
A. Marcus and W. Wang (Eds.): DUXU 2017, Part I, LNCS 10288, pp. 3–18, 2017.
DOI: 10.1007/978-3-319-58634-2_1

like planning software [3,4]. The theory of technology dominance [5] (studied and tested in accounting and taxation, e.g. [6–8]) discusses how both experienced and novice decision makers may become reliant on decision aids. In the case of novice users, they end up not acquiring domain expertise at all and as a result, they come to rely on the decision aid, whereas, in experienced users, there is a de-skilling effect due to over-reliance on the decision aid when the task complexity, decision aid familiarity, and cognitive fit are all high. A study on cab drivers' reliance on GPS units concludes that it causes atrophy of drivers' hippocampus [9]. Our ability to read long articles has decreased, owing to bite-sized information readily presented over the Internet [10]. A series of recent experiments indicates that the ready availability of information online weakens our memory [11]. Architects seem to have lost their sense of scale due to employing computer-aided designing over paper-drawing [12]. The shortcomings of spell-checker software discussed in [13] exemplify *automation complacency*, i.e., the user becomes less vigilant about system's output due to a false sense of confidence in the system's accuracy [1]. Simply knowing that an experience has been photographed with a digital camera weakens a person's memory of the experience [14].

2   Need for Redesign

We see a need to propose a new set of design principles in the wake of growing evidence on the negative impact of prolonged use of technology. This is because traditionally human-computer interaction (HCI) has emphasized on usability, optimization, and efficiency, in order to reduce cognitive overload on the user with a task at hand. This approach increases the overall productivity of users, but it also makes them offload their innate capabilities onto the plethora of 'smart' devices surrounding them. Borgmann introduces the concept of 'devices' in his 'device paradigm' and describes them as highly commoditised and disengaging us from our surroundings [15]. He argues that as result of using devices, skilled engagement with one's environment is no longer required. Hence the satisfaction of adeptly completing a task is now replaced by passive consumption of technology. One may argue that engagement with digital technologies could increase certain capabilities of the user that are directly related to the interaction with technology. For example, because of working more on a PC, one's typing skills in terms of speed, would improve. However, spell-check and autocorrect software functionality may actually reduce the user's inherent spelling abilities.

Unlike the more observable and immediate physical effects of over-reliance on technology, the cognitive effects are likely long-term, thus may be more difficult to discern and reverse when they have become observable. How should technology be (re)designed so as to reduce the negative effects of on users' cognitive abilities when used over time? Many of the design guidelines/heuristics such as Nielsen's heuristics [16] and Shneiderman's Golden Rules [17] focus on designing for efficiency and usability, as these have been the main aims and goals of many consumer hardware/software products in the past. As we spend increasingly longer hours interacting with IT devices, this trend is expected to increase, thus a shift of design approach is a timely and necessary endeavor.

In the next section, we summarise some alternative points of view on designing for usability and how they address the limitations of the efficiency/productivity- and user satisfaction-focused interactions which we have been aiming for today. Then in Sect. 4, we summarise our design exercises that consider some of the commonly-used applications today and come up with artefacts that may support minimising the negative cognitive effects of use over time. Section 4 also reports the findings from a half-day workshop with 21 young participants who discussed and gave feedback on the designed artefacts. Section 5 then extracts from the design exercises and the findings from the workshop, the common and essential factors and concepts that may serve as principles for any future designs to ensure minimal negative long-term consequences in the use of any interactive application.

3 Discussion of Related Work

There is increasing discussion in the HCI community about design approaches that run counter to accepted design practices. In this section, we highlight four related design approaches that may inform how we can come up with principles for helping designers consider how long-term use of their artefacts could maintain and even improve users' unassisted abilities and reduce negative impacts of over-reliance.

3.1 The Philosophy of "slow" Technology

Hallnas and Redstrom [18] explore creating 'slow technology' for supporting reflection over efficiency in performance. They describe slow technology as one where the user "takes time to: learn how it works, understand why it works the way it works, apply it, see what it is, find out the consequences of using it." While such slowness is considered to be bad design as it could cause user frustration, it could be intentionally leveraged to provide opportunities for the user to reflect on/while using the technology.

This philosophy has been applied in a variety of applications. Hessenwahl and Klapperich [19] compare the experiences of brewing coffee in automated and manual ways and recommends an "experience-centred design" of everyday automation. If response time of search systems were to be compromised, while the perceived quality of results may be low, in certain scenarios the actual search results may be of greater value to the user, as discussed in [20]. A reflective approach for motivating people to increase their physical activity has been discussed in [21].

3.2 "Hard-to-use" Interfaces

There is growing evidence that sometimes what is traditionally viewed as "usability issues" may actually benefit the user sometimes [22]. The work of

Cockburn et al. [23] discusses how user interfaces that require more user effort improve users' spatial memory and benefit the learning of spatial tasks. However, this extra effort has to be *meaningful* and *discretionary* i.e. the user is not mandated to go through additional effort, but willingly chooses to do so [24]. Pierce and Paulos' work [25] is aimed at studying what affordances can be provided through counter functional things and intentionally designed limitations. This approach of introducing "counter functionality" takes "hard-to-use" systems to an extreme by suggesting the opposition or even omission of functionality to actually provide the feature.

3.3   (In)appropriateness of Technology and "Undesigning"

Baumer and Silberman [26] discuss a series of questions aimed to help design practitioners to gauge the appropriateness of using technology to solve problems in specific contexts. They ask designers to consider if a problem can be solved using a "low-tech" or even non-technological solution. When designers choose to provide a technological solution, they have to consider if the solution does more harm than the good it provides. Finally, designers have to ascertain if the technology they choose solves the actual problem, or just a representation of the problem that can be solved by that technology.

Pierce [27] proposes "undesigning of technology" i.e. elimination of design, to negate the harmful effects of technology, on social and environmental issues, through design. One of the design elimination approaches discussed in this paper is the use of persuasive design. While the approach is generally thought of as persuading users to behave in an intended manner, Pierce proposes the use of self-inhibition, that is, designing technology that inherently inhibits its own usage. The author also explains how the principles of persuasive design (discussed in the next sub-section) can in fact be applied to dissuade undesirable user behaviour or attitudes.

3.4   Persuasive System Design and Gamification

Persuasive system design and persuasive technologies have been extensively used for promoting behaviour change for health and safety [28], supporting self-management of health [29], promoting sustainable behaviours [30], help overcome substance addiction [31], in web-based learning environments [32], and even for contributing to crowd-funding campaigns [33].

The persuasive system design (PSD) framework proposed by [34] discusses design principles for *primary task support* (including guiding users in moving closer to attaining desired behaviour/attitude, providing tailored and personalised content and services, and tracking users' performance over time), *dialogue support* (such as praising and rewarding target user behaviour, and providing suggestions that aid users in performing target behaviour), *system credibility support* (through third-party endorsements and verification), and *social support* (by creating opportunities for competition, cooperation, social comparison, and recognition among users).

The use of game elements to persuade user behaviour/attitude in intended direction has been studied by [41]. Gamification can be defined as "the application of lessons from the gaming domain to change behaviors in non-game situations" [35]. Gamification concepts (such as those discussed in [36]) have been employed to promote healthy behaviour [37], in education [38], to increase performance of elderly and disabled workers in production environments [39], and even in enterprise software use [40].

There is considerable overlap between gamification concepts and persuasive design principles, specifically those corresponding to dialogue and social support. Also, understanding the inevitable trade-offs incurred when serious situations are gamified (e.g. time efficiency and short-term productivity vs. sustained engagement and fun) and the strategies to strike the right balance, seem to share similar considerations for trade-offs in designing technologies that promote users' cognitive efforts while at the same time ensure a reasonable level of usability.

4   Redesign Exercise and Feedback Session

Drawing from some of the techniques and theoretical concepts discussed in the previous section, we conducted a series of design exercises to re-design commonly-used applications today, specifically calculator, spell-checker, scheduling/to-do list, GPS navigation app, and app marketplace. They illustrate how the interaction could be designed in such a way that may reduce the negative effects of over-reliance on them and possibly even to increase the users' cognitive ability while using them, while at the same time supporting the task that the users want to achieve.

To validate our proposed design approach and to elicit feedback on various aspects of the redesigned applications, we undertook a design studio approach (similar to the methodology described in [42,43]) and conducted a half-day feedback workshop with 21 participants. Demographics of the participants were: ages between 18 and 23; 11 females and 10 males; nationalities included Cambodian, Chinese, Filipino, Indonesian, Japanese, Malaysian, Mongolian, Myanmarese, Singaporean and Sri Lankan.

The workshop was conducted with users of this specific age-group as they are considered to be "digital natives" who have been using IT applications and devices throughout their lives and hence are at high risk of over-reliance on technology and yet may not be aware of how it could adversely affect their cognitive abilities/skillset over time. By engaging users from a breadth of countries with varying levels of technological adoption and attitude towards tech-use, we obtained a more balanced feedback on the acceptability of our design approach.

The participants were divided into five groups of four/five users and moved around each design artefact. Each artefact had a dedicated facilitator walking the participant group through the redesign and rationale. Participants were encouraged to ask questions and discuss the design implications among other members of their group. In addition, they provided individual and anonymous feedback on each artefact through post-it notes. At the end of the workshop we collated the feedback received and identified common themes for each and across all artefacts.

4.1 GPS Navigation App

Instead of providing turn-by-turn directions, the GPS navigator makes the user look out for landmarks and cues that help to retain and even improve the driver's situational awareness (Fig. 1).

In this redesign, instead of providing very specific, detailed, step-by-step instructions, we provide leeway for users to figure out intermediary steps on their own. When the usage situation repeats over time, instead of providing the entire set of instructions, we encourage users to recollect from their memory, as much as possible, before intervening and revealing the instructions. The GPS app has been redesigned such that it exhibits *self-inhibition* through the use of gamification elements such that the lesser the users require the app's assistance for navigation, the more they progress through levels. (See Fig. 6 in Sect. 5 for explanation in the context of extracted design principles.)

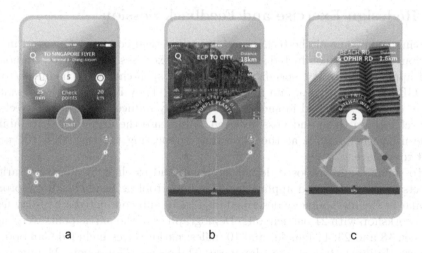

Fig. 1. Redesigned GPS app: Provide spatial cues instead of detailed directions. (a) Upon indicating the destination, an overall route with major enroute landmarks is visualised. (b) As the user drives by the landmarks, photos of the landmark scenes are displayed. (c) Instead of providing turn-by-turn instructions using length measurements, spatial cues are used so that users may recollect from memory during subsequent trips.

Feedback: The redesigned GPS navigation app met with unanimous positive feedback from the participants. They felt it is good to have the role of the GPS navigation app relegated to that of *sous*-navigator who only helps when the driver explicitly asks, rather than actively directing the driver. In fact, one participant commented "I like how it brings technology to its assistive role, to be there when I really need it, while letting me use my own memory otherwise."

4.2 Calculator

We have designed a calculator app (see Fig. 2) which, when invoked for simple calculations, elicits a 'guesstimate' from the user. The app then reveals the actual answer and indicates how accurate the user's guess was. We have used the concept of *counter-functionality* whereby, the user, who wants an accurate answer immediately with minimal effort, is asked to first try to 'guesstimate' the value. We believe the extra effort is *meaningful* and *discretionary* as the user is provided the option to skip this step and directly obtain the calculated value. Finally, the system provides tips on how to guess better, corresponding to PSD framework's design principle on providing *suggestions* for system-human dialogue.

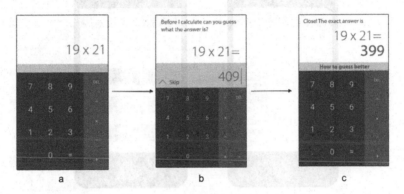

Fig. 2. Redesigned calculator: Encourage the user to 'guesstimate' arithmetic calculations before revealing the actual answer. (a) User types in query. (b) Instead of displaying the answer immediately, the system asks the user to estimate the answer, while also providing the option to "skip". (c) The system then responds how close the estimate is, and reveals the correct answer.

Feedback: Participants welcomed the approach of asking them to attempt to calculate values on their own first. However, they acknowledged that they may sometimes be in situations where accuracy and timeliness are of the essence. Hence they liked the feature to quickly switch between 'ability' and 'accuracy' modes. Some participants suggested identifying and designing for specific usage scenarios where the 'ability' mode is strictly enforced and tips and hints are displayed everyday, for example, in education. Participants also wanted to see some kind of analytics to understand how their "guessing accuracy" has improved over time.

4.3 Scheduling App/to-do List

In this redesigned calendar/scheduling app (see Fig. 3) the user is made to recollect the agenda and timing of the day's meetings, instead of being informed by the app. The user is presented with the timings for the events/appointments of the day and a list of possible events. (The number of events is more than the number of time slots.) The user is required to match the timing with the event that is scheduled for that time, in order to see the actual appointments for the day.

By making the user match the day's meetings with their corresponding times, we hope to encourage users to *reflect* on those events when they go through the extra step. By *praising* the user for correctly matching the tasks and timings, the redesign supports system-human dialogue principle of the PSD framework.

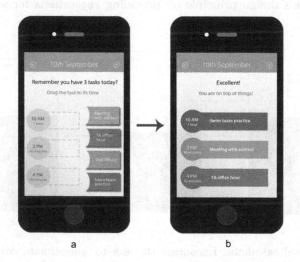

Fig. 3. Redesigned scheduling app: Help users in recollecting meetings and agendas, instead of reminding them. (a) When the app is opened, the user is asked to drag and drop the main events to the correct time slots. (b)The correct schedule is then shown, thereby confirming the user's answers.

Feedback: Participants saw the redesigned interaction as opportunities for reflecting on the events/meetings. Some even suggested adding more dimensions, like testing the user on facts relating to the meetings or using photographs to "involve more senses." The interaction could be gamified through incentives, points, or unlocked features. However, a few participants felt that planning/scheduling should not be complicated and should remain in the form of passive notifications or popups.

4.4   Spell-Checker

Figure 4 shows how a text-writing application (e.g. email or word-processor) could be redesigned such that the user is informed of the presence of error in the text, without being shown the exact error and the correct solution. The user

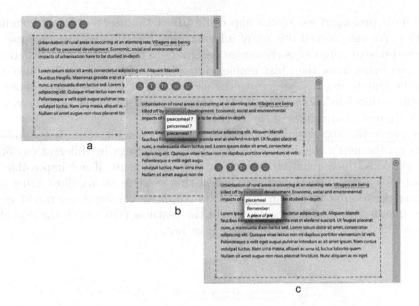

Fig. 4. Redesigned spell-checker: (a) The sentence with incorrect spelling is highlighted, as a whole. (b) When the user identifies the misspelt word, spelling variations are presented for the user to choose the correct spelling. (c) Upon choosing a word, the system reveals the answer.

would thus have to first identify the error, then decide on the correction and finally, learn ways to remember the correct form.

The proposed redesign can be considered *slow* and *hard-to-use* as the user is required to spend some effort in pinpointing the exact error and then choosing the correct version. However, the additional effort followed by hints and suggestions should improve error prevention and users' recall.

Feedback: While participants liked how the redesigned spell-checker makes them identify and correct the mistake on their own rather than auto-correcting, they felt the redesign could be extended to cater to different learning abilities of individuals, some through examples, some through mnemonics, and others through explicit repetition of words that are always misspelt by the user. One participant suggested displaying a summary of mistakes the user had made, as recap, when the user saves and closes the document.

4.5 App Marketplace

Given the innumerable number of apps, how can we ensure that users actually choose those that are beneficial to them despite the perceived extra effort in using those apps?

We propose that, in addition to the existing information like app ratings, customer ratings and reviews, app marketplaces should also display information about how prolonged use of the app could affect the user's different cognitive abilities. We have named this set of information "UX2.0 index" as we hope our proposed design approaches encourage designers to think about user experience design as being more than just usable, compelling, and emotive, but also consider the long-term consequences to the users. Similar in approach to those for enforcing ethical behaviour-design [44], the proposed elements support *system credibility* design principles of the PSD framework.

In Fig. 5, the app download page pertains to a section that shows possible effects on the user's cognitive skills over time, in ratings by different cognitive abilities/skills. Such quantitative ratings may be difficult, if not impossible, to measure for a newly developed app, but in this exercise we are illustrating how the consideration of long-term use and its cognitive consequences might eventually manifest so that it becomes one of the features from which the potential users could decide whether to purchase it or not.

Fig. 5. Redesigned app marketplace: On the lower-right side of the screen, the page provides the ratings in 5 cognitive abilities/skills (arithmetic, memory, visual and spatial, language and interpersonal) and explanations on how prolonged use of the app may affect users' cognitive abilities

Feedback: Participants felt that rather than discouraging them from choosing apps that are harmful for them, the information in app marketplace could actually encourage app designers and developers to create apps that rate highly on the UX2.0 index, thereby indirectly designing better for cognitive abilities. Some participants suggested including limiting access to apps by age, based on effect on cognitive abilities. Others advocated allowing users to make their choice and potentially only displaying warning messages, like similar labels on cigarette packs. A couple of participants raised the issue of reliability of UX2.0 index rating and suggested having a credible organisation or institution to review and rate apps based on the index parameters.

5   Moving Towards Design Principles

From our review of literature, design exercise, and the user feedback for our designs we extract a set of general considerations as the step towards establishing design principles intended to help designers consider how long-term use of their artefacts could maintain and even improve users' unassisted abilities and reduce negative impacts of over-reliance.

One of the designed artefacts, the GPS navigation app, has gone through more rigorous discussions and thus covers wide principles and categories we considered. We ended up redesigning the GPS app more fully. We present our design principles, along with illustrations of how apply them, through the redesigned GPS navigation app, which we call "GPS2.0".

1. Consider whether the domain you are designing for and the technology and interactions you are designing, have long-term effects on users' cognitive abilities. Determine which abilities will be affected and how.
2. Allow users to switch easily between a mode in which the principles are implemented (*ability* mode), and a mode in which speed, efficiency and accuracy are the main goals (*accuracy* mode). Leave the choice of using the *ability* or *accuracy* mode to users, as some may not be concerned with effects of prolonged technology use, but warn them of the potential consequences.
   In Fig. 6d and e, the user is able to easily switch between *GPS2.0* mode where there is more wholesome interaction offering some room for exerting more mental effort, and *normal* GPS mode in which the system provides turn-by-turn instructions. When the system operates in *normal* mode it displays a warning message about potential harm to user's spatial abilities.
3. *Show, don't tell*: Don't show full solution but find a way to help users find the solution themselves by:

   – Suggesting a more wholesome/physical/natural way of solving
   – Giving minimal amount of information, in the form of appropriate hint or quiz to guess or reflect first
   – Highlighting user's error, rather than auto-correcting

   In Fig. 6a the system displays a general overview of the entire journey, akin to physical map, and minimal information in terms of expected duration, number of main decision points/landmarks and total distance of the journey. In Fig. 6b–d landmarks and visual cues (i.e. expected scenery or view during the drive) are used to inform and confirm users about driving directions, rather than the traditional way of turn-by-turn instructions and distance measurements.

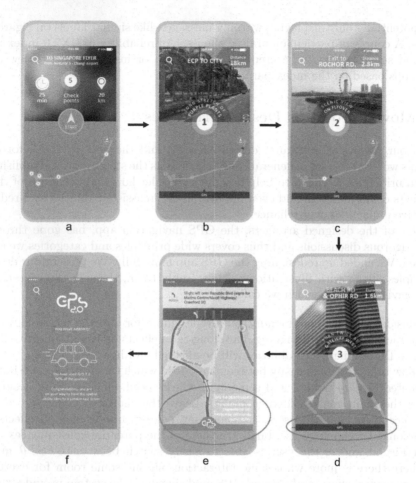

Fig. 6. GPS2.0: Proposed design principles applied for redesigning GPS navigation app

4. Hints should not be repeating the same pattern but changing.
   When the user requires directions for the same route repeatedly, do not provide the entire set of hints. Encourage users to recollect from their previous experience(s) of driving through the same route. Only if they explicitly request assistance or appear to be lost, provide the hints/suggestions. Even then, change the nature or pattern of hints.
5. Introduce gamification elements like (a) rewards (b) progression through levels and (c) competition, to ensure sustained use of the app.
   As seen in Fig. 6f, the system uses gamification concept of levels and progression, to encourage users to drive unassisted by GPS as much as possible. In this particular example, the user has used the app in *GPS2.0* mode for a great part of the journey, thereby attaining the level of "London cab driver" (whose spatial navigation skills are well-known [45]).

6. Encourage users to exercise their abilities through data analytics to show how the abilities progress over time.

The GPS2.0 app tracks how well the user is able to navigate (a) without assistance of the app and (b) using *GPS2.0* mode instead of *normal GPS* mode. This information is used in conjunction with gamification elements to encourage users to continue using their inherent abilities, as shown in Fig. 6f.

6 Conclusion

In this paper, we have established the necessity for approaching user experience design from the perspective of reducing and preventing over-reliance on technology, and maintaining and possibly even improving users' cognitive abilities when used over time. Through investigation of literature on recent design discussions in the HCI community, persuasive systems, and gamification, we have derived a set of design principles to help designers consider how long-term use of their artefacts could maintain and even improve users' unassisted abilities and reduce negative impacts of over-reliance.

The principles encourage users to keep using their own unassisted cognitive abilities in completing a task while also allowing them to get an immediate task solution. This is an important facet that manifests in the changed tone from the existing design guidelines. To address the dichotomy between the two modes (i.e. *ability* versus *accuracy*, as described in Sects. 4 and 5), we continue to explore by expanding the concepts and principles introduced in this paper into a spectrum for determining the appropriate tradeoff/balance point(s). We hope that our proposed design approach generates discussions to start the awareness in the HCI community.

Acknowledgments. This work was supported by the Singapore Ministry of National Development and National Research Foundation through Future of Cities project at Lee Kuan Yew Centre for Innovative Cities, SUTD (Grant Number L2NICTDF1-2014-1). We would like to thank Singapore Technologies Endowment Program who helped in organising the design feedback workshop during Ecosperity Young Leaders Dialogue 2016, and the international student delegates who participated in the workshop.

References

1. Carr, N.: The Glass Cage: How our Computers are Changing Us. W. W. Norton & Company, New York (2015)
2. van Nimwegen, C.: The Paradox of the Guided User: Assistance Can be Counter-Effective. Utrecht University (2008)
3. Burgos, D., van Nimwegen, C.: Games-based learning, destination feedback and adaptation: a case study of an educational planning simulation. In: Games-Based Learning Advancements for Multi-Sensory Human Computer Interfaces: Techniques and Effective Practices, Information Science References, Hershey, PA, pp. 119–130 (2009)

4. van Nimwegen, C., van Oostendorp, H.: The questionable impact of an assisting interface on performance in transfer situations. Int. J. Ind. Ergon. **39**(3), 501–508 (2009)
5. Arnold, V., Sutton, S.G.: The theory of technology dominance: understanding the impact of intelligent decision aids on decision makers' judgments. Adv. Acc. Behav. Res. **1**, 175–194 (1998)
6. Hampton, C.: Determinants of reliance: an empirical test of the theory of technology dominance. Int. J. Acc. Inf. Syst. **6**, 217–240 (2005)
7. Masselli, J.J., Rickets, R.C., Arnold, V., Sutton, S.G.: The impact of embedded intelligent agents on tax-reporting decisions. J. Am. Taxation Assoc. **24**(2), 60–78 (2002)
8. Dowling, C., Leech, S.A., Maroney, R.: The deskilling of auditors' abilities: an empirical test of the theory of technology dominance. In: The 2nd Asia-Pacific Research Symposium on Accounting Information Systems (2006)
9. Maguire, E.A., Gadian, D.G., Johnsrude, I.S., Good, C.D., Ashburner, J., Frackowiak, R.S., Frith, C.D.: Navigation-related structural change in the hippocampi of taxi drivers. Proc. Nat. Acad. Sci. **97**(8), 4398–4403 (2000)
10. Carr, N.: Is Google Making Us Stupid? (2008). http://www.theatlantic.com/magazine/archive/2008/07/is-google-making-us-stupid/306868/
11. Sparrow, B., Liu, J., Wegner, D.M.: Google effects on memory: cognitive consequences of having information at our fingertips. Science **333**(6043), 776–778 (2011)
12. Caicco, G.: Architecture, Ethics, and the Personhood of Place. University Press of New England, Hanover and London (2007)
13. Galletta, D.F., Durcikova, A., Everard, A., Jones, B.M.: Does spell-checking software need a warning label? Commun. ACM **48**(7), 82–86 (2005)
14. Henkel, L.A.: Point-and-shoot memories: the influence of taking photos on memory for a museum tour. Psychol. Sci. **25**(2), 396–402 (2014)
15. Borgmann, A.: Technology and the Character of Contemporary Life. University of Chicago Press, Chicago (1984)
16. Nielsen, J.: Usability Engineering. Morgan Kaufmann Publishers, San Francisco (1994)
17. Shneiderman, B., Plaisant, C., Cohen, M., Jacobs, S., Elmqvist, N., Diakopoulos, N.: Designing the User Interface: Strategies for Effective Human-computer Interaction, 6th edn. Pearson Addison Wesley, Boston (2016)
18. Hallnäs, L., Redström, J.: Slow technology-designing for reflection. Pers. Ubiquit. Comput. **5**(3), 201–212 (2001)
19. Hassenzahl, M., Klapperich, H.: Convenient, clean, and efficient?: the experiential costs of everyday automation. In: Proceedings of the 8th Nordic Conference on Human-Computer Interaction: Fun, Fast, Foundational, pp. 21–30 (2014)
20. Teevan, J., Collins-Thompson, K., White, R.W., Dumais, S.T., Kim, Y.: Slow search: information retrieval without time constraints. In: Proceedings of the Symposium on Human-Computer Interaction and Information Retrieval (2013)
21. Lee, M.K., Kim, J., Forlizzi, J., Kiesler, S.: Personalization revisited: a reflective approach helps people better personalize health services and motivates them to increase physical activity. In: Proceedings of the 2015 ACM International Joint Conference on Pervasive and Ubiquitous Computing, pp. 743–754 (2015)
22. Riche, Y., Henry Riche, N., Isenberg, P., Bezerianos, A.: Hard-to-use interfaces considered beneficial (some of the time). In: CHI 2010 Extended Abstracts on Human Factors in Computing Systems, pp. 2705–2714 (2010)

23. Cockburn, A., Kristensson, P.O., Alexander, J., Zhai, S.: Hard lessons: effort-inducing interfaces benefit spatial learning. In: Proceedings of the SIGCHI Conference on Human Factors in Computing Systems, pp. 1571–1580 (2007)
24. Kelly, R., Gooch, D., Watts, L.: Technology appropriation as discretionary effort in mediated close personal relationships. In: Collaborative Appropriation: How Couples, Teams, Groups and Communities Adapt and Adopt Technologies, in Conjunction with CSCW 2016 (2016)
25. Pierce, J., Paulos, E.: Counterfunctional things: exploring possibilities in designing digital limitations. In: Proceedings of the 2014 Conference on Designing Interactive Systems, pp. 375–384 (2014)
26. Baumer, E.P., Silberman, M.: When the implication is not to design (technology). In: Proceedings of the SIGCHI Conference on Human Factors in Computing Systems, pp. 2271–2274 (2011)
27. Pierce, J.: Undesigning technology: considering the negation of design by design. In: Proceedings of the SIGCHI Conference on Human Factors in Computing Systems, pp. 957–966 (2012)
28. Purpura, S., Schwanda, V., Williams, K., Stubler, W., Sengers, P.: Fit4life: the design of a persuasive technology promoting healthy behavior and ideal weight. In: Proceedings of the SIGCHI Conference on Human Factors in Computing Systems, pp. 423–432 (2011)
29. Win, K.T., Mullan, J., Howard, S., Oinas-Kukkonen, H.: Persuasive systems design features in promoting medication management for consumers. In: Proceedings of the 50th Hawaii International Conference on System Sciences (2017)
30. Mustaquim, M.M., Nyström, T.: A system development life cycle for persuasive design for sustainability. In: MacTavish, T., Basapur, S. (eds.) PERSUASIVE 2015. LNCS, vol. 9072, pp. 217–228. Springer, Cham (2015). doi:10.1007/978-3-319-20306-5_20
31. Lehto, T., Oinas-Kukkonen, H.: Persuasive features in web-based alcohol and smoking interventions: a systematic review of the literature. J. Med. Internet Res. **13**(3), e46 (2011)
32. Daud, N.A., Sahari, N., Muda, Z.: An initial model of persuasive design in web-based learning environment. Procedia Technol. **11**, 895–902 (2013)
33. Wang, B., Lim, E.T., Van Toorn, C.: Gimme money! designing digital entrepreneurial crowdfunding platforms for persuasion and its social implications. In: Proceedings of the 20th Pacific Asia Conference on Information Systems (2016)
34. Oinas-Kukkonen, H., Harjumaa, M.: Persuasive systems design: key issues, process model, and system features. Commun. Assoc. Inf. Syst. **24**(1), 28 (2009)
35. Robson, K., Plangger, K., Kietzmann, J.H., McCarthy, I., Pitt, L.: Is it all a game? understanding the principles of gamification. Bus. Horiz. **58**(4), 411–420 (2015)
36. Cugelman, B.: Gamification: what it is and why it matters to digital health behavior change developers. JMIR Serious Games **1**(1), e3 (2013)
37. McCallum, S.: Gamification and serious games for personalized health. In: Proceedings of the 9th International Conference on Wearable Micro and Nano Technologies for Personalized Health (2012)
38. Muntean, C.I.: Raising engagement in e-learning through gamification. In: Proceedings of the 6th International Conference on Virtual Learning (ICVL), pp. 323–329 (2011)
39. Korn, O.: Industrial playgrounds: how gamification helps to enrich work for elderly or impaired persons in production. In: Proceedings of the 4th ACM SIGCHI Symposium on Engineering Interactive Computing Systems (2012)

40. Herzig, P., Strahringer, S., Ameling, M.: Gamification of ERP systems-exploring gamification effects on user acceptance constructs. In: Multikonferenz Wirtschaftsinformatik, pp. 793–804 (2012)
41. Fogg, B.J.: Persuasive Technology: Using Computers to Change What We Think and Do. Morgan Kaufmann Publishers, San Francisco (2003)
42. Reimer, Y.J., Douglas, S.A.: Teaching HCI design with the studio approach. Comput. Sci. Educ. **13**(3), 191–205 (2003)
43. Lindstrom, J.: Design Studios: The Good, the Bad, and the Science (2011). http://www.uxbooth.com/articles/design-studios-the-good-the-bad-and-the-science/
44. de Oliveira, R., Carrascal, J.P.: Towards effective ethical behavior design. In: CHI 2014 Extended Abstracts on Human Factors in Computing Systems, pp. 2149–2154 (2014)
45. Maguire, E.A., Woollett, K., Spiers, H.J.: London taxi drivers and bus drivers: a structural MRI and neuropsychological analysis. Hippocampus **16**(12), 1091–1101 (2006)

User Operational Design Thinking

Peipei Cai[✉]

Beijing Baidu Netcom Science Technology Co., Ltd., Beijing, China
caipeipei@baidu.com

Abstract. It is necessary to accept new users, retain old users, keep users active, promote user consumption, and restore the loss of users, after all websites and products are released online. User operations are almost the core work of the development of each site or product. So what is the core content of user operation? The answer is opening source (to pull new users), throttling (to prevent loss of users), promoting activity (to enhance user activity), Promoting payment (to stimulate the user to pay conversion). In fact, none of the above contents is easy to achieve. So we must apply the basic knowledge of the user operations, combined with the user experience knowledge, to create the operational design thinking. The operational design thinking can help the sites or products to obtain a good user experience.

Keywords: User experience design · User operations · Opening source · Promoting activeness

1 Introduction

Product design is a long and escalating process which includes the following steps, first of all combining the user needs with the market demands, secondly a series of development, testing, releasing online, and then understanding the product's results through the data feedback, and finally improvement and optimization.

Operation is of great importance for the success of a product. When the product design and development are completed, the operation can help the product to propagate, promote the user to use, and improve the user retention. So operational design is very important to make the product live better and longer.

The user experience is a design behavior that runs through the entire product lifecycle. As the user experience designers, we must fully understand the operational knowledge, master the design of operational thinking, and design products to meet users' needs, in different user operating stages. Products can run better and longer once they meet the needs of users.

The operations include three aspects: content operations, user operations, and event operations. This paper is mainly about the user operations, which is most closely integrated with the user experience and has greatest guiding value for the user experience design. Mastering the user operational design thinking can help us to improve the quality and value of the user experience design.

A. Marcus and W. Wang (Eds.): DUXU 2017, Part I, LNCS 10288, pp. 19–27, 2017.
DOI: 10.1007/978-3-319-58634-2_2

2   The Importance of the User Operations

It is necessary to accept new users, retain old users, keep users active, promote user consumption, and restore the loss of users, after all websites and products are released online. User operations are almost the core work of the development of each site or product. The content operation, the activity operation, and the evaluation of the KPI are all determined by the user operations. Besides, the discussions of the user scale, the user payment, operation data health, as well as other factors are all in fact contained in the work of user operations. In general, the user operations include the following items:

- First of all: We must fully understand the user structure of our products. For example, among our users, are men more or women more? How old are they? Which provinces are they in? How about their education levels? What are they interested in? Are these data above possible to create common user types?... ... These are the basic data for user analysis.
- Second: We must understand the scale of the users. How many new users? How many old users? What is the number of the daily growth? What stage are the users at in their life cycles? When clearing these questions, we can understand the stage of our website and product, as well as the stage of our users. Then we are able to select the appropriate user operation method.
- Finally: We must know and understand the data of the user behavior on our website. By analyzing the data, we can understand why the users come? Why the users leave? Why the users active? Why the users retained? Only by understanding these user behaviors, we can use different operating strategies to attract new users, to active old users, to restore lost users, etc.

Therefore, the core contents of user operations are the opening source (to pull new users), the throttling (to prevent loss of users), the promoting activity (to enhance user activity), and the promoting payment (to stimulate the user to pay conversion). In fact, none of the above contents is easy to achieve. So we must apply the basic knowledge of the user operations, combined with the user experience knowledge, to create the operational design thinking. The operational design thinking can help the sites or products to obtain a good user experience. Referring to the following figure (Fig. 1).

- Opening source: When the users use the product at the first time, we need to ensure that the user experience is very good in order to attract them to stay.
- Promoting users' activity: In order to make users like our products and continue using our products, we must divide the users into sub-groups, and provide them different quality services based on their different interests.
- Promoting payment: On the basis of users' psychology, we should seize the needs of the core users, let the user use the paid features, and then guide the user to pay for the features.
- Throttling: In order to find the possibly lost users in advance, we should analyze the behavior of the lost users, and do some operations to recall them.

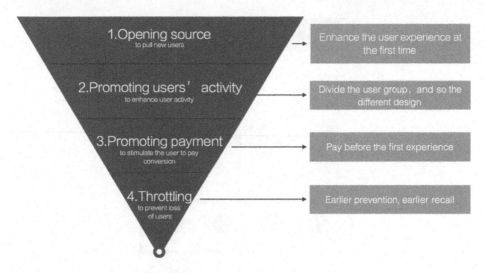

Fig. 1. User operational design thinking

3 User Operational Design Thinking

On the basis of the knowledge of the user operations and the knowledge of user experience, the user operational design thinking can help us to improve the user experience, to design the satisfactory products, and to follow the law of the user operations.

3.1 Opening Source (Enhance the User Experience at the First Time)

The purpose of opening source is to expand the number of users. The main tasks include expanding the registration channels and enhancing the registration rate. From the perspective of user experience, how to reduce the login threshold is the focus problem for the designers at this stage. The purposes are to allow users to smoothly and quickly complete the registration process and to improve the rate of successful registration. Especially for a new product, we must reduce the registration threshold in order to obtain more users.

3.1.1 Lower Login Threshold - Third Party Authorization Login

After years of development, the registration of Internet products has been very mature. Besides the registration way of the product itself, there will be other ways to register, such as binding registration. Binding registration allows the user of other products to quickly log on our products by the authorization account. This approach can significantly reduce the cost of obtaining the users. For example, the current common login page, refer to the following figure, prompts users to use the accounts of Sina microblogging, QQ, and WeChat to directly login the website, which can quickly increase the user numbers, especially for the new products. Referring to the following figure (Fig. 2).

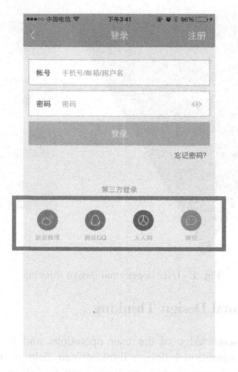

Fig. 2. Third party authorization login

3.1.2   Lower Login Threshold - Account Exchange

Many companies not only have one product, but a product group, which are closely related products. In this case, it is necessary to make full use of any product account to get through the group of the products in order to reduce the threshold of registration.

For example, Baidu has a number of apps such as Baidu on the phone, Baidu map, Baidu Nuomi, Baidu take-away, Baidu reading, etc. In order to reduce the login threshold, Baidu uses the account exchange. The user logged in an app, and his account information will be recorded. When the user login Baidu's other apps in the same phone, it will be prompted whether to use the recorded account to login. Referring to the following figure (Fig. 3).

This approach greatly reduces the login threshold, and enhances the success rate of the login. Baidu's products fully share account resources between each other.

3.1.3   Lower Login Threshold - Product Optimization

With the advent of the age of the mobile Internet, everyone has a mobile phone number. Mobile phone number is not only convenient to contact, but also very convenient to remember. So mobile phone number has gradually become a very important account information.

It will be more convenient using mobile phone number to register in the app than using the mailbox to register. Referring to the following figure (Fig. 4).

Fig. 3. Baidu account exchange

Fig. 4. Using mobile phone number to register

3.2 Promoting Users' Activity (Divide the User Group, and so the Different Design)

The needs of users are very diverse:

- Although each site has the clear positioning and the specific user groups, the users are still very different. So the demands from the users are certainly different.
- Each user has a specific life cycle (including start-up, growth, active, recession). The users starting to use the product at the different time, will be in different stages; Or the users starting to use the product at the same time but having different growth rates, will also be in different stages. In different life stages of the user, the demands for natural products are also different.

In summary, regardless of the user's own differences or their different stages, the user's needs are different. So we have to divide the users into groups. For different user characteristics of different groups, we must do the different designs in order to enhance the users' activity. Referring to the following figure (Fig. 5).

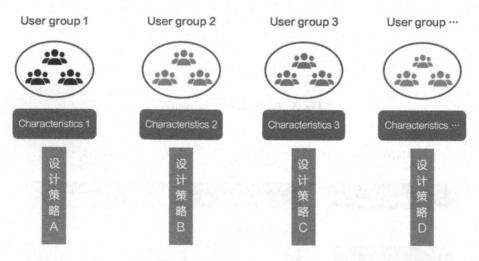

Fig. 5. The different user groups

In the process of categorizing the user, we found that different types of user group account differently. The groups with large proportion are named with important user groups. For these user groups, we should do a special treatment to meet their particular needs.

For example, the education group, the largest user group, which accounts for 40.8% in the whole number of users of Baidu Library. They have great demands for viewing and downloading the educational documents. So we specifically design and deliver educational VIP for them. The original solution that users can view and download documents 10 times within a month without the limitation of document types is upgraded to 15 times a month only with educational documents. For the educational user group, the membership value is increased by 1.5 times at the same price. While after releasing the new solution, the VIP income is increased with 4.1%, and the ARPU is increased with 3.6%. Referring to the following figure (Fig. 6).

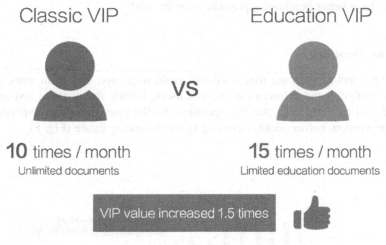

Fig. 6. Classic VIP vs Education VIP

3.3 Promoting Payment (Pay Before the First Experience)

On the basis of users' psychology, we should seize the needs of the core users, let the user use the paid features, and then guide the user to pay for the features. Referring to the following figure (Fig. 7).

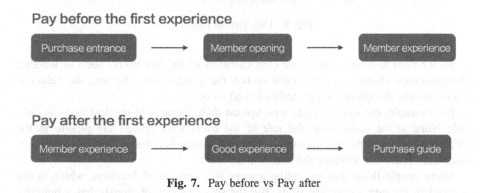

Fig. 7. Pay before vs Pay after

The role of the user experience is important to stimulate users to pay for the services provided by the products. For example, many products have a membership system. We can only use the corresponding privileges after purchasing members, while if we do not buy members, we can only see a bunch of cold copies of the presentation.

Please remember that: The users' purposes of using the products are not to buy members, but to meet their specific needs. So a good experience process is: The user can try to use the membership functions. After that, if they are satisfied with the service, they will buy the members. Although this process delays the purchase of members, the purchase behavior will be more effective, have higher purchase success rate, and have better purchase experience after the trial.

3.4   The Throttling

Throttling refers to keep the user scale and avoid user loss. The main work mainly includes analyzing the behaviors of the lost users, finding the possible lost users in advance, and recalling users through operation. So the core of the user experience is: earlier prevention, earlier recall. Referring to the following figure (Fig. 8).

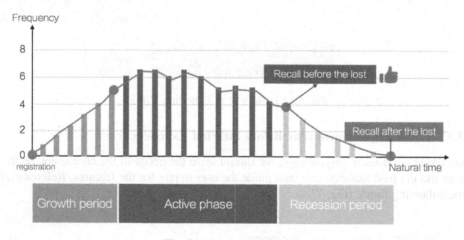

Fig. 8. User growth model

So we need to analyze the same characteristics of the lost users. Such as whether the registration channels are the same or not, the gender ratio, the age, the behavior characteristics, the interest characteristics, and so on.

For example, the rate of users who upload their pictures in the lost users is only 20%, while at the same time, the rate of the users who upload the picture in the remaining users is 80%. So uploading the head picture is a very important indicator, which can determine whether the user will be lost.

Many people think that uploading avatars is a very small function, which is not involved in the user's core functions. But the small picture obviously has a butterfly effect. For example, in the SNS virtual community, the avatar photos allow others to understand our preferences at the first glance. If it is a true picture, the user will be very easy to be recognized by their friends. So the avatar photo is very important to build their user relationships.

In summary, first of all, we need to find the same performance of the lost users. Once the users show these performance, it indicates that these users having the trend to be lost. We need to recall these users in advance.

4   Conclusion

After releasing a new product, it is necessary to attract new users, retain old users, keep users active, promote user consumption and restore the loss of users. It can be seen that user operation has become the core of the online products. On the basis of the operational knowledge and the user experience knowledge, the user operational design thinking can guide the user experience design, help us to design the satisfying products and to follow the law of the user operations.

Acknowledgements. Thanks again to Operation methodology created by Professor Zhang Liang, which gives me deep thinking of Internet Operation.

References

1. Liang, Z.: Operate from Scratch. CITIC Publishing House, Beijing (2015)
2. Pu, J.: How to do user operations. http://jingyan.baidu.com/article/d3b74d6489b749 1f76e6094d.html
3. Data Resource. http://tongji.baidu.com
4. Baidu Library. http://wenku.baidu.com
5. Baidu Register. https://passport.baidu.com/v2/?reg&tt=1486360368057&gid=6BC6F60-3CF5-4D84-A5AA-9B85ACBB98CC&tpl=pp&u=%3A%2F%2Fpassport.baidu.com%2F
6. Baidu Login. https://passport.baidu.com

Disappearing Boundary

Wai Ping Chan[✉]

School of Design, China Central Academy of Fine Arts, Beijing, China
marco@cafa.edu.cn

Abstract. With the breakthrough of the confinements of materials by Screen Technology, it has ushered in another kind of expression mode, which is detached from the sense of distance featured by technology and is fused with the realistic world. The appearance of the screen media which surpasses the definition of papers but has costs lower than paper would once again subvert the human visual experience and life habits. As a kind of new means of visual language, since the 1960s, interface design has brought the world brand new design concepts and design norms. The human beings' entry into the intelligent era has been much more rapid than expected, and this has brought design tremendous impacts and challenges, but has also brought the designers boundless possibilities. Under the influence of visual language for interface designs, designers wonder how to conduct designs and in reverse it would aid such an era to a certain place. The Author proposes that in the visual language for interface designs there exists a developmental trend from "fear to be unseen" to "fear to be seen"; meanwhile it is also proposed that the visual language for interface designs features profound effects and behavior planning on the conventional graphic design. This Paper holds that there would be no development of interface design without the screen, and the development map of the interface designs would put forward new requirements on the development process of the screen. It can be said that the screen has shaped the temperament of the modern technological society featuring constant fusion and merging. The appearance of the screen established a boundary, but this boundary possesses boundless integration and merging ability, and this is not only manifested in the externalized substance, but is more manifested in people's hearts. The boundary between substances is disappearing.

Keywords: Screen technology · Interface design · Graphic user interface

1 From "Fear to Be Unseen" to "Fear to Be Seen"

From "Fear to be Unseen" to "Fear to be Seen", and what such a process of simplification indicates is the elevation of the users' abilities... The Author.

When tracing the development of the scroll bars in the visual language for interface designs during the desktop era, we would discover that there exists a process of simplification, but this process does not simplify for the mere purpose of simplification, and neither is it a transformation of the aesthetic angle on the visual organs. The Author names this process a process from "fear to be unseen" to "fear to be seen"; for the users of the Xerox Star era in 1981, many people failed to understand that the world of screen

© Springer International Publishing AG 2017
A. Marcus and W. Wang (Eds.): DUXU 2017, Part I, LNCS 10288, pp. 28–44, 2017.
DOI: 10.1007/978-3-319-58634-2_3

is something that can scroll ahead in an unlimited way. The world can scroll ahead without any limits; in the era of viewing TV, the users were only responsible for receiving the signals transmitted from the screen. However, in front of a PC, if no command is given, it would have no response of any kind, and a scroll bar is just one of the most important breakthroughs in the visual language for interface designs. In order to enable the users to understand and use such a function, the design of its visual images involved being fearful of not being seen by the users, and the rolling direction of the arrow was a metaphorical expression with the arrow being pushed upward from downward and moved from upward to downward. However, such a metaphorical expression incurred some changes in the scroll bar design of the Apple Lisa interface language in 1983, and under the guidance of direct perception and clearance and no need for more considerations, moving upward means the upward moving of the page and moving downward means the downward moving of the page. In 2007, in the visual language for interface designs of iPhone iOS, the arrow for scroll bars was eliminated. This indicated that with the popularization of the PCs, under the long-term influence of the visual language for interface designs, users' comprehension of the operations of the interface has been substantially elevated, and without the excessive interpretations of the visualized language, the users are able to understand the screen can be scrolled, so the indicative role of the scroll bar's functions were lowered, and its visual images gradually subsidized; when necessary, users would take the initiative to find it, and its function only indicates the position of the current scrolling (Fig. 1).

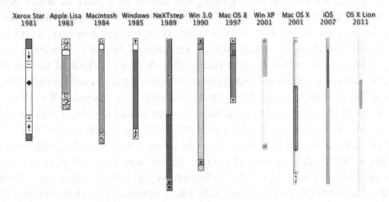

Fig. 1. The scroll bar development from 1981 to 2011

It took two-third of the 20th century for the PCs to be transformed from their gigantic sizes to the desktops, from military applications to civilian uses, from super users to individuals, from the mechanical moving to the intelligence of the screen interface. At present, desktops, notebooks, and palm PCs coexist. Not only can PCs assist you in doing your jobs, learning and entertainment, they can even help you at any time. People no longer need to worry about the differences in applications brought about by the changes in sizes. Regardless any forms, the similar interfaces and the same applications are operated.

PCs have made our modern living become so unconventional; however, what is the thing that integrates such seemingly disorderly life needs? It is the screen, and the visual language for interface designs. The interface created by the screen is just like an all-mighty pocket, while the visual language for interface designs contains and integrates people's constant life needs on the same platform, and this process is still in progress. The fusion ability of the screen interface has failed to reach its limits.

On one hand, portable PCs have been transformed into today's notebook PCs along its own route of development; on the other hand, it sped up the advent of palm PCs, and quickened the appearance of palm PCs, thus enhancing the development of the screen interfaces of smaller sizes; this was closely associated with the advancement of the screen technology. The emergence of such a group of flat screens as LED made the screen sizes more flexible.

1.1 Interfaces Without Any Need for Thinking About Operations

The inception of the "Palm PCs" concept was not aimed at making "smaller PCs"; instead, it made endeavors to explore the "handwriting PCs". SketchPad was just a model of the handwriting PC, which was invented in 1963 by Ivan Sutherland by American computer scientist as well as the pioneer of the Internet. The Author holds that the Sketchpad which had initially solved the problem of handwriting entry should be the father of palm PCs. This is because only with the emergence of handwriting entry that people would imagine regarding the screen as a piece of waste paper and hold it in hand and make entries in the mode of writing with a pen. What SketchPad used was already a kind of touch screen interactive technique; however, it was not until the 21st century that such a touch Screen Technology began to gradually enter the ordinary families; the crucial element lied in that there was a lack of the flexible and changeable screen technologies and application software that could match them.

SketchPad enabled its inventor Ivan Sutherland to be awarded the 1988 Turing Award. What is noteworthy is that the fact an invention of the 1960s was awarded the highest award in computer technology indicated that the importance of that invention was not substantiated until the 1980s. The end of the 1980s was the golden era for the development of the flat screen technology, and it was also the golden era for the development of interfaces. Upon the sufficient preparation of technology, SketchPad provided a multitude of PC developers with a new orientation of development. Such an event is a verification of the Author's viewpoint: The SketchPad with pen entry was an infancy of the modern palm PCs, with the only difference being that such a pen was now replaced by the finger. Its emergence has re-written the interactive relation between the humans and the screen. We should know that before its advent, people were only able to communicate with a screen through the mode of the intervention of a third party. Its emergence provided humans and the screen with a "touch" type interaction relation, and such a kind of new relation is bound to guide human beings in advancing towards an intelligent era that is freer and broader.

The working goal of Ivan Sutherland for the invention of SketchPad was a hope that the users could have better communication with the PCs and the communication speed could also be substantially elevated. Indeed, there was nothing that was more direct the "touch-response" type communication. However, there was also a regret, i.e. SketchPad still failed to accomplish the entry of texts. The "Light-Pen" it used to be a kind of photosensitive input device; it allowed the users to conduct operations on the CRT screens and get direct responses; however, such a device was not sensitive enough to express more detailed things, such as words as well as complicated images; what is more, it failed to manipulate the sizes of the entry contents. Despite all these, this was only a new start; during the end of the 1980s, under the stimulation of the screen technology as well as the development of technologies, SketchPad began to be valued or even led to the advent of a new term that matched it Pen Computing".

It took about 3 decades for the desktop PCs to develop to palm PCs. During this period, there were technological developments, and also the users' expectations and adaptations. GUI has played an important role, and it was the popularization of GUI that sped up the users' quests for palm mobile smart terminals.

From the end of the 1980s to the early 1990s, prior to the advent of Palm, some embryonic forms of the tablet PCs had emerged, such as GRIDpad, Workslate, Momenta, Go, Casio Zoomer, Sony Magic, as well as Apple Newton, which was a model of the Apple, and these tablet PCs all adopted the interactive mode of pen entry; nevertheless, most of them were not clearly positioned and were highly priced; although their hardware was meticulously made, their functions failed to match it; most importantly, the user interface designs were not ideal and failed to entice users; they all came to a demise on the market.

What are the PCs that can represent the future? Jeff Hawkins, who developed GRiD Compass as well as GRIDpad holds that the desktop PCs, as the personal computers, are still too over-sized, too complicated and too power-consuming for the future, and the PCs needed by everyone should be a small type electronic device, which can be placed in a handbag or even the pocket.

The extended meaning of the word Palm means the palm, and Jeff Hawkins defined the success of Palm on size, price as well as speed. The link that connected these four items was the "interface". For a desktop, there should be a distance of at least 60 cm between the users and the PCs for viewing; however, for a palm device, the viewing distance was greatly reduced, so it was inevitable to adjust the interface. Palm's GUI was guided by the rapid online of the cursor, and the users' most commonly used functions are placed on the most conspicuous positions. In order to avoid the misoperation caused by the numerous and small keys, efforts were also made on the Palm to reduce the number of buttons on the hardware, with the conversion to the use of a set of virtual keyboard and handwriting pen was used for entry, and it did not take long to realize the replacement of the writing pen with the finger.

"The differences of Palm's GUI with the desktop are not only manifested in such an interactive mode as "Navigation", but also in such a variety of aspects as the characteristics of the menus, reading experience, active control and accessibility. Prior to the advent of the handwriting era, Palm had found one possibility of solution for the development of palm PCs. Palm also had a highly featured interface configuration, i.e. the command shortcuts, as well as some special combinations of Graffiti. They enabled the users to bypass the menus and rapidly execute the commands. Such an approach; on one hand, they elevated the efficiency of the skilled users, but, on the other hand, it required the users to memorize more things.

1.2   From WIMP to FIMS

Since the 1990s, the expansion of Microsoft Windows exerted tremendous amount of pressure on the Apple. However, the situation saw a fortunate turn in the early 20th century. In January, 2007, Steve Jobs released the iPhone on the MacWorld Conference, announcing the formal advent of the era of the smart cell phone GUI. It was indicated by the previous statements of the Apple that the iPhone team used to intend to rely on the original mature interface system; however, the reason for their original abandoning was something of great interests. However, the Author holds that the crucial reason of the problem lied in the "screen". From desktop to palm, the screen's sizes had been changed, and the interactions among humans must have a mode that can adapt to these changes (Fig. 2).

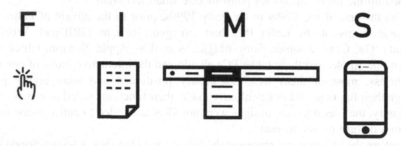

Fig. 2. From WIMP to FIMS (F represents Finger, I represents Icon, M represents Menu and S represents the Screen)

The Author holds that the visual language for interface designs under the popularization of the smart cell phones had seen some changes, and transformation from the screen viewing mode and the operation mode exerted real-time changes on the principles of the visual language for interface designs. The Pointer (P) in WIMP had totally vanished in the smart cell phones, and the language mode of the interface designs of the windows (W) had also become extremely vague, or had even vanished, with them replaced by the users' finger (F), and the users' fingers becoming the most important element for interactions with the screen; the emergence of windows was also replaced by the sizes of the screens themselves, so users no longer consider the contents of different windows and only need to be concerned about the contents that are ongoing on the current screen. The users can manipulate the screen with the near-perfect "pinching, extending, shortening and expanding" and "inertial scrolling", thus making the application programs more natural and more real-time. This is a gigantic step forward. The geniuses of the Apple Company creatively subverted the human perception of machines. It enabled "humans" to be closer to children; we all know that when the children perceive this world at the initial stage, the direct responses brought about by the "touching" could usually bestow upon them a sense of achievement and they can obtain an incentive for "continuing".

In 1993, the Apple Company used to promulgate a 415-page *Human Interface Guidelines*.[1] When renewing the OS, the Apple conducted revisions on this "*Guidelines*". Through the revision process, we can see the developments and changes in from human interface visual language for interface designs over the past 20 years. In 1995, the established "Human Interface Principles" pointed out for the users the development orientation of human interface in the future for the Apple. The users here mainly referred to the then program developers and the interface designers. This principle was divided into a total of 11 parts, namely: Metaphors, Direct Manipulation, See-and-Point, Consistency, WYSIWYG, User Control, Feedback and Dialog, Forgiveness, Perceived Stability, Aesthetic Integrity as well as Modelessness.

After the birth of iPhones, the Apple leaped into the era of iOS, with the original "principles" being unable to fully support the development of human interface visual language for interface designs. Therefore, in 2008, the Apple started the gradual adjustments on the "principles", and Perceived Stability, Modelessness, Forgiveness and Mental-Model, etc. were abolished, with the additions of "Explicit and Implied Actions". Soon, after the release of iOS 4, See and Point also disappeared from the iOS' "principles". There had also been substantial changes in the rankings of the various items of the "principles", and I the list of "principles" released in 2015, "Aesthetic Integrity" had been ranked top, with "Metaphors" and "User Control" ranked the last ones.

Through such changes, the Author holds that during its development the visual language for interface designs has been transformed from the concepts of technology and functions to the concepts of providing higher quality, from the mode of guiding, constructing and encouraging the users' uses to the elevation of the users' conscious uses, from the interactions of human-machine interface to the interactions of human-machine content. Such items that have disappeared in the list of "principles" as detectability, feedback, evoking and consistency were not useless in the true sense; the only difference is that with the elevation of the users' abilities, those items have become trivial.

For the current vast PC users, the important thing is not the indications of functions, but rather "viewable" and "usable" contents, as well as the interactions with these contents. In the latest iOS 9, we can easily see such changes. Deference Principle display of UI should facilitate the users in better comprehending the contents and have interactions with them, rather than dispersing the users' concentration on the contents themselves. Clarity Principle requires that the texts of various fonts should be clarified and legible, the icons be precise and conspicuous, and the excessive modifications should be eliminated so as to substantiate the key points so as to drive the designs with content functions. Depth Principle encourage the sense of levels of vision as well as the interactive animations, and these would bestow upon the UI new vigor and facilitate the users in better comprehending and elevating the users' sense of pleasure during the application process.

Under iOS, the visual language for interface designs is limited, and this is the possibility that was brought about by the technologies and behaviors which was

---

[1] Apple Computer Inc. (1993). *Macintosh Human Interface Guidelines*, Addison-Wesley Professional.

provided by the iOS. This possibility makes the job of interface designers transformed into the interface designs for various kinds of application programs. The visual language of the application programs would impact the executions of the background programs, and it would also affect the users' behaviors, or even influence the contents of the programs. The iOS provides each APP with a uniformed platform, thus enabling them to substantiate the core functions, and manifest the associations, and meanwhile bring the users direct and detailed experience and the impressions with rational modifications. The point of the drive APP interfaces lies in the content and functions, rather than in precedents and the various prior hypotheses. Aesthetic Integrity does not simply mean how pretty an APP interface is, but rather refers to whether the APP's out-appearance is perfectly combined with the functions. The APPs used for handling the practical jobs are usually the simplified and modified UI elements, and its importance lies in the tasks themselves, and they are transmitted to the users in such a way, and it is the unification of this APP in objectives and features. If the contents are not considered and only the bazaar and flaring interfaces are provided, this would cause the users to fail to comprehend them and give rise to a mood of displeasure and contradiction. The consistency in the mode of interface language is to ensure the users can make references to the relevant knowledge and experience in the previous uses. This item does not serve as an encouragement for copying, but rather the sufficient utilization of the experience advantages brought about by normalization and hipping. Direct Manipulation allows users to directly manipulate the objects on the screen and it is no longer necessary to accomplish them via the operation of a third-party control. This is extremely important for the users' dedication in the tasks themselves, and can more easily help the users comprehend and imagine the outcomes of the operations. The screen's "multi-touch technology" enables the users to truly experience the convenience of direction operations. Through the means of gesture operation, the mouse is discarded and the keyboard light medium, thus bestowing upon the users more sense of intimacy, as well as a sense of control for the interface. Feedback is a response to the users' operations, thus enabling the users to be assured that their own requests are being processed. Users hope that when operating the controls, they can receive real-time feedback; in case the operation process is lengthy, it would be necessary to constantly display the progress of the renewed operations. Metaphor refers to the reflection of the virtual world to the realistic world, with a "folder" being a typical example' in the true world, people use folders to holding things. Therefore, in PCs, the placements of files into folders can be rapidly understood. There are also many examples of metaphors: for example, in the gaming, the dragging, rolling and sliding of objects; the sliding of bidirectional switches; the rolling of pictures; and selections conducted through a selector, etc., which enable the users to control them. User Control refers to the users' sufficient Authority, but meanwhile assists the users in avoiding the perilous outcomes. Sufficient Authorities can help the users better familiarize, comprehend and memorize them, but this is not at the sacrifice of devastation. For the mistaken and dangerous operations, it is very important for the users to have a chance to halt and return to a certain phase.

The current visual language for interface designs have drawn humans and the machine to a highly close position. The machine would also make responses according to the humans' desires, and this is also the objective for human beings' constant promotion of technological innovation and the interface developments. Under such a condition, the job of interface design has become more complex and much broader, because it has tasted the benefits, and the users with elevated abilities would have more demands so as to satisfy their ceaseless demands for living.

In contrast to iOS' standardized visual language for interface designs, for a long time Android has retained in the developments of the functions and applications. The users' interface GUIs were accomplished by the various manufacturers of cell phones themselves; therefore, we would see different cell phones have different modes of visual languages for interface designs. However, the behavioral modes were mostly the mimics of the iOS. In 2014, Google released the design language texts for "Material Design", thus specifying an orientation for the developers and designers of Android. In contents, this "Material Design" which is similar to the Apple's *Human Interface Guidelines*" also featured its own characteristics. Seen from the objectives, "Material Design" was aimed at providing the cell phones, tablet PCs and desktops and "other platforms" with a broader "out-appearance and sensation". What was established by Google was a rather broad framework rather than a uniformed platform. It only included three design principles, namely "metaphors", "sharpness·image·thoughtful-ness", as well as "significant animation effects". "Metaphor" means the construction of a "substantial metaphor" through the construction of systematic dynamic effects and the rational utilization of space. The unconventional sense of touching is the basis for the substance, and this inspiration originated from the research on paper and ink. Such a principle of Android is forward-looking, and it is believed that with the technological advancements, it will have an enormous future perspective for applications. The stimulations of the surfaces and edges of the substances can provide a visual experience based on the true effects, and the familiar sense of touching can incite the users to rapidly have comprehension and cognition. The diversity of the substances would also provide more and rich design effects with practical significance. Meanwhile, the sim-ulations of "light effect, surface texture and sense of motion" can better interpret the intersection relation, spatial relations as well as trajectory of motion between the substances. What is implied in "sharpness·image·thoughtfulness" means that in the handling of the basic elements, aided by such conventional printing designs as layout, grids, space, proportions and color configuration and image applications. These basic graphic design norms have direct experience to follow in such aspects as delighting the users, constructing the visual hierarchies, visual meaning as well as visual focusing. Through the meticulous selections of colors, images as well as the fonts and blanks that are proportional, it creates a distinctive and vivid visual language for user interface, thus providing the users with an operational guidance and entice the users to be immersed in it. Meanwhile, Google held that "meaningful animation effects (abbre-viated as animation effects)" not only can give effective hints and guide the users' behaviors; in addition, they can change the sense of touching of the integral designs. Meaningful and rational "animation effects" can make the substance changes look more consistent and smoother, and they can make the users more dedicated to the changes that are talking place and will take place.

The visual language for interface designs has become the most important compo-nent of the mobile palm PCs, and without an excellent interface language, even there is a faster, better and more stable system, its function cannot be brought into play. When the screen definition of cell phones has reached the equivalent level of the definition of the desktop PCs, or is even higher, users would prefer to use cell phones, because it has broken through the limitations of locations, while its control mode is more direct and rapid. In contrast to PCs' development, the development of touch screen smart mobile devices was just a phenomenon in the past few years; however, many people would discover that we have become used to such an interactive mode as touching; sometimes, we would unconsciously use gestures on the desktop PCs. It was the touch type screen technology that has cast the current era in which the interface is prevalent.

1.3   Aesthetic Integrity

Prior to the advent of the screen, its important value lied in "displaying" and "reproduction". The impacts brought about by it were: it turned out that not only are we able to reproduce the "reality", we can also reproduce the "reality" dynamically. It means of interactions with humans is that we can decide to view or not to view them, as well as what contents to view within a limited scope. As for the contents that are seen, they are predetermined, and they are not determined by the wills of an individual user. At this time, the interface is "the hard interface", with twisting, pressing and drawing being the main stream. For each user, these actions have represented "modernity". In the novel *Gulliver's Travels* created by Jonathan Swift in 1726, the plot that surpassed the reality was still a kind of groundless and far-fetched illusions. However, the sci-fi writer Jules Verne of the 19th century had already begun considering the future "reality". The screen provides such imaginations with a perfect platform, and sci-fi movies are an important category of the movie families. Incredible future, machine wonders, mad scientists, stars and space, etc. through such movies, people predict the future. The development of the screen technology has shortened the distances between these predictions and the reality.

When the screen has become a standard configuration for PCs, the interactive mode of "input-response" closely associates the PCs and the users. From military applications to business and civilian uses, the scope of users has been constantly expanded. The hard interface was transformed to the soft interface. The development of the interfaces better conforms to the expectations of single users, and with the establishment of the GUI concept, the users' abilities have been gradually enhanced, and conversely, this has impacted the development direction of the technology. With the impressive elevations of such core elements of the screen technology as "pixel", "definition", "color gamut", "viewable area", "contrast" and "response time", the degree of freedom that can be manifested by the interface has become increasingly bigger, the colors clearer and brighter, the sizes more flexible and changeable, and the operations simpler and more convenient. The boundary between the PC design and substance design is disappearing. Anything that can be imagined can almost be turned into reality. However, designs still can be distinguished as being good or poor; then, what are the norms for judgments?

The Author holds the opinion that design does not exist in an isolated way, and all the designs are the methods for problem solutions under various restraints. For the boundaries, when a technology is still at the initial stage, the excessively high design requirements are nothings but "far-fetched ideas"; technological advancement and technological orientation will be the fundamentals; when technologies have developed to a certain extent, the space provided for "designs" will be expanded, and at this time, the importance of "designs" will be substantiated. This is because fundamentally speaking, technological developments need APPs, and no matter where the APPs are used, there will be a need to the subjects of APPs, i.e. the users; the users' needs are the service subjects of "designs". During the initial period of the interface development, the engineers were the first ones to appear and were the most important roles; but interestingly, at the crucial links of the interface developments, we could all see the figures of the designers and artists. It was due to their participations that the GUIs could have been manifested in a more ideal way. At present, engineers and designers are cooperating in various means; however, through the event that amendment of the *Human Interface Guidelines* by the Apple listed Aesthetic Integrity on the top rank, we shall have a new positioning of the role played by the designers in the interface development. By GUI, graphs is placed before the users, and the graphs with adequacies and Aesthetics are the preconditions of the user interface and they are the reliance for the users' comprehensions; and they are an important basis for the elevation of the users' experience. In the views of the Author, those designers who can design ideal interfaces should be interdisciplinary; on one hand, they should be highly aware the extent of technological development and know the bottom lines of the technological realizations; on the other hand, they also should grasp the users' demands and are capable of providing the users with more functions.

Current designers can already use better techniques, but there have been no fundamental changes in the nature of designs and it still stands on top of the art and practicality. People with a grasp of art history all know that there was nothing that had not totally existed before and people have always been standing on the shoulders of the giants, with reliance of the previous experience, and some of the experience is close to the present, while others are distant; the flashing of inspirations usually had some trigger points. The screen is a virtual window, while the interface is a desktop in imagination, and we would place some images on the desktop and to a large extent, they originated from people's habits of sorting and classification. This can be exemplified by a simple example, i.e. why are artists used to do paintings using the pixel points on the he screen? It is quite simple that fundamentally speaking, rugs, embroidery and mosaic are all arts that are created using the alignments of points. Such truth is not only reflected in the subjects of art history, it also has similar manifestations in such a multitude of humanity disciplines as sociology, history and information communication. As pointed out by Marshall McLuhanin his work *Understanding media*: The content of each medium is another kind of medium[2]. Its intrinsic connotation means that the media would become increasingly, and would have hierarchies with the sequences of history. The older medium was always the content of a newer medium. For example, as a relatively "older" medium, movies are always the topics and contents of the "new" media TV and the PCs. What they interpreted is just such a principle. A good design is a product of the synthetic actions of the social environment

---

[2] Marshall McLuhan (1964). *Understanding Media: The Extensions of Man*, Signet Books.

and technological developments, users' needs and aesthetics, and the medium itself is not the whole content. What is important is that the designers must be aware what they are able to do, what people need, as well as what kinds of tools can be used.

Users are positioned in the front end of the interface, and, using the existing entry modes—the mouse, keyboard, monitor and touch screen for operating the various kinds of modes of interfaces–WIMP interface, web-based interfaces, gesture-based interfaces, and voice-based interfaces, etc. in the various kinds of PC terminals—PCs, TV sets, smart cell phones, and tablet PCs, the application programs are run. On one hand, whether an application program can benefit the users has to do with the modes of input and output; most importantly, it is related to the interfaces. Technologies have provided the interface's degree of freedom with space, the primary the technology, the smaller the space, and the greater the gas from the users; the higher the technology, the greater the design space of the interfaces, and the closer of its relation to the users. At present, in contrast to the past, the screen technologies closely associated with interfaces have been developed to a certain height, with the confinements on interface design gradually diminished, and this has deepened the users' dependence on the interfaces, thus manifesting the greater importance of excellent interface designs. Meanwhile, the interfaces' connotation and denotation have also been expanded. In the era when the PCs were still the auxiliary tools of personal jobs, the interfaces included the interfaces for the desktops and programs.

Under such a condition, it is held by the Author that the current development of interfaces should follow several principles. Firstly, it involves "simpler and more direct", and everyone is equal in front of science and technology; the job of a designer should be making efforts to enable more users to experience the convenience of technology, so efforts should be made to avoid any designs that could result in the users' perplexities. Users can no longer need to save the complicated instructions, and can effectively use the interfaces when driving, walking and queuing. People do not need to abandon the various kinds of screens to be able to return to the simple living, for these screen interfaces will become simpler and more direct and more integrated, and the "enthusiasts of electrical appliances" and the "old antiques" will all find modes that suit their needs. Secondly, it involves being "safer and clearer feedback", and the users no longer need to worry about the leakage and losing of data. The accident incidence of users when using these screen interfaces will be reduced. Meanwhile, the era of big data has brought the users with convenience, but also panics, and the association of the online identity and the real identity will become closer; the protection of privacy and the safety of interface operation should be one direction for the future. Thirdly, it means a "cleaner environment", and users can be more dedicated to the interface operations without being disturbed by irrelevant events, unless they intend to do so. At the same time, the program association will be enhanced so as to prevent the users from making constant searches in the complex structures. Fourthly, it is the "more coordination of the interface and contents", without the sensation of the interface's existence and better utilization of its content should be a higher state of the interface designs. Design is not aimed for being more obvious, more substantial' excessive beautifying will not necessarily bring about better outcomes; but conversely it means you have a commanding view from a vantage ground and it involves disrespect for the users.

1.4 An Opportunity for New Breakthroughs

The word "medium" is the translation of the English word "medium", and its Latin source was "Medius", which denotes "being in the middle", and contains the meaning of "communication". Historically, its concept has been rather complex, and the connotation of "medium" we use today was established in the 1960s, which was an important period for the development of TV sets and PCs. In Chinese, it is translated into "Mei Jie", which is a highly adequate wording. By "Mei", according to *Zhou Li*, a classical book in ancient China, "it is something that brings together two things of different kinds; as for the wording "Jie", according to *XunZi*, a classical book I ancient China, "When the dukes meet, you serve as a Jie". Such two wording ideally interprets the connotation of this expression meaning "being in an important intermediate position and features the function of communication". In a broad sense, languages, literature and music are all media; however, since they were not established ad inherited by the social organizations, they are called "informal media".

As seen by the Author, within the visible scope, screen technology will have parallel development along such three directions as "material revolution", "display revolution" and transformation of operational mode". Through the decades of development, there is no doubt about the 2-D display capacity of the screens; the emergences and applications of multiple touching and press control have also brought the advantages of the screen's "touch" operational mode into extreme. Within a few years, the screen will still rely on "glass" as the medium, becoming bigger, thinner, lighter, more durable, brighter and clearer. It will also try some changes in shapes, such as bending and folding. The ePaper has appeared, and this mainly a monitor that adopts the technique of electrophoresis Display, EPD, and can be as thin as a piece of paper, and can be bent and erased. It is quite possible that it will play an important role in the not-too-distant future. If its industry can replace paper, it will greatly enhance the conversation of energy, and people will be able to bid a farewell to the embarrassment and frustrations of having to find a cell phone everywhere; the PCs will be fused with the office environment, thus saying good-bye to a computer configuring mode featuring "the mainframe-screen-keyboard-mouse".

The operational mode of the screen would also see changes accordingly, and multi-touch and press touch will be realized in a greater scope. With the assistance of the "gestures", the screen will become more intimate with humans. As n important organ for the using of tools by humans, the hand receives the direct commands of the brain and such behaviors as expansion, shrinking, sliding, clicking, pressing and trial are closer to the instincts, probably, just like the Author, you have often heard people mention that the current children seem to be born for the PCs, and they feature innate strong controllability on the PCs. In fact, the PCs have found a mode to be more intimate with the humans. The PCs have finally become a tool that differ from automobiles and they need no drivers' license, and even children can use them for conducting learning and having amusement. As the aids of "gestures", the development perspective for voice control can also be seen, with the Apple iOS already having the voice assistant SIRI; although it still has flaws in the aspect of voice identification, it has certainly made s gigantic leap forward in the aspect of voice control technique. Regarding voice input, voice companion and voice control, etc., voice will become another bright spot for the screen following the gestures. Regarding the aspect of screen displays, it is quite obvious that 2-D has already failed to satisfy the market needs, and 3D effects would be a better option. This should be a beneficial transition to the all-rounded transformation to the "full image".

With the technology with "glass" as the screen being developed into an extreme value, within a period of time, people would rack their brains to expand the screen's extensions, and anywhere with glass will be screens, such as car windows, household windows, mirrors and photo frames. People can watch news while brushing their teeth; and in the social public areas, there will no longer be a need to hang the display panels high on the wall; and for the buildings themselves, even all the plugs for the electrical power, telephone and the Internet will disappear, and all the wall surfaces are composed of a material similar to a e-screen; all the electrical appliances have wireless power supplies, and lighting fixtures will disappear, for the ceiling and any a wall surface will become a lighting device; in addition, t is possible to create different lighting effects according to the setups of the programs. Finally, a day will come when people will consider abandoning the substantial body of the "screen". What is noteworthy is that the glass material mentioned in this Paper does not specifically denote the glass in the sense of physics, but rather the glass surfaces and they may also be transparent films.

With the abandonment of the "glass" screens, the conventional tablet substances will gradually come to demise, with the "Virtual Reality" being the best alternative. Currently, such a trend has begun to be substantiated, and "Virtual Reality,VR" and "Augmented Reality, AR" are the products that symbolize the future. The emergence of the VR concept was actually in the 1980s and it refers to a technique that can cast a 3-D dynamic scene; through the users' substantial behaviors, it can enable them to be engrossed in the scene. Such a technique features strong practical significance and can provide assistance to such a multitude of fields as urban planning, training of special professions, and the protection and restoration of tangible and intangible cultural relics. Currently, there have been relevant products on the market, such as Oculus Rift, which is mainly applied in gaming so as to elevate the users' experience of being in the scene in gaming. Oculus Rift uses a head-mounted display device and it has accumulated some experience in the casting of realistic scenes. Its development is only a matter of time. The technique of Augmented Reality, AR involves the integration of the virtual images into the realistic scenes and can also support the users in having interactions with them. In contrast to VR, there are some variations in the users' senses of existence.

For the AR, the virtual images are combined in a realistic scene nod what people perceive is still the reality, the only difference being that the reality was added new "furniture", such as interface, operations, data, texts and the contents that the users intend to view. It does not make the users in other locations; instead, it only "augments" the users' status of current existence, and the Reality Goggles of BMW MINI and Google Glass, as well as the Hololens of the Microsoft are just the techniques of this kind. Take the Reality Goggles as an example, when the glasses are worn, not only a user's personal information can be displayed, it can also display such auxiliary contents as speed, navigation and telephone alarm, and even through the cameras mounted on the cars, a user can also realize the "transparent eyes" and have a full view of the actual situations inside and outside the vehicle. For VR, people's experience is fused with the virtual scenes and is totally detached with the surrounding realistic world.

Under guidance, human senses are transformed from reality to fiction. People are no longer seated at the door for viewing; but rather open the door and walk into it. It is quite probable that this will be the ultimate morphology for the future transformation of the screen. Through the reconstruction of a world, human beings would bring about a substantial leap-forward for their life experience, and they can be placed in the space to view the vast galaxies; they can also be placed in the ancient time to see the migration of the dinosaurs. In contrast to AR, VR has a stronger sense of immersion; in comparison to VR, AR features a greater degree of freedom. Therefore, in the future, AR's application scope will be much broader and enduring, while VR will possess obvious advantages in some specific fields. Regardless AR or VR, their speeds of development have become increasingly faster. Nevertheless, for the present, they are nothing more than the trial products of a handful enthusiasts or technicians. Their main resistance stems from the PCs' ability to have real-time rendering of HD images, for only when this problem is solved, the users can sense the existence of the VR scenes and would incite the revolution of the developments of the screen and the interface.

GUI, as a derivative of the screen technology and the means of the visual language of the interface visual language, will walk onto a new path of development by taking the changes of screen technology as an opportunity. Firstly, its key point will be somewhat shifted, walking from "desktop" to contents. With the constant elevation of the users' abilities, the desktops themselves no longer seem too important, and the important things are the contents contained in them. APP interfaces will replace the desktops and become the main topic for desktop developments. How can payments be simpler and safer, how can the various APPs be better connected and have mutual benefits, how can the APPs be better compatible in different equipment and different systems, and how can socialization be become more convenient and swift? Such questions are the issues faced by the interface designs within a certain period of time. This is not the future, and it is already the "present continuous tense". If we are more careful, we will discover that: when we turn on a PC or use a cell phone, the time for retention on the screen has been constantly reduced; usually, we retain on various APP interfaces. After the screen had made a breakthrough in the limits of materials, the boundary formed by the interfaces will not disappear within a certain period of time; this is because the gate for the association of the virtual world and the realistic world still relies on the interfaces to conduct indexing for the construction of a virtual world. By then, the interface designs will be conducted centering on the virtual reality, and under AR, if we want to discard a file, maybe we only need to stretch our hand to grab it and throw it into a virtual waste basket. But under the VR condition, what we are faced with may be one after another door, and if we have taken a wring way, then we can turn around and walk out of it. Despite this fact, the mode of interface language will see some changes, and people can find another kind of mode for association with the virtual world; and people can also walk ahead amid a virtual maze. Such a way s bound to exist, such as voice control, gesture, face identification and motion capture. Through more effective means, it is possible to covey commands and obtain responses, and the language of the graphic interfaces will lose a great field.

In the future, a brand new interface design language will be needed for coping with the connections and interactions between the realistic world and the virtual world. Under the influences of the changes of technologies and the interface structures, the interface design language shall be transformed from a passive state to an active state, and this is because the mode needed for people's expressions will become more direct, such as calling, and, under the principle of Aesthetic Integrity, the interface design language should have its own coping strategies, such as the reduction in the concerns about the machine's vibrations, but rather attach importance to the users' intensity; reduction of the concerns about the brightness of the screen, but rather attach more importance to the brightness of the users' environment, reduction of the smoothness on the screen interface, but rather attach more importance to users' sense of touching on the screen; reduction of concerns on the sense of speed of the interface, but rather attach more importance to the users' time of response; reduction of the concerns on the interface's graphic designs, but rather attach more importance to the designs of fonts; reduction of concerns on the colors on the interface, but rather attach more importance to the interface's dynamic effects; reduction of finger input, but rather attach more importance on voice entry; reduction of the human-machine interactions, but rather attach more importance to the interactions between humans. The human-human interactions are the fundamental element, while fundamentally speaking the human-machine interactions aim to solve the various kinds of limitations for the human-human interactions; and the interface design language should become more intelligent, and big data analyses and the trial experience and error calculation shall be used for determining what kinds of ways of communications are needed by the users.

2 Conclusion: The Disappearing Boundaries

With the breakthrough of material limits by the screen technology, it has ushered in another expression mode, which is detached from the alienation of science and technology and integrated with the realistic world. The emergence of screen medium with definitions superior to that of paper and costs lower than that of paper would once again subvert human visual experience and life habits. The breakthroughs made in the multi-dimensional projection technology and air projection technology enable the users to truly return to the desktops and have interactions with the virtual world by manipulating the realistic world. Metaphor is no longer used; instead, the intuitive appearance is used, and this would result in a world which is more realistic than the reality, thus enabling the users to view the true illusions which were originally invisible and intangible.

Human body would become an important interface, and the operations of this interface would be extended from the screen, human hands to the entire human body, and the various parts of the body might become the interfaces that can be operated, and this would bring about new needs for the developments of the interfaces, and the emergence of new visual language for interface designs, Meanwhile, the linkage trend between the interfaces began to be substantiated, and the body movements would be interlinked with visions, thus forming a truer interaction. In the process of processing the interface visual contents, our brains are bound to become smoother, stabilized and enclosed. People would become more habitual and dependent on the interactions of the three-dimensional true space, while the space for two-dimensional virtual interfaces would be phased out or retained in a certain corner. The interface language in the three-dimensional space would thoroughly alter the existing form of images, with images and objects gradually becoming convergent in visual experience and their differences diminished. This would lead result in people's neglects of the images or the out-appearances of substances, and turn to the process and outcomes of the interactions. Designers' job would accordingly have important changes, and become more real-time, synchronized with the users and step towards the interactive experience with the users.

"Display is operation" has guided the visual language for interface designs onto a path of rapid development and reshaped the jobs of the designers; the metaphoric method has cast the currently most prevalent the visual language for interface designs— GUI, and the "WYSIWYG (What you see is what you get)" that is advocated by it, after successfully bringing human beings to an era in which everyone can use the PCs. Will reach an era of "WYGIWYT (What you get is what you think)", and this would alter the status in which the interface language has an over-reliance on vision. The current visual language for interface designs based on graphs will also need to have some new changes; the language for interface designs is bound to be changed at a faster speed, for the development trend of the screen technology has permeated into different fields; however, such a screen is not necessarily one with vision as the center, but rather one with the user as the center; just like the current scroll bars, screens will also be fearful of being seen.

The jobs of the future architects no longer simply involve conducting designs with eyes, but rather need to regard senses of hearing and touching as the important elements of designs. The roles of such undeveloped sensations will even surpass vision itself. In addition to senses of smell and taste, the Author holds that the path for the interactive combination of the senses of smell and taste has not emerged. The changes in the design contents will bring about new professions, with Somatosensory Designer being one of them; the interactive language design with human body as an interface will become a main stream, and with the body as an interface, this will provide the users with a real-time, audio-visual mode for communication with the virtual world. "Somatosensory Designers" will make attempts to blur the boundary between the virtual world and the realistic world. In other words, the paramount job of a "Somatosensory Designer" lies in the simulation of the perceptions of the virtual world into the realistic world; such designs will be unprecedented, with the screen and the interface becoming the link of these two worlds; this will fundamentally elevate the position of interface design in the design field, become an important orientation of development for the future of designing and the language for interface design that is closer to people's needs will become the key point.

With the constant deepening and expansion of intellectualization, most users would reach a height of high automation and independent thinking in the perception of graphic interface, the operating system would regard the contents as the main body and the distributions and positions of the language for interface designs would retreat and be gradually fused into the content. The language concepts of definition and pixels would disappear or become no longer important, and the screen technology would push definition to the extreme limits of the human being, or even surpass the definition needed by human beings themselves; the screen proportions and viewing distance that have made breakthroughs in the material limits are the important job items for the designs of the interface language. The fundamental reason for human-machine inter-action is to return to the high-efficiency communication between persons, and the users' needs are the sole prime mover for the developments of technology and the design languages.

The Author holds that the screen technology and interface visual language it created has shaped our current way of living. Its development is bound to exert important impacts on the development of the design language of interfaces and it is the key for the solutions of the various kinds of problems caused by the revolution of human visual experience. The advent of the screen established a boundary, but such a boundary features boundless abilities of fusion and merging, and this is not only manifested in the externalized substance, it is more manifested in people's hearts. The boundary between substances is disappearing and the boundary between the substances has been broken. Accordingly, the boundary between the social industries is also disappearing, with the new commercial modes constantly emerging. The boundary between humans and the virtual world is also disappearing, and there have been drastic changes in the way people view this world as well as living modes. The breakthroughs of these barriers and the disappearances of such boundaries made our living more efficient and convenient and this is an opportunity that has been brought to the world by the screen and the visual language for interface designs; our jobs, and regardless it is engineers or designers, what they need to do is to sufficiently utilize such an opportunity and have constant expansions so as to benefit more users, thus truly realizing the universal equality in front of technologies.

Reference

1. McLuhan, M.: Understanding Media: The Extensions of Man. Signet Books (1964)

Investigating User Interpretation of Dynamic Metaphorical Interfaces

Kenny K.N. Chow[✉]

School of Design, The Hong Kong Polytechnic University,
Kowloon, Hong Kong
sdknchow@polyu.edu.hk

Abstract. This paper describes an approach to analyzing interpretation of a kind of dynamic, metaphorical interface, which shows contingent changes over time provoking imagination and reflection, so named "lively". Grounded in the concept of animacy, blending theory, and embodied interaction, the approach integrates interpretive analyses with empirical studies. It includes a protocol of cognitive processes in two stages of use facilitating researchers to speculate the user experience of a lively artifact, to craft interview questions inviting participants to retrospectively express their thoughts and feelings during use, and finally to summarize possible interpretations constituting verisimilar design narratives. To demonstrate, three exemplary lively artifacts are examined in the laboratory.

Keywords: Embodied cognition · Embodied interaction · Blending theory · Sensorimotor experience · Reflective design · Liveliness

1 Introduction

When a user interacts with an interface, one understands the perceived feedback based on different actions at different moments of use differently. When an Apple Watch user rolls up the digital crown and sees listed contents on the display moving up accordingly, he or she intuitively assumes rolling down the digital crown will bring the contents down as well. The action and feedback looks similar to controlling a rotary knob connecting to a mini scroll "inside" the watch. On the other hand, rolling up the digital crown at the home screen of the watch will zoom in to an app icon in the center incrementally. The user can hold the zooming by pausing the roll action, or even zoom out and in casually with the finger sliding down and up aimlessly. This gives the user an illusion of moving the viewpoint toward or away from the center app icon. In either case, the user understands digital operation logic through metaphorical mapping of familiar sensorimotor experiences from mundane physical operations, resulting in different interpretations (i.e., rolling a scroll vs. moving the viewpoint).

Some interface metaphors are dynamic. They show contingent changes over time, which provoke extended or "shifted" interpretations at higher cognitive levels. An example is the mobile phone NEC FOMA N702iS (designed by Oki Sato and Takaya Fukumoto). It features a "water-level" battery meter, which is displayed on the phone's screen as an image looking like water. Holding the phone, the user is allowed to tilt it,

© Springer International Publishing AG 2017
A. Marcus and W. Wang (Eds.): DUXU 2017, Part I, LNCS 10288, pp. 45–59, 2017.
DOI: 10.1007/978-3-319-58634-2_4

resulting in animation that the water seemingly flows to react (see Fig. 1). The sensorimotor experience resembles swaying a container filled with liquid, giving the user an immediate sense of a water-filled phone. At a later time, the water level, indicating the battery level, drops and causes the user to become curious. One may infer that the water is gone and start to worry. It is like having insufficient drinking water for a journey. This extended interpretation builds on metaphorical projections from water to electricity, from drinking to consuming, which may lead to user reflection on one's own behavior.

Fig. 1. The water image displayed on the phone flows in response to a user's action in real time.

We call this kind of dynamic, metaphorical interface "lively". This paper describes the theoretical grounding of the liveliness framework and a methodology for collecting and analyzing user interpretation of lively artifacts in hope of bridging the interpretation gap between designers or researchers and users.

2   Related Concepts

The notion of liveliness is related to the concept of animacy, blending theory, as well as embodied interaction and reflective design.

2.1   Animacy with Contingency

Animacy refers to people's concept separating animate from inanimate. In cognitive science, it is a kind of image schema [1]. Lakoff [2] and Johnson [3] introduce the idea of image or embodied schemata, which are spatial structures and/or dynamic patterns recurring in our bodily experiences (e.g., things up above are usually more difficult for one to access and so more precious) and underlying many entrenched, basic concepts in our minds (e.g., GOOD is UP). Lakoff and Johnson [4] raise numerous evidences from everyday life via what they call "conceptual metaphors" (e.g., we say and see something good as "high quality"). Mandler [1] and Turner [5] (pp. 20–22) point out that animacy is a complex image schema of observed movements, including self-motion, which can be irregular and unpredictable, as well as contingent motion, whose link to other happenings may not be obvious, thus eliciting curiosity or even wonder. Contingent change, a broader view than motion, is a key quality of liveliness, which prompts one to interpret and imagine.

2.2   Blending: Emergent and Embodied

While embodied schemata and conceptual metaphors explain the bodily basis of entrenched concepts like animacy, Gilles Fauconnier and Mark Turner's blending (aka conceptual integration) theory [6] extends to explicate the dynamic, emergent nature of our thoughts (in which metaphor is regarded as a kind of asymmetric static blend). The notion is built on ideas including mental spaces [7] and frames [8, 9]. Mental spaces are "small conceptual packets" that an individual constructs for local understanding and action [6] (p. 40), representing particular scenarios as perceived, imagined, or remembered. A mental space typically contains elements of the scenario and relations between them, which are structured by background knowledge from long-term memory called "frames" [10] (p. 21). One accesses a frame from long-term memory and fills in local information as elements to form a mental space. By integrating two or more mental spaces with analogical mappings between corresponding elements and relations, new "blended" meaning is generated. Blending is emergent that the output of one blend can become input to another new blend, forming a conceptual integration network. Fauconnier and Turner regard metaphor as a kind of asymmetric static blend [11] and point out many cases of emergent blends in everyday life [6].

Blending is also pervasively embodied in many situated sensorimotor experiences, like throwing crumpled paper into a trashcan as if shooting a basketball through the hoop [12], and operating the computer desktop like manipulating things on a task table [13]. Blending, as an analytical instrument, is useful in analyzing or predicting possible imagination prompted by lively artifacts, which feature dynamic metaphorical mapping of familiar, mundane experiences.

2.3   Everyday Experience in Interaction and Reflection

The idea of blending with familiar sensorimotor experiences and scenarios from everyday life for meaning making and imagination resonates with Paul Dourish's proposal of embodied interaction [14]. Drawing on notions from phenomenology, including Martin Heidegger's "being-in-the-world", Dourish emphasizes meaning creation through the use of interactive artifacts based in the everyday world (p. 126). Designing interactive systems should consider people's familiar, everyday experiences, such as physical habits or social practices, in pursuit of meaning. Although meaning can be multiple and design is open to user interpretation [15], embodied interaction, with its emphasis on the everyday world, seems to provide frames for multiple, yet not completely open, interpretations in the use of interactive artifacts. The everyday world, we believe, also provides interpretive frames for imaginative blends to take place when lively artifacts evoke familiar experiences.

Multiple interpretations entail different assumptions and perspectives, which may lead to different levels of reflection. Fleck and Fitzpatrick [16] delineate reflection into four levels. The ground level is just describing actions or happenings, which is not reflective. The first level is providing explanations or justifications for actions taken in events. The second level is considering different reasons, hypotheses, or perspectives. The third level is asking fundamental questions and challenging personal assumptions, leading to a change in practice. Finally, the fourth level is considering a wider context including social or ethical issues. Everyday experience integrated in lively artifacts enables imaginative blends in users, which can be elaborated at multiple levels of understanding, from inference, imagination, to reflection.

3 The Cognitive Processes in the Liveliness Framework

Lively artifacts trigger different levels of interpretation at different moments of use. Users first understand the initial operation logic of a system via an immediate blend with a familiar sensorimotor experience from a mundane physical operation. Yet, the blended experience continues to change, which seems curious and prompts elaboration or shifting of the initial interpretation at a later time. For researchers to conduct interpretive analyses, the user experience of lively artifacts can be delineated in two stages, each of which involves four cognitive processes, resulting in different levels of understanding.

At the initial stage of use, immediate understanding of operation comes about:

1.1 Perceiving affordances – The user perceives something do-able with motor action and then acts on the interface.
1.2 Receiving quick feedback – The user receives quick sensory feedback based on the action taken, forming an experience at the sensorimotor level.
1.3 Triggering immediate blends – The sensorimotor experience looks familiar to the user, triggering an immediate blend with a past experience, yielding an imaginary concept of the operation.
1.4 Becoming second nature – After repeated use, the operation becomes second nature. Gaps between action and feedback are bridged by the blend and become unnoticed.

At later stages of use, the artifact provokes further imagination and extended interpretation:

2.1 Noticing contingent changes – The user perceives changes over time, and becomes curious about the meaning in accordance with the imaginary concept in 1.3.
2.2 Invoking interpretive frames – The user invokes a frame from memory, which includes a remembered or imagined scenario with similar changes.
2.3 Elaborating metaphorical blends – The remembered or imagined scenario is analogically mapped with the imaginary concept in 1.3 plus the changes. Both become inputs to the next blend, yielding an imaginary scenario elaborated from the imaginary concept.
2.4 Reflecting on the situation – Through invoking different frames, the user reviews possible explanations for the situation, which invite one to see from different perspectives.

4   Researcher Interpretation

To demonstrate the methodology, several lively artifacts, including the water-level interface, a messaging website (SnowDays), and an art-game (Passage), are examined. The study of each artifact starts with researchers' interpretive analysis, followed by experience prototyping and laboratory experiments involving users.

4.1   The Water-Level Mobile Interface

At the initial stage of use:

1.1 Perceiving affordances – The user perceives the subtle water movement on the interface of the phone in hand, and impulsively tilts the phone to see if the water is reactive.

1.2 Receiving quick feedback – The user sees the water moving in response to the tilt, forming a sensorimotor experience.

1.3 Triggering immediate blends – The tilt action and the reactive water movement look similar to the everyday act of holding a bottle of water. The phone is mapped to the bottle, the water graphics (including the waves and bubbles) to the real water. The immediate blend is an imaginary action of moving the water trapped inside the phone. The main gaps include the lack of weight-shifting during the tilt.

1.4 Becoming second nature – After receiving several incoming calls, the user gets used to shaking the phone for bubbles to cancel. The operation becomes second nature. The gaps like lack of weight-shifting become unnoticed.

At a later stage of use:

2.1 Noticing contingent changes – The user notices the drop in water level, and wonders how and why the water is gone.

2.2 Invoking interpretive frames – The drop prompts the user to invoke a frame about consumption. The user attributes the drop to battery consumption in which the level descends gradually without the act of drinking.

2.3 Elaborating metaphorical blends – With the consumption frame, the user sets up a mental space of a remembered or imagined scenario like having not enough water, food, or gasoline for the rest of a journey. The battery power is analogically mapped with the limited resource left. A possible metaphorical blend results in a parable that the "juice" in the phone is insufficient for today.

2.4 Reflecting on the situation – In the parable, the user understand he or she has consumed too much "juice". The user feels anxious and may try to "save the juice".

4.2   The SnowDays Website

SnowDays (snowdays.me) is a messaging website whose front page depicts a snowy scene in which each falling snowflake has been previously crafted by a web visitor

Fig. 2. Moving the mouse pointer over a snowflake opens a close-up view of it.

(with the tool provided by the site). When making a snowflake, one may leave a message "inside" it, and the recipient is notified. When a visitor gazes at the graphical scene and moves the mouse pointer over a particular falling flake, a close-up view of the flake pops up (see Fig. 2). One feels like catching and examining it. When the visitor uses the given tool to make a new flake, it is like doing folded paper cut.

At this initial stage, the cognitive processes include:

1.1 Perceiving affordances – The visitor sees an animation of paper folding and becomes aware that he or she is able to draw lines to "cut", by dragging the mouse pointer.

1.2 Receiving quick feedback – The visitor sees the six-sided symmetric graphic resulted from his or her drawing in real time. The coupling of action and perception forms the sensorimotor experience.

1.3 Triggering immediate blends – The folding of paper, drawing, symmetric graphic, and then typing messages all look familiar to the user, evoking the childhood memory of making origami cutouts or greeting cards. The symmetric graphic is mapped to the physical paper, drawing by mouse to cutting by scissors, and typing messages to writing messages. The immediate blend is an imaginary operation of crafting origami cutouts to send out over the Internet. The main gaps include the lack of physical action while sending the handicraft (just by clicking).

1.4 Becoming second nature – After crafting a few snowflakes, the user feels a sense of control. One becomes accustomed to the drawing dexterity and unaware of the gap between drawing on the touchpad and cutting with scissors, because of the immediate blend. The operation becomes second nature, and the user can focus on the creation process.

In fact, one may revisit the page, appreciate falling flakes, and respond any time. The background of the scene changes in color according to the time of day at the visitor's geographical region. At this later stage, the cognitive processes include:

2.1 Noticing contingent changes – The user notices the background color of the scene has changed, and feels amazed that the time of day in the virtual scene matches that in the user's time zone.

2.2 Invoking interpretive frames – The user invokes a frame about live broadcast, assuming that the virtual scene is current and live, just like live video streaming of a real nature scene.

2.3 Elaborating metaphorical blends – As the virtual snowfall is current, the falling flakes are newly created. The myriad different flakes in the virtual scene newly crafted by different people are analogically mapped with the countless, varied pieces emerging in the nature. One possible metaphorical blend yields an imaginary scenario that many people are currently making and presenting their crafts.

2.4 Reflecting on the situation – Through this frame, the user sees many different people currently in the show. One may want to make flakes and join now.

4.3 The Passage Game

Passage is an expressive art-game created by independent game designer Jason Roher. It presents the metaphor, "life is a journey," literally as a main horizontal walkway with many branches and obstacles (see Fig. 3). A player starts the game with a character walking alone. The character sprite (the on-screen graphic)'s screen position shifts toward the right at regular time intervals. The right end of the screen are purposely blurred and unfolded only when the character moves toward it. When the character bumps into a companion, the couple walks hand in hand and becomes unable to pass through many passageways and collect treasures, though still able navigate the major passage.

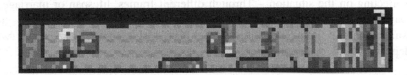

Fig. 3. A screenshot of passage showing a horizontal walkway with obstacles and the blurry right end.

At this initial stage of play:

1.1 Perceiving affordances – The pixel-graphic style suggests that the player uses the arrow keys on the keyboard or touchscreen to move the character up, down, left, or right.

1.2 Receiving quick feedback – The player sees the character moving in accordance with the key pressed or tapped. The coupling of pressing an arrow sign and seeing the corresponding movement forms the sensorimotor experience.

1.3 Triggering immediate blends – The four directional movements are a two-dimensional simulation of our everyday walking. The sliding of the character is mapped to one's strides, sliding right is moving ahead, moving up or down is turning left or right. If the character sticks with the companion, some passageways down south become too narrow to pass through. The width of the graphics is mapped to the physical width in the real world. The immediate blend is an imaginary possible walk around passageways and corners in the maze.

1.4 Becoming second nature – Just after a few strides and turns, one knows well the ability of walking through a passageway or not, with or without the companion. The user feels a sense of control.

Meanwhile, the character is depicted as increasingly older (going bald and grey, becoming hunched, etc.). The character's moving speed (the player only presses a key and has no control of the speed) is also decreasing. In 5 min, no matter what the player has done, the character sprite reaches the right end of the screen and dies. At this later stage of play, the cognitive processes include:

2.1 Noticing contingent changes – The player notices the subtle changes in the character appearance. More importantly, the slow motion makes the user feel hard to move and wonder what happens to the character.

2.2 Invoking interpretive frames – The curious changes prompt the user to invoke a frame about lifespan, in which every person is getting older and older as time goes by. It is the same for the character.

2.3 Elaborating metaphorical blends – Since the character is getting old and finally dies, the journey in the maze means his life. The right end is analogically mapped with the future, the left end is the past, the main horizontal straight walkway is the stable, typical type of life, the winding narrow passages down south is different alternative, adventurous styles of life, and the journey companion is the life companion. One possible metaphorical blend is that marriage limits possibility. In the scenario with a companion, a person cannot pass through many branches to explore and collect rewards.

2.4 Reflecting on the situation – Through different frames, lifespan or marriage, the player understand there are limitation or constraints. Marriage brings you a companion yet limits possibility. One may feel blessed or regretful, which depends on his or her attitude.

5 User Experience Studies

Laboratory experiments were conducted on each artifact or its prototype with one participant at a time. Each participant was involved in a set of activities, followed by an in-depth semi-structured interview. The activities, which took place in a usability study room, were designed to let participants experience the artifacts or prototypes for a period of time. We paid attention to what participants perceived, acted, felt, and thought via observations and interviews. Some findings of the studies have been published elsewhere [17, 18]. This paper is not to delineate the experiments in details, but to summarize major empirical findings in comparison with interpretive analyses for discussion.

5.1 The Water-Level Mobile Interface

20 participants (6 females and 14 males, 6 at the age between 18 and 25, 9 between 25 and 35, and 5 above 35) were involved. Each participant was asked to stay alone in a sitting room environment with a given iPhone with an audio content, which was intended to engage the participant. The phone came with a simulated implementation of the water-level interface. The participant was asked to cancel any incoming calls from

"Unknown caller" by shaking the phone. The participant was also reminded to "pay attention to the interface, which showed the battery level" (in exact wordings). The water surface started at a level of 70% on the screen and continuingly descended to the bottom in only 16 min.

5.2 The SnowDays Website

17 participants (12 females and 5 males, 10 at the age between 18 and 25, 6 between 25 and 35, and 1 above 35) were involved. Each participant was introduced to the website on a notebook computer and allowed to explore for a couple of minutes with think-aloud protocol. The participant was then asked about the first impression of it. The participant then spent 5 to 10 min to create a snowflake with the web tool, and send it to a real person. The interview then started. Lastly, the participant was required to re-visit the website at some other night, followed by answering another set of questions online

5.3 The Passage Game

The participant set is the same as that of SnowDays. Each participant played Passage for two rounds on a tablet computer. After each round, one had to describe the passage and differences between the two if any.

5.4 Major Findings

Interviews were semi-structured according to the outline of cognitive processes in two stages of use. We then transcribed all interviews and identified participants' quotes as chunks of expression and information. According to the corresponding interview questions, sometimes with individual participants' free digressions, and their contents and semantics, the quotes were categorized as signals of various cognitive processes and clustered into different cognitive phenomena, as seen in the following tables with example quotes (Tables 1, 2 and 3).

6 Discussion

Comparing the empirical findings with the researcher's interpretive analyses, we uncover the interpretation gap at different stages of use.

6.1 The Water-Level Mobile Interface

At the initial stage of use, 17 participants have thought of liquid containers implying hand interactions, while 10 participants have imagined fixed containers (some have mentioned both kinds). The lack of hand interactions in some interpretations is

Table 1. Participants' responses to the water-level interface, clustered into various cognitive phenomena.

Cognitive processes	Major responses
1.1 & 1.2	Tilted the phone arbitrarily and found the movement of the on-screen graphics (e.g. the blue line) seemingly responding to the phone orientation
1.3	Imagining liquid containers with hand interactions: – "Glass/cup/bottle of water", "juice box" – "Spirit level" – "Water inside goggles when swimming" – "Glass ball toys with water and maybe snowflakes inside" Imagining liquid containers without hand interactions: – "Fish tank/bowl", "aquarium" – "Swimming pool" – "Lava lamp"
1.4	Hesitant for a second about the first ring. Tried with the way and magnitude of shaking in order to cancel it. After the first call, reacted quickly by shaking the phone
2.1 & 2.2	Noticed the level drop and invoked different frames Leaking or draining: – "The line drained, ..." – "Pulling the plug of the sink and water drains" From draining to time passing: – "Hourglass" – "Deadlines, time is less and less, and one still has a lot of things to do"
2.3	Imagining drinking: – "I'm consuming the water" – "Drinking a glass of juice using straw" Imagining eating: – "Similar to a jar with lots of candies, and as you pick the candies, it gets empty" Imagining intangible consumption: – "Money becomes less and less with everyday shopping and eating" Imagining virtual consumption: – "Fighting games – energy bar to show how much energy the player got"
2.4	Imagining replenishment after consumption: – "Like hourglass, it's been empty out; I think if we flip it over, it will refill" – "Had I shake the phone longer, it'd have filled up the water!" Tried to save the battery: – Putting the phone horizontal to save the battery as "this turned the screen off" – Turning down the volume "to stop the water from leaking"

probably due to incomplete modalities represented by the interface. The interface shows visuals reactive to hand movements, yet there is no sound or force feedback. While the current mobile phone products have limitations in simulating the sense of

Table 2. Participants' responses to SnowDays, clustered into various cognitive phenomena.

Cognitive processes	Major responses
1.1 & 1.2	"Checking" the patterns and messages of different flakes, but not everyone excited
1.3	Remembering handicraft done in childhood with others, sticking on windows: – "In kindergarten, teacher would teach to fold the paper, cut and make snowflakes and stick on the window" Imagining putting up decorations: – "Traditional decoration for New Year, 'flowers on the window'" Imagining making a gift: – "It is more about putting thoughts rather than buying a gift"
1.4	Said they "catch" the flakes Excited about creating own flakes using the web tool: – "Extremely excited, entirely open to process of making"
2.1, 2.2	Noticed the color change in the background and assuming it was night. Invoking frames related to live connection: – "The virtual environment keeps changing with the real world"
2.3	Thinking of individual uniqueness: – "Some new snowflakes created by others … much more unique and meaningful" – "They represent many people on the world. Each one is unique"
2.4	Thinking of showing among people: – "Like the leaves on a wishing tree that everyone who uses this website can see what you wrote on it" – "It's a platform for strangers to view the artworks of others and make compliments although they don't know each other"

weight-shifting due to water flow, adding the sound of water flow can be a means to enhance the sensorimotor experience of moving a water-filled phone.

At later stages, due to the aforementioned nuances in initial interpretation, the frames invoked to explain the water-level drop are also varied. 12 participants have thought that the drop was a result of leaking, draining, or indicatively time passing as seen in an hourglass, which are different from the researcher interpretation. Meanwhile, 11 participants could associate with consumption, although the materials might be varied from beverage to food and even money. Whether it is leaking or consuming, changes over time are important to making such meaning.

6.2   The SnowDays Website

At the initial stage of use: Speaking of the flakes, 10 participants mentioned handmade decorations to be put up on windows, while only 6 participants mentioned handmade gifts. This shocking difference from the researcher interpretation may be because participants saw their creations immediately being shown in the snow scene, while the

Table 3. Participants' responses to passage, clustered into various cognitive phenomena.

Cognitive processes	Major responses
1.1 & 1.2	In the first round, wandering, feeling bored, confused In the second round, mildly excited about exploring the maze
1.3	Imaging exploring a city, an unfamiliar place, etc. – "Like exploring a city or when I am lost or unfamiliar to the place" Thinking of romance: – "Like falling in love with a totally random stranger" Thinking of companion: – "If you go out to eat as two people, you have to consider the other; if you go alone, you have more freedom and choices"
1.4	Get used to the navigation: – "With two persons, it was difficult to go to some places as they were too narrow"
2.1 & 2.2	Noticed the character's hair was changing in color, walking slower, hunched over, implicitly invoking the lifespan frame: – "Hair changed colors, character got bald, slowed down after the girl character died - definitely ageing"
2.3	Mapping journey companion to life companion: – "When you are alone, you are free, have more freedom but with wife and baby, have more responsibilities and also have to respect their thoughts" Mapping the passage to the life journey: – "Forward means no obstacles, no bonus, going down you get obstacles but you also get bonus" – "Left is more like going down the memory lane and right is future"
2.4	Reflecting on marriage: – "Marriage is like taking drugs. If you fall in love, you are like taking drugs. You are addicted to something or someone … The girl in the game was like a burden" On life companion: – "It is like a cooperation. You have lot of difficulties to face; you need a partner with something in similar, same aim for life so that you can cooperate" On life and death: – "Sad and helpless as it makes me think about death"

sent messages only received acknowledgment much later. Although both the falling flake and the message were processed immediately by the website, one's perception and attention are overwhelmed by the prominent snowfall scene, rather than by the message delivery. Perceived immediacy in feedback plays a crucial role at this immediate level of understanding.

At later stages of use, most participants noticed the color change in the background of the snow scene and assumed it was live and current. There was not much discrepancy from the researcher interpretation. On elaborating the metaphorical blends, 4 participants thought of individual uniqueness and 3 participants saw flakes as visible expression. The central thought seems to be about making one's unique expression visible to others. In other words, the idea of sending the flake to someone was further diluted and unnoticed. Instead, showing off to the public became major. This meaning is possible only when one revisits the website after some time and notices the changes.

6.3   The Passage Game

At the initial stage of use, only 4 participants could associate the maze exploration with their experiences of going to an unfamiliar place. Others probably just saw it another mundane maze game, until some unexpected changes emerged in their avatars. Their attentions were conversely caught by the coupling with another character and the walking hand-in-hand.

At later stages of use, a majority, 11 participants, was able to tell their avatars were getting old, not only because of the changing appearance, but surprisingly also due to the slowing down walking speed. The registration of the slowing down of the character is a much more noticeable change than the whitening hair or hunching over. The latter is limited by the pixel graphics representation, which could be less obvious to some users. The former conversely gives a direct change in the moving speed in response to the same user action (just pressing the key). This simple variation in displacement over time elicits powerful, embodied sense of decreasing motility in users, prompting the lifespan frame and enabling the metaphorical imagination.

7   Design Implications

After the discussion about the nuances between researcher and user interpretations, we come up with additional design guidelines or recommendations to narrow the gap.

Guideline 1: Aware of Limited Modalities in Sensory Feedback
Designers have to be aware of what forms of sensory perception are possible. Due to technical constraints or resource limitation, common sensory feedback today includes visuals, sounds, or vibrations. Other parameters like surface texture, temperature, and weight, are largely missed out. For the water-level interface, without a shift of gravity some participants could not associate the experience with hand interactions. While adding weight-shifting effect to a mobile phone may not be feasible, designers can add extra audiovisual effects to cover up the gap. For example, adding a straw in the interface reminds users of "drinking".

Guideline 2: Animate the Feedback for Meaning
Not only should feedback be quickly perceivable, the feedback that is crucial for meaning making has to be prominent, for example, by animating it. In the water-level interface, the reactive graphic representing the water surface flows continuously. In SnowDays, user action of sending a flake is immediately followed by the flake falling in the snow scene, rather than the message flying toward the recipient. This is the reason why our participants could not associate it with sending handmade gifts to someone; instead they were engrossed in the immediate presenting of their creations in the open space, which evoked the memory of putting up paper cutouts on windows.

Guideline 3: Changes in Intuitive, Interactive Forms
Changes may take many different forms. They can emerge in the visual, like the descending line in the water-level interface, the changing background color in SnowDays, or the changing appearance of the character in Passage. Other dimensions, like movement and interactivity, should also be considered. For example, the character in Passage starts to move slower in response to user action after "getting old". This changing speed scale between control and output proved intuitive to the participants in our study. To make the changes easy to notice and interpret, designers may consider more intuitive, interactive forms.

8 Conclusion

Lively artifacts enable interactions that are reminiscent of people's familiar sensori-motor experiences for understanding from the operational level to the reflective level. The changes in the processes of use look curious, prompting one to invoke different frames to explain them. Through reframing, one elaborates the initial blend and looks at things from different perspectives. This paper articulates the theoretical framework of liveliness and describes the analysis methodology, followed by demonstration. As the post-structuralist argument goes, meaning is never given, but instead made by readers, viewers, users, and people. Yet, as designers/researchers, we should not just leave interpretation completely open. We can speculate and collect possible interpretations with user participation, identify the intended meaning, and then try to narrow the spectrum. By comparing interpretive analyses and empirical results from user experience studies, in accordance with the proposed cognitive processes protocol, designers/researchers can identify the design components that probably influence interpretation.

Acknowledgments. We thank all the participants, and all publications support and staff, who wrote and provided helpful comments on previous versions of this document. We gratefully acknowledge the grant from Hong Kong General Research Fund (PolyU 5412/13H).

References

1. Mandler, J.M.: How to build a baby: II. Conceptual primitives. Psychol. Rev. **99**(4), 587–604 (1992)
2. Lakoff, G.: Women, Fire, and Dangerous Things: What Categories Reveal About the Mind, p. xvii, 614 p. University of Chicago Press, Chicago (1987)
3. Johnson, M.: The Body in the Mind: The Bodily Basis of Meaning, Imagination, and Reason, p. xxxviii, 233 p. University of Chicago Press, Chicago (1987)
4. Lakoff, G., Johnson, M.: Metaphors We Live By, p. xiii, 276 p. University of Chicago Press, Chicago (2003)
5. Turner, M.: The Literary Mind, p. viii, 187 p. Oxford University Press, New York (1996)

6. Fauconnier, G., Turner, M.: The Way We Think: Conceptual Blending and the Mind's Hidden Complexities, p. xvii, 440 p. Basic Books, New York (2002)
7. Fauconnier, G., Mental Spaces: Aspects of Meaning Construction in Natural Language, p. xlvi, 190 p. Cambridge University Press, Cambridge (1994)
8. Minsky, M.: A Framework for Representing Knowledge, Cambridge, Mass (1974)
9. Fillmore, C.J.: Frames and the semantics of understanding. Quaderni di Semantica **VI**(2), 222–254 (1985)
10. Coulson, S.: Semantic Leaps: Frame-Shifting and Conceptual Blending in Meaning Construction, p. xiii, 304 p. Cambridge University Press, Cambridge (2001)
11. Fauconnier, G., Turner, M.: Rethinking metaphor. In: Gibbs, R.W. (ed.) The Cambridge Handbook of Metaphor and Thought, pp. 53–66. Cambridge University Press, New York (2008)
12. Coulson, S., Fauconnier, G.: Fake guns and stone lions: conceptual blending and privative adjectives. In: Fox, B., Jurafsky, D., Michaelis, L. (eds.) Cognition and Function in Language. CSLI, Palo Alto (1999)
13. Imaz, M., Benyon, D.: Designing With Blends: Conceptual Foundations of Human-Computer Interaction and Software Engineering, p. xi, 229 p. MIT Press, Cambridge (2007)
14. Dourish, P.: Where the Action is: The Foundations of Embedded Interaction. MIT Press, Cambridge (2001)
15. Sengers, P., Gaver, B.: Staying open to interpretation: engaging multiple meanings in design and evaluation. In: DIS 2006 Proceedings of the 6th Conference on Designing Interactive Systems, University Park, Pennsylvania, USA (2006)
16. Fleck, R., Fitzpatrick, G.: Reflecting on reflection: framing a design landscape. In: OZCHI 2010, Brisbane, Australia (2010)
17. Chow, K.K.N., Harrell, D.F., Wong, K.Y., Kedia, A.: Provoking imagination and emotion with a lively mobile phone: a user experience study. Interact. Comput. **28**(4), 451–461 (2015)
18. Chow, K.K.N., Harrell, D.F., Kedia, A., Wong, K.Y.: A cognitive and interpretive approach to imaginative and affective user experiences: two empirical studies of lively interactive artifacts. In: IASDR 2015, Brisbane (2015)

Thinking in Interdisciplinary Design Teams
Based on Workshop

Ying Hu[✉], Ying Li, and Xing Du

Hunan University School of Design, Changsha, China
dkm88@163.com

Abstract. The era we are facing today, pushing design to the process of paradigm shift, the transformation of thinking is particularly important, so mindset shifting become an inevitable problem. In order to study the shifting of mindset, this research launched a "fair-themed" extending over 2 days' workshop. Four teams solving a service design problem in workshop have been studied, which providing us with the empirical observation of how teams change their mindset from industrial thinking to service thinking. Firstly, we find the trigger point and push point of mindset shifting, and then we examine the factors work on (spur, accelerate or delay) this process. Multiple, coordinated research methods, including spot observations, structured interviews, oral analysis were used. we would like to provide a reference for cultivating the interdisciplinary talents in the information era.

Keywords: Mindset shifting · Transformation nodes · Interaction behavior · Knowledge sharing · Boundary spanning

1 Introduction

Service Design is an emerging, new holistic, multi-disciplinary, integrative field focused on the creation of well thought through experiences using a combination of intangible and tangible mediums. Service design as a new domain, emphasizes multidisciplinary cooperation in order to make it possible to innovative and competitive co-creation, and with the characteristics of brand-new, strong integrity. It combines different methods and tools from various disciplines. It is a new way of thinking as opposed to a new stand-alone academic discipline. Service design as a practice generally results in the design of systems and processes aimed at providing a holistic service to the user. This cross-disciplinary practice combines numerous skills in design, management and process engineering [1].

Service design in essence is a kind of design thinking mindset. Industrial thinking is characterized by tangible, visible, product-related, and dominated by function and visual performance. While, service thinking is intangible, invisible, emphasizing service flow process, whole system, and putting user experience in the first place. The era we are facing today, makes the design into the process of paradigm shift, which requires designers to change design thinking from tangible to intangible. It is in essence a change of design thinking. Therefore, whether in the field of design or in the field of education, the transformation of thinking is particularly important, so mindset shifting

© Springer International Publishing AG 2017
A. Marcus and W. Wang (Eds.): DUXU 2017, Part I, LNCS 10288, pp. 60–70, 2017.
DOI: 10.1007/978-3-319-58634-2_5

becomes an inevitable problem. A mindset is dynamic. It tends to expand into complexity by a widening process and shrink into simplicity by a narrowing process. Switching from one set of cognitions to another is a universal nature of human mind, although there are marked differences in the nature and extent of switching as a function of, among other factors, cultural imperatives [2]. The thinking process of designers is one of the most important issues in design research [3]. The thinking activity of designers is a brain activity, which can not be directly observed and described; Trying to analysis the thinking process and mindset of designers, difficulties occur because we have no direct measures to inspect the process in the designer's brain. Besides the implicity, design thinking also has complex, fine-grained, dynamic features. This bringing huge challenges to the research of design thinking.

The creation of innovative service design often requires the exploration and integration of dynamic and diverse knowledge from multiple domains, disciplines and contexts among specialists. In the field of service design, it is widely acknowledged that design teams increasingly include participants from different domains who must explore and integrate their specialized knowledge in order to create innovative and competitive services. These participants come to the design situation with pre-existing patterns of work activities, specialized work languages. Participants' unique past experiences, specialized work language, and differences in work patterns, perceptions of quality and success, organizational priorities, and technical constraints may cause them to challenge or contest one another's contribution. This phenomenon, characterized as 'contested collaboration' [4], can lead to conflict and has a negative impact on the quality of the design process and design outcomes. Design participants need to explore and integrate these differences. Thus communication, including integration of specialized knowledge and negotiation of differences among team participants, has emerged as a fundamental component of the design process. Human communication is a dynamic process in which one person consciously or unconsciously affects the cognition of another through materials or agencies in symbolic ways. The effectiveness of design communication becomes critical for designers in sharing design information, in decision-making and coordinating design tasks. The necessity of communication is based on the possibility of different cognition of representations by different participants as well as conveying new information [5]. Thus, good team communication can promote the transformation of design thinking. Language-based communication has been argued to play a principal role although the structuring of communication as scaffolds for knowledge construction has never been measured directly [6].

During the design process, team participants often sharing knowledge about the current (and evolving) task, service context, design context, stemming from their past knowledge. Participant's knowledge sharing behaviors (KSBs), making the experience or knowledge of one unit transmitted to the other unit. And knowledge sharing is considered as a process in which one unit is affected by the knowledge and expertise of another unit. Sharing knowledge is an important process in enhancing organizational innovativeness and performance. A research was conducted by Rivera-Vazquez et al. [13] to investigate overcoming cultural barriers for innovation and knowledge sharing [7]. To a certain extent, it will accelerate the transformation of the design thinking of the whole team and affect the final design output. The concept of knowledge sharing is getting more and more attention in the research and practice of knowledge management

[8]. Wang et al. [12] aimed to study the impact of knowledge sharing on firm performance and the mediating role of intellectual capital. Kumar and Rose [14] examined the factors that contribute to knowledge sharing behavior, Kamaşak and Bulutlar [15] explored the effects of knowledge sharing on innovation [7]. The sharing of system structure and task knowledge positively and significantly influence task performance and group performance, whereas interpersonal relationship knowledge sharing positively and significantly influences group performance.

2   Method

In this paper, our purpose is to find factors works on the mindset shifting by launching and focusing on the "fair-themed" extending over 2 days' workshop, which provided us with the empirical observation of how teams change their mindset from industrial thinking to service thinking and its influential factors (spurred, accelerated or delayed the mindset shifting process).

2.1   Participants

A total of 17 graduate students (mean age: 22.764 years, SD: 0.831, male: 5, female: 12) participated in the workshop extending over 2 days. All participants (come from different design backgrounds, including Industrial Design, Visual Communication Design, Furniture Design and Mechanical Design, Automation, etc. mainly major in industrial domain) had no service design background and were divided into four groups (g1 to g4), g1, g2, g3 each consisting of four participants, g4 five participants, and were required to design a service system based on the theme of "fairness". No participant was assigned any particular role in the task.

2.2   Procedure

The main purpose of this workshop is to find how participants and groups change their mindset from industrial thinking to service thinking, and factors accelerated or slowed this transformation process. To spur the transformation of mindset, the teacher will preach some basic features, introduce some tools and methods, and related knowledge of service design to participants. Besides, give comments on each group's design outcomes of each stage. This "fair-themed" workshop is divided into the following stages:

Stage 1, Case Finding Period: Participants were required to find unfair cases in the field of service design.

Teacher A preached "individual-stakeholders-local community-society", guided participants change their design concerns from individual to stakeholders and local community, even to society and the world, take more considerations about the system and service ecosystem. Teacher B preached "product & experience & service" (PES) flow chart, intended to change participants' focus from product itself to user experience, and then transit from user-experience centered mindset gradually to a service ecosystem that users and service providers are both satisfied. Besides, introduce brainstorming methods to participants.

Stage 2, Pain Point and Context Period: Participants used brainstorming to make a deeper exploration, to dig out the situation and pain points behind these unfair cases. Made clear of problem scope and generated preliminary design opportunities.

Two teachers (A+B) made comments on the outcomes of each group in stage 2. Introduce Customer Journal Map, Value Statement to participants.

Stage 3, Solution and Rank Period: Participants took comprehensive consideration of all kinds of stakeholders, and used Customer Journal Map, proposed solutions revolve around the problem scope, and write Value Statement of solutions. Then made a comparison and rank among those various solutions and choose the optimal one.

Two teachers made comments on the solutions of each group in stage 3. Introduce story board and business canvas methods to participants.

Stage 4, Complete and Perfect Solution Period: Completed and perfected the selected solution, submitted the final design.

Two teachers made comments on the final solutions of each group in stage 4.

PS: There were presentations after each stage, each group presented their periodical outcomes.

2.3 Date and Analysis

This study applies grounded theory to examine the factors involved in the process of mindset shifting. Grounded theory is emphasized that conclusion must be traced back to the original data, must be based on empirical facts. In this research we utilized data from actual workshop and participants to develop systematic theories. Firstly, we collected all the original documents (such as sketches, brainstorming maps, power point slides, etc.), and we also recorded the video of each group's presentation (there were presentations after each stage, 4 * 4 totally 16 segment videos). Secondly, we took the approach of spot observation (real time and dynamic observation of each group's design process), some findings were observed and recorded in time. Thirdly, we conducted 30 min. long structured interviews with 8 participants (each group selected 2 participants) at the end of this workshop. This 'retrospective' research aimed to examine each group's design process and mindset shifting more deeply. Examples of studies that have taken this approach include Curtis et al. [9] Peng [10]. Finally, we used "oral analysis" approach to analyze the aforementioned interview materials.

3 Results

In this study, we use the aforementioned methods to examine the process of mindset shifting and factors worked on this process in the real workshop. The members of the four teams come from different design backgrounds, mainly from industrial design, and no one from the service design background. Thus they must to break the original industrial mindset and transform to service thinking mindset to give a satisfying service solution. After empirical observations combine with deep analysis of dates, we primarily find that all groups have successfully transformed into service design thinking mindset through this workshop. While the speed and quality of the transformation of each group is not the same. There are some factors can accelerate or slow mindset shifting process, and affect the quality of transformation, and thus affect the final design outcomes.

Figure 1 shows each groups' mindset transformation process in workshop.

GROUPS	ISLS	PES	Brainstorming	Comments	Customer Journal Map	Value Statement	Comments	Story Board	Business Canvas	Comments
G1	▶	☺	▶	▶	▶	▶	▶	▶	▶	▶
G2	▶	▶	▶	☺	▶	▶	▶	▶	▶	▶
G3	▶	▶	▶	▶	▶	▶	☺	▶	▶	▶
G4	▶	▶	▶	▶	▶	▶	▶	▶	▶	▶

☺ Trigger point   ▶ Driving point

Fig. 1. Four groups' mindset transformation process in workshop

3.1 The Drive Point and Trigger Point of Mindset Shifting

Figure 1 shows that there are two key nodes which play an important role in the process of mindset shifting. One is "Driving point", a quantitative transformation node, which means service design mindset to be continuously strengthened while original thinking mindset to be weakened. Another is "Trigger point", a qualitative transformation node, means completely jumping out of the original mindset and growing into service mindset. Figure 1 also shows that the trigger point and driving point of each team are very different and the speed of mindset transformation is not the same.

G1's trigger point was spurred by teacher's preaching of PES flow chart (Product-Experience-Service). In case finding period, G1 mainly found product-related cases, focusing on the unfair situations caused by product itself. After the preach of PES, G1 gradually transited to service design thinking, they understood that product is one part of the service flow, is a touch point of service eco-system. Thus G1 gradually considered design problem with the system thinking. For G2 and G3, their mindset shifting was both spurred by teachers' comments. After stage 1 and stage 2, they all failed to transform their mindset to service thinking. Their mindset was still limited in the area of product design. Pain points and contexts that G2 had proposed, were all focused on the improvement or redesign of one product, falling into the black hole of product. While G2 started the transformation process after listening to teachers' comments on their outcomes of Pain point and Context period. Instead of transformation, G3 continue caught into "product" black hole until the end of stage 3, when teachers gave comments on their design solutions. G4, before case finding period, G4 participants searched the definition of service design and gathered some existed service cases, applied this definition and cases to their own design scheme in later design process. Thus, at the beginning of this workshop, G4 already started to use service thinking to solve unfair service problems. Therefore, G4 had no clear trigger point in this work-shop. Moreover, because they were too dependent on the searched definition and cases, their mindset was framed, showing low activity. Driving Point can strengthen service design thinking and accelerate transformation process. Tools such as customer journal map and business canvas, helped participants to think design problems with service thinking.

Figure 2 shows mindset shifting process of four groups.

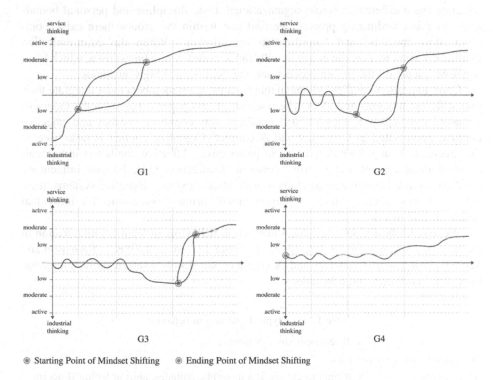

⊚ Starting Point of Mindset Shifting   ⊚ Ending Point of Mindset Shifting

Fig. 2. Mindset shifting process of four groups

We also find that G2 and G3 both caught into the "product" black hole at the beginning, and their trigger point were all teachers' comments. There existed industrial design thinking and service design thinking at the beginning, and then completely transformed into the service design thinking. However, the trigger point of G2 is earlier than G3, and service thinking is more active than G3. What factors affect the rate and quality of transformation of thinking in the team?

3.2   Intragroup Interactions in Design Collaboration

In order to study factors that affect the speed of mindset shifting, we use oral analysis to analyze structured-interview materials, and combine with the natural observation of participants' behavior in workshop. Authors took communication and interaction behaviors among team members as the breakthrough point. Participants' unique past experiences, specialized work language, and differences in work patterns, etc. may cause them to challenge or contest one another's contribution. This phenomenon, characterized as 'contested collaboration'. Team members need to coordinate and integrate these differences across organizational, task, discipline and personal boundaries. In this coordinating process, we find that within the groups there exist 'communication conflicts' and 'coordination breakdowns'. When the communication conflict escalates to a certain extent, it will lead to coordination breakdown, which has a negative impact on the design process and the quality of design outcomes.

Communication conflicts are inevitable because team members must integrate their own different thoughts and ideas. The research of this paper is based on the theory of Amason and Sapienza, they divided conflicts into cognitive conflict and affective conflict, abbreviated as C conflict and A conflict. Cognitive conflict is task-oriented disagreement arising from differences in perspective. Affective conflict is individual-oriented disagreement arising from personal disaffection [11]. Factors influencing conflicts include communication skills of individuals, existing incentive systems, team emotional atmosphere, different representational formats, and norms for individual behavior, and mores.

We eventually dig out five typical interaction behaviors of team communication in the context of design situation. As shows in Table 1. And on the basis of Amason and Sapienza's research (C conflict and A conflict), we deeply analyze those interaction behaviors' attributes and orientations.

Table 1. Five typical interaction behavior

		A, B represent some person(s)
No-communication breakdown		
PS	Idea persuade	A attempt to change B's thoughts, attitudes, aims at letting B accept A's idea. Result usually shows that A's idea are reserved while B's discarded
IG	Idea integration	A, B integrate their own existing idea through discussion and coordination
		Result usually shows that the generation of idea (A+B)
CB	Idea co-building	A, B have no idea, but through cooperation, construct a new idea together
		Results usually shows that the generation of brand-new idea C
Appear communication breakdown		
IR	Idea ignorance	Have no interests on others' idea or proposal, A, B have no mutual interaction, develop independent
AT	Idea attack	Blindly deny other's views

Orientations: The reason behind behavior is divided into cognition-oriented or emotional-oriented.

Attributes: In order to distinguish the role of those intragroup interactions, we further analyze attributes behind them. We concluded that there are three attributes, respectively:

1. Aggressive, usually time-consuming and inefficient, such as Idea Persuade.
2. Constructive, foster productive, conducive to the creation of more good ideas, promote the design process, such as idea integration, idea co-building.
3. Conflictive, the ideas or actions of one are either resisted by or unacceptable to another. Usually leads to friction, disagreement, or discord arising within a group. Such as idea ignorance, idea attack.

Based on the time axis of the workshop, intragroup interactions of 4 groups are showed in Fig. 3.

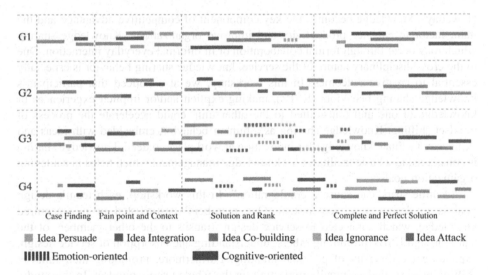

Fig. 3. Intragroup interaction behaviors of 4 groups

Results show that the high-performance group, they have more complex interactive behavior network, and constructive behavior is always interwoven within it. Moreover, frequency and intensity of constructive behaviors were significantly better than that of ordinary groups. Besides, most of this constructive interactions are cognition-oriented, few is based on emotion.

On the contrary, interactions within ordinary group, often shows high frequency on idea persuade, idea ignorance and idea attack. Besides, intragroup communication conflicts are mainly emotional oriented. However, emotional oriented interaction often leads to lengthy and invalid arguments, and further leads to tension, confrontation, hostility and other negative emotions in group. The most typical one is G3, in stage 2, pain point and context period, team members start to appear aggressive and conflictive interactions, but those are mainly based on cognitive orientation. While in stage 3, solution and rank period, constructive interactions are disappeared and replaced by emotional oriented aggressive and conflictive interactions (mainly idea persuade, idea attack and idea ignorance), accompanied with coordination breakdowns. This high frequency of emotional based aggressive and conflict interactions leads to bad atmosphere within group. The result is that group splits into two opposites, the two parties dispute and do not compromise.

High frequency of emotional oriented aggressive and conflictive interactions, and low frequency of cognitional oriented constructive interactions, may explain why G2's mindset shifting process is faster and better than G3. In this part, we conclude that emotional oriented interactions can hinder the shifting of mindset, and constructive interactions can improve design efficiency and influence the final design outcomes.

3.3   Knowledge Sharing

Nowadays, knowledge becomes the key component of competitive advantage and the main factor to enhance productivity and improve organizations. Knowledge sharing which may occur through formal collaboration or in informal everyday interaction. Due to the cross disciplinary nature of the service, knowledge sharing behavior is especially essential to creative outcomes. In this workshop, we also noticed that participant's knowledge sharing behaviors (KSBs), making explicit and/or implicit experiences or knowledge of one unit transmitted to the other unit, could accelerate the process of mindset shifting. Knowledge sharing as a human behavior, embedded with ideas and skills, can facilitate knowledge for innovation at workplace. Indeed, knowledge sharing is considered as a basic facilitator for knowledge management which helps in achieving organization goals.

"A little spark can cause a conflagration". In this workshop, each team's design goal is to design a service system. One members' past-existed or new-acquired knowledge, which connected to service design, transits to the other members of the team through KSBs, promoting others' understanding and absorption of service design, expanding the diversity of personal thinking. Furthermore, promoting their mindset shifting process, and eventually impacting on the whole team's mindset. In this study, we found that in high-performance group, their KSBs were significantly abundant than ordinary groups. The most typically is G1, the amount of KSBs is significantly higher than other groups. And one member of G1 has participated in a service project, her KSBs greatly promote the whole team's mindset shifting. And these frequently KSBs also improve the quality of thinking transformation.

Thus, we concluded that the more frequencies of knowledge sharing behavior and the more complex of sharing network, the faster the process of mindset shifting. While, the thin spread of application domain knowledge will inhibit the transformation of team's mindset and affect the design output.

3.4 Boundary Spanning

In this workshop, participants are asked to think outside the box of industrial design and think about the design problem with service thinking. That means participants must jump out the circle of industrial design and jump into the circle of service design. And we define this behavior as "boundary spanning". Research also shows that groups who have trans-boundary movements tend to have higher thinking activity than those who haven't. The most typical is G4, at the beginning of this workshop, G4 already started to use service thinking to solve unfair service problems. Thus this group did not go through boundary spanning, unlike other groups with multiple switching from industrial domain to service domain (or from service domain to industrial domain). G4 participants searched the definition of service design and gathered some existed service cases, applied this definition and cases to their own design scheme in later design process. However, we find that G4's mindset seems to be framed and level of thinking activity is low, the reserve strength for innovation are weak. Although G4 is the first group to complete the process of mindset shifting, while the quality of the mindset shifting is inferior to other groups.

Results from these studies positively relate high boundary spanning activity to high project performance. Groups who have gone through boundary spanning, could understand the difference between service design and industrial design more deeply, and the final design output is more inclined to service, and with higher quality. Instead, non-boundary spanning groups, their thinking activity shows inactive, and their final outputs is inferior to high-boundary spanning groups.

4 Conclusion

In this research we utilize data from actual workshop, design participants to develop systematic theories. In this "Design for fairness" workshop, 4 teams' mindset shifting process are studied. Firstly, we find that all groups have successfully transformed into service design thinking mindset through this workshop. And there are two key nodes which play an important role in the process of mindset shifting. One is "Driving point" and another is "Trigger point". Moreover, the trigger point and driving point of each team differed significantly and the speed of mindset transformation is not the same. Then we further analyze intragroup communications and interactions, dig out five typical interaction behaviors of team communication in the context of design situation, 3 attributes (aggressive, constructive, conflictive) and 2 orientations (emotion-oriented, cognition-oriented). Results show that the efficiency and effective of mindset shifting significantly are influenced by intragroup communications and interactions. High frequency of constructive interactions, low frequency of aggressive and conflictive interactions will promote the efficiency of mindset shifting. Besides, emotion-oriented interactions are negatively correlated, cognition-oriented interactions are positively with the shifting effectiveness. In this workshop, we also noticed that the more frequent knowledge sharing behavior and the more complex the sharing network, the faster the process of mindset shifting. Finally, results from these studies positively relate high boundary spanning activity to high project performance and high mindset transformation.

There are some limitations. First, as the sample size of this study consisted of only 4 groups, significant findings should be interpreted with caution. Moreover, the efficiency and effectiveness of various trigger point and driving point was not well researched and requires further study. However, our results are instructive for mindset shifting, and bear implications for training and practice in education and design related fields. We would like to provide a reference for cultivating the interdisciplinary talents in the information era.

Acknowledgement. Grateful thanks to all participants of this workshop. Their time, active participation and valuable feedback greatly assisted the development of this research. And we also thank Colin M. Gray, assistant Professor, Purdue University, his participation and meticulous guidance during this workshop. This research is supported by National Science and technology support program (2015BAH22F02) and Hunan Province Education Science "13th Five-Year" program (XJK016QGD003). We also gratefully acknowledge their financial support.

References

1. Stickdorn, M.: This is service design thinking (2011)
2. Sinha, J.B.P.: Psycho-social Analysis of the Indian Mindset. Springer, Berlin (2014)
3. Stempfle, J., Badke-Schaub, P.: Thinking in design teams - an analysis of team communication. Des. Stud. **23**(5), 473–496 (2002)
4. Sonnenwald, D.H.: Communication roles that support collaboration during the design process. Des. Stud. **17**(3), 277–301 (1996)
5. Chiu, M.L.: An organizational view of design communication in design collaboration. Des. Stud. **23**(2), 187–210 (2002)
6. Dong, A.: The latent semantic approach to studying design team communication. Des. Stud. **26**(5), 445–461 (2005)
7. Masa'deh, R.: Knowledge Sharing Capability: A Literature Review, vol. 4. Social Science Electronic Publishing (2016)
8. Yi, J.: A measure of knowledge sharing behavior: scale development and validation. Knowl. Manage. Res. Pract. **7**(1), 65–81 (2009)
9. Curtis, B., Krasner, H., Iscoe, N.: A field study of the software design process for large systems. Commun. ACM **31**(11), 1268–1287 (1988)
10. Peng, C.: Exploring communication in collaborative design: co-operative architectural modelling. Des. Stud. **15**(1), 19–44 (1994)
11. Amason, A.C., Sapienza, H.J.: The effects of top management team size and interaction norms on cognitive and affective conflict. J. Manage.: Official J. South. Manage. Assoc. **23**(4), 495–516 (1997)
12. Wang, Z., Wang, N., Liang, H.: Knowledge sharing, intellectual capital and firm performance. Manag. Decis. **52**(3), 230–258 (2014)
13. Rivera-Vazquez, J., Ortiz-Fournier, L., Flores, F.: Overcoming cultural barriers for innovation and knowledge sharing. J. Knowl. Manage. **13**(5), 257–270 (2009)
14. Kumar, N., Rose, R.C.: The impact of knowledge sharing and Islamic work ethic on innovation capability. Cross Cult. Manage. **19**(2), 142–165 (2012). doi:10.1108/13527601211219847
15. Kamaşak, R., Bulutlar, F.: The influence of knowledge sharing on innovation. Eur. Bus. Rev. **22**(3), 306–317 (2010). doi:10.1108/09555341011040994

Digitization of the Design Thinking Process Solving Problems with Geographically Dispersed Teams

Christoph Lattemann[1], Dominik Siemon[2], David Dorawa[1(✉)], and Beke Redlich[1]

[1] Jacobs University Bremen, Bremen, Germany
{c.lattemann, d.dorawa, b.redlich}@jacobs-university.de
[2] Braunschweig University of Technology, Brunswick, Germany
d.siemon@tu-braunschweig.de

Abstract. In a globalized world, collaboration within geographically dispersed team members is becoming more important due to the possibilities given by information systems and the increase in productivity of knowledge workers. Design Thinking is a creative innovation method that is originally performed to enable participants to collaborate successfully in analog workshops. By referring to this initial situation, we hypothesize that a virtual Design Thinking platform can be at least as effective for generating creative innovations as an analog one, if the platform and the underlying processes are designed in an adequate way that enables collaboration and communication.

The key question in this research is, consequently, how a virtual Design Thinking platform should be designed to enable effective real-time communication and collaboration like in regular face-to-face Design Thinking workshops.

As the guiding approach for our methodology, we apply a Design Science Research approach. In the first section of this paper, we introduce the problem statement as well as a detailed motivation of our research project. Following, we present latest research on telework, virtual collaboration, and Design Thinking as the underlying foundation for our propositions. In section three, we introduce our methodological research approach, introducing our artifact – a virtual Design Thinking platform – and finally presenting our case study and survey results. Subsequently, we discuss the findings vis-à-vis recent research findings and draw conclusions. We can reveal that our virtual Design Thinking platform is applicable for virtual collaboration and team members can produce a valuable, creative and innovative solution in less time than working face-to-face.

Keywords: Design Thinking · Innovation · Virtual teams · Collaboration

1 Introduction

Due to the continuous development of information systems (IS), digitization is shifting the workforce towards an economy that generates value through digital work [1]. Furthermore, information and communication technologies (ICT) enable remote work.

© Springer International Publishing AG 2017
A. Marcus and W. Wang (Eds.): DUXU 2017, Part I, LNCS 10288, pp. 71–88, 2017.
DOI: 10.1007/978-3-319-58634-2_6

Research show that remote work increases knowledge workers' work-life balance and productivity, saves time on commuting to work, decreases pollution and attracts qualified workers across the world [2, 3]. The primary reason why knowledge workers support remote work is based on the empirically proven fact that it increases productivity, job satisfaction, employee's time flexibility and lower expenses [2].

In a globalized, ICT supported work environment remote work of geographically dispersed teams is becoming more important [4]. To cope with contemporary requirements for collaboration, ICT tools, which support virtual teamwork are becoming a necessity for companies [5–8]. Research show that remote work performs over regular office work, when there is a need for uninterrupted concentration on one task [3].

De Vreede and Briggs [9] state that collaborative processes must be strictly designed, so that teams can achieve a common goal. Hence, remote teams need structured collaborative processes in order to develop an innovative solution for the customer relating to the common goal that needs to be achieved [9]. Design Thinking (DT) is one strictly designed, user-centered, creative and collaborative innovation method that has proven to be successful during analogue face-to-face co-work settings [10, 11]. A user-centered innovation collaborative method, such as DT, lowers the risks of creating unwanted results and consequently, risks concerning the implementation of innovations are reduced [12].

To guarantee that a DT team performs well, specially trained moderators/coaches must set up, organize, and guide the team in a sound way [10, 13]. However, coaching and moderating in a virtual environment is much more complex than in a face-to-face environment, and it require adequately designed supporting ICT tools (platform) and functionalities [14]. In this paper, we propose that virtually performed DT can, despite the difficulties that come with virtual collaboration, be as effective as DT performed in an analog environment, if adequately designed supporting ICT tools are used. In order to test this proposition, we develop and test the effectiveness of a virtual DT platform.

As the underlying approach for our paper, we follow the principles of Design Science Research (DSR) [15] by structuring our research accordingly: – introduction, literature review, method, artifact description, evaluation, discussion, and conclusions. DSR has proven its applicability in IS and guarantees a general approach to develop and evaluate artifacts [16]. Consequently, the introduction is followed by the review of relevant research in related fields, which are in this case telework, virtual collaboration, and Design Thinking. The research streams and their findings serve as a foundation for the development of the artifact and formulation of propositions. The section is followed by the presentation and explanation of our methodological approach. Following the seven guidelines of DSR, we introduce and evaluate our artifact – a virtual DT platform. The evaluation is based on a case study and a survey.

In the closing section, we discuss our findings vis-à-vis prior research findings. Eventually, we conclude and give answer to our key research question: How effective can a virtual DT platform perform compared to face-to-face Design Thinking?

2 Related Work

In order to build an appropriate artifact and to define the propositions of our research project, related work is reviewed. To gain insights, we present and discuss research findings on remote work/telework, virtual collaboration, and Design Thinking. These three perspectives will be discussed separately and fuse our research framework.

2.1 Remote Work/Telework

Martin and MacDonnell [17] define telework as the "substitution of communication technology for work-related travel [...it...] can include work from home, a satellite office, a telework center or any other work station outside of the main office [...]" [17, p. 603].

Due to the advancements of IS, people can work from a distance and still be within the structure of an organizational framework of a company [18]. Harpaz [18] states that a ""telecommuter" can structure his/her work tasks and working life in many ways – dependent on the nature of the work, the organization, the customer-base, etc." [18, p. 75]. The difference between "telecommuters" is a variable degree of "remoteness" – "the ratio of time spent on organizational premises versus the time spent at home" [18, p. 75]. Remote work and telework are interchangeable terms which appoint to employees, who work from a distance, while being connected via ICT within the organizational framework of a company [2, 18, 19].

One of teleworks primary advantages is the potential increase in productivity which can range from 10% to 40% on average [2]. The main reason for an increase in productivity is that teleworkers can choose their working hours flexibly without any disturbances from colleagues [2] and time lost for travel [18]. But telework comes also with disadvantages, such as no separation between home and work, a need for self-discipline or the over-availability syndrome [18]. Apart from the high increase in productivity, an organization faces also some risks when letting employees telework such as a possible loss of commitment, investment in training and new supervising methods [18]. Harpaz [18] concludes that advantages of telework outweigh the disadvantages. Furthermore, not only single teleworkers, but virtual teams, composed of teleworkers, can outperform normal (non-virtual) teams [19].

2.2 Virtual Collaboration

Collaboration is considered when at least two or more people are working on the same problem to achieve a shared goal [20]. According to Nunamaker [21], collaboration encourages to be more creative and therefore innovative solutions can be presented. In the past, collaboration has been geographically determined to one physical place. With recent technological advancements, it has been possible to collaborate remotely and simultaneously [21, 22].

The fast paced business environment needs individuals who are able to generate innovative ideas in order for companies to remain competitive on the global market [23].

One way to enhance the generation of creative ideas, is the implementation of ICT that fosters idea generation within a company [23]. During a controlled experiment, Massetti [23] has found out that ICT enhance the creative performance of individuals, while generating more novel ideas than with a pen and paper. Teams connected virtually together via ICT are called "virtual teams" [24] and the process is called "virtual teaming" [24]. Virtual teams, who are focusing on the customer's needs while generating great solutions in the today's competitive economy, have high chances of succeeding [24].

Voigt and Bergener [25] argue that the majority of creative work is done in teams, rather than by individuals. Companies are understanding creativity as a competitive advantage and strategic asset [26] and that is why they often choose to apply ICT to enhance creative collaboration [27]. From an IS perspective, a focus is set towards designing systems which are supporting teams at developing creative ideas [25]. In order to create such a system that focuses on the development of creative ideas, De Vreede and Briggs [9] state that collaborative processes must be strictly designed, so that teams understand each phase of the collaborative process and can achieve a common goal. Such a collaborative and strictly designed innovation process can be referred to as Design Thinking [10].

2.3 Design Thinking - A Method for Innovation Management

DT is a creative and user-centered innovation method to solve complex/wicked problems within multidisciplinary teams [28–30]. Due to the fact that DT is a human/user-centered problem solving approach, empathy is the foundation since it reveals the core needs and real problem statements [28, 31]. During the entire DT process, a focus is set towards the user's needs, starting with understanding and observing the problem and the user, redefining the problem statement from a user perspective, continuing with the generation of ideas and ending with the creation of a product, service or process that is tested [29]. For each phase there exist multiple methods and tools that can be applied to enhance the creation of new ideas, understand the problem or prototype [1]. Additionally, the DT approach inherits a mindset, which acts as a framework of requirements to secure the quality of a DT process [32, 33]. The DT mindset involves aspects such as user-centeredness, creativity, iteration, multidisciplinarity, creativity, co-creation and space aspects, etc. [10, 28, 34–37]. Especially, while performing DT workshops, the design of the space and surroundings, such as moveable furniture, tools and materials, visualization of new ideas foster creativity [37].

Design Thinking Process and Process Features. Due to its popularity, we have chosen to focus on the DT process approach based on Stanford's d.school, which includes the phases "Empathize", "Define", "Ideate", "Prototype", and "Test" [38]. During the first phase "empathize", it is important to observe the behavior of users and gain empathy for their problem by communicating with them. This phase helps understanding the potential user, for whom teams are developing a new product, service, or processes [35]. After collecting a wide spectrum of insights and needs from potential users, information must be focused to formulate a clear problem statement during the second phase "define". Hence, a clear definition of the problem serves as a guideline for the multidisciplinary DT team to generate creative ideas from the user's perspective [35]. The key process features of the third phase "ideate" are to generate a wide spectrum of diverse and creative ideas without boundaries and judgement by other team members at the beginning and to focus on a few ideas at the end of the idea generation process [35]. During the fourth phase "prototype", the development of a prototype begins that allows interaction, because during the last phase "test" new insights may be gathered by observing the user's interaction with a prototype. After testing the prototype, the multidisciplinary team(s) may realize that the problem has not been defined correctly or the prototype needs an improvement and the phases can be repeated due to DT's iterative process.

During "empathize", "define", "ideate", and "test" communication within the team and with the user is very important to gain empathy, understand the problem, and communicate while discussing ideas. This interactive communication is considered as an important feature of DT [39]. While generating ideas, the "DT team" needs to organize, share and develop their ideas, hence, collaboration and creativity are key features in this phase. During the development of prototypes interaction among the team members [10] is needed. In summary, four key features of DT can be extracted as relevant for our research: communication, developing creativity, collaboration, and interaction. These four key features must be supported by a virtual Design Thinking (VDT) platform. While designing an artifact for VDT (the VDT platform), two perspectives need to be considered - management and technology [40].

The discussion on remote work/telework, virtual collaboration, and DT indicates that wicked problems can be effectively solved by virtual teams, who collaborate on a VDT platform. This finding guides us to our research questions: Can a VDT platform outperform face-to-face Design Thinking? What is an adequate design of a virtual DT platform to effectively support virtual DT teams?

2.4 Propositions in Regards to a Virtual Design Thinking Platform

In this section, propositions are derived from the presented findings.

In a globalized and highly competitive economy, companies need creative individuals and teams to remain or grow the company's market share with the creation of demanded goods [23]. The modern workforce prefers telework when a task demands a high level of concentration [3]. To achieve a common goal, a virtual team needs a structured collaborative process [9]. To further guarantee a high level of competitiveness, company's innovations (product, service, process) must be user-centered and of high relevance [23, 41]. Cronin and Tayler [41] state that the quality of a good is measured in relation to consumer satisfaction. DT is a user/customer-centered approach that focuses on the development of innovative and desired goods by the customer [12]. We therefore derive the following proposition:

1. *A virtual Design Thinking platform supports dispersed and remote teams at achieving satisfactory innovations for their customer.*

ICT allows people to work remotely on projects [18]. Guthrie [42] states that high-involvement work practices increase job satisfaction and also productivity. People who work remotely have the chance of improving their time management skills and be more productive [18]. Sandmann [2] confirms the increase of productivity in telework and states that an increase in productivity between 10% and 40% on average can be expected, when people are working remotely. Individual teleworkers can be connected via ICT to form a virtual team [19]. Due to an increased level of productivity and structured collaboration via ICT using DT a shared goal can be faced [10, 11]. Based on these findings, we derive the following proposition:

2. *A virtual Design Thinking platform increases a remote team's productivity/ efficiency at innovating.*

In the remainder of this paper, we will test these propositions.

3   Methodology

As the guiding approach for our methodology, we apply Design Science Research (DSR) [40]. DSR has proven its applicability in IS and provides a structured approach to develop and evaluate artifacts [16]. Our methodological approach is based on the seven guidelines of DSR [40], shown Table 1.

Table 1. Design science research guideline by Hevner (Source: Hevner [40, p. 83])

Guideline	Description
Guideline 1: Design as an artifact	Design-science research must produce a viable artifact in the form of a construct, a model, a method, or an instantiation
Guideline 2: Problem relevance	The objective of design-science research is to develop technology-based solutions to important and relevant business problems
Guideline 3: Design evaluation	The utility, quality, and efficacy of a design artifact must be rigorously demonstrated via well-executed evaluation methods
Guideline 4: Research contributions	Effective design-science research must provide clear and verifiable contributions in the areas of the design artifact, design foundations, and/or design methodologies
Guideline 5: Research rigor	Design-science research relies upon the application of rigorous methods in both the construction and evaluation of the design artifact
Guideline 6: Design as a research process	The search for an effective artifact requires utilizing available means to reach desired ends while satisfying laws in the problem environment
Guideline 7: Communication of research	Design-science research must be presented effectively both to technology-oriented as well as management-oriented audiences

Following the seven guidelines, we introduce and evaluate our artifact – a VDT platform. The evaluation is based on a case study and a survey. Because there is limited research on the digitization of a DT process, we chose an exploratory case study to test and improve our artifact. A case study is suitable, when the aim of a contribution is to answer "how" and "why" questions and if the behavior of the involved participants cannot be manipulated [43]. The developed artifact is tested under controlled quasi-real conditions with a geographically dispersed team. The principle research rigor of DSR (guideline 5) is to determine how well an artifact works or does not work, in order to enable the development of new artifacts study [40]. The explanatory case study is focused to answer the questions of how well our artifact works [43].

The designed artifact in this contribution (guideline 1) can be considered an instantiation, "type of system solution" [40, p. 77], which can demonstrate the feasibility of a VDT platform [40]. We have analyzed the process features of each DT phase in respect to communication, development of creativity, collaboration, and interaction and derived the required features for an adequately designed VDT platform. We did not develop new ICT tools but we assembled suitable existing ICT tools for virtual communication, collaboration, creative work, and interaction into the virtual DT platform based on Voigt's and Bergener's framework [25]. A detailed description of the VDT instantiation is presented in the next subsection.

Guideline 2 of the DSR refers to the relevance of the problem [40], which can be solved with a technology-based approach as described in the introduction of this paper. We evaluated our artifacts (guideline 3) by conduction an explanatory case study under quasi-real conditions (see Subsect. 3.2) [40]. Additionally, we performed a survey to compare the findings from the case study with the participant's opinion about various factors, such as the quality of the result, pace of work, quality of communication, required skills to participate or the efficiency of virtual collaboration.

The contribution of our research (guideline 4) is to show that geographically dispersed teams can innovate as effectively as face-to-face teams, by using a VDT platform [40]. Our case study will answer how a virtual Design Thinking platform should be designed to enable effective real-time communication, collaboration, creative work, and interaction like in regular face-to-face Design Thinking workshops. The findings are presented in this section.

Guideline 6 of the DSR framework states, that not all means (infrastructures), ends (utility and constraints) and laws (cost and benefit constants) can be considered while designing an artifact since it is infeasible, but it should be focused on the utilization of available means, ends and laws [40]. That is the reason why we assemble already existing, easy accessible (Internet) and free-of charge ICT tools, in order to design the artifact of the VDT platform. While designing the artifact of the VDT platform both perspectives have been considered - management and technology (guideline 7) [40].

In the following subsection, we present and explain our artifact for a VDT platform.

3.1 Virtual Design Thinking Platform (Artifact: Instantiation)

Guideline 1 (design as an artifact) of DSR requires the instantiation of a viable artifact [40]. Voigt and Bergener [25] identified a framework for the development of systems for creative group processes. We have chosen Voigt's and Bergener's framework [25] because a creative group process is inherent in DT and the framework stresses the importance of communication, group collaboration and to develop a new services or products (prototypes). Voigt and Bergener [25] also argue that teams are more creative than individuals. In order to enhance creativity, ICT are often applied [27]. Furthermore, virtual teams can outperform offline teams [19]. Our VDT artifact is focusing on enabling the development of any type of innovation, such as service, product or process, while the geographically dispersed team members are collaborating on an ICT platform. Further, our VDT-artifact combines various access-free internet communication, collaboration, and interaction tools, which foster creativity. The requirements for our IS tools have been derived from the four key process features of DT: communication, creative work, collaboration, and interaction. The artifact of our VDT platform and its supporting IS tools for each DT phase is shown in Fig. 1.

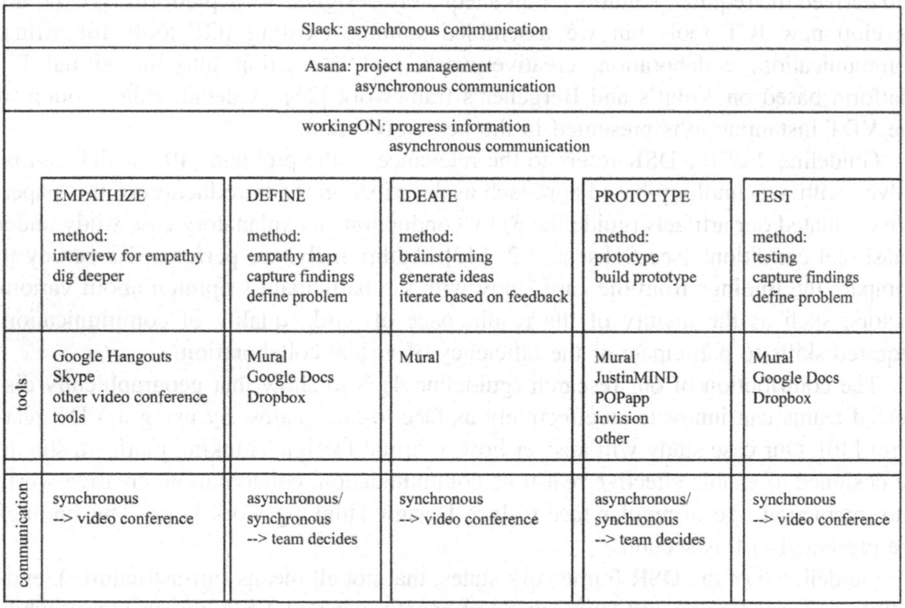

Slack: asynchronous communication				
Asana: project management asynchronous communication				
workingON: progress information asynchronous communication				
EMPATHIZE	DEFINE	IDEATE	PROTOTYPE	TEST
method: interview for empathy dig deeper	method: empathy map capture findings define problem	method: brainstorming generate ideas iterate based on feedback	method: prototype build prototype	method: testing capture findings define problem
tools Google Hangouts Skype other video conference tools	Mural Google Docs Dropbox	Mural	Mural JustinMIND POPapp invision other	Mural Google Docs Dropbox
communication synchronous --> video conference	asynchronous/ synchronous --> team decides	synchronous --> video conference	asynchronous/ synchronous --> team decides	synchronous --> video conference

Fig. 1. Our virtual design thinking platform artifact

Communication is an important key feature of the whole DT process. Virtual teams can apply synchronous (real-time) and asynchronous (non real-time) communication [44, 45]. Virtual synchronous communication can be conducted by using for example video conferencing [46].

According to guideline 6 of DSR, the artifact should be focused on the utilization of available means (infrastructures), ends (utility and constraints) and laws (cost and benefit constants) [40]. This is why we assemble existing free to use ICT tools for our VDT platform. In the following, the applied ICT tools, which were applied in all DT steps, will be described.

We identified three ICT based communication and collaboration tools, which are used throughout all five DT phases. We suggested Slack [47] as a tool for all asynchronous communication in the group, e.g. for tracking project updates. Slack [47] has been chosen because it is a free-to-use software, and it is a widely-known tool for text-based synchronous and asynchronous communication. We introduced Asana [48] as a project management tool for remote teams. It has been chosen because it makes teams more efficient, makes team's goals clear, and reduces communication efforts [48]. The platform workingON enables a minimalistic status reporting on each task [49]. It has been chosen because of its easy-to-use functionality and usability (status reporting) which is needed for structured teamwork.

In the following, we will describe ICT tools, which are applicable in each individual DT phase.

Tools for the "Empathize" phase. In the emphasize phase, team members have to get familiar with the problem at hand, immerse in the life of others and build up empathy with users (user-centered-approach). To do so, synchronous communication is necessary. Documentaries in form of written text, photos, and videos need to be developed, shared and explained within the group. In our case study, the groups were free to choose their preferred tool for their synchronous communication. However, we proposed video conferencing tools for communication such as Google Hangouts [50] and Skype [51].

Tools for the "Define" phase. In the define phase, an asynchronous and synchronous communication is necessary since teams may decide to discuss their observation together or write down their comprehension of the problem individually. Suggested ICT tools that support participants to share their written information are the following ones: Mural (for sharing unstructured information, such as pictures or audio files), Google Docs (for written text documentations) and Dropbox (for sharing files). Mural is a digital whiteboard [52]. Google Docs can be used to virtually collaborate simultaneously or asynchronously [53]. Dropbox enables file sharing [54]. These ICT tools have been suggested to be used, because they offer simultaneous and asynchronous collaboration, are easy-to-use, are widespread, and are (in their basic versions) free of charge.

Tools for the "Ideate" phase. The ideation phase is a highly interactive and creative phase. Within this phase ideas are collaboratively developed. Mural [52] enables virtual collaborative and creative work. This virtual whiteboard is free-of-charge and can be used in an intuitively way. Google Hangout was suggested for synchronous communication [46].

Tools for the "Prototype" phase. The characteristics of the given problem and of the possible innovations (product, service, process) define the prototyping phase and the applied methods. The methods, which can be applied in this phase range from rapid prototyping, over website mock ups to virtual role plays (just to name a few). For the development of apps and website mock ups, we suggested to use JustINMIND [55], POP app [56] or invision [57]. For visual 3D-prototypes the groups were free to use any suitable computer aided design software, which suits best their needs and experiences.

Tools for the "Test" phase. The goal of the test phase is to present and review the prototype. In principle, user insights are recorded (video, photo, text) and shared. We suggested to use the same ICT tools for asynchronous communication as in the emphasize phase, i.e. Google Hangout were suggested to be applied.

3.2   Design Evaluation: Case Study

By following the DSR methodology, we evaluated our proposed artifact within an exploratory case study under quasi-real conditions [40]. We constructed a survey to capture the group member's perceived effectiveness of our artifact [58]. A total of seven people have participated in the case study, which consisted of six male design team participants and one male assignment provider (acts as the customer). All design team participants are between 23 and 26 years old. The assignment provider is 45 years old. The design team participant's backgrounds are in computer science, crash simulation engineering, patent law, production system engineering, business administration and mechanical engineering. The assignment provider is a professor of aeronautical engineering. The case study has been limited to three days and all participants have been located at different places across Germany.

Case study structure. We recorded an instructional video where the work team explain DT and the purpose of this study, in order to minimize the need for moderation and coaching in the DT process. In the beginning of the case study, the group members needed to watch the instructional video and the group was introduced to the initial assignment (problem to be solved).

The task of the DT team was to come up with an innovative idea on how to advertise a specific communication platform used by the International Forum for Aviation Research (IFAR) to the IFAR employees and external project partners. The NASA and the German national aeronautics and space research center (DLR) use the social network platform, called IFARLink, to connect scientists and executives and discuss upcoming topics in aviation.

During the "Empathy" phase, the assignment provider introduced the task to and discussed the task with the team. In the "Define" phase, the team members individually formulated their understanding of the assignment before they collaboratively discussed their understandings by using video conferencing. In the "Ideation" phase, the team used the virtual whiteboard Mural to conduct brainstorming, and to cluster and to select ideas.

As the final idea, the group agreed on the development an infomercial video to introduce and advertise the IFARLink platform to the end-users. In the "Test" phase, the script for the video was shown to the assignment provider (customer) via internet (available at https://www.ifarlink.aero/video) and discussed by the support of video conferencing to iterate the solution. Finally, the infomercial video was presented the board members of IFAR.

After the completion of this case study, each group member had to fill out a questionnaire with 38 items. The assignment provider/customer received a specific questionnaire to gather information about his prominent role during the DT process.

The next section covers the design of the two questionnaires.

3.3   Questionnaire and Data Analysis

For each of the five phases of the DT process, questions were derived based on the guidelines by Porst [59] and Fink [58] to determine if the VDT platform (our artifact) supported creative group work (communication, collaboration, interaction). Before the virtual group work started, two control questions were asked about the team members' preferred way of communication, collaboration, and interaction in group work. Further, this question helped to determine if the experiences with the VDT platform changed group members' opinion about their preferred way of communicating, collaborating, and interacting in team work.

The questionnaire was divided into six sections. Section 1 listed items about the perceived quality of the result of the VDT. Section 2 of the questionnaire had questions about the required skills to use the VDT platform and to communicate, collaborate and interact in a creative way via ICT. The questions in section 3 asked about participants' perceived effectiveness of the virtual collaboration. The fourth sections contained questions about the workflow and continuity. Section 5 contained items to get information about group members' perceived level of satisfaction of the results and quality of the outcome. Section 6 listed question about the perceived quality of the communication within the team.

We furthermore asked about the group members' experiences with the suggested ICT tools, with the applicability, the usefulness, and the degree if support for creative work in each single phase of the DT process. To do so, we referred to questions from the Creativity Support Index (CSI) [60]. The CSI covers six dimensions "Enjoyment, Exploration, Expressiveness, Immersion, Results Worth Effort and Collaboration" [60, p. 21] with two questions each.

As the "assignment provider" was not directly involved in group work but in communication and coordination task, we established another questionnaire to get information about the assignment providers' experiences with digital collaboration, and experienced difficulties. To get information about these experiences, qualitative, open-ended questions were asked [61].

3.4   Data Analysis and Results

We conducted a three-staged analysis method to gather qualitative data [61], including data reduction, data display, and conclusion drawing. In order to achieve a data reduction, we abstracted and transformed the answers into insights based on the answers from the group members. The answers were clustered on a whiteboard, patterns were analyzed, and conclusions were derived in a narrative approach.

Face-to-face or virtual collaboration. Four group members preferred direct, non-ICT based collaboration, two participants expressed their perception that "offline" collaboration leads to better collaboration. Two group members were indifferent in their opinion about the effectiveness of offline and ICT-based group work. One person answered that the process itself is very structured and motivates people to collaborate and only focuses on the problem to find a good solution.

Necessity of Skills. The participants have been asked about the skills that are necessary to complete the DT process. According to the answers, basic computer skills are necessary to be able to set up all ICT tools and to be able to perform virtual group work. Two out of six group members think that for a virtual DT communication is as important as a creative and structured thinking.

Efficiency of virtual collaboration. Four out of six participants answered that results are not achieved in a faster way in a face-to-face environment (in comparison to a virtual setting). The results show that ICT tools foster creativity, which leads to a faster solving of given problem and the sharing of information is faster in a virtual environment. However, two out of six group members think that results could be achieved faster in a face-to-face setting, due to less technical issues and non-verbal communication.

Quality of the results. All six group members expressed that the VDT leads to better results (in comparison to face-to-face settings), although the expressed reasons for this vary.

Quality of communication. Conference calls are perceived by three out of six group members as good as face-to-face communication, as there was "no noticeable difference in workflow" and that everybody was able to see each other. The other three group members missed non-verbal communication and mentioned slow Internet bandwidth as a limiting factor for virtual communication.

Work flow and continuity. Four group members mentioned that catching up with the group progress has not been a problem because everybody was able to see what other participants did in the meantime, due to asynchronous communication.

Empathize phase. All of the participants answered that they would not understand the problem better while being in person. The group members stated that they were able to ask questions in the same manner and with the same effectiveness as in face-to-face meetings.

Define Phase. The participants stated that they did not experience any difficulties in defining the problem and collectively formulating the problem digitally. One participant stated that there is less pressure to understand everything related to the problem, because ICT tools and IS-based methods help to understand the details. In general, all team members appreciated how well the problem was defined in the virtual, remotely conducted "Define" phase.

Ideate phase. The following table presents the results of the CSI analysis with the software Mural (Table 2).

The results show that the digital whiteboard Mural succeeded at enhancing creativity according to the CSI by Cherry and Latulipe [60] as all CSI scores are way above 50%. Digital whiteboards, such as Mural, support idea generation and support creativity in the process. Nevertheless, two group members mentioned that they had problems with organizing their ideas.

Prototyping Phase. The team decided to continue to work with Mural in the prototyping phase to write a script for the informational video (prototype). Five team

Table 2. CSI results for mural as a creativity support tool based on Cherry and Latulipe [60]

Six dimensions of creativity support	Results
Exploration	86.66%
Enjoyment	83.93%
Expressiveness	73.85%
Immersion	80.18%
Results wirth effort	91.02%
Collaboration	89.28%

members mentioned that they were not able to prototype the idea in any better way in person, because the tool provided a good overview of the process and the progress.

Test Phase. All participants mentioned in the questionnaire that gathering feedback in person would not lead to any better results than with the digital-based solution. Furthermore, the team members were very satisfied with the test phase, because they had a common understanding of the solution.

Data Analysis of Assignment Provider. The assignment provider (customer) stated that he prefers to use a virtual communication and collaborate platforms for group work, since it offers him the freedom of location choice. He experienced no quality loss in any regards.

4 Discussion

Our research aims to find out how effective a VDT platform can perform in comparison to face-to-face DT. In this paper, we firstly introduced our motivation, problem statement and methodology. We structured this paper along the logic of DSR and, therefore, started with an examination of related research that builds the theoretical foundation for (a) our artifact/VDT platform and (b) the derivation of propositions, which allow to the answer our research question [2, 9, 40, 42]. Within Sect. 3, we introduced our methodological approach based on the seven DSR guidelines and started with the introduction of our artifact, continued by the presentation of our evaluation approach, a case study and a survey [15]. Within this section, we fuse the findings from the related work. Our research results prove proposition 1, i.e. a VDT platform supports remote teams at achieving satisfactory results for their customer.

Our artifact is a digital representation of the creative innovation method Design Thinking (DT). DT follows a structured logic of five iterative phases. Design Thinker's values are driven by a specific open, collaborative and creative mindset for group work. This is in line with De Vreede and Briggs [9], who state that virtual teams are in need for a structured, collaborative process to achieve a common goal [9].

The results of the case study and the survey, with particular regard to the stated satisfaction of the assignment provider [41], prove that the VDT platform supports remote teams at achieving satisfactory results for their customer (which is in our case the assignment provider). Therefore, our proposition 1 is supported.

Proposition 2 – A virtual Design Thinking platform increases a remote team's productivity/efficiency at reaching goals.

The VDT platform supports remote-based Design Thinking by providing adequate ICT tools. Due to the results from our case study and survey, the participants using the VDT platform confirm that their perceived level of efficiency in virtual collaboration was higher in comparison to face-to-face interaction. The answers of the survey reveal that the VDT platform supports a more structured collaboration that leads to reaching goals more efficiently, which is in line with De Vreede and Briggs [9]. This is also in line with recent findings that remote work/telework leads to a higher productivity/ efficiency of reaching goals in general [2, 18]. Additionally, the evaluation revealed that team members focus more on the task when using the VDT platform, which affects the efficiency of collaboration. This can be traced back to a "high-involvement work practice", which – according to Guthrie [42] – increases productivity and efficiency. Hence, our proposition 2 is supported.

However, our findings show that the majority of participants prefer face-to-face collaboration instead of virtual collaboration, which is due to a lack of non-verbal communication and technical issues that interrupted the workflow.

To summarize, we can state that our artifact – the VDT platform – is a viable solution to effectively do Design Thinking in a virtual way. Nonetheless, there is room for improvement concerning the satisfaction of virtual team performance and over-coming technical difficulties.

5   Concluding Remarks and Outlook

Through the continuous process of digitization and development of information systems (IS), work is increasingly performed virtually [1]. The use of ICT in companies allows individuals and teams to perform remote work/telework and thereby create values. This, on the one hand, leads to more flexibility in time management and productivity of workers but, on the other hand, requires adequate ICT to allow and support virtual collaboration [2, 3, 9]. The need for ICT supported collaboration for remote work of geographically dispersed teams is gaining importance and companies are challenged to keep up pace with this contemporary necessity [4]. Furthermore, companies require innovative products, services and/or processes to satisfy customer's needs and to achieve success [23, 24]. Design Thinking (DT) is a creative innovation method that is originally used in analog team settings to develop innovative products, services and/or processes [10–12]. The DT process, DT methods and DT mindset together form a strictly designed procedure that is targeted towards user-centered innovations. To meet contemporary business requirements, our research project aimed at enabling virtual teams to perform DT in a geographically dispersed setting with the support of a newly design VDT platform. We set up an artifact that follows the requirements of DT with the support of existing platforms and tools. In this research paper, we present our research of the evaluation of our artifact, which is based on the research question: How effective can a VDTplatform perform compared to face-to-face DT?

In this paper, we firstly introduced our motivation, problem statement and methodology. We structured this paper based on DSR, and therefore, started with an examination of related work that builds the theoretical foundation for (a) our artifact/VDT platform and (b) the definition of propositions that enable the answering of our research question. Within Sect. 3, we introduced our methodological approach based on the seven DSR principles [40] and started with the introduction of our artifact, continued by the presentation of our evaluation approach, a case study and a survey. Our propositions – a VDT platform supports remote teams at achieving satisfactory results for their customer and a VDT platform increases a remote team' s productivity/efficiency at reaching goals [2, 18] – are confirmed based on the examination of related research work and our findings from the evaluation. Nonetheless, our evaluation revealed that a lack of non-verbal communication and challenges with technical issues downgrades the performance of our VDT platform in comparison to face-to-face interaction.

Concluding, we can reveal that DT can be virtually performed without any loss of efficacy in comparison to face-to-face DT. Nevertheless, there is room for improvement of the VDT platform. A fully automated platform would probably lead to positive effects on the workflow and the effectiveness of virtual DT collaboration. Hence, further research is needed.

Our paper has several limitations that need to be considered for future research. The digitization of DT entails the adherence of all DT requirements. For upcoming research, the effectiveness of the VDT platform also needs to be evaluated concerning the level of (team) creativity within the process and of the solution itself. Furthermore, there are several approaches for DT phase sequences, which can be tested. The number of participants within the case study is restricted, additionally future research could be conducted to test how the virtual DT process works with participants from different backgrounds, different levels of computer skills, more multidisciplinary, multicultural, diverse gender settings and different ages in the team constellation. Additionally, the influence of altered timeframes for DT performance could be tested as well as potential differences when developing products, services or processes.

Acknowledgement. This paper is part of a project called DETHIS – Design Thinking for Industrial Services, funded by the German Federal Ministry of Education and Research (BMBF); Grant # 02K14A140.

References

1. Keuper, F., Hamidian, K., Verwaayen, E., Kalinowski, T., Kraijo, C.: Digitalisierung und Innovation: Planung - Entstehung - Entwicklungsperspektiven. Springer, Wiesbaden (2013). (in German)
2. Sandmann, P.: Telearbeit - Impulse für eine zukunftsfähige Regionalentwicklung? Fallbeispiele aus dem Silicon Valley und Los Angeles für "Lernende Regionen no. 34." (2000). (in German)
3. Vilhelmson, B., Thulin, E.: Who and where are the flexible workers? Exploring the current diffusion of telework in Sweden. New Technol. Work Employ. **31**, 77–96 (2016)
4. Daniels, K., Lamond, D., Standen, P.: Teleworking: frameworks for organizational research. J. Manag. Stud. **38**, 1151–1185 (2001)

5. Bailey, D.E., Kurland, N.B.: A review of telework research: findings, new directions, and lessons for the study of modern work. J. Organ. Behav. **23**, 383–400 (2002)
6. Butler, E.S., Aasheim, C., Williams, S.: Does telecommuting improve productivity? Commun. ACM **50**, 101–103 (2007)
7. Gibson, C.B., Gibbs, J.L.: Unpacking the concept of virtuality: the effects of geographic dispersion, electronic dependence, dynamic structure, and national diversity on team innovation. Adm. Sci. Q. **51**, 451–495 (2006)
8. Raffaele, C., Connell, J.: Telecommuting and co-working communities: what are the implications for individual and organizational flexibility? In: Sushil, C.J., Burgess, J. (eds.) Flexible Work Organizations, pp. 21–35. Springer, India (2016)
9. de Vreede, G.J., Briggs, R.O.: Collaboration engineering: designing repeatable processes for high-value collaborative tasks. In: Proceedings of the 38th Annual Hawaii International Conference on System Sciences, p. 17c (2005)
10. Brown, T.: Change by Design: How Design Thinking Transforms Organizations and Inspires Innovation. Harper Collins, New York (2009)
11. Kolko, J.: Design Thinking Comes of Age. https://hbr.org/2015/09/design-thinking-comes-of-age
12. Müller, R.M., Thoring, K.: Design thinking vs. lean startup: a comparison of two user-driven innovation strategies. In: Leading Innovation Through Design, pp. 151–161 (2012)
13. Lattemann, C., Fritz, K.: Learning integrative thinking. Presented at the Society for Information Technology & Teacher Education International Conference, 17 March 2014
14. Unger, D., Witte, E.H.: Virtuelle Teams—Geringe Kosten, geringer Nutzen? Zur Leistungsverbesserung von Kleingruppen beim Problemlösen durch elektronische Moderation. Gr. Organ. **38**, 165–182 (2007). (in German)
15. Gregor, S., Hevner, A.: Positioning and presenting design science research for maximum impact. Manag. Inf. Syst. Q. **37**, 337–355 (2013)
16. Peffers, K., Tuunanen, T., Rothenberger, M.A., Chatterjee, S.: A design science research methodology for information systems research. J. Manag. Inf. Syst. **24**, 45–77 (2007)
17. Martin, B.H., MacDonnell, R.: Is Telework Effective for Organizations? A Meta-Analysis of Empirical Research on Perceptions of Telework and Organizational Outcomes. ResearchGate
18. Harpaz, I.: Advantages and disadvantages of telecommuting for the individual, organization and society. Work Study **51**, 74–80 (2002)
19. Townsend, A.M., DeMarie, S.M., Hendrickson, A.R.: Virtual teams: technology and the workplace of the future. Acad. Manag. Exec. **12**, 17–29 (1998)
20. Martinez-Moyano, I.: Exploring the dynamics of collaboration in interorganizational settings. Creat. Cult. Collab. Int. Assoc. Facil. Handb. **4**, 69 (2006)
21. Nunamaker, J.F., Briggs, R.O.: Introduction to collaboration systems and technology track. In: 2015 48th Hawaii International Conference on System Sciences, p. 1 (2015)
22. Redlich, B., Siemon, D., Lattemann, C., Robra-Bissantz, S.: Shared mental models in creative virtual teamwork. In: Proceedings of the 50th Hawaii International Conference on System Sciences (2017)
23. Massetti, B.: An empirical examination of the value of creativity support systems on idea generation. MISQ. **20**, 83–97 (1996)
24. Bergiel, B.J., Bergiel, E.B., Balsmeier, P.W.: Nature of virtual teams: A summary of their advantages and disadvantages. Manag. Res. News **31**, 99–110 (2008)
25. Voigt, M., Bergener, K.: Enhancing creativity in groups – proposition of an integrated framework for designing group creativity support systems. In: 2013 46th Hawaii International Conference on System Sciences (HICSS), pp. 225–234 (2013)

26. DeFillippi, R., Grabher, G., Jones, C.: Introduction to paradoxes of creativity: managerial and organizational challenges in the cultural economy. J. Organ. Behav. **28**, 511–521 (2007)
27. Briggs, R.O., De Vreede, G.-J., Nunamaker Jr., J.F.: Collaboration engineering with ThinkLets to pursue sustained success with group support systems. J. Manag. Inf. Syst. **19**, 31–64 (2003)
28. Brown, T.: Design thinking. Harv. Bus. Rev. **86**, 84–92 (2008)
29. Buchanan, R.: Wicked problems in design thinking. Des. Issues **8**, 5–21 (1992)
30. Johansson-Sköldberg, U., Woodilla, J., Çetinkaya, M.: Design thinking: past, present and possible futures. Creat. Innov. Manag. **22**, 121–146 (2013)
31. Bellet, P.S., Maloney, M.J.: The importance of empathy as an interviewing skill in medicine. JAMA **266**, 1831–1832 (1991)
32. Lawrence, C., Tuunanen, T., Myers, M.D.: Extending design science research methodology for a multicultural world. Presented at the IFIP Working Conference on Human Benefit through the Diffusion of Information Systems Design Science Research (2010)
33. Lindberg, T., Köppen, E., Rauth, I., Meinel, C.: On the perception, adoption and implementation of design thinking in the IT industry. In: Plattner, H., Meinel, C., Leifer, L. (eds.) Design Thinking Research, pp. 229–240. Springer, Heidelberg (2012)
34. Seidel, V.P., Fixson, S.K.: Adopting design thinking in novice multidisciplinary teams: The application and limits of design methods and reflexive practices. J. Prod. Innov. Manag. **30**, 19–33 (2013)
35. d.school: bootleg bootcamp (2011). https://dschool.stanford.edu/wp-content/uploads/2011/03/BootcampBootleg2010v2SLIM.pdf
36. Taura, T., Yamamoto, E., Fasiha, M.Y.N., Goka, M., Mukai, F., Nagai, Y., Nakashima, H.: Constructive simulation of creative concept generation process in design: a research method for difficult-to-observe design-thinking processes. J. Eng. Des. **23**, 297–321 (2012)
37. Grots, A., Pratschke, M.: Design thinking — Kreativität als Methode. Mark. Rev. St Gallen. **26**, 18–23 (2009). (in German)
38. The Making of a Design Thinker - Metropolis Magazine, October 2009. http://www.metropolismag.com/October-2009/The-Making-of-a-Design-Thinker/
39. Brereton, M., McGarry, B.: An observational study of how objects support engineering design thinking and communication: implications for the design of tangible media. In: Proceedings of the SIGCHI Conference on Human Factors in Computing Systems, pp. 217–224. ACM, New York (2000)
40. Hevner, A.R., March, S.T., Park, J., Ram, S.: Design science in information systems research. MISQ. **28**, 75–105 (2004)
41. Cronin Jr., J.J., Taylor, S.A.: Measuring service quality: a reexamination and extension. J. Mark. **56**(3), 55–68 (1992)
42. Guthrie, J.P.: High-involvement work practices, turnover, and productivity: evidence from New Zealand. Acad. Manage. J. **44**, 180–190 (2001)
43. Baxter, P., Jack, S.: Qualitative case study methodology: study design and implementation for novice researchers. Qual. Rep. **13**, 544–559 (2008)
44. Mabrito, M.: A study of synchronous versus asynchronous collaboration in an online business writing class. Am. J. Distance Educ. **20**, 93–107 (2006)
45. Schoberth, T., Schrott, G.: Virtual communities. Wirtschaftsinformatik **43**, 517–519 (2001). (in German)
46. Berge, Z.: Interaction in post-secondary web-based learning. Educ. Technol. **39**, 5–11 (1999)
47. Slack: Slack: Where work happens https://slack.com/
48. Use Asana to track your team's work & manage projects • Asana. https://asana.com/dot
49. WorkingOn. https://www.workingon.co
50. Google Hangouts. https://hangouts.google.com/

51. Skype | Kostenlose Anrufe an Freunde und Familie. https://www.skype.com/de/. (in German)
52. Suarez-Battan, M.: Mural. https://mural.co/
53. Dekeyser, S., Watson, R.: Extending Google Docs to Collaborate on Research Papers
54. Dropbox. https://www.dropbox.com/
55. Prototyping tool for web and mobile apps – Justinmind. https://www.justinmind.com/
56. POP - Prototyping on Paper | Mobile App Prototyping Made Easy. https://marvelapp.com/
57. Free Web & Mobile Prototyping (Web, iOS, Android) and UI Mockup Tool. https://www.invisionapp.com/
58. Fink, A.: How to Ask Survey Questions. Sage, Thousand Oaks (2002)
59. Porst, R.: Question Wording-Zur Formulierung von Fragebogen-Fragen (2000). (in German)
60. Cherry, E., Latulipe, C.: Quantifying the creativity support of digital tools through the creativity support index. ACM Trans. Comput.-Hum. Interact. **21**, 21:1–21:25 (2014)
61. Appleton, J.V.: Analysing qualitative interview data: addressing issues of validity and reliability. J. Adv. Nurs. **22**, 993–997 (1995)

Processless Design Extended

Joon-Suk Lee[✉]

Virginia State University, 1 Hayden Street, Petersburg, VA 23806, USA
joonsukl@acm.org

Abstract. Technologies increasingly inhabit ever more mundane and personal settings, a fact that has caused some designers to reflect upon the emergent, inaccessible nature of context. Recently, *processless design* has been proposed as an important alternative to existing design thinking. *Processless design* argues that by intentionally leaving out processes, or minimally embedding processes in system design, designers might be able to come up with systems that are more open to different interactional possibilities. In this paper, we extend the *processless design* idea, and propose *customizable processes* and *appropriable opportunities* as two key design ramifications of the original *processlessness* concept. We argue that *processless design* supports the ability of users to construct more spontaneous, opportunistic and meaningful experiences *in situ.*, and that *processlessness* is the key in designing educational technologies for increasing student learning, and in making it possible to account for promoting teacher adoption during the design time.

1 Introduction

Years ago, Weiser foresaw the future as technologies would become so pervasive and ubiquitous that they would disappear into the fabric of everyday life [12]. Indeed, the use of wireless handheld devices such as mobile phones, PDAs, and tablets is no longer bound to work places, but becoming increasingly integrated into every aspect of our lives, promoting socio-cultural reformations from within. In the field of education, the influx of digital technologies opened up new forms of educational opportunities such as mobile learning and distance learning, while it also instigated reformation of centuries-old classroom learning [11].

Over the years, an increasing number of educational technologies have been designed, developed and deployed by designers and researchers, yet the discussion of whether or not the technology is beneficial to education is still inconclusive. Technologies proven to produce positive increases in student learning in experimental settings have shown limited success in actual classroom adoption [1,14]. Longitudinal studies also report incompatible findings. For instance, Dynarski et al. [4] report that they did not find either an increase or decrease in student learning after a year-long study testing the effectiveness of Reading and Mathematics software in classrooms whereas Roschelle et al. [7] report strong classroom learning gains from a large-scale, multi-year investigation of deploying SimCalc in multiple classrooms.

© Springer International Publishing AG 2017
A. Marcus and W. Wang (Eds.): DUXU 2017, Part I, LNCS 10288, pp. 89–99, 2017.
DOI: 10.1007/978-3-319-58634-2_7

Noticing such discrepancies, Dickey-Kurdziolek and Tatar [2] assess the difficulties in educational technology design, and point out that a strategy of "design(ing) for student learning, and then find(ing) ways to increase teacher adoption later [2]" is bound to produce ineffective classroom technologies. They suggest that technology designers need to consider the *design tensions* [9] between "designing for the student experience" and "designing for teacher adoption" in design time. Roschelle et al. [7] contend that the key to the successful deployment of classroom technology is not just about designing novel technologies, but is more about creating "interventions that deeply integrate professional development, curriculum materials, and software in a unified curricular activity system [7, p. 874]." Yet, both Dickey-Kurdziolek and Tatar [2] or Roschelle et al. [7] do not explicitly show how to design educational technologies that can increase student learning while promoting teacher adoption, or that can easily be integrated with the professional development and curriculum materials.

Every school, every classroom and every teacher is unique and probably has very different demands and requirements for technology use in the classroom. This multifarious nature of classroom context makes designing classroom technologies which can easily be integrated to a number of different existing curricula, while meeting individual teacher's local needs a formidable task. Furthermore, even for the same school, same classroom and same teacher, the use of technologies is always being continually defined and negotiated in the classrooms in the moment. That, in turn, makes *context* not only illusive and slippery, but also central and critical in interactive system design [3]. In a similar vein, context is central and critical in educational technology design as well.

In order to demystify *context* and account for ever-changing *context* in the design process, researchers have introduced different design ideas. For instance, Höök et al. suggest making the representation of systems' internal mechanisms transparent to users as a way to enable user appropriation [5]. Dourish lists three approaches for supporting continually manifested and interactionally defined context in system design [3]. He argues for making systems that display their context and support "deep customization" at the architectural level. In addition, he proposes separating information from the structure in which the information is organized. More recently, drawing on *Zensign*, the idea that what we leave out of a design is as important as what we put in it [10], Lee et al. [6] have proposed *processless design* as an important alternative to existing design thinking. *Processless design* argues that by intentionally leaving out processes, or minimally embedding processes in system design, designers might be able to come up with systems that are more open to different interactional possibilities. Yet, Lee et al. [6] do not explicitly discuss design considerations relating to the process of leaving out processes in design.

In this paper, we extend *processless design*, and discuss *customizable processes* and *appropriable opportunities* as two key design ramifications of the original *processlessness* concept. We concur with Lee et al. [6] in believing that *processless design* can support the ability of users to construct more spontaneous, opportunistic and meaningful experiences *in situ*. We further argue that *processlessness* is the key in designing educational technologies for increasing student learning, and in making it possible to account for promoting teacher adoption during the design time. We present a sample design case that demonstrates how the design embodying *processlessness* can eventuate in an increased adoptability for multiple educational settings.

2   Processless Design Extended

2.1   Processlessness

Lee et al. [6] recount that *processless design* does not suggest that interactional process is located solely in the artifact, and hence fully defined by the artifact's built-in features. Process as a larger phenomenon is always interactionally defined, managed, negotiated and recreated in the moments of use. People and artifacts co-define process as they constantly reconfigure each other in situ [8,13]. Yet, by trying to encode and rigidify the processes at design time, designers might be depriving individuals of opportunities to create more diverse, tailored, and appropriate processes in situ. In this sense, *processless design* is not about removing processes from holistic human-nonhuman interactions, but rather it is about redistributing some of the process-making activity to the users, times and places in which the artifacts are enacted.

2.2   Customizable Processes

While *processless design* values removing processes from digital artifacts as the primary design principle, building technologies devoid of any process at all is not practical, if not entirely infeasible. That is, when we design digital artifacts, even in the *processless way*, we are destined to put a certain amount of processes into the design. In that respect, we contend that the subsequent auxiliary principle in *processless design* is the user customizability of the embedded processes. Designers need to provide ways in which users can replace or supplement any built-in processes.

Dourish points out that, in information technology design, it is important to separate information from the structure in which the information is organized [3]. On top of that, *processless design* proposes separating processes from the structures in which processes are organized. By modularizing processes and making processes replaceable and customizable, designers can incorporate processes into the digital artifacts in the *processless way*.

2.3   Appropriable Opportunities

By minimally embedding processes in digital artifacts, and preparing the embedded processes to be easily customizable, designers not only create interaction technologies, but also fabricate new possibilities for user interactions around the built artifacts. Designers, especially educational technology designers, however, also need to take a step further and attempt to design holistic user experiences. With what they provide or do not provide through technology designs, educational technology designers need to create interventions that integrate (1) individual teacher's needs, (2) existing curriculum materials and (3) different use practices.

When leaving out processes in technology design, designers are not delegating their responsibilities to the users. "Whatever designers leave out, the users will fill in" is not the philosophy of *processlessness*. Designers should always consider what it means to leave out certain processes in technology design, and think about how users will or will not be able to appropriate interactional possibilities created by the design. Thus when leaving out any processes in design, designers should not consider themselves as practicing *not-designing*, but instead see themselves as designing interactional possibilities beyond the artifacts as well as the affordances for unfolding users' activities.

In sum, designers practicing *processless design* should consider putting minimal processes in the digital artifacts. When embedding any processes, they should consider making the processes easily customizable. When leaving out any process, they should consider the consequences of not embedding the process.

3   ESL Password: An Example

In this section, we present ESL (English as a Second Language) Password as a sampler applique of ESL class activities, and demonstrate how the three design principles of *processlessness* are embodied in technology design.

3.1   Software

ESL Password is a multi-user parallel distributed game activity. It resembles a television game show from the 60's in which a presenter is given a target word or phrase and asked to use words that would get the guesser to say the target. For example, a presenter can say "it's raining cats and ...?" to make the guesser say "dogs." Guessers are allowed to ask presenters questions and actively engage in the game. If the guesser cannot guess the word, the presenter may "pass" and move on to the next word. Thus, the original game involves two roles, that of the presenter, who knows the word or phrase, and that of the guesser, who does not. These roles are filled by exactly one person at a time. There is also a third role, that of audience, filled by many people. The audience is told the target word or phrase and is therefore presumably more allied with the presenters' than the guessers' experiences. Although the audience role is tacit in the game description, this role is quite important. The original T.V. game was arguably designed as much or more for the audience as for the players. (Indeed to whom else would a television show be targeted if not for the studio audience and for home viewers?).

Inspired by the fact that the rules of the game obligate participants to speak, we developed ESL Password (Fig. 1) for people learning English as a second language. Users can choose to take one of three roles. Different helping mechanisms were added to help ESL students with their roles.

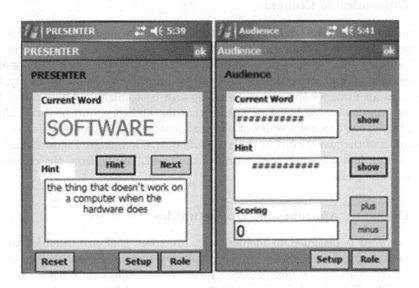

Fig. 1. ESL Password - PDA version

The system is used to deliver words/phrases for the players as well as to provide hints. Presenters can fetch words or phrases on their devices as well as retrieve a dictionary definition of the word. Guessers can access six different kinds of hints from the system. These are machine-generated hints such as an anagram, the length of the word, or the revelation of random letters.

In order to grant the audience access to the information available to presenters and guessers, the audience mode has an option to display both the given words and the hints given for the guessers. In addition, in order to nudge the audience to take an active role in the game play, the audience is given an option to keep track of the scores for the current game.

3.2   Embedding Minimal Processes

Two main processes embedded in the software are a word-delivery system with built-in English dictionary and hinting mechanisms. These two functionalities represent two embedded processes that automate different user tasks in the non-digitized version of gaming activity. For instance, a word-delivery system is a substitute for a flashcard that displays different words/phrases. We could have designed the activity to require one dedicated player to flip the flashcard for the presenter. Our design rationale for automating the flashcard and the card flipping task is rather obvious; the flashcard flipping task requires an additional role without adding any value to the game. Hinting systems provide mechanisms for balancing task difficulty levels for non-native speakers.

3.3   Customizable Contents

Two embedded processes in ESL Password are both user customizable. Users can replace the built-in dictionary with custom built ones. This is a key feature in ESL Password since teachers would need to customize the words list, and possibly the presenter hints prior to using ESL Password in the classroom. Similarly, the hinting mechanisms for the guessers are also user customizable. Users can either use computer generated hints, or author textual, auditory, and pictorial hints. For instance, one can use a series of pictures depicting the given word or even a translation of the given word in the guesser's native language. Figure 2 shows a pictorial hint and a Korean translation of the word, 'apple' from the children's version of the game.

3.4   Designing Appropriable Opportunities

ESL Password is designed to include only processes that are essential to the game play. For instance, without a word-delivery system, ESL Password activity itself regresses to the non-digitized form of the gameplay. Without hinting systems, ESL Password is no more than an automated flashcard. Two features we intentionally left out in designing ESL Password are scoring and encoding user roles. While we have user interface for marking, increasing and decreasing scores, no process has been embedded in the software. In addition, even though

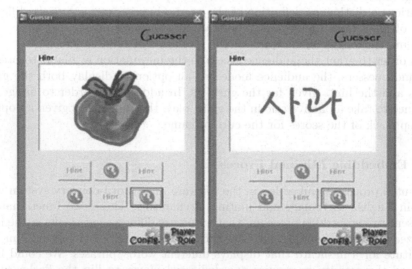

Fig. 2. Pictorial and Korean guesser hints from children's version

we support three user roles by providing different user interfaces for the different roles, we do not explicitly encode the roles in the software. Users can always switch to different user modes at any given time. The enacting and regulating of user roles is left to the users to decide, manage and negotiate in the course of acting out the gameplay.

4   ESL Password in Action

ESL Password has been deployed on multiple occasions and has been tested with a variety of student groups and settings. In this section, we report on two occasions in which ESL Password was used in distinctively different ways.

4.1   English Language Institue

As a first attempt to deploy ESL Password in a classroom setting, researchers conducted three game sessions with students at the English Language Institute at Virginia Tech on three different days. With help from the teachers at the institute, we were able to get consent from students to video record the sessions. The vocabulary lists as well as the logistics of the game were modified to accommodate class curriculum and schedule.

The teachers administered ESL Password activities in three different ways. Some teachers, prior to using ESL Password, had used a whiteboard as a medium for the game activity. Students were asked to pair up with another student. The pairs were then asked to play the traditional version of the game. Guessers were seated in the front row facing backwards while presenters were seated in the second row facing the whiteboard. When a teacher wrote a word on the board, all the presenters tried to explain the word to their partner guessers. The pair who got the correct answer first won a game-point (It was up to the teacher to decide whether to wait for other pairs to finish guessing the word or to continue on to the next word).

When teachers used ESL Password, students were asked to form presenter/guesser/audience triplets or quadruplets (two audience participants). As with the traditional game mode, teachers in this setting also controlled the game play. They decided when to move on to the next word and also changed dictionaries if needed.

When a teacher initiated the game play, a randomly selected word from a dictionary was displayed on all the presenters' PDA screens. Instead of looking at the whiteboard for a word, presenters were able to use their handheld devices to look at the given word. All the presenters tried to explain the word to their partner guessers. The team that got the correct answer first was given a game point. The teacher clicked on the next-word button when she decided to go on to the next word.

ESL Password was tested in two different conditions. In an "audience without PDAs" condition, only presenters and guessers were given handheld devices. No handheld devices were given to the audience. In an "audience with PDAs" condition, the audience members used the handheld devices to monitor the team's activity. When a guesser chose to use the "audience help," the guesser asked the audience for help. In this case, the audience was expected to explain the word on the behalf of the presenter.

It was quite interesting to see that audience members who had access to shared visual information (participants with PDAs) were more likely proactive in participating in the game activity than audience members who did not have access to the information. For instance, Fig. 3 portrays a scene in which a presenter holding a PDA looks at the guesser, while a guesser looks at her PDA screen, possibly trying to get a guesser hint. It is probable to assume that these two are actively engaged in the task at hand. However, two audience participants, Audience A and Audience B, withdraw themselves from the activity to look at the font of the classroom, most likely to look at the teacher. Indeed, researchers observed that a majority of audience members tended to focus on the teachers instead of engaging in the game activity when they did not have access to the shared information.

The two audience participants from Fig. 3 changed their behaviors drastically when they were given access to the shared information. As shown in Fig. 4, once given his own PDA, Audience A actively opted in, also taking on the role of presenter even though the rules clearly stated audience members can only step into the game when a guesser chose to use "audience help." This change of the behaviors among audience members is worth noting since it signifies that shared visual information not only results in helping peripheral participants learn, but also triggers in peripheral participants significant attitude changes toward participation in the activity. In addition, it also shows how different actitivy designs impact students' behaviors differently, and how students appropriate the given opportunities to redesign their activities.

4.2   Women in Computing Day

The Association for Women in Computing (AWC) is a student-run, non-profit organization at Virginia Tech. Every year, AWC holds a keystone event, Women in Computing Day (WCD) in which AWC invites local junior high school female students and introduces various computing technologies to inspire them to pursue computing careers.

As a part of the event, we held four Password gaming sessions. Each session lasted about 45 min and there were 8 to 11 students in each session. Students were first briefed on the game rules and PDA devices were distributed. Students were free to choose their roles (presenter, guesser or audience). One of our research team members, supervised the game play sessions.

Since students were native English speakers, we prepared a special dictionary designed for the event. The dictionary consisted of 55 words and each word had a definition and two guesser hints.

When we deployed the system, students quickly adopted and created their own versions of the game. Instead of having one presenter, one guesser and several

Fig. 3. An ESL Password session held at English Language Institute - audience w/o shared visual info

Fig. 4. An ESL Password session held at English Language Institute - audience with shared visual info

Fig. 5. A password puzzle session held during women in computing day event

audience members, students divided into groups of presenters and guessers. Multiple presenters usually took turns explaining, while teams of guessers shouted out possible answers. It was notable that the students were able to appropriate their own activities without the supervision of a teacher (or, in our case, of a supervising researcher). Figure 5 shows a puzzle session held during the event.

5   Conclusion

In this paper, we extended *processless design*, and proposed *customizable processes* and *appropriable opportunities* as two key design ramifications of the original *processlessness* concept. We presented a sample design case that demonstrates how the design embodying *processlessness* can result in supporting different use scenarios in multiple educational settings.

We believe that *processless design* supports the ability of users to construct more spontaneous, opportunistic and meaningful experiences in situ. Moreover we also believe that *processlessness* is the key in designing educational technologies for increasing student learning, and in making it possible to account for promoting teacher adoption during the design time.

References

1. Convery, A.: The pedagogy of the impressed: how teachers become victims of technological vision. Teach. Teach. **15**(1), 25–41 (2009)
2. Dickey-Kurdziolek, M., Tatar, D.: Discussion of the educational technology design problem. In: Proceedings of Alt.CHI (2012)
3. Dourish, P.: What we talk about when we talk about context. In: Proceedings of UbiComp (2004)
4. Dynarski, M., Agodini, R., Heaviside, S., Novak, T., Carey, N., Campuzano, L., et al.: Effectiveness of Reading and Mathematics Software Products: Findings from the First Student Cohort. U.S. Department of Education, Institute of Education Sciences, Washington, D.C. (2007)
5. Höök, K., Karlgren, J., Waern, A., Dahlback, N., Jansson, C., Karlgren, K., Lemaire, B.: A glass box approach to adaptive hypermedia. User Model. User-Adapt. Interact. **6**(2–3), 157–184 (1996)
6. Lee, J.S., Branham, S., Tatar, D., Harrison, S.: Processlessness: staying open to interactional possibilities. In: Proceedings of Designing Interactive Systems (2012)
7. Roschelle, J., Shechtman, N., Tatar, D., Hegedus, S., Hopkins, B., Empson, S., Knudsen, J., Gallagher, L.P.: Integration of technology, curriculum, and professional development for advancing middle school mathematics: three large-scale studies. Am. Educ. Res. J. **47**(4), 833–878 (2010)
8. Suchman, L.: Human-Machine Reconfigurations: Plans and Situated Actions. Cambridge Univ. Press, Cambridge (2007)
9. Tatar, D.: The design tensions framework. Hum.-Comput. Interact. **22**(4), 413–451 (2007)
10. Tatar, D., Lee, J.S., Alaloula: Playground games: a design strategy for supporting and understanding coordinated activity. In: Proceedings of Designing Interactive Systems (2008)
11. Tatar, D., Roschelle, J., Vahey, P., Penuel, W.R.: Handhelds go to school: lessons learned. IEEE Comput. **36**(9), 30–37 (2003)
12. Weiser, M.: The Computer For The 21st Century. Scientific American (1991)
13. Wertsch, J.: Mind as Action. Oxford Univ. Press, Oxford (1998)
14. Zhao, Y., Frank, K.A.: Factors affecting technology uses in schools: an ecological perspective. Am. Educ. Res. J. **40**(4), 807–840 (2003)

The Categorization of Document
for Design Thinking

Tingyi S. Lin[✉] and Min-Zhe Yi[✉]

National Taiwan University of Science and Technology, Taipei, Taiwan
tingyi@mail.ntust.edu.tw, minzhe_yi@126.com

Abstract. Documents are closely related to our daily life, from morning papers to various corporate reports, and even to site maps issued by tourist attractions. Before the advent of the Internet in the 1970s, documents were certain physical objects on which significant text and graphic symbols were drawn, written, printed or shown in a way to be visible. With the emergence of the Internet, the presentation of documents has become diversified. Traditional physical documents are gradually replaced by digital documents and those changes have altered how we communicate to each other. Although documents are so important, many documents attract less attention from users due to the lackluster content and to many perplexing problems in information structure, graphic symbols, layout. Document design has accumulated considerable practical experience and design methods nowadays. The design category has also been widening. Digitization can bring freer presentation and wider communication to documents; paper documents also have advantages in reading habits, execution efficiency and convenience. No matter how the information is presented, being easy to understand, being easy to use and creating a pleasant reading atmosphere are still the common goals of all the document designs. On this basis, it is essential to pay great attention on the various of document for different requirement.

The accuracy and appropriateness of the collected data will affect not only the designers' judgment on users' needs but also the result of design thinking. Design thinking is the methodology of the whole idea and design. It means seeking different possible solutions to different design themes and thinking differently. Design thinking in document design provides the possibilities of document innovation and reconstruction for designers. In the process of design thinking, it is necessary to explore the core needs of users from a large number of research data. Classifying existing documents can help designers clearly know their design objects and better target them during the data collection to obtain valuable design suggestions. In order to categorize document for better design and further research, this study aims to (1) extensively collect existing document samples and classify them, and (2) analyze the spatial coordinate distribution and illustrate design features of these documents.

There were 153 document samples collected and screened. The original samples were filtered by excluding with highly similar content and forms. It turned out that 54 representative samples were selected and were analyzed with the KJ Method. Five document types were concluded, including (1) Indicative document: introduce the use of a product or guide users to complete a task. (2) Retrieving document: users seek the information they need from a complex set of information according to visual cues in the document. (3) Dialogical

© Springer International Publishing AG 2017
A. Marcus and W. Wang (Eds.): DUXU 2017, Part I, LNCS 10288, pp. 100–113, 2017.
DOI: 10.1007/978-3-319-58634-2_8

document: there are repeated interactions between users and documents. The document here can be seen as an intermediary; through the document, users talk with the man or the computer at the other end. (4) Feedback Document: Users provide a direct and prompt one-way information on the feedback sheet. (5) Expository document: The document only informs users of the relevant information, without any further interactions with users. The results show that clustering existed in the spatial distribution of these documents in the process of chart making, with which the pattern of readability and interactivity of those sample documents are shown on the distributed plot. The next phase of this project is to further investigate design rules of thumb in document categories. Further research will be continued to perceive useful instruments for executing design practices. Design cases and practical techniques will be extensively inquired for design consultation together with the hidden relationships discovered from this project.

Keywords: Categorization · Document design · Visual design · Design thinking

1 Introduction

Documents are closely related to our daily life, from morning papers to various corporate reports, and even to site maps issued by tourist attractions. Before the advent of the Internet in the 1970 s, documents were certain physical objects on which significant text and graphic symbols were drawn, written or printed (Kimball and Hawkins 2008). With the trend of digitalization, some physical documents are gradually replaced by digital documents. For example, the invention of the e-mail leads to the gradual decline of handwritten letters, and this change alters the way we communicate to each other. Today, breaking the limit of paper, document designers can create various styles and can add more features to their documents by using modern computer technology. Aligning with multi-media such as combining text, animation and sound altogether on a cross-platform is possible. The new technology gives users in this century a fresh new experience that they would not have ever. Knowledge acquisition is no longer limited by geographical space and information presentation also becomes abundant. The information derived from text, image, sound and all those from the multimedia works provides people a full understanding of the world. The advantages of the digital age are obvious. Even in preschool nowadays, the use of computer (including IPAD) as an educational tool is becoming the norm. Moreover, several researchers are promoting that e-learning should become a part of children's lives and kindergarten teachers should also make good use of digital products to improve children's learning ability (Wachob 1993; Backingham and Scanlon 2003). Although the external forms of documents always change, the essence of physical documents and digital documents is identical. When we read a physical document or a web page, the content must have been appropriately established so that significant information could be gotten (Kimball and Hawkins 2008).

In the mid to late twentieth century, the design world has begun to realize the importance of documents to society and carried out a series of studies on good document and visual designs. Document design is a process that organizes significant visual symbols together in a comfortable and easy way to help readers find content of interest (Carliner 2006, p. 2). Many areas also regard document design as part of information design. For example, Schriver (1997) argued that document design followed the ideas of information design to arrange words and pictures and thus to help people achieve goals in their work (p. 10). Horn (1999, pp. 15–16) pointed out that information design was a process that integrated information by means of science and art to facilitate the effective use of information. It mainly contains three purposes– (1) to make the content of the document more accurate, more easy to understand and easy to transform into action; (2) to make the human-computer interaction more simple, natural and pleasant; and (3) to make people more comfortable in the process of finding a path. On the basis of definition, this study sets forth that the document is an entity or a digital carrier for systematic integration of various types of information; and document design aims to create more efficient and accurate information communication between documents and users so that users can understand the content.

Today, document design has accumulated considerable practical experience and design methods. The design category has also been widening. While digitization can bring freer presentation and wider communication to documents, print-based documents have advantages in reading habits, execution efficiency and convenience. It is the common goals of all the document design works, in any form, need to be designed in a way to be ease of understanding, to be ease of using, and to be pleasure in use. However, various forms of document require different design treatments and strategies. For example, site maps should help visitors determine their current locations and find out the optimal path to the destination. Instructional materials require designers, engineers and technical writers to closely cooperate in order to translate professional terms into understandable languages. In order to strengthen the theoretical base to meet the complex needs of design practices, combining methods from design thinking provides the possibilities of document innovation and reconstruction for designers.

Design thinking is the methodology of the whole idea and design. It means seeking different possible solutions to different design themes and thinking differently. Brown (2008) pointed out that the design thinking was a people-oriented design spirit and method which considered not only people's needs and behaviors, but also technological and commercial feasibilities. In the process of design thinking, it is necessary to explore the core needs of users from a large number of research data (Institute of Design at Stanford, n.d. 2015). The accuracy and appropriateness of the collected data will affect not only the designers' judgment on users' needs but also the result of design thinking. With this concern, this study aims to classify the existing documents so that designers are able to clearly know and better target their design targets–

1. Extensively collect existing document samples and classify them.
2. Analyze the spatial coordinate distribution and investigate the design features of document types.

2 Literature Review

2.1 The Development of Document Design

Document design requires designers (or authors) to consciously organize information and help users recognize, understand and use documents effectively. Though differences exist between physical and digital documents in the presentation of information, both of them convey meaningful information and guide people's reading behaviors by integrating various visual elements. The earliest pattern can be traced back to 30,000 years ago when Chauvet Cave was created in France. These prehistoric marks and patterns cover cave paintings, cliff drawings, petroglyphs as well as any picture or symbol carved in the natural rock surface (Visocky O'Grady 2008). Empiricists believe that these symbols at that time were used to record people's daily hunting or used as a teaching tool in introducing prey's local features to new hunters (Kleiner 2009). The plain language movement prevailing in the United States in 1970s can be regarded as the sprout of modern document design. The purpose of the movement is to remove recondite, confusing and insulting words in tables, leaflets and brochures so that government documents can be easier to understand. Similar movements have also affected the UK, Australia, New Zealand and many other countries. In Britain, for example, the government held plain English awards to encourage institutions to participate in the competition with their office documents in order to promote the vernacular movement (Moss 1987). William Playfair (1759–1823) was a Scottish engineer whose inventions such as bar charts, line graphs and pie charts had a profound impact on the humanities, mathematics, engineering and geography. He believes that any numerical information can be converted into charts and lines. Compared with a long list of statistics, a well-designed chart can provide more information and stronger visual impact. Nowadays, information visualization has become one of the main ways to convey quantitative information in books, newspapers and magazines. Even TV stations have used various kinds of information visualization to attract the audience (Parks et al. 2006). Among those important milestones in the history of information design, International System of Typographic Picture Education (ISOTYPE) was founded by the Viennese philosopher and sociologist Otto Neurath (1882–1945) in 1920s. Considering people's low educational level at that time, Neurath hoped to establish a global educational system that would use symbolic patterns to explain complex economic problems and gradually develop into a "world language" without words. Neurath pointed out that the symbols must be clear enough and as free as possible from the help of words. Sufficient recognition should exist among symbols and thus there was no need to name all the symbols. In addition, symbols should also be concise enough to write in the limited line spacing of letters (Neurath 1936). Although ISOTYPE did not succeed as Neurath expected in the end, the various graphic symbols we see today in public places have been all deeply affected by this system.

Before the widespread use of the term "document design", Ladislav Sutnar (1897–1976) had written down many works related to catalog design, book design, and exhibition design. Sutnar was an interior designer and exhibition designer worked in New York World's Fair in 1939. Although having scheduled a short stay, he had to stay in America due to the war sweeping to his hometown. He found a new way to design information for business with his friend Knud Lönberg-Holm (Palacio and Vit 2011). To make it easy to find desired products from catalogs, Sutnar & Lönberg-Holm developed a design system by which each item in catalogs was cross-referenced with company names, industries and product names. They believed that heavy information could be classified by color, shape and graphic symbol to facilitate people's information searching, reading and remembering. To improve the reading experience of magazines, Sutnar tried to change the original single page browsing into double-page spread that not only made magazines more interesting but also enhanced the continuity of information (Clifford 2013).

In the mid to late 20th century, the term document design began to be used in industries and universities. Since document design is a branch of information design, journals (*Document Design* was merged to *Information Design Journal* in 2004) and associations (e.g. Information Design Association (IDA), International Institute for Information Design (IIID)) related to information design also undertake the promotion and research of document design and promote the professionalization of document design. A set of scientific design process is gradually established in document design. From pre-design research to user testing, the whole process fully embodies designers' increasing attention to users and the environment. The development of document design is largely attributable to two aspects. First, people's increasing requirements for accurate and convenient communication become the internal driving force promoting the sustainable development of document design. Second, science and technology updates become the external conditions for the diversified forms of document design. Under the combination of the two aspects, document design continues to improve and always pursues the efficiency of information transmission.

2.2 Basic Concepts and Applications of Classification

The basic concept of classification is to establish the relationship among different types and classify them into more subclasses for distinguishing. Classification means classifying animals and plants into different categories according to their external similarities such as calls and home range in biology. The American Library Association (ALA) has expressed that "classification" has three different but interrelated meanings in the practical application of libraries. Firstly, from the basic meaning of the word, classification is a behavior related to classifying or making classification schemes. Secondly, classify files to distinguish different topics and contents. Finally, documents (including books and other materials) will be placed on shelves or listed in the library catalog according to classification results (Wedgeworth 1993). Tan et al. (2013) argued that the main task of classification was to assign undefined items to well-defined categories. In their examples, e-mail headers could be used as a basis for computers to judge spams; cells could be classified into benign or malignant ones according to the scanning results of NMR; and galaxies could be classified into spiral or elliptical ones according to their shapes.

Classification is a ubiquitous thing in every field. With the development of the times, it continues to produce new forms. Design, as a discipline, appeared in the 20th century when the classification of disciplines was still changing continuously. Science and technology innovation diversified the tools and presentation of design, so new design types emerged. For example, with the rising of the industrial revolution, people began to make mass production with machines and design activities also stepped into the industrial design stage. Likewise, with the popularity of computers, human-computer interface design also appeared. Sanders and Stappers (2008) classify design disciplines from different perspectives into–(1) commercial design, industrial design, spatial design, fashion design and others by "product" as this classification considers the similarity of the designs/products of these disciplines. (2) service design, information design, emotional design, and others by "purpose" for those designers work not only for consumers but also for human society. For example, service design is the integration of design, management, engineering techniques and many other fields; it can be tangible or intangible and its purpose is to provide more enjoyable and available service experience for users in different contact points.

3 Research Methods and Procedures

Classifying existing documents is the preparation for design thinking and innovative solution seeking. It can help designers target data during searching. A common classification method is to assign undefined items to well-defined categories (Tan et al. 2013). For example, classify according to document carriers (such as paper, screen, and metal) or expression forms (such as text, symbol, and image). Since every items can only be assigned to a predefined category, current classification is clear but results in creativity and exploration lacking. In order to break the traditional thinking and to update the categories, this study uses the KJ Method to classify existing documents. Scupin (1997) pointed out that the KJ Method allowed researchers to collect data and conclude a relatively wide range of topics; then the data could be classified according to the relationship among them. The classification without pre-specified category is conducive to break the status quo and has become an important method for the academic research and business analysis on unknown fields.

The KJ Method is named after Jiro Kawakita who devised this method based on his years of experience and his geographical expeditions in the Himalayas in Nepal in the 1960s. This study refers to the following steps proposed in the KJ Method (Scupin 1997) to collect, classify and analyze document samples–

(1) Label making: Extensively collect various documents and screen them; ensure the discrimination among samples and then convert all the images into text description on cards; randomly shuffled the cards.
(2) Label grouping: Sort all the cards into different groups according to the functional attributes of documents until all the cards have been used. Then sort these cards into the middle group, the large group and even families in the same way.
(3) Chart making: Break the sorted cards apart and place them into the X-Y plot respectively according to the level description developed by this study.
(4) Verbal explanation: According to the coordinates shown at the previous step, make logical statements to analyze the spatial distribution and design features of these documents. The illustrations of the four steps are shown in Fig. 1.

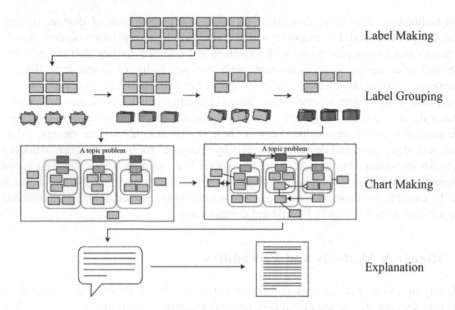

Fig. 1. Four Steps of the KJ Method (Viriyayudhakorn 2013)

4   Data Analysis and Discussion

There were 153 document samples collected and screened. The original samples were filtered by excluding with highly similar content and forms. It turned out that 54 representative samples were selected and were analyzed with the KJ Method (See Fig. 2).

4.1   Step 1: Label Making

All the samples were converted into cards in this step and were prepared to benefit next step for label grouping. Samples were converted into descriptive texts on cards to minimize the interference factors in reading images and to truly identify and process data through text. This approach has also long been used in the KJ Method. Researchers accurately wrote down the functions of these samples on cards according to their observation. For example, Sample 01 was an airplane flight manual and its function description was "teach passengers how to use safety equipment in airplanes". Sample 02 was a curriculum vitae and its function description was "introduce job seekers' background to interviewers". Sample 03 was a shopping site and its function description was "Display all kinds of goods online and provide ordering service". The rest of the cards were labelled by analogy.

Fig. 2. Selected fifty-four research samples

4.2   Step 2: Label Grouping

Researchers then integrated these cards from bottom to top at the second step, spread out these cards and read them, then drew out the cards with the same attribute to sort into a small group until all the cards had been used. In the course of sorting, if there was any card that could not be clearly sorted, it would be put back and sorted into a separate group. The grouping of middle and large groups was made in the same way. It turned out that five document types were summarized (Fig. 3) and named according to their features. Detailed description is as follows:

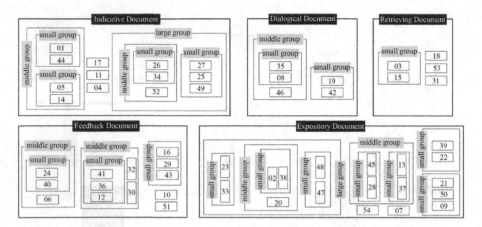

Fig. 3. Five document types from label grouping

(1) Indicative document: Introduce the use of a product or guide users to complete a task. For example, users can learn the functions of each button from mobile phone manuals before use.

(2) Retrieving document: Users seek the information they need from a complex set of information according to visual cues in the document. For example, when consumers browse shopping sites, they can click the pictures of their favorite products to learn the details (price, style, manufacturer, etc.).

(3) Dialogical document: There are repeated interactions between users and documents. The document here can be seen as an intermediary. Users talk to the person or communicate with the computer at the other end. If it is a person at the other end, the document could be a social media, or so to speak. If it is a computer, the document could be a "Help" document to answer the input questions by the computer.

(4) Feedback document: Users provide a direct and prompt one-way information on the feedback sheet. For example, people fill in the name, home address, telephone number and other personal information according to the requirement of questionnaires.

(5) Expository document: The document only informs users of the relevant information, without any further interactions with users. Expository documents are often overlooked due to their few interactions with readers, but the information in the documents may be very useful and this type is also one of the most common document types. For example, monthly bank statements allow clients to know their economic situation. The humble clothing hang tags can contain a lot of information such as size, manufacturer, material, washing method and storage method.

4.3   Step 3: Chart Making

At this step, the sorted data were organized into a X-Y plot that directly shows the pattern of interactivity (X-axis) and readability (Y-axis) among collected samples. Both axes had tick marks. The interactivity was classified into 8 levels from low to high and the readability was classified into 4 levels from high to low. The corresponding level description (Table 1) was developed after discussion with five design experts (two university design teachers and three senior designers from industry). The level of each sample was determined by two coders who had reached a consensus based on the level description. While the coordinates of the sample were obtained, and the relationship among different document types were easily shown (Fig. 4).

Table 1. Document level description

Level	Level description of interactivity
1	Users need to read the documents for some reason. For example, tourists read street signs to orient themselves
2	Attracted by the visual design, users casually browse the document
3	Interested in some of the contents, users read the document selectively
4	Users are willing to read all the contents of the document
5	Users can complete a certain task after reading the document such as tuning channels or adjusting volume by using the TV remote
6	Users provide a simple information feedback according to the prompt of the document such as grading (Check the box in Likert Five- or Seven-Point Scale)
7	Users provide more complex information feedbacks according to the prompt of the document such as filling out personal suggestions
8	Users make repeated communication with the document. For example, users use the Help document of a software program to input questions and get answers
Level	Level description of readability
1	There is very little original information (e.g. dressing room sign) or the contents have been refined by designers to a very streamlined level that users can immediately understand
2	Necessary text information is retained. Difficult information in the original data is also optimized by using symbols, diagrams and illustrations
3	All the original data of the document are retained but an effective information structure is built to help users understand it
4	No optimizations are made by designers so users have to interpret the document by themselves

4.4   Step 4: Verbal Explanation

The above chart (Fig. 4) shows that clustering existed in the spatial distribution of these documents, and the interactivity and the readability of documents that in the same type have internal consistency. The spatial distributions of these document types are as follows:

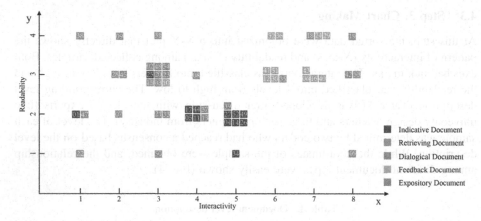

Fig. 4. The relationship among different document types shown in a X-Y plot

(1) Indicative document: These documents are mainly distributed in the middle part of the plot; the interactivity is average and the readability is comparatively low. For those documents with indicative and instructional purposes, designers usually simplify the complex operation steps into diagrams as a great strategy with which to assist novices to learn. Let us take the sample 26 as an example. This document is a low power prompt of mobile phone and its purpose is to guide users to complete the charging action. The content of the document consists of text and symbols. Text information is more detailed. It tells users to immediately charge the cell phone or exit some applications to save power. In addition, the charging time may increase if the cell phone is at the same time in use. Plug and battery icons are designed in an intuitive way to tell users to charge the cell phone and such graphic symbols increase readability.

(2) Retrieving document: These documents are mainly distributed in the middle and upper part of the plot. The readability is relatively low. Text is the main content of these documents. Users have to select what they need from a lot of information by their own judgment. For instance, sample 15 is an email interface which allows users to select the email they want to read from the list. In the searching process, users can read emails in sequence from the very beginning, or quickly find out the target ones by inputting keywords or selecting a certain contact.

(3) Dialogical document: These documents are mainly distributed in the right part of the plot. The interactivity is relatively high because users need to input information before getting feedback from the device. The interaction may be repeated. Sample 35 is the user login interface of Google. Users need to input registered accounts and passwords to use Google service. If the account or password is wrong, a prompt will appear to tell users to retry or to retrieve password. This process can be regarded as a conversation between human and documents. If users forget the password, they have to answer the preset questions to confirm their identities. Then the number of human-computer conversation will increase.

(4) Feedback document: Feedback documents are basically online or physical forms and happen to be mainly distributed in the upper right part of the plot.

The interactivity of feedback document is naturally high since it requires users to fill in the information. Sample 16 is a mailing label for airmail parcel post, for example. The boxes in red are designed for post office to use (e.g., zip code, delivery date, delivery cost) and the ones in blue are for general public (e.g., sender's and receiver's names, addresses, and telephone numbers… etc.). The information in red boxes, for staff in postal office to use, are in more detail and with more professional terms. On the contrary, the rest area tends to be designed in a friendly way for the general public to sufficiently use. Few clarification notes are also added on at several places to assist users to fill in their answers.

(5) Expository document: The information of expository document tends to explain or describe something. The interactivity of this kind of documents is relatively low due to the users of this document only read but no need to provide feedback. The distribution is mainly on the left part of the plot, obviously. As most of the expository documents focus on information integrity and accuracy, there are few deep refinements for the original data. Taking an ATM transaction receipt as an example (Sample 20), this document contains fairly small space but covers much information such as withdrawal, transfer, and balance inquiries… etc. A clear information structure is established to highlight key points in such a limited space.

Furthermore, there are four samples (Sample 01, 22, 38, and 47) in the space with very weak interactivity ($x = 1$) in Fig. 4. The one-way delivery purposed documents are either notification or warning messages with which no feedback is asked from users. For example, Sample 22 is a food preservative pack, with striking font and color (usually red) to warn people not to eat it. On the other hand, high interactivity is required when users need to provide complex feedback, and human-computer inter-activities are the regular basis nowadays. Four samples (19, 42, 46, and 53) show extremely strong interactivity ($x = 8$) on the plot. Sample 42 is a Calendar App in mobile phones. Users can key in various information such as date query, filling in to-do items and setting time and reminders. The machine records the information simulta-neously. Reminder sends alarm when it is activated. There are four samples (22, 34, 46, and 50) show their high readability on the plot ($y = 1$). They are either simplified enough for ease of reading, or visualized in a way for ease of understanding. For example, Sample 34 is a warning pattern on the product packaging. It reminds workers to keep one side up during transport in case of damaging the product. The document includes only arrows and the text in capital, THIS SIDE UP, for high awareness. There are nine samples (09, 18, 19, 24, 29, 31, 32, 36 and 38) in the space with very low readability ($y = 4$). Most information of these documents presents in text form. Users hardly grasp the idea and interpret the information when it gets complex and lacks of a well-designed presentation.

5 Conclusions and Recommendations

Precise management and specification of document types can assist designers to carry out data collection and to stimulate new ideas. Sample documents were classified with the KJ Method to conclude into five document types, including indicative document, retrieving document, dialogical document, feedback document and expository document. The plot showed that clustering existed in the spatial distribution of these documents in the process of chart making, with which the pattern of readability and interactivity of those sample documents are shown on the distributed plot. According to the graphic analysis, this paper puts forward the following suggestions to improve the interactivity and readability in document design. First of all, it is important to keep the coherence of logical thinking when we design the high interactivity documents, as well as keep away the unnecessary visual elements in order to avoid the interruption of obtaining information. Secondly, not only the effectiveness, but the efficiency of information design in the document is equally important. Research shows that users, especially younger kids or Asians, may lose their confidence if they cannot understand the document (Schriver 1997), or just give up in searching and waiting if they fail to acquire information in time. Thirdly, users' interests and desire in using the document can be stimulated through design thinking from an information design viewpoint, especially to the documents with low interactivity (e.g. expository document). With this notion in mind, documents have to be more friendly for people to use. For instance, technical diagrams and terms are mostly acceptable to professionals as they have been trained. For the general public, however, the overloaded complex information may result in a wrong judgment. It is therefore necessary to set up a reasonable information structure to guide users to find the information they need.

Based on the categorization of document design in this study, further research will be continued to perceive useful instruments for executing design practices. The next phase is to investigate design rules of thumb in document categories with the essence of design thinking embedded within. Together with the hidden relationships discovered from this project, design cases and practical techniques will be extensively investigated for design consultation.

References

Backingham, D., Scanlon, M.: Education, Entertainment, and Learning in the Home. Open University Press, Philadelphia (2003)

Brown, T.: Design thinking. Harvard Bus. Rev. **86**(6), 84–92 (2008)

Carliner, S.: Current challenges of research in information and document design. In: Carliner, S., Verkens, J.P., de Waele, C.A.E. (eds.) Information and Document Design: Variety on the Research, pp. 1–24. John Benjamins, Amsterdam (2006)

Clifford, J.: Graphic Icons: Visionaries Who Shaped Modern Graphic Design. Pearson Education (2013)

Horn, R.E.: Information design: emergence of a new profession. In: Jacobson, R. (ed.) Information Design, pp. 15–33. MIT Press, Cambridge (1999)

Institute of Design at Stanford (n.d.). An introduction to design thinking process guide. https://dschool.stanford.edu/sandbox/groups/designresources/wiki/36873/attachments/74b3d/ModeGuideBOOTCAMP2010L.pdf. Accessed 16 Jun 2015

Kimball, M.A., Hawkins, A.R.: Document Design: A Guide for Technical Communicators. Bedford/St. Martin's, Boston (2008)

Kleiner, F.S.: Gardner's Art Through the Ages: A Global History. Thomson Wadsworth, Boston (2009)

Moss, W.: The plain English campaign: a interview. Res. Pract. Adult Literacy **4**, 1–6 (1987)

Neurath, O.: International picture language: the first rules of isotype (1936). http://imaginarymuseum.org/MHV/PZImhv/NeurathPictureLanguage.html. Accessed 16 Jun 2015

Palacio, B.G., Vit, A.: Graphic Design, Referenced: A Visual Guide to the Language, Applications, and History of Graphic Design. Rockport Publishers, Beverly (2011)

Parks, H., Musser, G., Trimpe, L., Maurer, V., Maurer, R.: A Mathematical View of Our World. Cengage Learning (2006)

Sanders, E.B.N., Stappers, P.J.: Co-creation and the new landscapes of design. Co-design **4**(1), 5–18 (2008)

Schriver, K.A.: Dynamics in document design. Wiley, New York (1997)

Scupin, R.: The KJ method: a technique for Analyzing data derived from Japanese ethnology. Hum. Organ. **56**(2), 233–237 (1997)

Tan, P.N., Steinbach, M., Kumar, V.: Introduction to Data Mining. Addison-Wesley, Boston (2013)

Viriyayudhakorn, K.: Creativity Assistants and Social Influences in KJ-Method Creativity Support Groupware (Unpublished Doctoral's Thesis). Japan Advanced Institute of Science and Technology, Ishikawa (2013)

Visocky O'Grady, J.: The Information Design Handbook. How Books, Cincinnati (2008)

Wachob, R.: Young minds soar with technology. Comput. Teach. **20**, 53–55 (1993)

Wedgeworth, R.: World Encyclopedia of Library and Information Services. American Library Association, Chicago (1993)

Internet Product Design Is the Whole Design Around the "Product Strategy"

Chao Liu[✉]

UX Department, Baidu, Beijing, China
Liuchao05@baidu.com

Abstract. The first step in the design of Internet products is "product strategy" design. "Product strategy" is the core features of the product design. This article tells how to design a scientific product strategy, how to use the "product strategy" to produce "product features", how to design a "graphical interface" based on the "product strategy", how to choose "operation" and "delivery channel" based on "product strategy" through the Chinese Internet well-known cases that the author personally experienced. All aspects are evaluated around the "product strategy". The success or failure of the product is the success or failure of the "product strategy".

Keywords: China internet domain · Products design · User experience design

1 Introduction

China's Internet market competition is very intense. BAT [1] and other giants adhere to their own mainstream business while also try to innovate a variety of projects. With the popularity of Internet technology and the call of the Chinese government, a large number of traditional enterprises have begun to do the Internet products. But in reality 93% [2] of the new products will disappear within 5 years (According to data statistics of Baidu promotion). The author finds that the failure of most products is because of the product core direction is not clear or the implementation process of local links and product core are out of line. (Through the designers' interview by Baidu UX academy on small and medium-sized company.) So the author will discuss the influence of "product strategy" and "product strategy" on other factors, in order to discuss the design of Internet products is a whole design concept.

A. Marcus and W. Wang (Eds.): DUXU 2017, Part I, LNCS 10288, pp. 114–121, 2017.
DOI: 10.1007/978-3-319-58634-2_9

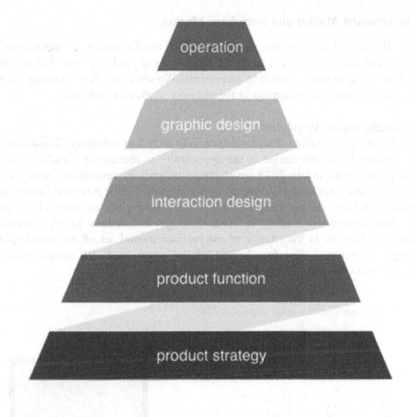

2 How to Design the "Product Strategy"

We will do a very important analysis before doing any products: How big the market is, is it the incremental market or shrinkage market, the market share of competitors, what the user needs, what advantages we have. And finally we have the possibility of holding a certain market share.

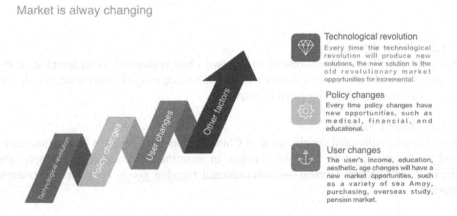

2.1   Incremental Market and Shrinkage Market

First of all, we first analyze the product involved in the market is incremental or shrinkage: The key to success is to do the right thing at the right time. The so-called correct time is the industry market in increments. We often use the following ways to predict whether there is an increase in the industry market opportunities:

2.1.1   Technological Revolution

Every technological revolution will produce new technical solutions. The new technology solution is the old market is the opportunity to increase the market. Such as Android phone broke out in 2013 smart phone technology revolution. New android users do not know what kind of APP they need to install? So the APP that recommends the application have the potential market. It has become the entrance of company mobile App distribution market. It needs average 1–2 dollars to recommend to download an App. So in the change of market incremental set off by mobile phone technology revolution a, the first benefit of the company is 91 mobile assistant. Eventually Baidu bought it for $1 billion 900 million.

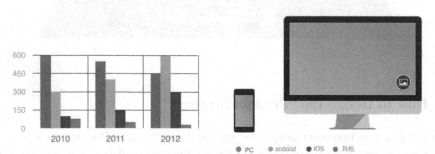

The increments of 91 mobile assistant APP

Recommend a variety of APP grab head, 91 mobile assistant is called app distribution entrance.

From the data, PG users use a large number of long time to the wireless device migration, wireless user growth rate surge, the time of android users are 3 times than IOS from 2010 to 2012. So that we can infer the new user mobile phone download app is a phased outbreak just need, because all app are new. The class of mobile assistant app is recommended into the app traffic entrance.

2.1.2   Policy Changes

For example, China's liberalization of the two-child policy led to an increase in the market for child care services. China's population tends to age in the future, which will lead to future growth in the pension market.

2.1.3   User Changes

For example, with rapid development of Chinese economic, People's income increases and aesthetic improves. And the changes in consumer upgrade. For example, the demand for overseas tourism and international branded goods is in the incremental market.

2.1.4   The User's Needs Pain Points

We have to understand the user after understanding the market increment. The key to research users is to find out the needs of users. We often put some users that think fun and interesting as a user needs pain points, such as somatosensory games of Xbox360. Most of the users to buy this product will not be more than 2 weeks. Eventually they back to the handle game. There are also recent meteor VR games. Users use less time. How to determine the needs of users just need it. There are actually two ways. First we can see the user on this demand is a long-term existence or not. Such as the various levels of human needs in the Maastian theory. In fact, many Internet products can correspond to this system. The second method is that we can see that if the user they want to find alternatives when the thing do not meet this demand. For example, The author once asked the user of a mobile phone UI design to improve in 2010 show, many users said it was not cool when looking at the mobile phone interface of UI animation, but they never try to find alternatives. But when the user found the phone text was too small to see clear. There are users to find a magnifying glass to see this mobile phone. This point that the real needs of the mobile phone UI design pain point is too small, not cool enough.

3   Competitive Analysis

First of all we have to know the market share of competitors. Second, we must know the characteristics and advantages of competitors which is the key to producing our "product strategy". For example, "Hungry" take away (China local food delivery company) the pursuit of single and cheap restaurants, which gives Baidu Takeaway opportunities. Baidu takeout main concentrate on quality and brand restaurants. Although the restaurants of Baidu Takeaway are less than "Hungry", it has won the white-collar group of market space.

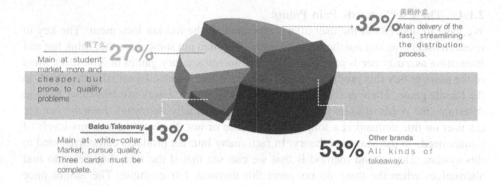

4 Core Strengths

The core step of "product strategy" is to understand their own advantages. What we are good at determining our "product strategy". We can think from the following aspects:

4.1 Industry Advantage

After 2015, China has been very difficult to produce pure Internet companies. Many new Internet companies are actually "Internet +" companies, that is, the enterprises and teams that have certain advantages in the traditional business use Internet technology and methodology to generate new products. Such as the catering industry department master, laundry industry, such as e bag washing.

4.2 Technical Advantages

Such as Baidu produces Baidu unmanned vehicles, Baidu degree and other artificial intelligence products, in artificial intelligence on the accumulation of technical advantages.

4.3 Capital Advantage

DIDI taxi rapidly occupy the majority of China's taxi travel market through financing advantages. Let v as the financing advantage through the subsidies in the field of television has rapidly become a first-line brand.

4.4 Branded Advantages

Baidu, Tencent, Alibaba and other companies in the well-known brands in the Internet finance occupy a reputation advantage.

5 "User Research" Is Consistent with "Product Strategy"

When we establish the "product strategy" through the above methodologies, any part of the team's work should be carried out around the "product strategy". First of all, what we must do is the user research, which is the key link through the product research and development. There are many ways for user research, we don't discuss here. The most basic requirements of these methods are "research target users", while the standard of "target user" is determine by the "product strategy".

6 Graphic User Interface Design Is Consistent with "Product Strategy"

Graphical design of the product contains a lot, in addition to the user interface, but also include the product VI system, as well as offline operation of the material (portable display, billboards, etc.). These designs must be unified in order to allow users to remember. The uniform style must be consistent with the emotion expresses of the product strategy. The series of Baidu bear is to increase the warmth and temperature for serious technology, which is the mascot of Baidu employees. So its color and style has always been lively and fun. Baidu college entrance examination "product strategy" with large data to help high school students simulate and forecast tests so the visual style the semantics combine youth inspirational and technology.

7 Interaction Design Is Consistent with "Product Strategy"

"Product strategy" is essential which involves every aspect of the product. For example, we design mobile phone products APP interactive navigation framework to make navigation Tab (Fig. 1), the average distribution (Fig. 2), or that the middle one, even the Fig. (3) in the sidebar. In fact, there is no this standard of "product strategy", all of them are right, they are also wrong. Figure 1 the average allocation is equal to the switching frequency for each channel. Figure 2 it emphasizes the middle one, which indicates that the channel logic in the middle is different from that of the other. Figure 3 in the sidebar shows that there is only a common channel, the other can be hidden.

Fig. 1.

Fig. 2.

8 The Product Promotion Is Consistent with Product Strategy

Product design and product operation is inseparable. Product marketing promotion also has a lot of methodologies and verification methods. But these methodologies, just like user research, must be based on "relevance" to promote this foundation. While the standard of "relevance" of is still "product strategy."

Fig. 3.

9   Discussion

To sum up, the core product design is the "product strategy" design. If the "product strategy" is not considered maturely or not been initially verified, do not carry out other aspects of the work blindly. And when there are many team members or the length of the project from the initial time is very long, the team manager must observe and consider whether there is a link from the product "product strategy" to the other direction. It is possible to win in the market only all the links strive to a scientific "product strategy".

1. Majority UI designers are artists background in China, how to make these artists have rational product thinking?
2. The core competitiveness of Internet products is technology, how to make design more valuable in Internet products?
3. If everything revolves around the core of "product strategy", how do product managers focus on the details of the user experience?

References

1. Baidu, Alibaba, Tencent
2. http://www.cyzone.cn/a/20151006/281109.html

Reflection on Exploring and Designing Generation Y Interaction Qualities

Wei Liu[✉]

Beijing Normal University, Beijing, China
liuwei.dk@gmail.com

Abstract. This paper addresses the main findings of a research project on Generation Y interactions, including reflection on the research questions, the conceptual framework, the research framework and designing for interaction qualities. The perspective of this research underwent two big changes through understanding and designing Generation Y interactions. First, we started with demographics, which changed to styles of interaction. Secondly, we worked with interaction qualities instead of function qualities, developed a way to specify them for office situations, and used and evaluated them in design.

Keywords: Interaction qualities · Generation Y · Reflection · Office work

1 Introduction

The rapid development of information technology in the past decade has enabled the introduction of a number of new communication tools and platforms in everyday life, such as instant messaging, podcasting, blogging and social networking. These tools offer people new ways of interacting, enabling them to create, retrieve and broadcast large amounts of digital information, using a great variety of devices, techniques and media. As a result of this constant stream of information, people have become more socially active as well as become more capable and ready to integrate their virtual world with their physical world, using highly interactive devices, such as mobile phones, laptops and multi-touch tablets.

So far, however, this kind of interactive behavior has mainly manifested itself in people's private context, while in the more public work context the rich interactions that all these new technologies are offering do not seem to be supported to a great extent yet. Whereas office applications have increased sometimes dramatically in functionality, the ways of interacting with all these functionalities have evolved much more slowly [17]. As a consequence, most office work is thus still done through the ubiquitous, almost 40-year old, set-up of keyboard, display and mouse, which only supports limited behaviors, such as keyboard tapping and mouse clicking.

This lack of richness in interaction is becoming more evident, now that a new generation of workers is quickly entering the market. This so-called Generation Y, born in the 1980s and early 90s, are digital natives [21, 25], who have experienced digital technology their entire lives. Thus they have developed new ways and habits of interacting with their (digital) world, putting very high demands on the applications, services, devices and networks that enable and support these interactions.

A. Marcus and W. Wang (Eds.): DUXU 2017, Part I, LNCS 10288, pp. 122–133, 2017.
DOI: 10.1007/978-3-319-58634-2_10

An interesting challenge therefore presents itself to designers and researchers: How to bring the qualities of the interactions [13, 14, 23] that people currently experience in the private context of their homes and friends into the more public context of their offices and colleagues?

This challenge is taken on through a number of studies, in which the following research questions were addressed:

1. What are Generation Y styles of interaction in home life and office work?
2. What are the interaction qualities that make up Generation Y styles of interaction?
3. How are these interaction qualities experienced within home and office context?
4. What are opportunities to design office tools or services that support Generation Y styles of interaction?
5. How are the interaction qualities of these new designs experienced?

Figure 1 shows the research framework, which distinguishes three major components: (1) people (Generation Y), (2) technology and (3) context (home vs. work). On the intersections of these three components are the interactions that are at the core of the research.

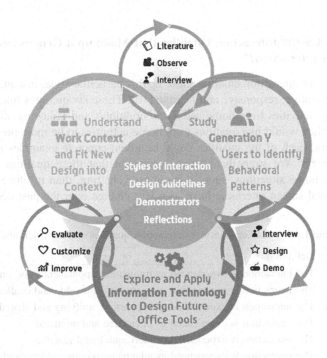

Fig. 1. The research framework

2   The Research Questions

The starting point of this research was formed by the research questions as listed in the introduction. In the remainder of this section, the author discusses what answers were found.

2.1   'What Are Generation Y Styles of Interaction in Home Life and Office Work?'

The literature review showed that Generation Y has experienced a different state of technology and ways of (social) interaction than the generations before them, e.g., in that they grew up online, and experience mobile devices and social media as the natural condition of life. We gathered a set of examples of activities representative of what people currently do in their home and office context, and found that they could be grouped into a style of interaction [1, 18], which we have labeled as 'Generation Y'. We also noticed that this style of interaction seemed to be more prominent in the home situation than in the office context.

2.2   'What Are the Interaction Qualities that Make up a Generation Y Style of Interaction?'

Table 1 shows six interaction qualities make up this particular style: instant, expressive, playful, collaborative, responsive and flexible [10]. These six qualities functioned well in categorizing activities from home and work situations, and in having office workers describe how they would like qualities from home activities to be more present in their work situations. Each of the qualities could be given concrete examples in the home and work context. We strengthened the impression that these qualities were better represented in home situations, such as gaming or chatting, than in office conditions, where traditional screen interfaces have seen less change over the past decade.

Table 1. The six Generation Y interaction qualities and their definition

Qualities	Definition
Instant	The interaction is experienced as immediate, spontaneous and on the spot
Playful	The interaction is experienced as engaging, enjoyable and challenging
Collaborative	The interaction is experienced as supportive, unifying and shared
Expressive	The interaction is experienced as open, free and animated
Responsive	The interaction is experienced as alert, quick and reactive
Flexible	The interaction is experienced as adaptable, accommodating and adjustable

2.3 'How Are These Interaction Qualities Experienced Within the Home and Office Context?'

The six interaction qualities were used as criteria to assess and compare the experience of user interactions in the home and work context. Playful, expressive, responsive and flexible seem to give good directions for improving interactions at work, while instant and collaborative showed less opportunity. The latter, however, but may have been because of the choice of the particular office activities. The above might suggest a straightforward solution for improving interactions at the office: bring in the Nintendo Wii and the Microsoft Kinect controls, and social media. In practice, however, not all workers are Generation Y people, not all are digital natives, and the office equipment has to support collaborations between different people. For that reason, designing for Generation Y qualities is more subtle (and more limited) than just bringing in devices and techniques that Generation Y is familiar with.

2.4 'What Are Opportunities to Design Office Tools or Services That Support Generation Y Styles of Interaction?'

The interviews and discussions showed that the six interaction qualities made sense to users and designers alike. However, mostly designers would pick up the names of the qualities, whereas users tended to refer to examples that were given. This may be because designers are more used to talk about interactions and qualities as abstract things, whereas other people will refer to their direct experiences. The six interaction qualities together, with their corresponding guidelines, could be used by the author, and by design students with some success to design and enrich new types of user interactions in the work context. However, although they supported discussions and gave direction, this depended a lot on where in the design process they were used. In order to demonstrate Generation Y interactions, a pair of YPhone prototypes were designed and developed.

2.5 'How Are the Interaction Qualities of These New Designs Experienced?'

In the evaluation, the YPhone prototype worked in demonstrating Generation Y interaction qualities, transferring the Generation Y style of interaction from home to work. Moreover, the evaluation results indicated that the interactions would fit into work contexts and enrich people's work situations. And we found that the qualities could be fitted in the Hassenzahl model of qualities [5]. Most participants recognized the intended user-product interaction qualities, except for instant and collaborative.

3 The Conceptual Framework

The Besides finding (partial) answers along the directions of the research questions, the research helped sharpen our understanding of how interaction qualities might be instrumental in design processes. It turned out to be important where the qualities are positioned, both in the solution space of what is evaluated or designed, and in the design process.

3.1 Interactions Between Context and Product

Interactions do not exist by themselves. They are situated on an activity level between the context of use level and the functional and product level. The interaction between user and products lies between these two, and the interaction qualities at this level are connected to the other two levels. At the Why level, a person has an urgent reason to consult a colleague over the phone. At the What level, he does this by using the designed product, a phone. And in between is the interaction where he uses the phone toward the goal.

Both these levels are hurdles for interaction designers. Many interaction designers see their main focus on designing 'the concept', i.e., that there are things like urgent consultations and who is involved in these. For many, the interaction and its qualities only come into view after the functional problems are being solved. In the student projects, this problem surfaced most visibly. Many struggled so hard with designing interactive technology that they were satisfied when 'the button was pushable and could start the show', showing difficulty in mustering the sensitivity to consider 'whether the button was big, small, quick, slow, etc.'. Even when we tried to have them focus explicitly on the qualities by restricting the solution space to a pre-given context (i.e., the Pong game), the students pushed toward modifying the context (i.e., the pirate ship Pong) or a modality (i.e., the stereo audio Pong), with limited explorations along axes of interaction qualities [12].

In their defence, interaction qualities can easily be confused with functional qualities of a product [16, 20]. In the evaluation of YPhone, we found that the playful, expressive, responsive and flexible interaction qualities implemented in YPhone were experienced well in a lab context and in a work context, but the instant and collaborative qualities were experienced less. It may well have been that respondents found it difficult to assess whether YPhone's interactions were experienced as instant and collaborative, because the activity of making a phone call is being perceived as instant and collaborative by nature, i.e., talking in real time with somebody else.

3.2 Interaction Qualities in the Design Process

The above difficulties suggest that interaction qualities are most helpful at guiding design actions during detailing rather than conceptualization. Possibly, designers should first solve the issues of context and product level before attending to interaction qualities to tweak, tune and polish them in subsequent iterations. This implies that the design should first be grounded in scenarios, storyboards and first functional proto-types, before the part of solution space is opened up where interaction qualities can help. Earlier research prototypes, e.g., those by Frens [4] and Wensveen [27] were also fully functional.

3.3 Qualities, Words and Experience

As noted earlier, the six interaction qualities were readily picked up by designers to discuss activities and products, and served well as labels for groups of collected activities for respondents in research. However, giving only the names and a verbal definition or description to student designers had only limited value. Often stories, memories, demonstrations and examples, were needed to give guidance. One reason for this is that the qualities are more abstract than product qualities like 'soft', 'yellow' and 'curved' that designers have been used to deal with: interaction qualities are essentially relations (between user and product), depending highly on dimensions like time (fast or slow), proximity (close or distant) or amplitude (small or big), that manifest themselves in bodily experiences. For each of these, the symbolic nature of language is a limited means of expression and communication.

In order to support designers in working with interaction qualities, they may need to develop not only a vocabulary, but also a 'sense', a repertoire along these dimensions. Designers could then pick one or more interaction qualities from such a repertoire of examples, and use these as a benchmark against which they later could compare their designs.

Tools for exploring interaction qualities are also needed. For classic product qualities, such as the color of a display, many simple and sophisticated tools exist. But the subtlety of flicking the magnet ball in YPhone requires fine-tuning resistance, friction and stability, which can currently only be done by careful craft, i.e., repeatedly cutting the running groove with appropriate tools. New developments in 3D printing may well prove important in enabling such explorations, e.g., by creating a series of variations of running grooves for testing their motion qualities.

4 Designing for Interaction Qualities

Traditionally in design, products were designed to look beautiful and to function well. These products were created by combining technology trends, software capabilities and product functions rather than focusing on the application and experience of user interactions in a specific context. Since two decades ago, IT products have become interactive and with the maturing of interaction design as a discipline, attention is gradually shifting from designing quality of aesthetics and function to designing qualities of interaction. The focus there becomes managing relations, such as trust and experience, along longer stretches of time and in more complex environments.

This research contributes to the existing body of knowledge in this domain by taking the notion of interaction qualities from theory to practice and bringing Generation Y interaction qualities from home to work. Although other researchers and designers know how to start designing from a functional perspective, designing using interaction qualities is new. Previous work [4, 22, 23, 27] sees interaction qualities as analytical tools and inspirational instruments, and would fit them into user experience, which addresses user feelings, memories and expectations from interacting with the interfaces. In this research, interaction qualities, as a new strength in guiding design, are about what experience a user can get with a design through actively engaging with a product, system or service. They can help designers give specific emphasis when designing the interactions they want their product to evoke.

We believe that interaction qualities can serve as a tool to guide the design process, especially in tuning interactions that have been chosen. The six interaction qualities become a set to guide designers in realizing Generation Y interactions. They are a key set for this research and are helpful to guide designers, but not a complete set (e.g., the playful quality may extend to cheerful, engaging and passionate qualities) for reaching out every detailed aspect describing user-product interactions.

Are there only six interaction qualities? In our studies, six interaction qualities were sufficient to categorize the set of activities we found in the home and work context, and all six had some value in giving direction to designers. But the ease in which these six qualities could be fitted into the Hassenzahl model [5] may be a sign that there may not be a complete set. It may even be questioned if making a complete set would be useful, given the observation that none of the six qualities were identical to the ones in the Hassenzahl model. Rather, the most important lesson may be to direct the designer's attention to interaction qualities as something that can (or should) be designed, and to point out how the solution space can be explored, possibly by showing a repertoire of solutions that instantiate each quality.

5 Reflection on the Approach

In this section the author reflects on methods used in this research on Generation Y interactions.

5.1 Literature and Interviews

In the first part of the project, literature study, contextual interviews were the main methods. Although the literature helped with identifying Generation Y demographics, lifestyles and behaviors, little was found on the specific level of interactions.

The open-ended nature of face-to-face interviewing was assisted by generative toolkits and guided tours through the users' home and work environment served to identify the interactions, and to derive a model. Previous work [2, 3, 6, 29] shows that interviewing and designing with a toolkit can engage users in a user-centered design process and support them in activities such as sharing experiences, building skills and implementing ideas. In this research, the toolkit [10] served as a trigger to overcome the difficulties of getting people to talk about interactions. It helped prompt the participants to recall concrete experiences and to think about how they experience certain contexts and interactions [19, 24, 28]. This evoked the participants to make comparisons on interactions between the home and work context. Because the design of the interview boards and the activities was somewhat ambiguous, the boards mainly served to help the participants talk about memories and opinions, rather than answer specific questions. This enabled us to discuss possible conflicts and differences in perspectives, and to cluster the interpretations based on the transcripts, field notes and the notes. A consequence of this openness was that the interpretation of individual cards and terms varied. Although the placement of the cards on the boards might be regarded as ratings on 7-point scales, a statistical analysis was not possible. Rather, the analysis focused on interpreting what the participants said to explain their placements.

5.2 The Value of Doing Design as Part of the Research

Research offers methods to conduct studies and to gain knowledge on a current state of affairs. In order to study a state of affairs that does not yet exist, we can bring that state into being, which requires an act of design. In research through design, both the resulting prototype and the act of designing itself can contribute to that new understanding. The prototype can be evaluated in the setting, with regular methods of study. In the act of designing, the designer-researcher is confronted with the difficulties of realizing the theoretical ideas into the real world. Reflecting on the design decisions also provides understanding, which is more difficult to capture than the results that are visible in the prototype. In this research project, the author's own design iterations [11, 12] and his involvement in student projects provided continuous occasions to reflect on and reconsider the value of the interaction qualities in guiding him or the students, and to collect examples of situations where the qualities are best represented. Although this process was not documented explicitly, it contributed implicitly to the progress of the research.

5.3 Prototypes and Evaluations

Prototypes [11, 12, 26] were built with an iterative design process and with the intent to demonstrate Generation Y interactions. It was worthwhile to build prototypes such as YPhone, because such prototypes enabled the participants to experience interaction qualities implemented in a design (in the same way in the same evaluation settings). Considering all the techniques used in the design process, ranging from sketching, storyboarding to play-acting, demonstrating a new design with a working prototype was the most important. By designing and building prototypes, different aspects were integrated from theory and practice. By setting out and demonstrating prototypes that cover interaction qualities, feedback from users, peers and experts was gathered. Prototypes make it possible to communicate complex results through demonstration. They guide users in imagining different office situations by demonstrating interactions and user scenarios. This is valuable, as users do not only reflect on an envisioned experience, but on an embodied experience, when they are immersed in the experience by touching and operating the prototypes.

For the controlled in-lab evaluations [9], the evaluation questionnaire borrowed was based on the Hassenzahl model, which was proved to work well for assessing interaction qualities [5]. This worked because it addressed the right interaction qualities, which are the Generation Y interaction quality word pairs and the qualities in the Hassenzahl model. In other research through design projects [4, 22, 27], the researchers primarily focused on controlled in-lab and longitudinal studies to evaluate a main hypothesis. Compared with their approaches, the approach followed in this research has a broader range of involving user, experience and context. This was essential to capture the real-world user experiences in the work context. This helped form and improve our understanding of how to design office tools with Generation Y type of interaction. Figure 2 shows user experience of the YPhone prototype.

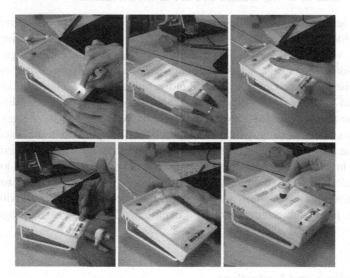

Fig. 2. The participants experienced YPhone and evaluated the design based on their experiences

6   Discussion

This research project was started with the aim of finding guidelines for practitioners to design 'the next generation interfaces for office use'. We aimed the work to be both useful for practitioners and design researchers. In this section the author suggests recommendations for each group.

6.1   For Office Tool Developers

At this moment (beginning of 2017) there still aren't too many examples of office tools being fully integrated with new interactions (e.g., Generation Y interactions) and new technologies (e.g., high-tech sensors and actuators). The few notable exceptions are mostly conceptual designs, which are not broadly experienced and adopted by office workers. To point a direction for developers, like Exact, who care about supporting office situations with new tools, applications and services, starting out projects from user-centered perspectives and from the interaction perspective are recommended. One direction that could be explored is to gamify specific ways of working, which apply elements such as training, practicing, competing and rewarding within the design of applications. The interaction qualities approach can enhance this by promoting designs that are not just game-like in a structural sense of taking turns and earning rewards, but, e.g., also more playful as an experience.

6.2   For Design Practitioners, Educators and Students

The six interaction qualities can help designers develop products that fit with the new interaction styles that have entered our lives in the last decade. These qualities indicate directions, present examples, and provide relevant dimensions to evaluate a design. On the basis of the experiences, the author recommends that the qualities are applied after a basic design direction has been chosen, i.e., both a context and a product. The qualities help in improving the how of the interactions, but provide less guidance during the earlier phases where the goals and the interactions are chosen. Moreover, it is recommended that the designer chooses some examples of existing interactions to exemplify the design directions, so that he or she can make intuitive use of his bodily experiences, rather than going 'by the name of the quality' alone. Building a personal collection of 'inspiring examples of qualities' may serve the designers in future projects. Such a collection may also prove of value for education.

For design students, it is important gain a feeling for the difference between interaction qualities, context and product level. Such a feeling can be fostered by design exercises in which the product and context are clearly fixed, and in which the qualities are systematically varied. Such exercises can also deliver rich examples to guide others, as they have done for classic design parameters such as color and lifestyle.

6.3   For Design Researchers

This research studied how a specific set of qualities can be identified and put to use in designing products. The research was mainly exploratory and qualitative, and served to highlight opportunities and pitfalls. We can claim that we now understand the specifics of the new generation of devices better, and have provided means to find such qualities, evaluate their presence in existing products and prototypes of new products, and guide designers toward improving those qualities in their designs. But in none of these can we claim to have provided the final word. It is not unthinkable that an extra quality is still found. Also, the complexities of context and product level also provide some difficulties in presenting the qualities as ready-to-use tricks.

Future research may validate the qualities in more controlled conditions. But more urgently, it would be helpful if the repertoire of qualities is mapped out with examples into a collection that researchers, but also practitioners, educators and students, can use.

Such a repertoire may convey the subtlety and richness of Generation Y experiences. It can be a tool to assist designers in exploring the solution spaces that underlies the qualities. Optimally, such a tool should itself be instant, expressive, playful, collaborative, responsive and flexible.

Acknowledgement. The publication of this research project was supported by the Fundamental Research Funds for the Central Universities.

References

1. Arvola, M.: Interaction design qualities: theory and practice. In: Proceedings of the 6th Nordic Conference on Human-Computer Interaction: Extending Boundaries, pp. 595–598. ACM Press, New York (2010)
2. Boess, S., Saakes, D., Hummels, C.: When is role playing experiential?: Case studies. In: Proceedings of the ACM Conference on Tangible Embedded Interaction (TEI), pp. 279–282. ACM Press, New York (2007)
3. Buxton, B.: Sketching User Experiences: The Workbook. Morgan Kaufmann, San Francisco (2014)
4. Frens, J.W.: Designing for rich interaction: integrating form, interaction and function. Doctoral dissertation. Eindhoven University of Technology, Eindhoven (2006)
5. Hassenzahl, M.: The interplay of beauty, goodness, and usability in interactive products. Hum. Comput. Interact. **19**, 319–349 (2004)
6. IDEO (2014). http://www.ideo.com/work/virtual-wallet-interactive-banking-experience
7. Keller, A.I.: For inspiration only, designer interaction with informal collections of visual material. Doctoral dissertation. Delft University of Technology, Delft (2005)
8. Koskinen, I., Zimmerman, J., Binder, T., Redström, J., Wensveen, S.: Design Research through Practice, 1st edn. Morgan Kaufmann, San Francisco (2011)
9. Liu, W., Stappers, P.J., Pasman, G., Taal-Fokker, J.: Evaluating generation Y interaction qualities in an office work context. In: Extended Abstracts of the ACM SIGCHI Conference on Human Factors in Computing Systems (CHI). ACM Press, New York (2014)
10. Liu, W., Pasman, G., Taal-Fokker, J., Stappers, P.J.: Exploring 'Generation Y' interaction qualities at home and at work. J. Cogn. Technol. Work **16**(3), 405–415 (2014)
11. Liu, W., Stappers, P.J., Pasman, G., Taal-Fokker, J.: YPhone: applying generation Y interactions into an office context. In: Proceedings of the ACM SIGCHI Conference on Computer Supported Cooperative Work (CSCW). ACM Press, New York (2013)
12. Liu, W., Stappers, P.J., Pasman, G., van der Helm, A., Aprile, W., Keller, I.: Interactive Pong: exploring ways of user inputs through prototyping with sensors. In: Proceedings of the ACM SIGCHI Conference on Ubiquitous Computing (UbiComp). ACM Press, New York (2012)
13. Locher, P.J., Overbeeke, C.J., Wensveen, S.A.G.: Aesthetic interaction: a framework. Des. Issues **26**(2), 70–79 (2010)
14. Löwgren, J.: Articulating the use Qualities of Digital Designs. Aesthetic Computing. MIT Press, Cambridge (2006). pp. 383–403
15. Martin, F., Roehr, K.E.: A general education course in tangible interaction design. In: Proceedings of the ACM Conference on Tangible Embedded Interaction (TEI), pp. 185–188. ACM Press, New York (2010)

16. Norman, D.A.: Emotion and design: attractive things work better. Interactions 9(4), 36–42 (2002). New York: ACM Press
17. Oxygen Report: Generation Y and the workplace annual report. Johnson Controls (2010)
18. Øritsland, T.A., Buur, J.: Interaction styles: an aesthetic sense of direction in interface design. Int. J. Hum. Comput. Interact. 15(1), 67–85 (2003)
19. Pasman, G., Boess, S., Desmet, P.: Interaction vision: expressing and identifying the qualities of user-product interactions. In: Proceedings of the International Conference on Engineering and Product Design Education, pp. 149–154 (2011)
20. Preece, J., Roger, Y., Sharp, H.: Interaction Design: Beyond Human-Computer Interaction, 2nd edn., pp. 181–217. Wiley, Hoboken (2007)
21. Prensky, M.: Digital natives, digital immigrants. On the Horizon 9(5), 1–6 (2001)
22. Ross, P.R., Wensveen, S.A.G.: Designing aesthetics of behavior in interaction: using aesthetic experience as a mechanism for design. Int. J. Des. 4(2), 3–13 (2010)
23. Rullo, A.: The soft qualities of interaction. ACM Trans. Comput. Hum. Interact. 15(4) (2008)
24. Sanders, L., Stappers, P.J.: Convivial Toolbox: Generative Research for the Front End of Design, pp. 224–225. BIS Publishers, Amsterdam (2013)
25. Spiro, C.: Generation Y in the workplace. Defense AT&L (2006)
26. Stappers, P.J.: Teaching principles of qualitative analysis to industrial design engineers. In: Proceedings of the Conference on Engineering & Product Design Education (2012)
27. Wensveen, S.A.G.: A tangibility approach to affective interaction. Doctoral dissertation. Eindhoven University of Technology, Eindhoven (2005)
28. Whyte, W.: Advancing scientific knowledge through participatory action research. Sociol. Forum 4(3), 367–385 (1989)
29. Zimmerman, J., Forlizzi, J., Evenson, S.: Research through design as a method for interaction design research in HCI. In: Proceedings of the ACM SIGCHI Conference on Human Factors in Computing Systems (CHI). ACM Press, New York (2007)
30. Woolfolk, A., Winne, P.H., Perry, N.E.: Social cognitive and constructivist views of learning. In: Educational Psychology, pp. 329–370. Pearson Canada, Toronto (2009)
31. Zimmerman, J., Forlizzi, J., Evenson, S.: Research through design as a method for interaction design research in HCI. In: Proceedings of the SIGCHI Conference on Human Factors in Computing Systems. ACM Press, New York (2007)

Design-Based Evidence Collection
and Evidence-Based Design (DEED) Model

Caitlyn McColeman[1(✉)], Robin Barrett[1,2], and Mark Blair[1,2]

[1] Department of Psychology, Simon Fraser University, Burnaby, Canada
caitlyn_mccoleman@sfu.ca
[2] Cognitive Science Program, Simon Fraser University, Burnaby, Canada

Abstract. The DEED (design-based evidence collecting and evidence-based design thinking) model offers a structure in which designers and scientists can effectively support one another in the development of both design and knowledge. The model offers one possible implementation of the applied and basic combined strategy to research [1]. DEED offers a design strategy that

(1) immediately - supports design; in the
(2) short term - supports organizational/collective improvements; and in the
(3) long term - adds to general knowledge to support society as a whole
(4) all while ensuring that researchers do not interrupt the design process, and
(5) scales well for small and large organizations.

This paper introduces the DEED model, its stages, and explores the distinction between design thinking and the design thinking process. The DEED model is an example of the latter, and is a strategy to gain deep knowledge by building on contemporary design strategies. The DEED model anticipates potential points of concern between designers and scientists working in collaboration and offers a structure to support risk-taking and innovation in a manner that may not be typical of a design process with researcher involvement. DEED offers a robust strategy to incrementally increase general knowledge, and to pointedly improve design.

Keywords: Design thinking · Collaboration · Work-flow · Innovation · Qualitative and quantitative research · Applied and basic research combined

1 Introduction

What may once have a useful distinction between science, humanities, and design now marks a shallow boundary between blending pursuits. Science had served to understand the natural world [2], but "natural" performance now also includes computer-mediated behaviour. In our lab, we collect video game data in order to better understand human learning [3–5], and although the end goals of our research differ from game designers and humanities researchers, these goals are achieved through similar means. Understanding the domain, the user, and the context are critical to all three pursuits. These overlapping pursuits create opportunity for all parties to achieve understanding together beyond what each field could do on its own.

© Springer International Publishing AG 2017
A. Marcus and W. Wang (Eds.): DUXU 2017, Part I, LNCS 10288, pp. 134–151, 2017.
DOI: 10.1007/978-3-319-58634-2_11

Building on this, we present the DEED (Design-based evidence collection and evidence-based design thinking) process model to implement the "Applied and Basic Combined" approach [1]. The DEED model is an extension of a basic agile design strategy, which retains critical design stages to support rapid prototyping and development. The novel contribution of DEED as a design thinking process model is the built-in research stages. Findings from the research stages inform the product/service under development, and can be shared among the organization to support progress across multiple, related projects. Additionally, the basic findings that come out of research can be used to learn about the natural world generally, over a longer time scale.

The model maintains separate stages to support independent thought, and connects those stages to support systematic collaboration. Sensitive to the concerns of some designers, the DEED model constrains research to a subset of the process and ensures that creatives and developers have sufficient space to innovate. Anyone can use the DEED model, from a single entrepreneur to a large, established organization with multiple specialists or departments for each stage. While basic science usually strives to understand fundamental principles, applied science more typically focuses on practical solutions to problems. On the journeys to their respective goals, though, applied and basic science often share methodology, resources, skills and sub-goals such as collecting data or understanding the ways that different variables play a role in outcomes. Combining basic and applied science [1] is critical for the research stages in the DEED model, where the data from the design process can be leveraged to make general inferences, but also can be used to directly inform the product or service under development. The proposed model explicitly includes research as part of the design process, and implicates design as being integral to the research process. This is **evidence-based design thinking**: it values research to ensure that the design works. Larson describes the design process itself as experimental (2005), and building off this sentiment, the DEED model encourages design and research teams to use both qualitative and quantitative methods in the *Collaborative Gear* (see Fig. 1). The Collaborative Gear (modified from [6]) contains specific stages dedicated to research, which makes it easier for the design team to support and inform researchers about concerns or risks taken during the content creation stage that researchers can then explore. With this emphasis on team work, the DEED model affords a safe way to take design and innovation risks. This DEED framework encourages designers to actively participate in the research process and researchers to understand more completely the design decisions upon which their test object is built. Similar stages already exist in most rapid prototyping design models; paper sketches and low-fidelity prototypes are the basis for early qualitative research, while high fidelity prototypes are the basis for later quantitative research. DEED formalizes the role of both qualitative and quantitative research as being valuable steps throughout the design process (Table 1).

Design will benefit from this arrangement long term as researchers learn more about behaviour outside of traditional laboratory tasks and can apply it back to future design iterations. Using basic research to eliminate inviable approaches saves time and effort from being spent on methods which produce less accurate or even misleading results. To do this, basic research needs data which can only be provided with the help of the design team: this is **design-based evidence collection**. By constraining the

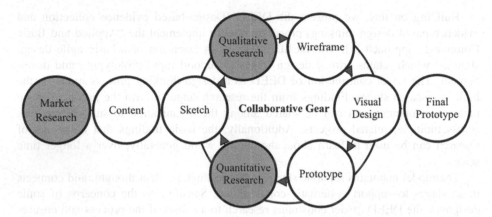

Fig. 1. The DEED model, schematic. The DEED design process begins with market research, and concludes with a final prototype. Research is built in to the design process, which offers evidence to inform rapid iterations (immediate), information to share among partnering projects in an organization or community (short-term), and data to increment scientific progress (long-term). The DEED model is an agile, rapid-prototyping design process.

Table 1. Summary of primary contributions of the DEED model

	Feature	Cost	Benefit (example)
1	Agile design process	Basic design process replication; no additional costs	Rapid iteration, flexible, increased risk/reward payoff
2	Research contributions	On-boarding researchers; resources to support their methods	Nuanced feedback to inform iterations for the project; increases organizational and general knowledge
3	Knowledge development	Communication of findings (time, resources)	Funding partnerships; progress in general society for extending science's reach
4	Dedicated design stages	Supporting each stage (time, resources)	Avoid groupthink; support creative risk taking
5	Scalable	Included with other features	Young organizations can add specialists as they grow; small companies can have one person acting in multiple roles

contribution of a researcher to specific stages in an adapted agile design strategy, it's unlikely that research impedes innovation, but more likely that the researcher maximizes intellectual gains by being involved in the design process. Including research as part of the rapid prototype stage offers an opportunity for designers and researchers to collaborate and communicate over each iteration to foster more effective collaboration strategies [7]. If designers are sensitive to the goals of more basic research, they can support information gathering in natural environments that are specifically designed to allow users to achieve their goals unimpeded. In doing so, researchers gain insight into the natural behaviour of people to better understand cognition and decision making.

The DEED process supports both knowledge discovery and effective design through:

(a) market research
(b) content creation
(c) repetitions of the Collaborative Gear
(d) final prototype

Organizationally, a project manager can set a threshold for key performance indictors (e.g. enjoyability, efficacy measures). These are measured in the quantitative research test, where, should the results of user testing suggest the key performance threshold is met, the cycle advances for the final time. In each round, the researcher's responsibility is to ensure that the data required to perform their research is available. The test is both a test of the product and of the process. The design structure can be made leaner by constraining the maximum number of cycles and participants [8], or it can be made more research-intensive by setting more sensitive advancement thresholds.

The DEED model includes nine distinct stages (see Fig. 1): market research, content creation, sketching, qualitative research, wireframing, visual design, proto-typing, quantitative research and the final prototype. Market research and content development precede the Collaborative Gear which contains everything from sketching to quantitative data, all of which can be repeated as needed to reach a threshold that is established by the design team or a product manager. The threshold can be defined by key performance indicators as indicated by the design problem. Indeed, the design process should only enter the Collaborative Gear if it is discovered that there is a real problem for which a solution can be attained. If meeting that goal can be quantified or measured qualitatively, that is an ideal measure for which the progression to the final prototype might be allowed. The stages of the model are explored in more detail below in Sect. 5.

2 Motivation

"Contemporary research teams get a further boost from fresh ways of using the Web, social media, and visual communications tools that amplify collaborations [1]."

- B. Shneiderman

The DEED design process model, if applied widely, offers benefits spanning immediate product improvements and general, societal-level advantages of a well-informed populace. Our initial motivation, as cognitive psychology researchers, was an academic one: to better understand human cognition. Our experience with programming experiments to be as user-friendly as possible, and collecting video game data to inform real-world motivated behaviour made it clear that human-computer interaction problems are similar to human cognition problems. Both domains share methods, equipment, and populations of interest; both domains have a lot to offer each other.

2.1   Practical Considerations

Having someone with knowledge of the scientific method as an integrated part of the design team is advantageous. A team member who knows about strategically manipulating critical components of interest over rapid iterations, can help to inform causal claims between them. Simultaneously implementing all of the test group's user feedback, and/or corrections for observed usability problems is poor practice. Changing everything at once does not inform the scientist or the designer as to the actual source of the user frustration or the usability error. Changing one feature at a time and observing its effect is much more informative. The scientist may generalize the findings to support or refute a scientific theory. The designer will know what to do in future work.

Further, making step-by-step iterations avoids problems of "throwing the baby out with the bath water", in that there might be a really useful feature that users are not interacting with because of some co-occurring issue. If the feature is excluded based on observation of a group of people who ignored it for a myriad of potential reasons, the interface may not be as strong as it could be. For example, a search feature on a website might not be easy to find in the first design iteration (a placement flaw, or aesthetic issue, perhaps). Removing it entirely would be poorly advised; when instead, having it placed more effectively or tweaking its appearance could make it accessible.

Extreme caution is advised in overriding the intuitions of artists to align with potentially relevant scientific claims, though. Throughout history, artists and poets have communicated real psychological phenomena through their art work, sometimes making observations about human perception which would not be studied scientifically for some time after their discovery in artistic mediums. Brunelleschi knew how to invoke depth perception in a two-dimensional painting in 1415 [9]. Oculomotor vergence, the underlying mechanism enabling this phenomenon, was not even a topic conversation for another four and a half centuries in the scientific community [10]. With the rapidity of both artistic and scientific advances, and the openness of communication the information age affords, this latency between artistic insight and scientific principles is expected to shrink moving forward [11]. With this in mind, artists may shed light on interesting behavioural phenomena exhibited by their audiences before scientists are even looking that direction. Squashing artistic pursuits might harm scientific advancement as odd or interesting phenomena may be entirely overlooked if the artist does not have room to explore their own domain.

To this point, it should be clear that designers and researchers are well positioned to help each other. A solution to the potential tension between researchers and designers on a team is to make the role of both explicit: researchers and designers share the same ultimate goal in better understanding the user's experience. The focus within that goal differs, and that difference is a productive one.

2.2   Theoretical Background

Applying concepts from psychological science to industry problems seems like a relatively straightforward problem at first pass: learn something about people, check that it happens consistently, and communicate it to the industry to fold it into design strategies or into products that consider human psychology. It's probably never that clean. Learning about human behaviour in the lab does not often allow for confident predictions about analogous behaviour in the wild. Learning about human behaviour in the lab does not even offer much confidence about predicting human behaviour in the lab. A large-scale replication effort by the 270 contributors of the Open Science Collaboration repeated 100 psychological studies. A meagre 36% of the replication efforts yielded significant p values in the direction that were originally reported [12][1]. If direct replications of experiments fail more often than not, it's unsurprising that industry applications of psychological findings may fail to meet their mark. It's important for scientists to make their data open so these verifications are made possible, even if — or especially when — working with design and industry partners.

The replicability of psychological findings aside, another concern with their application is that the scalability of the findings is tenuous. Even the Posner cuing task, a mainstay in attention labs, suffers when the cues are changed to be more realistic [13]. Central cues appear to draw reflective attention when they're arrows or eyes, regardless of how predictive they are. There's a reaction time advantage for when a left-pointing arrow predicts a target to appear on the left side of the screen, even when that arrow is only helpful on 50% of trials. This counters the assumption that cues will draw attention only when they're actually predictive of the target location. Having eyes and arrows rather than boxes as a cue is hardly a big step in scaling a problem up, yet the paradigm appears to break down even with these minor manipulations.

Another issue of applying basic attention findings to interfaces are cases where real-world problems have multiple modes of stimulation. Findings of visual attention do not necessarily scale cleanly to multimodal interfaces. Saccades are modified by congruent tactile stimulation [14], such that eye movements are made to a target more quickly when matched with a tactile stimulus in the same direction. Learning is supported by multi-modal integration, as evidenced by participants' reduced timing errors when provided with auditory and visual feedback rather than visual feedback alone [27]. Applying attention findings to interface design isn't always a multimodal problem, but most interfaces are improved with the integration of an auditory component and much of what we know about visual attention is based upon findings isolating the visual modality.

From the design side, it's challenging to test the efficacy of scientifically-principled features if the test groups assessing early versions of an interface or game are unaware of their own limitations. People are apt to overestimate their cognitive and perceptual abilities, thinking that they would notice items manipulated in a change blindness task even when observers all fail to do so [15]. Participants involved in alpha testing of an interface might be frustrated with informative components of the display and deem them unnecessary even though these extra sources of information may minimize inattentional blindness, change blindness or other quirks of the visual system.

---

[1] It should be noted that there are limitations in this massive replication attempt, and the failure to replicate may not be quite as dire as it was stated in the original report. Psychology does, nonetheless, have some serious work to do to improve the robustness of our findings.

Participants' metacognitive failures in overestimating their abilities might mean that an alpha testing group tells the design team that a component of the design is unnecessary, and so the responsive development team might opt to eliminate it during the next iteration. These same interface elements or design choices that are maligned by participants and subsequently excluded may actually help people avoid failures of the visual system - failures that most of us think we're above committing. If feedback of this sort from test groups is implemented, it's critical that a new test group is run through the newest design iteration before it goes live, to avoid the possibility that these metacognitive failures lead to the exclusion of helpful features and accidentally lead to a catastrophic usability flaw.

Among metacognitive failures there are three "illusions of visual bandwidth" [16]: overestimations of breadth, countenance, and depth. The overestimate of breadth is the misguided assumption that viewers can simultaneously observe all of the details of a scene. Overestimating countenance is the mistaken belief that observers will attend to more of the screen than they do, thinking that a person viewing a display will look at all of its elements, for example. Finally, the overestimate of depth refers to the assumption that attention to an object yields a detailed and robust encoding of it. Awareness of these common errors might support interface and game design by providing strategically redundant sources of information for particularly important events, or invoking a parsimonious strategy in deciding what to include in an interface. Further, arming a design team with this list of illusions of visual bandwidth might help them weight the feedback provided by test groups to avoid unprincipled or reactionary design decisions on later iterations of an interface.

3   Design-Based Evidence (DE) Collecting

Basic research based upon video game data is the best current example of design-based evidence collecting. This is the case in our own lab, where records of StarCraft 2 actions are used to inform us about cognition [3]. StarCraft 2 is a video game, and so the environment with which users interact is a designed one. What makes StarCraft 2 a good example case for design-based evidence collection is that the designers of the game record data from users that can be effectively leveraged for science. While the primary of goal of the designers was probably not to support science, the incidental design decisions the StarCraft 2 team made opened up opportunities for research projects with the resulting game data: the design decisions supported evidence collection.

In game design, challenges are purposely introduced to make specific subsets of the experience harder; in StarCraft 2, for example, players cannot see the whole game environment at once. As researchers who are interested in studying information access patterns, we are able to use the player behaviour in response to that game design decision to tell us about how people access information in dynamic environments [4, 5]. If designers are sensitive to the goals of researchers, they can support information gathering in natural environments by recording valuable data from users interacting with their design.

One important goal of human-computer interaction design is to reduce unnecessary friction, so the user may easily focus on their task. In basic laboratory tasks of human cognition, our goal is similar: we try to manipulate some quality of the environment so that the only difference between groups is the quality we changed. Should we find a difference between the groups, we can then attribute it to the manipulation and infer that the manipulation caused the difference. If, however, the task is unnecessarily complicated, it requires additional cognitive processing to simply interact with the experiment the evidence we collect in response to that experiment is influenced, in part, by the intuitiveness of the experiment interface and so some of the differences in participants' behaviour is a function of the interface rather than the manipulation. This stymies the scientists' understanding of cognition. All of this is to say that the human-computer interaction designs that successfully reduce the friction between the users and the computer get closer to the users' genuine cognition, and provide a cleaner look at natural behaviour. Should these designers choose to record data from their users and share records of user behaviour with scientists, they would contribute invaluable data to understanding cognition. In doing so, everyone involved gains insight into the natural behaviours of people and basic scientists are able to use recorded information to better understand cognition.

In addition to the quality of data arising from expertly designed interfaces, there is an issue simply of quantity. Most studies in psychology include about 25 people per experimental condition. Expertly designed websites, apps, games and other interfaces invite orders of magnitude more users than a typical psychology study. The sheer quantity of data, above and beyond its potentially superior quality, offers more room for research insights. User experience researchers conducting A/B or MVT (multivariate) tests to quantify the efficacy of design choices can also be testing a critical hypothesis for the foundations of human cognition without knowing it. History has shown before that artists have insights about the existence of phenomena well ahead of scientists that aim to explain them. Sharing information between designers and researchers will serve to help scientists keep up and symbiotically move our understanding of human cognition and effective human computer interaction forward.

4 Evidence-Based Design Thinking (ED)

One way to apply findings from basic science to improve interfaces is to use data collected by users of similar interfaces, have scientists build models of their behaviour, and use the resulting models to predict how people will perform in the interface of interest. Borji, Lennartz, and Pomplun recorded people playing video games, and created a series of models to predict their attention patterns and behaviours during driving game play [17]. The authors were able to predict where people would look depending on the state of the game they were in and general properties of the play environment. Improvements to these types of models on the scientific end can save time and research energy on the industry end. Scientific models can also help to inform designers where to put valuable information in a display, so as to improve the usability of the interface.

Some task interfaces have fostered masterful performance in their users. Perhaps the most consistent inter-generational one is the car. Dashboards, keys, and practically everything under the hood changes often, but the actual practice of driving, at some degree of abstraction, is not terribly different today than it was nearly a century ago. Novice drivers display different eye movement patterns than experienced drivers [18]. Novices look ahead of the car more often, and make fewer lateral eye movements. This is attributed to the propensity of expert drivers to scan their environment for potential hazards more often. Typifying eye movement patterns to discern the level of expertise of the user is a strategy that astute designers may consider using in developing their own interfaces. This would allow us to employ scientific principles in interface design.

Front facing cameras on personal laptops are nearly good enough to act as coarse eye trackers, should a good algorithm to support real-time data cleaning and eye position relative to viewing angle and head distance be made available. Assuming the inevitable capacity to use built-in hardware to measure eye position, and a corpus of sample eye movement patterns from people at different level of skills with a software program, the interface could unfold features as the user displays behavioural and attentional patterns consistent with the next level of task mastery or the inferred goals of the user. Making such interface adjustments in service of a goal and in response to data is evidence-based design thinking.

User centered design can be better informed by researchers focused on human behaviour, performance and experience. Cognitive science is just this. In includes people like social psychologists, behavioural economists, and marketing researchers who are effective for performing early market research. Qualitative research is experiencing a resurgence in the social sciences, and is an important tool in getting the most information out of low-fidelity, sketch-based testing. It is a way to get a fuller sense of a real user and to rely less on contrived personas that may oversimplify the design problem space [19]. Cognitive scientists are poised to effectively test computer mediated behaviour. Generations of cognitive scientists have done just that, but perhaps with less of a mind to generalizability than the user experience tester may require training to be sensitive to. Designers who support cognitive researchers will benefit from this investment long term as researchers learn more about behaviour outside of traditional laboratory tasks.

5 The DEED Model Stages

The DEED (design-based evidence collection & evidence-based design thinking) model serves research and design alike. By opportunistically gathering data from well-designed interfaces, research can gather insight into human cognition. By opportunistically applying research findings, designers can make informed design decisions. In the DEED model, these specialists can more directly support each other's work by sharing in the main goal of designing a good interface. In DEED, science and design can serve each other as a natural consequence of the stages and their processes.

The DEED model encourages the researcher to act during specific stages in an adapted agile design strategy. This balances the value added by a researcher with the chance that the research impedes design innovation and brainstorming, which has been a concern for some designers. Additionally, having explicit stages dedicated to research makes it easier for all members of the design team to support or query the researcher(s) about concerns or unknowns. If a designer wishes to try something outlandish, the researcher can help to determine whether or not it works after the designer has had a chance to implement it. Having this safe organizational structure within which to take risks has the added benefit of supporting innovation. A designer who may have previously opted not to try something unconventional for fear that it would not work can more safely explore that idea in this DEED framework, since the research stages will catch design decisions that interrupt usability.

The stages of the DEED model feed forward more than backward, but a researcher might have suggestions for which user behaviours to record to make the best possible test case. For design-based evidence collection to work effectively, it's important that the researcher is able to make requests for data, so long as those requests for data do not impede the design decisions. Rapid prototyping is supported by this model structure and including research as part of the rapid prototype stage offers an opportunity for designers and researchers to collaborate and communicate over quick iterations to foster more effective collaboration [7].

Generally, social psychologists, behavioural economists, and marketing researchers are more effective in early qualitative research stages as they are best suited to extract the most information out of low-fidelity, sketch-based testing paradigms. In later stages, cognitive scientists are poised to effectively test quantitative, computer mediated behaviour. At any research stage, fundamental concerns can be illuminated and the design process can revert one step to address them.

Market Research
What is it? Market research is the process of finding a need to meet. In the very simplest (and perhaps most powerful) cases, finding a need of one's own that is not met by product and services acts as market research. Market research will inform the design team about what success looks like. The team can use information from this stage and their prior experience to establish the qualities of the minimally viable product before moving on through the DEED model.

Who does it? In smaller enterprises, market research is conducted by individuals who identify a need to be met. In larger enterprises, market research can be a more formal pursuit wherein social psychologists, economists, business and marketing practitioners, and other social scientists identify trends, gaps and qualities of demographics that a potential product or service could benefit.

Why do it? Human computer interaction is effectively informed by the human's experience of a product or service. Market research introduces the human into the equation. Without market research, the audience is underspecified and any work conducted on a product might miss an important group of people that otherwise might benefit from the development process. The results of market research can suggest whether the idea is pursued at all. If the need is minimal or insufficient, knowing that and deciding not to pursue the idea saves a lot of time and energy that would otherwise be spent on a great product for which no users exist. The better a potential user is understood, the greater the probability of success.

Content

What is it? Content is what your product or service is about. There are as many answers to "what is content?" as there are ideas for apps, games, and websites, but it includes the information that's necessary to convey to users to get the main idea. For example, a website: the content would include the working title, the main pages, the ideas for headings, the general navigational structure, and the copy for a sample post. Some ideas about the information architecture should also be part of content generation.

Who does it? The content will traditionally be most closely associated with the person who motivated the project in the first place. However, content can be generated in larger organizations by having copy-writers, developers and designers all working together to create.

Why do it? Most human-computer interaction involves transferring information. Without having content by which to start design iterations, the human-computer interaction design problem is fundamentally lacking. Content, in a lot of ways, is the *why* of good design while the rest of the DEED model describes the *how* of good design.

5.1   The Collaborative Gear

Sketch

What is it? A sketch can be as informal as a pen and paper drawing, outlining how the content from the previous stage would be presented to a user. Sketches are low-fidelity prototypes, on paper or in software, that represent the structure and the general presentation of content.

Who does it? A sketch can be done by anyone with access to pen and paper, and earlier sketches will probably arise as a natural consequence of content generation. It is important to make the sketch an explicit stage, though, lest it not be natural for a particular person or team to draw out their ideas. While it's nice to have someone with drawing talent perform a sketch, anyone who is able to approximate shapes can perform this step.

Why do it? Without a sketch, knowing how content is organized and presented can be very difficult. Sketches reduce sources of potential error between collaborators in content generation, because team members can see it start to take shape and recognize assumptions they were making that hadn't come up in conversation during content generation. Additional iterations of the design process result in additional sketches demonstrating possible design solutions in response to feedback from previous stages. Subsequent stages build upon improvements reflected in the sketch.

Qualitative Research

What is it? Qualitative research is a relatively unconstrained method in which data is collected from people. It includes things like open ended questions or talk-aloud verbal protocol procedures.

Who does it? Qualitative methodology is enjoying a resurgence of interest in the social sciences. Many anthropologists, psychologists, historians, human resource specialists and people with similar training are effective qualitative researchers. In recent years, students out of user experience design programs are encouraged to learn and use qualitative research methods to explore their design practices.

Why do it? Qualitative research offers a good opportunity to "dive deep" into a user's experience. Open-ended questions and talk-aloud protocols invite opportunities to discover experiences that arise in response to design decisions that were unintended. Placing a search box at the bottom of the website page might invite anger in response, for example, and it might be difficult to know to ask that question unless you ask a research participant to talk through their experience while navigating the low-fidelity prototype developed in the previous stage.

In later iterations, especially for larger firms with more resources, qualitative research can add value in knowing how different audiences might respond to an existing product. For example, scaling social media to communities with different cultural norms might require tweaks to the user experience that were not indicated by experience of the original audience. These types of opportunities for innovation arise in response to qualitative research like ethnographic studies, a new set of talk-aloud procedures and interviews.

Wireframe

What is it? A wireframe improves upon a sketch, or revisits design decisions that didn't fare well in previous iterations. While a sketch is low-fidelity prototype, a wireframe is a higher-fidelity step toward a working prototype and considers properties that are necessary for implementation. For the website example, the wireframe invites the use of a grid to plan where images and content will be placed. Wireframes are typically digitized, and represent site components through boxes and grids (at least for two-dimensional interfaces).

Who does it? Wireframes are well within the wheelhouse of user experience designers, business analysts and user interface specialists. It is wise to have a wireframe upon which a developer can start to work or inform their plan, and so someone with some experience or understanding of the subsequent stages in development is a good person to have on wireframing.

Why do it? Wireframes clarify the structure for navigating between different content elements, work to meet one level of the users' needs (namely - the structural interaction needs), and to plan the interaction design generally.

Visual Design

What is it? Visual design is all of the work that bridges a wireframe to a working prototype. If the wireframe was lower fidelity, then visual design will be the process of folding in content, aesthetic decisions, considerations for accessibility, etc. The visual design step will include everything that creates the "look and feel" of the product or service. User interfaces will be fleshed out in this stage, and graphic design decisions are firmed up.

Who does it? Graphic designers, interface designers, user experience designers, branding specialists can all be part of this process.

Why do it? Products and services developed with the end user in mind can make the interface simpler to use and increase the probability of repeated users, or loyal customers as the case may be. Ideas that are well-thought out, but poorly implemented can be abandoned prematurely if the design does not accurately capture the value added by the content.

Prototype

What is it? A prototype is a sample of the product. It can be an early draft of what the team thinks the final version will be, or it can be snippet of the overall experience. The prototype accurately represents the type of content conveyed by the product, how that content is accessed, and the navigation between elements.

Who does it? Prototypes are typically finalized by developers, but may be developed in concert with designers and engineers.

Why do it? The prototype is the product. Without a prototype, the team has nothing. The better question to ask is, "why can't I stop here?" which is a crucial concern for design thinking generally. How can a team know when their design is ready to ship? The (admittedly underwhelming) answer is that it depends on what the expectations of the users and the design team are. If a product is distributed as an early alpha test version, the expectations might be lower, and so the first couple of prototypes might actually go live to a select group of people. However, for most design problems, the first prototype will not be the final one. One way to determine when iterations stop is to have a critical quantitative research question (e.g. time to gather information from the website your team is developing). When that value reaches a desired threshold, the product might go live. Better still, there may be multiple measures in addition to a team consensus, and until all measure are met and the team agrees the product is ready to ship, the product goes through more iterations of the Collaborative Gear.

Quantitative Research

What is it? Quantitative research is studying performance indicators or research questions in a way that can be numerated. Counting successful attempts at solving a problem with the product is an example of quantifiable research. Larger firms with more resources might choose to include more advanced metrics like eye tracking, mouse tracking, response time analysis, survey data, etc. to quantify how effective the product is at meeting the need of the users in the most user-friendly way possible. In each round of testing, the researcher's responsibility is to ensure that the data required to perform their scholarly and their design research is available. The test is both a test of the product and of the process.

Who does it? Quantitative research is traditionally conducted by people with some statistical training and some programming knowledge. People from more technical disciplines in the social sciences, engineers, data scientists and engineers are all among those who would be effective quantitative researchers.

Why do it? Qualitative research is great for diving deep into a few people's experiences, while quantitative research is good for getting a general sense of many people's experiences. Quantitative research can be a deep-diving pursuit, too, though: having people come in to the lab and performing careful observation of their experience with the prototype can offer insight that users may not even be aware of. For example, eye tracking data can provide an index of arousal (or stress) that might not be brought up by the users themselves. Additionally, if a user consents to have data collected while they engage with the product under development, the researchers can query particular parts of the interaction process without explicitly asking the participant about their experience, thereby avoiding expectancy effects that might come up through qualitative research. Using both approaches, then, offers the most robust understanding of the user's experience, and thereby assesses the extent to which the product does its job effectively.

Final Prototype

What is it? The final prototype is the version that reaches the threshold established by the design team or the product manager. It's version that the end user sees.

Who does it? The final prototype is the collective output of everyone on the design team, though a developer is likely to be the last person to touch it.

Why do it? Until the final prototype is released, the product is an idea. When the final prototype ships, the design team might keep an eye on user reviews and responses and begin the DEED model again with their eyes on the next version of the product. In that next iteration, then, the market research is largely provided by the responses of people after engaging with the final prototype of the first product.

One Good DEED Deserves Another

Organizationally, a project manager can set a threshold upon which the development cycle is closed. This is effectively set after the quantitative research test, where, should the results of user testing suggest below-threshold differences to the earlier sketch, the cycle advances for the final time, and user experience testing acts as checks and balances. We suggest that the quantitative research stage is a good place to end iterations of the Collaborative Gear. While some products or services are better evaluated qualitatively, many will be suited for some quantifiable metric of success. If the results of the research suggest that the design is sufficiently close to the metrics defining desirability, feasibility and viability then the next step is to prepare the final prototype.

In DEED, the design team should talk about what success looks like and establish the qualities of the minimally viable product prior to the first iteration of the Collaborative Gear (i.e. at the close of market research). The researchers can then discuss how to assess success, in a manner informed by everyone involved in design. A project manager might decide that the product or service will never be fully completed, and set a threshold of minimal change that would trigger release of the final prototype. Naturally, if the iterations are showing no improvement, the team will be having conversations about whether the design is ready to go or ready to be abandoned. Having set ahead of time the minimum number of changes per prototype supports (a) rapid development and (b) efficient use of resources by avoiding endless cycles of the same design. Efficiency and agility, in this regard, are informed by both designers and researchers. The DEED design process can be made leaner by constraining the maximum number of cycle through the process, or it can be made more research-intensive by setting more sensitive advancement threshold.

The start of the DEED model might be the end of an earlier iteration through the full process. Large firms, like established game design companies or big tech departments, might iterate multiple versions of a product. The DEED model can be chained (DEED model 1 for version 1.1; DEED model 2 for version 1.2, etc.) by setting interactive goals during design and development. In these environments, the output of the whole design process naturally leads to the input of the next version. As soon as a website goes live by achieving sufficient success to close out the first iteration of the DEED model, for example, the team can begin brainstorming improvements based on what is working well, and how they might want to expand it to offer different solutions to different problems.

This design model can work for teams of any size that have interest in both extending knowledge and improving design. A single person could feasibly play the role of market researcher, qualitative researcher, and wireframer, but naturally, people who specialize in each of these roles are desired if resources allow. Keeping these stages separate encourages some autonomy and exploration within each of the stages. Some room for independent innovation is important, and helps to assuage concerns of "groupthink" arising [26] from having every team member entirely invested in every step of the process. Keeping ideas from teammates hinders progress, however, so the DEED model does keep the output of these stages connected, and encourages effective communication between team members of the connected parts of the DEED process.

In DEED, the design thinking process is a way to manifest design thinking generally. We think it's useful to disambiguate design thinking *as a mindset* versus the design thinking processes *as a set of steps*. While design thinking is a solution-based approach to a problem, a design-thinking process is a set of steps required to get to that solution. The DEED model is an example of such a process. In addition to being helpful in its own right, we hope that the DEED model sets a precedence of approaching of design thinking and its implementation as separable ideas.

6 Design Thinking

Before email really caught on as a communication tool, there was a time where new mail notifications were going unnoticed and messages were left unread. At the time, the notification was a prominent arrow on top of inbox to indicate a new message. In the original design of this email software, it was generally underused and users insisted that emails they had received had not been available until they were pointed out by support staff, despite having been sent days in advance. A clever designer implemented a "You've got mail" component to the notification, which assuaged concerns about mail going unnoticed [16]. The now antiquated "You've got mail" notification appears to be polarizing, garnering some retro appreciation wherein people today have it set as their phones' email notifier while others start conversation threads on forums about how awful it is to overhear it. To not have included that message, though, might have meant that email remained ineffective as a communication tool; a tool that'd be missed by the people sending and receiving 196,400,000,000 emails [20] each day. This innovation is an example of design thinking in action.

Design thinking is a phrase that seems to be used more often than it is explained. Like many community-based phrases, the people who use design thinking know what they mean by it, but it's difficult to explain to people outside of design circles. In an attempt to lower the barrier to entry so more people can employ it, we have provided an exposition of what design thinking is. Perhaps more critically, in this section we disambiguate design thinking from its implementation: the design thinking process.

The DEED model is an example of a design thinking process. While design thinking is more of a framework, or a way to approach problems, the design thinking process is a set of steps to apply that way of thinking. Put simply: design thinking is the *why*, and the design thinking process is the *how*.

Design thinking is difficult for formally define. Mootee makes clear the issue of defining it: "[t]here is no single, unifying, common definition of design thinking" [21]. Many subscribers of design thinking define it as a mentality toward problem solving, while others see design thinking as a "toolbox" to be used in organizational settings to improve the collaborative process [22]. As one report on the matter points out, both sets of language are used by different organizations to define design thinking as both a toolkit, and as a mental trait [23]. Among their sample, there is a tension between those who see design thinking as a *descriptive* element whereby practitioners would identify as design thinkers, while others would view design thinking in *prescriptive* terms as something to be used by a group of collaborators. This tension results in a vagueness of terminology which risks "Design Thinking" turning into a buzzword, rather than as a serious concept to implement in business models.

Both the prescriptive and descriptive ideas of design thinking have merit, but would benefit from being differentiated. We distinguish between design thinking (descriptive, and as a mindset), and the design thinking process (prescriptive, and as a set of steps to find solutions). Design thinking, is the mindset of approaching problems openly, generally, creatively and considers the genuine use case of the product under development. A design thinker then keeps the three constraints of desirability, feasibility, and viability [24] in mind as they work through the brainstorming process. When it comes to the actual application of the design thinking process, steps are taken by a team or individual to find desirable, feasible and viable solutions. This often means iterating through prototypes to maximize all three. In this sense, a practitioner of the design thinking process can assess their design against measures of desirability, feasibility and viability. With this separation of mindset (design thinking) and practice (the design thinking process), much of the uncertainty associated with design thinking is reduced.

The DEED model presents a case example of how the design thinking process can be applied, while also helping to collect valuable information.

7 Conclusion

The symbiotic relationship between science and design has been noted before [1]. Making the roles of both scientists and designers necessary components of a design process solidifies the relationship between them, and supports improvements in both product design and general knowledge. Larger firms have more opportunity to support each stage, while smaller ones might have to simplify the process; but allowing for a step in the design where someone asks themselves what their results tell them about their understanding of the world generally — beyond the product and beyond the market — gives them an opportunity to (a) advance human knowledge, (b) consider the longer term impact of their work, and (c) consider related gaps that their product might fill.

The DEED model is one strategy to implement the "applied and basic combined" research approach [1], and comes at a critical time. Science is struggling with a rising "post truth" rhetoric and socio-political hurdle at the same time where a record number of Ph.Ds are graduating to find a small academic job pool [25]. Design, however, is enjoying a surge in popularity, and innovation is among the most valued qualities in businesses. While opportunities to work in basic science may be shrinking, applied science and design benefit from that research, and so this model offers a method by which information can be collected by basic scientists for immediate application and general theorizing.

The DEED model is a design thinking process that offers a balance between including research and evidence in the design process while ensuring that designers have space and support to innovate. The DEED model encourages the researcher to act during specific stages in an adapted agile design strategy. This balances the value added by a researcher with the chance that the research impedes design innovation and brainstorming, which has been a concern for some designers. It immediately supports the design of a single product/service by virtue of its agile design properties; it supports the growing body of knowledge in an organization or community; and it supports the understanding of the natural world by contributing to scientific findings. It is an alliance of people, methods, and complementary goals that, when combined, benefit the product, the organization, and the society as a whole.

Acknowledgements. We would like to thank members of the Cognitive Science Laboratory who offer their time and talents to developing projects. Thanks especially to Steve DiPaola, and Thomas Spalek, whose questions and guidance encouraged the development of this material.

References

1. Shneiderman, B.: The new ABCs of Research: Achieving Breakthrough Collaborations. Oxford University Press, Oxford (2016)
2. Cross, N.: Designerly ways of knowing: design discipline versus design science. Des. Issues **17**, 49–55 (2001)
3. Thompson, J., Blair, M., Chen, L., Henrey, A.: Video game telemetry as a critical tool in the study of complex skill learning. PLoS ONE **8**, e75129 (2013)
4. Thompson, J., Blair, M., Henrey, A.: Over the hill at 24: persistent age-related cognitive-motor decline in reaction times in an ecologically valid video game task begins in early adulthood. PLoS ONE **9**, e94215 (2014)
5. Thompson, J., McColeman, C., Stepanova, K., Blair, M.: Using video game telemetry data to research motor chunking, action latencies, and complex cognitive-motor skill learning. Top. Cogn. Sci. (2017). http://onlinelibrary.wiley.com/journal/10.1111/(ISSN)1756-8765/earlyview
6. Mayer, L., Rauch, S., Daukaeva, K., Henwood, L.: Agile design. Lecture from RED Academy, Vancouver (2015)
7. Carlgren, L., Elmquist, M., Rauth, I.: Exploring the use of design thinking in large organizations: towards a research agenda. Swed. Des. Res. J. **1**, 47–56 (2014)
8. Nielsen, J.: Why you only need to test with 5 users. www.nngroup.com, https://www.nngroup.com/articles/why-you-only-need-to-test-with-5-users/
9. Op-Art.: Op Art History Part I: A History of Perspective in Art. www.op-art.co.uk, http://www.op-art.co.uk/history/perspective/

10. Enright, J.: Art and the oculomotor system: perspective illustrations evoke vergence changes. Perception **16**, 731–746 (1987)
11. Schaller, R.: Moore's law: past, present and future. IEEE Spectr. **34**, 52–59 (1997)
12. Open Science Collaboration: Estimating the reproducibility of psychological science. Science **349**, acc4716 (2015)
13. Kingstone, A., Smilek, D., Ristic, J., Friesen, C., Eastwood, J.: Attention, researchers! It is time to take a look at the real world. Curr. Dir. Psychol. **12**, 176–180 (2003)
14. Colonius, H., Diederich, A.: Multisensory interaction in saccadic reaction time: a time-window-of-integration model. J. Cogn. Neurosci. **16**, 1000–1009 (2004)
15. Levin, D., Momen, N., Drivdahl, S., Simons, D.: Change blindness blindness: the metacognitive error of overestimating change-detection ability. Vis. Cogn. **7**, 397–412 (2000)
16. Varakin, D., Levin, D., Fidler, R.: Unseen and unaware: implications of recent research on failures of visual awareness for human-computer interface design. Hum. Comput. **19**, 389–422 (2004)
17. Borji, A., Lennartz, A., Pomplun, M.: What do eyes reveal about the mind?: algorithmic inference of search targets from fixations. Neurocomputing **149**, 788–799 (2015)
18. Underwood, G., Chapman, P., Brocklehurst, N., Underwood, J., Crundall, D.: Visual attention while driving: sequences of eye fixations made by experienced and novice drivers. Ergonomics **46**, 629–646 (2003)
19. Peterson, M.: The problem with personas. blog.prototypr.io. https://blog.prototypr.io/the-problem-with-personas-82eb57802114#.yum1nufsg
20. Radicati, S.: Email statistics report, 2013–2017. http://www.radicati.com/wp/wp-content/uploads/2013/04/Email-Statistics-Report-2013-2017-Executive-Summary.pdfl
21. Mootee, I.: Design Thinking for Strategic Innovation: What they can't Teach You at Business or Design School. Wiley, Hoboken (2013)
22. Johansson-Sköldberg, U., Woodilla, J., Çetinkaya, M.: Design thinking: past, present and possible futures. Creativity Innov. Manag. **22**, 121–146 (2013)
23. Schmiedgen, J., Rhinov, H., Koppen, E., Meinel, C.: Parts without a whole? The current state of design thinking in organizations. Study Report 97 from Hasso-Plattner Institute for Technical Software Systems at Potsdam University (2015). ISBN: 978-3-86956-334-3
24. Brown, T.: Change by Design: How Thinking Transforms Organization and Inspires Innovation. HarperBusiness, New York (2009)
25. Schillebeeckx, M., Maricque, B., Lewis, C.: The missing piece to changing the university culture. Nat. Biotechnol. **31**, 938 (2013)
26. Nemeth, C., Nemeth-Brown, B: Better than individuals. In: Group Creativity: Innovation Through Collaboration, pp. 63–84 (2003)
27. Doody, S., Bird, A., Ross, D.: The effect of auditory and visual models on acquisition of a timing task. Hum. Mov. Sci. **4**, 271–281 (1985)

Information Behaviour in Design;
A Conceptual Framework

Farnaz Nickpour[⊠]

Design Department, Brunel University London, Uxbridge, UK
farnaz.nickpour@brunel.ac.uk

Abstract. Designers draw on a significant volume and range of information throughout the design process. This could include information on people, materials, markets, processes, etc. However, not all this information is effectively communicated to and used by designers. In order to provide designers with information that is useful, useable and engaging for them, it is important to understand why designers use information, what information they use and when and how they use it. This will be collectively referred to as 'information behaviour' in this paper.

Keywords: Information behaviour · Designers · Designers' information behaviour

1 Introduction, Motivation and Scope

'Information behaviour' is defined as "how people need, seek, give and use information in different contexts" (Pettigrew et al. 2001, p. 44). The many technological, social and cultural changes and developments in recent decades have highlighted the role and importance of information and information behaviour. The increased volume and diversity of information together with improved access to it have brought up terms such as information society (Webster, 2006; Kidd 2007) and consequently information overload (Hwang and Lin 1999). This has subsequently increased the importance of study of information behaviour and the significance of understanding the user of information when designing and developing information systems, products and services (Hepworth 2007).

In design, similar to other fields, designers draw on a significant volume and range of information throughout their design process. This could include information on people, materials, markets, processes, etc. This information is collectively called 'design information' and is described as referring to features of design including functions, material selections, process of manufacturing, etc. (Li and Ramani 2007). A review of the nature of design practice, current uptake of design information, and some emerging areas in design, identifies both opportunities and problems in regards to designers' information behaviour. These key issues and emerging opportunities, either way, highlight the need for study of information behaviour in design and underline the important role this could play in facilitating better uptake of design information and improving current design practices. Some of these challenges and opportunities include:

A. Marcus and W. Wang (Eds.): DUXU 2017, Part I, LNCS 10288, pp. 152–162, 2017.
DOI: 10.1007/978-3-319-58634-2_12

- **Designerly ways of knowing**

In his book 'Designerly Ways of Knowing', Cross (2006) makes the case for building a network of arguments, articulation and evidence for the particular nature of design behaviour and activity. He argues "If we want to develop a robust, independent discipline of design - rather than let design be subsumed within paradigms of science or the arts - we need to make evidence for 'designerly ways of knowing'." (Cross 2006, p. 3)

- **Limited understanding of designerly ways of knowing**

A conventional lack of interest in the study of designers' information behaviour and their ways of knowing and doing has been noticeable. This could be due to the fact that in design, focus has typically been on the 'end-product' to be delivered by the designers, rather than the 'process' they went through. This brings up the notion of 'Black-Boxing' (Jones 1970), describing lack of knowledge of the design process, focus on the 'input' and 'output', and limited understanding of designers' information behaviour.

- **Emerging design approaches and abundance of information**

New design approaches such as people-centred design (Wood 1990; Darses and Wolff 2006), inclusive design (Keates and Clarkson 2004), and user-led innovation (Dibben and Bartlett 2001) have emerged. These design approaches bring with them a wealth of new and existing design information (specifically on people) that needs to be effectively communicated to designers, if they are to be successfully adopted. This highlights the need to better communicate not only the existing but new and diverse sets of design information to designers.

- **Growing number of information tools aimed at designers**

The ever-increasing volume, range and diversity of design information and the growing demand for better ways of using it in order to facilitate existing and new design approaches, has led to more information systems and tools being designed and developed aimed at designers. Such information tools have a broad range and format including books, handbooks, online tools, CD packages, cardsets, etc.

- **Limited use of information tools and resources in design**

Despite all the design information available, there is evidence that this information is not effectively used by designers in practice (Mieczakowski et al. 2010; Law et al. 2008; Burns et al. 1997). Also, various studies of designers show the use of design tools and resources is currently limited and not effective within the design industry (Green and Jordan 1999; Restrepo and Christiaans 2004; McGinley and Dong 2009). The minimal use of information tools and resources by designers could have various reasons. Study of designers' information behaviour would be one first step to address these issues.

A brief review of major design challenges and opportunities highlighted the need for and importance of studying information behaviour in design. However, there is currently a lack of a holistic and methodical understanding of designers' information behaviour. Therefore a research was carried out to provide a structured understanding of information behaviour in design, leading to a systematic way for investigation, analysis and reflection on designers' use and requirements of information. It was hoped that through this, the limited understanding of designerly ways of knowing could be improved, new and existing design approaches were better supported and their uptake by designers was facilitated, and the design and development of new information tools was better informed.

- **Scope of research**

In studying designers' information behaviour, this research specifically focused on a number of areas and aspects as listed below.

- **Industrial design and product design**

Design is a wide-ranging term that could encompass many different disciplines. In this research, two specific design disciplines i.e. industrial design and product design were focused upon.

- **Practicing designers**

Student designers and design practitioners have different needs, attitudes and criteria when approaching a design task (Ahmed et al. 2003) and thus different information behaviour. This research focused on practicing (as opposed to student) designers as key users of information in the real-world practice of design.

- **People information**

Design information encompasses various types of information. This research focused on 'people information' as a major type of information used throughout the design process. Here, people information is broadly defined as 'all types of information that help designers better understand people and their context'.

2   Methodology and Methods

After the review of a number of relevant social sciences and design research methodologies, and based on the nature of the information behaviour study and its aims and objectives, a specific research methodology was designed. The general research methodology adopted an integrative approach to existing research methodologies where the general elements of DRM (Blessing and Chakrabarti 2009) and Case's stages of research process (2008) were applied and Robson's (2002) research methodology was also implemented in specifying research methods and techniques of data collection and analysis.

The study adopted a convergent methodology (Goodman et al. 2006) through employing a number of research methods. The research triangulation (Jick 1979; Creswell and Clark 2007) approach was adopted in order to enable cross examination (Cheng 2005) of the results of the studies. Thus, the initial framework outlined based on literature analysis and synthesis was planned to be revised, evaluated and detailed in an iterative cycle through three types of complementary studies, i.e. interviews with designers, observations of designers and a survey with designers and design researchers. Studies varied in terms of breadth, depth, level of control, scope and generalisability (Henn et al. 2006). Through using a variety of methods, approaches and participants along with the literature analysis and synthesis, validity and reliability (Gray 2004) of research was hoped to be improved. Figure 1 presents the schematic research methodology adopted by this research. Table 1 presents a breakdown of studies and relevant methods used in the second stage of the research.

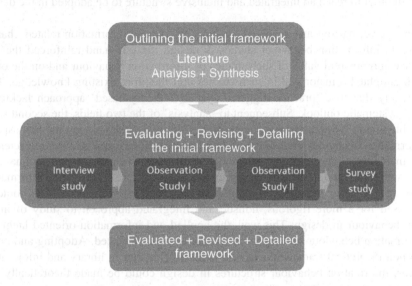

Fig. 1. Research methodology in this research

Table 1. Research strategies and methods adopted for this research

	Study 1: Interview with designers	Study 2: Observation of designers	Study 3: Observation of designers	Study 4: Survey with designers & researchers
Type of research	Qualitative + Quantitative	Qualitative	Qualitative	Quantitative + Qualitative
Data collection methods	Semi-structured interview + Ranking questionnaire	Marginal participant observation + Online questionnaire (multiple-answer questions)	Recognised outsider observation + Online questionnaire (multiple-answer questions)	Online survey (open questions for comments & multiple-answer questions)
Data analysis methods	Qualitative + Statistical analysis	Qualitative analysis	Qualitative analysis	Statistical + Qualitative analysis
Number of participants	9	5 (1 project)	19 (3 teams)	Refinement: 89
				Evaluation: 89
				Detailing: 66

3 Results and Findings

3.1 Literature Analysis + Synthesis

An illustrative review of knowledge of information behaviour was carried out on the library and information sciences and design respectively. The existing knowledge of information behaviour in these two fields was then analysed. The key identified aspects and facets of information behaviour in these two fields were then synthesised and linked in order to reach an integrated and inclusive structure to be adopted in the design field.

Several yet narrow and scattered attempts to address information-related charac-teristics in information behaviour studies in design, on one hand reinforced the sig-nificance and inherent value of such studies of information behaviour and on the other hand highlighted a major gap in such studies and therefore existing knowledge. This was mainly due to a 'practice-triggered' yet not 'theory-based' approach lacking a holistic systematic outlook. Subsequent to 'analysis' of the two fields, the second stage in the literature investigation was 'synthesis' of the two fields, linking the key aspects of information behaviour in design with key facets of library and information sciences in an integrative approach. The inherently distinctive terminology and language of design and library and information sciences in addressing and investigating information behaviour resulted in identification of different focus and various aspects. This could be synthesised for a more rigorous, holistic and integrated approach to study of infor-mation behaviour in design. This way, the applied and information-oriented language of information behaviour in design was maintained yet enhanced. Adopting and being built upon theoretical frameworks of information behaviour in library and information sciences, information behaviour structures in design could be made theoretically rig-orous and comprehensive.

The initial set of information dimensions derived from the analysis and synthesis of literature in fields of design and library and information sciences formed the 'Initial Information Framework' for information behaviour in design. Figure 2 shows the process of synthesis of information behaviour facets (in library and information sci-ences) with information dimensions (in design), resulting in an integrated set of information dimensions for information behaviour in design.

The identified information dimensions in design included 'type', 'format', 'source' and 'attributes'. These were aligned with the three facets of information behavior identified as key in information sciences i.e. information 'need', 'seeking' and 'use'. The 'type', 'format' and 'attributes' dimensions were in line with the 'need' facet, while the 'source' dimension related to 'seeking' facet. The 'format' dimension was also in line with the 'seeking' facet, thus it was located in the borderline between need and seeking facets. However, the 'use' facet did not have a parallel in the identified information dimensions. Therefore in merging the two sets, 'use' was included as a dimension to the initial information framework in design. As a result, the proposed initial framework included five dimensions i.e. 'type', 'format', 'source', 'attributes' and 'use'.

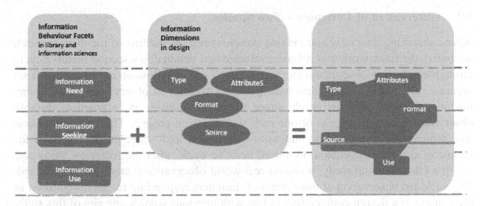

Fig. 2. Synthesis of 'Initial Information Framework' for information behaviour in design

3.2   Interviews with Designers

This study built on the findings from the literature analysis in two areas of library and information sciences and design. The initial information framework was implemented in this study and evaluated, refined and detailed. Using interviews and ranking questionnaire with nine selected UK-based design companies each of the five dimensions of the initial framework were explored and further detailed them by identifying sub-dimensions to each. Also, head designers' responses to five selected design support tools in form of comments and numerical ranking in order of preference were collected.

This study showed that practicing designers' use of existing formal anthropometric information and tools (i.e. books, handbooks, software packages, online sources, etc.) in design companies is currently very limited. The research also highlighted the dominant role of experimental methods in sourcing practicing designers with people information. Practicing designers perceive and evaluate such sources as more effective and useful compared to referring to existing anthropometric sources. Designers' opinions on ergonomics tools varied and it was difficult to achieve consensus in terms of designers' preferences on such tools. However, most desired and preferred tools had a number of information attributes in common which included, accommodating experiential information, seamless integration with other tools designers typically use, high visual and graphic qualities and intuitive and simple presentation of information. It was concluded that the problems with the existing anthropometric information, included not only lack of 'usability' and 'desirability', but also lack of 'usefulness'. The above situation made it an imperative to get an in-depth insight into designers' information needs, seeking and use in order to provide them with better information and tools. Based on the designers' suggestions and preferences, there is potential for information tools to be designed and developed specifically for designers (Nickpour and Dong 2010). This has to be done by carefully adopting designers' inherent information behaviour; needs, seeking and use - and by adapting existing information to fit that.

3.3   Observation of Designers – Two Studies

After conducting interview and ranking questionnaire (as the first of the three research methods), the framework was refined, evaluated and detailed in a second iterative cycle through conducting observation together with self report follow-up questionnaire. Two separate real- world field studies were partaken in order to observe designers' information behaviour. The first study aimed to 'observe designers in practice' through observing the design process of one real- world design project. The 'use' dimension was refined and changed into 'intensity' dimension and 'stage' was suggested for inclusion as a new dimension. In a third iterative cycle, after the Interview study and the first Observational study, a second real-world observational study was conducted. This included observation of three teams of designers responding to one design brief in the context of a design competition. In line with previous studies, the aim of this study was also to refine, evaluate and detail the information framework. The newly included 'stage' dimension was also to be further investigated and evaluated.

Findings from both observational studies confirmed both conflicts and interrelations between various dimensions of the information sought and used by designers throughout the design process. There was conflict of demands in regard to some aspects of information, specifically there was some divergence between 'format', 'type' and 'attributes' of people information designers sought. Some significant interrelations were also observed between various dimensions of framework in particular 'purpose' with 'source' and 'type', also 'type' with 'format' and 'qualities'. Discover and Define stages of the design process were when the people information was most heavily sourced and used, this suggests more focus is needed on designers' information behaviour (explicitly people information) at the front-end of the design process.

3.4   Survey of Designers and Design Researchers

As the last of the three triangulated research methods, a survey was conducted with designers and design researchers aiming at refinement, evaluation and detailing of the information framework. An online survey was designed and completed by 90 participants overall (67 participants detailing the framework and 90 participants evaluating and refining the framework).

The web-based survey evaluated, refined and detailed the information framework. The framework was evaluated as comprehensive and useful yet complex and needing further clarity on its purpose. This was expected as the framework was intended to be primarily evaluated by design researchers rather than designers (though designers were one main group of respondents).

The results regarding refinement of the framework suggested further consideration for three main aspects:

- Visual representation of the framework
- The relationship between its dimensions
- The terminology used to communicate the framework. The dimensions with an unclear terminology included 'Attributes', 'Intensity', 'Purpose', and 'Type' versus 'Format'.

Figure 3 shows the Information Framework based on interview and observational studies and the suggested refinements to the framework based on survey study.

Purpose | Source | Content | Presentation | Quality | Intensity | Stage

Fig. 3. Information Framework based on interview, observational studies and survey results

4 Conclusion and Further Work

4.1 Conclusion

The outcomes of the four studies led to a refined and verified version of the information framework that included seven key dimensions (i.e., 'purpose', 'source', 'format', 'type', 'attributes', 'stage' and 'intensity') of people information that designers use in a design process. These seven dimensions are summarised below:

Purpose - *Why information is used.*
Source - *How information is sourced.*
Type - *What type of information is used.*
Format - *What representation of information is used.*
Attributes - *What the qualities of information are.*
Stage - *When information is used.*
Intensity - *What range and depth of information is used and how frequently.*

The research reported in this paper has made three contributions to the knowledge in this field:

1. The research has enhanced the knowledge of information behaviour in design through creating a novel information framework which is comprehensive, integrated and systematic.
2. The research has enhanced understanding of designers' use of people information throughout the design process by detailing the seven dimensions of the proposed information framework.
3. The research has facilitated investigation and communication of design information used by or aimed at designers, thus facilitating information design and development of information systems.

4.2 Further Work

Having revisited the core focus of this research and its boundaries, a number of areas to be explored are discussed here. Information behaviour is an under-explored area in design.

Outlining and detailing the information framework was one initial step towards understanding and modelling designers' information behaviour in a systematic and comprehensive way. This brings forward a number of opportunities for further research to be carried out, a number of which are listed below.

- **Developing a model of information behaviour in design.** This research resulted in the creation and detailing of a framework for studying information behaviour in design. Findings suggested a number of key refinements to the information framework. These included terminology, visual presentation, and linkage and hierarchy. While a framework identifies the elements that should guide analysis of a phenomenon, a model is defined as a set of assumptions about underlying processes between the elements which cause that phenomenon. Thus, a model is more complete and complex in its explanation of a phenomenon compared to a framework which focuses on "capturing the variation and dimensionality of a phenomenon with the fewest dimensions" (Miller 2006, p. 6). A model of information behaviour in design could be developed building on the existing information framework. This could be a significant additional contribution and a step forward in the under- explored area of information behaviour in design.

- **Comparative study of student and experienced designers' information behavior.** This research focused on detailing the information framework based on empirical studies of practicing designers, focusing on people information. However, as Ahmed et al. (2003) and Cross (2006) clarified, student designers and experienced designers have different needs, attitudes and criteria when approaching a design task, and thus different information behaviour. A comparative study of student and experienced designers' information behaviour adopting the information framework could shed light on similarities and differences between these two groups. This could provide a foundation for any further applications and connections between the two groups.

- **Comparative analysis of observed and self-reported information behaviour in design.** Adopting research triangulation, this research collected data on both observed and self-reported information behaviour of designers through observational studies alongside interview and survey. Also, within the observational studies, designers were furthermore asked to self-report on their information behaviour to complement the observations. The results from the above confirmed differences between the observed and self-reported information behaviour. A further comparative study could contrast these two aspects. This could further the understanding of similarities and differences between designers' observed and reported information behaviour and thus extend the knowledge of information behaviour in design.

- **Research on information intensity.** 'Intensity' was one novel and complex dimension of the information framework. It was first replaced with 'use' dimension in the initial framework and was further detailed and refined through three empirical studies. 'Depth', 'range' and 'frequency' were identified as three constituents of this dimension and semantic differential scale was adopted as the method for measuring and assessing each. As study results showed a high level of variance, further research is suggested to be carried out in terms of scaling methods for each constituent, weighting of each constituent, and also proposing an overall assessment for intensity dimension as a whole. Future research could focus on detailing and further developing this dimension, as one key dimension of the information framework that directly addresses information use.

- **Cultural differences in designers' information behavior.** This research had a western focus on studying designers' information behaviour in that the sample for interview, observational studies and the survey was largely UK-based (all nine interviewees, 22 out of 24 participants in the two observational studies, and 32 out of 64 survey participants were UK-based). This would give a western orientation to the collected data on designers' people information behaviour. Adopting the information framework from this work, further research could explore and examine the role and significance of cultural differences in designers' information behaviour and how culture would influence designers' information needs, seeking and use.

References

Ahmed, S., Wallace, K.M., Blessing, L.T.: Understanding the differences between how novice and experienced designers approach design tasks. Res. Eng. Des. **14**(1), 1–11 (2003)

Blessing, L., Chakrabarti, A.: DRM, a Design Research Methodology. Springer, London (2009)

Burns, J.A., Stanley, L.G., Stewart, D.L.: A projection method for accurate computation of design sensitivities. In: William, W.H., Panos, M.P. (eds.) Optimal Control: Theory, Algorithms and Applications, pp. 40–66 (1997)

Case, D.O.: Looking for Information: A Survey of Research on Information Seeking, Needs and Behavior. Academic Press, Amsterdam (2008)

Cheng, L.: Changing Language Teaching through Language Testing: A Washback Study, pp. 72–85. Cambridge University Press, Cambridge (2005)

Creswell, J.W., Clark, V.L.: Designing and Conducting Mixed Methods Research. Sage, Thousand Oaks (2007)

Cross, N.: Designerly Ways of Knowing. Springer, London (2006)

Darses, F., Wolff, M.: How do designers represent to themselves the users' needs? Appl. Ergon. **37**(6), 757–764 (2006)

Dibben, P., Bartlett, D.: Local government and service users: empowerment through user-led innovation? Local Gov. Stud. **27**(3), 43–58 (2001)

Goodman, J., Langdon, P.M., Clarkson, P.J.: Providing strategic user information for designers: methods and initial findings. In: Clarkson, J., Langdon, P., Robinson, P. (eds.) Designing Accessible Technology, pp. 41–51. Springer, Heidelberg (2006)

Gray, D.E.: Doing Research in the Real World. Sage Publications, London (2004)

Green, W.S., Jordan, P.W. (eds.): Human Factors in Product Design: Current Practice and Future Trends. Taylor & Francis, London (1999)

Henn, M., Weinstein, M., Foard, N.: A Critical Introduction to Social Research. Sage Publications, Wiltshire (2006)

Hepworth, M.: Knowledge of information behaviour and its relevance to the design of people-centred information products and services. J. Documentation **63**(1), 33–56 (2007)

Hwang, M.I., Lin, J.W.: Information dimension, information overload and decision quality. J. Inf. Sci. **25**(3), 213–219 (1999)

Jick, T.: Mixing qualitative and quantitative methods: triangulation in action. Adm. Sci. Q. **24**, 602–611 (1979)

Jones, J.C.: Design Methods: Seeds of Human Futures. Wiley- Interscience, Chichester (1970)

Keates, S., Clarkson, P.J.: Countering Design Exclusion: An Introduction to Inclusive Design. Springer, London Ltd (2004)

Kidd, P.T.: European Visions for the Knowledge Age: A Quest for New Horizons in the Information Society. Cheshire Henbury, Macclesfield (2007)

Law, C.M., Yi, J.S., Choi, Y.S., Jacko, J.A.: A systematic examination of universal design resources: Part 1, heuristic evaluation. Univ. Access Inf. Soc. **7**, 31–54 (2008)

Li, Z., Ramani, K.: Ontology-based design information extraction and retrieval. Artif. Intell. Eng. Des. Anal. Manuf. **21**, 137–154 (2007)

McGinley, C., Dong, H.: Accessing user information for use in design. In: Stephanidis, C. (ed.) UAHCI 2009. LNCS, vol. 5614, pp. 116–125. Springer, Heidelberg (2009). doi:10.1007/978-3-642-02707-9_13

Mieczakowski, A., Langdon, P.M., Clarkson, P.J.: Investigating designers' cognitive representations for inclusive interaction between products and users. In: Langdon, P., Clarkson, J., Robinson, R. (eds.) Designing Inclusive Interactions, pp. 133–143. Springer, London (2010)

Miller, C.R.: Ph.D. dissertation: The tholian web: The political/institutional context of regional cluster-based economic development, Virginia Polytechnic Institute and State University, United States (2006)

Nickpour, F., Dong, H.: Developing user data tools: challenges and opportunities. In: Langdon, P., Clarkson, J., Robinson, P. (eds.) Designing Inclusive Interactions, pp. 79–88. Springer, New York (2010)

Pettigrew, K.E., Fidel, R., Bruce, H.: Conceptual frameworks in information behavior. Ann. Rev. Inf. Sci. Technol. **35**, 43–78 (2001)

Restrepo, J., Christiaans, H.: Problem structuring and information access in design. J. Des. Res. **4** (2), 1551–1569 (2004)

Robson, C.: Real World Research. A Resource for Social Scientists and Practitioner-Researchers. Blackwell Publishers, Oxford (2002)

Webster, F.: Theories of the Information Society, 3rd edn. Routledge, London (2006)

Wood, D.: Ergonomists in the design process. In: Ergonomic Design for the Consumer. Proceedings of the 26th Annual National Conference of the Ergonomics Society of Australia, Adelaide, pp. 125–132 (1990)

Four Biases in Interface Design Interactions

Alamir Novin[✉] and Eric M. Meyers

School of Library, Archival and Information Studies,
University of British Columbia, Vancouver, Canada
{alamir.novin, eric.meyers}@ubc.ca

Abstract. In a time when fake news has captured the attention of the broader public, and claims of algorithmic manipulation make us question everyday sources of information, it is essential that we unpack the ways our thinking and perception interacts with search engine results. Cognitive biases can be created from the common heuristics a person applies to process new information about a topic. These biases can contribute to difficulties in inferential thinking. In this paper, we focus on four potential sources of bias rooted in cognitive psychology that relate to information presentation in search, and unpack how they may affect the way people express their nascent understanding of a topic. Our study used a population-based experiment with 60 undergraduates at a large research university. Our findings suggest that the design of a search interface may cause a user to misapply heuristics, which can be linked to these cognitive biases. We conclude with recommendations for interface designers as well as those who mediate search practices in educational settings.

Keywords: Cognitive bias · Interface design · Information interaction · User experience · Search engines

1 Introduction

The way search algorithms present information influences our opinions (Belkin et al. 2009; Epstein and Robertson 2015). Information presentation likely affects the quality of student thinking and knowledge creation, particularly when students demonstrate and report relying heavily on the authority of search engines (Hargittai 2010; Meyers 2012). In an age of increasing science skepticism, people require both tools and critical thinking skills to evaluate the new scientific information they encounter in everyday life. According to the National Science Board, the public's primary form of science education is via the medium of search engines, but while the Internet increases the public's access to scientific information it also increases access to misinformation (2014). Therefore, it is worth questioning the level of critical thinking that people apply when selecting sources on a search engine results page (SERP) (Guo et al. 2010; Höchstötter and Lewandowski 2009). Within the SERP there are algorithmic biases that can influence user behaviour (Epstein and Robertson 2015). A search engine's algorithm presents a hierarchical list of what it deems would be the most important. However, the list may be limited by the way search engines qualify relevance over other contextual factors (Kelly 2009; Shiri and Zvyagintseva 2014). The presentation of a hierarchical list visually removes all intellectual relationships between each item in

© Springer International Publishing AG 2017
A. Marcus and W. Wang (Eds.): DUXU 2017, Part I, LNCS 10288, pp. 163–173, 2017.
DOI: 10.1007/978-3-319-58634-2_13

the list (Tufte 2006) and the algorithm behind Google's document ordering is ambiguous to even Google's search engine developers themselves (Cellan-Jones 2016). Whether the top result on Google is there because it is the most relevant, useful, popular, current, or the most hyperlinked is unknown to users. As a result, users remain unaware of the hidden biases in search engines (Gerhart 2004).

2 Background: Cognitive Biases Work

To understand the role of bias in constructing meaning from search engines, we draw on research in cognitive science, in particular theories of judgment and decision making. Cognitive biases and heuristics affect the way people perceive and process new information about a topic – particularly when the learner has to process conflicting or non-intuitive information (Tversky and Kahneman 1974). While dozens—some scholars identify as many as 53 different kinds—of cognitive biases contribute to difficulties in inferential thinking (Hilbert 2012; see also Kahneman 2013) for a survey of the literature), we look at four that we believe are directly related to Search Engine use in learning situations, namely: (1) Priming effects, (2) Anchoring, (3) Framing, and the (4) Availability Heuristic.

2.1   Priming Effects: How Our Familiarity with Google's Interface Biases Against Alternative Perspectives

Immediately after we perceive an object with our eyes a "stimulus is facilitated if it matches a prime previously seen in the same context" (Kahneman et al. 1992). A priming effect in user interfaces occurs when the repeated use of a layout automatically directs our eyes to information (Ware 2013). This creates a cognitive bias whereby we are influenced by certain cues (Kahneman et al. 1992). Scholars observed that Google's algorithm is biased towards presenting mainstream sources that users find familiar (Diaz 2008; Gillespie 2010). While efficient, users may automatically disregard unfamiliar sources that represent minority views (Braun and Gillespie 2011; Hindman et al. 2003; Rieder and Sire 2013).

2.2   Anchoring Effects: How Information at the Top of the SERP Creates Bias

Anchoring occurs when we are biased towards the first value we perceive in a set of data (Tversky and Kahneman 1974). The first result in a SERP can affect the user's impression of the importance of the next result (Lauckner and Hsieh 2013). This is problematic for SERPs because it affects the level of critical thinking that is applied to all other search results.

2.3   Framing Effects: How the Multiple Top Results Work Together

The Framing Effect is a cognitive bias that occurs when peoples' choices are dependent on the way information is presented (Kahneman 2002). Framing is not about unavailable information, but about *whether* the presentation makes us care about competing views and *how* (Scheufele and Tewksbury 2007). For example, if a SERP represents two perspectives but the first perspective dominates the top results in a SERP, then it is seen as more valuable than the second (Epstein and Robertson 2015; Lauckner and Hsieh 2013).

2.4   Availability Heuristic: How the Availability of Sources Marginalizes Challenging Perspectives

An availability heuristic bias occurs when a person's estimate is influenced by the ease of a person's recall of immediate information (Tversky and Kahneman 1974). With SERPs, non-expert may feel satisfied with more simplistic summaries of information (Browne et al. 2007). However, this is problematic when non-experts casually browse lesser known controversies that require greater cognitive effort from the user to understand.

All of these constructs represent kinds of cognitive "short cuts", techniques that we employ, either consciously or not, to ease our cognitive load when resolving information problems. These factors contribute to judgment errors in information seeking, but can also affect the extent to which new information leads to the development or revision of conceptual structures.

3   Methods

We explored a common science controversy on the subject of biofuels and *advanced* biofuels. While biofuels are increasingly common, the general population is less familiar with the various methods by which such fuels are produced, and the scientific disagreements related to the consequences of this production. The "food vs fuel" controversy, for example, is related to the use of agricultural land to produce matter (such as corn for ethanol) that competes with cropland dedicated to staple crops for human consumption or feed crops for animals. Sixty participants were recruited from a large public research university for this study, 91% had little to no knowledge of the topic prior to their recruitment.

The sample included students ages 18–30, with roughly equal gender distribution (45% female). Participants were then asked to read and rank five search results followed by a second questionnaire on their knowledge of biofuels. The results were presented to participants in four different ways, and order balanced. Students were asked to write their own summary of Biofuels using search results with brief summaries (~ 25 words); they were then provided with longer summaries (~ 100 words). The task goal was to write a brief explanation of biofuels as though they were writing for a colleague.

Our analysis looked at the participant rankings and resulting written explanations for four different kinds of cognitive bias, specifically priming, anchoring, framing, and the availability heuristic. We using a combination of observed behaviours as well as coding of the written work to make inferences about which type of bias provided the most robust explanation for the participants' choices. We did not, however, isolate the biases as discrete variables. Given this, there are some obvious limitations to our analysis.

4 Findings

4.1 Document-Genre Effects on Scoring

When analyzing the effects of document-genre on scoring (Fig. 1), we found that participants strongly favoured Wikipedia over all other websites for its generally objective perspective. As one participant explained, it was "the perceived neutrality of Wikipedia that links as a basis" for completing the assignment. While this finding agrees with past literature, we note it here because despite its reputation Wikipedia can contain biases that misrepresent information. As we explained, earlier, Wikipedia's Biofuels article does not present information neutrally on its interface when it relegates criticisms of biofuels into a weblink at the bottom of its page.

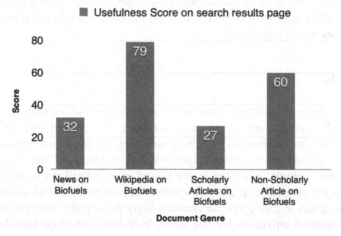

Fig. 1. Scores on usefulness of Wikipedia article on "Biofuels" in comparison to other sources (reported in percentages).

4.2 Document Order Effects on Write-up

The authors of the study were interested in how the document order affected how information was used by the students in their writing. When document-genre was controlled for, we found that the higher an article that mentions the biofuels controversy was presented on a search engine's results page, the more likely the controversy is mentioned in their write up. When the top result on a SERP was a source that explicitly mentioned the biofuel controversy, 73% of the participants mentioned the controversy in their write-ups. However, if it was place elsewhere on the SERP then the number would fall to 41%. For example, a participant who had the controversy mentioned at the top of the SERP wrote: "Biofuels are basically fuels that comes from starch based plants such as corn or soy. However, because of this it takes up farmland which raises food prices. This can be really devastating to poor countries/those in poverty because they cannot afford the food." In contrast, most participants who did not have the controversy mentioned at the top of the SERP did not mention the controversy. Instead, they would focus on what corn biofuels were.

A Pearson chi-square test was performed to analyze whether a topic's position on the results list was related to students mentioning the topic in their explanations. A relationship was found between whether a group had a controversial topic anchored at the top of a SERP and the number of participants that mention the controversy in their write up, $X2$ $(1, N = 42) = 4.1067$, $p = 0.043$. The association between rows (groups) and columns (outcomes) is statistically significant (Table 1).

Table 1. Chi square comparison of write-ups between group with anchored results vs. groups without.

	Number of participants that mention controversy in their write-up	Number of participants that do not mention controversy in their write-up	Total
Group with controversy anchored at top	11	4	15
Groups without controversy anchored at top	11	16	27
Total	22	20	42

When the controversial source appeared at the top of the search results, students were more likely to incorporate this information in their written responses, as opposed to the controversial information appearing lower in the search results page. As we will explain in the Discussions section the differences between the two groups may indicate anchoring effects are causing cognitive bias.

4.3   Document-Genre Effects on Write-up

This study was also interested in how information was used by students and whether there were any document-genre effects on the writing. To examine this, we compared the write-ups of participants that received the conflicting source on the topic of advanced biofuels in different document-genres; we compared the group who was provided the academic document-genre of the conflict against the group who had the non-academic document-genre of the conflict. The automated textual analysis for word frequency revealed that three key terms "food price", "production", and "land" were mentioned frequently in the write-up for the group with the academic document-genre of the advanced biofuel conflicting source. However, for the group that was provided the non-academic version of the conflicting source the key terms were "new", "generation", "focus", and the perspective of "scientists". The words in this latter group related directly to the conflicting source on advanced biofuels (i.e., a "new" "generation" of biofuels and the current "focus" of many "scientists"). For example, one participant from the group provided the non-academic genre of advanced biofuels wrote: "Scientists are becoming aware of the food issues and have come up with other ways to obtain biofuels. There are 4 'generations' of biofuels each with different types of materials used. Algae seems to be a promising source of biofuels." However, the type of sentences that focused on advanced biofuels appeared less frequently in the write-ups of participants who received the academic document-genre of advanced biofuels. Instead, the frequent words of the participants who were provided an academic document-genre) were more focused on the old generation of biofuels (i.e., its "land" "production" and raising of "food price").

Furthermore, participants who were provided a non-academic document-genre of advanced biofuels created more comprehensive arguments. This likely occurred because for someone to explain why a biofuel is "advanced" they must first contextualize the topic by (1) first explaining what biofuels are, then (2) explaining the controversy of biofuels that are derived from corn, and then (3) explain that advanced biofuels address the controversy by focusing on biofuels that do not use land (4) and provide an example of a non-corn biofuel, such as algae. The group that received the academic document-genre sources never mentioned this fourth point about algae. In our post-hoc analysis we suggest the fact that these two groups focused their write-ups towards two different types of biofuels can be explained by framing effects causing cognitive biases.

4.4   Document Order Effects on Scoring

We presented participants with a source with an academic document-genre that was challenging because it was scientific in language and low-ranking on the SERP. When users were presented with the source on the SERP the users did not view the information as useful and gave it a very low score (Fig. 2). However, when participants were asked to read a large excerpt of the same result, its usefulness received a much higher score (Fig. 2). As we will explain in the Discussions section this increase in score may be due to a participant's initial reluctance to apply cognitive effort on a scholarly source at the bottom of a SERP and the availability-heuristic may be causing a cognitive bias.

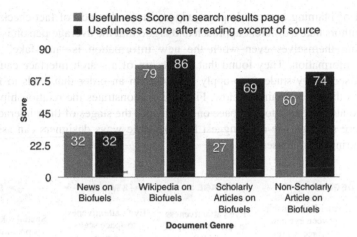

Fig. 2. Comparison between score of SERP results before and after reading excerpts of the sources.

5 Discussion

The current president of the United States, Donald J. Trump, has accused a few mainstream news outlets of distributing fake news, the outlets include *New York Times, CNN*, and "any negative polls are fake news, just like the CNN, ABC, NBC polls in the election" (Trump 2017). Trump's ongoing remarks on the issue are creating public discourse on the topic. The public, including scholars, are interested in the effect of "fake news" online and how web-services and algorithms can fact-check against them. There is no question that certain facts are more valid than others, that certain information sources are more careless with the validity of the facts, and that people are capable of critically-thinking and weighing the validity of certain arguments based on those facts against others. However, there are several assumptions in the argument "fake news affects people's judgement and should be fact-checked" that ought to be clarified: What counts as "fake"? What counts as "news"? Which web-services are to be trusted with "fact-checking"? Most importantly, do people assume that *they themselves* are on the side of the fact-checkers and its *other* people that are susceptible to "fake news"?

Even if all these prior concepts were clarified, at its core the concept of "news fact-checker" websites on its own is paradoxical because information cannot be both "new" and an "established fact" that can be checked. Because new information and established facts are distinct, new information must always have *some* degree of disagreement from prior information. Therefore, when "news fact-checkers" compare these two distinct pieces of information they will never find complete agreement (unless the information is not actually new). Fact-checker websites have and do check old facts, which can be a useful service. However, it is also the case that "new" information is generally useful when it updates, challenges, or changes what was once thought as established fact.

Instead of blaming a person's poor judgement on the lack of fact-checking websites, the authors take a different approach and argue that the average person is at risk of misinforming themselves even when the new information is "non-fake" scientific sources of information. They found that the design of a search interface causes competent post-secondary students to apply heuristics in an order that leads to four cognitive biases that are explained below. Figure 3 demonstrates the relationship between a user's eye-attentiveness to the space on a page and the stages of their interaction. For each of these sections, we also suggest four possible ways designers can assist users with countering these biases.

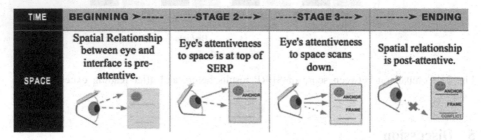

Fig. 3. Relationship between a user's eye-attentiveness to space on a page and interaction time

Stage 1: When a user first sees a SERP, the spatial relationship between their eye and interface is *pre-attentive* (i.e., the eye subconsciously looks for patterns (Ware 2013). In this stage, the user may experience a cognitive bias known as *Priming* (i.e., the repeated use of a layout automatically directs our eyes to information that is familiar rather than relevant (Tversky and Kahneman 1974). The authors tested for the scenario where SERPs provide sources that are familiar to users, but are not comprehensive. Our study found that users preferred less comprehensive sources, but this behavior affected their work output. We suggest that designers consider how to design an interface that facilitates these user heuristics so that they can discover counter primed information. For example, an interface can visually demarcate sources that function as counterpoints, falsifications, or conflicting information.

Stage 2: In the next stage, eye-tracking software reveals that a user's attentiveness focuses on the top of a SERP (Hotchkiss et al. 2010). In this stage, the user may experience a cognitive bias known as *Anchoring* (i.e. when we are biased towards the first value we perceive in a set of data (Tversky and Kahneman 1974). Users often over trust the top result in a search (Hullman and Diakopoulos 2011; Lauckner and Hsieh 2013; Meyers 2012) Our study argues that a SERP's hierarchical list over-emphasizes the top result over other results because features such as "I'm Feeling Lucky" and the Answer Box single out a dominant perspective for users when none exists. For instance, an opinion-piece might have anchoring effects on a user while they search for an academic source. Designers might counter this bias by allowing users to choose a standard for the document-genres they retrieve.

Stage 3: In the next stage, a user's eye scans down a page looking for patterns (Ware 2013). In this scenario, the user may experience a cognitive bias known as Framing (i.e., when peoples' choices are influenced by the manner information is presented (Kahneman 2002)). A SERP interface might not intentionally frame, but it might mistake conflicting results as irrelevant and rank them lower. Our study found that this process can frame a debate by narrowing the multiple perspectives that can contextualize a controversy. Interface designers might counter this bias by allowing users to "scan the landscape" of information before focusing on an area. A low-ranked website may seem out of place, but it can be a valuable resource that negates prior assumptions in a query. A quick scan by users will double-check that nothing was missed.

Stage 4: The final spatial relationship between a user's eye and the interface is post-attentive, whereby the user's attention is drawn away from the interface. In this scenario, the user may experience a cognitive bias known as the Availability Heuristic (a person's estimate is influenced by the ease of a person's access to information over subsequent information (Tversky and Kahneman 1974)). Our study found that when a SERP presents sources that contain language that is difficult to understand without context, users may skip the answer for sources that do provide familiar responses that scaffold their prior knowledge. Designers might counter this bias by allowing for multiple users to collaborate on a query with the intention of attaining multiple-perspectives on information. Scholars have expounded on the numerous benefits of collaborative searching (Dillenbourg and Baker 1996; Foster 2010; Hansen et al. 2015; Morris 2013; Twidale et al. 1997). Searching with colleagues or sharing results to discover multiple-perspectives on findings and search strategies can lead to a wider range of useful results.

6 Conclusion

The authors draw from a long scholarly debate between various information scientists and cognitive science labs to argue that the analysis of observations can determine which cognitive-biases provide the best explanatory power. For example, current public discourse is interested in the effect of "fake news" online and how web-services and algorithms can fact-check against them. However, this approach (1) assumes that we have a clear idea of how an individual's cognition works, (2) assumes that "fact-checking" removes biases and (3) removes the individual from their social context. The authors take a different approach and argue that the average intelligent student is also at risk of misinforming themselves even if the sources are "non-fake" scientific information. Instead of removing a person from context and checking for cognitive-biases on an interface, this paper addresses this issue from the opposite angle suggested by recent scholars. This paper first used a *population-based survey experiment* to work outside of the lab and within the context of a student library. Second, it created a work task that did not merely observe how students ranked the relevancy of information but how they used the information. It then altered basic interface variables for different groups of users (74 participants total) and then analyzed which cognitive-biases provided the best explanatory power for our observations. By doing so, the paper determined that the interface design can influence the way a user interacts with a search interface. It also found the design of a search interface causes a user to misapply heuristics when they use that information. Finally, it argues that four cognitive biases can explain why the heuristics were misapplied.

Acknowledgments. The authors gratefully acknowledge the student participants who provided their time and attention to this study, as well as anonymous reviewers whose comments and suggestions improved the quality of this paper.

References

Belkin, N.J., Cole, M., Liu, J.: A model for evaluation of interactive information retrieval. Presented at the Proceedings of the SIGIR 2009 Workshop on the Future of IR Evaluation, pp. 7–8 (2009)

Braun, J., Gillespie, T.: Hosting the public discourse, hosting the public: when online news and social media converge. Journalism Pract. **5**(4), 383–398 (2011)

Browne, G.J., Pitts, M.G., Wetherbe, J.C.: Cognitive stopping rules for terminating information search in online tasks. MIS Q. **31**, 89–104 (2007)

Cellan-Jones, R.: Six searches that show the power of Google (2016). http://www.bbc.com/news/magazine-36131495

Diaz, A.: Through the Google Goggles: sociopolitical bias in search engine design. In: Spink, A., Zimmer, M. (eds.) Web Search: Multidisciplinary Perspectives, pp. 11–34. Springer, Berlin (2008)

Dillenbourg, P., Baker, M.: Negotiation spaces in human-computer collaborative learning. In: Proceedings of the International Conference on Cooperative Systems, pp. 12–14 (1996). http://ses.telecom-paristech.fr/baker/publications/ArticlesBakerPDF/1996/1996EtAl-e.pdf

Epstein, R., Robertson, R.E.: The search engine manipulation effect (SEME) and its possible impact on the outcomes of elections. In: Proceedings of the National Academy of Sciences, 201419828 (2015). https://doi.org/10.1073/pnas.1419828112

Foster, J. (ed.): Collaborative Information Behavior: User Engagement and Communication Sharing. Information Science Reference, Hershey (2010)

Gerhart, S.: Do web search engines suppress controversy? First Monday **9**(1) (2004)

Gillespie, T.: The politics of "platforms". New Media Soc. **13**(3), 347–364 (2010). https://doi.org/10.1177/1461444809342738

Guo, Q., White, R.W., Dumais, S.T., Wang, J., Anderson, B.: Predicting query performance using query, result, and user interaction features. Presented at the Adaptivity, Personalization and Fusion of Heterogeneous Information, pp. 198–201. Le centre de hautes etudes internationales d'informatique documentaire (2010)

Hansen, P., Shah, C., Klas, C.-P. (eds.): Collaborative Information Seeking. Springer International Publishing, Cham (2015). http://link.springer.com/10.1007/978-3-319-18988-8

Hargittai, E.: Digital Na(t)ives? Variation in internet skills and uses among members of the "Net Generation". Sociol. Inq. **80**(1), 92–113 (2010). https://doi.org/10.1111/j.1475-682X.2009.00317.x

Hilbert, M.: Toward a synthesis of cognitive biases: how noisy information processing can bias human decision making. Psychol. Bull. **138**(2), 211–237 (2012). https://doi.org/10.1037/a0025940

Hindman, M., Tsioutsiouliklis, K., Johnson, J.A.: Googlearchy: how a few heavily-linked sites dominate politics on the web. Presented at the Annual Meeting of the Midwest Political Science Association, vol. 4, pp. 1–33. Citeseer (2003)

Höchstötter, N., Lewandowski, D.: What users see–structures in search engine results pages. Inf. Sci. **179**(12), 1796–1812 (2009)

Hotchkiss, G., Sherman, T., Tobin, R., Bates, C., Brown, K.: Search engine results: 2010. Enquiro Search Solutions 1–61 (2010)

Hullman, J., Diakopoulos, N.: Visualization rhetoric: framing effects in narrative visualization. IEEE Trans. Vis. Comput. Graph. **17**(12), 2231–2240 (2011)

Kahneman, D.: Maps of bounded rationality: a perspective on intuitive judgment and choice. Nobel Prize Lect. **8**, 351–401 (2002)

Kahneman, D.: Thinking, fast and slow (2013)

Kahneman, D., Treisman, A., Gibbs, B.J.: The reviewing of object files: object-specific integration of information. Cogn. Psychol. **24**(2), 175–219 (1992). https://doi.org/10.1016/0010-0285(92)90007-O

Kelly, D.: Methods for evaluating interactive information retrieval systems with users. Found. Trends Inf. Retrieval **3**(1–2), 1–224 (2009)

Lauckner, C., Hsieh, G.: The presentation of health-related search results and its impact on negative emotional outcomes. In: Proceedings of the SIGCHI Conference on Human Factors in Computing Systems, pp. 333–342. ACM (2013). http://dl.acm.org/citation.cfm?id=2470702

Meyers, E.M.: Access denied: how students resolve information needs when an ideal document is restricted. In: Proceedings of the 2012 iConference, pp. 629–631. ACM (2012). http://dl.acm.org/citation.cfm?id=2132316

Morris, M.R.: Collaborative search revisited. In: Proceedings of the 2013 Conference on Computer Supported Cooperative Work, pp. 1181–1192. ACM (2013). http://dl.acm.org/citation.cfm?id=2441910

National Science Board: Science and Engineering Indicators. National Science Foundation, Arlington, VA (2014)

Rieder, B., Sire, G.: Conflicts of interest and incentives to bias: a microeconomic critique of Google's tangled position on the Web. New Media Soc. (2013). 10.1177/1461444813481195

Scheufele, D.A., Tewksbury, D.: Framing, agenda setting, and priming: the evolution of three media effects models. J. Commun. **57**(1), 9–20 (2007). https://doi.org/10.1111/j.1460-2466.2006.00326.x

Shiri, A., Zvyagintseva, L.: Dynamic query suggestion in web search engines: a comparative examination. Presented at the Proceedings of the Annual Conference of CAIS/Actes du congrès annuel de l'ACSI (2014)

Trump, D.J.: Any negative polls are fake news, just like the CNN, ABC, NBC polls in the election. Sorry, people want border security and extreme vetting [microblog], 6 February 2017. https://twitter.com/realdonaldtrump/status/828574430800539648

Tufte, E.R.: Beautiful Evidence. Graphics Press, Cheshire, Conn (2006)

Tversky, A., Kahneman, D.: Judgment under uncertainty: heuristics and biases. Science **185** (4157), 1124–1131 (1974)

Twidale, M.B., Nichols, D.M., Paice, C.D.: Browsing is a collaborative process. Inf. Process. Manage. **33**(6), 761–783 (1997)

Ware, C.: Information Visualization: Perception for Design, 3rd edn. Morgan Kaufmann, Waltham (2013)

Fire in the Kitchen: The Campfire Experience that Led to Innovation in Human Product Interaction

Marlen Promann[✉]

Purdue University, West Lafayette, USA
marlen.promann@gmail.com

Abstract. User experience (UX), with practical roots in Renaissance and theoretical beginnings in Modernism, is a contemporary design practice concerned with how users are impacted by their interaction with a product or a service. As design thinking has shifted from form based arts and crafts toward user-centered and user-serving profession, so have its methods locked in on user-centric research and validation tactics. Yet, something crucial seems to have been lost in the process – that of direct first hand experiences as triggers of user empathy that reveals their latent desires for speculative innovation. As such, UX is facing a philosophical conundrum: while it seeks to serve the experiential needs of others, it has come to reject experiences as its primary source of insight and inspiration. This article discusses the experience-centric design process of *Black Flame*, a novel induction cooktop product interaction. The case serves as a philosophical call to self-reflection and action to the HCI, Design and Information Systems communities to embrace *empathy, speculation* and *design activism* as avenues via which to advance human-technology interactions and the increasingly ubiquitous forms of experience.

Keywords: User experience · Human computer interaction · Interaction design · Speculative design · Empathetic design · Design philosophy

1 Introduction

Understanding users experiences (UX), that is, their needs, expectations and desires with a product or service is a critical issue for a variety of professions, but especially for designers and product managers who are responsible for customer satisfaction [1].

The tradition for design to support aesthetically, ergonomically and interactively defined experiences is long, but it has evolved from a top-down designer-artist creative practice to a more bottom-up and analytical user service. Undoubtedly, its growing reliance on user centric research and validation methodologies, such as interviews and contextual observations, have allowed designers to complement their personal gut-feelings and preferences with feedback and insight directly from the end-users they are designing for. This is crucial for the User Centered Design (UCD) method that has shifted designers' attention away from the material artifact to the user and their fluid state of experiencing the world.

© Springer International Publishing AG 2017
A. Marcus and W. Wang (Eds.): DUXU 2017, Part I, LNCS 10288, pp. 174–185, 2017.
DOI: 10.1007/978-3-319-58634-2_14

Importantly, UCD has increased the methodological rigor of the design practice and reduced some of the designer-bias inherent in many of the objects still prevalent in our everyday life. The new focus on UX is raising new questions about how the product meets their expectations, needs, wants, moods and even latent desires and gives them a particular experience over time, many of which have remained unanswered. Indeed, despite the general agreement that its focus on the interactions between people and products (i.e., touch points), and the experience that results from that interaction (across the touch points over time) is what makes it unique [1], the definition of UX has remained inconclusive [2].

Current discussion is mostly centered on how UX differs from usability, by means of separating the many different facets of experiences, such as "*physical, sensual, cognitive, emotional, and aesthetic*" to define how the product impacts the users (i.e., gives a user an experience) [1] (p. 261). A number of design guides have been proposed in an effort to systematically assist the application of UCD processes, yet they tend to focus either on the product [3], the user [4] or the inter-mediating interaction between the two [1], not on the resulting experiences. How are user experiences understood, defined and so designed are questions still in need of answers.

The present article is not seeking to provide these answers. Rather, it serves as a philosophical call to pause, reflect and rethink the way UX is researched and designed. To better understand what UX is today, a brief review of its practical and theoretical histories is offered. While interlinked, the two can still be seen as two distinct strands of UX thinking. An experience centric design process of *Black Flame*, a novel human-product interaction, is used to discuss the current limitations of UCD method and what it could learn from the UX practice in the wild. The *Black Flame* case illustrates the current UX conundrum: namely, designers are designing experiences in response to users' current ways of doing things without explicitly leveraging their own experiences of the manifold issues and joys present in this world.

2 User Experience Design in the Wild

User experience (UX) is a seemingly new design approach of the UCD method, yet its foundational principles of *utility* (i.e., useful, beneficial) and *usability* (i.e., ease of use, learnability) can be traced all the way back, to Da Vinci's inventions during the Renaissance. What is more recent in the UX context perhaps (not in history in general) is the analytical consideration for *aesthetics* (i.e., beauty), *emotion* (i.e., strong feelings) and *affect* (i.e., impression) as opportunities to *delight* (i.e., pleasure) users.

Utility and usability stem from the ergonomic concerns of the 1900s Industrial Revolution, where principles of *effectiveness* (i.e., achieving the desired results) and *efficiency* (i.e., minimized cost or burden) drove workplace innovations often attributed to industrialists like Winslow Taylor and Henry Ford. Both of these men optimized work for their employees and ignited research into workers' relationship with their tools (i.e., human factors).

While Ford was driven to increase production volumes and lower prices for his always black T-Models, General Motors' Alfred Sloan differentiated from Ford by pioneering the now standard way of segmenting the consumers of the car market:

'a car for every purse and purpose' [5]. To counter Ford's utility driven value proposition, Sloan offered consumers a number of aesthetic options with varying affect appeals, capturing the many desires of the different consumer segments. Years later, Toyota's human centered production processes shifted the focus from pure efficiency to workers' experience, igniting a debate on how to better the human-technology interaction via design, and design workers experiences to optimize their work efforts.

In the 1950s, the American industrial designer Henry Dreyfuss reflected on his successes and failures in his now classic text *Designing for People*: "*When the point of contact between the product and the people becomes a point of friction, then the industrial designer has failed. On the other hand, if people are made safer, more comfortable, more eager to purchase, more efficient - or just plain happier - by contact with the product, then the designer has succeeded*" [6] (p. 24). In his binary definition of success, Dreyfuss captured the two-fold requirements of UX, namely the baseline need for *usability* (i.e., the meeting of the user needs and expectations) and added value of *joy* (i.e., the exceeding user expectations), which is referred to as *delight* [3] in the contemporary UX literature.

In the 1970s, Walt Disney capitalized on his efforts to achieve delight by his '*Imagineering*' principle, which meant to leverage new and emerging technologies to fascinate, surprise and mesmerize people (i.e., what is now known as the *joy*-offering Disney World) [7]. Together with Bob Taylor and his research on mouse controlled graphical user interfaces (GUI) at the Xerox PARC, the two men laid the groundwork for what UX in practice was about: the design of unimaginable experiences with novel computer technologies.

In the 1990s Don Norman professionalized the UX design discipline when he became Apple's first User Experience Architect. While his book *The Design of Everyday Things* championed cognitive usability and ergonomic functionality over aesthetics [8], Steve Jobs led Apple products remain the epitome examples of balancing usability and aesthetics in mutually reinforcing ways, granting Apple unprecedented market success.

Indeed, by the end of the twentieth century, *utility* and *usability* were no longer enough to define and understand user experiences. The 1996 ISO 9241-11 [9] usability standard was upgraded to a ISO 9241-210 [10], a UCD standard for interactive systems that accounts for users experience as pleasure that results from "*the presentation, functionality, system performance, interactive behavior, and assistive capabilities of an interactive system, both hardware and software, [... but also] the user's prior experiences, attitudes, skills, habits and personality*" [11] (p. 161).

With the proliferation of user-product touch points, consideration for the users' experiences has grown more important. Where usability became a necessity, the need to differentiate has encouraged speculation of alternative possibilities and embracing users latent desires for joy and imagination.

Yet, systematic ways on how to balance considerations of usability and artistic aesthetics as a unified UX effort have remained difficult to achieve. Currently, the industry is complementarily blending user-centered UX researchers with designer-artist '*imagineers*' as the crucial duos offering the best experiences to their users.

3   User Experience Research in Academia

Contrary to practice in industry, UX is a newer consideration in design thinking in the academic context, but it has struggled with the same essential dilemma of balancing utility and beauty. Throughout the centuries, design theory has shifted its focus from *form* to *function* and to *communication*, and is only recently discussing the viability of *experiences* as the object of design-theoretical analysis.

Early academic thinking on design is rooted in Modernist movements of the late 19th century. In the aftermath of the industrial revolution, design writings were underlined by a social shift: moving from *decorative arts* that bore no direct utility to society, to *usability* that had an agenda to enhance the well-being of people through material objects. Bauhaus design school's systematic practical and theoretical research into the formal, technical and economic informed their Modernist paradigm of *form follows function* [12]. As such, Modernism marked the shift where design stopped being concerned with *form* and became obsessed with *interaction* (i.e., the ways of using, doing, and ultimately, of living).

With the turn of the century, design writing became more concerned with *usability* and perceived *ease of use*. In an effort to make a design easy to understand, interpret and therefore use, something that was not always common among the Bauhaus work, design became a matter of semiotics, where artifacts were messages of usability and utility framed as a form of visual communication. In Smith and Tabor [13] words: *"the fundamental training and skills of artist-designers lie in detecting, creating, and controlling cultural and emotional meanings"* (p. 40).

Today, the discussion has moved beyond communication of messages and meanings. UX has become an established field of research at the intersection of Design and Human Computer Interaction (HCI) [14] with a conceptual discussion centered on how design can embed and convey certain *action potentials* (i.e., affordances) that result in some positive *impact* (i.e., experiences). Herein, design is no longer focused on the physical or symbolic forms of material objects, or the end-users *per se*, but rather on the users' experiences with it at the motor, task and goal levels [11] over time and across different emotional states.

Many different frameworks have been proposed to systematize the manifold nuances that create user experiences. Forlizzi and Battarbee [1] attempted to define experiences with interactive systems as a two-tiered framework of *quality* (usability, cognition and expression) and *depth* (interaction, experience and co-experience with other users). Desmet and Hekkert [3] proposed *aesthetics*, *meanings* and *emotions* as the three variables needed to guide design and evaluate human-product interactions that could account for users affective responses to the experiences studied. A number of affordance based frameworks have also been proposed to better address *user needs* [11] or to leverage *aesthetics* to communicate action potentials [15].

In complement to the UX practice in industry, controlled experiments have proven beauty's mediating role in perceived usability [16]. As such, *aesthetics* and *affordances* are increasingly recognized among HCI, UbiComp and Design researchers as important for designers to provide effective ways of interaction through artifacts. Xenakis and Arnellos' [15] theoretical model is a unique effort to connect the two by leveraging interaction aesthetics as detection mechanisms for action possibilities (i.e., affordances). Hornecker and Buur [4] provided concepts for enhancing *social* and *collaborative* experiences via tangible interaction technologies.

The models have raised many criticisms and have hardly led to easily actionable and generalizable design methods. On a fundamental level, a distinction can be drawn between *holistic* and *reductive* approaches of UX that are rooted in complexity embracing phenomenology and complexity reducing cognitive psychology, respectively [17] (p. 1). The former focuses on the complex interplay between the many experience-defining variables about the user (e.g., emotion, intellect and sensation), their action, context and time. While invaluable to advancing our understandings of the many complexities associated with user experiences, they are difficult to use as design guides. To this end, the latter approach aims to simplify the holistic perspective, by chunking the variables into independent parts that are easier comprehend.

A number of situated research activities have been proposed to help designers position themselves in the shoes of their intended users and assist them in better understanding the experiences that they seek to design [1]. Yet, with the exception of pure ethnography, social scientific research methods have fallen short in granting designers direct experiences of what they are designing. Redström [18] has articulated the problem that *"with its ambition to create a tight fit between object and user, the development seems to point to a situation where we are trying to optimize fit on the basis of predictions rather than knowledge, eventually trying to design something that is not there for us to design"* (p. 124).

Despite the manifold efforts the relatively new research field lacks the prescriptive tools to guide efforts to research and design experiences. We are faced with critical questions about what it means to design user experiences (vs. products)? What information do we need? How do we go about getting the necessary knowledge? These are crucial questions to answer, unless we are prepared that our work might result in the old problem of offering users *"experiences that they do not wish"* [11] (p. 160).

4   Discussion: Bringing a Fire into the Kitchen

Black Flame is a novel induction cooktop prototype that emulates a campfire experience by utilizing spatial bodily interaction as its heating control. It serves as an illustrative case for how designers' personal experiences (vs. the much embraced UCD) can lead to novel human-product interactions and should be considered as a potential source for insight (into users latent desires), inspiration (for experience empathy), and speculative innovation, especially in the banal and naturalized context of the everyday.

4.1   First Hand Cooking Experiences

In the summer of 2015, three women: an electrical engineer, industrial designer and a user experience designer –, all working for Whirlpool Corporation in Benton Harbor, MI, came to share a variety of first hand cooking experiences that led them to innovate a novel human-product interaction.

After working their daytime job roles the women convened to cook and dine together. While collaborative cooking was joyous, it increased the already frequent number of cooking related incidents with the classic electric cooktop (see Fig. 1). The common issues that occurred included burning the food, over boiling and spilling, forgetting burners on, melting plastic cooking utensils, and perhaps most frequently, burning one's fingers by touching hot surfaces or foods.

This was not surprising since stovetops are deemed a classic usability issue, alongside microwave interfaces, camera menu options and other products that suffer from the same complexity, feedback and mismatch issues for decades. However, the issues became more prevalent as more people joined the cooking effort. This was thought to have happened for two main reasons: attention had shifted from cooking to social conversation, and with more people executing tasks, it was difficult to preserve an overview of what was going on with the different pots and pans. The main interface flaws of the electric stovetops include the following:

- **Disconnected controls**: The heat controlling knobs of the burners are positioned above the stove top, separate from the actual cooking surface. This made it difficult to know which knob controls which burner and resulted in common errors.
- **Time delay between input and output:** It takes time for burners to get red and hot. This resulted in meats being placed on a pan too early and not getting seared.
- **Lack of feedback:** While the burners turn red when they are in the process of heating and there is nothing placed on them (good safety), they do not stay red while 'on', when a pot is on it, or when it is already cooling but still too hot for touch. This led to burned fingers, pots and melted kitchen utensils.
- **Inflexible heating areas:** Despite the varying sizes, burners are often too large (e.g., when boiling a few eggs) or too small (e.g., when using a square griddle pan). This caused safety hazards when over boiling water splashed off the burner and cooking issues when the griddle pan had to be moved around to heat its corners.
- **Inefficient spatial layout:** An associated issue is the inefficient placement of the burners in each corner of the cooktop and none in the middle. A wok pan's wide radius and high edge makes it too large to fit on back burners and a potential safety hazard on a front burner. Again, most burners are too large for wok's small base.
- **Arbitrary and inconsistent temperature references:** While numeric control is easy for users to remember over repeated use, they are arbitrary and inconsistent from one stove to another, causing usability issues during new encounters.
- **Socio-spatial limitation:** Despite the increasingly open plan living setting cooking by the cooktop always locks the chef in the kitchen, excluded from the social conversations of other family members or guests.

Comparatively, when taking a weekend camping trip to the Dune Lake Campground on the shore of Lake Michigan, the women experienced a similarly social and collaborative, yet far less stressful and more intuitive cooking experience around the campfire. While the oven offers many more functions with much more ease than setting up a campfire, there was something immensely intuitive about how one could control the heat when cooking above live campfire (Fig. 2). The main experience defining campfire features included the following:

Fig. 1. Cooktop in the kitchen where shared dinners took place, Beckwith Hall, MI.

Fig. 2. Dinner and smores at the campfire, Dune Lake Campground, MI.

– **Direct control:** Cooking a sausage or a smore on a stick above a campfire flame offers users no other control but a direct distance based interaction with the flame.
– **Live input and output:** The direct correlation between moving one's food closer and burning it, or keeping it too far away and not cooking it enough, is an intuitive relative interaction space between the chef (input) and the static campfire (output).
– **Multisensory feedback:** Campfire cooking leverages the human sensors more than stovetop cooking does: one can feel the heat of the fire, sees the impact of the fire on the food, smells the food getting ready, and hears the sizzles of a sausage.
– **Food awareness:** Besides the lid-less pan, most indoor cooking hides the food in pots and pans eliminating the option for visual feedback as the food changes and becomes ready. This visual feedback is readily available when cooking over a fire.
– **Smooth spatial workflow:** While the tactical motion of moving food closer or away from oneself is similar to the motions one makes on the stovetop, campfire contextualizes the interaction in meaningful hot-cold spatial orientations.
– **Social inclusion:** Cooking around a campfire is an inherently social activity, where everybody gathers around the fire to cook and eat together. The circular, inward facing, slow and more seamless cooking experience is socially inclusive.

4.2   Black Flame: A Novel Human-Product Interaction

The contrasting experiences with the stovetop and the campfire resulted in a critical realization that the long internalized and accepted ways of cooking are not how things should be. While the self-experienced problems with the cooktop resulted in insights that most UCD methods could have captured; the campfire experience was unique in two crucial ways:

1. It offered designers a point of comparison that granted them the *empathy* to see and question the already normalized issues of current cooktops that they were so accustomed to in their everyday life.
2. It directly informed their *speculative alternative considerations* for the new cooktop design. It triggered a series of experimentations regarding form and embodied interactions that would have not been considered otherwise.

While the first hand campfire experience informed alternative ways on how to approach a potential solution, the tactics of sketching, prototyping and user testing remained the same when validating the speculative designs (Fig. 3). *Black Flame*, is a working prototype of an induction cooktop that uses the visual pattern of a Fibonacci spiral as an analogy to a real fire (Fig. 4): its dense center serves as the heart of the fire, while its widening curve correlates with cooling temperatures one would experience as they would pull their food away from the fire.

Fig. 3. *Black Flame* cooktop agile and user centered prototyping process.

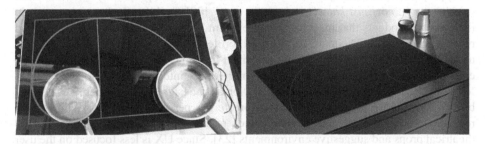

Fig. 4. *Black Flame* prototype melting butter at different speeds and visual mock up.

Noteworthy features include:

- **Ergonomic motion:** The Fibanocci curve across the *Black Flame* cooktop allows users to conveniently leverage the natural and smooth left-right hand curvature to move their pots and pans between higher and lower temperatures (Fig. 4).

- **Spatial temperature control:** Instead of knobs, *Black Fire* emulates the campfire experience by leveraging the spatial positioning, guided by the Fibonacci curve, as proxy for temperature control. For instance, to melt butter the user would briefly place it at the heart of the curve (fast melt), and swiftly slide it to the other side to keep the butter melted without burning it (see Fig. 4 for an illustration).
- **Spatial temperature feedback:** There is no need to double check if the temperatures for each burner is correct at any given time. The position of the pots on *Black Flame* conveys that information via spatial layout. In general, most cooking would start on the high end and end all the way on the low end where the pots and pans could be 'kept warm', eliminating the trouble of having to lift pots and pans away from the cooktop because the burners are still too hot and would burn the food.
- **Maximised heating area:** Similarly to some existing induction cooktops, like Gaggenau, *Black Flame* was designed to leverage many small coils laid out in a honeycomb grid. As such, *Black Flame* is a cook anywhere surface where each coil would turn on efficiently when recognizing a pot or a pan above them.

4.3   UX Conundrum: Experiencing Experiences to Create Experiences

Black Flame serves as an unconventional innovation that stemmed from designers' unique first hand experiences that triggered their empathetic feelings and critical speculations to simplify the currently complex ways and unnecessary social norms related to cooking. If to acknowledge human discourse not as a meaning framed in form, but rather, as an interaction [19], then experiences could be seen as a form of discourse. Drawing on *Black Flame's* experience centric design, the two ways in which first hand experiences could inform designers and research about experiences include empathetic comparison and speculative design.

Experiencing situations first hand that are similar, but not the same as their users' experiences, could grant designers an ***empathetic comparison*** to help them gain a *"deep[er] understanding of the user's circumstances and experiences, which involves relating to, [...not] just knowing about the user"* [20] (p. 440). Such insight can help them create products that meet users' more latent needs. While there is a widespread recognition in the UCD context, of the need for designers to be empathetic towards the users, their methods to achieve it have remained limited. The design literature discusses empathy as a limited quality of the designer (one's intuitive ability to establish an 'emotional connection' with another [21]), or as a design process where such sensibility is trained [20] via communication (e.g., personas and storytelling) and role-playing techniques, such as 'experience prototyping' [22] that is supported by theatrical props and suggestive environments [23]. Since UX is less focused on the user and more interested in understanding their behavioral and experiential existence, experience-based empathy can help designers understand situations from fresh angles.

Indeed, varied experiences and especially their correlations can trigger critical curiosity and capability for *"speculative design [which] serves two distinct purposes: first, to enable us to think about the future; second, to critique current practice"* [24] (p. 11). Similarly, speculative design is currently a collection of exploratory design efforts that commonly borrow experiences and references from unconventional sources to inform novel "*use[s] of technology, aesthetics, behavior, interaction and function of the designed artifact*" [24] (p. 11). In the case of *Black Flame*, designers were triggered by the initially unrelated campfire experience, which informed their speculative approach to alternative realities for the current cooktop solution. Designers are essentially called upon to part-take in design activism by experiencing situations and life as users and responding to it, whether pragmatically, philosophically or other means.

The current UX conundrum is the phenomenon of the design theory closing a full circle on its historic trajectory. What started as elite artistic concern about beauty, craft and form, had become increasingly democratized and methodical, through Modernism. The shifting focus from aesthetic artifacts to useable products that serve user needs is facing the already familiar artist-designer dilemma in design theory.

Concern for users' overall experience with the product has shifted the designers' attention to experiences, which are too complex and difficult to understand and design for with existing UCD methods. Dunne and Raby's [25] call for designers to look to varying experiences, other disciplines and sources as artistic inspiration to speculate, is the latest effort to bridge the artistic '*Imagineering*' and Norman's usability. It is important to not entertain the pre-UCD definition of a designer who was seen as the all-knowing visionary and a creative talent who should define our lives for us [26].

When pursuing innovation, it is important to have an understanding of the end-users and their problems, via empirical, observational and other methods. At the same time, as cases from history have shown, designers should also able to ignore customer inputs. Ford's adherence to his speculative vision of the mass-market car was key to his early successes. It turned to his failure when he failed to respond to the changing marketplace, where people no longer wanted faster horses but desired different cars with financing options [5]. Ford's failure was not his failure to listen or understand his customers, but in his refusal to keep testing his original vision against reality via UCD.

5 Conclusion

UX is facing a conundrum: while it seeks to serve the experiential needs of others, it has yet to embrace experiences as its source of insight and inspiration. Design practices at the periphery, namely empathetic and speculative design, have been exploring opportunities to better embed designers in experiential situations. But make no mistake, reducing the designer-bias and pre-empting false assumptions by user-validation has been a crucial journey in design history, one that has led to the success of many products and services that served real user needs, wants and desires.

As UX definitions, processes and thinking mature, so too, should its methods. There is a need for ways to understand, define, and study the 'magical' and 'artistic' of designers and their processes. Researchers have explored the differences between novice and expert designers [27] and traced links between UX frameworks and design practices [28]. But, questions about how to derive experiences from experiences have remained in need of an answer. Looking at experiences as a human discourse could point to possible ways forward.

Acknowledgements. The three authors of *Black Flame* were Marlen Promann, Eva Ross and Rachael Acker. They were awarded the Whirlpool Corporation's internal Bravo Gold Award in August 2005.

References

1. Forlizzi, J., Battarbee, K.: Understanding experience in interactive systems. In: Proceedings of the 5th Conference on Designing Interactive Systems: Processes, Practices, Methods, and Techniques, New York, NY, USA, pp. 261–268 (2004)
2. Lallemand, C., Gronier, G., Koenig, V.: User experience: a concept without consensus? Exploring practitioners' perspectives through an international survey. Comput. Hum. Behav. **43**, 35–48 (2015)
3. Desmet, P., Hekkert, P.: Framework of product experience. Int. J. Des. **1**(1), 57–66 (2007)
4. Hornecker, E., Buur, J.: Getting a grip on tangible interaction: a framework on physical space and social interaction. In: Proceedings of the SIGCHI Conference on Human Factors in Computing Systems, New York, NY, USA, pp. 437–446 (2006)
5. Vlaskovits, P.: Henry ford, innovation, and that 'Faster Horse' quote. Harvard Bus. Rev., 29 August 2011. https://hbr.org/2011/08/henry-ford-never-said-the-fast
6. Dreyfuss, H.: Designing for People. Allworth Press, New York (2003)
7. Dickerson, J.: Walt disney: the world's first UX designer. UX Mag. Article no. 1083, 09 September 2013
8. Norman, D.: The Design of Everyday Things: Revised and Expanded Edition, Revised Edition edn. Basic Books, New York (2013)
9. ISO 9241: Ergonomic requirements for office work with visual display terminals (VDTs)-Part 11: Guidance on usability. Institutional Organization for Standardization (ISO), Switzerland (1996)
10. Bevan, N.: International standards for usability should be more widely used. J. Usability Stud. **4**(3), 106–113 (2009)
11. Pucillo, F., Cascini, G.: A framework for user experience, needs and affordances. Des. Stud. **35**(2), 160–179 (2014)
12. Gropius, W.: Principles of Bauhaus production. In: Bauhaus Dessau: Principles of Bauhaus Production, pp. 95–97. Bauhaus, Dessau 1975 (1926)
13. Smith, G.C., Tabor, P.: The role of the artist-designer. In: Winograd, T. (ed.) Bringing Design to Software, pp. 37–61. ACM, New York, NY, USA (1996)
14. Hassenzahl, M., Tractinsky, N.: User experience - a research agenda. Behav. Inf. Technol. **25**(2), 91–97 (2006)
15. Xenakis, I., Arnellos, A.: The relation between interaction aesthetics and affordances. Des. Stud. **34**(1), 57–73 (2013)
16. Tractinsky, N., Katz, A.S., Ikar, D.: What is beautiful is usable. Interact. Comput. **13**(2), 127–145 (2000)
17. Blythe, M., Hassenzahl, M., Law, E., Vermeeren, A.: An analysis framework for user experience (UX) studies: a green paper. In: Towards UX Manifesto, vol. 2, pp. 1–5 (2007)
18. Redström, J.: Towards user design? On the shift from object to user as the subject of design. Des. Stud. **27**(2), 123–139 (2006)
19. van Dijk, T.A.: Discourse as Social Interaction. SAGE, London (1997)
20. Kouprie, M., Visser, F.S.: A framework for empathy in design: stepping into and out of the user's life. J. Eng. Des. **20**(5), 437–448 (2009)

21. Battarbee, K., Koskinen, I.: Co-experience: user experience as interaction. CoDesign **1**(1), 5–18 (2005)
22. Buchenau, M., Suri, J.F.: Experience prototyping. In: Proceedings of the 3rd Conference on Designing Interactive Systems: Processes, Practices, Methods, and Techniques, New York, NY, USA, pp. 424–433 (2000)
23. Keller, I., Stappers, P.J.: Presence for design: conveying atmosphere through video collages. CyberPsychology Behav. **4**(2), 215–223 (2001)
24. Auger, J.: Speculative design: crafting the speculation. Digit. Creativity **24**(1), 11–35 (2013)
25. Dunne, A., Raby, F.: Speculative Everything. The MIT Press, Cambridge (2013)
26. Tonkinwise, C.: How we intend to future: review of anthony dunne and fiona raby, speculative everything: design, fiction, and social dreaming. Des. Philos. Pap. **12**(2), 169–187 (2014)
27. Akin, O., Ahmed, S., Wallace, K.M., Blessing, L.T.M.: Understanding the differences between how novice and experienced designers approach design tasks. Res. Eng. Des. **14**(2), 1–11 (2006)
28. Law, E.L.-C., Hassenzahl, M., Karapanos, E., Obrist, M., Roto, V.: Tracing links between UX frameworks and design practices: dual carriageway. In: Proceedings of HCI Korea, South Korea, pp. 188–195 (2014)

User Participatory Methods for Inclusive Design and Research in Autism: A Case Study in Teaching UX Design

Debra Satterfield[1](✉) and Marc Fabri[2]

[1] California State University Long Beach, Los Angeles, USA
debra.satterfield@csulb.edu
[2] Leeds Beckett University, Leeds, UK
m.fabri@leedsbeckett.ac.uk

Abstract. User participatory design is considered to be one of the best methods for understanding the needs of a target audience and creating high quality, well designed solutions to meet their needs. For many design students, the principles of participatory design in the creation of new user experiences are part of their curriculum. However, the involvement of disabled persons into the user experience design (UXD) process can be difficult in an educational setting. Often persons with autism and cognitive disabilities are excluded from user experience data collection due to their lack of sufficient cognitive ability and language skills to participate in these research methods in meaningful ways. Further, educators may shy away from involving this group due to institutional regulations and ethical concerns. This paper presents a case study introducing design students to inclusive UXD strategies and observing autistic children, using an approach called the "Connectivity Model". The model avoids the requirement for complex ethical clearance by facilitating observations via recorded videos. We present outcomes and evaluate the model against the most pertinent needs of these children.

Keywords: Participatory design · Autism · Design education · Higher education · User experience design · Serious games

1 Introduction

Working with actual target audience groups in university design courses is often difficult because of the time involved in creating user experience design (UXD) research protocols and gaining approval to conduct the study with actual users. Further, disabled persons are protected from certain types of user research in the United States and other countries thus making their participation in UXD research even more difficult. However, there is great value in considering the needs of this user group as there can be particular design challenges, and outcomes can be revealing and rewarding. In order to include these user groups in testing or observations, the research methodology must go through intense scrutiny to ensure their rights as a protected population as indicated by the relevant Institutional Review Board (IRB) or Ethical Approval process. In addition,

© Springer International Publishing AG 2017
A. Marcus and W. Wang (Eds.): DUXU 2017, Part I, LNCS 10288, pp. 186–197, 2017.
DOI: 10.1007/978-3-319-58634-2_15

children under the age of 18 are not able to give consent and an assent process must be used along with the typical consent forms given to the parent or guardian.

Because of this complicated and potentially lengthy review process, including these audiences in the research process for students in a UXD course is difficult. However, without meaningful input from these persons in the design process – amongst the input from other stakeholders – the resulting products and services may not adequately meet their specific needs and preferences. Further, it is highly beneficial to students to learn together in an environment that closely resembles the real-life equivalent, which in this case is conducting research with autistic people. Such situated learning aids students' progress by creating a community of practice (Lave and Wenger 1990).

Therefore, we consider it highly beneficial to teach design students how to be IRB compliant in their research and at the same time use methods that consider input of the autistic target audience in ways that are sensitive to their needs, do not violate their human rights, and allow participation in appropriate and meaningful ways (cf. Satterfield et al. 2016). This paper will present and evaluate such a model of participatory UXD for autism that can be incorporated into university design courses.

1.1 A Case for Early Intervention

The US Center for Disease Control (CDC 2012) found that one in 68 children aged 8 years old have an autism spectrum disorder (ASD). While no intervention has yet been shown to reduce the prevalence of ASD, the CDC recommends that early support and intervention might maximize the ability of children to function and participate in their community. In addition, initiation of school-based services prior to formal school entry might aid educational progress. Chez (2008) noted that autism does not typically shorten the lifespan, therefore society needs to prepare for long-term support of these children as they grow to adulthood. We argue that improving early intervention and quality of life, improving social impairments in communication and awareness of others, and potentially reversing some aspects of these autistic behaviors at a neurological level will benefit everyone.

1.2 Identifying Key Challenges

Satterfield et al. (2013) found that parents and teachers of children on the autism spectrum were in strong agreement when identifying the most difficult social, communication and behavioral issues facing these children. Both participant groups were asked to complete an online survey and rate the importance of the children's social skills (6 questions), communication skills (7 questions), and behavioral skills (7 questions) when performing their roles in taking care of the children, on a 1–5 Likert scale. The most important skills (average ranked 4.5 or higher by both parents and teachers) identified were:

1. The ability to avoid or control "tantrums", "melt downs" or "acting out."
2. The ability to understand that other people have feelings.
3. The ability to understand social situations.

4. The ability to understand the thoughts, words, and communication of other people.
5. The ability to use age appropriate speech and/or language for communication.

In a large-scale qualitative study, Wittemeyer et al. (2011) found that enabling autistic persons to have control and make their own choices is a key factor in reaching a "good outcome" for their adult life. With regards to parents' aspirations for their autistic children, the top priorities were:

1. Emotional wellbeing (25%);
2. The ability to build social relationships (25%);
3. Employment (22%); and
4. Developing independent living skills (19%);

Generally, any intervention that aims to support autistic children and prepare them for adult life ought to therefore focus on some or all of abovementioned key challenges.

1.3 Participatory Design

Human-centered design approaches have long advocated for the active involvement of users in the design process in order to gain a clear understanding of user and task requirements (Maguire 2001). This may be in the form of interviews, focus group, prototype testing and final system evaluation. Participatory design takes this further by considering the user not simply as a source of information or evaluator of the final product, but as an active contributor of design ideas and a decision-maker in the design process (Sanders and Stappers 2008). There is a growing body of research concerned with involving people on the autism spectrum in the design of products targeted at this group.

Much of the participatory design literature in this field focuses on adequately representing the needs and requirements of children (Börjesson et al. 2015), people with learning difficulties or communication impairments, teenager and young people (Fabri and Andrews 2016), or those with difficulties imagining how they themselves or others might use the product (c.f. Millen et al. 2010; Coons and Watson 2013). Children can be informants or design partners in the process (Druin 2002), with parents and teachers often acting as proxies, experts or facilitators (Börjesson et al. 2015). There is a clear need for UX designers to understand how to follow a participatory design process that is both sensitive to the characteristics of the user group and evidence-based.

1.4 Training the Next Generation of Designers

Universities have a duty to prepare future UX designers in the best possible way for the challenges of design practice – especially where the end product needs to be highly inclusive and accessible. The importance and feasibility of a practice-based approach has been shown before (Fabri 2015; Lugmayr et al. 2011). Going through the participatory design process with disabled or neuro-diverse users presents particular challenges as it requires students to be open to the needs, limitations and preferences of this group. Commonly held assumptions about users may not be valid (cf. Fabri and Andrews 2016), and UXD students need to learn how to involve autistic target audiences in meaningful and ethical ways. In order to do this, the design students need to have a firm understanding of how to conduct such research.

In this paper, we will investigate how the Connectivity Model, a participatory design research method developed by Kang and Satterfield (2009), can be used in a university context. We will embed the method into the UXD teaching curriculum of a university design course for senior students. In particular, we will explore the effectiveness of specific research tools in helping students identify the needs of an autistic target audience. We also demonstrate a method of using the Connectivity Model UXD data collection tools with a carefully selected series of videos on a YouTube channel of ASD and classroom situations as an alternative to in-person ethnographic observations. This gives the advantage of eliminating a need for a complicated IRB and access to a classroom with the appropriate student population for this type of observation. This greatly increases the ability to teach UXD for ASD in a university setting that might otherwise lack such access for students to observe ASD.

2 The Connectivity Model

The connectivity model is a UX research method that collects data in social, emotional, behavioral and motivational areas. It was developed for the inclusion of persons with cognitive disabilities and autism into the user experience design cycle as part of a participatory design process (Kang and Satterfield 2009). The model analyzes user data based on socially and emotionally appropriate practices in relation to the community of the target audience. It further considers physical constraints such as ability in the areas of physical, cognitive, and developmental areas and combines this into the optimal design zone.

This design zone takes into consideration not only what a particular person or group can do, but also what they prefer or desire to do in their daily lives. The model encourages the designer to develop deep empathy for the end user before starting the creative design process. In this respect, it is not unlike the early stages of Design Thinking approaches (cf. IDEO 2015) which advocate a deep inquiry into a user's motivations, abilities, concerns, dislikes and personal preferences. The Connectivity Model combines methods from Kansei Engineering (Nagamachi 1999) and Activity Theory (Engeström 1993) and incorporates audience analysis in the areas of physical and cognitive abilities and primary motivating factors. *Kansei Engineering* is an evaluation methodology that focuses on how people respond emotionally to products, packages, and brand experiences. It addresses the question of why people like a product, package, or brand in terms of its sensory and tactile properties. Activity Theory (AT) was developed by Russian psychologist Lev Semenovish Vygotsky. It provides a framework for evaluating how social, cultural, and historical conditions influence people. The Connectivity Model applies the combined metrics into a cohesive method of analysis and to the design of artifacts, environments and experiences for persons from all ability levels.

3 The Play•IT Design Project

Play•IT is the title of a pilot study assignment in a university design course for senior students. It was offered as a way to investigate the design of UXD data tools and their use by students as a way to collect and analyze UXD data for use in studio projects. Here, it acts as the case study for evaluating a participatory design method.

The objective of the Play•IT project is to design an educational game that mediates social interactions between typical children and children on the autism spectrum. The emphasis is on creating a designed solution that addresses the social, communication and behavior skills needed by children with autism as they interact and play with their neurologically typical peers on an equal basis.

Play•IT was taught in Fall 2016 as part of an online course, DESN 482: Research Methods for Inclusive UX Design at California State University Long Beach. The class focuses on research methods, design for social inclusion, and design for behavioral change. DESN 482 is an upper division, fully online course in a 4-year design major. The online format was chosen because it offers many options to students in the areas of content delivery, access to digital information and a minimized bias in the classroom with regard to race and gender (Satterfield and Kelle 2016).

The course uses inclusive UXD tools and strategies to identify differences in social, ethical, and physical abilities in multiple target audiences. It also takes into consideration the importance of age appropriateness and stylistic appeal to both the child with disabilities and to the typical peers (cf. Satterfield 2010).

3.1 Project Requirements

The solutions students create for the Play•IT project had to meet the following requirements:

1. It had a primary target audience of children ages of 6 and 12 years old;
2. Accommodate the social, ethical, and physical issues face by all constituent groups including peers, teachers, and parents;
3. The project solution must be age appropriate and interesting to both the child with autism and to their neurologically typical peers;
4. It must not be designed or branded as an "autism" or "disabilities" product;
5. It must have learning outcomes that are beneficial to both constituent groups.

Students were expected to design and prototype all interfaces, objects, spaces and other essential elements to demonstrate the functionality of their final solution. The project goals were:

1. Incorporate multi-sensory data into a UXD solution;
2. Incorporate information design for multiple audiences;
3. Create a visually dynamic solution that appeals to multiple audiences; and
4. Incorporate a fun UXD solution with social, emotional and behavioral learning experiences.

3.2   Course Structure

Lectures. Ethnographic information was given through a series of lectures on autism, the Connectivity Model, audience analysis, motivation, behavior modification techniques, and branding. Students were also required to complete the IRB training for social and behavioral research (cf. Satterfield 2016). Guest lectures with parents of children with autism were included into the online weekly meetings. The students were required to write out questions for the parents prior to their guest presentations and then submit the completed questions and answers based on the information from the presentation.

Data Gathering. Students were asked to collect ethnographic data by observing and analyzing pre-selected YouTube videos from a variety of natural and school settings, complemented by insights from a literature review. Using a worksheet based on the Connectivity Model (Fig. 1), students recorded the autistic and typical child behaviors they observed. This was done by using a YouTube channel with videos edited for the purpose of allowing students to observe and record both typical and ASD children. The data from these ethnographic observations was then used to inform the final Play•IT design solutions by connecting the UXD research findings and letting this inform user personas, journey maps, and design solutions for the final project.

Connectivity Model UX Worksheet	
Positive Social Issues	Negative Social Issues
Positive Emotional Issues	Negative Emotional Issues
Positive Behavioral Issues	Negative Behavioral Issues
Physical Conditions	Motivational Issues

Fig. 1. The connectivity model data collection worksheet.

Assessment. Class assessment was done via weekly assignments posted to an online course management tool. Students were required to login once a week for live lectures, project evaluation, and group critiques. Students participated in additional active learning or constructed learning experiences such as making a video of themselves demonstrating a favorite toy and discussing why it was fun or educational. They also posted discussions of favorite online games for children. Students were required to complete and document the following aspects of their research and design:

1. Identify and research multiple target audiences,
2. Develop a series of user personas;
3. Complete the IRB test and generate interview questions for a parent
4. Conduct ethnographic observations with the Connectivity Model worksheet;
5. Create a design with sketches, and low, mid and high fidelity prototypes; and
6. Demonstrate the game play and educational content.

4   Results

The final projects were constructed as high fidelity prototypes. Students were encouraged to choose a method of final construction that best demonstrates their concept and thoroughly document it through photos or digital images. A process book was created to document their UXD research including user personas, compilation of research questions and interview data, ethnographic observations and data interpretation.

4.1   Student Project 1: Perry Penguin

Perry Penguin (Fig. 2) is a multi-sensory game designed using the Connectivity Model to incorporate textures, colors, and sounds into a fun, learning environment. A snowball is used to bowl over the penguins and to identify the related colors and two-term concepts.

Fig. 2. Perry Penguin game solution for Play•IT

4.2   Student Project 2: Tumi Turtle

Tumi Turtle (Fig. 3) is a tabletop game interface that allows children to play both individually or in groups. The turtle has a screen on the top and a projector that displays onto a wall for groups to interact. Color, sound and interactivity are incorporated into table.

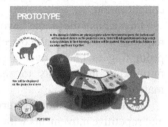

Fig. 3. Tumi Turtle is a multi-purpose game table.

4.3   Student Project 3: Tree Haus

Tree Haus (Fig. 4) is a pre-school classroom designed to incorporate sensory spaces and break away areas for all children to work in large or small groups based on their sensory needs and tolerances.

Fig. 4. Tree Haus inclusive classroom.

5   Connectivity Model Analysis

The information collected in the Connectivity Model assesses social, emotional, physical, motivational and behavioral data. In the following paragraphs we will analyse and evaluate the model by focusing on student project 1: Perry the Penguin. This project acts as an example that represents characteristics of all three projects.

In a self-assessment of Perry the Penguin using the Connectivity Model data, the student identified several social goals achieved by the design. The game can be played solo or with friends or family. It promotes positive social behaviors through sharing, waiting, and turn taking. It allows the child to help reset the pins for another player or for themselves. It creates a learning experience by matching numbers, shapes and colors of birds to mat. It provides opportunities for organizing the penguins off the ice rink matt in different patterns, understanding and following directions given by game play cards or parents.

Emotional goals were also identified. When playing the game, everyone can celebrate when one player knocks over pins as an emotional reinforcement. If the game is played with a sibling or friend, it creates a friendly competition and encourages collaboration.

Physically, the game involves hand-eye coordination and the fine motor skills required to hold the ball correctly and to stand the pins up. It uses language and verbal prompting to knock over a certain pin. It incorporates hand-eye coordination and mimicking movements to succeed. A variety of textures help kids learn tactile matching.

Behaviorally it requires turn taking, knocking down the pins indicated on the card, and repetitive movements with each successive turn. Pins can be gently tossed back and forth or set up in a specific pattern as indicated by the playing cards. By watching other people take their turns, children can learn the game play.

Winning the game and hearing positive feedback sounds when the birds fall over or when you place them on the correct color or number is motivational.

It is socially motivating and promotes learning through interacting with peers in a fun, safe, and entertaining environment. The textures and colors on the penguin characters are both tactilely and visually stimulating.

This game can be played solo or collaboratively with peers. The game is not branded as a "disability" game. The different colors, textures, shapes, and positive sound reinforcements are learning aids for any child within the 3–4 year old range. Overall it does not stand out as a product created for kids with disabilities, but as a fun game that anyone can play and learn.

6   Discussion

Students were introduced to data-driven, user participatory research for inclusive design through a series of lectures, a YouTube channel with videos, and class discussions on data driven processes. The IRB test was a useful introduction to the ethics and strategies for social and behavioral research. By allowing students to write and address questions to parents they were able to glean useful qualitative data to inform their designs. Access to the YouTube videos gave students a much clearer understanding of the exact behavioral and communication issues in autism than can be understood by only reading about the condition. The combination of lectures, videos and person interviews provided a well-balanced and informative set of data for the Play•IT project.

The lack of face-to-face engagement between student designers and autistic children is a limitation of the approach, whilst also being its defining strength. By definition, participatory design ought to include face-to-face interactions. The application of video observations provides an alternative way for designers to develop empathy for users. Information gathered from parents complemented the video observations, with parents taking on the roles of both proxies and experts.

The Connectivity Model UX research tools effectively helped students identify the social, emotional, behavioral, physical and motivational needs of target audiences both with autism and those who are neurologically typical. Lectures on the Connectivity Model combined with the worksheets appeared to provide a clear method for conducting ethnographic observations. Students were introduced to each aspect of the model and shown examples of what that specifically looks like in a natural setting. By using carefully selected videos, students were able to play the videos multiple times in order to take notes on both the frequency and context of social, emotional, physical and behavioral actions demonstrated by the people in the videos.

The UXD strategies used in the Play•IT project were considered to be successful in this pilot study. All students were able to conduct the UXD research and apply it to their designs. It was used in initial design stages to inform the concept of the project. At later design stages, the video observations and parent interview data was useful in making specific refinements to the designs. By recording these answers in a meaningful way during the parent interview and during the video observations, students were able to find and retrieve the answers that they needed to make decisions about the experience design.

Additionally, this method can be easily implemented in both online and traditional university classes. It does not require lengthy IRB approvals and will allow students to experience what it is like to do actual site observations. By allowing the students to practice developing and asking survey questions, they had the opportunity to gain valuable UXD skills in qualitative research and focus group administration.

7 Future Research

Future research will examine whether an increased awareness of user participatory design strategies produces UX design solutions with a greater connection to the needs of target audiences both with autism and those who are neurologically typical. The Play•IT project will be replicated in other design programs and with different project parameters to test the effectiveness of the UXD methods outlined by the Connectivity Model and the use of online and digital resources. We also hope to be able to expand the scope to include other cognitive and physical disabilities.

References

Börjesson, P., Barendregt, W., Eriksson, E., Torgersson, O.: Designing technology for and with developmentally diverse children: a systematic literature review. In: Proceeding of 14th International Conference on Interaction Design and Children (IDC 2015), pp. 79–88. ACM, New York (2015). doi:10.1145/2771839.2771848

Börjesson, P., Barendregt, W., Eriksson, E., Torgersson, O.: Diverse Children - A Systematic Literature Review (2014)

Center for Disease Control: Prevalence and Characteristics of Autism Spectrum Disorder Among Children Aged 8 Years—Autism and Developmental Disabilities Monitoring Network, 11 Sites, United States (2012). http://www.cdc.gov/mmwr/volumes/65/ss/ss6503a1.htm. Accessed 14 December 2016

Chez, M.G.: Autism and Its Medical Management: A Guide for Parents and Professionals. Jessica Kingsley, London (2008)

Coons, K., Watson, S.: Conducting research with individuals who have intellectual disabilities: ethical and practical implications for qualitative research. J. Dev. Disabil. 19(2), 14–24 (2013)

Druin, A.: The role of children in the design of new technology. Behav. Inf. Technol. 21(1), 1–25 (2002)

Engeström, Y.: Developmental studies of work as a testbench of activity theory. In: Chaiklin, S., Lave, J. (eds.) Understanding Practice: Perspectives on Activity and Context, p. 67. Cambridge University Press, Cambridge (1993)

Fabri, M.: Thinking with a new purpose: lessons learned from teaching design thinking skills to creative technology students. In: Marcus, A. (ed.) DUXU 2015. LNCS, vol. 9186, pp. 32–43. Springer, Cham (2015). doi:10.1007/978-3-319-20886-2_4

Fabri, M., Andrews, P.C.S.: Human-centered design with autistic university students: interface, interaction and information preferences. In: Marcus, A. (ed.) DUXU 2016. LNCS, vol. 9747, pp. 157–166. Springer, Cham (2016). doi:10.1007/978-3-319-40355-7_15

IDEO: The Field Guide to Human-Centred Design, IDEO, San Francisco (2015)

Kang, S., Satterfield, D.: Connectivity model: evaluating and designing social and emotional experiences. Paper presented at International Association for Societies of Design Research (IASDR) Conference, Rigors and Relevance in Design, Seoul, Korea, 18–22 October 2009

Lave, J., Wenger, E.: Situated Learning. Cambridge University Press, Cambridge (1990)

Lugmayr, A., Jalonen, M., Zou, Y., Libin, L., Anzenhofer, S.: Design thinking in media management education - a practical hands-on approach. In: Proceedings of 4th Semantic Ambient Media Experience (SAME) Workshop in Conjunction with the 5th International Convergence on Communities and Technologies, Brisbane, Australia (2011)

Maguire, M.: Methods to support human-centred design. Int. J. Hum.-Comput. Stud. 55, 587–634 (2001). doi:10.1006/ijhc.2001.0503

Millen, L., Edlin-White, R., Cobb, S.: The development of educational collaborative virtual environments for children with autism. In: Proceedings of the 5th Cambridge Workshop on Universal Access and Assistive Technology, Cambridge (2010)

Nagamachi, M.: Kansei engineering; the implication and applications to product development. In: 1999 IEEE International Conference on systems, Man, and Cybernetics, vol. 6, pp. 273 – 278 (1999)

Sanders, E., Stappers, P.J.: Co-creation and the new landscapes of design. CoDesign 4(1), 5–18 (2008)

Satterfield, D.: Ethics in service design for children with autism and cognitive disabilities. In: Abramsky, S., Ahram, T., Karwowski, W. (eds.) Advances in Intelligent Systems and Computing. Advances in The Human Side of Service Engineering, vol. 494, pp. 63–72. Springer, Cham (2016). doi:10.1007/978-3-319-41947-3_7

Satterfield, D.: Play•IT: a methodology for designing and evaluating educational play experiences for children with cognitive disabilities. Paper presented at 7th International Conference on Design & Emotion, Chicago, Illinois, 4–7 October 2010

Satterfield, D., Kang, S., Lepage, C., Deering, H., Ladjahasan, N.: Childhood autism: comparison between impressions of parents and educators. In: Proceedings of International Meeting for Autism Research (IMFAR) 2013, San Sebastian, Spain, 1–4 May 2013

Satterfield, D., Kang, S., Lepage, C., Ladjahasan, N.: An analysis of data collection methods for user participatory design for and with people with autism spectrum disorders. In: Marcus, A. (ed.) DUXU 2016. LNCS, vol. 9746, pp. 509–516. Springer, Cham (2016). doi:10.1007/978-3-319-40409-7_48

Satterfield, D., Kelle, S.: Ethical issues in online education. In: Advances in Intelligent Systems and Computing Advances in the Human Side of Service Engineering, pp. 257–266 (2016). doi:10.1007/978-3-319-41947-3_24

Wittemeyer, K., Charman, T., Cusak, J., Guldberg, K., Hastings, R., Howlin, P., Macnab, N., Parsons, S., Pellicano, L., Slonims, V.: Educational Provision and Outcomes for People on the Autism Spectrum. Autism Education Trust, London (2011)

Constructing Cognitive Pattern in Design Thinking Based on Complementary Perspective

Xiaoxian Wang[✉]

School of Design Arts and Media, Nanjing University of Science
and Technology, 200, Xiaolingwei Street, Nanjing 210094, Jiangsu, China
11048456@qq.com

Abstract. Design thinking is a phase of thinking fast with high-intensity, and cognition phase is also a very complicated process, in which the perspective of observing and pondering on design matters often directly affects the process and results of design. Some distinguished scholars have provided different perspectives for us to understand the world around us, such as E. H. Gombrich's "Reflections on Main Project", Rudolf Arnheim's "Vision is Thinking", Michel Foucault's "The Eyes of Power", and Heinrich Wolfflin's "Reflections on Form", among others.

In the long-term design practice and research, from the "Complementary Perspective", the author finds that the cognitive intention is rooted in the Chinese traditional thoughts and culture, and perceives the objective world with a unique way. As Lao Tzu said, "Distinguishing the right from the wrong is the basic rule of life". From the opposite side, we should observe, analyze, and understand the design matters in a thinking mode of "tackling both extremes" to break through the limitation of one-way thinking. In the dynamic activities of opposition and complementation, noting the rheology between the opposite and the complementary relationship behind enables us to "sense" the "phenomenon" that others analyzing architecture failed to sense, which can help the design cognition become more comprehensive and the innovation deeper.

"Complementary Perspective" aims at broadening design thinking, constructing, organizing and creating a more comprehensive cognitive pattern based on the diversity, unity, and integration of design, contingency of decision, and varieties of possibilities in problem solving. Specifically, Complementary Perspectives include positive perspective, and opposite perspective; common-seeking perspective, and difference-seeking perspective; ego perspective, and non-ego perspective; ordered perspective, and disordered perspective; and traditional perspective, and prospective perspective, and among others.

Keywords: Complementary perspective · Cognitive pattern · Design thinking and method · Innovation capability

1 Introduction

In this digital information era of rapid development, with the progress of science and technology, the internet has witnessed the explosive development while various aspects in people's lives have witnessed revolutionary changes, including production modes,

© Springer International Publishing AG 2017
A. Marcus and W. Wang (Eds.): DUXU 2017, Part I, LNCS 10288, pp. 198–215, 2017.
DOI: 10.1007/978-3-319-58634-2_16

living, reading, and information exchange. When the screen came into people's sight instead of the paper, the old mode to obtain information, which is passive, linear, and unidirectional, was eliminated. Reading on the screen via digital media, the information is decomposed, included, produced, stored, and transmitted in the form of "digits". People selectively screen the information. They are both the receiver and the publisher of information. The involvement of new media forms, not only provides more presentation modes and methods for visual communication, but also contributes to a visible, audible, sensible, touchable, and movable world of information. New media forms interact with the traditional ones and accelerate the change of our design thinking and methods. Our ideas have been changed that we stop chasing the unpredictable cause-and-effect relationship but to focus our attention upon the correlation between things [1]. Within such a big background, the author deeply feels that we need to view and think problems from a more open, diversified, systematic, and related perspective, and diversified media forms actually provide us with a more diversified stage for design. From print media to digital media, as a matter of fact, all sorts of information dissemination media are involved in a dynamically changing system. In the process of contact, confliction, and communication with each other, they achieve self-perfection by interaction, complementation, and self-regulation, and therefore produce new changes to meet the demand of information communication under new conditions. It is a proposition for us to know how to comprehensively use the diversified media methods for visual information communication, which is proposed by the era. Whether problems confronted in design are on paper or on screen, static or dynamic, unidirectional or interactional, humanistic or scientific, tangible or intangible, and passive or active, they have been more complex than ever meanwhile the phenomenon of complementarity and the demand for complementarity have been increasingly evident. On the other hand, in the actual design practice and research work, especially at the idea creation stage, we always find that a complementary relationship is left finally between the seemly opposite content and forms, or even between mutually exclusive ideas and systems. The series of phenomena and problems arouse author's thinking: there exists a complementary relationship between the seemly opposite things. Therefore, the author "complementarily" comprehended the cognition of "complementary" existences in various domains through the source tracing for "complementarity", and learnt that complementarity can be regarded as not only a law of nature, a type of philosophical idea, a scientific principle, and a means, but also a type of design thinking and method.

2 Concept of "Complementarity"

2.1 Philosophical Thinking Sources of "Complementarity"

When Pythagoras with his school put forward the ten pairs of "opposites" constructing the universe, that is, finite and infinite, odd and even, one and many, right and left, man (male) and woman (female), dynamic and static, straight and curving, light and shade, good and evil, and square and rectangle, the description for the interaction between opposites was unclear and just focused on the "opposition". Until Heraclitus gave his idea in his words that "on the circumference, the end point is the starting point", as well as "ever-living fire" and "the flux of river", the implication of being "opposite and complementary" or "unity of opposites" had been firstly expressed. Heraclitus said, "They do not know how the opposites can be complementary. The power of opposition can contribute to harmony, just like the bow and the lyre". The "opposition" in his words actually means "conversion". He not only clearly put forward the idea of being opposite and complementary, but also pointed out that only opposites can contribute to harmony in this theory. For the western philosophy, Heraclitus is the father and founder of this theory.

In China, Lao Zi, known as "the founder of Chinese philosophy", often masterly summarized concepts of things with opposite and complementary words. For example, he said, "All in the world know the beauty of the beautiful, and in doing this they have (the idea of) what ugliness is; they all know the skill of the skillful, and in doing this they have (the idea of) what the want of skill is. So it is that existence and non-existence give birth the one to (the idea of) the other; that difficulty and ease produce the one (the idea of) the other; that length and shortness fashion out the one the figure of the other; that (the ideas of) height and lowness arise from the contrast of the one with the other; that the musical notes and tones become harmonious through the relation of one with another; and that being before and behind give the idea of one following another", and "Who knows how white attracts, Yet always keeps himself within black's shade, The pattern of humility displayed, Displayed in view of all beneath the sky". In which, Lao Zi showed a type of relative thinking method and his words "are strictly true seem to be paradoxical". However, upon the description for a certain thing, it obtains a kind of unity with another aspect, and they are interdependent, mutually included, integrated, and interpenetrated, so as to be unified and consistent. Thus, the flow and conversion of opposite concepts are included in the judgement for the same concept. The view on empty and fact in the foresaid words "existence and non-existence give birth the one to (the idea of) the other" together with the view on beauty and ugliness of the conversion between goodness and evilness, has brought a profound influence on the development of Chinese design.

Moreover, Confucius mentioned "tackling both ends" in The Analects, which means think of the problem from two aspects, and then you can solve it. In On Leveling All Things, Zhuangzi also tell us how to know something entirely and comprehensively, "There is nothing which is not this; there is nothing which is not that".

However, the author thinks the best interpretation for complementarity is The Book of Changes which says "Dao contains one Yin and one Yang". "All things leave behind them the Obscurity [Yin] (out of which they have come), and go forward to embrace the Brightness [Yang] (into which they have emerged), while they are harmonised by the Breath of Vacancy." [2] Yin and Yang became one in an opposite and complementary relationship. They are opposite and rooted in each other while waxing and waning with each other. When both of them achieve the extremes, they will convert into each other. Yin and Yang, a pair of complementary notions, have been widely used into various aspects such as the universe nature, structures, relationships, the root (internal reasons) of changes (including creation, metaplasia, and birth and death), and laws. As a matter of fact, it is a complementary dialectical idea. The cosmic philosophy characterized by the opposite but unified organic integrity where "all the things can be separated into two and combined into one" has been a basic idea, instructing people to observe and learn about the world for two thousand years.

Li Zehou is the one who introduced the concept of "complementary" into Chinese philosophy research. He said in his book *The Course of Beauty* that "Complementation between Confucianism and Taoism" is a basic clue of Chinese thoughts for two thousand years. But he failed to interpret the concept of complementarity. Confucianism represented by Confucius and Mencius, and Taoism represented by Laozi and Zhuangzi, are different and opposite, but actually are complementary to each other for harmony. Here, the word "complementary" largely means the infiltration and coordination between the opposites rather than the exclusion and confliction. It is this very pair of opposite and complementary thoughts that contributes to prosperous cultures in Chinese history.

Thus, it can be seen that from the very beginning of Chinese and Western philosophical thoughts, sages managed to interpret notions of things and expressed their ideas with the concept of "complementarity" simultaneously. In philosophical thoughts, coexistence of both sides is the premise of "complementation" which includes opposites and complements. They turn into the complement of each other in the process of contradiction, movement, waxing and waning, and conversion, and therefore become more complete. "Complementarity" is a related, dynamic, and developmental concept. As a broader thinking framework, complementarity exists in various domains such as traditional Chinese medicine, painting and calligraphy, literature, poetry, and building.

2.2   Linguistic Application of "Complementary"

Language has been applied in a typical complementary way from its very beginning. (Niels Bohr, 1960) However, human's thinking method is realized by means of language, and people think of problems with the opposite and complementary mode unconsciously. Just like what mentioned by Confucius, "tackling both ends", we can often learn the nature of things more comprehensively, which exactly explains why there are so many scholars at all times and in all over the world using the complementary relationship to interpret basic theories, including shape and spirit, empty and fact, sparsity and density, pen and ink, beauty and ugliness, nature and charm, adoption and discard, and similarity and dissimilarity in painting and calligraphy; appearance and morality, appearance and nature, sensibility and rationality, one and many, dynamic and static, novelty and rigor, elegance and popularity, generalization and change, and style and character in the aesthetics domain; opposition and unification, symmetry and equilibrium, rule and freedom, and contrast and reconciliation in the law of beauty in form; and the five pairs notions of art styles raised by Wolfflin, that is, Linear und Malerisch (linear and picturing), Fläche und Tiefe (plane and deep), geschlossene Form und offene Form (closed form and open form), Vielheit und Einheit (identity and diversity), and Klarheit und Unklarheit (clearness and ambiguity).

Wittgenstein said the language you select determines your thinking mode, and the selected thinking mode determines your life style. There are two weak points in Chinese language. One is that our concepts are ambiguous, and the other is that our logic is weak, [3] which lead to the lacking in rational thinking and meticulous scientific logical thinking in Chinese people's thinking mode. Chinese people lack the exploration for "seeking the truth", but think highly of "pragmatism"; put emphasis on the intuition and experience as well as general feelings, and study objects roughly, which easily results in ambiguous concepts; lack the deep thinking for perceptual material and the precise analysis for things, but prefer the summarization of experience and general description. Just as what mentioned by Lin Yutang in his book *My Country and My People,* "Here enter the survivals of savage in Chinese thinking. Unchecked by a scientific method, 'intuition' has free room and often borders on a mere play of words or on some fantastic association of thought." In this way, the abundant perceptual thinking in Chinese thinking mode and the strong imagination have been developed, and therefore this type of perceptual thinking mode has been rooted in Chinese culture and life styles.

2.3 Philological Paraphrase for "Complementary"

The word "complementary" in Ci Hai is paraphrased as supplementary or replenishing; (things) complement each other. Here, as it mentioned, "each other" means it is bidirectional. A one-way dependency between A and B cannot be said as a complementary relationship. Being complementary means two items are different from each other but make a good combination, which becomes more complete.

Therefore, there are three stipulations for being complementary: be bidirectional; preserve the nature of themselves; and overcome their own weak points by learning from each other's strong points. Thus, both of them can benefit from each other in complementation. Coexistence of the two items is the premise of complementarity whose role is for a more complete combination.

2.4 Knowledge of the "Complementary" Principle

The Danish physicist Niels Henrik David Bohr is the first person who clearly put forward the concept of "complementary". In 1927, Bohr raised the "complementary principle" for explaining the major feature of quantum phenomenon – wave-particle duality. He thought microscopic particles have two features which are exclusive but complementary – particle property and wave property. In experiments, the two phenomena cannot be completely described with a unified image, but both particle property and wave property are indispensable for the description of quantum phenomenon. The two properties must be combined together for the complete description. Therefore, the quantum phenomenon must be described with the method in which the two properties are exclusive but complementary to each other. The scientific method of creation is characterized by complementarity, interaction, dialectical thinking, and comprehensiveness. Bohr thought the complementary principle can be regarded as a universal philosophical principle and used as a boarder thinking framework to solve problems in various domains such as psychology, linguistics, biology, mathematics, chemistry, anthropology, and national culture. He also managed to reveal other forms of complementary relationships in his research. The complementary principle shows us the interaction between objects in research and observation tools from a scientific perspective. Although the phenomena observed in different experimental conditions are seemed to be so opposite, they are indispensable parts for learning the objects completely. The author believes it actually reveals the integration of knowledge and enables us to observe with different perspectives in the actual design practice, especially in the process of design thinking, and thus deepen our cognition. It is uneasy for us to deepen our thinking with research perspectives in the same direction, but the complementary perspective may enable us to have comprehensive and thorough knowledge in research.

2.5 Analysis of the "Complementary" Methodology

In 2001, Lu Yuntao, a professor in Southwest University for Nationalities, put forward the "complementary theory" from the epistemological perspective. He demonstrated the common existence of complementation in the nature world, social life, and thinking domain, and analyzed the mechanism of complementary existences: ①The universe is a unity, in which each part are interrelated. Each part in the unity inevitably possesses a complementary relationship with each other. ②Each component within things seeks balance all the time. Complementarity is an important method to achieve balance. The imbalanced tendency of some components can eliminate the weak points by learning from each other's strong points, and therefore approach balance, which gives us the epistemological meaning, and some enlightenments for knowing the world: ①The world is diversified. ②Everything is good for something. ③Nothing and nobody in the universe can be self-sufficient without others [4].

In 2002, Professor Liu Dachun, a Chinese scholar, introduced the complementary philosophical concept into methodology for research. Based on the comparison of methodology in his monograph *Scientific Activity Theory, Complementary Methodology*, he found a macroscopic law related to methodology – "Complementary Methodology", which evidently shows with multiple perspectives, the occurrence of the methodological thinking system cannot be avoided, the content or forms of which are exactly opposite (exclusive). However, during conflicts and confrontations, they will finally reveal a certain complementary relationship [5]. It is the first time for Chinese scholars to introduce complementarity into methodology for research.

In 2011, Professor He Xiaoyou introduced the complementary philosophical concept into the design domain for research. He put forward the **"Complementary design method"** and managed to establish an interrelated design thinking mode. This type of relationship is seemed to be opposite, but to some extent complementary. In other words, with the complementary perspective, the exclusive ideas may show a certain type of complementarity. When we think of these problems dialectically, our innovative thinking can be more comprehensive and thorough under its guidance [6]. It is the first time for the design methodology research to have a specific concept of "complementary design method".

3 "Complementary" Perspectives

Designers use the thinking tools to develop relationships with the target world and form a certain type of cognitive structure schema shown as specific understanding for their own design activities, which is the cognitive structure of design thinking methods.

In the design research, we "see" the "phenomenon" which cannot be seem in other thinking frameworks with the cognitive intention based on the "complementary understanding". Laozi said, "All things leave behind them the Obscurity [Yin], and go forward to embrace the Brightness [Yang]", which exactly refers to the philosophical structure of the universe. Yin and Yang are opposite and interdependent, and cannot present themselves without each other, which emphasize the interrelation between all the things in the universe rather than the isolated status. "Interrelation" refers to an opposite and interdependent relationship. At the actual design innovation stage, designers need to handle the problems from an "interrelation" perspective like Yin and Yang rather than an isolated perspective. We shall "tackle both ends" with the "complementary perspective" upon observation, seeing from not only the opposite side but also the interdependent side.

From the complementary perspective, based on the diversity, unity, comprehensiveness, contingency of selection behaviors, and multiple possibilities of problem solving, one can expand the design thinking, and construct, organize, and create a more profound cognitive mode. In detail, complementary perspectives include: forward or reverse perspectives; commonness-seeking and difference-seeking perspectives; self and non-self perspectives; ordered and unorderly perspectives; and traditional and future perspectives.

3.1 Cognitive Mode of Forward or Reverse Perspectives

Positive orientation based on the forward perspective. Forward perspective, also called positive perspective, refers to a kind of presupposition adopted for observed objects or considered "problems", which is good, correct, valuable, meaningful, and positive. One may find the advantages and value in observed objects or considered "problems" with the positive perspective. It is a transcendental thinking direction of positive value.

In daily life, we basically use the forward perspective for those accepted valuable, good, correct things. As a matter of fact, it only adds grace to what is already beautiful with the positive perspective, which makes a little difference. Under this condition, designers are required to think of problems with the "forward perspective" at any time, especially for the cases when everybody thinks it impossible to be positive, which actually can be regarded as a kind of creative thinking. The positive thinking upon negative things, indeed is dialectical to some extent. For example, we can turn "waste" into "wealth" with the forward perspective, including household articles made of straws, fine photo frames, and fruit baskets made of old magazines. The thinking mode of the forward perspective enables us to comprehensively evaluate the value of things, actively explore the potential value of things, or develop new values which are useful

Fig. 1. Coca-Cola 2nd Lives

for us. With emotions being input, design culture being endowed, and social responsibilities being delivered, ordinary things also can be classic (Figure 1).

Subversive creativeness based on the reverse perspective. Reverse perspective, also called negative perspective, is opposite to forward perspective. The word "negative" is similar to "reverse", which means thinking from the opposite or reverse side, and finding, analyzing, and answering the problems in the reverse direction of common thinking. It shows a thinking mode different from the normal forward perspective, which is anti-traditional, anti-conventional, and anti-habitual. Lao Zi said, "The movement of the Tao by contraries proceeds" [7]. The plain dialectics in his words tells us a creative thinking method – seeking from the reverse side, with which one can always achieve success with original ideas and break the rules. One can start from a subversive idea at the early stage of thinking to develop a hypothesis on the reverse side: "What if…not…?"

Complementation between forward and reverse perspectives. Anything has its opposite side. The opposition between objective existences provides two different thinking directions including positive and negative directions, and inspire the dialectical thinking of designers. Thus, the thinking cognition becomes dialectical and comprehensive.

When we think of design objects, or design "problems", we can start with the "forward perspective", determine the design value, and observe and analyze the problems under the guidance of positive thinking in order to achieve the unity of the design content and forms and obtain logical design results. Experience tells us that it is very common for most of people to think about solutions for problems firstly, so it is necessary to expand our thinking in multiple directions and collect the information as much as possible under the positive, active, and valuable guidance of the "forward perspective". If one thinks of problems with the "reverse perspective", the rules can be broken while the traditions can be subverted with the reverse thinking, and we may obtain some novel ideas. It is contrary to the normal and proper practice, but is reasonable and conforms to the righteousness (Fig. 2).

In the process of cognizing design thinking objects, the key is to develop the type of complementary thinking habit at the creation stage, and therefore we can think of thinking objects immediately from forward and reverse perspectives. Thus, we are able to have relatively profound and comprehensive cognition and knowledge for such "problems" and may find different ways and suitable pointcuts to effectively solve the problems.

Fig. 2. Mind mapping of forward and reverse perspectives

3.2   Cognitive Mode of Commonness-Seeking and Difference-Seeking Perspectives

Finding universal connections between things based on the commonness-seeking perspective. With the commonness-seeking perspective, we are required to seize some common points between two or more things, phenomena, ideas and concepts in order to connect the dramatically different things, phenomena, ideas, and concepts for generating new creative ideas.

Finding connections between things is the starting point of the commonness-seeking perspective. We aim to finding the common ground and similarities between different things and connecting them with its thinking results. By introducing the analogical and associative thinking, we are provided with the cognitive basis and thus obtain new creative ideas. With the cognitive purpose, on one hand, we can have a clear concept of design thinking objects; on the other hand, the audience can know well about unfamiliar things, which will arouse their sympathetic responses. In various connections, the greater the superficial difference, the more amazing the connections, when they are connected within the commonness-seeking perspective.

The print advertisement of "ABSOLUT" Vodka is a typical example of the "commonness-seeking perspective". The shape of its bottles is very distinctive, which has been shown in hundreds of print ads. You can find it if you are careful. The bottle shape combined with various natural regions, cultures, and living scenes in print ads, contributes to this extraordinary design idea and the classic "ABSOLUT" (Figure 3).

Fig. 3. A series of "ABSOLUT" ads. A classic work in advertisement design using the isomorphic technique

Finding distinctions of creativity based on the difference-seeking perspective.
With the difference-seeking perspective, we are required to find solutions of problems
with divergent thinking which features adaptability and flexibility. We need to get rid
of the accepted knowledge and old experience upon consideration, break though the
limitation of logical thinking and linear thinking, focus our attention on "what else it
may be" other than "why", and therefore put forward creative ideas, views, and
solutions. From the difference-seeking perspective, design thinking is differentiated,
distinctive, experimental, individualized, and diversified, divergent thinking can be
used profoundly while the adaptability and flexibility can bring the diversity in design.

Design ideas need to be distinctive, so all those excellent designers are characterized with the "difference-seeking perspective." For example, the topic of the 2003
Alliance Graphique Internationale (AGI) meeting in Helsinki was "Chair" and the AGI
had invited its members for creation as shown in Fig. 4. On the same chair model, we
can see that designers had their own perspectives different from each other, which gave
birth to various types of amazing chairs.

Fig. 4. Members' design: "skin of chairs", 2005 (designed by Yu Bingnan, Wang Xu, An
Shangxiu, Liu Xiaokang, and Stefan Sagmeister (from left))

**Complementation between commonness-seeking and difference-seeking perspec-
tives.** The key for developing commonness-seeking and difference-seeking perspectives is to think by means of association, analogy, and divergence. The former
(commonness-seeking perspective) features the reconstruction of the commonness in
order to obtain the concept of thinking objects. The latter (difference-seeking perspective) emphasizes the change of perspectives for receiving novel results of thinking
(Figure 5).

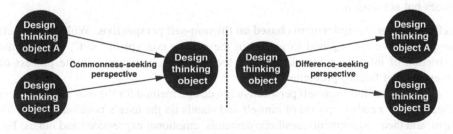

Fig. 5. Mind mapping of commonness-seeking and difference-seeking perspectives

At the stage of cognition, the "commonness-seeking perspective" can be used to fully know about the observed objects and find the commonness between things, so one can have profound knowledge of "notions" of objects, find common relations between various kinds of things to arouse association and perform isomorphism, and turn the unfamiliar into the familiar. Thus, we can well prepare for the translation of visual images. The "difference-seeking perspective", on the contrary, is complementary to the former. At the stage of observation, with the difference-seeking perspective, objects can be observed from different points of view, and therefore unique characteristics of which can be found. In the process of visual image interpretation, the familiar is turned into the unfamiliar, with which one can achieve success with some original ideas. With the two perspectives, one can have comprehensive knowledge of observed objects and find solutions based on actual cases.

3.3   Cognitive Mode of Self and Non-self Perspectives

Experiencing design perception based on the self perspective. In the design thinking, self perspective refers to the design perception experienced from designers themselves. Based on the interpretation of themselves for observed objects, designers can produce the pieces evidently featured with their own styles. This type of design generally fails to follow those popular design styles, yet it is popular for its unique and distinction and thus can lead the design trend of the era. The self perspective of design mentioned here, mainly features designer's own subjective consciousness and evident personal design style.

"Body writing" of Stefan Sagmeister, "potato series" of Gunter Rambow, "word games" of Zhu Yingchun, and "free curves" of Luigi Colani are good examples to show the resonance between the designer and the audience can be achieved with the self perspective. It is partially because designers are also audiences and users. We live in the similar social environment and are confronted with similar problems, so we can focus on ourselves and directly show our own feelings and experience. In particular, the word "self" refers to the ordinary people who can find the common ground with others in daily life and have personal demands similar to others, and thus they can create designs accepted by others. In addition, extremes shall be prevented in the self perspective. The job of designers is to design the items which can be accepted by the public rather than something with extreme individualism which otherwise may be art pieces but not design.

Reflecting user's requirements based on the non-self perspective. With the non-self perspective, we are required to get rid of the narrow concept of "self", and also the restriction of inherent personal concepts, feelings, and standpoints in the process of observing and finding problems.

As a matter of fact, non-self perspective is a design method for the user's requirement research. One needs to get rid of himself and stands on the user's position to think for them, and their requirements, aesthetic demands, emotional expressions and others. For commercial projects, when a designer cognizes design thinking objects with the non-self perspective, he is propelled by commercial interests, and needs to have a kind of humanistic concern. For example, the brand concept of Muji, raised by Ikko Tanaka, is rooted in the life style and aesthetic awareness of Japanese people. It is Shinzo Higurashi who firstly came up with this brand name, and Mr. Ikko Tanaka accepted and used it. Ms. Ichiko Koike also put forward the slogan, "quality and cheap". As a result, Muji provides batches of customer-friendly and affordable products with simple styles and natural texture. Since 1980, Muji has achieved so many good results, which is known by Japanese and the rest of the world. From its founder Ikko Tanaka and Ichiko Koike to Hara Kenya and Naoto Fukazawa, Muji has influenced people's life style with its products which are "fine enough in this way", its attitude of "WORLD MUJI" and its "good enough living" style, and thus owns a great number of loyal fans.

In addition, in another case, that is, when design thinking objects are things, animals or plants, with the non-self perspective, we can observe and analyze them in another interesting way. The examples include "Language of Ant" of Zhu Yingchun, "Drawing of Tree" of FSC, and "Thinking of Apes" of Hiroki Taniguchi.

Complementation between self and non-self perspectives. Self and non-self perspectives are a unity of contradiction. The conclusions obtained from the two perspectives are different as shown in Fig. 6.

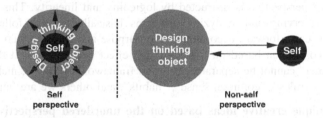

Fig. 6. Mind mapping of self and non-self perspectives

With the self perspective, designers tend to solve problems with their own consciousness, understanding, requirements, and aesthetic preferences. However, as a member of the society, the designer is living in a similar environment and life style as that of other people and confronted with similar problems, moreover, has almost the same physiological structure like others. Thus, they obtain consonance with the self perspective meanwhile their design always features strong individual awareness and styles. But designers shall never only pay attention to their own consciousness, they need to find balance between the subject and the object and build a bridge between the visual information and its receiver for free communication. On the other hand, with the non-self perspective, designers need to get rid of the role of self, and be user-centered and neutral to design for "He". They need to solve problems with an objective, just, rational, and effective attitude based on requirements, aesthetic standards, living styles, and even reading habits of users. Design with the non-self perspective is more similar to research, which is more rational and logical than the self perspective. Purposes and results of the self perspective are aimed to meet requirements of a certain group. In the actual design thinking process, there is indeed no absolute self and non-self perspectives, because they are interwoven with each other in most cases with their own focuses and are complementary to each other for target groups in design.

3.4   Cognitive Mode of Ordered and Unorderly Perspectives

Forming systematic design based on the ordered perspective. With the ordered perspective, designers are required to observe and analyze design thinking objects strictly based on a certain logical principle, demonstrate concepts and solutions practically in order, analyze the nature from the phenomenon, put emphasis on the logicality, and recognize the inevitabilities to ensure creative points in design can be performed and completed as planned.

For the ordered perspective, the author thinks it includes two types of order: One is "natural" order; another is "man-made" order.

Nature is a type of order. "The structure of any nature shape is inevitable while the connotation of which is self-known" [8]. We choose to observe a certain objective target from the outside to the inside, cognizing it from appearance, shape, texture, and material to structure, organization, and laws. The step of observing "from the outside to the inside" itself is a kind of ordered perspective. On the other hand, for the man-made order, this kind of "ordered perspective" is actually developed based on people's design practice and activities and established as a systematic mode of design, such as "systematic visual image design" put forward by an American designer Lance Wyman.

The ordered perspective is instructed by logicality and linearity. This type of perspective for observing and analyzing problems basically has the following major characteristics: carry forward according to the purpose and the plan step by step, and generate the conclusion based on the cause-and-effect relationship. At the cognition stage, the "order" cannot be separated from the frameworks in mind, including "concepts", "laws", "rules", "common sense", "habits", and others we are familiar to.

Obtaining unique creative ideas based on the unordered perspective. With the unordered perspective, designers are required to observe and analyze design thinking objects without the established frameworks and traditional modes in mind, break out "laws", "rules", "principles", "common sense", "habits", and other like things, get rid of the restriction of logical mind and linear thinking to free their imagination and feelings in order to arouse the imagination and achieve better creative effects with intuition. The following aspects are important in the thinking process: ①know the dominant concept; ②find different ways to observe things; ③get rid of the orderly linear thinking; ④be good at using contingent factors and seize the inspiration of "epiphany". Compared with the "lateral thinking" put forward by Edward de Bono, it has different approaches but achieves equally satisfactory results.

The design thinking with the unordered perspective features divergent thinking. Epiphany, inspiration, and imagination are the impetuses which gives birth to the unordered perspective. The design thinking with the unordered perspective to some extent is rebellious and revolutionary. Designers with which dare to break the rules and regulations, shake off the constraints of habits, experience, principles, laws, and regulations, and catch up with sudden changes and skips in the thinking direction of the thinking process.

Interaction and cooperation between ordered and unordered perspectives.
Ordered and unordered perspectives have different thinking methods upon observation

as shown in Fig. 7. For the ordered perspective, it is the logic that controls the whole thinking; for the unordered perspective, the logic is on stand-by. With the ordered perspective, designers are required to observe and think based on some certain thinking routes, within a specific range, and according to a certain established rule, which stresses on learnt experience and knowledge, and generate creative ideas by reconstructing the old experience and knowledge. In this way, the given demands of the public can be satisfied with creativeness, but designers fail to make a breakthrough in design forms which are relatively similar to each other. However, using this perspective for creativity, designers can study and express profoundly on things, and design can be easily systematic. Unordered perspective is unpredictable and applied upon thinking. Designers with which need to get rid of established knowledge and old experience, break the rules, be good at seizing the occasional ideas, expand the cognitive range, and come up with creative ideas, opinions and solutions. The application of cognition mode basically follows divergent thinking and depends on designer's intuition and inspiration. In the creative process of design, in most cases, the ordered is included in the unordered. Once creative points are found in the unordered, ordered steps for moving forward are taken gradually. The unordered is required in the ordered. Only with the interaction and cooperation of both perspectives, the best solution can be provided.

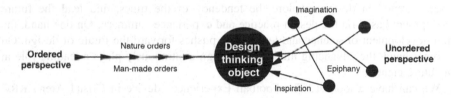

Fig. 7. Mind mapping of ordered and unordered perspectives

3.5 Cognitive Mode of Traditional and Future Perspectives

Adding innovation to Chinese forms with the traditional perspective. With the traditional perspective, one inspects the origins and development of things and concepts from the dimension of history in order to master the past and know better about the present. In the design thinking, the traditional perspective requires us to take in the wisdom from traditions, through traditional forms to observe the thinking mode, traditional culture, reading habits, living styles, traditional design ideas, craft skills and materials, and communication media, and to design based on it so as to enlighten the modern innovative design. Meanwhile, we need to make it clear that thinking with the traditional perspective is not to fully follow and conservatively copy traditions and transplant symbols, but to discard what has outlived its time and develop the new, to follow the tide of the times, and to explore the interaction between inheritance and innovation, nationalization and internationalization, traditional methods and modern science and technology based on the current living style, so as to revitalize the design.

At present, there are many designers with the traditional perspective among the famous designers of visual communication design. For example, Chinese designer Jin

Daiqiang appeals "to integrate the Chinese and the West, and poetize the design"; Chen Shaohua points out that "traditional factors are effective tools for communication"; Chen Youjian delivers "charm of the east and melody of the west" in his works; Han Zhanning thinks about "traditional images"; Lu Jingren shows "implication" which is peculiar to Chinese people and also presents his "humility and low profile" in his works. He holds an attitude of "inheriting the spirit and expanding the forms" towards the traditional culture; and Zhu Yingchun "seeks for experience from traditions" in book design.

With the traditional perspective, one can find innovation inspiration and visual elements in the traditional culture. The process of which is not to simply transplant symbols and reproduce images, but to integrate traditional elements and traditional culture spirits with current design based on the exploration for traditional thinking modes, traditional culture, and traditional living styles and to endow the design with new ideas and the spirit of the times. In other words, it is a way to inspire innovation design with traditional wisdom. In the actual design expression, we need to pay attention to the interaction between traditional methods and modern science and technologies, in order to achieve "inheriting the spirit and expanding the forms".

Exploring the developing tendency based on the future perspective. With the future perspective, designers think of the developing tendency of things and concepts in the future to seek for the transcendence in design. They are required to measure the current "trend" in design, explore the tendency of the times, and lead the future development based on the design practice and experience summary. On one hand, the rapid development of science and technology pushes forward the future of design. On the other hand, the advancing thinking of design continuously plays a leading role in our future creation.

We can have a look at "The Football Experience" device in Cristal Arena KRC Genk as shown in Fig. 8. It shows the cases of sport injuries with life-sized 3D dummies. The device comes into "life" with the touch-sensitive interface and the friendly interactive design as well as pictures, images, short films, words, and cartoons. The interactive experience enables sport injuries as the content of popular science to be easily understood. With the future perspective, the visual information communication becomes increasingly interesting.

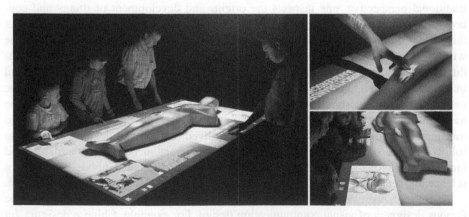

Fig. 8. "The Football Experience"/ART + COM

The future perspective is mainly experimental, prospective, and scientific, which features forward thinking. We cannot avoid the great influence on every aspect of people's life brought by computers, and must put emphasis on the combination of science and technology and humanity. Artificial intelligence will definitely be a development tendency in the future while the visual communication design domain also plays a leading role in the change. However, designers with the future perspective need to make the world be more higher-technology and also more human again. In the interrelation of human – information – environment, designers also need to think how to show the ecological view and make our lives better with design!

Penetration and integration between traditional and future perspectives. Traditional and future perspectives are varied according to time dimensions as shown in Fig. 9. In the modern society, people's requirements for interaction of information communication have been higher and higher, design methods take lessons from and are integrated with the science and technology domain, and computer software programs, holographic display, and artificial intelligence have been increasingly grafted into design, the application scope of which has been expanded to virtual vision from physical presence. Design modes in the future will be more free and personalized, just as mentioned by David Carson, "I believe that the next graphic design approach comes from other non-design fields". Looking into the future based on the traditional culture, we can make design be more adaptable to the modern society with acceptable methods of information communication.

Fig. 9. Mind mapping of traditional and future perspectives

Traditional culture and modern design, even future design are supposed to be penetrated into each other and integrated with each other. For the traditional culture, we should deeply probe into its charm of history, philosophical ideas, culture spirits, and traditional wisdom other than simply transplant the symbols. The future design is also probably rooted in the thinking with the traditional perspective. It is now an important task for Chinese designers to think about this pair of perspectives and also an inevitable problem which cannot be avoided in seeking an innovation path for Chinese design.

4 Conclusion

The fast speed of the aging of the population makes people concern more about old people's health conditions. The improvement of sleep quality can directly affect their health status. This paper mainly analyzed the sleep quality of the elderly from the perspective of physiology and furniture. However, there are many factors that can influences their sleep quality such as mental condition 'daily habits' interpersonal relationship and economic status. When designing furniture for the elderly, we must have a clear understanding of their needs and design products that are fit for their use so as to improve their quality of life.

"Complementary understanding" provides us with a cognitive mode to cognize the universe in philosophy. The paper introduces it into design and gives cognitive modes of five pairs of complementary perspectives for observing, analyzing, and summarizing design problems, so as to have profound and comprehensive knowledge of design thinking objects.

Constructing the cognitive mode with the "complementary" perspective, basically is an activity for cognizing objective items under the guidance of dialectical thinking. With the cognitive mode, we can avoid the defect of failing to profoundly and comprehensively conduct the research in the same research perspective, observe objects with opposite, exclusive, and contradictory "complementary" perspectives, and master objects in a dynamic, developing, associated, and comprehensive way. In thinking activities of design, we can arouse the thinking and design intelligence, boost the creativity with the convergence and divergence of thinking, abstract summary and specific description, scientific rational thinking, and intuitive epiphany, and therefore achieve the purpose of creative design.

The purpose of the "complementary" perspective is to observe objects from different points of view, discard the old visual and perceptual experience, break the obsolete rules and regulations, and find innovative points in design for constructing new rules. This process is as follows: selection – breakthrough – reconstruction. The cognitive mode of forward and reverse perspectives can help us break thinking barriers from the opposite side and obtain the "impossible" creativity; the cognitive mode of commonness-seeking and difference-seeking perspectives enables us to have profound and comprehensive knowledge upon the commonness and individuality of design thinking objects, and lay a foundation for the translation and generation of visual images through heterogeneous assimilation and homogeneous alienation together with analogy and association; the cognitive mode of self and non-self perspectives requires designers to recognize the difference perspectives between themselves and design targets. In most cases, changes of the neutral position and perspectives in design can bring different design ideas and concepts; the cognitive mode of ordered and unordered perspectives tells that the nature world is the best source of design inspirations. Designers can cognize design thinking objects between nature and artificiality, regulations and freedom, and rules and imagination. The cognitive mode of traditional and future perspectives enables us to view from different time dimensions, appeal to protect and actually take in the traditional culture, continuously explore new directions in design, and lead the future of design, which makes design indeed adapt to people's life style in a more reasonable and perfect way.

The digital information era is calling for an associated, integrated, systematic, and diversified thinking mode of design. We need to cognize problems in design from multiple perspectives, and solve them with comprehensive methods. With the cognitive modes of the "complementary" perspective, we can dialectically think about the complementarity between contradictory ideas meanwhile our innovative thinking ability can be developed comprehensively and profoundly.

Acknowledgements. The authors are grateful for the financial support provided by "the Fundamental Research Funds for the Central Universities". (No.30915013107)

References

1. Mayer-Schnberger, C.: Big Data: A Revolution That Will Transform How We Live, Work, and Think. p. 29. Zhejiang People's Publishing House, Hangzhou (2013). Sheng, Y., Zhou, T
2. Yang, C., Tai, J.: Philosophy, p. 3. Xue Lin Press, Shanghai (2003)
3. Chu, Y.: Criticism of the Chinese People's Thinking, p. 135. People's Publishing House, Beijing (2011)
4. Lu, Y.: Complementary theory. J. Southwest Nationalities Coll.·(Philos. Soc. Sci.) **22**(3), 61–68 (2001)
5. Liu, D.: Scientific Activity Theory, Complementary Methodology, pp. 297–298. Guangxi Normal University Press, Guilin (2002)
6. He, X.: On the methodology of complementary design. J. Nanjing Art Coll. (Art Des.) **20**(3), 34–36 (2011)
7. Chapter 40 of Tao Te Ching, see details in [Wei] Wang Bi's Annotation on Lao Zi's Tao Te Ching. Proofread by Lou, Y. Zhonghua Book Company, Shanghai, p. 113 (2011)
8. Xiaoyou, H.: Problems in Design, p. 34. China Architecture & Building Press, Beijing (2003)

Aesthetics and Perception in Design

U-index: An Eye-Tracking-Tested Checklist on Webpage Aesthetics for University Web Spaces in Russia and the USA

Svetlana S. Bodrunova[✉] and Alexander V. Yakunin

St. Petersburg State University,
7-9 Universitetskaya nab., St. Petersburg 199004, Russia
{s.bodrunova, a.yakunin}@spbu.ru

Abstract. *Background.* Understanding the relations between user perception and aesthetics is crucial for web design. But it is frequent in today's graphic and media design that rules, established by practitioners even before the advent of Internet and still untested empirically, are taught at design schools and widely used for online interface design. So far, there is no well-established linkage between the in-class recommendations and our empirical knowledge on usability, for which design plays a role just as crucial as web projecting. Will webpages that are better from the designers' viewpoint perform better in terms of usability? And can one have a list of recommendations tested empirically?

This is especially important for large-scale organizational web spaces where design plays a huge role in brand recognition and visual unity. Large web spaces need complex ergonomic assessment both on the level of selected nodes and on that of architecture/navigation. Of many large web spaces, university portals suit best for elaboration and pre-testing of such a methodology, as they serve various publics, contain sub-domains, and often face criticism for their user-unfriendly design and messy structure.

Objectives. We aim at creating a two-level usability expert test for a large web space that would be based on design recommendations tested empirically, thus eliminating the necessity of tech-based assessment of newcoming products. In this paper, we elaborate the node-level methodology. For this, basing on leading design literature, we create a page usability index (U-index) for 'good' design that provides quantitative measurement for traditional design decisions on the micro- and macro-level of a web page. Then, we test by eye tracking whether 'better' design (corresponding to higher U-index values) favors a particular pattern of content consumption – not 'random search' but more efficient 'reading'.

Research design. To check whether web design measured qualitatively correlates with perception of web pages as tested by eye tracking, we first define target nodes by collecting the hyperlink structure and constructing web graphs for three web spaces of the biggest universities in the USA and Russia (Harvard University, Moscow State University, St. Petersburg State University). For this, we combine web crawling and web analytics. Second, we construct the U-index with the maximum value of 22. Third, to assess user perception of the target web pages, we create a series of tasks on information search and measure three test parameters (number of eye fixations, duration of fixations, and saccade length) and their derivatives, as well as heat maps. To avoid bias in quantitative

© Springer International Publishing AG 2017
A. Marcus and W. Wang (Eds.): DUXU 2017, Part I, LNCS 10288, pp. 219–233, 2017.
DOI: 10.1007/978-3-319-58634-2_17

measurement, we use two eye trackers (one head-fixed, one stationary) to test the results in parallel. Fourth, for finding correlations between U-index and eye-tracking results, descriptive statistics (Spearman's rho and Cramer's V) is used.

Results. First of all, our results suggest that various types of eye tracking hardware produce very different test results; this implies that eye tracking research always needs pre-testing. Second, we see that heat maps may be very suitable in express assessment of the web design quality, which speaks in favor of preserving some eye tracking tests in the final methodology. Third, we see substantial difference between Russian universities and Harvard: the latter, indeed, shows that features of web design correlate with eye tracking experience of the assessors, while for the Russian university websites, even after their repeated attempts of redesign, it remains unclear whether web design contributes to better user experience. For Harvard, the web pages with a higher usability index tend to facilitate 'reading' instead of 'search'. Fourth, micro-level elements of the layout seem to contribute more to the general index and, thus, may deserve bigger attention of web designers.

Keywords: Web usability · Web design · Aesthetics · Eye tracking · U-index

1   Literature Review

Algebra and harmony: linking aesthetic parameters of web design to user experience. Inter-relation between web usability and web aesthetics is believed to be one of the major research areas within web usability studies (Hassenzahl and Monk 2010; Bargas-Avila and Hornbæk 2011). In 1990s – early 2000s, the first 'aesthetics vs. interface usability' studies by Kurosu and Kashimura (1995) and Tractinsky et al. (2000) showed that visual appearance casts independent impact upon user perception of their interaction with interfaces. Later, many studies showed the influence of aesthetics on perception of usability (Ben-Bassat et al. 2006; Thüring and Mahlke 2007) and overall user impression (Schenkman and Jönsson 2000); the latter work even stated that the best predictor for the overall user judgment on a website was its aesthetic appeal. But till today, there is no clear answer whether and, more important, in what way aesthetics on the whole or its particular aspects are linked to web usability. As Tuch et al. (2012) have noted, several later studies have proved the linkage itself, while others showed there was no direct relation between the two.

There are, to our viewpoint, several reasons for the absence of clear answer to this 'beautiful and/or usable' dilemma – despite the fact that there is growing evidence of the positive answer to it (Sonderegger and Sauer 2010). At least partly, it lies in the 'lack of experimental studies manipulating aesthetics and usability as independent variables' (Tuch et al. 2012, p. 2). Also, most works that explore the linkage and may state causal relations between aesthetics and usability, use the data that are correlational by nature (Tractinsky et al. 1997; van Schaik and Ling 2003, 2008; Hassenzahl 2004; De Angeli et al. 2006), and 'the causality is solely a matter of theoretical reasoning and cannot be tested by existing data' (Tuch et al. 2012, p. 2). While we do see a problem with causality/correlations, we would argue that the first problem – the lack of experimental studies – seems to be a bigger one. In our viewpoint, it partly lies in the fact that, today, web design comprises the areas of design activity as different as prototyping, layouting, graphic design, and web architecture&navigation. Partly due to this, it seems hard to establish a clear set of measurable variables that could be tested via objective means like eye tracking.

The majority of works that claim testing the web design actually test architectural and navigation problems. This comes from early academic works on web design (see Goldberg et al. 2002 as one of the earlier examples setting this trend), but in many today's web agencies prototyping/layouting and graphic design for web are considered different professions; working with page structural elements lies somewhat in between, as the set of necessary elements is defined by account managers and prototypists, while their visual appearance and relative visual salience is the designers' area of responsibility. But this duality in the understanding of what is actually analyzed by eye tracking tests is virtually never addressed in academic works. Thus, a line of studies have focused on menu layouting (McCarthy et al. 2004; Leuthold et al. 2011) as a 'design' element. Similarly, some studies have looked at the page elements that are most attractive for specific audiences, calling them 'design elements', which are actually page structure ones. Thus, Djamasbi et al. (2010) have shown that 'a main large image, images of celebrities, little text, and a search feature' are the design elements that attract Generation Y audience. But among the elements named, there are no graphic design ones as such. Many works assess layouting features (Buscher et al. 2009).

A sub-area that comes closer to linking graphic design and web usability testing is heuristic evaluation (Nielsen 1994; De Kock et al. 2009). The works in this research zone provide multiple criteria for heuristic evaluation (see the Multiple Heuristic Evaluation Table excerpts, De Kock et al. 2009, p. 131). But as this method is based on expert evaluation, the way the assessment criteria are formulated ('all the text in black font is easy to read', 'the graphics convey information clearly') cannot be applied for objective measurement of design features.

Also, there's a range of works that test the so-called first user impression; in the 2000s, it was shown that the 'good' design (as measured by users) raises the level of user satisfaction (but not the efficacy of information search; Phillips and Chaparro 2009). The authors even claimed that visual appearance had a long-lasting impact upon user satisfaction, since design perceived as better helped maintain the positive impression even after user interactions with manipulated pages. Another study (Lindgaard and Dudek 2002) also found that, even if user satisfaction dropped significantly after running flawed web pages, the aesthetic perception remained high. Reinecke et al. (2013) inter-changed the independent and dependent variables and tried to predict users' first impressions by correlating them to perceived visual complexity and colorfulness; a similar effect on 'what is usable is beautiful' was discovered by Ilmberger et al. (2008). But these studies are united by seeing aesthetics as just 'high/low', 'good/poor' (e.g., Moshagen et al. 2009). Even the famous study by Lavie and Tractinsky (2004), despite complicated methodology, results in measures like 'clean', 'symmetrical', 'pleasant', or simply 'aesthetic' design. Studies in related areas also used the 'attractive/non-attractive' division, rather than measurable parameters (see, e.g., Sonderegger and Sauer 2010; Quinn and Tran 2010).

Some works, though, provide a closer look at some single design elements. Thus, in their famous study 'Eyetrack III' of early 2000s, the Poynter Institute have hinted that smaller case and shorter headlines would lead to higher usability results (Outing and Rual s.d.). Lindgaard (2007), as many other colleagues afterwards, focused on color and color combinations, while Cyr et al. (2010) have stated cross-cultural differences in the impact of color on user experience. Bernard, Chaparro and Thomasson, as early as in 2000, have stated that whitespace amounts play a role for subjective user satisfaction, rather than for task performance; later works (Coursaris and Kripintris 2012) further proved the mid-level of whitespace as a significant factor in raising user experience data.

More systemic works that try to catch a variety of aesthetic features of web design are, i.e., found in two other literature streams. One of the research areas worth looking at is the one on visual complexity of websites and various types of images. Thus, we take into account the work by Pieters et al. (2010) where they state and describe the 'design complexity' (as distinguished from 'feature complexity'), as well as show that design complexity raises, not lowers, the efficacy of ad perception. The criteria of design complexity provided by the authors are, again, non-measurable; but the authors make an attempt to measure it in terms of yes/no, and we will partly follow this logic. But perhaps the stream of literature and experiments that comes closest to objectivization of web aesthetics is the one that derives from the works by Ngo and colleagues (Ngo 2001; Ngo and Byrne 2001; Ngo et al. 2000, 2003 and others). Thus, based on them, Purchase et al. (2011) have elaborated 14 aesthetic parameters like balance, equilibrium, symmetry etc., all measured (0:1), and showed their relevance for user experience. This work is a rare attempt to bring objective measurement into the highly subjective area of aesthetics.

But what these works still lack is the relation between specific graphic design and layouting recommendations, on one hand, and user experience, on the other. Till today, qualitative assessment of web pages remains largely detached from the literature for graphic designers and web designers where practical advices in color, spacing, lineage and other artistic aspects were discussed by design gurus. This paper aims at finding correlations between qualitative assessment of design of web pages and eye-tracking results for the same web pages, thus (possibly) linking the existing tradition of graphic design to today's understanding of web usability and its metrics. In other words, we would like to test whether recommendations provided in today's design manuals are, indeed, relevant and may be combined in a checklist of sustainable and testable recommendations.

University websites as the testing ground: 5-step usability assessment for large organizational web spaces. Among various types of websites, large web spaces (e.g. web portals of large organizations) remain under-researched in terms of user satisfaction in both ergonomics and web architecture and navigation. Today, analysis of web efficacy has reached the level when it is possible to analyze not only individual web pages but large web segments that include hundreds of thousands of pages; in most cases, they can be reconstructed as networks via web crawling (Blekanov et al. 2014). They represent web clusters where the same design pattern needs to be replicated but also necessarily changes for sub-domains and within the page hierarchy.

Thus, large web spaces, especially web portals of large organizations, may represent suitable objects for elaboration and testing of comparative methodology of assessment of efficacy of web design. In this research zone, web analytics is intertwined with design, engineering psychology, and micro-ergonomics. Thus, for such research objects, web metrics and usability metrics should be viewed as two inter-dependent and interweaved sets where dependencies are still to be checked and tested.

Among large web spaces, university web spaces represent a special cluster and suit well for our analysis, as they serve very different publics, are multi-task, contain sub-domains and often evoke criticism for their messy structure and user-unfriendly design. Moreover, they are available to the researchers full-time, which made university websites a popular research object. University websites have become a usual object for both single-country (Zaphiris and Ellis 2001; Hasan 2012) and cross-cultural comparative web usability tests. Our novelty here is that we treat the university website as a web space where the basic design elements are responsible for brand recognition despite the differences between schools and colleges inside a university, as well as presence of many additional pages within university web clusters. For this paper, we still focus on the core websites of the universities (the main-domain sites) but aim at expanding the research to the 'web space' level.

We have selected the web spaces of Moscow and St. Petersburg State Universities as the two largest universities in Russia, and also Harvard University website known for its minimalistic design; we expect the latter to work in a way as a benchmark for our assessment of the two Russian universities.

2 Research Design and Methodology

For large web spaces, we propose a complex usability test based on three steps. Step 1: selection of key nodes for analysis (by web crawling and web analytics), Step 2: ergonomic (page-level, or node-level) tests, Step 3: architecture and navigation tests (for the detailed account, see Bodrunova et al. 2016). In this paper, we focus on Step 2 and use Step 1 for page sampling. Also, in order to pre-test the suggested methodology, we will introduce a comparative component into the study.

A special role in any web space belongs to key architectural and network nodes; their usability and navigation through them must be looked at with special attention. We will focus on testing the key nodes comparable in terms of their position in graphs and the main website menus (that is, the nodes that were meant to become key pages and are, indeed, performing these roles).

For Step 1 (selection of web pages), a web crawler with specialized modules was tested (Blekanov et al. 2012) and adapted. As a result of web crawling for the three universities, three web graphs were reconstructed. Based on them, we have singled out comparable pages. We have included into pre-testing high-rank web pages only, as based on their network centrality data: a page had to belong to top pages by at least one of SNA centrality metrics for all three universities, to be comparable in its overall structure and aims to its counterparts and, third, to play an important role in the structure of the university website.

The following pages were chosen (15 pages altogether): homepage; university news; university structure (+ contacts of the faculties/institutes/personnel); scientific life (coverage of main scientific events); university life (announcements and short news-like coverage).

For Step 2a (qualitative assessment). Despite their importance, elements of graphic design traditionally considered responsible for readability and user friendliness of a media interface (and used, e.g., in newspaper layouting), were not tested well enough, neither individually nor as a complex. These elements are parts of the so-called composite-graphic model (further referred here as CGM), or, in a simpler and less precise way, a layout (which is the result of application of the CGM to a particular page). To overcome the term mess existing in today's literature and described above, we will use CGM as a referenced-to whole that comprises page-level and element level components. We state that there is no agreed methodology of CGM usability testing.

As stated in Sect. 1, most researchers focus on just one or several aspects of visual organization of a page and formulate dependencies that relate user experience to particular elements of CGM. But we take into account the integrity of a web project; this implies a certain hierarchy in designers' decision-making. Thus, based on works by Velichkovsky (2010), we have divided CGM's visual organization into two levels. The macro-level comprises composition, color, zonation, and page-level spacing and deals with heterogeneity, content combination, and visual saliency of layout elements; micro-level comprises individual-block parameters, typography, inter-line spacing, and syntagmas and deals with readability and cognition speed.

For single page assessment, we have elaborated a qualitative index of usability for a web page (GCM usability index, or U-index) based on a wide range of literature on traditional newspaper design, digital news design, web design, and perception theory. We focus not only on the works of graphic design gurus as Arnheim or Berlyne but also on over a dozen today's popular design and web design manuals.

In the U-index, we have also combined the findings of those who analyzed the layouting features and the scarce findings on the web graphic design. On the macro-level, we have taken into account notion of website visual complexity and cognitive load (Pieters et al. 2010; Wang et al. 2014), as website complexity seems to play a role exactly for the mode of webpage consumption: high-complexity websites, counter-intuitively, tend to facilitate the 'reading' mode (see below; Wang et al. 2014). In the test tasks, both levels were taken into consideration.

The index includes the following categories:

- macro-level: overall type of layout; layout module structure; vertical spacing; page zonation; creolization of the layout;
- micro-level:
  - syntagma: line length, line length in title block, leading (inter-lineage spacing);
  - typography: contour contrast, tone&color contrast with background, font adaptivity, x-height, font&line length combination.

Each of the 13 chosen parameters were given values (0; 1) or (0; 1; 2). The overall maximum index of a page equals to 22.

Our goal is to test the U-index on the whole, as well as on the macro-and micro-levels. In future, individual parameters of the U-index are to be tested; but we first wish to prove that there is, in general, a link between user experience and the index.

For Step 2b (quantitative test), we have elaborated the information search tasks for each page based on the existing practices of usability testing (Broder 2002; Rose and Levinson 2004), as well as on the pre-assumption that there are two modes of a user's interaction with a page: that of *search* and that of *reading*, as suggested by Velich-kovskiy (2010). The mode of 'reading' is desirable, while the mode of 'search' is not, as in the existing studies 'reading' implies focused studying of target content, while 'search' implies random looking for it on a page. The tasks we designed were oriented to finding a piece of target content, not to in-depth understanding or long-term memory on it, as such tasks let assess how quickly 'search' transforms into 'reading' and whether 'reading' dominates. Thus, five tasks were elaborated, each one adapted for three different pages; we made sure they were comparable in each case. So far, the task complexity as an intervening factor was not tested within our pre-test.

The testing methods we use are heat maps and metrics of eye movement. Among the latter, eye fixations are assessed, most often by three metrics (Salvucci and Goldberg 2000; Poole et al. 2004): the number of fixations, their duration, and saccade length (the distance between two fixation dots on the monitor). We explore the 'search'/'reading' modes by these metrics as well as their derivatives.

Two new derivative metrics that we suggest are calculated as mean deviations of the main eye movement metrics. Thus, while mean fixation length provides hints on overall mean readability of the page, mean fixation length deviation tells whether the layout is the same throughout the page, or some parts of the content are consumed faster than others. Similarly, mean saccade length deviation hints to the dynamics of 'search'/'reading', thus enriching our knowledge on the overall content consumption pattern described by the average saccade length. Lower deviations would tell of the 'reading' pattern, while higher deviations would be a sign of 'search'.

Then, we have introduced several more comparative elements into our research design and sampling.

First, as several recent works have stated that only fixations over 300 ms count, we created two datasets for each university – namely, the one with all the fixations of eye motion and the one with the fixations of 300+ ms. Thus, we will analyze the eye tracking results comparing the samples of all fixations and of fixations of 300+ ms.

Second, we will compare the results of the two eye tracking methods: the quantitative measures (number of fixations, fixation duration, saccade length, and the derivative metrics) vs. heat map assessment. We further elaborated the latter quantitatively and included five metrics in our study:

overall number of red spots on the screen (in N -> 0; 1; 2);
number of red spots close to the target element (in N -> 0; 1; 2);
size of the maximal red spot closest to the target element (in mm -> 0; 1; 2);
intensity of the biggest red spot closest to the target element (qualitatively -> 0; 1);
diameter of the maximal red spot closest to the target element (in mm - > 0; 1; 2).

Third, to be able to recommend the U-index to professional designers, we wanted to ensure that the results of assessment are not hardware-dependent and that any eye tracker would produce similar results. Two eye trackers (one stationary and one 'unobtrusive' with head fixation) were used. Two groups of four assessors each performed the same search tasks on one of the two eye trackers.

Thus, as heat maps were tested on the first eye tracker only, for each of the 15 pages chosen, 13 qualitative and 10 to 15 quantitative/mixed-method variables were assessed. Of the 13 variables in U-index, 3 figures were formed (for micro-level, macro-level, and their combination). Thus, the pre-test sample includes 40 entries with a single web page as the unit of analysis; 20 entries were measured by 18 variables each, and other 20 by 13 variables (excluding heat map analysis). All data on eye movement were assessed twice – within all-fixation and 300+ ms samples. For the resulting variables and research design overview, see Table 1.

Table 1. Testing the U-index: the research design and variables

U-index, general (Uigen)	U-index, macro-level (Uimac)	U-index, micro-level (Uimic)

vs.

Variable category	Variable sub-category	Fixations			Variable category	All fix.
		All	300+			
Number of fixations	Number of fixations (Nfixall)	x	x		Overall N of red spots (Nrspots)	x
Fixation duration	Average fixation duration (Dfixall)	x	x		N of red spots near target (Ntar)	x
	Mean duration deviation (Dfixmall)	x	x		Max red spot size (Maxsize)	x
Saccade length	Average saccade length (Savall)	x	x		Max red spot intensity (Maxint)	x
	Mean length deviation (Sdevall)	x	x		Max red spot diameter (MaxD)	x

Eye tracker 2				
Variable category	Variable sub-category	Fixations		
		All	300+	
Number of fixations	Number of fixations (Nfix300)	x	x	
Fixation duration	Average fixation duration (Dfix300)	x	x	
	Mean duration deviation (Dfixm300)	x	x	
Saccade length	Average saccade length (Sav300)	x	x	
	Mean length deviation (Sdev300)	x	x	

After the eye tracking test, we have looked for correlations between independent (U-index) and dependent (eye tracking) variables applying two different statistical metrics – Spearman's correlation metric and Cramer's V cross-tabulation metric.

3   The Research Hypotheses

H1. We consider eye trackers to be equivalent in their capacity of measuring user-interface interaction efficacy. Thus, two assessor groups will provide similar results.

H2. We consider web design to cast impact upon user interaction experience. Thus, U-index (measured on micro-level, macro-level, and on the whole) will correlate with user experience metrics.

H3. In our opinion, efficient design should facilitate the 'reading' mode. Thus, we hypothesize that, on the pages with better CGM (that is, with higher U-index), subjective user experience will be more like 'reading', not like 'search'. That is, it will have:

lower number of fixations;

lower mean fixation duration;

lower mean fixation duration deviation;

lower mean saccade length;

lower mean saccade length deviation;

bigger and more intense 'heat' grouped around the target elements.

H4. Despite the existing literature, we do not expect the results for all-fixation sample to differ from the 300+ ms one.

H5. Due to its minimalistic design, Harvard will perform better than the Russian universities in all the aspects.

4   Conduct of Pre-test

For the pre-test, each assessor was asked to conduct 15 tasks (one task for each page), where the tasks for each page type were identical. Average session duration was between 30 and 40 min. As the tasks were similar but language-dependent, all the assessors were native Russian speakers with good command of English as well (EILTS 6 or higher). The eye tracking procedures took place in soundproof rooms. The same supervisor assisted at the procedures. The groups were homogeneous in terms of age (Master students) and were slightly familiar with all the three websites before the test.

5   Results

All in all, application of descriptive statistical metrics has returned the following results (only significant, marked bold, and slightly insignificant, marked italic, values are included). Please see Table 2 for Spearman correlation for groups 1 and 2, and Table 3 for Cramer's V for groups 1 and 2.

H1 proves to be wrong. As evident from the Tables 2 and 3, we have discovered high differences in the results that we received from the two groups of assessors. This brings in new premises for future eye tracking research of web interfaces, as it is not

Table 2. Spearman correlations for groups 1 and 2

Group 1:

		Nfixall	Nfix300	Dfixall	Dfixmall	Dfix300	Dfixm300	Savall	Sdevall	Sav300	Sdev300	Nrspots	Ntar	Maxsize	Maxint	MaxD
Harvard	Uigen											0,483*	0,722***			0,504*
	Uimac												0,628***			0,659***
	Uimic	-0,387 (p=,092)				0,393 (p=,086)							0,605**			
MSU	Uigen															
	Uimac															
	Uimic															
SPbU	Uigen												-0,411 (p=,072)			
	Uimac															
	Uimic												-0,384 (p=,095)			

Group 2:

		Nfixall	Nfix300	Dfixall	Dfixmall	Dfix300	Dfixm300	Savall	Sdevall	Sav300	Sdev300
Harvard	Uigen	-,747**	,644**	,761**		,547*	,776**	-,652**	-,667**		,736**
	Uimac	-,696**	,447*	,679**		,514*	,465*	-,471*	-,529*		
	Uimic	-,609**	,597**	,648**		,474*	,776**	-,699**	-,631**		,736**
MSU	Uigen										
	Uimac										
	Uimic										
SPbU	Uigen			,437 (sig.0,053)				-,467*			
	Uimac										
	Uimic	-,483*		,543*				-,549*			

only the quality of eye tracking data that are of concern (Holmqvist et al. 2012) but also the nature of the eye tracker itself that matters. Our suggestion for continuation of our own research is to use the 'unobtrusive' eye tracker – not because it has produced more substantial results but due to its unobtrusive nature.

H2, as we see, looks partly proven. Eye tracker 1 seems to reject it, except for the heat maps, and with the latter, only Harvard shows significant correlations for three of five variables. But eye tracker 2 shows that nearly all kinds of the suggested variables form significant correlations with the U-index for Harvard, and the traditional all-fixation-encompassing variables make it for SPbU; the results are also partly supported by Cramer's V. This, first of all, provides the premises for future research, as the U-index seems to have relevance, at least in the case of one university (Harvard). Then, we need to know why MSU, SPbU and Harvard produced so different results; other factors, perhaps, need to be taken into consideration, as we definitely see that there is an overall cause of a dramatic difference between Harvard and MSU in terms of

Table 3. Cramer's V cross-tabulation for groups 1 and 2

Group 1:

		Nfixall	Nfix300	Dfixall	Dfixmall	Dfix300	Dfixm300	Savall	Sdevall	Sav300	Sdev300	Nrspots	Ntar	Maxsize	Maxint	MaxD
Harvard	Uigen															
	Uimac											,725*	0,569 (p=,086)			
	Uimic															
MSU	Uigen					,901 (p=,067)						,701**				
	Uimac											,683 (p=,069)				
	Uimic											,720**				
SPbU	Uigen															
	Uimac	,968 (p=,065)														
	Uimic	,968 (p=,060)														

Group 2:

		Nfixall	Nfix300	Dfixall	Dfixmall	Dfix300	Dfixm300	Savall	Sdevall	Sav300	Sdev300
Harvard	Uigen		,760***			,886**	,690***				,632**
	Uimac		,655**								
	Uimic		,849***			,968***	,690***			1,000***	,632**
MSU	Uigen										
	Uimac										
	Uimic										
SPbU	Uigen										
	Uimac		,901**								
	Uimic										

correlation between the U-index and assessors' performance, be it the overall minimalist style of the Harvard web design or some other outer factor. But we also need to notice that language must, evidently be excluded as such a cause, as web design features seem to facilitate the assessors' performance, but in English – contrary to expectations, as the assessors were Russian native speakers. So far, we can say that traditional metrics (that is, all-encompassing number of fixations, fixation duration, and saccade length) worked for two universities on eye tracker 2, and 300 + metrics did so only for Harvard, as well as deviation metrics introduced by us. At the same time, we cannot help noting that the mean deviation metrics also worked well for eye tracker 2, especially in case of 300+ ms metrics. This may mean that mean deviations may be used to detect not only the direct efficacy of eye motion (e.g. timing of eye motion) but also more sophisticated patterns of content consumption.

H3 is also partly proven, and our results bear the logic of the 'reading' pattern, especially in case of Harvard. For this university:

for heat maps, *H3* is supported, as the U-index is higher if:
more red spots are there on the screen;
more red spots surround the target content;
diameter of the major red spot near target is bigger.

For quantitative metrics, the situation is more nuanced than we hypothesized. Thus, indeed, higher U-index correlates with lower overall number of fixations, as well as lower saccade length and its mean deviation. That is, efficient pages are consumed with fewer 'stops' and smaller 'jumps' around the page. But at the same time, as soon as we take into account only 'long stops' (fixations of 300+ ms), the bigger number of fixations and saccade length, the better. Taken together with the fixation duration, these metrics form the 'reading' pattern, while big numbers of short fixations and short saccades form the 'random search' pattern.

H4, as seen from *H3*, is wrong; moreover, the case of Harvard shows that both overall and 300+ ms fixations metrics need to be taken into consideration in the usability tests, as they relate to different patterns of user-interface interaction, if taken together with other metrics.

H5 proves right on available data but definitely needs further research. Thus, on the whole and on micro-level, Harvard shows stronger correlations between qualitative assessment and eye tracking results. This may mean that Harvard needs smaller improvement of design to get the same user efficacy; also, design has a bigger chance to cast impact upon user-interface interaction within the university web space. Taking into consideration absence of clear picture for MSU and almost the same picture for SPbU, we conclude that design of the Russian university websites has smaller impact upon user experience and, thus, must be less efficient than that of Harvard.

6   Conclusion

So far, our results suggest that, at least in some cases, there is linkage between qualitative 'designer' understanding of efficient web design and user experience in content consumption. For Harvard, we have discovered that web pages more efficient from the designer viewpoint tend to have the 'reading' pattern (relatively small number of long fixations quite distanced from each other) and not the 'search' pattern (a lot of short fixations with short 'jumps' between them). This means that the U-index (after more testing and fine-grained research) may become a practical instrument for web designers and experts in practical web usability tests. Also, we have discovered the necessity to combine the variables to describe 'search' and 'reading' patterns in a more nuanced way.

But at the same time our results for the Russian universities show that web design might be irrelevant for assessors' performance on search tasks; counter-intuitively, native Russian speakers demonstrated a more solid pattern of interaction with the American website, rather than with the Russian ones. Further research is needed to define the factor that prevents web design from casting impact upon user experience in the latter cases.

Acknowledgements. This research has been supported in full by Russian Foundation for Basic Research, research grant 15-01-06105 (2015–2016) 'Elaboration of webometric and ergonomic models and methods of analysis of efficacy of web presence of large organizations'.

References

Bargas-Avila, J., Hornbæk, K.: Old wine in new bottles or novel challenges: a critical analysis of empirical studies of user experience. In: Proceedings of the 2011 Annual Conference on Human Factors in Computing Systems, pp. 2689–2698. ACM (2011)

Ben-Bassat, T., Meyer, J., Tractinsky, N.: Economic and subjective measures of the perceived value of aesthetics and usability. ACM Trans. Comput. Hum. Interact. **13**(2), 210–234 (2006)

Bernard, M., Chaparro, B., Thomasson, R.: Finding information on the web: does the amount of whitespace really matter. Usability News **2**(1), 1 (2000)

Blekanov, I.S., Sergeev, S.L., Martynenko, I.: Construction of subject-oriented web crawlers using a generalized kernel. Sci. Tech. Bull. St. Petersburg State Polytech. Univ. **5**(197), 9–15 (2012)

Bodrunova, S.S., Yakunin, A.V., Smolin, A.A.: Comparing efficacy of web design of university websites: mixed methodology and first results for Russia and the USA. In: Proceedings of the International Conference on Electronic Governance and Open Society: Challenges in Eurasia, pp. 237–241. ACM (2016)

Broder, A.: A taxonomy of web search. SIGIR Forum **36**(2), 3–10 (2002)

Buscher, G., Cutrell, E., Morris, M.R.: What do you see when you're surfing?: using eye tracking to predict salient regions of web pages. In: Proceedings of the SIGCHI Conference on Human Factors in Computing Systems, pp. 21–30. ACM (2009)

Chaparro, B., Bernard, M.: Finding information on the web: does the amount of white space really matter? In: Proceedings of the Tenth Annual Usability Professionals' Association Conference (2001). http://psychology.wichita.edu/surl/usabilitynews/W/whitespace.htm

Coursaris, C.K., Kripintris, K.: Web aesthetics and usability: an empirical study of the effects of white space. Int. J. e-Business Res. (IJEBR) **8**(1), 35–53 (2012)

Cyr, D., Head, M., Larios, H.: Colour appeal in website design within and across cultures: a multi-method evaluation. Int. J. Hum Comput Stud. **68**(1), 1–21 (2010)

De Angeli, A., Sutcliffe, A., Hartmann, J.: Interaction, usability and aesthetics: what influences users' preferences? In: Proceedings of the 6th ACM Conference on Designing Interactive Systems, pp. 271–280. ACM (2006)

De Kock, E., Van Biljon, J., Pretorius, M.: Usability evaluation methods: mind the gaps. In: Proceedings of the 2009 Annual Research Conference of the South African Institute of Computer Scientists and Information Technologists, pp. 122–131. ACM (2009)

Djamasbi, S., Siegel, M., Tullis, T.: Generation Y, web design, and eye tracking. Int. J. Hum. Comput. Stud. **68**(5), 307–323 (2010)

Goldberg, J.H., Stimson, M.J., Lewenstein, M., Scott, N., Wichansky, A.M.: Eye tracking in web search tasks: design implications. In: Proceedings of the 2002 Symposium on Eye Tracking Research & Applications, pp. 51–58. ACM (2002)

Hasan, L.: Evaluating the usability of nine Jordanian university websites. In: 2012 International Conference on Communications and Information Technology (ICCIT), pp. 91–96. IEEE (2012)

Hassenzahl, M.: The interplay of beauty, goodness, and usability in interactive products. Hum. Comput. Interact. 19(4), 319–349 (2004)

Hassenzahl, M., Monk, A.: The inference of perceived usability from beauty. Hum. Comput. Interact. 25(3), 235–260 (2010)

Holmqvist, K., Nyström, M., Mulvey, F.: Eye tracker data quality: what it is and how to measure it. In: Proceedings of the Symposium on Eye Tracking Research and Applications, pp. 45–52. ACM (2012)

Ilmberger, W., Schrepp, M., Held, T.: Cognitive processes causing the relationship between aesthetics and usability. In: Holzinger, A. (ed.) USAB 2008. LNCS, vol. 5298, pp. 43–54. Springer, Heidelberg (2008). doi:10.1007/978-3-540-89350-9_4

Kurosu, M., Kashimura, K.: Apparent usability vs. inherent usability: experimental analysis on the determinants of the apparent usability. In: CHI 1995: Conference Companion on Human Factors in Computing Systems, pp. 292–293. ACM (1995)

Lavie, T., Tractinsky, N.: Assessing dimensions of perceived visual aesthetics of web sites. Int. J. Hum. Comput. Stud. 60(3), 269–298 (2004)

Leuthold, S., Schmutz, P., Bargas-Avila, J.A., Tuch, A.N., Opwis, K.: Vertical versus dynamic menus on the world wide web: eye tracking study measuring the influence of menu design and task complexity on user performance and subjective preference. Comput. Hum. Behav. 27(1), 459–472 (2011)

Lindgaard, G.: Aesthetics, visual appeal, usability and user satisfaction: what do the user's eyes tell the user's brain? Aust. J. Emerg. Technol. Soc. 5(1), 1–14 (2007)

McCarthy, J.D., Sasse, M.A., Riegelsberger, J.: Could i have the menu please? An eye tracking study of design conventions. People and Computers XVII — Designing for Society, pp. 401–414. Springer, London (2004)

Moshagen, M., Musch, J., Göritz, A.S.: A blessing, not a curse: experimental evidence for beneficial effects of visual aesthetics on performance. Ergonomics 52(10), 1311–1320 (2009)

Ngo, D., Samsudin, A., Abdullah, R.: Aesthetic measures for assessing graphic screens. J. Inf. Sci. Eng. 16(1), 97–116 (2000)

Ngo, D., Byrne, J.: Application of an aesthetic evaluation model to data entry screens. Comput. Hum. Behav. 17(2), 149–185 (2001)

Ngo, D.: Measuring the aesthetic elements of screen designs. Displays 22(3), 73–78 (2001)

Ngo, D., Teo, L., Byrne, J.: Modelling interface aesthetics. Inf. Sci. 152, 25–46 (2003)

Nielsen, J.: Heuristic evaluation. In: Nielsen, J., Mack, R.L. (eds.) Usability Inspection Methods, pp. 22–62. Wiley, New York (1994)

Nielsen, J.: F-shaped pattern for reading web content. Jacob Nielsen's Alertbox (2006). http://www.nngroup.com/articles/f-shaped-pattern-reading-web-content/

Outing, S., Rual, L.: The Best of Eyetrack III: What We Saw When We Looked Through Their Eyes. Poynter Institute (not dated). http://poynterextra.org/eyetrack2004/main.htm

Phillips, C., Chaparro, B.: Visual appeal vs. usability: which one influences user perceptions of a website more. Usability News 11(2), 1–9 (2009)

Pieters, R., Wedel, M., Batra, R.: The stopping power of advertising: measures and effects of visual complexity. J. Mark. 74(5), 48–60 (2010)

Poole, A., Ball, L.J., Phillips, P.: In search of salience: a response time and eye movement analysis of bookmark recognition. In: Fincher, S., Markopolous, P., Moore, D., Ruddle, R. (eds.) People and Computers XVIII-Design for Life: Proceedings of HCI 2004. Springer, London (2004)

Purchase, H.C., Hamer, J., Jamieson, A., Ryan, O.: Investigating objective measures of web page aesthetics and usability. In: Proceedings of the Twelfth Australasian User Interface Conference, vol. 117, pp. 19–28. Australian Computer Society (2011)

Quinn, J.M., Tran, T.Q.: Attractive phones don't have to work better: independent effects of attractiveness, effectiveness, and efficiency on perceived usability. In: Proceedings of the SIGCHI Conference on Human Factors in Computing Systems, pp. 353–362. ACM (2010)

Reinecke, K., Yeh, T., Miratrix, L., Mardiko, R., Zhao, Y., Liu, J., Gajos, K.Z.: Predicting users' first impressions of website aesthetics with a quantification of perceived visual complexity and colorfulness. In: Proceedings of the SIGCHI Conference on Human Factors in Computing Systems, pp. 2049–2058. ACM (2013)

Rose, D.E., Levinson, D.: Understanding user goals in Web search. In: Proceedings of WWW 2004, pp. 13–19 (2004)

Salvucci, D.D., Goldberg, J.H.: Identifying fixations and saccades in eye-tracking protocols. In: Proceedings of the 2000 Symposium on Eye Tracking Research & Applications, pp. 71–78. ACM (2000)

Shenkman, B.O., Jönsson, F.: Aesthetics and preferences of web pages. Behav. Inf. Technol. **19** (5), 367–377 (2000)

Sonderegger, A., Sauer, J.: The influence of design aesthetics in usability testing: Effects on user performance and perceived usability. Appl. Ergon. **41**(3), 403–410 (2010)

Thüring, M., Mahlke, S.: Usability, aesthetics and emotions in human–technology interaction. Int. J. Psychol. **42**(4), 253–264 (2007)

Tractinsky, N.: Aesthetics and apparent usability: empirically assessing cultural and methodological issues. In: CHI 1997: Proceedings of the SIGCHI Conference on Human Factors in Computing Systems, pp. 115–122. ACM (1997)

Tractinsky, N., Katz, A.S., Ikar, D.: What is beautiful is usable. Interact. Comput. **13**(2), 127–145 (2000)

Tuch, A.N., Roth, S.P., Hornbæk, K., Opwis, K., Bargas-Avila, J.A.: Is beautiful really usable? Toward understanding the relation between usability, aesthetics, and affect in HCI. Comput. Hum. Behav. **28**(5), 1596–1607 (2012)

Van Schaik, P., Ling, J.: The effect of link colour on information retrieval in educational intranet use. Comput. Hum. Behav. **19**(5), 553–564 (2003)

Van Schaik, P., Ling, J.: Modelling user experience with web sites: usability, hedonic value, beauty and goodness. Interact. Comput. **20**(3), 419–432 (2008)

Velichkovskiy, B.M.: Research on cognitive functions and today's technologies [Issledovanie kognitivnykh funktsiy i sovremennye tekhnologii]. Bull. Russ. Acad. Sci. **80**(5–6), 440–446 (2010)

Wang, Q., Yang, S., Liu, M., Cao, Z., Ma, Q.: An eye-tracking study of website complexity from cognitive load perspective. Decis. Support Syst. **62**, 1–10 (2014)

Zaphiris, P., Ellis, R.D.: Website usability and content accessibility of the top USA Universities. In: WebNet, pp. 1380–1385 (2001)

An Association Analysis Between Content Topic and Appeal Type of Infographics

Tzu-Fan Hsu[(✉)]

Department of Commercial Design,
Chung Yuan Christian University, Taoyuan City, Taiwan
nightshift1943@gmail.com

Abstract. Infographics become viral on the internet and social media, offering people visual information in an easy way to consume and share. The design, story, and data all play an important role in infographic. However, the latter two were less explored than the first one. Hence, this study conducted an association analysis between the two variables, "content topic" and "appeal type" from the infographics which received more than 10000 page views on Visual.ly. The study comprised the two phrases. Phase 1 aimed to classify the categories for both the two variables by card sorting and cluster analysis. Next, association analyses were performed in phase 2 to discover the connections between the two important factors of infographics. The results were as follows. (1) The content type was divided into the four categories: "statistical data", "original insight", "life issues" and "development progress". (2) Web infographics adopting "rational appeal" were more than those adopting "emotional appeal". (3) A significant association did exist between content type and appeal type. Rational appeal was usually used with the contents of statistical data, and emotional appeal was usually applied in the topics of development progress and life issues. Overall, the findings could serve as a foundation for further studies in infographic, and enable designers to enhance users' experience in visual communication.

Keywords: Infographic · Content topic · Appeal type

1 Introduction

1.1 Background Information

Infographics is a visual representation of knowledge to convey message in a quick and concise way. With the coming of digital age, internet becomes an important platform for people to communicate with each other, leading that a new breed of infographic has evolved to be for mass communication in blogs or social media and been an excellent tool for commercial marketing in recent years (Rendgen and Wiedemann 2012). To fit within a width of web media, this new infographic turns into a long and skinny form (Lankow et al. 2012).

Infographics is a combination of information and graphic, meaning that both are the main elements. Compared to graphic, information issue is less explored in the field of infographic. Slembrouck (2011) pointed out that information consists of graphic, data,

© Springer International Publishing AG 2017
A. Marcus and W. Wang (Eds.): DUXU 2017, Part I, LNCS 10288, pp. 234–247, 2017.
DOI: 10.1007/978-3-319-58634-2_18

and storying, implying that the latter two factors are essential to probe into the information aspect of infographic. From the viewpoint of commercial profit, peoples' attentions mean huge potential of economic value, resulting that attention turns into a crucial and rare resource (Davenport and Back 2002). Hence, infographic with stunning visuals is applied widely in social media platform. Laskey et al. (1995) pointed out that effects of communication are influenced by content and appeal of product. In contrast to infographic, these two properties are quite similar to data and storytelling. The former is the theme of selected content, and the latter is an approach to guide people with a specific content to generate resonance. Therefore, this study took "content topic" and "appeal type" as the two factors to explore the info aspect of infographic. (Fig. 1).

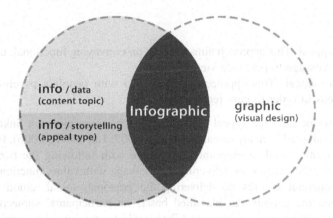

Fig. 1. Main factors of infographic

Advertisement is a typical application of information design. The message content conveyed through advertising usually focus on the characteristics, benefit, or features of the product or the service (Rotzoll et al. 1989). Except for informativeness, the entertainment is also necessary for content (Steinbock 2007). Hence, letting people has an experience with fun is an important issue in modern marketing in order to leave them with a message to take away. As for infographic, clarifying the categories of content topic people are interested in will provide valued references for academic research and design practice.

Moreover, appeal means an approach seeking to build a link between the content and viewers' resonance. Design and marketing staff attempt to achieve an effective communication through various appeal types (Hsiao 1991). In order to choose an appropriate classification for infographic, this study collected related scholars' viewpoints and integrated them in Table 1.

The numbers of types might be different; however, there is a general agreement in among most of them in classifying appeals: rational/emotional appeal, which is been widely used in related researches (Rothschild 1987; Ju 1995; Turley and Kelley 1997). Hence, it was took as basis of appear type in this study, and been described as followed.

Table 1. List of related appeal types

Scholar	Types
Vanghn (1980)	Think/Feel
Aaker and Norris (1982)	Informational/Rational/Image/Cognitive/Emotional/Feeling
Puto and Wells (1984)	Informational/Transformational
Snyder and DeBono (1985)	Functional appeal/Symbolic appeal
Rossiter and Percy (1987)	Positive/Negative
Johar and Sirgy (1991)	Utilitarian appeal/Value-expressive appeal
Kotler (1991)	Rational appeal/Emotional appeal/Moral appeal
Ju (1995), Turley and Kelley (1997)	Rational/Emotional

- Rational appeal: This approach aims to focus on conveying functional, utilitarian, or practical message to persuade viewers.
- Emotional appeal: This approach is concerned with people's psychological and social needs in order to gain recognition.

In order to measure the appeal type of various message media, a linker scale is a common tool adopted in many researches (Chen 2003; Lin and Tu 2006). For instance, Lin and Tu (2006) used seven-point Likert scale with following the two questions: (1) this commercial focuses on delivering the message with value, function, or benefit. (2) this commercial focuses on delivering the personal, social, emotional, humor message. Then the stimuli was classified based on participants' subjective scoring. Therefore, this study used seven-point Likert scale to measure the appeal type infographic adopted.

1.2 Research Questions

The survey and analysis of this study would clarify cognition of infographic, and enable designers to enhance users' experience in visual communication. Overall, the research questions were as follows.

1. Classifying the categories of content topic of infographic.
2. Survey on the proportion of appeal type adopted by infographic.
3. Examining the association between content topic and appeal type.

2 Experiment

2.1 Method

Classification is a method to explore construction of knowledge. The process of assigning the stimuli into groups by similarities can enable the clarification of commonality and differentiation among groups. Hence, the methodology of this study was as follows.

1. A card sorting was used as a tool to classify the content topic of stimuli by participants. Additionally, based on the angle of rational and emotional appeals, a seven-points of Likert Scale was adopted to measure the appeal type of stimuli by participants' subjective scoring.
2. The assignment results of all participants were analyzed by cluster analysis to find the commonality within each cluster and the differentiation among clusters. Both the dendrogram and agglomeration schedule were used to determinate the numbers of clusters. The former is a tree diagram for illustrating the arrangement of clusters, and the latter is a numerical summary descripting the combination process of the cluster of stimuli.
3. After classifying both the content type and appeal type of stimuli, an association analysis was performed to uncover the relationships between these two variables in order to identifies how content topic are associated with appeal type of infographics.

2.2 Stimuli

According to Alexa Internet top 500 sites analytics (Alexa 2015), Visual.ly is the infographic website with most page views in recent years. The infographics with more than 10000 views from Visual.ly Community were sampled as the stimuli.

To reduce variability and experiment overload, these stimuli were filtered and examined by the three reviewers with more than 6 years experiences in graphic design and infographic based on quality evaluation of design, communication, and visual storytelling (Kimura 2010). The reviewers assigned each stimulus to one of five options: "strongly agree", "agree", "neither agree nor disagree", "disagree", or "strongly disagree". A stimulus would be preserved if it obtained a "strongly agree" or "agree" score from at least two reviewers. Finally, 203 infographics were sampled as the stimuli for experiment.

2.3 Participants

To ensure reliability and validity of card sorting data, Gaffney (2000), Tullis and Wood (2004) recommend 30 as a proper number of participants. Thus, 30 senior undergraduates in design related courses from Chung Yuan Christian University took part in the experiment. All were 22 years old, gender balanced, and obtained a certificate of high-intermediate level of General English Proficiency Test.

2.4 Variables

The definitions of the variables were as follows.

1. Content topic: it refers to a theme conveyed by infographic. The content topic of each stimulus is determined by classification using card sorting and cluster analysis by all participants.

2. Appeal type: it refers to an approach to develop a link between information and the people's approval. "Rational appeal" and "emotional appeal" are two broad types (Ju 1995). The appeal type of each stimulus is determined by cluster analysis on subjective scoring using seven-point Likert scale by all participants.

2.5 Procedure

The procedure of experiment was as follows.

1. Apparatus: An ACER Laptop (Intel i7-3612 Processor, 4096 MB RAM, 15-inch screen, resolution of 1366 * 768 pixels) was prepared with ACDSee Pro 2 software for participants to view, rearrange, and classify stimuli.
2. Procedure: The experiment was preceded by appointment. Before each experiment, the researcher gave out the instructions regarding classifying stimuli into groups based on similarities of content topic and scoring appear type by seven-point Linkert scale in the questionnaire. When there were no further questions, the experiment was begun without time limitation.
3. Data registering: Upon completion of the experiment, the researcher registered the stimuli in all clusters. Moreover, an interview was conducted and recorded if the participant's reasons for assigning and scoring stimuli in order to clarify each group characteristics and differences in the clustering process.

2.6 Statistical Analysis

Following these procedures, 30 valid data sets were obtained and then analyzed by cluster analysis to build a clustering hierarchy based on distance or similarity of observations. The analysis procedures were as follows.

1. Distance matrix: The data of card sorting were to be converted into a distance matrix, a numerical form of data which could be analyzed through cluster analysis. Parser for Cluster Data, from the Computer Aided Kansei Engineering (CAKE) software by Chuang and Chen (2004) was used as the tool to convert the collected data into distance matrix.
2 Cluster analysis: The distance matrix obtained through CAKE was then analyzed by the hierarchical clustering function of SPSS software for cluster analysis, generating the classification results.
3. Chi-square test: Finally, the frequency distribution of stimuli was build based on the classification results, and calculated for association between the two categorical variables: content topic and appeal type.

3 Results

3.1 Cluster Analysis of Content Topic

In order to classify the content type, the process of cluster analysis was represented in the two forms. One is a dendrogram, which is a tree structure of clustering process rescaled into a range from 0 to 25. The other is an agglomeration schedule table, showing (1) the stage of clustering order and cluster of stimuli to be merged at each stage, (2) the coefficient registering distance as stimuli were merged, and (3) the difference of coefficient values between its stage and next stage. Usually, the maximum difference was considered to be an indicator to stop clustering (Huang 2000). Thus, this study adopted the stage of maximum difference as the critical point to decide the number of content type.

The agglomeration schedule was summarized in Table 2, which extracted the stages of first clustering in each cluster and when the stage clustering stopped. When the stimulus 6 were merged into the group of stimulus 3 at stage 199, the difference between stage 199 and 200 registered the maximum of 18.192, revealing it as the critical point to stop clustering.

Table 2. Summary of agglomeration schedule of content type

Stage	Cluster combined		Coefficients	Difference	Stage cluster first appears		Next stage
	Cluster 1	Cluster 2			Cluster 1	Cluster 2	
1	200	203	0	0	0	0	4
5	182	140	0	0	0	0	16
11	158	76	0	0	0	0	19
37	28	68	0	0	0	0	45
199	6	3	16.070	18.192[*]	196	196	200

[*]Maximum of difference

Meanwhile, four clusters were found after the combination of stimulus 6 and 3 in the dendrogram (Fig. 2). Hence, four categories of content types, cluster I, cluster II, cluster III, and cluster IV were classified by all participants. Subsequently, the clusters were named after the combination characteristics according to the clustering results and the participant interviews.

1. Cluster I: Totaling 107 stimuli in this cluster. It accounted for 52.7% of sampled infographics. The common theme of which was various research survey or issue coverage with huge volumes of statistic data. Such as "Facebook vs Twitter", it made various comparison of the percentage distribution among users background and online activity between these two iconic social medias. The content of infographic tended to be more informative than entertaining. Thus, this cluster was named as "statistical data".

2. Cluster II: Totaling 21 stimuli in this cluster i.e., 10.3% of sampled infographics. Except for collecting the data, this cluster aimed to offer a proper interpretation from

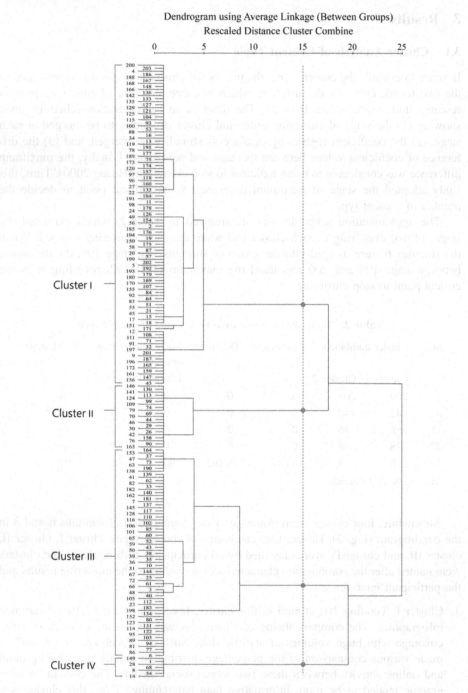

Fig. 2. Dendrogram of content topic

the result of comparisons. Such as "Social vs. Search", it distinguishes the differences between these two online methods measure up on their own. Most people prefer social media over search marketing. However, this infographic told us that combing these two would lead to more powerful results. Thus, this cluster was named as "original insight".

3. Cluster III: Totaling 68 stimuli in this cluster. It took up 33.5% of sampled infographics. The content of this cluster covered the familiar daily topics and social phenomena. Such as "Should I Text Him", it told us that sometimes people's minds and their decision-making skills are just not up to par. Then, this infographic helped us navigate the tricky waters of whether or not we should go ahead and hit send in a funny way. This content of infographic tended to be more entertaining than informative. Thus, this cluster was named as "life issues".

4. Cluster IV: Totaling 7 stimuli in this cluster i.e., 3.4% of sampled infographics. The content of this cluster focused on a series of results for the evolution process of a particular topic. Such as "The subjective timeline of the best gift ever", it reflected on a long history of boy's and girl's amazing holiday gifts - then and now. Thus, this cluster was named as "development progress".

3.2   Cluster Analysis of Appeal Type

The issue of appeal has been explored in the fields of advertising and communication (Laskey et al. 1995; Ju 1996; Lin and Tu 2006), and rational/emotional appeal is generally accepted. Hence, this study classified the appeal type of stimuli based on the distribution of participants' subjective scoring, instead of card sorting assignments task. From the summary of agglomeration schedule in Table 3 and dendrogram in Fig. 3, the assignments was divided into the two clusters, containing 127 and 76 stimuli respectively.

Table 3. Summary of agglomeration schedule of appeal type scoring

Stage	Cluster combined		Coefficients	Difference	Stage cluster first appears		Next stage
	Cluster 1	Cluster 2			Cluster 1	Cluster 2	
1	12	198	0	0	0	0	4
7	19	37	0	0	0	0	38
201	1	3	3.152	12.505*	199	197	202

Subsequently, Table 4 showed that the means of cluster with 127 stimuli and that with 76 stimuli were 6.126 and 2.329, revealing that the former cluster was stimuli of rational appeal, and the latter cluster belonged to emotional appeal. Hence, infographic adopted rational appeal (62.6%) more than emotional appeal (37.4%).

Additionally, a t-test was performed to examine if a differences between the scoring of rational appeal (6.126) and that of emotional appeal (2.329). From the summary in

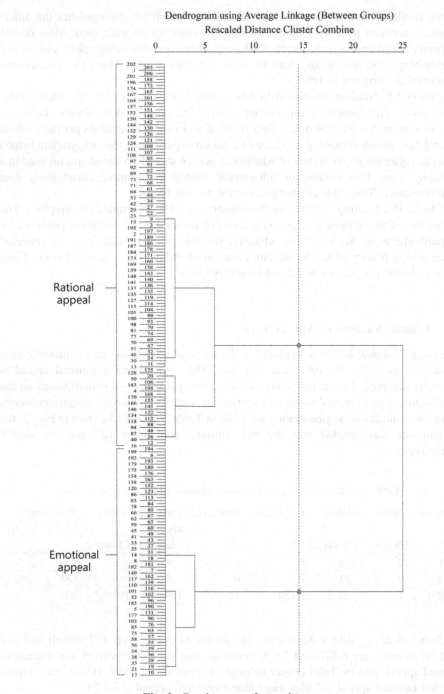

Dendrogram using Average Linkage (Between Groups)
Rescaled Distance Cluster Combine

Fig. 3. Dendrogram of appeal type

Table 4. Summary of descriptive statistics of appeal type

Appeal Type	Counts	Mean	SD.	Percentage
Rational appeal	127	6.126	.823	62.561%
Emotional appeal	76	2.329	.750	37.438%

Table 5. Summary of t-test of appeal type

	95% Confidence interval of the difference		t	df	Sig.
	Lower	Upper			
Appeal score	.017	.027	8.376	29	.000

Table 5, a significant difference existed (t = 8.376, p < .05), offering a support for the validly of classification result.

3.3 Association Analysis Between Content Topic and Appeal Type

According the previous classification results of content topic and appeal type, the assignments of stimuli were integrated in Table 6. Then this study conducted a chi-square test to evaluate association between the two variables. From the test summary in Table 7, it showed that an association significantly existed ($\chi2 = 25.883$, p = .000).

Table 6. Cross tab of appeal type and content topic

		Appeal type		Total
		Rational	Emotional	
Content topic	Life issues	31	37	68
	Statistical data	24	83	107
	Original insight	12	9	21
	Development progress	1	6	7
Total		68	135	203

Table 7. Chi-square tests

	Value	df	Asymp. Sig. (2-sided)
Pearson Chi-square	25.883[a]	3	.000
Likelihood ratio	26.394	3	.000
Linear-by-Linear association	.506	1	.477
N of valid cases	203		

The two types of rational appeals and emotional appeals were 62.6% and 37.4%, revealing that both obtain a considerable proportion. Further incorporating the factor of content topic into account, it was found that significant difference existed among the percentages of content topics by appeal types. From the statistical results in Table 8, it signified that rational appeal was adopted usually by statistical data (77.6%) of content topic, and emotional appeal was used usually with development progress (85.7%) and life issues (54.4%).

Table 8. Content topic by appeal type

			content topic				total
			life issues	statistical data	original insight	development progress	
appeal type	rational	Count	31a	83b	12a, b	1a	127
		% within content	45.6%	77.6%	57.1%	14.3%	62.6%
		% within appeal	24.4%	65.4%	9.4%	0.8%	100.0%
		Residual	-11.5	16.1	-1.1	-3.4	
	emotional	Count	37a	24b	9a, b	6a	76
		% within content	54.4%	22.4%	42.9%	85.7%	37.4%
		% within appeal	48.7%	31.6%	11.8%	7.9%	100.0%
		Residual	11.5	-16.1	1.1	3.4	
total		Count	68	107	21	7	203
		% within content	100.0%	100.0%	100.0%	100.0%	100.0%
		% within appeal	33.5%	52.7%	10.3%	3.4%	100.0%

4 Discussion and Conclusions

4.1 Content Topic and Appeal Type of Infographic

Based on survey of current status and statistical analysis on popular infographics, this study classifies the four categories of content topic: life issues, statistical data, original insight, and development progress.

According to the point that the theme of message property has the two aspects of informativeness and entertainment (Scharl et al. 2005; Steinbock 2007), the four categories of content topic can be reorganized as Fig. 4(a). It clearly reveals that proportion of informative message (black area) in the content topic of infographic is larger than that of entertaining message (gray area). Moreover, the survey of appeal type is depicted in Fig. 4(b), showing that rational appeal adopted by infographics is more than emotional appeal.

In order to clearly explain the effects between the content topic and appeal type, this study rearranges the association results in Table 9. Kotler (1991) indicated that

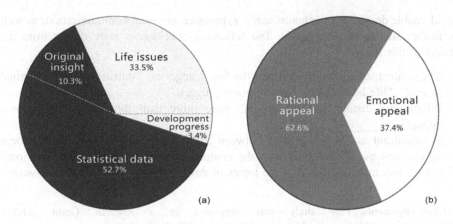

Fig. 4. Pie charts of content topic and appeal type

Table 9. Summary of association between content topic and appeal type

		content topic (informative)		content topic (entertaining)	
		statistical data	original insight	life issues	development progress
appeal type	rational	●	○		
	emotional		○	●	●

message in rational appeal usually conveys in a way of logic, reason, and benefit. It corresponds with the survey results that statistical data of content type has a high ratio in informative theme of infographics.

Furthermore, emotional appeal focuses on the pursuit of personal or social emotional needs (Snyder and DebBono 1985). From the content topic survey and participant interviews, it shows that life issue is usually full of delight and entertainment, and development progress often emphasis the features which is related to potential target group. It provides a possible explanation for the high proportions of these two content topics in emotional appeal.

Lastly, original insight is the only one that does not tend to favor neither rational nor emotional appear among all types of content topic.

5 Conclusions

Infographics offer people visual information in an easy way to consume and share, becoming a viral phenomenon on the internet and social media. Hence, this study conducted a survey on popular infographics using card sorting and cluster analysis for classification. Then an association analysis was performed to examine the interaction between the two factors of "content topic" and "appeal type". Overall, the findings could enable designers to enhance users' experience in visual communication, as well as further studies in infographic. The following conclusions were drawn from the results of this study.

1. The content topic was divided into the four categories: "statistical data", "original insight", "life issues", and "development progress".
2. Infographics using "rational appeal" were more than those using "emotional appeal".
3. A significant association existed between content type and appeal type. Rational appeal was usually adopted with the contents of statistical data, and emotional appeal was usually applied in the topics of development progress and life issues.

Acknowledgements. This study was supported in a research Grant (MOST 105-2410-H-033-034) from the Ministry of Science and Technology, Taiwan.

References

Aaker, D.A., Norris, D.: Characteristics of TV commercials perceived as informative. J. Advertising Res. **22**(2), 61–71 (1982)

Alex Website: 'Top 1,000,000 Sites' (2015). http://www.alexa.com/topsites. Accessed 31 December 2015

Chuang, Y.L., Chen, L.L.: Computer aided Kansei engineering with XML technology (Technical report no. NSC 92-2411H011007). Taiwan National Science Council, Taipei (2003)

Chen, C.C.: The influences of advertiser credibility and appeal type on advertising effects, unpublished Master's thesis. National Dong Hwa University, Taiwan (2003)

Davenport, T.H., Beck, J.C.: The Attention Economy: Understanding the New Currency of Business. Harvard Business Review Press, Boston (2002)

Gaffney, G.: What is card sorting? (2000). http://infodesign.com
http://www.infodesign.com.au/usabilityresources/design/cardsorting.asp. Accessed 12 October 2012

Hsiao, F.F.: Introduction of Commercial Marketing. Yuan-Liou Publishing, Taipei (1991)

Huang, J.Y.: Multivariate Statistical Analysis: An Introduction. China's Economy Enterprise Institute, Taipei (2000)

Johar, J.S., Sirgy, M.J.: Value-expressive versus utilitarian advertising appeals: when and why to use which appeal. J. Advertising **20**(3), 23–33 (1991)

Lin, L.Y., Tu, K.M.: The influence of brand concept images and advertising appeals on advertising effectiveness: the moderating effects of involvement level. Tamsui Oxf. J. Econ. Bus. **15**, 77–108 (2006)

Ju, F.G.: Strategic analysis of advertising emotional appeals strategy. J. Advertising Res. **5**, 85–112 (1995)

Kimura, H.: Infographics. Seibundo Shinkosha Publishing, Tokyo (2010)

Kotler, P.: Marketing Management: Analysis, Planning, Implementation and Control, 7th edn. Prentice-Hall, New Jersey (1991)

Laskey, H.A., Fox, R.J., Crask, M.R.: The relationship between advertising message strategy and television commercial effectiveness. J. Advertising Res. **35**(2), 31–39 (1995)

Puto, C.P., Wells, W.D.: Informational and transformational advertising: the differential effects of time. In: Kinnear, T.C. (ed.) NA - Advances in Consumer Research, vol. 11, pp. 638–643. Association for Consumer Research, Provo (1984)

Rendgen, S., Wiedemann, J.: Information Graphics. Taschen, Cologne (2012)

Lankow, J., Ritchie, J., Crooks, R.: Infographics: The Power of Storytelling. Wiley Inc., Hoboken (2012)

Rossiter, J.R., Percy, L.: Advertising, Communications and Promotion Management. McGraw-Hill Book Company, New York (1997)

Rothschild, M.L.: Advertising: From Fundamentals to Strategies. Heath, Lexington (1987)

Rotzoll, K., Haefner, J.E., Sandage, C.J.: Advertising and the classical liberal world view. In: Hovlan, R., Wilcox, G. (eds.) Advertising in Society. NTC Publishing Group, Lincolnwood (1989)

Slembrouck, P.V.: Analyzing the top 30 infographics on visually (2012). http://www.scribblelive.com/blog/2012/05/14/top-30-viral-infographics/. Accessed 21 April 2015

Snyder, M., DeBono, K.G.: Appeals to images and claims about quality: understanding the psychology of advertising. J. Pers. Soc. **49**, 586–697 (1985)

Steinbock, D.: The Mobile Revolution: The Making of Mobile Services Worldwide. Kogan Page, London (2007)

Tullis, T., Wood, L.: How many users are enough for a card-sorting study? In: Proceedings of UPA 2004, Minneapolis (2004)

Turley, L.W., Kelley, S.W.: A comparison of advertising content: Business to business versus consumer services. J. Advertising **26**(4), 39–48 (1997)

Vanghn, R.: How advertising works: a planning model. J. Advertising Res. **20**(5), 27–33 (1980)

Automatic Information Loss Detection and Color Compensation for the Color Blind

Sung Soo Hwang[✉]

School of Computer Science and Electronic Engineering,
Handong Global University, Pohang, Republic of Korea
sshwang@handong.edu

Abstract. Graphic designers utilize colors or various combinations of colors to express information effectively. However, the information expressed by colors may be lost when viewers are color blind. This paper presents a system for the color blind which can minimize information loss by automatic information loss detection and color compensation. The proposed system is operated in a mobile device, and for hardware and software independency, it periodically takes a screenshot. To test possible information loss, the system generates the simulated model of the screenshot and applies the equivalent segmentation algorithm to the screenshot and the simulated model. The possible information loss is then estimated by measuring the ratio between the number of groups in the original design and that in the simulated model. When possible information loss is detected, color compensation is applied to the screenshot. For inexpensive computation, a color compensation algorithm which does not require color space transformation is utilized. Simulation results show that the proposed application enables color vision deficiencies to receive information expressed by colors.

Keywords: Universal design · Information loss detection · Color compensation · Mobile device · Color blind

1 Introduction

Graphic designers utilize colors to express various information effectively. This is because utilizing colors gives a large amount of information and insight for general users. Unfortunately, the information expressed by colors may be lost when viewers are color blind. A person with color blindness has the decreased ability to see color differences, mainly due to the fault in the development of one or more of the three sets of color sensing cones in the eye. Figure 1 shows several examples of these infor-mation losses. When they are viewed by a person without color blindness, graphic designs such as Fig. 1(a) and (c) are easy to notice. When they are viewed by the color blind, however, Fig. 1(a) and (c) become vague ones like Fig. 1(b) and (d). Even though a certain amount of information loss is inevitable, it can cause serious problems if the information expressed by colors is critical. Hence, it is desirable to minimize theses information loss.

These information losses can be prevented by two ways. First, special tools can be utilized to notify designers, during the design process, that the use of certain colors

© Springer International Publishing AG 2017
A. Marcus and W. Wang (Eds.): DUXU 2017, Part I, LNCS 10288, pp. 248–257, 2017.
DOI: 10.1007/978-3-319-58634-2_19

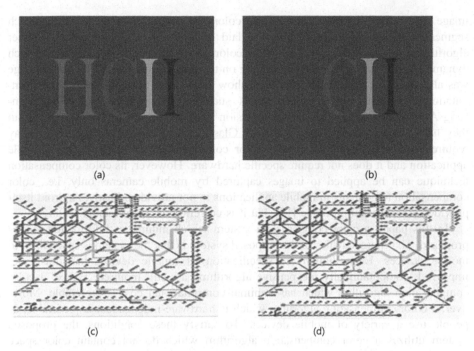

Fig. 1. Examples of information losses caused by viewers and display condition. (a)(c) Original graphic design (b)(d) Graphic design viewed by a person with color blindness

should be avoided to minimize the information loss. That is, the information loss depending on the characteristics of viewers is estimated beforehand. One way to achieve this goal is to generate the simulated models of an original graphic design and visually checking each simulated model. A similar platform is currently provided by Adobe Systems Inc. [1]. They consider the information loss caused by color blindness, and they let graphic designers preview their arts in the same way that a colorblind individual would see it. However, it can be tedious to test every graphics designs. Moreover, the platform provided by [1] does not measure the quantitative information loss. This makes it difficult to select one design among several graphic design candidates which are designed to minimize information losses. To deal with these problems, an image analysis tool was proposed which quantitatively estimates information losses caused by viewers [2]. This method measured information loss by measuring the reduction of color contrast, since the contrast of colors is related with providing objective information.

Another way of minimizing information loss is to compensate colors in a graphic design so that a person with color blind can see the design clearer. Several color compensation algorithms have been proposed and Daltonization method is one of them [3]. It compensates colors by utilizing color differences between the original image and the simulated image. Note that color differences are measured in RGB color space. An algorithm which utilizes image segmentation and confusion line was proposed [4]. This algorithm first applies image segmentation by utilizing hue component of an input image. Then the algorithm compensates colors of the input image such that each segmented region of the input image is laid on different confusion lines. Another algorithms compensates colors in HSV color space [5], and an algorithm which dynamically compensates colors depending on the color differences of the input image was also proposed [6]. These algorithms show satisfactory results, but they are computationally expensive. Several products such as Enchroma Glasses [7], Samsung AMOLED Display [8], and Imagovision [9] have been introduced as well, but they have several limits. Both Enchroma Glasses and Samsung AMOLED Display require specific hardware to provide color compensation. Imagovision is a mobile application and it does not require specific hardware. However, its color compensation technique can be applied to images captured by mobile cameras only, i.e., color compensation to contents in mobile applications is not provided. Lastly, Android itself provides color correction mode [10], but it is currently an experimental feature.

In this paper, a color compensation system which minimizes information loss is proposed. The characteristics of the proposed system is that the system is specialized to mobile devices. Even though the specification of mobile devices has drastically improved, computationally inexpensive algorithms are still required. Hence, a color compensation algorithm which has minimal computational cost is preferable. Moreover, a color compensation algorithm which is hardware-independent is preferable, as people use a variety of mobile devices. To satisfy these conditions, the proposed system utilizes a color compensation algorithm which do not contain color space conversion. The proposed system also performs color compensation only when information loss is estimated. And for hardware-independency, the system periodically takes a screenshot and compensate colors of the screenshot.

This paper is organized as follows. In Sect. 2, the proposed method is explained. In Sect. 3, the proposed method is evaluated by several graphic designs. And I conclude in Sect. 4.

2   The Proposed System

2.1   System Overview

Figure 2 illustrates the overview of the proposed system. The proposed system periodically takes a screenshot. Then the system estimates information loss of the screen-shot. For this purpose, the proposed system generates the simulated model of the screenshot and applies the equivalent segmentation algorithm to the screenshot and the simulated model. When possible information loss is detected, color compensation is applied to the screenshot. For inexpensive computation, a color compensation algorithm which does not require color space transformation is utilized.

Among various color blindness, I focus the case when viewers are protanopic. Note that the proposed system can easily expanded to other types of color blindness. To generate the simulated model, simulation model proposed by H. Brettel et al. is used [11].

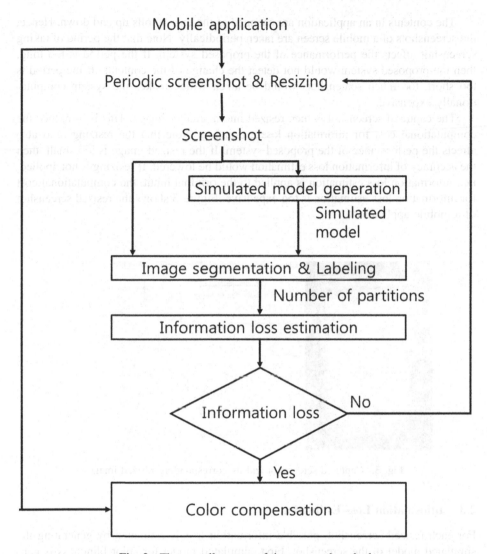

Fig. 2. The overall system of the proposed method

2.2 Periodic Screenshot and Image Resizing

In order to estimate possible information loss, the contents shown in a screen should be accessed in pixel-by-pixel basis. However, for security purpose, mobile operating systems do not allow an application to access images of other applications. To solve this problem, I take screenshot of the contents of an application and analyze the captured screenshot. Screenshot can be taken by either utilizing APIs mobile operating systems provides, or utilizing rooting. I assumed that most users do not prefer rooting, and hence, screenshots were taken by utilizing APIs. To be more specific, Media Projection API was utilized, as experiments were conducted in Android phones.

The contents in an application are changed as the user scrolls up and down. Hence, the screenshots of a mobile screen are taken periodically. Note that the period of taking screenshot affects the performance of the proposed system. If the period is too long, then the proposed system would not detect the change of the contents. If the period is too short, too much screenshots would be taken which makes the system computationally expensive.

The captured screenshot is then resized into a smaller image. This is to reduce the computational cost for information loss estimation. Note that the resizing ratio also affects the performance of the proposed system. If the resized image is too small, then the accuracy of information loss estimation would be lowered. If resizing is not applied, i.e., information loss estimation is applied to the original input, the computational cost for information loss estimation is too expensive. Figure 3 shows the resized screenshot of a mobile application.

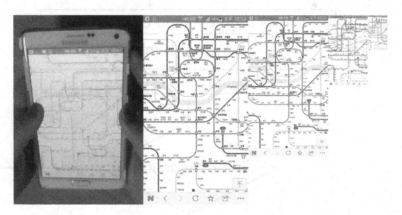

Fig. 3. Captured screenshot and its corresponding resized image

2.3   Information Loss Estimation

For each resized screenshot, possible information loss is estimated by generating the simulated model of the screenshot. First, simulated model for color blindness is generated by using the method proposed in [11]. Normal color vision is trichromatic and any color stimulus can be specified by three cone responses and all colors visible to the color-normal observer are included in a three-dimensional color space. For dichromatic observers, however, any color stimulus is initiated by two cone responses, and all colors that they can discriminate are included in a two-dimensional color space. For instance, to imitate color appearance for a person with protanopia, a color stimulus Q represented in RGB color space is transformed into LMS space as (1).

$$\begin{pmatrix} L_Q \\ M_Q \\ S_Q \end{pmatrix} = \begin{bmatrix} 0.1992 & 0.4112 & 0.0742 \\ 0.0353 & 0.2226 & 0.0574 \\ 0.0185 & 0.1231 & 1.3550 \end{bmatrix} \begin{pmatrix} R_Q \\ G_Q \\ B_Q \end{pmatrix} \tag{1}$$

Then by using Eq. (2), a color stimulus Q in LMS space is projected onto the reduced stimulus surface for protanopia.

$$
\begin{pmatrix} L'_P \\ M'_P \\ S'_P \end{pmatrix} = \begin{bmatrix} 0 & 2.02344 & -2.52581 \\ 0 & 1 & 0 \\ 0 & 0 & 1 \end{bmatrix} \begin{pmatrix} L_Q \\ M_Q \\ S_Q \end{pmatrix} \tag{2}
$$

Finally, by using Eq. (3), it is again transformed into RGB color space.

$$
\begin{pmatrix} R' \\ G' \\ B' \end{pmatrix} = \begin{bmatrix} 0.0809 & -0.1305 & 0.1167 \\ -0.0102 & 0.0540 & -0.1136 \\ -0.0003 & -0.0041 & 0.6935 \end{bmatrix} \begin{pmatrix} L'_P \\ M'_P \\ S'_P \end{pmatrix} \tag{3}
$$

Figure 4 illustrates simulated models for protanopia.

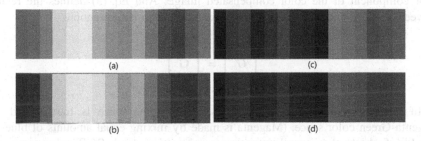

Fig. 4. Simulated model generation and segmentation results. (a)(b) original graphic design and its simulated model for protanopia (c)(d) segmentation result of (a) and (b)

Secondly, the resized screenshot the simulated model is partitioned into several regions. For the simplicity of the algorithm, color thresholding is utilized. I uniformly quantize each color component into multiple levels. And a color in a pixel is assigned to a certain level depending on its color components. Hence, colors that fall into the same level are considered as the same color. For labeling (i.e., counting the number of regions in a design), a blob counting method proposed in [12] is used. Figure 3 also illustrates the result of segmentation for the original design and the simulated model.

Finally, the information loss of the original graphic design is estimated. As a result of segmentation, each image is partitioned into several groups. Even though equivalent segmentation method is used, the number of groups is different and the number of groups in the simulated model tends to be smaller than that in the original design. This is because some colors become undistinguishable to protanopic. Thus, by measuring the ratio between the number of groups in the original design and that in the simulated model, the information loss can be estimated. Let N_O, N_S be the number of the segmented regions in the original design and the simulated model, respectively. When the number of segmented regions differs, information loss is estimated to be occurred, and it is computed by Eq. (4).

$$\text{Information Loss} = 1 - \frac{N_S}{N_O} \tag{4}$$

2.4   Color Compensation

After estimating information loss, the system applies color compensation to a screenshot in which possible information is detected. This is done by checking information loss: if information loss is bigger than a pre-defined threshold, the system determines that the input screenshot has information loss. The proposed system utilized the color compensation algorithm proposed in [13]. For the completeness of the paper, I briefly explain the algorithm. The color compensation algorithm proposed in [13] replaces a RGB color component users cannot perceive with perceivable color component. Let R, G, B be RGB color component of the input image and R', G' ,B' be RGB color component of the color compensated image. And Eq. (5) defines the relation between R, G, B and R', G', B' if users are assumed to be protanopic.

$$\begin{pmatrix} R' \\ G' \\ B' \end{pmatrix} = \begin{pmatrix} R \\ G \\ R \end{pmatrix} \tag{5}$$

In other words, for protanopic users, RGB color space is transformed into Magenta-Green color space. (Magenta is made by mixing equal amounts of blue and red) Fig. 5 shows the example of color compensation. Each RGB color component value of the left image in Fig. 5 is R = 178, G = 76, B = 47. By applying color compensation, each RGB color component value of the right image becomes R = 178, G = 76, B = 178. If users are assumed to be Deuteranopia, Eq. (6) defines the relation between R, G, B and R', G', B'.

$$\begin{pmatrix} R' \\ G' \\ B' \end{pmatrix} = \begin{pmatrix} R \\ G \\ G \end{pmatrix} \tag{6}$$

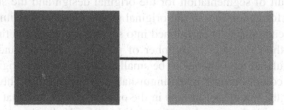

Fig. 5. An example of the color compensation algorithm utilized in the proposed system (Color figure online).

In other words, RGB color space is transformed into Red-Cyan color space. (Cyan is made by mixing equal amounts of blue and green)

3 Experimental Results

For the evaluation of the proposed system, the proposed system was run by an Android smartphone (Samsung Galaxy Note 4). The performance of the proposed system can be varied by the interval of the periodic screenshot and the resolution of the resized screenshot. Table 1 shows the operating time of the proposed system depending on the resolution of the resized screenshot. The resolution of the original screenshot was 1440 × 2560, and 1/2 means half the resolution of the original screenshot, i.e., 720 × 1280. As Table 1 indicates, the operating time was decreased as the resolution of the resized screenshot was decreased. When the screenshot was not resized, it takes about 3 min just for detecting information loss. When the screenshot was resized into one-thirty-second of the original size, it takes 0.13 s for detecting information loss. Note that the computing time for color compensation is constant for every resolution of the screenshot. This is because the resized screenshot is used for information loss detection only and color compensation is applied to the original size of the screenshot. From this experiment, one might think that the screenshot should be resized to one-thirty-second of the original size since it detects information loss the fastest. However, when the resolution of the resized screenshot was too small, the information loss detection algorithm can be unreliable. Hence, we set the resolution of the resized screenshot as 9 0 × 160, which is one-sixteenth of the original size. At this resolution, the operating time of the proposed system was 0.75 s. This means the interval of the periodic screenshot should be longer than 0.75 s. In this paper, we set the interval as 1 s. As the interval was set as 1 s, the proposed system currently can cover static or less dynamic contents such as news and blog contents.

Table 1. The operating time of the proposed system depending on the resolution of the resized screenshot (seconds)

	Resolution					
	Original	1/2	1/4	1/8	1/16	1/32
Information loss detection	185.24	49.54	11.75	2.54	0.60	0.13
Color compensation	0.15	0.15	0.15	0.15	0.15	0.15
Total	185.39	49.69	11.90	2.69	0.75	0.28

After setting the interval of the periodic screenshot and the resolution of the resized screenshot, the proposed system was tested by using one image, one mobile application [14], and one website [15]. Figure 6 shows the test images. And the threshold for information loss was set to 0.5. When the proposed system is running, a notification message is generated at the top of the screen when possible information loess is estimated. And the system provides a color-compensated image when a user clicks the notification message. Figure 6 also shows the process. In case of the test

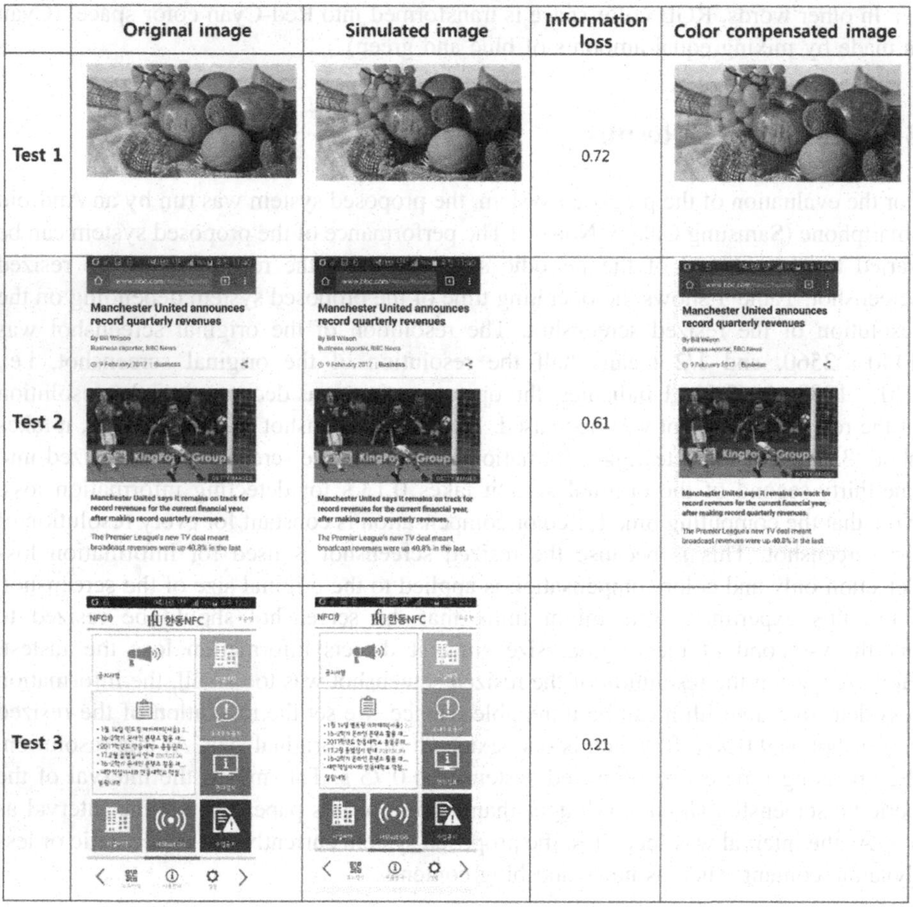

	Original image	Simulated image	Information loss	Color compensated image
Test 1			0.72	
Test 2			0.61	
Test 3			0.21	

Fig. 6. Simulate results. Test 1 is tested by using an image, test 2 is tested by a website, and test 3 is tested by a mobile application.

image and the test website, information loss was detected, and color compensation was performed. However, for the test mobile application, information loss was not detected and color compensation was not performed.

4 Conclusion

In this paper, a color compensation system for the color blind which can minimize information loss is proposed. The proposed system is operated in a mobile device, and it consists of automatic information loss detection and color compensation. For information loss detection, the proposed system periodically takes a screenshot. Then the simulated model of the screenshot is generated and applies the equivalent segmentation algorithm to the screenshot and the simulated model. By analyzing the number of segmented groups in each image, the information loss is finally estimated.

When information loss is detected, color compensation with inexpensive computational cost is applied to the screenshot. As the proposed method automatically detects information loss and color compensation is applied adaptively, I believe that the proposed system can prevent the color blind from missing information expressed by colors.

As future works, a more elaborate information loss algorithm will be studied. And a color compensation algorithm which compensates colors of an image depending of the contents of the image will be studied. Lastly, a more computationally inexpensive algorithm will be studied so that the proposed system can cover more dynamic contents.

References

1. http://blogs.adobe.com/adobeillustrator/2009/04/new_tools_for_color_making_you_1.html
2. Hwang, S.S.: Robust design: an image analysis tool for analyzing information loss caused by viewers and environments. In: Marcus, A. (ed.) DUXU 2016. LNCS, vol. 9748, pp. 159–166. Springer, Cham (2016). doi:10.1007/978-3-319-40406-6_15
3. Han, D.I., Park, J.S., Choi, J.H.: A novel color transfer method for protanopia and deutanopia using the enhanced daltonization process. In: Proceeding of the Fall Conference of the Institute of Electronics and Information Engineers, pp. 201–202 (2009)
4. Han, D.I., Park, J.S., Choi, J.H.: A novel color conversion method for color vision deficiency using color segmentation. J. Inst. Electron. Eng. Korea 48(5), 37–44 (2011)
5. Kim, H.J., Cho, J.Y., Ko, S.J.: Re-coloring methods using the HSV color space for people with the red-green color vision deficiency. J. Inst. Electron. Eng. Korea 50(3), 237–238 (2013)
6. Park, J.S., Han, D.I.: An enhanced color conversion method for color blindness people using the dynamic color transformation. In: Proceeding of the Summer Conference of the Institute of Electronics and Information Engineers, pp. 176–177 (2010)
7. http://enchroma.com/
8. https://youtu.be/hAcHSwmGBMY
9. http://www.imagovision.co.kr/
10. https://support.google.com/accessibility/android/answer/6151850?hl=en
11. Brettel, H., Viénot, F., Mollon, J.D.: Computerized simulation of color appearance for dichromats. J. Opt. Soc. Am. 14(10), 2647–2655 (1997)
12. Gonzalez, R.C., Woods, R.E.: Digital Image Processing, 3rd edn. Pearson, London (2008)
13. Kwak, K.H., Jun, Y.C., Choi, S.I., Shin, H.J., Hwang, S.S.: A mobile color-compensating application using RGB color compensation algorithm. J. Korea Multimedia Soc. 19(12), 1936–1942 (2016)
14. Handong Global University: Handong Global University Smart Campus Application (Version 2.1.1) [Mobile Application Software]. https://play.google.com/store
15. http://www.bbc.com/news/business-38904511

Research on the Form Design of Mini Car in Perceptual Consumption Times

Xinhui Kang[✉], Minggang Yang, Weiwei Yang, and Yixiang Wu

School of Art, Design and Media,
East China University of Science and Technology,
NO. 130, Meilong Road, Xuhui District, Shanghai 200237, China
nbukxh@163.com

Abstract. Except for the basic function to replace walk, current customers also desire mini car can reflect the trends of the time. So it has been an important consideration for enterprises to meet customers' emotional needs. The research will understand the preference for mini car production among different age groups of consumers in depth by Miryoku engineering theory. Evaluation Grid method provides a way to analyze attractive factors of the products among related researches on Miryoku engineering, which extracts the median original evaluation (customers' demands), the lower specific reason (product details) and the upper abstract reason (users' emotions) by deep interviews to experts and thus sorts out the structure network map of the evaluation of the products from respondents. At last, the quantification theory I establishes a functional relationship between the abstract upper emotions and the specific design details in the kansei data, and analyzes the influence weight among the attractive factors. Four attractive factors related to mini car were concluded. Among such attractive factors as "fashionable", "delicate" and "elegant", red car color maximally stimulates the consumer's positive emotions while the thick car body has the greatest negative correlation with the "light" attractive factor. The innovation method proposed by this research can rapidly obtain user's needs, shorten the overall operation steps and improve the development efficiency. Meanwhile, the method can be effectively used in other industrial product designs.

Keywords: Product design · Kansei engineering · Miryoku engineering · Quantification theory type I · Minicar · Form design

1 Introduction

Car has a long history, the French who liked to use gas invented the gas car, the British who were proud of Watt invented the steam car driven by a steam engine. It was the internal-combustion engine, which produced power by the detonation between the volatile fuel and air, started the car times indeed. Consumers' needs on car were only the function of instead of walking during the material poverty period, even buying cars was an entertainment of the high-society people. Ordinary people have had cars with the development of modern science and technology as well as the improvement of quality of living. Customers choose their favorite style among various car categories on the market according to the work demand, interests, personality characteristics and

© Springer International Publishing AG 2017
A. Marcus and W. Wang (Eds.): DUXU 2017, Part I, LNCS 10288, pp. 258–271, 2017.
DOI: 10.1007/978-3-319-58634-2_20

values. The function difference among new products introduced by major manufacturers has been increasing ambiguous. Fashionable appearance, comfortable driving experience have been the key factors of successful marketing. As household bulky item, car reflects or symbolizes the status of consumers. Customers regard the products as their own specialty to represent themselves.

The consumers behavior is divided into 3 basic stages by famous marketing master Kotler Philip [1]: the first stage is the consumption of amount that people pursue the merchandise they can afford to buy and buy; the second is the consumption stage of quality, which means seeking genuine goods at a fair price, distinctive and high-quality merchandise; the third is perceptual consumption stage which pays attention to the emotional experience of shopping and interpersonal communication, it takes the personal preference as the standard of purchase decision and gives more emphasis on "emotional value" than "functional value". Therefore, in the age of perceptual consumption, everyone has the tendency of subjective perceptual consumption. They hope to enjoy the shopping process. They pursue grade, status and a sense of pleasure from the heart. In recent years, mini car has been paid attention to and loved by more and more people under the environmental-friendly design concept, their fashionable and sunny style especially caters to the aesthetic taste and cultural quality of young group.

Due to the features of flexibility and agility and compact appearance, The mini car (Fig. 1) can meet the consumer's various requirements such as work and leisure. Different from the mechanical and calm appearance of commercial vehicles, the appearance of mini car can be freely matched according to the preference of users to achieve easy replacement as phone covers. As household transportation mini car is very suitable for mini life, housewives can buy food, go shopping, pick up kids and take them on short distance driving on the mini car through the mini street. It can effectively relieve a serious problems such as difficult driving and hard parking in the first-tier cities which have the problems of traffic jam. At the same time, with the increase of life cost and work competitive pressure, urban white-collar workers can purchase their favorite transport in the mini-car market where the price is relatively low and the quality is fine. After one day's tired work, stylish and cute appearance of mini car can relieve the user's inner pressure. Meanwhile, the rising oil prices and pressure brought by family expenses have opened up new market demand for mini car. Customers' demands on products have been improved from the satisfaction of material to psychological and emotional levels. The first impression of the new product appearance greatly affects the consumer's purchase preferences. The form, color and material of new product reflect the appearance style of product, the basic function and operation and brand influence, so the attractive appearance of the mini car will lead to consumer recognition and emotional resonance. Therefore, how mini car design can attract captious consumer and exploring the inner attractive factors of the customers have been focused on research by the car designers and related practitioners.

This study mainly discusses the consumer's preferences for the shape of mini car in the age of perceptual consumption and establishes new emotional needs of consumers in the new era. By using Kansei Engineering methods user's feeling and emotion can be converted into specific design specification. The Kansei Engineering technology which originated in Japan in 1970s can provide reference in the early stage of new product's development and design [2]. At last, the abstract upper emotional vocabulary

Fig. 1. Smart (source:http://china.smart.com/)

and lower specific design elements in the experimental data were analyzed using quantification theory type I. In the research, the functional relation between the customers' emotional intention and design elements was concluded, in addition, the weight relation of influence among attractive factors was analyzed. The paper expected to provide the related industries with mini car and designers a designing reference to improve the attraction to customers when developing new products.

2 Literature Review

2.1 Kansei Engineering

Kansei Engineering was developed as a consumer-oriented technology for new product development. It is defined as "translating technology of a consumer's feeling and image for a product into design elements" [3]. In 1998, the Japanese Institute of Kansei engineering was established, and the Miryoku engineering became part of it. Miryoku engineering was a research developed by Masao Inui and Japanese scholar Junichiro Sanui in referring to the book The Psychology of Personal Constructs written by clinical psychologist Kelly, which provides the designers a method to make the customers' fuzzy perceptual cognition become specific when executing product development [4]. It was understood that some ways to choose products by customers and the experience of successful product design can catch the products' attractive essence, thus a design full of attraction would be created. The method clearly discussed the similarity or difference relationship in the comparison between object A and B mainly by individual interviews, thus the individual qualities of target objects were sorted out. The attraction factors will be the key points to successful products if they can be obtained in the products design and development as well as applied and transformed to actual product aspects, so the extraction of charm has been worked on finding by many designers in the design process.

The Evaluation Grid Method provides an analytic approach to product attractive factors with theory basis among the related researches in Miryoku Engineering, providing stimulation according to the category of the theme and in the form of depth interviews to know the customers' feeling about the products' charm, making the participants have obvious feeling difference after the comparison of preference degree among participants, so the participants' original concept to the subject will be known, thus leading to the participants' more definite analyzing the original evaluation concept and connecting its upper abstract concept with lower specific description, and then a network diagram of participants' evaluation structure of products will be sorted out.

The theoretical basis of the Miryoku Engineering is mainly in the following three points: basic theory, modeling (Research and analysis) and design [6]. As shown in Table 1.

Table 1. Theoretical basis of Miryoku Engineering (Sources: Ujigawa, 2000)

Area	Peculiarity	Concept and theory	Method
Basic Theories	Definition		
	Recognition	Inclusive recognition	
		Pattern recognition	
	Learning	Fashion, Character goods	
	Value system	Reference groups	
Modeling	Structure identification	Depth interview	Evaluation grid method
			Paired comparison
	Parameter identification	Composite effect	Regression analysis
			Conjoint analysis
	Segmentation	Cluster analysis	
	Forecasting	simulation	
Design	Planning	On-site thinking	Scenario marking
	Design Strategy	Positioning	Cognitive Map
	Materializing	Prototype creation	User participation

2.2 Quantification Theory Type I

Theory of quantification, as a branch of multivariate analysis, began in the 1950s. Originally it was only applied in "sociology of measurement". With the extensive application of electronic computers after the sixties, it was increasingly applied in the field of natural science [7]. Japanese scholar Chikio Hayashi first invented four non-parametric theory of quantification, which can easily handle quantitative data by multivariate analysis [8]. Quantification theory type I are extensively applied in relevant researches of Kansei engineering. Designers regard consumers' perceptual evaluation as criterion variable and design elements as explanatory variables respectively. The relationship between the two variables is established by the regression equation, which guides the creative workers' designing. To improve customers' satisfaction, Schütte and Eklund [9] took the rocker switch on the vehicle as example to describe the product areas from the physiological and semantic perspective by kansei engineering method, meanwhile collected the data from 71 persons to carry out linear regression analysis in the dimensional matrix of quantification theory I. The results provided design reference to the three major car manufacturers in Sweden. Qiu and Omura [10] applied quantification theory I and factor analysis to carry out perceptual evaluation experiment on name card design as well as introduced the establishment of the emotion design system by the characteristic combiner automatically generating design combination. On the basis of quantification theory I and principal component analysis. Bahn and Lee [11] proposed developing and using an emotional design framework to identify important emotional characteristics of users and systematically integrate them into product design attributes. Zhang and Vertiz [12] proposed that automobile interior coordination has got more and more attention by customers. Kansei engineering is an emotional way to quantify the relationship between design elements and customers' emotion. This paper continued the previous research findings of indoor coordination of commercial trucks as well as investigated and surveyed the user's emotions in the several visible elements of commercial truck by category classification method. Quantification theory I was applied in this paper to describe the relationship between visible kansei image and design elements. The results showed that the truck driver's "elegant" and "preference" feelings are strongly affected by the trimmed material, shape, color, window size and map bags. The results also showed the difference between the different emotions of the truck drivers and design engineers.

3 Research Subject

Mini-car (Fig. 1) is an important branch and application of the automobile family and it plays an important role under the social background of energy shortage and environmental pollution. Therefore, this case study takes the front styling of mini car as example. With the gradual maturity of basic technology and manufacture, the function difference of different cars is getting smaller and smaller. Consumers shift the focus of attention from the function to the emotion. This enables users to pay more attention to the appearance of the car and psychological and emotional satisfaction. Mini car with trendy appearance can better realize the convenience of urbanism.

4 Research Method and Process

The research combined qualitative with quantitative method to explore the form design of mini car. The experiment can be divided into two stages. In the first stage, ten high-involvement experts were selected to determine the original reasons of preference and aversion by the evaluation grid method of Miryoku engineering. The abstract upper factors and specific lower factors were asked to sort out the structural map of evaluation. In the second stage, the quantitative linear regression method was used to analyze the influence relationship and the weights of the factors of various strata in the previous stage.

4.1 Miryoku Engineering Method

4.1.1 The Collection of Experimental Samples

As the size of mini car is big, the pictures were presented to the respondents in order to collect the true feelings of consumers. 18 clear mini cars with a front 45° angle were selected from network, magazines, related journals and other channels. Meanwhile, the background color and emblem mark were removed by photoshop in case of the emotional and visual interference. The picture size is 21cm × 30cm (Fig. 2).

Fig. 2. Revised picture of the mini car sample

4.1.2 The Selection of Respondents

The collected sample pictures in observation are not enough to evaluate the preferences of mini car from the perspective of consumers. The driving experience, age, the plan and wish to buy mini car were very focused on in selecting respondents. The following five experts were determined after considering the life background of the consumers (Table 2) (Fig. 3).

Table 2. Group of tested experts

Name	Age	Profession	Driving experience
Miss Wang	24	Animation designer	3 years
Miss Qiao	33	Real estate marketing manager	11 years
Mr Zeng	29	Dress designer	7 years
Mr Fan	37	Enterprise white-collar	5 years
Miss xie	28	College teacher	5 years

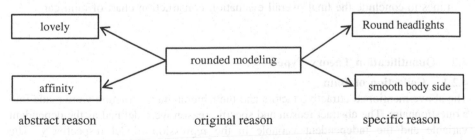

Fig. 3. A single evaluation project construction chart

4.1.3   The Procedure of Evaluation Grid Method

1 Interview equipment and personnel preparation
After determining mini car as research theme, the interview samples such as product pictures, text were printed and then placed on the table. There were one main questioner, one record person and one photographic video person.
2 Identifying the original evaluation items
The respondents were interviewed in-depth individually with the above-mentioned data. The respondents were asked to compare 18 mini cars and explain the original reasons for preference. For example:
Ask 1: "What do you think of Sample 13 as compared with Sample 17?"
Answer: "I prefer sample 17."
Ask 2: "why do you prefer sample 17?"
Answer: "because it's rounded"
3 Asking the relationship between the upper and lower levels
After determining the original reasons for preference, the upper abstract reason (Ladder up) and the specific details characteristics of its composition (Ladder down) were asked.
(1) Ladder up: The upper abstract reason of the original evaluation project "rounded modeling" obtained from the second procedure was unceasingly asked.
Ask 3: "why do you prefer "rounded modeling"
Answer: because "rounded modeling" looks very lovely and affine
(2) Ladder down: Basing on "rounded modeling", the respondents were unceasingly asked the specific design elements to analyze the physical property for reference.
Ask 4: What design factors make you feel "rounded modeling"?
Answer: "the smooth body side" and "round car headlights"
A median original evaluation project was sorted out in the above two steps. A three-level architecture of upper-level abstract reason and lower-level concrete reason is in the following.
4 Sorting out personal evaluation construction chart
All the evaluation construction projects of the respondents can be asked in turn according to above steps. A complete evaluation construction chart of each respondent can be concluded by three-tier connection and arrangement.
5 Sorting out the overall evaluation construction chart
Simplifying and classifying the personal evaluation construction chart of all respondents. Gathering the overlapping vocabulary and calculating the overlapping times to conclude the final overall evaluation construction chart of mini car.

4.2   Quantification Theory Type I

4.2.1   Collection of Data

The above-mentioned attractive factors and their hierarchical structure were made into a questionnaire. The abstract reason and specific reason were defined as the dependent variable and the independent variable in the regression model respectively. The semantic vocabulary of the abstract reason is determined to be "fashionable" "refined" "elegant" and "dexterous". A point table with five orders from –2 to 2 was carried out by SD semantics [13] to quantify the customers' psychology feelings of the 18 mini cars. Design items are the body color, body proportions and car headlamps. The design category was determined as Table 3. The questionnaires were distributed in the network, and 100 data were collected. Finally, the final score was perceptually evaluated by averaging method. The perceptual evaluation matrix shown in Table 4 was obtained.

Table 3. Classification of design elements

Item	Category		
Body color (X1)	Blue (C11)	Red (C12)	Gray (C13)
Body proportions (X2)	Square modeling (C21)	Mellow modeling (C22)	Honest modeling (C23)
Headlamps (X3)	Round (C31)	Square (C32)	Organic form (C33)

The main reasons why the customers prefer mini car as well as the weight relation between the attractive factors and the design elements were calculated by Quantification theory I. Category score, complex correlation coefficient, coefficient of determination and partial correlation coefficient can be concluded by statistical analysis. Their calculation methods and representative significances will be briefly described in the following.

(1) Category score: category score are on behalf of the relationship between the lower specific design elements and the median original evaluation. High value means the lower has a higher impact on the median. Meanwhile, the category score has positive and negative points. Positive values have positive impact on the median while negative values may have a negative impact. The calculation is as (1). Assume that the following linear model is followed by the reaction between the baseline variable and each item and category.

$$y_i = \sum_{j=1}^{m} \sum_{k=1}^{r_j} \delta_i(j,k) b_{jk} + \varepsilon_i, i = 1, 2, \ldots, n. \tag{1}$$

b_{jk} is a constant term which only depends on category of project. ε_i is a random error in the i sample

(2) Multiple correlation coefficient R: The multiple correlation coefficient represents the overall influence of multiple variables on a dependent variable. Its value represents the correlation, which is used to measure the accuracy of the prediction. Sugiyama [14] proposed the relationship between the R coefficient and the reliability in the relevant research. As in Table 5:

Table 4. Kansei valuation matrix

Sample		Design elements									Evaluation value of kansei vocabulary			
NO.	picture	Body color (X1)			Body proportion (X2)			Car headlamp (X3)			fashionable	delicate	elegant	Dexterous
		C_{11}	C_{12}	C_{13}	C_{21}	C_{22}	C_{23}	C_{31}	C_{32}	C_{33}				
1		1	0	0	0	1	0	0	0	1	2.38	2.75	2	3.75
2		0	1	0	1	0	0	0	1	0	3.25	3.75	3.13	3.13
3		1	0	0	0	0	1	0	0	1	2.25	2.5	2.38	2.13
⋮		⋮	⋮	⋮	⋮	⋮	⋮	⋮	⋮	⋮	⋮	⋮	⋮	⋮
18		0	0	1	1	0	0	0	0	1	2.13	2.63	2.38	2.38

Table 5. The relationship between R value and reliability

R value	Reliability
0.00–0.19	Predictive values showed a low correlation
0.20–0.39	Predicted values are correlated
0.40–0.69	Predictive values are strongly correlated
0.70–1.00	Predictive values are strongly correlated

The accuracy of the prediction can be measured by the multiple correlation coefficient of the sample R (namely the correlation between the predicted value and the measured value), which can be calculated by formula (2).

$$r = \frac{\sigma_{\hat{y}y}}{\sigma_{\hat{y}}\sigma_y} = \frac{\sigma_{\hat{y}}}{\sigma_y} = \sqrt{\frac{\sum_{i=1}^{n}(\hat{y}_i - \bar{y})^2}{\sum_{i=1}^{n}(y_i - \bar{y})^2}} \tag{2}$$

(3) The coefficient of determination (the square of the multiple correlation coefficient): The coefficient of determination is a modified value, which presents the interpretation amount of the total variation and is an important indicator to measure whether the forecasting ability of the model and the regression equation are effective or not. In this research, it is the degree of the charm of mini cars being explained by the abstract adjectives. Higher value means the charm of mini cars can be more strongly affected by this feeling, the probability of occurrence of the prediction error can be also reduced.

(4) Partial correlation coefficient: higher partial correlation coefficient means this category effects more on the upper abstract vocabulary and the median primitive evaluation contributes more to the adjectives. In order to calculate the partial correlation coefficient, each item was regarded as a variable and formula 3 was regarded as the quantitative data of the i sample in the j item. In this way the correlation coefficient between an item and another item, item and the dependent variable as well as the correlation matrix R can be concluded, on the basis of which the partial correlation coefficient can be calculated.

$$x_i^{(j)} = \sum_{k=1}^{r_j} \delta_i(j,k)\hat{b}_{jk} \quad i = 1, 2, \ldots, n; j = 1, 2, \ldots, m \tag{3}$$

5   Analysis and Results

5.1   Hierarchy Architecture of Mini Car

Five experts expressed their own preferences for mini car, as well as the upper abstract reasons and lower specific reasons for preference by Evaluation Grid Method (EGM) of Miryoku engineering. The overall evaluation construction figure after sorting is as Fig. 4. It can be found that "body color and texture", "body ratio" and "car headlights" are more likely to arouse consumers. Among the original reasons of "body color", "beautiful red", "colorful", "distinct color block" and "bright texture" were analyzed by customers. The upper abstract reasons of "body color and texture" include "fashion", "athletic" and "lovely". In the second stage of the experiment, the abstract reasons were transformed into kansei vocabulary to score the high-involvement group. The original and specific reasons of the evaluation construction chart were translated into item and category respectively. The importance degree and relationship of the two were analyzed by quantification theory type I.

5.2   Quantification Theory Type I Analysis

The appearance charm design of mini car was analyzed by quantification theory I. Quantification theory type I is a commonly used research tool that transforms kansei image into design elements. The established mathematic model predicts the kansei

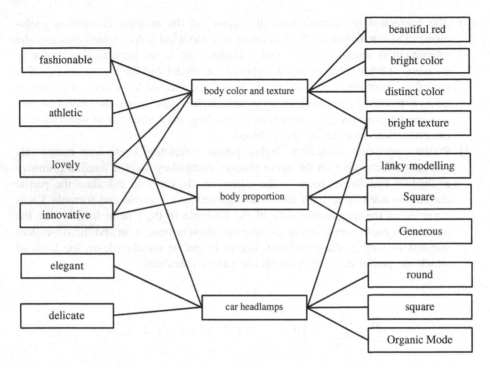

Fig. 4. The overall evaluation construction chart of the experts

evaluation of consumers more accurately. 100 people were surveyed in the network and 87 valid questionnaires were collected. The effective rate of the questionnaire was 87%. The corresponding complex correlation coefficient, constant term, partial correlation coefficient and category score of various perceptual adjectives of mini car are shown in Fig. 5. R is the complex correlation coefficient between the predicted and measured values. R^2 is the decision coefficient. R and R^2 of "fashionable" is 0.8369 and 0.7 respectively. R and R^2 of "delicate" is 0.8681 and 0.7536 respectively. R and R^2 of "elegant" is 0.8677 and 0.7529 respectively. R and R^2 of "dexterous" is 0.6626 and 0.439 respectively. It can be found that the first three adjectives have a very strong correlation while the last adjective has a stronger correlation by comparing the relationship between R value and the reliability. Consequently, the experimental data is true and reliable.

5.2.1 Analysis on "Fashionable" Attractive Factor

According to the calculation results of quantification theory I, the biggest partial correlation coefficient of "body color" is 0.8054, which shows the greatest influence on "fashionable" of mini car. "Body color" includes "blue", "red" and "gray". "Red" scored the highest, which indicates that red body color strongest stimulates the customers' "fashionable" emotion. While gray mini car category scored the lowest, indicating gray color may have a negative impact on the customers' "fashionable" emotion.

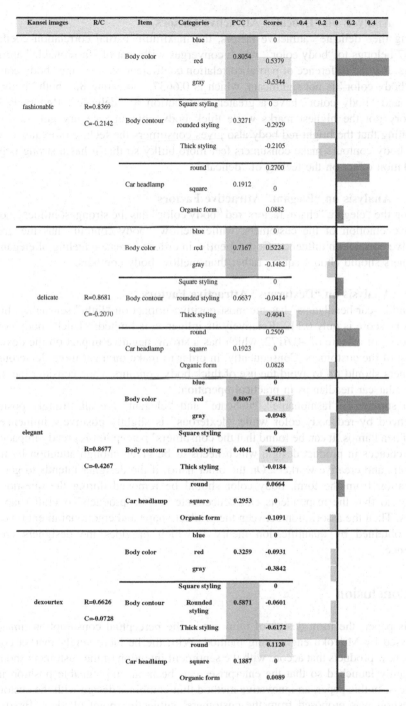

Kansei images	R/C	Item	Categories	PCC	Scores	-0.4	-0.2	0	0.2	0.4
		Body color	blue	0.8054	0					
			red		0.5379					
			gray		-0.5344					
fashionable	R=0.8369	Body contour	Square styling	0.3271	0					
	C=-0.2142		rounded styling		-0.2929					
			Thick styling		-0.2105					
		Car headlamp	round	0.1912	0.2700					
			square		0					
			Organic form		0.0882					
		Body color	blue	0.7167	0					
			red		0.5224					
			gray		-0.1482					
delicate	R=0.8681	Body contour	Square styling	0.6637	0					
	C=-0.2070		rounded styling		-0.0414					
			Thick styling		-0.4041					
		Car headlamp	round	0.1923	0.2509					
			square		0					
			Organic form		0.0828					
		Body color	blue	0.8067	0					
			red		0.5418					
			gray		-0.0948					
elegant	R=0.8677	Body contour	Square styling	0.4041	0					
	C=-0.4267		roundedstyling		-0.2098					
			Thick styling		-0.0184					
		Car headlamp	round	0.2953	0.0664					
			square		0					
			Organic form		-0.1091					
		Body color	blue	0.3259	0					
			red		-0.0931					
			gray		-0.3842					
dexourtex	R=0.6626	Body contour	Square styling	0.5871	0					
	C=-0.0728		Rounded styling		-0.0601					
			Thick styling		-0.6172					
		Car headlamp	round	0.1887	0.1120					
			square		0					
			Organic form		0.0089					

Fig. 5. Weight score of four attractive factors

5.2.2   Analysis on "Delicate" Attractive Factors

Among the "delicate" attractive factors, the maximum partial correlation coefficient 0.7167 belongs to "body color", which converges with that of "fashionable" attractive factors. But the difference of partial correlation coefficient between the "body contour" and "body color" is not significant, which is 0.6637, indicating that both "body contour" and "body color" have a greater contribution to "delicate". Red body color category got the highest marks while thick body contour category got the lowest, indicating that the bright red body also gives consumers the feeling of exquisite while thick body contours make consumers feel more bulky so that it has a strong negative correlation effect on the feeling of "delicate".

5.2.3   Analysis on "Elegant" Attractive Factors

Among the "elegant" charm factors, red "body color" has the strongest influence on the positive emotion of the customers, while mellow "body contour" has the greatest negative correlation influence. Consequently, in order to create a feeling of elegant, the designers should choose square rather than mellow body contours.

5.2.4   Analysis on "Dexterous" Attractive Factors

"Round", "car headlamps" has the most positive impact on "light" sensuality, but the category score is only 0,112. Relatively its influence is limited. "Thick" body contour category got a score of –0.6172, which has a strong negative impact on the dexterous feeling of the customers. Consequently, in order to make mini car more dexterous, the designers should try to avoid the use of thick body contours while consider the design of circular car headlamps in practical operation.

In summary, "fashionable", "delicate" and "elegant" are all strongly positively influenced by red body color while "dexterous" is slightly positively influenced by round headlamps. It can be found that the consumers' perception is greatly impacted by color choices in product design, which needs to be given enough attention by manufacturers and creative workers. On the other hand, if the designer intends to get more inspiration from the form, body color should be removed during the questionnaire survey so that the respondents can concentrate on the products' overall shape and details. Then the association between the product shape and emotional intention can be fully obtained by quantification theory I, which provides the designers creative reference.

6   Conclusion

In this paper, the form design of mini car in the perceptual consumption times was discussed by Miryoku engineering method. With the he increasingly market competition, new products that accord with the sentiment intention of the customers should be constantly launched so that the enterprises can be in an impregnable position in the business. In this paper, an innovative method that combines design with the customers' suggestion was proposed from the customers' subjective point of view. Firstly, the upper abstract, median original and lower specific reasons were analyzed by evaluation grid method of Miryoku engineering. Four attractive factors such as "fashionable", "delicate", "elegant" and "dexterous" were concluded. Then the influence degree of the median original reason (item) and the lower specific reason (category) was connected by statistical method, and the corresponding relation between the sensible vocabulary and the design elements is established by quantification theory I, which provides the designers with theoretical reference. With the customers' emotional needs become more and more earnester, this research method can effectively increase the market share of new products and reduce the listing risk, and also applies to the research and development of other industrial products.

References

1. Kotler, P.: Principles of Marketing. China Machine Press, Beijing (2013)
2. Nagamachi, M.: Kansei engineering as a powerful consumer-oriented technology for product development. Appl. Ergon. **33**(3), 289–294 (2002)
3. Nagamachi, M.: Kansei engineering: a new ergonomic consumer-oriented technology for product development. Int. J. Ind. Ergon. **15**(1), 3–11 (1995)
4. Asano, H.: Practice of Miryoku Engineering. Kaibundo, Tokyo (2001)
5. Sanui, J.: Visualization of users' requirements: introduction of the evaluation grid method. In: Proceedings of the 3rd Design & Decision Support Systems in Architecture & Urban Planning Conference, vol. 1, pp. 365–374 (1996)
6. Miryoku Engineering Forum, Miryoku Engineering. Kaibundo (Japanese), Tokyo (1992)
7. Dong, W., Zhou, G.: Quantitative Theory and its Application. Jilin People's Publishing House, ChangChun (1979)
8. Hayashi, C.: On the quantification of qualitative data from the mathematico-statistical point of view. Ann. Inst. Stat. Math. **2**(1), 35–47 (1950)
9. Schütte, S., Eklund, J.: Design of rocker switches for work-vehicles—an application of Kansei engineering. Appl. Ergon. **36**(5), 557–567 (2005)
10. Qiu, Q., Omura, K.: Developing a document creating system for affective design: a case study in card design. Kansei Eng. Int. **15**, 91–99 (2015)
11. Bahn, S., Lee, C., Nam, S., Yun, H.: Incorporating affective customer needs for luxuriousness into product design attributes. Hum. Factors Ergon. Manufact. **19**(2), 105–127 (2009)
12. Zhang, L., Vertiz, A.: Kansei engineering application on commercial truck interior design harmony. Soc. Automot. Eng. **109**(2), 514–520 (2000)
13. Osgood, C.E., Suci, G.J., Tannenbaum, P.H.: The Measurement of Meaning. University of Illinois Press, Champaign (1957)
14. Sugiyama, K., et al.: The Basic for Survey and Analysis by Excel. Kaibundo Publishing, Japan (1996)

The Effects of Website White Space
on University Students

Yu-Chun Liu[1,2(✉)] and Chih-Hsiang Ko[1]

[1] National Taiwan University of Science and Technology,
Taipei City 106, Taiwan
kirstieliu@gmail.com, linko@mail.ntust.edu.tw
[2] China University of Science and Technology, Taipei City 115, Taiwan

Abstract. The purpose of this study was to explore university students' web browsing experience, including usability preference, aesthetics and perceived value. The experimental samples were a set of four web pages with 45% and 55% of white space and from narrow to wide spacing. Thirty-five participants aged between 18 and 24 years were recruited by purposeful sampling to conduct the operational evaluation. It was interesting to note that even though the samples were centered around 50% of white space as previous studies suggested, three questions revealed significant differences: "I found the web page unnecessarily complex," "the layout appears too dense," "this web page would help me to feel acceptable." The result also indicated that most participants preferred more white space, which could help designers to design web pages more accurately in accordance with user preferences.

Keywords: White space · Web pages · Usability · Aesthetics · Perceived value

1 Introduction

The user's web browsing experience can be affected by various visual design elements such as font, font size, color, column, spacing and layout, which are directly proportional to the amount of information on the page. Each user group's acceptable amount of information loading is different and is limited by physical and psychological constraints. Too much page content may present obstacles to users.

The amount of information on web pages is related to usability, aesthetics and perceived value. There were considerable studies on subjective preference assessment of web design, such as visibility, accessibility [1], aesthetics, satisfaction, pleasurability, attractiveness, information complexity, performance, working memory, and visual fatigue [2–14]. The variables of these studies were design elements such as font style [15], column width [16], proportion [2], color [17, 18], symmetry [19, 20], icon [13, 21, 22], screen size [13] and length of table [23].

White space is also known as negative space and is accounted for a part of the web layout. It is usually an unobtrusive blank area. By measuring the amount of white space, one would be able to observe the complexity of web pages and the amount of information. Therefore, white space is an important factor on web pages browsing. This study explored white space in order to provide more effective, concise and pragmatic recommendations for web design.

© Springer International Publishing AG 2017
A. Marcus and W. Wang (Eds.): DUXU 2017, Part I, LNCS 10288, pp. 272–283, 2017.
DOI: 10.1007/978-3-319-58634-2_21

2 Literature Review

There were many studies focused on evaluation of web pages browsing experience. For examples, readability was influenced by the amount of words and white space [24]. White space was associated with aesthetics [3]. Aesthetic web pages accounted for 90% of web reliability. White space on web pages and its association with usability and artistry was analyzed and explored [25]. The relevance between white space of advertisement and consumer perception was discussed from a semantic perspective [26]. Three kinds of white space were used to study the aesthetics, efficiency, utility and satisfaction of web pages. The results suggested that the usability of a website was impacted negatively when white space increased over 50% [3].

2.1 White Space

White space is known as negative space, which occupies a part of the web layout and is usually an unattractive blank. There are also some in-between areas that can be called white space, such as lines, pictures, texts, graphics, edges, fonts, paragraphs, and color blocks. These are the space for reading content easily [27, 28]. There are other situations that create the feeling of white space, such as the same background color and a set combination of images. White space is not directly related to "white background" [29]. "White" is not mentioned as white color, but white means "sensibility" [30]. In addition, the advertisement area can be seen as white space by users [31, 32].

There are a lot of studies on web design and performance. The performance issue of web design can be determined by variables such as "position of main visual images," "ratio of texts and images," "composition," "text size," "layout," "frames," "types of hyperlink," "number of colors" and "background colors". Each variables are related to the white space of web pages [3, 25, 26, 31–33].

2.2 Usability

Usability is an important element in the field of web design. It is all web designers' responsibility to transfer information from specific web pages to users [34]. Sometimes, users feel frustrated while gaining information on the Internet. The process or website is not designed for user experiences could be the reason. It does not correspond to users' communicative and cognitive abilities [35]. "Usability" is a concept that focuses on building an easy-to-use web interface [21, 27, 36–39]. Inexperienced users and experienced users have different preferences [40]. The perception of usability is also influenced by users with different backgrounds [34]. People with disabilities may have more specific needs. Designers need to analyze the actual needs of the disabled so that they could adapt to information technology [41, 42]. Poor design of website makes users difficult to search information [43], and even harder to receive content from the website [44].

The state of people receiving and digesting information from the outside world is called "information load" [45]. "Information overload" occurred when the amount of information exceeds the limitation of people's processing capacity [46, 47]. In the era of information explosion, there are many anxious people concerning so much information that needs to be absorbed. While information overload is a common problem that becomes more and more serious, a variety of tools has been developed to simply information. For example, there are tools that summarize articles automatically to rescue people from information flows. "Summly" is one of the tools that summarizes text, websites, and documents from vast information. In addition, "Readability" is another tool that is built as a Google Chrome plugin. It can enhance the comfort and readability of web pages browsing. Yahoo plans to develop a homepage for the elderly with other universal design projects. These attempts allow users to browse the Internet more effectively.

2.3 Aesthetics

Visual aesthetics has been shown to critically affect a variety of constructs such as perceived usability, satisfaction, and pleasure [3, 5]. The aesthetic appearance of user interface and its influence on users' impressions and performance has long been neglected in the field of human-computer interaction [20]. In fact, visual aesthetics plays an important role in users' evaluations of IT artifacts and in their attitudes toward interactive systems [48]. When the same content is presented using different levels of aesthetic treatment, the content with a higher aesthetic treatment is judged as having higher credibility [44]. Symmetry of compositional elements significantly affects users' aesthetic ratings of interfaces [19].

Users can generate a first impression of a web page in a short period of time and that impression has effect on their subsequent behaviors [49]. One of the factors that may influence users to stay or go is the page aesthetics [44]. Visual clarity and visual richness are two important aesthetic dimensions. Visual clarity refers to clean, clear, and symmetrical designs; visual richness refers to creativity and originality aspects of websites [50]. The degree of visual complexity is also an important indicator of aesthetic preference, and people prefer a moderate level of visual complexity [51]. Responding to his recommendation about the amount of information, the moderate amount of information conveyed by the website allowed the eyes feeling comfortable without visual burdens and were generally more receptive [52].

Aesthetically appealing websites received higher ratings of perceived usability and trustworthiness than non-aesthetic websites. The website scoring high on expressive aesthetics shows a similar pattern of results to classical aesthetics [53]. The perception of complexity is highly subjective but may be reliably measured. Understanding the complexity of web pages as perceived subjectively by users is important to better design of user interface [54].

2.4 Perceived Value

Web pages are mostly relevant to business purposes. Whether web design could bring people a sense of value or not is related to whether consumers feel the value of goods.

The difference between perceived value and satisfaction is that the former is the feeling before buying and the latter is the evaluation after purchasing or using. Therefore, perceived value is more applicable to the Internet generation. It could be the basis for assessing the customer's feeling of goods or services on the web page before buying or not [55, 56].

Web design affects not only usability and aesthetics, but is also closely associated to business outcomes and is an increasingly important component of promotional strategy for many organizations. Important factors that appear to influence perceptions of home page complexity, including home page length, number of graphics, number of links, amount of text, and use of animation [57]. White space is an essential element in web design and plays an important role in the visual layout and brand positioning [28]. It could be a chance to develop a more valuable brand [58]. Designers could create a refined and elegant, high-quality and noble feeling for a high-class brand by using white space [58]. More white space equals a more luxurious brand and website [24]. When white space is used appropriately, it allows a page to create a general flow and balance, which in turn helps communicate the intent of the design by welcoming readers and inviting them to stay awhile [29]. It could in turn affect market power and further contribute to brand positioning.

Perceived value into four dimensions. (1) Emotional values: the utility derived from the feelings or affective states that a product generates. (2) Social value (enhancement of social self-concept): the utility derived from the product's ability to enhance social self-concept. (3) Functional value (price/value for money): the utility derived from the product due to the reduction of its perceived short term and longer term costs. (4) Functional value (performance/quality): the utility derived from the perceived quality and expected performance of the product [59].

According to literature reviews above, white space, usability, aesthetics and perceived value are related. There are tight relationships between users' initial perceptions of interface aesthetics and their perceptions of the system's usability. These relations endure even after actual use of the system [60]. In order to create a good user experience, it is important to understand the relation between aesthetics and usability, as well as the processes underlying this relation [61]. Designers need to understand the user's behavior more and require a variety of design elements to adjust the presentation of the interface. An affective response to the design's aesthetics may improve users' mood and their overall evaluations of the system [60].

Users of different ages and backgrounds are varied in visual load, working memory and memory load. For the purpose of meeting the needs of all ages, it is necessary to understand comprehensively user behaviors and preferences. By lowering the threshold of use, users could enjoy new network service with ease and convenience.

3 Methodology

Thirty-five university students aged from 18 to 24 years old were recruited by purposeful sampling to conduct the operation evaluation. The ETtoday news interface was chosen as the sample, which was the top brand of news websites in Taiwan. Four web page samples were designed with low (45%) and high (55%) percentage of white space. In order to make the experimental web pages similar to real news web pages, the percentage of white space was only slightly modified and centered around 50%.

The web pages were arranged in a random order in order to avoid the order effect of the experiment. The participants sat directly in front of the computer monitor and operated the task one by one. After the participants browsed the web pages, their affective data were collected by a questionnaire. In order to confirm the reliability and validity of the questionnaire and ease the burden on the participants, a pretest was given to a group of students who met the demographic criteria. Some questions in the questionnaire that had insufficient reliability were deleted before the formal experiment.

The percentage of white space was calculated by detecting the color of each pixel on the web page, the total white space count would be plus one if a point of white was found. Java syntax was used for the calculation program. The meaning of texts, images and other factors that might influence visual perception of the web pages were excluded, in order to explore user preferences to usability, aesthetics and perceived value of white space on the web pages. The participants' psychological amount of white space on different samples was also compared. The questionnaire was discussed and formulated for the study and was based on the System Usability Scale (SUS) [37], the aesthetic preference evaluation [5], and the perceived value evaluation [59]. The experiment adopted a five-point Likert scale from 1 (strongly disagree) to 5 (strongly agree). Figures 1, 2, 3 and 4 are the experimental web pages with two different percentages of white space and two spacing values.

Fig. 1. Sample A with 45% white space and wide spacing

4   Results

Most of the participants had up to 5 years of experience in using a computer. The results of previous studies suggested that medium percentage of white space around 50% was more favorable to the user. The results of this study indicated that the participants preferred 55% to 45% white space.

It was interesting to note that even though the web pages were centered around 50% of white space, three questions revealed significant differences. "I found the web page unnecessarily complex" in the section of usability resulted in a statistically significant difference (F = 3.818; df = 3, 136; p < .05). Post-hoc Tukey HSD tests showed that sample C (3.2) was significantly different from sample B (2.3) (p < .05). "The layout

Fig. 2. Sample B with 55% white space and wide spacing

Fig. 3. Sample C with 45% white space and narrow spacing

Fig. 4. Sample D with 55% white space and narrow spacing

appears too dense" in the section of aesthetics resulted in a statistically significant difference (F = 4.007; df = 3, 136; p < .05). Post-hoc Tukey HSD tests showed that sample C (3.7) was significantly different from sample A (2.8) (p < .05), and sample C (3.7) was significantly different from sample B (2.8) (p < .05). "This web page would help me to feel acceptable" in the section of perceived value resulted in a statistically significant difference (F = 3.310; df = 3, 136; p < .05). Post-hoc Tukey HSD tests showed that sample B (3.6) was significantly different from sample C (3.0) (p < .05), and sample A (3.6) was significantly different from sample C (3.0) (p < .05).

4.1   Psychological Amount of White Space

Toward a specific web page, different participants might have a dissimilar feeling of white space is referred to as psychological amount of white space. The participants preferred the samples designed with wider spacing under the same psychological amount of white space. Narrower layout stimulated lower psychological amount of white space. The psychological amount of white space had overall statistically significant difference (F = 13.292; df = 3, 136; p < .05). Post-hoc Tukey HSD tests showed that sample B (49.0%) and sample D (46.1%) with more white space were significantly different from sample A (32.7%) (p < .05). Sample B (49.0%) and sample D (46.1%) with more white space were significantly different from sample C (34.1%) (p < .05). The overall anticipated psychological amount of white space was 72%–87% less than original calculation.

4.2   The Time Spent on the Internet

It was assumed that experiences and preferences were affected by the time spent on specific activities. The experimental results could be different if the participants spent different amount of time on the Internet. There were four levels. (1) Users spent under two hours on the Internet daily. (2) Three to six hours daily. (3) Seven to twelve hours daily. (4) More than thirteen hours daily.

There was no statistically significant difference in usability. An ANOVA on the section of aesthetics was conducted to examine significantly higher scores. "The layout appears too dense" was highly significant (F = 4.048; df = 3, 136; p < .05). Post-hoc Tukey HSD tests showed that sample A (3.667) was significantly different from sample D (2.417) (p < .05) and sample B (3.357) was significantly different from sample D (2.417) (p < .05). "Everything goes together on this site" resulted in a statistically significant difference (F = 4.619; df = 3, 136; p < .05). Post-hoc Tukey HSD tests showed that sample D (3.542) was significantly different from sample B (2.750) (p < .05). "The layout is pleasantly varied" resulted in a statistically significant difference (F = 7.902; df = 3, 136; p < .05). Post-hoc Tukey HSD tests showed that sample C (3.042) was significantly different from sample A (1.917) (p < .05), sample D (3.500) was significantly different from sample A (1.917) (p < .05), and sample D (3.500) was significantly different from sample B (2.679) (p < .05). "The layout appears professionally designed" resulted in a statistically significant difference (F = 3.654; df = 3, 136; p < .05). Post-hoc Tukey HSD tests showed that sample C (3.167) was significantly different from sample A (2.167) (p < .05), and sample D (3.250) was significantly different from sample A (2.167) (p < .05). "This web page has an acceptable standard of quality" resulted in a statistically significant difference (F = 4.567; df = 3, 136; p < .05). Post-hoc Tukey HSD tests showed that sample C (3.375) was significantly different from sample A (2.500) (p < .05), and sample D (3.708) was significantly different from sample A (2.500) (p < .05). "This web page has poor workmanship" resulted in a statistically significant difference (F = 3.051; df = 3, 136; p < .05). Post-hoc Tukey HSD tests showed that sample A (2.917) was significantly different from sample D (1.958) (p < .05).

An ANOVA on the section of perceived value was conducted to examine significantly higher scores. "This web page is one that I would enjoy" resulted in a statistically significant difference (F = 5.803; df = 3, 136; p < .05). Post-hoc Tukey HSD tests showed that sample C (3.063) was significantly different from sample A (2.000) (p < .05), and sample D (3.458) was significantly different from sample A (2.000) (p < .05). "This web page is one that I would feel relaxed about using" resulted in a statistically significant difference (F = 3.714; df = 3, 136; p < .05). Post-hoc Tukey HSD tests showed that sample D (3.583) was significantly different from sample A (2.500) (p < .05), and sample D (3.583) was significantly different from sample B (2.804) (p < .05). "This web page would help me feel acceptable" resulted in a statistically significant difference (F = 3.937; df = 3, 136; p < .05). Post-hoc Tukey HSD tests showed that sample D (3.958) was significantly different from sample B (3.143) (p < .05). "This web page would make a good impression on other people" resulted in a statistically significant difference (F = 3.518; df = 3, 136; p < .05). Post-hoc Tukey HSD tests showed that sample D (3.583) was significantly different from sample A (2.583) (p < .05). "This web page would give its owner social approval" resulted in a statistically significant difference (F = 6.212; df = 3, 136; p < .05). Post-hoc Tukey HSD tests showed that sample D (3.833) was significantly different from sample A (2.667) (p < .05), and sample D (3.833) was significantly different from sample B(3.036) (p < .05).

4.3   The Frequency of News Browsing

User experiences and preferences were influenced by the frequency of news browsing. There were the following selections: one day a week, two days a week, three days a week, etc.... and every day in a whole week. An ANOVA on the section of usability was conducted to examine significantly higher scores. "I think that I would like to use this web page frequently" resulted in a statistically significant difference (F = 3.022; df = 5, 29; p < .05). "I thought the web page was easy to read" resulted in a statistically significant difference (F = 2.613; df = 5, 29; p < .05). "Everything goes together on this site" on the section of aesthetics resulted in a statistically significant difference (F = 2.750; df = 5, 29; p < .05). "This web page would make a good impression on other people" on the section of perceived value resulted in a statistically significant difference (F = 2.843; df = 5, 29; p < .05).

5   Discussion and Conclusion

User preferences are supported by experiences. In this study, factors that affect usability, aesthetics and perceived value of web pages were examined and different percentages of white space were evaluated. "I found the web page unnecessarily complex" in the section of usability, "the layout appears too dense" in the section of aesthetics, and "this web page would help me to feel acceptable" in the section of perceived value, resulted in a statistically significant difference. The result also indicated that most participants preferred more white space.

The sample web pages were generated by lorem ipsum, and images were replaced by grey color blocks, but the participants still felt that actual banner images should be there. It was the experience from the participants' original memory. Some participants did not interpret text spacing as white space and the psychological amount of white space was lower than actual calculation. This research provided a method to evaluate usability, aesthetics and perceived value of white space on web pages. It is hoped that in the future, designers could design web pages more accurately in accordance with user preferences. A variety of user preferences cannot be anticipated without further studies. There are a lot of website design standards such as WCAG (Web Content Accessibility Guidelines) while more and more network services are related to customization. In the future, white space could be the key factor to improve the user's web browsing experience.

References

1. Kumar, K.L., Owston, R.: Evaluating e-learning accessibility by automated and student-centered methods. Educ. Technol. Res. Dev. **64**, 263–283 (2016)
2. Chen, C.H., Chiang, S.Y.: The effects of panel arrangement on search performance. Displays **32**, 254–260 (2011)
3. Constantinos, K.C., Konstantinos, K.: Web aesthetics and usability: an empirical study of the effects of white space. Int. J. E Bus. Res. **8**, 35–53 (2012)
4. Baddeley, A.: Working Memory. Oxford University Press, Oxford (1986)
5. Moshagen, M., Thielsch, M.T.: Facets of visual aesthetics. Int. J. Hum Comput. Stud. **68**, 689–709 (2010)
6. Nielsen, J.: Designing Web Usability: The Practice of Simplicity. New Riders Publishing, Thousand Oaks (1999)
7. Pearrow, M.: Web Site Usability Handbook. Charles River Media, Rockland (2000)
8. Schleicher, R., Galley, N., Briest, S., Galley, L.: Blinks and saccades as indicators of fatigue in sleepiness warnings: looking tired? Ergonomics **51**, 982–1010 (2008)
9. Serhat, P., Seyma, K.C., Kursat, C.: Exploring the relationship between web presence and web usability for universities: a case study from Turkey. Program **50**, 157–174 (2016)
10. Shneiderman, B.: Designing the User Interface: Strategies for Effective Human-Computer Interaction. Addison-Wesley, Reading (1987)
11. Smith, A.L., Chaparro, B.S.: Smartphone text input method performance, usability, and preference with younger and older adults. Hum. Factors **57**, 1015–1028 (2015)
12. van Schaik, P., Ling, J.: The role of context in perceptions of the aesthetics of web pages over time. Int. J. Hum Comput. Stud. **67**, 79–89 (2009)
13. Yu, N., Kong, J.: User experience with web browsing on small screens: experimental investigations of mobile-page interface design and homepage design for news websites. Inf. Sci. **330**, 427–443 (2016)
14. Wang, L.T., Lee, C.F.: The study of user's favor on the complexity of vision for web pages using neural networks. J. Des. **8**, 89–102 (2003)
15. Sharmin, S., Spakov, O., Raiha, K.J.: The effect of different text presentation formats on eye movement metrics in reading. J. Eye Mov. Res. **5**, 1–9 (2012)
16. Ganayim, D., Ibrahim, R.: How do typographical factors affect reading text and comprehension performance in Arabic? Hum. Factors **55**, 323–332 (2013)

17. Bonnardel, N., Piolat, A., Le Bigot, L.: The impact of colour on website appeal and users' cognitive processes. Displays **32**, 69–80 (2011)
18. Michalski, R., Grobelny, J.: The role of colour preattentive processing in human-computer interaction task efficiency: a preliminary study. Int. J. Indus. Ergon. **38**, 321–332 (2008)
19. Bi, L., Fan, X., Liu, Y.: Effects of symmetry and number of compositional elements on Chinese users' aesthetic ratings of interfaces: experimental and modeling investigations. Int. J. Hum. Comput. Interact. **27**, 245–259 (2011)
20. Tuch, A.N., Bargas-Avila, J.A., Opwis, K.: Symmetry and aesthetics in website design: it's a man's business. Comput. Hum. Behav. **26**, 1831–1837 (2010)
21. Grobelny, J., Karwowski, W., Drury, C.: Usability of graphical icons in the design of human-computer interfaces. Int. J. Hum. Comput. Interact. **18**, 167–182 (2005)
22. Mertens, A., Brandl, C., Przybysz, P., Koch-Korfges, D., Schlick, C.M.: Design recommendations for the creation of icons for the elderly. Work **41**, 3519–3525 (2012)
23. Wang, Y.C., Yueh, H.P.: A usability study of jobsite layout. J. Lib. Inf. Stud. **12**, 109–134 (2014)
24. Schenker, M.: How to make whitespace work on the web (2014). http://www.webdesignerdepot.com/2014/07/how-to-make-whitespace-work-on-the-web/
25. Zhang, T.X.: Virtual and actual harmony: the intentional blank space of web design. Value Eng. **234**, 148–149 (2011)
26. Pracejus, W.J., Olsen, G.D., O'Guinn, T.C.: How nothing became something: white space, rhetoric, history, and meaning. J. Consum. Res. **33**, 82–90 (2006)
27. Morris, I.: White space: a perfect option for improving usability in web designs (2015). http://usabilitygeek.com/white-spaces-improving-usability-web-designs/
28. Gócza, Z., Kollin, Z.: Myth #28: white space is wasted space (2013). http://uxmyths.com/post/2059998441/myth-28-white-space-is-wasted-space
29. Maria, J.S.: Under the loupe #1: white space (2006). http://v3.jasonsantamaria.com/archive/2006/01/05/under_the_loupe_1 white_space.php
30. Hara, K.: White. Lars Muller, Zurich (2012)
31. Jia, Y., Huang, Y.: How negative space on shopping websites influences users' purchase behavior. In: International Conference on Chemical, Material and Food Engineering, pp. 668–671. Atlantis Press, Amsterdam, Beijing, Paris (2015)
32. Yeh, M.Y., Chuang, F.Y.: The effect of white space on print advertising: an exploratory study. NTU Manag. Rev. **21**, 295–314 (2001)
33. Zhou, H.: On white space of web design. **5**, 254 (2013). Xiao Zuo Jia Xuan Kan
34. Monaco, E.: Issues related to accessibility and usability in furthering the implementation of e-governance. In: 3rd International Conference on Education and New Learning Technologies, pp. 2427–2440. IATED Academy, Valencia (2011)
35. Gray, D.B., Hollingsworth, H.H., Stark, S., Morgan, K.A.: A subjective measure of environmental facilitators and barriers to participation for people with mobility limitations. Disabil. Rehabil. **30**, 434–457 (2008)
36. Auger, C., Leduc, E., Labbé, D., Guay, C., Fillion, B., Bottari, C., Swaine, B.: Mobile applications for participation at the shopping mall: content analysis and usability for persons with physical disabilities and communication or cognitive limitations. Int. J. Environ. Res. Public Health **11**, 12777–12794 (2014)
37. Brooke, J.: SUS: a quick and dirty usability scale. In: Usability Evaluation in Industry, pp. 4–7. CRC Press, Boca Raton (1996)
38. Kim, H.: A study on usability improvement of smart phone banking considering elderly users: focusing on usability test targeting elderly for money transfer procedure of busan bank smart phone banking app. J. Digit. Des. **15**, 123–132 (2015)

39. Oakley, N.S., Daudert, B.: Establishing best practices to improve usefulness and usability of web interfaces providing atmospheric data. Bull. Am. Meteorol. Soc. **97**, 263–274 (2015)
40. Schwarz, E., Beldie, I.P., Pastoor, S.: A Comparison of paging and scrolling for changing screen contents by inexperienced users. Hum. Factors **25**, 279–282 (1983)
41. King, W.R., He, J.: A meta-analysis of the technology acceptance model. Inform. Manage. **43**, 740–755 (2006)
42. ISO: Ergonomics of Human-System Interaction: Part 210: Human-Centred Design for Interactive Systems. ISO, Geneva, Switzerland (2010)
43. Vu, K.P.L., Proctor, R.W., Garcia, F.P.: Website design and evaluation. In: Handbook of Human Factors and Ergonomics, pp. 1323–1353. Wiley, Hoboken (2012)
44. Robins, D., Holmes, J.: Aesthetics and credibility in web site design. Inform. Process. Manage. **44**, 386–399 (2008)
45. Biggs, S.F., Bedard, J.C., Gaber, B.G., Linsmeier, T.J.: The effects of task size and similarity on the decision behavior of bank loan officers. Manage. Sci. **31**, 970–987 (1985)
46. Berghel, H.: Cyberspace 2000: dealing with information overload. Commun. ACM **40**, 19–24 (1997)
47. Wu, L., Zhu, Z., Cao, H., Li, B.: Influence of information overload on operator's user experience of human-machine interface in LED manufacturing systems. Cogn. Technol. Work **18**, 161–173 (2016)
48. Tractinsky, N., Cokhavi, A., Kirschenbaum, M., Sharfi, T.: Evaluating the consistency of immediate aesthetic perceptions of web pages. Int. J. Hum. Comput. Stud. **64**, 1071–1083 (2006)
49. Lindgaard, G., Fernandes, G., Dudek, C., Brown, J.: Attention web designers: you have 50 milliseconds to make a good first impression! Behav. Inf. Technol. **25**, 115–126 (2006)
50. Hoffmann, R., Krauss, K.: A critical evaluation of literature on visual aesthetics for the web. In: Proceedings of the 2004 Annual Research Conference of the South African Institute of Computer Scientists And Information Technologists on IT Research in Developing Countries, pp. 205–209. South African Institute for Computer Scientists and Information Technologists, Stellenbosch (2004)
51. Berlyne, D.E.: Studies in the New Experimental Aesthetics: Steps Toward an Objective Psychology of Aesthetic Appreciation. Hemisphere Publishing, Washington, D.C. (1974)
52. Berlyne, D.E.: Complexity and incongruity variables as determinants of exploratory choice and evaluative ratings. Can. J. Psychol. **17**, 274–290 (1963)
53. Sonderegger, A., Sauer, J., Eichenberger, J.: Expressive and classical aesthetics: two distinct concepts with highly similar effect patterns in user-artefact interaction. Behav. Inf. Technol. **33**, 1180–1191 (2014)
54. Song, G.: Analysis of web page complexity through visual segmentation. In: Jacko, J.A. (ed.) HCI 2007. LNCS, vol. 4553, pp. 114–123. Springer, Heidelberg (2007). doi:10.1007/978-3-540-73111-5_14
55. Hunt, H.K.: CS/D-Overview and future research directions. In: Conceptualization and Measurement of Consumer Satisfaction and Dissatisfaction, pp. 455–488. Marketing Science Institute, Cambridge (1977)
56. Oliver, R.L.: Measurement and evaluation of satisfaction processes in retail settings. J. Retailing **57**, 25–48 (1981)
57. Geissler, G.L., Zinkhan, G.M., Watson, R.T.: The influence of home page complexity on consumer attention, attitudes, and purchase intent. J. Advertising **35**, 69–80 (2006)
58. Boulton, M.: Whitespace (2007). http://alistapart.com/article/whitespace

59. Sweeney, J.C., Soutar, G.N.: Consumer perceived value: the development of a multiple item scale. J. Retailing **77**, 203–220 (2001)
60. Tractinsky, N., Katz, A.S., Ikar, D.: What is beautiful is usable. Interact. Comput. **13**, 127–145 (2000)
61. Tuch, A.N., Roth, S.P., Hornbæk, K., Opwis, K., Bargas-Avila, J.A.: Is beautiful really usable? Toward understanding the relation between usability, aesthetics, and affect in HCI. Comput. Hum. Behav. **28**, 1596–1607 (2012)

Research on the Effect of Visual Conventions on Perception and Inference

Ningyue Peng[1,2], Chengqi Xue[1,2(✉)], Haiyan Wang[1,2], Yafeng Niu[1,2], and Yingjie Victor Chen[3]

[1] School of Mechanical Engineering, Southeast University, Nanjing, China
{pengny, ipd_xcq}@seu.edu.cn
[2] Institute of Product Design and Reliability Engineering, Southeast University, Nanjing, China
[3] Department of Computer Graphics Technology in Purdue Polytechnic Institute, Purdue University, Indiana, USA

Abstract. Visual conventions are perceptually efficient graphic agreements with common-sense like referents and are commonly used in what we interact with in daily life. It becomes a studying-worthy issue on whether such conventions can enhance performances and reduce cognitive load when we perceive and reason about new knowledge. Furthermore, whether the visual conventions can affect experts, who have prior knowledge and design experience about different visual encoding principles the same degree as novice who have no background knowledge in this area, is another research focus in this study. Our research is carried out according to action features when we read visualizations. Four task features are extracted, based on which behavioral and eye-tracking measurement were conducted, that is data localization, simple and complex data comparison, and knowledge inference. Both expert and novice participants were enrolled in our experiment. The result indicates that conventional elements in visualizations can hugely improve performances in more complex tasks involving higher-level cognition, like making comparisons and reasoning about new knowledge. The performance improvement can be seen from shorter response time on achieving conclusions and higher accuracy rates. Meanwhile, cognitive load, which can be measured from shorter total fixation duration and fewer fixation counts in AOIs, is reduced through applying visually conventional features. No statistically significant difference is found in comparing perceptual and inferential outputs of expert and novice group. We draw conclusions that visual conventions in visualizations can better performance in relatively complex activities, and it can be equally perceived and acquired regardless of the user's knowledge background is. What we conclude in this study can be extended to areas of dynamic data visualization and layout design in the digital interface domain.

Keywords: Visual conventions · Perception · Inference · Prior knowledge · Eye-tracking · Visualization

© Springer International Publishing AG 2017
A. Marcus and W. Wang (Eds.): DUXU 2017, Part I, LNCS 10288, pp. 284–297, 2017.
DOI: 10.1007/978-3-319-58634-2_22

1   Introduction

Visualizations act as key media for perceiving, understanding, reasoning and interacting with the sheer volume of data and information in the Big Data era. Understanding what does the visualization mean, and how it creates meaning are paramount tasks for both audiences and designers. The essence of each visualization is not to provide information solely, but to act as a platform and inference start point from which the audience could frame new information and knowledge [1]. In other words, how we designers can make the visualization much clearly through visual representations and encoding methods is crucial for constructing the inference point for audiences. Among visual representations, acquired codes, together with perceptual cues can leverage readability, comprehensibility and familiarity of visualizations [2]. Visual conventions, the perceptually efficient graphic agreements that are shared by both the users and designers, can lead to faster recognition and less effort spent. Apart from this, the emergence of knowledge visualization [3] makes it a worthwhile issue to investigate the function of visual conventions and perceptual cues in the perception and inference when interacting with visualizations.

2   Background Work

Visual conventions and metaphors are indispensable factors in improving the efficiency for information discovery, extraction and transfer [4]. They make the diagrammatic representation superior to sentential one in aspects of searching and identifying data. Larkin and Simon [2] concluded that diagrammatic representations can make relations between individual elements more explicit, which facilitate and simplify perception and comprehension. Encoding forms, like color and size, do carry a lot of cultural conventions. For example, color includes many common emotional and aesthetic associations, and sizes can be used to represent the relative importance of entities [5]. As is depicted in Fig. 1(a), the size and lightness indicate the number of linkages the dot may contain; and in Fig. 1(b), the lightness of BLUE means the volume of rainfall in each month, which coordinate with the perceptual decoding conventions and become universally-used visual representations provided to the end user. These encoding forms are termed as visual representation conventions. But whether their associations with entities can be perceived depends largely on the context.

(a)   (b)

Fig. 1. Visual representation conventions in visualization design (Color figure online)

Abundant evidences in linguistic domain suggest that integration of visual conventions and metaphor facilitates comprehension. And user performance will suffer once violating these. Santa-Maria and Dyson [6] investigated what would happen in seeking information on websites that violate visual conventions, like putting the scroll bar on the left side. They found that user performances are far better when interacting with the convention-conforming websites than those in convention-violating ones. The efficiency of searching in latter context will get improved after trainings. Lai and Curran [7] defined the mapping process during the conventional or novel metaphor cognition as a process, not representation stored in the long-term memory. They used N400, the neural indicator of the ease of retrieval in lexical research domain, to depict the ease of retrieval and comparisons of concepts through conventional metaphors and metaphor-free contexts. However, effects of visual metaphors varied from novices and experts, as it would serve as a mental scaffolding tool for novices, despite that these metaphors help the reconstruction of their knowledge structure. Owing to the skillfulness for experts to consolidate their background knowledge, metaphors will greatly facilitate their retrieval of new knowledge [8]. Concepts of conventions and metaphors originate from linguistics, and researches emerge with the focus of visual language.

As uses of visual conventions and metaphors lead to the ease of memory retrieval and information extraction, it may also play an important role in visual inference, which is characterized by the use of spatial relations to highlight conceptual ones, to represent meaning, and chunk information for computational efficiency [9]. The inference process is a higher cognitive process, which is indicated by Wang et al. [10] in the Layered Reference Model of the Brain (LRMB) (Shown in Fig. 2).

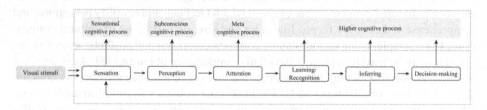

Fig. 2. Cognitive flow of perception and comprehension of visual stimuli

Entities in the upper dashed box are cognitive levels mentioned in LRMB, and entities in the bottom box depict the cognitive flow of perception and comprehension of visual stimuli, which consist of interdependent processes, with the former processes serve as basis for the latter ones.

Researches on inference in visualization demonstrate that these diagrammatic representations can improve reasoning, both in aspects of accuracy rate and inference time when compared with sentential representations. Bauer and Johnson-Laird [11] extended the conclusion drawn by Larkin and Simon [2] in target searching only, and found that more valid inferences and faster responses were made with diagrammatic representations. Grant and Spivey [12] found that attentional guidance can improve reasoning in a problem-solving task that relies on a diagram. They related attention capture theory with inference-making, but they discussed little about the mechanisms supporting the facilitation of making inferences. Fabrikant et al. [13] suggested that visually perceptual saliency corresponding to relationship of thematic relevance can affect viewing behavior and enhance the efficiency of spatial inference making, which can be manifested in eye-tracking data. Borgo et al. [14] investigated the impact of visual embellishment on visualization memorization, visual searching and concept grasping. Under the instruction of concept grasping, identification of key concepts within or behind visualizations were required. Despite the incremental difficulty, no higher-level of cognition was mentioned in their research. Mineshima et al. [15] explored the efficacy of Euler diagram in syllogistic reasoning and the checking of invalidity of an inference. They uncovered that the better performance of Euler diagram derived from the explicit visual representation of relational structures of elements.

Despite the fact that effect of visual representation on inference-making has been studied, little is known about the influence of visual conventions on perception and inference in visualizations. In addition, whether the influence is equivalent from expert to naïve users remain to be studied. That is why we focus on the effect of conventional metaphors in capturing, analyzing and reasoning about information in this study, and experimental data are compared between experts and novices. It is a worthwhile issue for visualization designers in order to create a more effective visualization and bring about more enjoyable user interactive experience.

3 Experiment Method

The study is based on the taxonomy of visual conventions, including color, spatial metaphor and some guidelines in Gestalt theory, like adjacency. These conventions are integrated into visualizations, which describe a context of certain topic.

3.1 Participants and Equipment

20 participants were enrolled from Department of Industrial Design and Department of Mechanical Automation in Southeast University. A classifying procedure, which is similar to Lee's in [8], was administered to identify all participants into expert and novice group.

Three questions were asked: (1) Have you ever had experience of reading diagrams or InfoViz (Information Visualization) before?; (2) Have you ever built diagrams in data analysis platform, like Excel or Tableau, etc.?; (3) Do you know some principles in interface design, including information encoding and data visualization, or combine those guidelines into your practice? Question (1) was designed to ensure that each participant has experience in reading diagrams, thus their experience should not be interferential variable. Question (2) was set to ensure that they are able to distinguish difference between two kinds of visualizations. For each time they choose the diagram format in the data analysis platform, they might keep in mind the relationship between the data category and visual representation format. The last question was to classify participants into two groups, with those being expert as well as having know-how knowledge of designing interface of visualizations in Expert Group, and those getting no prior experience in designing visualizations in Novice Group.

There were altogether 10 participants in Expert Group, and 10 in Novice Group. Their ages range from 19 to 27 (Mean$_1$ = 23.1, SD$_1$ = 1.66, Mean$_2$ = 21.7, SD$_2$ = 1.77), and all participants have normal or corrected-to-normal vision, without color blindness or weakness.

The experiment was carried out in the Ergonomics Lab of Southeast University, under the normal lighting condition (40 W daylight continuous current tungsten lamp). All the stimuli were presented, and both behavioral and eye movement data were collected by Tobii Studio 3.3.0. In addition, the display of visual stimuli was presented on a CRT monitor, of which CPU main frequency was 3.0 GHZ and display size was 17 in. (1280 pixels * 1024 pixels).

3.2 Procedure

Each participant underwent two blocks, and one block is featured by plain visualizations with no conventional representations; the other is featured by visual conventions. A randomized block experimental design was adopted in order to counteract the influence of block sequences. During the experiment, eye movement data were recorded by Tobii X2-30. Eye tracking indices including total fixation number, fixation duration were analyzed statistically. In order to get whether participants had made correct choices, their answers were recorded in the form of multiple choice.

Experiment tasks were chosen based on three main purposes or actions when interacting with info graphs [16] as is shown in Fig. 3. Participants would complete four tasks on each stimulus, and the four tasks were set according to the above-mentioned three

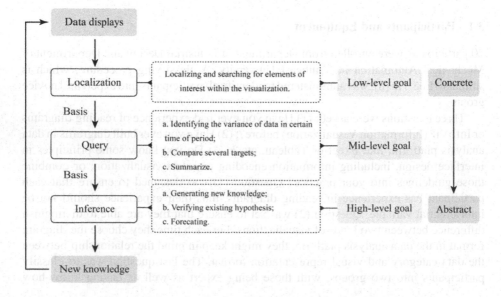

Fig. 3. Hierarchy of tasks in the interaction with visualization

actions. The example task instructions are listed in Table 1. In Task One, participants were instructed to localize the exact point in the visualization. In Task Two, simple comparisons between two values were required. While in Task Three, they were instructed to compare multiple pairs of values and even tendency of the data series, which is more demanding and complicated than Task II. In Task Four, participants were required to make inferences and get more abstract and potential information in those graphics. The general complexities of these four tasks are incremental.

Table 1. Examples of task instructions and the corresponding action categories

Task no.	Actions	Example of task instructions
Task one	Localization	Point out the range of precipitation in Feb. 2015
Task two	Query	Figure out the tendency of variance for precipitation in May 2014 and 2015
Task three		Compare the volume for which precipitation varied in May and Jun. from 2014 to 2015
Task four	Inference	Which month of 2016 carries the largest probability of waterlog?

Additionally, visualizations used in our experiment are elaborately designed, to achieve the equilibrium of both perceptual and cognitive loads across the stimuli. All the information depicted in the visualizations is extracted from daily life to ensure that participants are familiar with those contexts, like precipitation of City A or citation number of research topics in certain journal. However, hardly can they predict or infer from their prior knowledge without viewing the stimuli.

There are altogether 56 trials in two blocks, with 28 in each. Each stimulus has four trials in accord with corresponding four tasks. The experiment flow of one core experiment unit is established in Fig. 4. The task instructions were presented until participants pushing the button and indicating that they have finished reading and fully comprehended the instruction. Then, commentary about the visualization was displayed, providing background information of the following visualizations. The fixation marker followed, lasting for one thousand mini-seconds. Then the diagram was presented for infinite time until response was made. Multiple choices followed, to record the answer of each question. All 28 stimuli in each section were pseudo-randomized to ensure that in each pair, stimuli with visual conventions have exactly 50% chance to be displayed before plain stimuli, and vice versa. After participants finished each task, a 5 min break was set to ease tiredness.

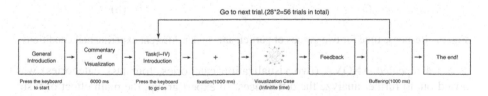

Fig. 4. Experimental flow for one block

4 Results

Behavioral, subjective and eye-tracking data were collected to compare subjects' performances of four individual tasks under conditions of visualizations with and without visual conventions. ANOVAs and paired t-test method were employed to compare whether there is significant difference between two experimental conditions; and whether performances vary significantly between expert and novice group.

4.1 Behavioral Data

Behavioral data includes response time and accurate rate under each condition for two groups. Among all the 20 subjects, two subjects' response time in Task Four in plain visualizations were rejected, for they asked question about task instructions during the presentation of diagrams. Their response time is replaced by the average response time of their group.

Response Time. As is shown in Fig. 5, both expert and novice groups responded in shorter time under visualizations without visual conventions in task one and two. These two tasks feature in localizing single or smaller amount data points than Task Three. However, performances under diagrams with visual conventions are better than those under without conditions in task three and four. These two tasks involve comparing multiple data points ($N > 2$) along the entire time span, and reasoning about abstract conclusion.

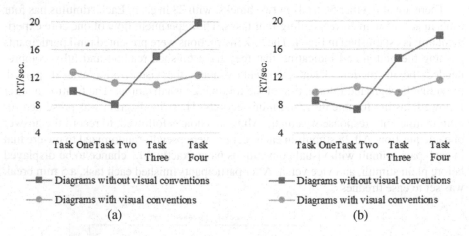

(a)   (b)

Fig. 5. Response time for two groups of participants under different experimental conditions

2 * 4 repeated ANOVA (two visualization categories, four task categories) was carried out to further analyze the differences. In expert group, the main effect of visualization category on response time is not significant ($F = 3.552$, $p = 0.064$, $\alpha = 0.05$, $\eta^2 = 0.049$), but task category exerts significant effect on response time ($F = 8.962$, $p = 0.000$, $\alpha = 0.05$, $\eta^2 = 0.115$). The interaction effect of diagram and task categories

is significant ($F = 18.180$, $p = 0.000$, $\alpha = 0.05$, $\eta^2 = 0.209$). In novice group, the main effect of visualization categories and task category on response time is significant $F_1 = 4.723$, $p_1 = 0.033$, $\alpha = 0.05$, $\eta_1^2 = 0.064$; $F_2 = 11.130$, $p_2 = 0.000$, $\alpha = 0.05$, $\eta_2^2 = 0.139$. The interaction effect of diagram and task categories is significant ($F = 11.425$, $p = 0.000$, $\alpha = 0.05$, $\eta^2 = 0.142$). The set of ANOVA result indicates that whether visualizations containing visual conventions or not may affect novices' response time considerably. Both expert and novice participants responded faster under visualizations with visual conventions than those without conventions in the last two tasks, which support the conclusion that conventional encodings can facilitate more complex tasks like comparison and knowledge inference. It should be noted that when the task is to localize specific data points, that is to say when the task is comparably easy to conduct, visualizations without conventional encoding will be more conducive.

Figure 5(a) and (b) *shows response time for expert and novice participants under conditions of two kinds of visualizations respectively.*

Accuracy Rate. Accuracy rates under different conditions are established in Fig. 6. It can be seen that accuracy rate of both expert and novice group gradually declined as task difficulty increasing in visualizations without visual conventions. However, accuracy rate of acquiring information from convention-conforming encoding diagrams showed an ascending tendency, from task one to task three. When it comes to task four, accuracy rate for those two groups of participants dropped remarkably. But expert group still outperformed novice group when there were visual conventions contained in the diagram in task three and four. According to Fig. 6, accuracy rate of novice participants in task three is higher with visually conventional diagrams than the one with plain visualizations. But the discrepancy narrowed in task four. What needs to mention is that accuracy rate of expert group in task four is higher than the one in the convention-free section. Paired t-test result indicates that experts' performance are significantly better in task four under conventionally encoding representations ($t = 2.813$, $df = 69$, **Sig.**(two-sided) $= 0.006$, $\alpha = 0.05$). But the difference does not reach to significance in task three for novice participants ($t = 1.270$, $df = 69$, **Sig.**(two-sided) $= 0.208$, $\alpha = 0.05$).

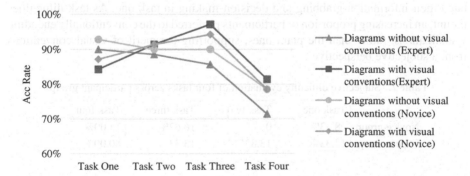

Fig. 6. Accuracy rate for two groups of participants under different experimental conditions

For expert participants, whether the visualization is plain or visually conventional make significant difference for accuracy rate ($F = 8.357$, $p = 0.005$, $\alpha = 0.05$). But the difference is not significant for novice ($F = 0.079$, $p = 0.780$, $\alpha = 0.05$). The interactive effect of representation category and task feature shares the same pattern, in which for expert groups, the interactive effect is significant ($F = 5.884$, $p = 0.018$, $\alpha = 0.05$), and it is not significant when for novice participants ($F = 2.162$, $p = 0.100$, $\alpha = 0.05$).

The result indicates that visual conventions contained in InfoViz carry little effect on novice participants' comprehension. However, it will significantly aid expert participants to correctly make inferences. When multiple data point's localization and comparisons were required, visualizations with visual conventions will help them to acquire information, reason about new knowledge and make decisions. Combining with the result of response time, novice participants can make more accurate options with less time spent when there are conventions in the visualization, so as to expert participants. This means that general performances of participants get improved in the conventional section. In another word, conventions will help participants to perceive information and make inference. But if the task is relatively simple, like localization of single data point, participants with common visualization will perform better. We hypothesize that the lower performance in task one and two when visual conventions were displayed may have something to do with unfamiliarity and the increase of perceptual load.

4.2 Subjective Data

Each participant would fill in the questionnaire as feedback after their completion of the entire experiment. In the questionnaire, five questions were listed: (a) Which section of representation facilitate your acquisition of information? (b) Which task is more difficult for you to answer? Question (c)–(e) corresponding to task one, task two and three, task four listed in Fig. 3 were set to get feedback of confidences of task completion across two groups.

Table 2 shows that the most majority of participants classified task four as the most difficult task to complete, validating the task arrangement in our research. Figure 7 shows the result of Question(c)–(e). Most participants claimed that plain visualizations facilitated their information-grabbing and decision-making in task one. As task difficulties mount, an increasing proportion of participants preferred to the conventionally encoding visualizations, rather than the plain ones, supporting the merit of visual conventions from a subjective perspective.

Table 2. Subjective difficulty evaluation of four tasks across participant groups

	Task one	Task two	Task three	Task four
Novice group	8.33%	0	16.67%	75.00%
Expert group	13.33%	13.33%	13.33%	80.00%

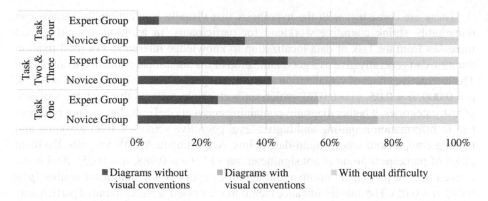

Fig. 7. Confidences of answering for participants with different visualizations

4.3 Eye-Tracking Data

Total Fixation Duration (TFD). The index of total fixation duration measures the sum of duration for all fixations within an AOI [17]. This index is often adopted in comprehension and evaluation of human cognitive process and also mental load. In our study, mean of total fixation duration for participants in two conditions of visualizations are presented in Fig. 8. For two groups, it is conspicuous from the figure that total fixation duration was less than that in without-convention diagrams in task three and four. ANOVA results indicate that main effects of visualization and task category are significant on total fixation duration across two groups ($F_1 = 16.782, p_1 = 0.000, \alpha = 0.05, \eta_1^2 = 0.015; F_2 = 19.394, p_2 = 0.000, \alpha = 0.05, \eta_2^2 = 0.050$). Paired t-test supports the significant difference between TFD in task one, two and task three, four ($Sig_{1\text{-}3\&4}$.(two-sided) = 0.000, $Sig_{2\text{-}3\&4}$.(two-sided) = 0.000, $Sig_{3\text{-}4}$.(two-sided) = 0.055, $\alpha = 0.05$;). No significant effect of participant groups is found, despite the gap depicted in Fig. 8.

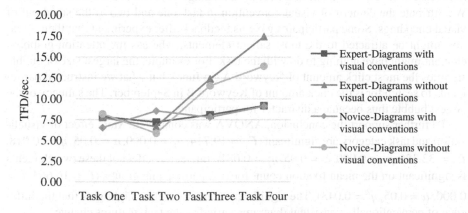

Fig. 8. Mean of total fixation duration for two groups in two conditions of diagrams

These are consistent with the hypothesis that visually conventional diagrams can remarkably shrink cognitive workload for participants. In addition, cognitive load increases from the task of data localization to knowledge inference. For total fixation duration can generally give us a good indication of the attentional allocation to an object. The interactive effect of visualization and task categories is also significant ($F = 9.724$, $p = 0.000$, $\alpha = 0.05$, $\eta^2 = 0.026$), which supports the hypothesis that with the variance of task categories, whether diagrams containing conventional encodings or not is important to information acquiring and higher-level cognitive activities, like reasoning and making comparisons among multi-data points. According to ANOVA results, the main effect of participant group is not significant on TFD ($p = 0.988$, $\alpha = 0.05$). And interactive effect of participant group and diagram category is not significant neither ($p = 0.848$, $\alpha = 0.05$). The non-significance means that knowledge background of participants exerts little implication when there is visual convention contained in the visualization. That is, visual conventions can be equally perceived for both expert and novice users. The finding deepens definition of visual conventions of perceptual agreements across users.

In spite of the fact that visualization format is marked as the covariate, we are surprised to find that the covariate also has an effect on total fixation duration ($F = 5.970$, $p = 0.015$, $\alpha = 0.05$, $\eta^2 = 0.005$). In our future study, we may focus on the interactive effect of different forms of visualization and visual conventions on information perception and knowledge inference.

Fixation Count (FC). The index of fixation count measures the times participant fixates on an AOI [17]. Mean fixation counts of expert and novice participants are established in Fig. 9. The mean fixation count varied across conditions with the same pattern as what is presented in Fig. 8. To be specific, mean fixation count, when visually conventional encodings were not presented in diagrams, was remarkably more than those in visually conventional diagrams. The advantage of visual convention is increasingly significant when it comes to task three and four, concerning more complex task features. However, in task one and two, the advantage of visual conventions weakened. We attribute the demerit of visual convention in task one and two to the stand-out of visual encodings. Some participants gave us feedback after experiment that their attention might be attracted to the most salient elements, whereas the attention-grabbing element might have nothing to do with the task. For example, the largest size of bubble signifies the most click amount of Keyword A (in June), but what we instructed participants to search for is the click amount of Keyword B in September. The saliency of the largest bubble thus became a distractor for participants.

To further support the conclusion, ANOVA was conducted. Main effect of visualization and task category are significant ($F_1 = 19.714$, $p_1 = 0.000$, $\alpha = 0.05$, $\eta_1^2 = 0.018$; $F_2 = 32.386$, $p_2 = 0.000$, $\alpha = 0.05$, $\eta_2^2 = 0.081$). Interactive effect of these two elements is significant on the mean fixation count for two participants groups ($F = 16.663$, $p = 0.000$, $\alpha = 0.05$, $\eta^2 = 0.043$). The significant interactive effect highlights that the influence of conventionally consistent diagrams varied as the task features change.

According to the theory that information can be further processed only when it was fixated, more fixation count in plain visualizations can lead to the conclusion that the

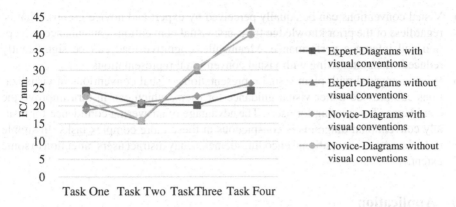

Fig. 9. Mean fixation counts for two groups in two conditions of diagrams

amount of information needed to get in-depth analysis is more than those in visualizations with visual conventions. The more the to-be-processed information is, the more cognitive load for participants will be, no matter what group of participants is, for the main effect of participant group is not significant ($F = 0.003$, $p = 0.960$, $\alpha = 0.05$, $\eta^2 = 0.000$). Another explanation for fewer fixation counts in convention-conforming visualizations is that these visual conventions provide more guidance for visual search and high-level cognition. As is shown in Fig. 6, accuracy rates of task three under with-conventions conditions are higher than those under without-convention conditions. In another word, fewer fixations were made but higher performances were achieved with these visual conventions. For two groups, the FC differences under two conditions during the completion of task two are significant according paired t-test result (Sig_1.(two-sided) = 0.012, Sig_2.(two-sided) = 0.019, $\alpha = 0.05$).

5   Conclusion

We measure performance and cognitive loads in dimensions of behavior and eye movement patterns. Eye-tracking measurement can be a good complement of behavioral experiment method, since it can qualitatively and quantitatively reflect cognitive loads for users. Future research will in-depth discuss effect of specific conventional representations on visual perception and new knowledge generation. Under conditions of plain and visually conventional visualizations in this study, following conclusion can be drawn:

- Visualizations containing visual conventions can facilitate multiple data points search, comparison and new knowledge inference. However, the advantage for visual conventions over plain visualization does not emerge when task is relatively simple, like searching for only single data. The advantage of conventional visualizations for more complex task manifests itself in shorter reaction time, higher accuracy rate, less total fixation duration and fewer fixation counts.

- Visual conventions can be equally perceived by expert and novice groups. That is, regardless of the prior knowledge for users, visual conventions can enhance perception and inference performance. Meanwhile, cognitive load can be significantly reduced when interacting with visual conventional representations.
- When compared with plain visual representations, visual conventions in visualizations can provide better visual guidance for users, which can in turn improve the confidence of answering for users. The advantage of answering confidence for visually conventional diagrams is conspicuous in these more complex tasks. In simple tasks, however, conventional encoding elements may distract users' attention to some extent.

6 Application

Applications of visual conventions are not restricted in static information visualization design. It can also be used in many areas of human-computer interaction. To name but a few, in area of data visualization, where sheer volume of data, coupling with high velocity variance are to be presented, visual conventions can be used to facilitate mining new knowledge from what we present dynamically to the end user. In addition, visual conventions can be considered as an effective way for layout designing in digital interfaces.

Acknowledgments. This work was supported by the National Nature Science Foundation of China Grant No. 71471037, 71271053.

References

1. Byrne, L., Angus, D., Wiles, J.: Acquired codes of meaning in data visualization and infographics: beyond perceptual primitives. IEEE Trans. Visual Comput. Graph. **22**, 509–518 (2016)
2. Larkin, J.H., Simon, H.A.: Why a diagram is (sometimes) worth ten thousand words. Cogn. Sci. **11**, 65–99 (1987)
3. Bertschi, S., Bubenhofer, N.: Linguistic learning: a new conceptual focus in knowledge visualization. In: Ninth International Conference on Information Visualisation, London, pp. 383–389 (2005)
4. Layton, R.A., House, R.A., Ohland, M.W., Ricco, G.: Promoting more effective communication of stories in the data. In: Frontiers in Education Conference, pp. 1–4 (2014)
5. Iliinsky, N., Steele, J.: Designing Data Vizualization, p. 66. O'Reilly Media, Inc., USA (2011)
6. Santa-Maria, L., Dyson, M.C.: The effect of violating visual conventions of a website on user performance and disorientation. How bad can it be?. In: Proceedings of the 26th Annual ACM International Conference on Design of Communication, Lisbon, pp. 47–54 (2008)
7. Tzuyin Lai, V., Curran, T.: ERP evidence for conceptual mappings and comparison processes during the comprehension of conventional and novel metaphors. Brain Lang. **127**(3), 484–496 (2013)
8. Lee, J.: The effects of visual metaphor and cognitive style for mental modeling in a hypermedia-based environment. Interact. Comput. **19**, 614–629 (2007)

9. Gattis, M., Holyoak, K.J.: Mapping conceptual to spatial relations in visual reasoning. J. Exp. Psychol. Learn. Mem. Cogn. **22**, 231–239 (1996)
10. Wang, Y., Wang, Y., Patel, S., Patel, D.: A layered reference model of the brain (LRMB). IEEE Trans. Syst. Man Cybern.-Part C Appl. Rev. **36**, 124–133 (2006)
11. Bauer, M.I., Johnson-Laird, P.N.: How diagrams can improve reasoning. Psychol. Sci. **4**, 371–378 (1993)
12. Grant, E.R., Spivey, M.J.: Eye movements and problem solving: guiding attention guides thought. Psychol. Sci. **14**, 462–466 (2003)
13. Fabrikant, S.I., Hespanha, S.R., Hegarty, M.: Cognitively inspired and perceptually salient graphic displays for efficient spatial inference making. Ann. Assoc. Am. Geogr. **100**, 13–29 (2010)
14. Borgo, R., Abdul-Rahman, A., Mohamed, F., Grant, P.W., Reppa, I., Floridi, L., Chen, A.M.: An empirical study on using visual embellishments in visualization. IEEE Trans. Visual Comput. Graphics **18**, 2759–2768 (2012)
15. Mineshima, K., Sato, Y., Takemura, R., Okada, M.: Towards explaining the cognitive efficacy of Euler diagrams in syllogistic reasoning: a relational perspective. J. Vis. Lang. Comput. **25**, 156–169 (2014)
16. Munzner, T.: Visualization Analysis and Design. CRC Press, Boca Raton (2014)
17. Tobii studio users' manual (2016)

Research on the Style of Product Shape Based on NURBS Curve

Zhangfan Shen, Chengqi Xue[(⊠)], Jing Zhang, and Haiyan Wang

School of Mechanical Engineering,
Southeast University, Nanjing 211189, China
{shenzhangfan, ipd_xcq}@seu.edu.cn

Abstract. To further study on the relationship between users' perception of style image and product shape features, a research method of product feature image based on the NURBS curve was proposed. The experimental study was conducted with the example of goblet. Firstly, the key control points impacting the shape features were extracted and a plurality of products 3D models were constructed. Secondly, five representative products and three key images were selected by the methods of hierarchical clustering and factor analysis. Then, the Kansei Engineering evaluation system of goblet was established, with which the subjects conducted Semantic Differential experiment for a thirty-three products with different shapes, and the data were analyzed by multiple regression analysis as well. Finally, the mapping model between the control points and Kansei images was constructed and its reliability was verified. This mapping model accurately reflected the relationship between the various control points and different style images, this research method can be applied to the modelling design of other products, which can help the designers grasp the product style accurately. This paper would play an important guiding role on product development and creative design.

Keywords: Style image · Shape features · NURBS curve · Semantic Differential

1 Introduction

As the key of emotional cognition of product design, style image becomes an important factor in the consumer markets, and it is of great significance to industrial product design [1]. In recent years, the perceptual technology based on semantic difference method has been widely used [2–5]. McCormack carried out a detailed method to evaluate the style of different kinds of industrial products [6]. Demirbilek discussed the key role of product characteristics and user emotions during the process of design [7]. Huang et al. studied the application of perceptual technology in aided product design system and developed a prototype system about self-adaptive product design on modularity [8]. Analysis plays a significant role during product design. Belaziz analyzed product shape by Kansei words and presented a form of features based tool to aid the integration of analysis during the design process [9].

© Springer International Publishing AG 2017
A. Marcus and W. Wang (Eds.): DUXU 2017, Part I, LNCS 10288, pp. 298–305, 2017.
DOI: 10.1007/978-3-319-58634-2_23

Besides, in previous Kansei Engineering studies, many researchers generally employed the concept of "items" and "categories" to develop a qualitative description of the overall product form in terms of its basic design features. Jindo describes the research and development work done on a design support system intended for use as a support tool in designing office chairs. Subjective evaluations were conducted using the semantic differential (SD) method to examine the relationship between users' personal assessments of office chairs and design elements [10]. Lai presented a new approach to determining the best design combination of product form elements for matching a given product image represented by a word pair. Grey relational analysis (GRA) model was used to examine the relationship between product form elements and product image [11].

However, the research of style image perception mostly stays on the entirety of products, lacking the study of points and lines which are the basic components of a product.

2 Background

In this paper, we studied the mapping mechanism between initial points and goblet style image based on NURBS curve. Firstly, the key control points impacting the shape features were extracted and a plurality of products 3D models were constructed. After that, five representative products and three key images were selected by the methods of hierarchical clustering and factor analysis. Then, the Kansei Engineering evaluation system of goblet was established, with which the subjects conducted Semantic Differential experiment for a thirty-three products with different shapes, and the data were analyzed by multiple regression analysis method. Finally, the mapping model between the control points and Kansei images was constructed and its reliability was verified.

The research of product design showed that lines are the key factor to determine the final shape of product. Therefore, we can control the shapes of product by adjusting the structural points which compose those lines. We took the shape of goblet as an example. According to the basic features and the design standard of goblet, the 3D models of goblet was created by 3D software and the NURBS curve was extracted as well. Figure 1 shows the nine control points which determine the shape of goblet. As the figure shows, P1, P2, P3 and P4 mainly control the shape of goblet head, while P5, P6 and P7 mainly control the shape of goblet body and P8 and P9 mainly control the shape of goblet foot. Obviously, these control points in the two-dimensional space are defined by X axis and Y axis. Any change of X or Y coordinates could lead to the change of product modeling.

3 Method

3.1 Create 3D Models

We invited five designers who have experience of more than six years of product design to adjust those nine control points to create a number of different goblet samples

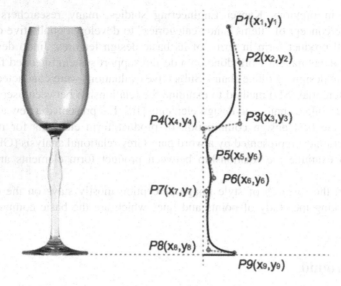

Fig. 1. The NURBS curve and control points of goblet

based on the numerical definition of the generic goblet form presented in Fig. 1. Five designers created total of fifty-nine 3D models with Rhinoceros 4.0 software developed by McNeel company. Figure 2 shows the total of thirty-three goblet samples we used in the experiment. User's image perception would be affected by different factors such as shape, texture, color, light, scene etc. [12, 13]. In order to exclude the influence of other factors we rendered those samples by applying the same color and texture in one scene.

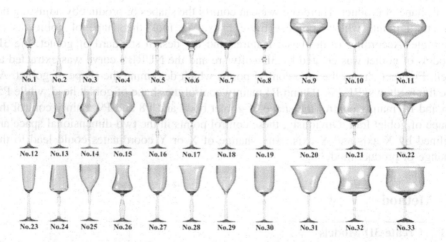

Fig. 2. The goblet samples used in the experiment

3.2 Select Appropriate Product Samples

Hierarchical Clustering was used to select appropriate product samples among so many models. As a result, all the samples were classified into five different groups and five representative samples were selected according to the Euclidean Distance. Figure 3 shows that No.29 was selected as the representative sample in the first group, No.16 was selected as the representative sample in the second group, No.23 was selected as the representative sample in the third group, No.11 was selected as the representative sample in the fourth group, and No.7 was selected as the representative sample in the last group.

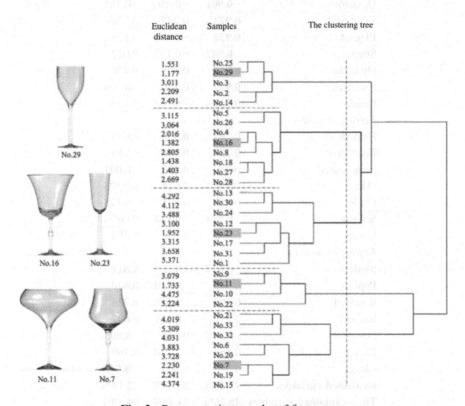

Fig. 3. Representative samples of five groups

3.3 Select Appropriate Product Image Descriptors

Consumers commonly use simple adjectives to express their perceptions of a product's image. As a result of consumers' personal values or preferences, these adjectives can provide an explicit representation of users' emotional response to a product's form [15]. Therefore, approximately one hundred adjectives in Chinese pertaining to goblets' form were collected from websites, magazines, papers and books. These adjectives were then sieved and twenty-six product image descriptors remained. As Table 1 shows, finally, the method of Principal Component Analysis was used to classify twenty-six adjectives into three style imageries (feeling of delicacy, feeling of unique and feeling of modern).

Table 1. The explained variance of 26 image descriptors

Product image	Factor A	Factor B	Factor C
Feeling of delicacy			
Luxury	**0.953**	0.237	0.103
Fancy	**0.869**	−0.214	0.430
Kingly	**0.816**	0.116	0.339
Ordinary	**−0.829**	−0.527	−0.176
Metabolic	**0.900**	0.114	0.421
Dexterous	**−0.901**	−0.056	−0.168
Emotional	**0.922**	0.207	0.326
Elegant	**0.932**	−0.635	0.139
Simple	**−0.982**	−0.172	0.077
Dynamic	**0.864**	0.008	0.476
Passionate	**0.929**	0.356	−0.006
Gentle	**0.765**	−0.231	0.465
Feeling of unique			
Individual	0.293	**0.955**	0.025
Innovative	0.224	**0.945**	0.219
Exaggerated	0.340	**0.933**	−0.031
Odd	0.144	**0.914**	−0.373
Fresh	0.455	**0.881**	−0.125
Solemn	−0.524	**−0.847**	0.065
Lovely	0.102	**0.788**	0.583
Feeling of modern			
Modern	−0.424	0.171	**0.811**
Popular	0.342	−0.420	**0.840**
Rounded	0.455	−0.088	**0.726**
Refined	0.212	−0.477	**0.697**
Powerful	−0.418	0.044	**−0.893**
Plump	0.556	−0.220	**0.760**
Classic	0.573	0.450	**−0.643**
Explained variables	**45.25%**	**29.23%**	**22.11%**
Total explained variables	**45.25%**	**74.48%**	**96.59%**

3.4   Image Perception Evaluation of Goblet Form

Thirty-six graduate students who major in product design were invited to evaluate all the thirty-three samples by the three style imageries in Kansei Engineering Evaluation System. As Fig. 4 shows, participants only need to observe the form of goblet model on the left side of the system interface, and then select a proper value of each image which represent their emotional response to the product's form. The data of each product sample data will be recorded automatically.

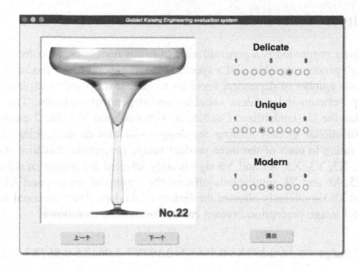

Fig. 4. Goblet Kansei engineering evaluation system

Table 2. Results of multiple linear regression analysis

Product form image	Unstandardized coefficients	Standardized deviation	Standardized coefficients	P value	Tolerance	Variance inflation factor
Delicate constant	5.144	0.555		0.000		
X2	−0.382	0.066	−0.914	0.000	0.450	2.223
X3	−0.186	0.049	−0.476	0.001	0.727	1.376
Y3	0.197	0.051	0.488	0.001	0.698	1.432
X5	−1.064	0.417	−0.352	0.017	0.598	1.671
X7	−0.867	0.389	−0.263	0.035	0.818	1.223
Y8	1.243	0.510	0.325	0.022	0.638	1.567
Unique constant	−1.945	0.253		0.000		
X1	0.428	0.122	0.647	0.002	0.433	2.322
X2	−0.434	0.113	−0.809	0.001	0.533	3.006
Y3	0.369	0.074	0.712	0.000	0.730	1.370
Y5	0.205	0.101	0.258	0.043	0.912	1.096
X6	1.212	0.423	0.381	0.008	0.832	1.202
Y8	1.811	0.729	0.369	0.020	0.668	1.497
Modern constant	7.229	1.115		0.000		
X1	−0.214	0.057	−0.406	0.001	0.803	1.246
Y2	−0.144	0.070	−0.228	0.041	0.789	1.268
X3	−0.116	0.047	−0.289	0.021	0.687	1.456
Y3	0.183	0.042	0.443	0.000	0.907	1.103
X5	−0.814	0.373	−0.262	0.038	0.659	1.518
X6	−0.871	0.269	−0.343	0.003	0.846	1.181

4 Results

Multiple linear regression is a generalization of linear regression by considering more than one independent variable, and a specific case of general linear models formed by restricting the number of dependent variables to one. It was used to explain the linear relationship between independent variables and dependent variables. The data presented within the Unstandardized Coefficients (UC) column of Table 2 can be used to construct functional models relating the design variables of the goblet form to an evaluative rating in each of the three product image perception domains. As Table 2 shows, X2, X3, Y3, X5, X7 and Y8 significantly affected the feeling of delicacy, X1, X2, Y3, Y5, X6 and Y8 significantly affected the feeling of unique, and X1, Y2, X3, Y3, X5 and X6 significantly affected the feeling of modern. The functional models for each product image perception domain can be formulated as follows:

"Delicate" image = 5.14-0.382X2-0.186X3+0.197Y3-1.064X5-0.867X7+1.243Y8

"Unique" image = -1.945+0.382X1-0.434X2+0.369Y3+0.205Y5+1.212X6+1.811Y8

"Modern" image = 7.229-0.214X1-0.144Y2-0.116X3+0.183Y3-0.814X5-0.871X6

Finally, as Table 3 shows, the mapping model between control points of NURBS curve and product style image was built, which means we could change specific control points to change the style image of goblets.

Table 3. The mapping relationship between control points and image

	Form image	
Delicate	Unique	Modern
$P2(x_2,y_2)$ $P3(x_3,y_3)$ $P5(x_5,y_5)$ $P7(x_7,y_7)$ $P8(x_8,y_8)$	$P1(x_1,y_1)$ $P2(x_2,y_2)$ $P3(x_3,y_3)$ $P5(x_5,y_5)$ $P6(x_8,y_8)$	$P1(x_1,y_1)$ $P2(x_2,y_2)$ $P3(x_3,y_3)$ $P5(x_5,y_5)$ $P6(x_8,y_8)$
With the decrease of X₂ X₃ X₅ X₇, the feeling of delicate increases.	With the decrease of X₂, the feeling of unique increases.	With the decrease of X₁ Y₂ X₃ X₅ X₆, the feeling of unique increases.
With the increase of Y₃ Y₈, the feeling of delicate also increases.	With the increase of X₁ Y₃ Y₅ X₆ Y₈, the feeling of delicate also increases.	With the increase of Y₃, the feeling of delicate also increases.

5   Conclusion

We proposed a numerical modelling method to define the mapping relationship between product form and style image. Taking goblets as example, we built the mapping model between the control points of NURBS curve and product style image. This model can accurately reflect the influence of each style image in the process of product modelling. It is also applicable to other product design area. This method can help designers to grasp better product style, which plays a crucial role in product development field.

Acknowledgments. This work was supported by the National Nature Science Foundation of China (Grant NO. 71271053, 71471037).

References

1. Xu, J., Wang, H.Y., Sun, S.Q.: Method of product generative design based on style evolution model. J. SE Univ. Nat. Sci. Ed. **42**(4), 654–658 (2012)
2. Xue, C.Q., Zhang, P., Zhou, L.: Computer-aided style design based on feature construction. J. SE Univ. Nat. Sci. Ed. **41**(4), 734–738 (2011)
3. Nagamachi, M.: Kansei engineering in consumer product design. Ergon. Des. **10**(2), 5–9 (2002)
4. Tanoue, C., Ishizaka, K., Nagamachi, M.: Kansei Engineering: a study on perception of vehicle interior image. Int. J. Indus. Ergon. **19**(2), 115–128 (1997)
5. Nagamachi, M.: Kansei engineering as a powerful consumer-oriented technology for product development. Appl. Ergon. **33**(3), 289–294 (2002)
6. McCormack, C.: Speaking the Buick language: capturing, understanding, and exploring brand identity with shape grammars. Des. Stud. **25**(1), 1–29 (2004)
7. Demirbilek, O.: Product design, semantics and emotional response. Ergonomics **46**(13), 1346–1360 (2003)
8. Huang, Q., Sun, S.Q., Pan, Y.H.: Product style recognition based on feature matching. China Mech. Eng. **14**(21), 1836–1838 (2003)
9. Belaziz, M., Bouras, A., Brun, J.M.: Morphological analysis for product design. Comput. Aided Des. **32**(5), 377–388 (2000)
10. Jindo, T., Shimizu, Y.: Development of a design support system for office chairs using 3-D graphics. Int. J. Indus. Ergon. **15**(1), 49–62 (1995)
11. Lai, H.H., Lin, Y.C., Yeh, C.H.: Form design of product image using grey relational analysis and neural network models. Comput. Oper. Res. **32**(10), 2689–2711 (2005)
12. Chou, C.J., Chen, K.: Creating product forms with preferred Kansei via formal features. J. Des. **8**(2), 77–88 (2003)
13. Chang, H.C., Lai, H.H., Chang, Y.M.: A measurement scale for evaluating the attractiveness of a passenger car form aimed at young consumers. Int. J. Indus. Ergon. **37**(1), 21–30 (2007)
14. Lai, H.H., Lin, Y.C., Yeh, C.H., Wei, C.H.: User-oriented design for the optimal combination on product design. Int. J. Prod. Econ. **100**(2), 253–267 (2006)
15. Chang, Y.M., Chen, H.Y.: Application of novel numerical definition- based systematic approach (NDSA) to the design of knife forms. J. Chin. Inst. Indus. Eng. **25**(2), 148–161 (2008)

A Quantitative Study of Emotional Experience of *Daqi* Based on Cognitive Integration

Min Xie, Liqun Zhang[✉], and Tian Liang

Institute of Design Management,
Shanghai Jiao Tong University, Shanghai, China
zhanglliqun@gmail.com

Abstract. In the Chinese aesthetic experience, *Daqi* is an important and representative emotional experience. However, it is not easy to express the *Daqi* in appropriate words. As the concept of complexity, how to measure and what is the concrete composition of *Daqi* are the focus of this paper. Based on cognitive integration of *Daqi*, this paper puts forward the quantitative research method of human emotional experience. This method first uses the text analysis to extract the representative vocabularies as the *Daqi* measurement indicators. Then Professional researchers grade the stimulants of the *Daqi* of multiple dimensions, calculate the proportion of *Daqi* indicators by SPSS factor analysis, and get a formula of *Daqi*. Finally, this formula is tested and refined by large-scale stimulus experiments. Cognitive quantitative method of emotional experience of *Daqi* is different from the previous emotional behavior analysis method and more conducive to analyze the deep causes and stimulating factors of emotion, enriching the depth and breadth of the emotional experience experiment. While the quantitative formula established by the research can be applied to product and visual design, sociology research and other specific areas, playing a guiding and testing role.

Keywords: *Daqi* · Emotional experience · Cognitive quantization · Stimulus experiment

1 Introduction

In recent years, emotional experience research has become a popular topic in sociology, computer science and other fields [1, 2]. Emotion refers to the subjective feelings or experiences of the individual [3]. Experience is the feeling, testing and introspection of the individual to the event [4]. Emotional experience refers to the individual subjective experience of emotion [5]. Scholars have become increasingly interested in the study of emotional experience, and the number of relevant research methods is growing. At present, the research methods of emotional experience are mainly text analysis [6] and emotional behavior analysis, such as sociological emotional vocabulary research methods, and EEG [7], eye movement detection methods [8] in the field of computer

© Springer International Publishing AG 2017
A. Marcus and W. Wang (Eds.): DUXU 2017, Part I, LNCS 10288, pp. 306–323, 2017.
DOI: 10.1007/978-3-319-58634-2_24

science. However, there are little research about causes, stimulating factors and specific components of emotion.

In the Chinese aesthetic experience, *Daqi*[1] is an important and representative emotional experience. Since ancient times, the demand for *Daqi* cognitive experience is remarkable. For example, the ancients will experience the *Daqi* in poetry and painting, and now people will experience the *Daqi* in music and film. However, it is not easy to express the *Daqi* in appropriate words. This paper studies the emotional experience of *Daqi*, and do the quantitative analysis of *Daqi* based on cognitive integration. The main contents are as follows:

- The intertextual vocabulary and word frequency related to *Daqi* were collected by text analysis. Then the professional researchers analyzed and correlated the relevant vocabulary, and the correlation score matrix of *Daqi* related words was obtained; The representative vocabulary were extracted as *Daqi* indicators through the multi-dimensional scale and cluster analysis.
- Getting high-quality and multi-category pictures as experimental stimulants through the network randomly. Professional researchers graded the stimulants of the *Daqi* of multiple dimensions, and got the data matrix of stimulants in different dimensions. By analyzing the results and professional awareness of the stimulants, *Daqi* indicators were selected and amended.
- The selected *Daqi* stimulants and indicators were subjected to large-scale stimulus experiments. The quantitative score matrixes of *Daqi* and *Daqi* indictors were obtained. Then calculating the proportion of *Daqi* indicators by SPSS factor analysis, and getting a formula of *Daqi*. Comparing the results of this formula with the score of *Daqi* in the stimulants experiments to test the accuracy of this formula. Finally, the cognitive quantification formula of *Daqi* was established.

2 Exploratory Research

Although the *Daqi* is a common emotional experience, since ancient times people use the word *Daqi* to express the views and feelings to a thing. *Daqi* is a kind of complicated emotional experience as well. There is currently no authoritative interpretation and evaluation criteria for *Daqi*. Therefore, in the early part of the study, this paper needs to carry out exploratory research. Through the literature research, researchers collect descriptions and vocabularies related to *Daqi* and expect to obtain representative vocabularies as *Daqi* indicators.

2.1 Data Collection

The literatures in this paper are collected from CNKI, Wanfang and authority comments on articles and paintings. The key word for searching the literature is *Daqi*.

---

[1] Whenever used in this paper, the word in italic and beginning with a capital letter is the professional word of experiment.

When the word *Daqi* appears in the article, the vocabulary or explanation associated with it is intercepted for analysis. Then the intertextuality and context of the *Daqi* are determined. Because there are a small number of relevant literatures related to *Daqi*, and professional and authoritative literatures need to be screened out, the literature and word frequency research all completed by the researchers, without the use of other tools or procedures for word mining.

Finally, 45 articles related to *Daqi* were sorted out, and 180 intertextual vocabularies of *Daqi* were arranged, including 150 synonyms and 30 antonyms.

2.2 Classification and Analysis of Keyword Frequency

Through literature research, all the *Daqi* related words are summed up and word frequency are calculated. Part of the vocabulary induction and word frequency statistics are as follows (Table 1):

Table 1. Part of the vocabulary induction and word frequency statistics

Keywords	Frequency
Daqi	40
Concise/Simple/Simplified/Concise/Refined	23
Grand/Magnificent/Broad	21
Elegant/Noble	15
Steady/Dignified/Solemn	12
Unaffected/Plain/Simple and unadorned	11
Large size/Wide and large/Large	9

Professional researchers summed *Daqi* related words up and calculated word frequency according to the words similarity. Finally, according to the results of the merger and the frequency statistics, the number of *Daqi* antonyms is small, and the corresponding *Daqi* isotropic words can be found. Therefore, this study extracts the representative words directly from the *Daqi* synonyms. The final number of vocabularies to be analyzed is 45. They are *Concise, Grand, Elegant, Solemn, Plain, Large-size, Delicate, Sturdy, Pure, Symmetrical, Uniform, Smooth, Generous, Full, Far-reaching, Aggressive, Round, Rough, Comely, Peaceful, Free and easy, Structured, Strong, Unadorned, Forceful, Rigorous, Vivid, Bold and unconstrained, Tall, Heavy, Deep, Quality, Magnificent, Exquisite, Sparse, Masculine, Sharp, Calm, Clear-cut, Magnanimous, Angular, Worth-looking, Upscale, Large dynamic range.*

2.3 Keyword Correlation Analysis

Although the *Daqi* related words were summarized to extract the keywords, the final number of keywords is 45. Taking the 45 words as *Daqi* indicators will lead to a huge experimental task. So these 45 keywords need to be reprocessed. Researchers will grade keywords by their correlation to get the correlation matrix between these key-words. Then SPSS tool is used to analyze the score results. After SPSS analysis, more appropriate and representative *Daqi* keywords will be extracted as the *Daqi* indicators.

Keyword Correlation Score. Under the hypothesis that *Daqi* related vocabulary search is extensive and representative, the experiment invites four professionals to grade the correlation between any two indicators of 45 *Daqi* keywords. The score is on a 9-point scale ranging from 'significant negative correlation' to 'significant positive correlation'. The scoring criteria are based on the professionals' understanding of the meaning of the vocabularies in the context and the interpretation in Modern Chinese Dictionary. The relevant portion of the score result is shown in Table 2.

Table 2. Part screen shot of keyword correlation score

	Concise	Grand	Elegant	Solemn	Plain	Large-size	Delicate	Sturdy
Concise	1	7	4	6	3	5	8	5
Grand	7	1	7	4	7	2	7	4
Elegant	4	7	1	2	4	5	2	7
Solemn	6	4	2	1	4	5	5	5
Plain	3	7	4	4	1	5	8	6
Large-size	5	2	5	5	5	1	5	4
Delicate	8	7	2	5	8	5	1	7
Sturdy	5	4	7	5	6	4	7	1
Pure	2	5	3	5	2	5	7	6

Keyword Correlation Matrix Analysis. SPSS software is used to analyze the key-words correlation matrix through multidimensional scale analysis, cluster analysis and factor analysis. The reliability analysis results are as follows (Table 3).

Table 3. (a) Reliability statistics of professional group 1; (b) Reliability statistics of professional group 2; (c) Reliability statistics of professional group 3; (d) Reliability statistics of professional group 4.

Reliability Statistics

Cronbach's Alpha	Cronbach's Alpha Based on Standardized Items	N of Items
.703	.738	45

a

Reliability Statistics

Cronbach's Alpha	Cronbach's Alpha Based on Standardized Items	N of Items
.663	.700	45

b

Reliability Statistics

Cronbach's Alpha	Cronbach's Alpha Based on Standardized Items	N of Items
.450	.497	45

c

Reliability Statistics

Cronbach's Alpha	Cronbach's Alpha Based on Standardized Items	N of Items
.855	.854	45

d

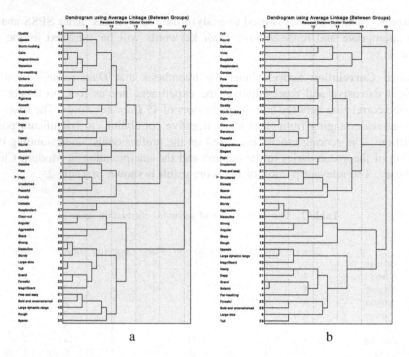

Fig. 1. (a) Dendrogram of professional group 1; (b) Dendrogram of professional group 2.

The reliability results of group 2 and group 3 are too low to be selected. and researchers compare the results of group 1 and group 4.

The results of the dendrogram show that the score matrix of group 1 is more hierarchical and iterative. The score result of group 4 shows that the correlation between the keywords is not high, and it is not conducive to conclude and extract keywords. So professional group 1's data is finally selected for analysis (Fig. 1).

Multidimensional scaling analysis can visually see the spatial distribution of all keywords, and cluster analysis shows the induction process between keywords. Combined with two kinds of analysis results, researchers can conclude and extract keywords scientifically (Fig. 2).

Finally, 16 words are extracted from 45 words as indicators for later experiment.

The 16 words are *Quality, Generous, Uniform, Smooth, Solemn, Full, Round, Elegant, Concise, Plain, Comely, Delicate, Angular, Strong, Grand, Bold and unconstrained* (Fig. 3).

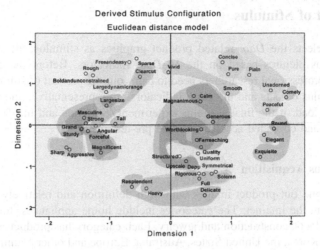

Fig. 2. Multidimensional scaling analysis of professional group 1

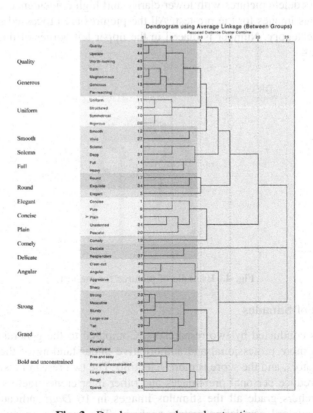

Fig. 3. Dendrogram and word extraction

3 Pre-test of Stimulus

This study selects the *Daqi* related product graphics as stimulus, allowing users to grade stimulus pictures based on the 16 *Daqi* indicators. Before the final stimulus experiment, professional researchers need to carry out the pre-test of stimulus to ensure that the stimulus objects and the *Daqi* indicators are representative, and reduce users' experimental load of the final stimulus experiment. Stimulus and the *Daqi* indicators are modified and corrected according to the pre-test result.

3.1 Stimulus Acquisition

Researchers find out product images with high definition and relatively pure content randomly from the internet. The categories include home appliances, furniture, transportation, artifacts, construction and jewelry. Each category has products selected from China, Japan Korea, the United States, Australia, Europe and other countries, to ensure comprehensiveness and richness of the stimulus.

Researchers delete pictures with lower clarity and high coincidence, and ultimately get 119 stimulus images for the pre-test. All the pictures are processed standardly and numbered by category. Number is placed in the upper left corner of the picture, from 001–119 (Fig. 4).

083

Fig. 4. Example of pictures for pre-test

3.2 Pre-test of Stimulus

The pre-test is conducted by two researchers. Compared to the general experimenter, research has a more professional and authoritative understanding of the stimulus and the *Daqi* indicators, and the score is more scientific. The two researchers work together to effectively reduce personal preferences and other interference factors.

The researchers grade all the stimulus images in 16 *Daqi* indicator dimensions obtained by keyword correlation matrix analysis. The specific operation is that the experimenters grade all the pictures in every *Daqi* indicator dimension on a 5-point scale ranging from 'low' to 'high'. Experiment photo is shown in Fig. 5 and data recording is shown in Table 4.

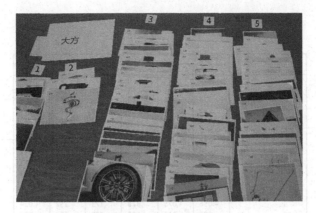

Fig. 5. Experiment photo

Table 4. Data recording

	A	B	C	D	E	F	G	H	I	J	K	L	M	N	O	P	Q
	ber of Pict	Quality	Generous	Uniform	Smooth	Solean	Full	Round	Elegant	Concise	Plain	Comely	Delicate	Angular	Strong	Grong	and unconsti
2	1	4	4	3	3	2	1	3	3	5	4	4	3	1	1	1	1
3	2	4	2	3	3	4	5	3	3	2	1	1	4	1	4	3	2
4	3	3	3	2	2	3	2	1	2	3	2	3	3	4	5	3	2
5	4	4	3	4	5	5	5	5	3	5	3	2	4	1	2	1	1
6	5	5	5	5	5	4	5	5	5	5	4	5	4	1	1	2	1
7	6	4	4	5	5	4	4	4	4	4	2	3	4	1	2	2	1
8	7	4	4	5	3	4	4	3	3	3	2	3	4	2	3	2	?
9	8	4	4	4	3	4	5	4	3	4	4	5	3	2	2	2	2
10	9	5	3	5	4	4	4	3	4	2	1	1	5	1	4	3	3
11	10	3	3	4	4	3	4	3	3	2	2	3	3	2	4	2	3
12	11	4	4	5	5	5	4	4	4	4	4	1	4	1	2	2	1
13	12	3	4	4	3	3	5	4	3	4	3	4	3	2	3	3	2
14	13	4	2	4	4	3	4	3	4	2	2	3	3	2	3	2	3
15	14	5	3	5	5	3	4	4	4	4	4	2	4	1	2	2	1
16	15	4	2	4	3	4	5	3	2	3	2	4	3	2	4	3	2
17	16	5	5	5	5	3	4	4	4	5	4	4	2	4	3	2	2
18	17	5	5	5	5	3	3	5	4	4	4	5	3	3	2	2	1
19	18	4	4	4	3	4	5	3	3	4	4	4	3	3	2	2	1
20	19	3	4	5	3	4	5	3	3	4	2	4	3	2	3	3	1
21	20	5	4	5	3	5	5	3	3	4	2	2	4	3	4	3	2
22	21	2	2	2	4	3	3	4	3	1	2	2	3	3	2	3	3
23	22	3	4	4	2	4	4	3	2	2	2	1	3	3	4	2	2
24	23	2	3	2	2	3	3	2	2	2	2	2	3	3	3	1	2

3.3 Analysis of Experimental Results

After the stimulus scoring matrix is obtained, the data is imported into SPSS for analysis. The result of reliability analysis is shown in Table 5.

Table 5. Reliability analysis of pre-test result

Reliability Statistics

Cronbach's Alpha	Cronbach's Alpha Based on Standardized Items	N of Items
.774	.740	16

Table 6. Factor analysis of pre-test result

Rotated Component Matrix^a

	Component					
	1	2	3	4	5	6
Quanlity	.891	-.018	-.050	.039	-.139	.017
Elegent	.862	.104	-.255	-.065	-.118	.005
Delicate	.774	-.358	.009	-.202	-.327	.052
Generous	.764	.364	.116	.175	.068	-.013
Uniform	.738	.146	.039	.451	-.003	.246
Round	.712	.160	-.448	-.025	.174	.257
Smooth	.684	.113	-.447	.156	.292	.236
Solemn	.676	.031	.305	.353	-.275	.153
Full	.589	-.176	.204	-.257	.335	.317
Plain	-.041	.880	-.084	.046	-.090	.024
Concise	.284	.848	-.034	-.127	.002	.035
Comely	-.031	.601	-.040	-.368	-.193	-.025
Strong	-.056	-.075	.878	.173	.152	-.034
Grand	.105	-.313	.191	.796	.197	-.099
Boldandunconstrained	-.157	-.204	.107	.178	.856	-.093
Angular	-.162	-.026	.078	.032	.086	-.938

Extraction Method: Principal Component Analysis.
Rotation Method: Varimax with Kaiser Normalization.
a. Rotation converged in 10 iterations.

The score of reliability analysis of the pre-test is 0.774, which does not reach 0.8. According to the majority of scholars' point of view on the SPSS reliability analysis, the reliability coefficient above 0.7 or more, means that the date needs to be modified a lot, but it still has its value [9, 10]. On the basis that the test data is still valuable, researchers continue to analyze the data by factor analysis (Table 6).

According to the results of factor analysis, when the number of common factor is 6, the total variance explained reaches 80%. The first common factor contains too many factors including *Quality, Elegant, Delicate, Generous, Uniform, Round, Smooth, Solemn* and *Full*. It is not conducive to extract the common factor. The common factor containing too many factors indicates that most stimulus tend to be consistent on these factor scores. It is necessary to increase the stimulus that get different scores in different dimensions.

Scores of the stimulus on 16 *Daqi* indicator dimensions can be regarded as the coordinate points in the 16-dimensional space. According to Euclidean distance formula, the distance between two vectors, a(x11,x12,...,x1n) and b(x21,x22,...,x2n) (n = 16) in 16 dimensions can be calculated as the following formula.

$$d_{12} = \sqrt{\sum_{k=1}^{n} (x_{1k} - x_{2k})^2} \tag{1}$$

Thereby the distance matrix between each two stimuluses can be obtained (Table 7).

Table 7. Partial screenshot of stimulus distance matrix

	A	B	C	D	E	F	G	H	I	J	K
1	ber of Pict	1	2	3	4	5	6	7	8	9	10
2	1	0	8.1240384	7.07106781	5.91607978	6.40312424	5.65685425	5.56776436	5.56776436	7.81024968	6.55743852
3	2	8.1240384	0	6	5.38516481	8.42614977	5.47722558	4.58257569	5.19615242	5.19615242	3.87298335
4	3	7.07106781	6	0	8.18535277	10.0498756	7.74596669	6.08276253	6.8556546	7.28010989	5
5	4	5.91607978	5.38516481	8.18535277	0	4.89897949	3	4.24264069	3.46410162	6.63324958	4.89897949
6	5	6.40312424	8.42614977	10.0498756	4.89897949	0	3.87298335	5.47722558	5.09901951	8.48528137	7.21110255
7	6	5.65685425	5.47722558	7.74596669	3	3.87298335	0	3	3.87298335	5.56776436	4.58257569
8	7	5.56776436	4.58257569	6.08276253	4.24264069	5.47722558	3	0	3.16227766	5.29150262	3.46410162
9	8	5.56776436	5.19615242	6.8556546	3.46410162	5.09901951	3.87298335	3.16227766	0	6.78232998	4.47213595
10	9	7.81024968	5.19615242	7.28010989	6.63324958	8.48528137	5.56776436	5.29150262	6.78232998	0	5.29150262
11	10	6.55743852	3.87298335	5	4.89897949	7.21110255	4.58257569	3.46410162	4.47213595	5.29150262	0
12	11	6.40312424	5.91607978	8.42614977	3.46410162	4.89897949	3	4.24264069	3.46410162	6	5.65685425
13	12	5.38516481	5.38516481	6.08276253	4	5.09901951	3.87298335	3.16227766	2.82842712	7.07106781	3.46410162
14	13	6.40312424	3.87298335	5.74456265	4.69041576	6.78232998	4.35889894	3.46410162	4.47213595	5.09901951	2
15	14	5.47722558	6.4807407	8.36660027	3.31662479	3.87298335	2.82842712	4.12310563	3.60555128	6.244998	5.56776436
16	15	7	3.87298335	5.19615242	5.29150262	7.07106781	5	3.74165739	4.47213595	6.4807407	3.16227766
17	16	5.83095189	7.07106781	8	4.12310563	4.35889894	3.74165739	4.35889894	3.60555128	6.70820393	5.74456265
18	17	5.29150262	8.24621125	8.24621125	5.19615242	3.60555128	4.24264069	5	5	7.54983444	6.08276253
19	18	5.29150262	6.164414	6.32455532	4.58257569	4.79583152	4.24264069	3.31662479	2.64575131	7.81024968	4.79583152

The results of SPSS analysis of stimulus distance matrix are shown as follows (Table 8):

Table 8. Reliability analysis of stimulus distance matrix

Reliability Statistics

Cronbach's Alpha	Cronbach's Alpha Based on Standardized Items	N of Items
.949	.959	119

The score of reliability analysis of stimulus distance matrix is 0.949, which is very high and great.

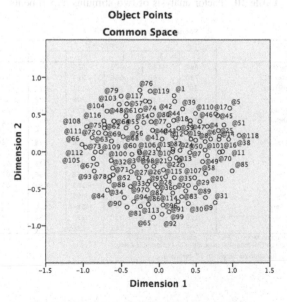

Object Points

Common Space

Fig. 6. Spatial distribution map of stimuluses

Spatial distribution map of stimulus obtained by Multidimensional scaling analysis is equally distributed. It shows that the 119 stimulus pictures are qualified for experiment. Researchers only need to increase some other stimuluses which will get different scores in different dimensions (Fig. 6).

3.4   Modify of Stimulus Pictures and *Daqi* Indicators

After discussion, Researchers increase the stimulus of lamps, furniture, utensils, jewelry and other types, intend to make these stimulus features get different scores in different dimensions. 48 stimulus images are final added and then do the stimulus experiment again.

SPSS analysis of the results of two stimulus experiments are carried out together. The results are as follows (Table 9).

Table 9. Reliability analysis of two stimulus experiments

Reliability Statistics

Cronbach's Alpha	Cronbach's Alpha Based on Standardized Items	N of Items
.723	.707	16

The reliability analysis score of the data gathered by two stimulus experiments is 0.723, which is slightly decreased.

Table 10. Factor analysis of two stimulus experiments

Rotated Component Matrix[a]

	Component					
	1	2	3	4	5	6
Quanlity	.861	.156	-.072	-.025	-.072	.097
Elegent	.780	.360	-.066	-.289	-.056	.038
Generous	.763	.003	.308	.135	.012	.209
Uniform	.731	.139	.210	.409	.092	.058
Solemn	.694	-.082	.045	.435	-.263	.246
Delicate	.665	.042	-.567	-.277	-.243	.027
Angular	-.049	-.797	-.082	.012	.216	-.125
Strong	.017	-.757	.037	.336	.218	.086
Round	.441	.725	.175	-.087	.099	.289
Smooth	.535	.642	.169	.032	.373	-.011
Plain	-.026	.058	.915	-.038	-.096	.020
Concise	.242	.121	.807	-.281	.093	-.053
Grand	.180	-.202	-.140	.805	.274	-.097
Comely	.100	.147	.441	-.584	-.050	-.261
Boldandunconstrained	-.170	-.241	-.010	.227	.854	.088
Full	.308	.177	-.063	.046	.073	.886

Extraction Method: Principal Component Analysis.
Rotation Method: Varimax with Kaiser Normalization.

a. Rotation converged in 17 iterations.

Six common factors are extracted by Factor analysis when the total variance explained reaches 80%. The sub-factors are more equally distributed compared to first stimulus experiment (Table 10).

The SPSS analysis of the stimulus distance matrix is then performed.

Table 11. Reliability analysis of stimulus distance matrix obtained by two stimulus experiments

Reliability Statistics

Cronbach's Alpha	Cronbach's Alpha Based on Standardized Items	N of Items
.972	.977	177

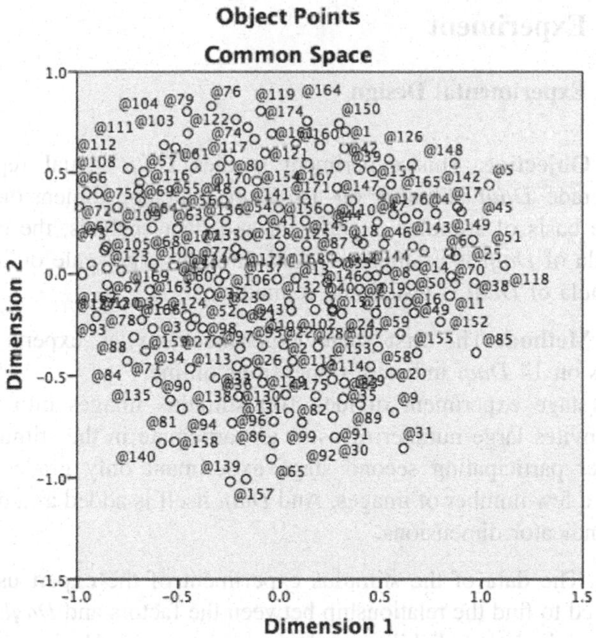

Object Points

Common Space

Fig. 7. Spatial distribution map of the total stimuluses

The Reliability analysis score is 0.972 and spatial distribution map covers more areas (Table 11). However, it is over upper on the whole, which means that some stimuluses need to be deleted (Fig. 7). Stimulus filter is based on Cluster analysis. The stimulus pictures with high density are extracted according to clustering order. Researchers ultimately delete 77 stimulus images based on the results of analysis and professional knowledge, and the final number of stimulus images is 100.

The selection and modify of stimuluses and *Daqi* indicators are the emphasis and difficulty of this research. Because the *Daqi* is difficult to describe and measure, the more relevant measurement indicators, the more describe can be comprehensive. However, taking the feasibility of the experiment into account, the number of stimuluses and indicators need to be controlled, and indicators should be easy understood and judged. The researchers conclude these factors with high degree of coincidence and no significant independence based on the results of pre-test. Judging by the results of factor analysis, *Round* and *Angular* are negatively correlated, and their scores have a negative correlation. *Angular* is a word with a characteristics of conflict. Researchers decide to delete the word *Angular* and retain the word *Round*. The scores of word *Quality* and *Generous* have a positive correlation. Comparing the measurability of two words, researchers retain the word *Quality*, remove the word *Generous*.

According to pre-test, the number of stimulus images is 100 and *Daqi* indicators for later stimulus experiment are *Quality, Uniform, Smooth, Solemn, Full, Round, Elegant, Concise, Plain, Comely, Delicate, Strong, Grand, Bold and unconstrained.*

4 Stimulus Experiment

4.1 Stimulus Experimental Design

Experimental Objective. This experiment studies *Daqi* visual representation of products and grade *Daqi* stimulus on 14 *Daqi* indicator dimensions obtained by pre-test. On the basis of stimulus experiment and data analysis, the cognitive quantification formula of *Daqi* is established. And through large-scale online user experiments, the formula of *Daqi* is tested and refined.

Experimental Method. The first stage experiment invites experts to grade 100 stimulus images on 14 *Daqi* indicator dimensions offline;

The second stage experiment divides 100 stimulus images into several groups randomly and invites large number of users to participate in the stimulus experiment online. The user participating second stage experiment only grades one group of stimulus within a few number of images. And *Daqi* itself is added as a dimension apart from 14 *Daqi* indicator dimensions.

Data Analysis. The data of the stimulus experiment of the expert users in the first stage are analyzed to find the relationship between the factors and *Daqi*. The analytical methods involved include reliability analysis, regression analysis, multidimensional scaling analysis, correspondence analysis, and so on. The analysis tools used are EXCEL and SPSS software.

After the large-scale experiment carried out by ordinary users on the second-stage online, researcher removes invalid data and substitutes the valid data of the stimulus objects in each dimension into the *Daqi* formula obtained by the expert user experiment. At last, researcher compares the data calculated by *Daqi* formula with user's score on *Daqi* dimension to test and refine the formula.

4.2 Stimulus Experiment of Expert Users

The experiment invites six graduate students from the design department to carry out experiments on behalf of the experts. At the beginning of the experiment, the researchers inform uses of experimental purpose, operational procedures and requirements.

The expert users grade all the stimulus images in 14 *Daqi* indicator dimensions obtained by pre-test. The specific operation is that the experimenters grade all the images in every *Daqi* indicator dimension on a 5-point scale ranging from 'low' to 'high'. The researchers then take photographs of the results and record them into the computer.

4.3 Get the Formula of *Daqi* Indicators' Contribution Proportion

For the six expert users' data obtained, SPSS analysis is used to detect data reliability. All subjects score between 0.6 and 0.8. The reason for not high score may be experimental task is huge, experimental time costs too long, and some *Daqi* indicators is difficult to judge intuitively. Taking the average of all the scores, the reliability score is 0.716, which is slightly higher than the individual experimenter's reliability score. Therefore, the average score of all experimenters will be analyzed as the final data.

The factor analysis of the average data shows that when the number of common factors is 5, the total variance of the common factor is 84.904%, and the factor is summarized as follows (Table 12).

It can be seen from the figure that the *Daqi* indicators contained in the common factor is relatively uniform and reasonable. Therefore, 14 *Daqi* indicators can be concluded into five categories of measurement indicators. According to the variance

Table 12. Rotated component matrix

Rotated Component Matrix[a]

	Component				
	1	2	3	4	5
Delicate	.850	-.085	-.349	.053	.158
Quanlity	.785	.296	-.033	.232	.301
Elegent	.779	-.186	.134	.434	.097
Boldandunconstrained	-.094	.931	-.058	.109	.061
Strong	.112	.776	-.110	-.413	.135
Grand	.094	.672	-.235	-.087	.524
Plain	-.295	-.045	.905	-.010	.064
Concise	.170	.017	.774	.360	-.283
Comely	.019	-.366	.764	.097	-.304
Round	.258	-.284	.128	.855	.039
Smooth	.468	.185	.300	.683	.040
Solemn	.394	.154	-.184	-.146	.822
Full	.102	.161	-.310	.466	.672
Uniform	.460	.442	.287	.246	.501

Extraction Method: Principal Component Analysis.
Rotation Method: Varimax with Kaiser Normalization.
a. Rotation converged in 10 iterations.

explained of common factors (Table 13), the contribution proportion of each common factors can be calculated and the formula is got as follows.

$$\mathbf{I} = 0.23187\mathbf{a_1} + 0.21431\mathbf{a_2} + 0.21301\mathbf{a_3} + 0.17421\mathbf{a_4} + 0.16660\mathbf{a_5} \quad (2)$$

a1, a2, ... a5 represent the common factors extracted from 14 *Daqi* indicators by factor analysis. a1 is on behalf of the common factor composed of *Delicate, Quality, Elegant, Bold and unconstrained*. a2 represents the common factor composed of *Strong, Grand*. a3 represents *Plain, Concise, Comely*. a4 is on behalf of *Round, Smooth*. a5 represents *Solemn, Full, Uniform*. Then researchers need to find out the suitable words to explain every common factor based on scientific induction and summary. Here researchers use *Delicate, Grand, Concise, Smooth* and *Full* to explain the common factors a1–a5. The preceding parameters represent the contribution of this common factor in the *Daqi* score.

Table 13. The variance explained of common factors

Total Variance Explained

Component	Initial Eigenvalues			Extraction Sums of Squared Loadings			Rotation Sums of Squared Loadings		
	Total	% of Variance	Cumulative %	Total	% of Variance	Cumulative %	Total	% of Variance	Cumulative %
1	4.602	32.874	32.874	4.602	32.874	32.874	2.756	19.687	19.687
2	3.687	26.336	59.211	3.687	26.336	59.211	2.547	18.196	37.883
3	1.969	14.064	73.275	1.969	14.064	73.275	2.532	18.086	55.969
4	.865	6.179	79.454	.865	6.179	79.454	2.071	14.791	70.759
5	.763	5.451	84.904	.763	5.451	84.904	1.980	14.145	84.904
6	.526	3.759	88.664						
7	.326	2.327	90.991						
8	.299	2.133	93.123						
9	.227	1.619	94.743						
10	.203	1.446	96.189						
11	.165	1.177	97.366						
12	.158	1.131	98.497						
13	.119	.853	99.350						
14	.091	.650	100.000						

Extraction Method: Principal Component Analysis.

4.4   Testing and Improvement of Formula

When the *Daqi* formula is determined, large-scale ordinary user experiments need to be carried out to verify the rationality of this formula. Due to the large number of stimulus, the whole experiment will take several hours if the user completes the whole experiment independently. Such a long time experiment will cause user to lose his patience and feel tired, and the accuracy of the experimental data will be affected as well. In order to reduce the intensity of the user's experiment and ensure the accuracy of the experimental results, researchers decide to divide stimuluses into several groups randomly. So that a user will only grade a small amount of stimuluses on 5 indicator dimensions and *Daqi* dimension. Under the premise that all ordinary users have a common understanding of stimuluses and 5 *Daqi* indicators, when the number of users reaches a certain amount, all users' data can be integrated and the integrated data can be used for post-analysis to verify and improve the formula.

The second stage experiment is intend to apply online experiment. Questionnaire will be issued as a web page. Each questionnaire will be assessed before it is integrated into background data. Finally, after the collection of a number of questionnaires, the integrated data is used for analysis.

The following Table 14 shows a partial screenshot of the integrated data. Due to time limitation, the large-scale user experiment is not completed yet. Now it is only a data analysis of small amounts of data.

Table 14. Partial screenshot of the integrated data

	A	B	C	D	E	F	G	H
1	Number of picture	Delicate	Grand	Concise	Smooth	Full	Daqi value	Daqi theoretical value
2	1	3	2	4	2.66666667	1.66666667	3.33333333	2.718496667
3	2	2.66666667	3.66666667	2.33333333	3.33333333	2.66666667	3	2.926113333
4	3	3	3	3.33333333	2.33333333	3	3.33333333	2.954863333
5	4	4	3	2	4.33333333	2.66666667	3.66666667	3.195606667
6	5	2.66666667	3.33333333	3.66666667	3.33333333	2.33333333	3	3.083156667
7	6	4	3.66666667	4	3.66666667	2	4	3.537293333
8	7	3	3.66666667	4	3.66666667	3.33333333	4	3.527556667
9	8	3	3	3	2.66666667	2.33333333	2.66666667	2.830863333
10	9	3.33333333	3.33333333	4	3.33333333	2.66666667	3.66666667	3.364273333
11	10	4.33333333	4	4.33333333	4	2.66666667	4.33333333	3.92616
12	11	3	3.66666667	1.33333333	2.33333333	3.66666667	3.33333333	2.782783333
13	12	3.33333333	3.33333333	2.66666667	2.66666667	3.66666667	3.66666667	3.13072
14	13	4.66666667	3.66666667	3.66666667	3	3.66666667	4.33333333	3.782396667
15	14	5	4	3.33333333	4.33333333	4	4.33333333	4.147933333
16	15	3.66666667	4	3.33333333	3.66666667	4	3.33333333	3.722633333
17	16	4	3.33333333	4.66666667	3	1.66666667	2.66666667	3.43619
18	17	3.33333333	4	5	3.66666667	1.66666667	3	3.611626667
19	18	3.66666667	3.33333333	4	3.33333333	2	3.33333333	3.330496667
20	19	2.66666667	2.66666667	5	4.66666667	2	3.33333333	3.401043333
21	20	3.66666667	3.33333333	5	3.66666667	2	3.66666667	3.601576667

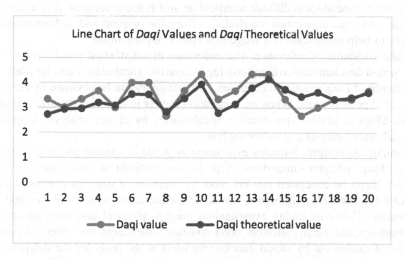

Fig. 8. Line chart of *Daqi* values and *Daqi* theoretical values

As shown above, scores of *Delicate, Grand, Concise, Smooth, Full* and *Daqi* is the average integrated score of large-scale user experiment. The *Daqi* theoretical value is calculated by *Daqi* formula. The correlation between *Daqi* values and *Daqi* theoretical values is analyzed, and the graphs are plotted (Fig. 8).

By comparing the line chart, it can be judged that whether there is a correlation between *Daqi* value and *Daqi* theoretical value. If there is a significant correlation between them, then the *Daqi* formula is established, and can be used as *Daqi* cognitive quantification tool. The correlation coefficient between *Daqi* value and *Daqi* theoretical value can be obtained from the correlation analysis, and the coefficient is substituted into the original formula, a more accurate *Daqi* cognitive quantification formula is modified.

$$D = \alpha I = \alpha(0.23187a_1 + 0.21431a_2 + 0.21301a_3 + 0.17421a_4 + 0.16660a_5) \quad (3)$$

D is the quantified *Daqi* value and α is the correlation coefficient between *Daqi* value and *Daqi* theoretical value. **a1, a2, ... a5** are common indicators which are *Delicate, Grand, Concise, Smooth and Full.*

5 Summary of Research Methods

Take the *Daqi* cognitive experience, which is the common emotional experience of Chinese people, as an example, this paper explore the quantitative study of emotional experience based on cognitive integration. The study method can be summarized as follows:

1. Conduct text study to collect intertextual vocabularies. Because the *Daqi* emotional cognitive experience is difficult to articulate and judge accurately, it is necessary to collect relevant intertextual vocabularies from the original and authoritative literatures to help understand and judge this emotional cognition.
2. Grade vocabularies' relevance. The collection of intertextual vocabularies need to be sorted and summarized, and the representative vocabularies can be used as the indicator of *Daqi* emotional cognition. The summary can be obtained by correlation grade of professionals. When the correlation matrix is acquired, the data is imported into SPSS to obtain representative vocabularies by cluster analysis, multidimensional scale analysis and factor analysis.
3. Stimulus experiment. Stimulus experiment is grade of specific physical pictures on each *Daqi* indicator dimensions. With the precondition of high quality of experiment, it can be concluded that the more the number of stimulus objects is and the wider the area *Daqi* indicators cover, the experiment result will become more accurate. However, taking experimental human, physical and time into account, stimuluses and *Daqi* indicators need constant assessment and filter. The data of pre-test carried out by expert user can be used as the basis for the deletion of the stimuluses and *Daqi* indicators. And the appropriate stimuluses and *Daqi* indicators will be used for the formal stimulus experiments. The formula of *Daqi* indicators' contribution is calculated by the formal experiment carried out by expert user. And the formula is tested and perfected by large-scale stimulus experiments carried out by ordinary user.

6 Conclusion

This paper explores the quantitative study of emotional experience based on cognitive integration. The study method includes three main steps: text research to collect intertextual vocabularies, vocabularies' relevance score and stimulus experiment. Cognitive quantification formula of emotional experience can be obtained finally.

The quantification formula of *Daqi*, which is validated and perfected, can be applied to specific fields such as field of product and visual design, sociology research and so on. As in the design field, the quantification formula of *Daqi* can help designers find the *Daqi* design path from different levels, and even turn the emotional indicators into design elements.

The quantitative research method of *Daqi* emotional experience explored in this study can be applied to other quantitative analysis of emotional experience which is difficult to measure directly. Compared with the previous emotional behavior analysis method, this method is more likely to find the deep factors and stimulus of emotion.

Because of the human, physical and time factors, this study is essentially an exploratory study of the quantitative study of emotional experience. On this basis, we can continue to cognitive quantitative research for the abstract indicators such as *Full* until all the indicators in the formula are easy to measure and judge.

References

1. Canli, T., Zhao, Z., Brewer, J., Gabrieli, J.D., Cahill, L.: Event-related activation in the human amygdala associates with later memory for individual emotional experience. J. Neurosci. **20**, RC99 (2000)
2. Zimmermann, P., Guttormsen, S., Danuser, B., Gomez, P.: Affective computing—a rationale for measuring mood with mouse and keyboard. Int. J. Occup. Saf. Ergon. **9**, 539–551 (2003)
3. Fox, E.: Emotion Science Cognitive and Neuroscientific Approaches to Understanding Human Emotions. Palgrave Macmillan, Hampshire (2008)
4. Gover, M.R.: The Embodied Mind: Cognitive Science and Human Experience. Mind, Culture, and Activity, vol. 3, pp. 295–299. Taylor & Francis, New York (1996)
5. Carstensen, L.L., Pasupathi, M., Mayr, U., Nesselroade, J.R.: Emotional experience in everyday life across the adult life span. J. Pers. Soc. Psychol. **79**, 644 (2000)
6. Tausczik, Y.R., Pennebaker, J.W.: The psychological meaning of words: LIWC and computerized text analysis methods. J. Lang. Soc. Psychol. **29**, 24–54 (2010)
7. Liu, Y., Sourina, O., Nguyen, M.K.: Real-time EEG-based human emotion recognition and visualization. In: 2010 International Conference on Cyberworlds (CW), pp. 262–269. IEEE (2010)
8. Lemos, J.: System and method for determining human emotion by analyzing eye properties. Google Patents (2006)
9. Nie, N.H., Bent, D.H., Hull, C.H.: SPSS: Statistical Package for the Social Sciences. McGraw-Hill, New York (1970)
10. Green, S.B., Salkind, N.J., Jones, T.M.: Using SPSS for Windows Analyzing and Understanding Data. Prentice Hall, Upper Saddle River (1996)

6   Conclusion

This paper explores the quantitative study of emotional experience based on cognitive inferences. The study method includes three main steps: text research to collect emotional vocabulary, vocabulary relevance score and stimulus experiment. Eventually, quantification formula of emotional experience can be obtained finally.

The quantification formula of Dmut, which is validated and perfected, can be applied to specific fields such as field of product and visual design, sociology research and so on. As in the design field, the quantification formula of Dmut can help designer find the Dmut design path from different levels and even turn the emotional indicators into design elements.

The quantitative research method of Dmut emotional experience explored in this study can be applied to other quantitative analysis of emotional experience which is difficult to measure directly. Compared with the previous emotional behavior analysis method, this method is more likely to find the deep factors and stimulus of emotion. Because of the further physical and unique factors, this study is essentially an exploratory study of the quantitative study of emotional experience. On this basis, we will continue to explore quantitative research for the abstract indicators such that we sure that all the indicators in the formula are easy to measure and judge.

References

1. Canli, T., Zhao, Z., Brewer, J., Gabrieli, J.D., Cahill, L.: Event-related activation in the human amygdala correlates with later memory for individual emotional experience. J. Neurosci. 20, RC99 (2000)
2. Zimmermann, P., Guttormsen, S., Danuser, B., Gomez, P.: Affective computing – a rationale for measuring mood with mouse and keyboard. Int. J. Occup. Saf. Ergon. 9, 539–551 (2003)
3. Boyd, D.: Emotion, Revised: Cognitive and Psycho-scientific Approaches to Understanding Human Emotion. Palgrave Macmillan, Hampshire (2008)
4. Simon, Herbert: The Cartesian Mind. Cognitive Science and Human Experience. Mind Culture and Activity, Vol. 6, pp. 293–299. Taylor & Francis, New York (1999).
5. Cochrane, A.L., Fitzpatrick, M., Maio, G.: The ethical, the emotional experience in everyday life across the adult life span. J. Pers. Soc. Psychol. 79, 644 (2000).
6. Turek, A., R.: Pennebaker, J.W.: The psychological meaning of works. LIWC and computerized text analysis method. J. Lang. Soc. Psychol. 29, 24–54 (2010).
7. Liu, Z., Sourina, O., Nguyen, M.K.: Real-time EEG-based human emotion recognition and visualization. In: 2010 International Conference on Cyberworlds (CW), pp. 262–269, IEEE (2010).
8. Larson, J.: Science and method for determining human emotion by analyzing eye properties. Google Patents (2006).
9. Nie, N.H., Bent, D.H., Hull, C.H.: SPSS: Statistical Package for the Social Sciences. McGraw-Hill, New York (1970).
10. Green, S.B., Salkind, N.J., Akey, T.M.: Using SPSS for Windows: Analyzing and Understanding Data. Prentice-Hall, Upper Saddle River (1999).

User Experience Evaluation Methods and Tools

Bringing Content Understanding into Usability Testing in Complex Application Domains—a Case Study in eHealth

Simon Bruntse Andersen[(✉)], Claire Kirchert Rasmussen,
and Erik Frøkjær

Department of Computer Science (DIKU), University of Copenhagen,
Universitetsparken 1, 2100 Copenhagen, Denmark
simon.b.andersen@outlook.com, erikf@di.ku.dk

Abstract. A usability evaluation technique, Cooperative Usability Testing with Questions of Understanding (CUT with QU) intended to illuminate users' ability to understand the content information of an application is proposed. In complex application domains as for instance the eHealth domain, this issue of users' content understanding is sometimes crucial, and thus should be carefully evaluated. Unfortunately, conventional usability evaluation techniques do not address challenges of content understanding.

In a case study within eHealth, specifically the setting of a rehabilitation clinic involving the participation of four physiotherapists and four clients in a period of 3.5 months, it was demonstrated how CUT with QU can complement conventional usability testing and provide insight into users' challenges with understanding of a new complex eHealth application. More experiments in other complex application domains involving different kinds of users and evaluators are needed before we can tell whether CUT with QU is an effective usability testing technique of wider applicability.

Performing CUT with QU is very demanding by drawing heavily on the evaluators' ability to respond effectively to openings and potential shortcomings in the users' content understanding. Evaluators need to train this interview/examination process in order to be able to reach a proper insight of the user's content understanding.

If CUT with QU after more research shows to be inadequate, the motivating research question behind this experimental study remains important: How can "content understanding" effectively be brought into usability testing in complex application domains?

Keywords: Understanding · Knowing · Usability testing · Cooperative Usability Testing · CUT with QU · Health informatics · Rehabilitation · Home-based training · Self-monitoring · Co-monitoring · Compliance · Field experiment

1 The Purpose of the Study

Conventional usability evaluation techniques as Think Aloud [7, 20], Heuristic Evaluation [21] and Cognitive Walkthrough [16, 27] are focusing on the users' ability to interact conveniently and effectively with the application. But in complex application

© Springer International Publishing AG 2017
A. Marcus and W. Wang (Eds.): DUXU 2017, Part I, LNCS 10288, pp. 327–341, 2017.
DOI: 10.1007/978-3-319-58634-2_25

domains this is usually not sufficient. Here users' understanding of the information content is often the main challenge—and the aspect of understanding is by nature difficult to uncover and evaluate.

Many examples of the importance of evaluating users' understanding can be found in the eHealth domain [2, 3, 8, 18], an application domain which certainly is complex. This is a result of the complexity of understanding the health care issue at stake combined with the challenges inherent in adapting possible treatments to the condition of the individual client. The complexity has to be understood both from the clients' perspective and the health professionals' perspective in order to successfully design and make use of new applications. To contribute effectively the clients must understand their role in the treatment when using the new application; the health professionals must learn the new possibilities offered by the application, and perhaps reconsider existing work practices.

In the current paper we propose a new usability evaluation technique targeting users' content understanding. The evaluation technique is developed and illustrated in a case study within eHealth, specifically in the setting of a rehabilitation clinic with the participation of physiotherapists and clients.

2   CUT with QU: The Proposed Usability Evaluation Technique

In order to uncover users' content understanding during usability testing, it is necessary for the evaluators and users to collaborate and discuss issues of understanding and potential misunderstanding. Therefore we have chosen to build upon a usability evaluation technique which has direct collaboration between evaluators and users as its core approach, namely CUT: Cooperative Usability Testing [9], a technique that we are familiar with and have used in many different application domains.

In CUT, users and evaluators are brought together in a constructive dialogue in order to understand usability problems. This happens through a video-recorded interaction session (IAS), where the test user performs relevant tasks with the application to uncover usability problems following a standard procedure, e.g. Think Aloud [7, 20] or Contextual Inquiry [4].

Then follows a cooperative interpretation session (IPS) based upon the video of IAS. The IAS video serves as a medium to supporting the test user and the evaluators to recall situations of interest raised during the IAS. In the IPS the evaluators and the test user identify and discuss the most important usability problems. The aim is not to reach a complete description of the usability problems. The aim is to establish a clear understanding of the most important issues, as the full descriptions are reached afterwards through analyses of the documentation in the form of video recordings and evaluators notes. Here affinity diagramming [12] is highly useful.

In "CUT with QU", the IPS is modified compared to CUT. The IPS is expanded with a set of key questions addressing the issues of content understanding (QU). Through the questions the user is invited to describe how the information from the application makes sense. We have approached this through a dialog with What, Why, and How questions adapted to the situation at hand.

How does the user interpret this information? Does the information fit with the user's prior understanding? Can the user make use of the information in new settings, et cetera? A great variety of questions can be raised; and the evaluator's experience, insight and creativity will be highly challenged in order to guide and manage such "questions of understanding".

Further, it must be realized that the evaluators will need to have solid domain knowledge at a level that goes beyond what can be expected by usual human-computer interaction experts. This proposal of bringing more domain knowledge into usability testing, also through the evaluators, will more generally contribute to the value and impact of the evaluation results as shown by Følstad [10, 11].

In Table 1, the questions of understanding, QU, related to the case study can be seen. These questions were develop during the interpretation sessions with our participants, but our key experience is that the most effective questions have to be grabbed situationally and adjusted to the individual participant. This is a very demanding evaluator capability, which must be refined through training. The video-recorded IPS will here be highly useful for the evaluators to analyze and evaluate their own performance.

Table 1. Six key questions challenging the issues of content understanding (QU).

QU no.	Key questions challenging the issues of content understanding (QU)/Examples
1	*How do you perceive this activity/facility?*
2	*Could it be done in a more intuitive way?*
3	*What are the consequences?*
4	*Why did you do as you did with this activity/facility?*
5	*Is this activity/facility relevant for you?*
6	*Could you suggest another way to do this activity/facility with a similar or improved effect?*

We have strived to build our questions of understanding on Gilbert Ryle's description of "knowing how and knowing that", as well as his ideas about understanding and theory building [25]; and on William James' work about "knowing" [15]. As expressed by James: "...the *relation of knowing* is the most mysterious thing in the world. If we ask how one thing can know another we are led into the heart of Erkenntnisstheorie and metaphysics. ... *There are two kinds of knowledge* broadly speaking and practically distinguishable: we may call them *respectively knowledge by acquaintance* and *knowledge-about* ... I am acquainted with many people and things, which I know very little about ..." [15, pp. 216–222].

For a thorough discussion of these complicated matters we recommend Peter Naur's book "Knowing and the Mystique of Logic and Rules" [19]. Here the reader can also find two metaphors, which are at the core of the proposed usability evaluation technique. These two metaphors describe key aspects of (1) human understanding and insight, and (2) how we as humans are able only to a very limited degree to express our insights directly, warning us how understanding and sharing insights are very difficult and time consuming. The metaphors go like this:

The Metaphor of Person's Insight. *"A person's insight is like a site of buildings in incomplete state of construction.* This metaphor is meant to indicate the mixture of order and inconsistency characterizing any person's insights. These insights group themselves in many ways, the groups being mutually dependent by many degrees, some closely, some slightly. As an incomplete building may be employed as shelter, so the insights had by a person in any particular field may be useful even if restricted in scope. And as the unfinished buildings of a site may conform to no plan, so a person may go though life having incoherent insights." [19, p. 215]

The Metaphor of a Person's Utterances. *"A person's utterances relate to the person's insights as the splashes over the waves to the rolling sea below.* This metaphor is meant to indicate the ephemeral character of our verbal utterances, their being formed, not as a copy of insight already in verbal form, but as a result of an activity of formulation taking place at the moment of the utterance." [19, p. 215]

Further, and down to earth, we have been inspired by Lavra Enevoldsen's classical series of textbooks titled "Read and Understand" (in Danish) [6]. These textbooks and her approach towards learning how to read have been in widespread use in Danish primary schools for decades. The textbooks are based on a set of small essays often supported by illustrations. After reading an essay and interpreting the illustration, the child is asked a number of questions. For some of the questions the answers are not explicitly to be found in the essay, but these questions can be answered clearly if the child has succeeded in reaching a coherent understanding from the reading and interpretation activity. The textbooks are typically used in a way where the child gives answers in written form. This approach of uncovering levels of understanding through a written dialog has been used in two comprehensive usability studies within HCI [13, 14]. The two studies are also concerned with complex application domains, namely information retrieval within programming [13], and reading activity and visualization [14]. These studies, however, did not directly—as this paper—emphasize the importance of focusing more generally within usability testing on the issue of content understanding.

3   The Context of the Case Study

In this section we briefly present the rehabilitation clinic and the application selected for the case study.

3.1   The Rehabilitation Clinic

The study took place in a Danish municipal rehabilitation clinic with 25 therapists employed. The starting point at the clinic was that the management of the municipal wanted to find out whether a new rehabilitation application intended for clients' home-training could increase the productivity.

This created a situation where we as researchers could support and engage the management of the clinic and the employees to participate in a pilot project uncovering the effects of the rehabilitation application. The first challenge was to establish an adequate understanding of the tasks of therapists, and to find therapists that were interested to participate. Here we succeeded to engage four early adaptors [24] with authority among colleagues, and they were involved in the planning of the pilot project with a time span of 3.5 months. These therapists recruited four of their clients with training needs fitting the rehabilitation application.

3.2   The Rehabilitation Application (RA)

The purpose of the rehabilitation application (RA) selected in the pilot project is to motivate the clients to follow their home-training program as defined by their therapist and stay compliant [17, 22, 23].

RA was studied in the version available February 2016. RA consists of a stretch sensor transmitting data to an app. The sensor consists of two parts, mounted on both sides of a latex free elastic band, held together by magnets. The app supplies the client with real-time biomechanical feedback of the training, and supplies the therapist with data tracking their clients' progress.

Figure 1 shows training exercise setup with RA placement on latex free elastic band. Figure 2 shows a screenshot of the therapist's training administration interface with facilities to define and specify exercises and therapy exercise dosage for a client. Figure 3 shows a screenshot presenting feedback data to the client about training performance. The feedback data consist of these measures: (1) compliance with therapy exercise dosage, (2) the number of repetitions performed, (3) time under tension (TUT), and (4) the force used to stretch the elastic band (pulling force).

4   Planning and Implementation of the Pilot Project

The pilot project was planned in three major stages, see Fig. 4.

The aim of *Stage 1* was "Knowing the Clinic". In order to understand the therapists' current work practices and their interaction with their clients we performed a number of Contextual Inquiries (CI) [4].

Stage 2, "Preparation of the Pilot Project" shows the action plan. Here we used the information from the contextual inquiries to make a detailed project description, and to prepare and communicate project activities and practical formalities to the participants. This included recruitment of participants who received an information letter describing their role along with consent forms. User manuals for RA and a plan for a workshop to introduce the therapist to RA were prepared. Based on this, a rehearsal was conducted in order to refine the experimental protocol.

During *Stage 3*, "Research data/Analysis", empirical data from the evaluation sessions with the four therapists and the four clients were collected. The sessions were video-recorded. Both therapists and clients assessed the usability of RA following the procedure of the System Usability Scale (SUS) questionnaires [5]. The empirical data was consolidated through affinity diagramming [12], SWOT analyses [26], and summarized in a final evaluation report [1].

Fig. 1. Training exercise setup with RA placement on latex free elastic band.

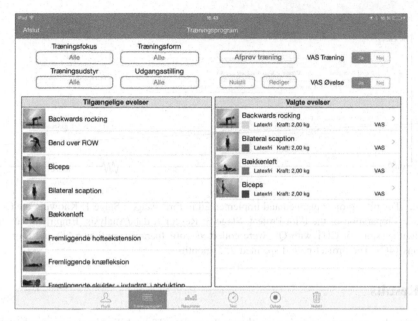

Fig. 2. The therapist administration interface. The top menu shows adjustable training parameters. The left menu shows a selection of the predefined training exercises. The right menu shows training exercises selected for a client's home-training program.

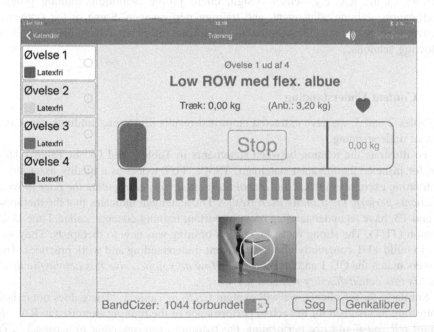

Fig. 3. The client feedback interface. The left menu shows the client's training exercises. The right window shows a visualization of training performance, i.e. number of repetitions, time under tension, and pulling force. Also a video of the training exercise can be activated.

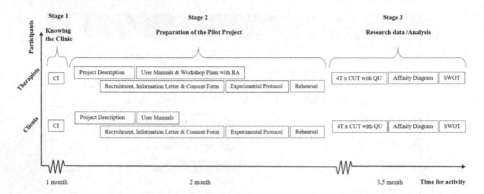

Fig. 4. The pilot project planned and implemented in three stages: Stage 1: Knowing the Clinic, Stage 2: Preparation of the Pilot Project, Stage 3: Research data/Analysis. Empirical data from the eight sessions of CUT with QU were collected, four therapist sessions (4T) and four client sessions (4C). The project period spanned 3, 5 months.

5   Results

Through the evaluation sessions with the therapists 36 usability issues were identified, with the clients 27 usability issues were identified. The usability issues were consolidated through affinity diagramming of the statements from the eight participants during their CUT with QU sessions. The usability issues were categorized according to the facilities of the RA, e.g. sensor design, client profile definition, training program specification, training adjustment, and training performance. Some of the statements uncover aspects of content understanding. Examples are extracted and discussed in the following sections.

5.1   Content Understanding

In Tables 2 and 3, we have extracted empirical results illustrating findings concerning content understanding.

To illustrate the relation between statements in Table 2 and QU in Table 1 let us take for instance the therapist statement, TS30: 'TUT works as a quality assurance of the training exercises in RA: *"It is a cool thing, that you can regulate the pace at which the clients perform the training exercises"* '. The statement indicates that the therapists, T1 and T3, have an understanding of an important training concept, called Time Under Tension (TUT). The strong focus of TUT in training was new to therapists. They were able to build TUT coherently into their current understanding and work practices. Their answers match the QU 1 and 5 (Table 1): *"How do you perceive this activity/facility?"* and *"Is this activity/facility relevant for you?"*.

Similarly for the clients, we will explain CS26 in Table 3: 'There does not exists a controlling mechanism for the actual performance of the training exercises in RA: *"RA cannot tell you if you are performing the training exercises right or wrong"* '. The statement indicates that the clients, C1, C2, C3 and C4, have a comprehensive

Table 2. Content understanding examples of therapist statements selected from the affinity diagrams. The first column specifies the statement number, e.g. TS04 indicating the therapist statement no 04. The Statement column describes the actual statement, followed by a quotation example. In the Participants column it is specified with an "X", which of the therapists that expressed the particular statement. TS04 was expressed by three therapists, T1, T2 and T4.

Statement no.	Statement	Participants			
Therapists		T1	T2	T3	T4
TS04	The administrative resources will increase when using RA in the beginning. After a periodic exposure, the treatment will be more efficient and decrease the administrative resources: *"The treatment process with RA takes a little longer in the beginning until you have tried it few times."*	X	X		X
TS17	There is a need for a search function in RA for finding a specific training exercise: *"It would be nice if you could search for a specific training exercise."*	X	X	X	X
TS19	RA is not compatible with non-elastic band exercises: *"Usually the training will be a combination of exercises with and without elastic band. But in case it is without elastic band it cannot monitor the client."*	X	X	X	X
TS30	TUT works as a quality assurance of the training exercises in RA: *"It is a cool thing, that you can regulate the pace at which the clients perform the training exercises."*	X		X	
TS31	The clients training is by default set to 8 a.m. in RA: *"It is unnecessary with a fixed training time, because it does not matter when the clients perform their training – they just have to perform it on the day itself"*	X	X	X	X

understanding, which extend far beyond the technical use of RA. The statement shows that the clients have approached the essence of the main challenges in RA and for rehabilitation in general. Their answers match the QU 1, 3, 5 and 6 (Table 1): *"How do you perceive this activity/facility?"* and *"What are the consequences?"* and *"Is this activity/facility relevant for you?"* and *"Could you suggest another way to do this activity/facility with a similar or improved effect?".*

5.2 Co-monitoring Versus Self-monitoring

Through the focus of content understanding by CUT with QU it became visible that the concept of self-monitoring should be questioned. Self-monitoring was initially an important goal of introducing the RA at the clinic in order to increase the productivity without losing quality. But both therapists and clients emphasized the importance of

Table 3. Content understanding examples of client statements selected from the affinity diagrams. The first column specifies the statement number, e.g. CS09 indicating the client statement no 09. The Statement column describes the actual statement, followed by a quotation example. In the Participants column it is specified with an "X", which of the clients that expressed the particular statement. CS09 was expressed by two clients, C1 and C3.

Statement no.	Statement	Participants			
Clients		C1	C2	C3	C4
CS09	RA is small and easy to carry around: *"It is nice that you can take RA with you and perform your training everywhere you like."*	X		X	
CS11	There is a need for performing the training after 12 a.m. in RA: *"Some days it is not until late in the evening that I have time to perform my training, because of a stressful day with lot of duties... Maybe a day could last for 28 h in RA."*	X	X		
CS18	Latex free elastic band is slippery and cause inaccurate rotation in the wrist: *"It is hard to hold on the elastic band when training – sometimes the hand slips."*	X	X		
CS25	The training exercises can be showed on video in RA:*"The videos are very easy to understand, and the text is a good guideline the first couple of times you perform the training exercises until they are permanent embedded."*	X		X	X
CS26	There does not exists a controlling mechanism for the actual performance of the training exercises in RA: *"RA cannot tell you if you are performing the training exercises right or wrong."*	X	X	X	X

collaboration, thus the idea of self-monitoring was partly misleading and should be balanced by a concept that we call "co-monitoring", see Tables 4 and 5. The fact that the aspect of co-monitoring became clear might be an effect of the explorative and collaborative evaluation approach.

In Table 4 and 5, we have extracted empirical results illustrating findings concerning co-monitoring. To illustrate the relation between statements in Table 4 and QU in Table 1, let us take for instance the therapist statement, TS34: 'The client has tried to train after 12 a.m. in RA: *"The training day stops at 12 a.m. in RA this means that you cannot cheat by performing yesterdays' training today. RA has a compliance cutoff, default at 12 a.m. which is not always appropriate – therefore we have to help them remembering"* '. The statement indicates that the therapists, T1 and T3, understand the content information behind RA's default settings concerning the principle of automatically compliance monitoring. It also illustrate that the therapists are beware of the importance of collaboration during a co-monitoring treatment processes in RA. Their answers match the QU 1, 3 and 5 (Table 1): *"How do you perceive this*

Table 4. Co-monitoring examples of therapist statements selected from the affinity diagrams. The first column specifies the statement number, e.g. TS03 indicating the therapist statement no 03. The Statement column describes the actual statement, followed by a quotation example. In the Participants column it is specified with an "X", which of the therapists that expressed the particular statement. TS03 was expressed by four therapists, T1, T2, T3 and T3.

Statement no.	Statement	Participants			
Therapists		T1	T2	T3	T4
TS03	Difficulties to see whether RA is activated or not because of its design: *"If we cannot see that RA is turned on we cannot be sure that it will monitor compliance correctly."*	X	X	X	X
TS34	The client has tried to train after 12 a.m. in RA: *"The training day stops at 12 a.m. in RA this means that you cannot cheat by performing yesterdays' training today. RA has a compliance cutoff, default at 12 a.m. which is not always appropriate – therefore we have to help them remembering."*	X		X	
TS36	RA automatically monitors compliance: *"I think it is a clever thing that the RA keeps track of the clients training."*	X	X	X	X

Table 5. Co-monitoring examples of client statements selected from the affinity diagrams. The first column specifies the statement number, e.g. CS07 indicating the client statement no 07. The Statement column describes the actual statement, followed by a quotation example. In the Participants column it is specified with an "X", which of the clients that expressed the particular statement. CS07 was expressed by three clients, C1, C3 and C4.

Statement no.	Statement	Participants			
Clients		C1	C2	C3	C4
CS07	Sometimes RA falls off the latex free elastic band during the training: *"When it happens either the training will be disturbed or the monitoring watchdog will be quiet."*	X		X	X
CS13	There is a need for a reminder function in RA concerning the therapy-prescribed exercise dosage from day to day: *"It could be smart, if you received a message on your phone, or the tablet made a noise when it is time for the daily training. In that way it is easier to adhere to the therapy-prescribed exercise dosage."*			X	X
CS15	RA can increase compliance in home training: *"I feel monitored and committed to do my daily training – kind of a watchdog effect."*		X	X	

activity/facility?" and *"What are the consequences?"* and *"Is this activity/facility relevant for you?"*.

Client statements in Table 5 is in addition to be coherently related to QU in Table 1 also coherently matched to therapist statement in Table 4 in the mind of co-monitoring and compliance aspects. To illustrate the relation between internal statements in Table 5 and QU in Table 1, let us take for instance the client statement, CS15: 'The application can increase compliance in home-training: *"I feel monitored and committed to do my daily training – kind of a watchdog effect"* '. The statement indicates that the clients, C2 and C3, expect RA to increase compliance in home-training. The "watchdog effect" was expressed with a twinkle in the eyes, and the gossiping RA seemed to be a motivating factor illustrating the importance of co-monitoring. Their answers match the QU 1, 3 and 5 (Table 1): *"How do you perceive this activity/facility?"* and *"What are the consequences?"* and *"Is this activity/facility relevant for you?"* The message of therapist statement TS34 match the client statement CS15, and so do the others.

6 Discussion

The case study taking place at a rehabilitation clinic during a period of 3.5 months has demonstrated how a combination of cooperative usability testing (CUT), and key questions concerning users' content understanding (QU) can complement conventional usability testing and provide insight into users' challenges with understanding and making use of a new complex eHealth application. This was established by extracting the statements concerning content understanding from our dialog with therapists and users. These statements were consolidated through affinity diagramming. We did not validate our results by having other researchers to do a similar task of extracting the relevant statements from our transcripts of key statements and make their independent data consolidation.

Using the QU in direct dialog between the evaluators and the clients and therapists was far from easy and straightforward. We had to modify the QU and gain experience through multiple iterations. Our performance as evaluators improved along with an increased understanding of the application domain, our ability to grab the interesting situations illuminating content understanding, and an increased familiarity with the vocabulary used by therapists and users. This experience matches what was to be expected, see Sect. 2 where the CUT with QU technique is described.

As a general result, both clients and therapists emphasized the importance of collaboration between client and therapist. The collaboration seemed important for the clients' motivation and compliance, which cohere with findings concerning the evaluated rehabilitation application (RA) by other researchers [23]. Thus, a widely used term "self-monitoring" for home-based training applications like RA is misleading. As a more appropriate term we propose the term "co-monitoring".

The usability evaluation technique, CUT with QU, has until November 2016 only been empirically studied in this case study, and in a few small laboratory style exercises with health informatics students. Thus the applicability of the technique is still an open question. It has to be studied in other complex applications domains involving more users and evaluators with different levels of domain knowledge before the technique can be claimed to be widely useful and effective. It would also be interesting to experiment with users giving written feedback to QU as this will reduce the highly demanding task of the evaluator to interpret and respond in direct dialog to the user's utterances concerning understanding issues.

7 Conclusion

We have proposed a new usability evaluation technique, called CUT with QU, which is targeting users' content understanding. The evaluation technique is developed from an understanding of human understanding and insight as described by William James [15], Gilbert Ryle [25] and Peter Naur [19], and from creative work by Danish teacher and textbook author, Lavra Enevoldsen [6]. These four authors agree that grabbing and extracting understanding as held by people is very complex. The understanding cannot be expressed fully, but can be approached effectively through a situationally focused dialog involving an interviewer/examiner with solid domain insight. This idea of how to illuminate content understanding has been integrated as a set of questions (QU) into the usability technique, CUT, Cooperative Usability Testing [9].

In a case study within eHealth, specifically the setting of a rehabilitation clinic involving the participation of four physiotherapists and four clients, it has been demonstrated how CUT with QU can complement conventional usability testing and provide insight into users' challenges with understanding and making use of a new complex eHealth application. Before claiming anything about the general applicability of CUT with QU, we need more experiments in other complex application domains and involving different kinds of users and evaluators.

Performing CUT with QU is very demanding by drawing heavily on the evaluators' ability to respond effectively to openings and potential shortcomings in the users content understanding. Evaluators need to train this interview/examination process in order to be able to reach a proper insight of the test user's content understanding.

If CUT with QU after more research shows to be inadequate, the motivating research question behind this experimental study remains important: How can "content understanding" effectively be brought into usability testing in complex application domains?

Acknowledgments. We are thankful to the four physiotherapists and four clients who showed an extraordinary interest and engagement making this case study possible. Especially, we are indebted to Lasse Andersen, physiotherapist. He was our key person in the relation to the clinic. Furthermore, we are grateful to the company BandCizer giving us access to the rehabilitation application used in the case study, and grateful to the rehabilitation clinic, Træningscenteret, Glostrup Kommune, Danmark. The management at Træningscenteret was open and supportive letting therapists and clients participate in this case study.

References

1. Andersen, S.B., Rasmussen, C.K.: BandCizer - Intelligent Elastic Band Training: A Case Study of a Rehabilitation Application focusing on Usability and User Experience. In: Danish, Bachelor thesis at Department of Computer Science (DIKU), University of Copenhagen (2016)
2. Andersen, T., Bansler, J., Kensing, F., Moll, J., Nielsen, K.D.: Alignment of concerns: a design rationale for patient participation in eHealth. In: 47th Hawaii International Conference on System Sciences (HICSS). http://dx.doi.org/10.1109/HICSS.2014.327
3. Ball, M.J., Lillis, J.: E-health: transforming the physician/patient relationship. Int. J. Med. Inform. **61**(1), 1–10 (2001). http://dx.doi.org/10.1016/S1386-5056(00)00130-1
4. Beyer, H., Holtzblatt, K.: Contextual Design: Defining Customer-Centered Systems. Morgan Kaufmann Publishers Inc., San Francisco (1998)
5. Brooke, J.: SUS - A Quick and Dirty Usability Scale: Usability Evaluation in Industry, pp. 1–7. Digital Equipment Corporation, Redhatch Consulting Ldt., Tayler & Francis Group, Reading (1986)
6. Enevoldsen, L.: Læs og forstå. ("Read and Understand", in English). Aschehoug, Denmark (1980)
7. Ericsson, K.A., Simon, H.A.: Protocol Analysis: Verbal Reports as Data. MIT Press, Cambridge (1984)
8. Eysenbach, G.: What is e-health? J. Med. Internet Res. **3**(2), e20 (2001). http://doi.org/10.2196/jmir.3.2.e20
9. Frøkjær, E., Hornbæk, K.: Cooperative usability testing: complementing usability tests with user-supported interpretation sessions. In: CHI 2005 Extended Abstracts on Human Factors in Computing Systems (CHI EA 2005). pp. 1383–1386. ACM, New York (2005). http://dx.doi.org/10.1145/1056808.1056922
10. Følstad, A.: Work-domain experts as evaluators: usability inspection of domain-specific work-support systems. Int. J. Hum. Comput. Interact. **22**(3), 217–245 (2007). http://dx.doi.org/10.1080/10447310709336963
11. Følstad, A., Hornbæk, K.: Work-domain knowledge in usability evaluation: experiences with cooperative usability testing. J. Syst. Softw. **83**(11), 2019–2030 (2010). http://dx.doi.org/10.1016/j.jss.2010.02.026
12. Gaffney, G.: Affinity Diagramming. Information & Design, Usability Techniques. Wiley, Indianapolis (1999)
13. Hertzum, M., Frøkjær, E.: Browsing and querying in online documentation: a study of user interfaces and the interaction process. ACM Trans. Comput. Hum. Interact. **3**(2), 136–161 (1996). http://dx.doi.org/10.1145/230562.230570
14. Hornbæk, K., Frøkjær, E.: Reading patterns and usability in visualizations of electronic documents. ACM Trans. Comput. Hum. Interact. **10**(2), 119–149 (2003). http://dx.doi.org/10.1145/772047.772050
15. James, W.: The Principles of Psychology, vol. 1, pp. 216–222. Henry Holt and Company, New York (1890). Reprinted in Dover Publications, Inc., New York (1950)
16. Lewis, C., Polson, P.G., Wharton, C. Rieman, J.: Testing a walkthrough methodology for theory-based design of walk-up-and-use interfaces. In: Chew, J.C., Whiteside, J. (eds.) Proceedings of the SIGCHI Conference on Human Factors in Computing Systems (CHI 1990), pp. 235–242. ACM, New York (1990). http://dx.doi.org/10.1145/97243.97279

17. McGirr, K., Harring, S.I., Kennedy, T.S.R., Pedersen, M.F.S., Hirata, R.P., Thorborg, K., Bandholm, T., Rathleff, M.S.: An elastic exercice band mounted with a BandcizerTM can differentiate between commonly prescribed home exercises for the shoulder. Int. J. Sports Phys. Ther. **10**(3), 332–340 (2015)
18. Mea, V.D.: What is e-Health (2): The death of telemedicine? J. Med. Internet Res. **3**(2), e22 (2001). http://dx.doi.org/10.2196/jmir.3.2.e22
19. Naur, P.: Knowing and the Mystique of Logic and Rules. Kluwer Academic Publishers, Dordrecht (1995)
20. Nielsen, J., Clemmensen, T., Yssing, C.: Getting access to what goes on in people's heads?: reflections on the think-aloud technique. In: Proceedings of the Second Nordic Conference on Human-Computer Interaction (NordiCHI 2002), pp. 101–110. ACM, New York (2002). http://dx.doi.org/10.1145/572020.572033
21. Nielsen, J., Molich, R.: Heuristic evaluation of user interfaces. In: Chew, J.C., Whiteside, J. (eds.) Proceedings of the SIGCHI Conference on Human Factors in Computing Systems (CHI 1990), pp. 249–256. ACM, New York (1990). http://dx.doi.org/10.1145/97243.97281
22. Rathleff, M.S., Thorborg, K., Rode, L.A., McGirr, K.A., Sørensen, A.S., Bøgild, A., Bandholm, T.: Adherence to commonly prescribed, home-based strength training exercises for the lower extremity can be objectively monitored using the bandcizer. J. Strength Conditioning Res. **29**(3), 627–636 (2015). http://dx.doi.org/10.1519/JSC. 0000000000000675
23. Riel, H., Matthews, M., Vicenzino, B., Bandholm, T., Thorborg, K., Rathleff, M.S.: Efficacy of live feedback to improve objectively monitored compliance to prescribed, home-based, exercise therapy dosage in 15 to 19 year old adolescents with patellofemoral pain-a study protocol of a randomized controlled superiority trial (The XRCISE-AS-INSTRUcted-1 trial). BMC Musculoskelet. Disord. **17**(242), 1–12 (2016). http://dx.doi.org/10.1186/s12891-016-1103-y
24. Rogers, E.M.: Diffusion of Innovations. Free Press of Glencoe, New York (1962)
25. Ryle, G.: The Concept of Mind. Penguin Books Ltd, London (1949). First published by Hutchinson (1949)
26. Sørensen, L., Vidal, R.V.V.: Getting an overview with SWOT. DTU Orbit – Research Information System (1999)
27. Wharton, C., Rieman, J., Lewis, C., Polson, P.: The cognitive walkthrough method: a practitioner's guide. In: Nielsen, J., Mack, R. (eds.) Usability Inspection Methods, pp. 105–140. Wiley, New York (1994)

The Use of Neurometric and Biometric Research Methods in Understanding the User Experience During Product Search of First-Time Buyers in E-Commerce

Tuna Çakar[1]([✉]), Kerem Rızvanoğlu[2], Özgürol Öztürk[2],
Deniz Zengin Çelik[2], and İrfan Gürvardar[3]

[1] Big Data Analytics Program, MEF University, İstanbul, Turkey
tuna.cakar@tunasc.com
[2] Faculty of Communication, Galatasaray University, İstanbul, Turkey
krizvanoglu@gmail.com, ozgurol@gmail.com,
denizzengincelik@gmail.com
[3] Gittigidiyor (Ebay Turkey) Inc. Co., İstanbul, Turkey
igurvardar@ebay.com

Abstract. Understanding user experience (UX) during e-commerce has been a relatively important research area especially in the last decade. The use of conventional methods in UX such as task-observation, in-depth interviews and questionnaires has already contributed for the measurement of the efficiency and effectiveness. This empirical study has aimed to make use of both conventional and neuroscientific methods simultaneously to provide a richer analysis framework for understanding the product search experience of the first-time buyers. The current work provides insights for the results from the combined use of conventional and neuroscientific-biometric methods in a UX study. Although this has been an exploratory study within a limited literature, the obtained results indicate a potential use of these methods for UX research, which may contribute to improve the relevant experience in various digital platforms.

Keywords: User experience (UX) · E-commerce · Product search · Decision making · Traditional user research methods · Neuroscientific methods · Neuroergonomics

1 Introduction

User experience (UX) is defined as "a person's perceptions and responses that result from the use or anticipated use of a product, system, or service" (ISO 9241-210 (2009)). This definition is directly related to the inner states of the experiencer in terms of both cognitive and affective dimensions. On the other hand, it covers the perception, evaluation and decision related to the product in use. It has been important to understand this integrated experience by examining different research methods and comparing these findings. The conventional methods including the surveys/questionnaires, think-aloud procedures and in-depth interviews have contributed considerably for

© Springer International Publishing AG 2017
A. Marcus and W. Wang (Eds.): DUXU 2017, Part I, LNCS 10288, pp. 342–362, 2017.
DOI: 10.1007/978-3-319-58634-2_26

understanding the problems during the use of internet sites for shopping. On the other hand, the use of neuroscientific and psychophysics methods, also mentioned as neuroscientific and biometrics in this text, has also grasped attention with the exciting idea of providing objective means of understanding cognitive and affective processes during the user experience under online environments (Chai *et al.* 2014). Despite the fact this idea has also strong limitations such that an attached device is usually necessary, it has been of interest for many researchers to explore such potential use in this interdisciplinary area of research. This empirical and exploratory study has aimed to understand the user experience of first-time buyers during e-shopping and specifically during product search in e-commerce via the use of neurophysiological and psychophysics research methods as well as the conventional methods. The main research scope is about understanding the potential negative factors, specifically obstacles, during e-shopping processes by both neurophysiological and conventional methods. We have also aimed to compare and to contrast the consistencies and differences between the findings of conventional and neurophysiological-biometric methods.

2 Theoretical Background

The current academic literature has provided two subcategories regarding the research on user experience evaluation methods. These are the subjective and objective evaluation methods. The former one generally relies on the self-reported data about the digital platforms presented whereas the latter one is not targeted at the perception of the user but rather the performance metrics such as total time spent on a web-site or the number of mouse clicks at a specific online medium allocate the main scale that is quantifiable and/or measurable (Hornbæk 2006). The objective measures have generally been referred to the use of eye-tracking method with the outputs such as number of fixations, total time spent on a specific Area of Interest (AOI). All these evaluation methods have been regarded as conventional user experience research methods by which generally a combination of these is preferred during research. Despite the fact these have been the dominant research methodologies used in UX research and professional projects, there are alternative techniques recently emerged involving neurophysiological and biometric/psychophysics methods. The use of neuroscientific and biometric methods has generally been referred to as neuromarketing or neuroergonomics but the former term covers different fields of application than user experience such as the assessment of TV advertisements, visual design tests, brand-adjective and in-store tests. The initial expectation from neuroscientific methods has been to provide a revolutionary change from conventional methodologies to neurophysiological and biometric methods. However, the obtained research findings obtained via conventional and neurophysiological methods has revealed that these methods should better be used as complementary methods to provide a more fruitful framework.

2.1 First-Time User Experience (FTUE)

The initial stages/steps of user experience on a software or an internet site has been defined as first-time user experience that involves signing up, the other configuration steps. Although one user might have an extensive experience with a similar product, he/she will have a FTUE with a new product regardless of how his/her previous experience will have an impact on this FTUE (Drenner et al. 2008). For assessing the usability of an e-commerce site, it is important to observe the behavior of first-time users/buyers who do not have any knowledge about the content/format of this web-site. Time effectiveness is one of the key factors for establishing a successful and long-term relationship between user and the service during FTUE. Time effectiveness has been defined as the effective use of time by the user to complete the given task within a considerably accepted range (Drenner et al. 2008). Thus, it inevitably depends on the complexity of the given task as well as the individual differences. The second factor is intuitiveness that refers to the usability of the presented software without any guidance that means the user can intuitively figure out what to do next without a need for external help. Thus, it is possible for researchers to assess several different factors including layouts, graphics, location of buttons and other features over the experiments done with FTUE to develop more user-friendly designs and to allocate the potentials problems/obstacles. The third factor is patience.

2.2 Subjective Measures

There are many different user evaluation methods including surveys, interviews, and contextual inquiry frequently used in user experience research done both in professional and academic studies (Law et al. 2009). Each method has different strengths and weaknesses but they are generally focused on obtaining information directly from the participants in which the verbal declarations are the main sources of information. Understanding the affects experienced by the users have been issued by Boehner as a critical component of the subjective interpretation and highly important for HCI research domain (Boehner et al. 2005). The emotional responses of the users have been collected retrospectively and directly from the users by which they are expected to state how they have interacted with the presented material/media. Although this is a common use in UX studies, it is widely accepted that the self-reports and other subjective measures are generally directed towards the best and worst experiences rather than providing a full account of the experience. Moreover, it has also been a critical issue that the participants could be influenced by the experimenters' demand so that they might not be delivering the correct information. For instance, the participants can positively be motivated towards the presented web-site with the belief that the experimenters are the designers of it thus they might not be glad to hear/receive negative feedback during the usability and user experience test. In addition to this, it has also been issued that participants might be willing to give the politically correct replies rather than giving the correct information that is not in line with the social norms (Ravaja 2004).

In-depth Interviews. In-depth interviews are mainly conducted for exploring the ideas, comments, perspectives of a small groups of people/participants on a given situation. In this respect, it was important to obtain the experiences, expectations, thoughts and suggestions of the participants about the operations, processes, and outcomes related to this e-commerce site. This type of detailed information composed of suggestions and expectations are useful in the sense to provide further explorations in more detail. The insights from in-depth interviews are commonly used to provide relevant context for understanding the data from other domains or sources. In-depth interviews are preferred over surveys, since they provide much more detailed information. Moreover, it might be preferable for participants when compared to surveys since they are more likely to be a relaxed and conversation-like way of data collection. However, there are also methodological limitations of this method that should be handled with care. First, the obtained responses from the interviews might be biased, since the participants might be looking for their own benefits. Secondly, the conduction of the interviews, transcription stage, and the evaluation of the responses might take too much time when compared to the analysis durations of the other methods. Thirdly, it is crucial to comfort the participant in the sense by an experienced interviewer that the participant could easily tell her opinions about the product or web-site of target. Moreover, the interviewer should not ask leading questions or should not give clues about his personal opinions and should fully attend the participant's interview. Fourthly, it is significant to recognize that the obtained results are mostly not generalizable due to the fact the sample size is generally small and random sampling methods are not performed. Thus, one should be precautious about reporting and presenting the obtained results and related conclusions.

Surveys. Surveys are tools for collecting information from the users about the experience they had while interacting with a website or software program. These tools contain set of questions to understand one's opinions, preferences, attitudes, and characteristics on a given item. The responses from the users will be directing the professionals or researcher to provide a more user-friendly version of the product or the service. The responses from a subset of the target population might be applied to a broader population. For the e-commerce research, there are three main issues regarding the usability of the website: (1) perceived ease-of-use, (2) satisfaction, and (3) perceived time.

Task Observation. Task observation is a frequently used research method that investigates the user during the experience of the presented product or service via online (or offline) observations by an expert. The expert identifies the potential factors that lead to the problems for instance during the use of the website in this context. These identifications regarding the UX could then be validated through the in-depth interviews and/or application of surveys. The task observation method is also critical and useful for understanding the implicit factors that could not be noticed by the user herself but the field expert can observe and identify the potential problems. These accounts from the observations are potentially beneficial for improving the usability of the target product or service.

There are a couple of neurophysiological and biometric methods that have increasingly been used by researchers as well as professionals in the field. The neurophysiological methods are the ones that collect data directly from the brain but the biometric methods have an indirect access to the brain activity. The most widely used neurophysiological methods include EEG/ERP, fMRI and fNIRS (optic brain imaging). On the other hand, the biometric methods involve galvanic skin response (GSR), eye-tracker (E-T), and heart rate (HR). In this study, EEG/ERP, eye-tracker and GSR methods were used for data collection. EEG/ERP method has generally been used for the valence/intensity of the experienced pleasantness (affect) with the calculation of Frontal Alpha Asymmetry (FAA). GSR has been used to detect the changes in the arousal dimension by measuring the electrical resistance of the skin. Eye-tracker has been used to keep track of the eye-movements of the participants thus the use of this method provided the potential explanations for the changes in neuroscientific and biometric indexes. The objective measures (as opposed to the subjective measures) are argued to have the advantage of providing continuous and quantitative output during the user experience. Moreover, the objective measures have also the advantage of not being dependent on any language (or any other verbal articulation). On the other hand, there are a couple of disadvantages of the objective methods such as the variations between subjects (due to individual differences), determination of the significant events especially in large datasets, and providing interpretations for the determined significant events (since different mental states might result with similar outputs). These pose challenging situations for the researchers making use of objective measures while trying to construct a reliable and replicable framework.

Time on Task (Reaction Time) Measure. Time on Task (ToT) measure has been a common measure specifically in UX research to infer/understand the easiness/difficulty of the given task (REF). Total time spent on a given task (for instance, the signing up process to a web-site) were calculated through the intervals between the initiation and completion of a given task. This measure is especially important to understand if a user spends excessive amount of time to complete a task.

The Valence of the Emotional State: Positiveness (FAA). The current academic literature indicates that frontal alpha asymmetry (FAA) can be used as a potential indicator for identification of the valence of emotions as depicted in several basic empirical studies (Briesemeister 2013). According to Davidson's model (1979), there is a hemispheric asymmetry regarding the alpha oscillations among the frontal channels. This neurophysiological model implicates that the left frontal cortex is more activated during the processing of positive affects whereas the left prefrontal cortex is responsible for the negative affect experienced (Davidson et al. 1979). This fundamental has extensively been used in neuromarketing and consumer neuroscience research. One of the main studies in the academic literature has targeted to address how the frontal alpha asymmetry can be used to dissociate between three similar versions of TV ads from the same brand (Ohme et al. 2009). The FAA approach has been used in wide range of applications from product design tests to TV advertisement assessments and to flavor tests (Tomico et al. 2008). One of the newest research and application domain has been suggested to understand the emotional states during user experience. The limited empirical evidence so far indicates that FAA can be a potential and useful index in human-computer interaction studies (Chai *et al.* 2014). As stated in the previous section, the results of the empirical study done by Chai *et al.* (2014) has shown that excellent user experience is correlated with a positive trend in FAA. On the other hand, it has also been revealed that negative emotional states have been correlated with the negative trends in FAA (Wheeler *et al.* 1993). One of the main neurophysiological paradigms of the current study is based on the use of FAA index through the inspection of first-time buyers during e-commerce. It was initially hypothesized that the participants will have negative peaks as they have difficulties during a given e-commerce task.

Arousal dimension of the Emotional states: GSR. Arousal has been another crucial dimension for determining the emotional state of the participants. The arousal level has been shown to be correlated with the galvanic skin response measure (GSR) that measures the electrical resistance of the skin through giving very low levels of amperes (at milliampere level) and measuring the voltage (Boucsein 2012). GSR is a psychophysics method that has been mentioned with different names in the literature as such: electrodermal response (EDR), psychogalvanic reflex (PGR), and skin conductance resistance (SCR). The GSR method has already shown to be correlated with sympathetic activity that is also demonstrated to be correlated with the emotional arousal (Westerink *et al.* 2008). Since GSR has been associated with the level of emotional arousal regardless of the intensity/direction of the emotion experienced, it has also been argued that various emotional states including fear, anger, orienting response might cause similar GSR reactions (Carlson 2013). On the other hand, it might be possible to infer about the processing difficulties of the participants relying on the signal peaks acquired from the GSR device (Carlson 2013). Arousal dimension has been crucial for this kind of studies mainly because of the activator aspect of the arousal such as being as a pusher for the fight-or-flight actions. In this respect, the detected peaks in the arousal dimension could be inferred as the instantaneous processing problems during e-commerce. However, one needs to be precautious during such inferences, since these peaks might also be caused by positive affect. In this respect, the findings from the FAA should also be evaluated as well as the contributions from the subjective measures.

2.3   Research Questions and Purpose

The main purpose of this study is to present and discuss the findings obtained by several different methods, which focus on understanding the product search experience of the first-time buyers in a desktop e-commerce web site. This empirical study mainly revolves around two main research questions: (1) What are the similarities/overlaps of the findings/results from conventional and neuroscientific/biometric methods? (2) What are the inconsistencies/differences and problems regarding the obtained results from these methods?

3   Methodology

This empirical study focuses on understanding the online shopping experience in desktop marketplace e-commerce website through the neuroscientific/biometric methods including EEG/ERP, eye-tracker, galvanic skin response (GSR), pulse rate (PR) as well as UX research methods such as task-observation, in-depth interview and survey.

3.1   Participants

The participants were all males, 24–35 years of age, right-handed, and actively working as professionals at least for 3 years. The participants were also required not to have done any online shopping via a specific web-site before. This requirement was significant to assess their first-time user experience (FTUE) in this specific web-site. They were also required not to use any psychiatric drugs in the last 6 months. The participants were informed about the aim and content of the experiment before the session starts. They were reminded that if they feel uncomfortable during the experiment, they might leave the experiment without any hesitation. The ethics approval for this study has been acquired from the Ethics Committee of Acıbadem University (Istanbul, Turkey).

3.2   Procedure

The participants were asked to sign up to this web-site, they were then to choose a specific item category to buy, to provide three concrete options for this category and then to purchase one of these options. These participants were motivated by a gift card of 250 TL (approximately 73 USD) as a contribution to their shopping task. In the post-test session, the participants were given a survey about the experiment and invited to an in-depth interview through a retrospective think-aloud protocol to be able to grasp their online shopping experience in more detail. The participants were instructed about the experimental task in detail.

The experimental session is composed of 4 different tasks: (1) signing in, (2) product search, (3) find 3 items of their interest & add to cart, (4) purchase one of these 3 items. The first task was that the participants were to login to this e-commerce site without any time limitation. For the second task, the participants were instructed to find a product category of their interest and they were asked to find three alternatives for this product category. Moderators reminded that it was important to reach the ticket limit of 250 TL to be able to activate the given tickets.

3.3   Conventional UX Research Methods

Test Evaluation. *Task-Observation.* A team of two researchers were responsible for the observation of the participants during task execution: A moderator and a facilitator. The test was led by a moderator and the task-execution was directly observed and recorded on a structured observation sheet by both the moderator and a facilitator.

Post-test Evaluation. *In-depth Interviews.* After the online recordings, the participants participated an in-depth interview by which their introspective judgments about their experience were asked and their replies were noted down. The participants were shown the related fields on the screen to enable them remember and actively participate in the interview session. The questions were generally centered at getting more about the experience of the participants in detail.

Surveys. A user experience questionnaire has been performed just after the in-depth interview session. The participants were asked to rate the perceived quality of their experience regarding different aspects. In this survey, three main aspects were questioned: (1) perceived ease-of-use, (2) satisfaction, and (3) perceived time. The participants were orally asked to rate the given aspect in 5-point Likert scale. The responses were noted down by the moderators.

3.4 Neurophysiological and Biometric Research Methods

Time-on-Task (ToT) Measure. Time-on-Task (ToT) measure has been a common measure specifically in UX research to infer and understand the degree of difficulty of the given task. ToT measures were calculated through the intervals between the initiation of a given task and completion of that task.

EEG Recording and Data Analysis. A 32-channel wireless dry-electrode EEG/ERP system, has been used to calculate Frontal Alpha Asymmetry (FAA) that has been claimed to be an indicator of approach/withdrawal tendencies of the participants. Thus, the valence dimension of the emotional experience has been estimated by these empirical outputs. The main scope has been to capture the instants with negative peaks including the issues related to personal information entry of the email addresses, log in to the email accounts, identity number and the issues related to the usability of the website including delay in the page loadings and unselecting items in the shopping cart.

The EEG data was continuously recorded from 32 scalp sites using dry electrodes mounted in an elastic cap arranged according to the 10–10 international placement system (g.Nautilus). The online reference was right mastoid (A2). The impedances of the EEG electrodes were below 50 kΩ. The EEG data were amplified with a bandpass filter of 0.01–45 Hz and digitized at 500 Hz. The recordings obtained from the prefrontal and frontal regions of the cortex (Fp1, Fp2, AF3, AF4, F3, F4, F7, and F8) were analyzed (Fig. 1).

Fig. 1. Wireless g.Nautilus 32-channel EEG/ERP device

The EEG data was processed using MATLAB 2014b and Fieldtrip. All the EEG data were DC corrected and re-referenced to linked mastoids offline. The filter was set to 40 Hz low pass and 0.1 Hz high pass. Then, the EEG data were epoched into periods of 500 points (i.e., 1000 ms). The power of alpha band (8–12 Hz) for each of the recorded electrodes was calculated for further analysis.

According to the previous empirical studies in the relevant literature (Ohme *et al.* 2010), the frontal alpha asymmetry (FAA) index was calculated as the difference between right-hemispheric data minus left-hemispheric data with the following formula (Davidson *et al.* 1979):

$$\text{ln (right alpha power)} - \text{ln (left alpha power)} \tag{1}$$

Due to the negative correlation between alpha power and brain activation, the positive score of the FAA index implies the dominance of left PFC and the negative score of the FAA index implies the dominance of right PFC. These neurophysiological and psychophysics outputs have been plotted in a video synchronized with screen recorder and eye-tracker. The obtained data has been statistically analyzed to find the significant peaks within the whole dataset. The voltage fluctuations above 200 microvolts per 250 ms and below 1 microvolts per 250 ms were excluded. The statistical analyses (parametric t-test for normal distributions) have been performed on the whole distribution of the data points calculated by FAA. The values at 95% significance level have been marked.

GSR Recordings and Data Analysis. Secondly, GSR method, as a measure of physiological arousal, has been used for exploring the changes in arousal dimension. The changes in arousal have already been issued with experience of difficulties while using an interface thus have been associated with frustration and stress. GSR recordings were performed via a mobile device (Shimmer) with a sampling rate 50 Hz. The fingers of the participants were cleaned with a soft cleaning gel. Then the device was plugged. The acquired data was filtered with a cut-off frequency of 0.3 Hz and with Butterworth filter of 10 Hz. The obtained continuous signal was detrended to eliminate the potential trend-related effects. The signal was then statistically analyzed to find the peaks throughout the whole distribution. Thus, the statistically significant peaks have been illustrated in a video of 250 ms frame (4 Hz). The obtained data has been statistically analyzed to find the significant peaks within the whole dataset. The values at 95% significance level have been marked and reported accordingly (Fig. 2).

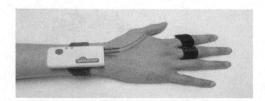

Fig. 2. Wireless Shimmer GSR device

Eye-tracking Records and Data Analysis. An eye-tracker device, Eye Tribe, has been used for data collection during the experiments. The eye-tracking data are important for understanding the trends in the EEG/FAA and GSR data. The eye-tracking data has been converted into heatmaps @4 Hz to be compatible with the other neurometric and biometric outputs.

4 Results and Discussion

4.1 Evaluation of the Findings from Conventional UX Research Methods

In this part, the findings obtained via different methods are summarized and demonstrated.

Evaluation of the Findings from the Task-Observation Stage. The product category menu on the left side appears as an initiator and navigator tool for the product search experience. Most of the participants (n = 14) attempted to make use of this menu especially in the very early periods of product search.

Search engine box, which provided autocomplete suggestions, was also used by most of the participants as a means for product search (n = 15). However, it was observed that only 4 participants preferred to use the search box as the first strategy to find the product they are looking for. Thus, as suggested by Baymard Institutes reports, the position, contrasts and size of the search field possibly affect the usage of this area. The remaining 11 participants preferred to search products through the category menu, but when they failed to find the desired product through the product category menu, they were inevitably forced to use the search engine box.

Some of the participants (n = 6) were also interested in the items that were presented in the main carousel in the categories. Specifically, a significant discount presented in the first slide of the carousel took their attention. Moreover, some of these participants made use of the navigator inside the carousel to change its content. However, the arrow buttons inside the carousel were not easily recognizable and appeared as a potential issue to be resolved.

One of the mostly observed behavior was that more than half of the participants (n = 11) were not able to notice the filter menu in the search results page due to the fact this menu is located below the category structure. Five participants could not see the filter menu during their entire product search process, whereas the remaining 6 participants could notice the filter menu far lately. This resulted in the insistent use of pagination and visiting the product search result screens one-by-one (n = 16).

One of the other aspects has been related to the use of filters. Only 9 participants directly head to the filter menu. Even by including the number of participants that noticed the filter menu late in their product search process, all the participants who used the filter menu (n = 15) limited their use with only three filters: Firsthand/ Second hand (*"Durum/Sıfır"*), free cargo (*"Kargo/Ücretsiz"*) and price range (*"Fiyat aralığı"*). Thus, our results on filter menu showed the importance of detailed and category specific filters as suggested by Holst (2016).

It was also remarkable that some of the participants (n = 4) were not able to see the arrow button to activate the price range filter after they entered the information to the relevant boxes. These participants expected to have an automatic activation of the filters as they entered the price ranges. It was also observed that the complementary features to support product search such as "sorting" and "viewing options" were used by none of the participants. Only one participant attempted to use the "viewing options" to see the product search results in a row based layout. This finding appeared as a potential limitation for an effective use of it by most of the participants.

Evaluation of the Findings from In-depth Interview Stage. The findings from the in-depth interviews are in line with the findings derived from the task-observation stage. A summary of the findings, which are accompanied by relevant quotes from the users, are presented in Table 1 below. The findings fell into five major categories: Browsing with the use of left-hand category menu, Search experience, Use of persuasive design features, Faceted-Browsing (Use of Filters), Product Listings (Product Search Results Page).

Table 1. Summary of the findings from the in-depth interview stage

	Positive insights	Frequency	Quotes
Browsing with the use of left-hand category menu	• Use of the product category menu on the left side as an initiator and navigator tool for the product search experience	11	• "I can easily find what I'm looking for according to product groups." (K1) • "It is very well classified, everything what I'm looking for is present... The menus on the left side are explanatory and detailed. Inside of the menu (mega drop-down), presence of photos during access of sub-categories is good." (K11)
Search experience	• Use of the search engine box which is supported by autocomplete suggestions	5	• "I can find products easily. Google search, let's think about such a culture. I wrote 'kol', consequently, everything related to "kol saati" was appeared. I liked it." (K5)
Use of persuasive design features	• Presenting discounted items in the first slide of the carousel	5	• "I view the carousels like this. There have been always very nice goods in that place." (K7) • "It is being today's deal and 40% discount attracted my attention. The price dropped to 259 TL from 429 TL." (K3)

(continued)

Table 1. (*continued*)

	Positive insights	Frequency	Quotes
Faceted-Browsing (Use of Filters)	• When noticed, although three filters were used frequently, the filters were valued	9	• "I like choosing search criteria (filters). The field that we can search, either fill it with special words or enter any criterion. The product that I intended to buy... Is it new? Is it in its own box? Even these are important for me." (K13)
	Negative insights	Frequency	Quotes
Faceted-Browsing (Use of Filters)	• Inability to notice the filter menu in the search results page due to the fact that this menu is placed/presented below the category structure	11	• "I could not find filtration. It was not clear." (K1) • "The website is nice but with few details, I could not find many goods that I am looking for, I intended to enter price range but I could not find." K6 • "Filter menu is shaded in color, it does not attract attention." (K12)
	• Inability to notice the filter menu resulted in the insistent use of pagination during the navigation through product search result screens	14	• "If I had been able to see the price range, I would not have gone until the page 24" (K11)
	• Frustration caused by the lack of auto-filtering which resulted in the ignorance of the filter activation button	4	• "When we click on checkboxes how it renews the process, I thought it will do it for price range, too. But, it did not. I realized the arrow below afterwards." (K7) • "Because I could not see the confirmation button "OK" after I enter the price range during filtering, I could not click on it. It should be clearer. Dark blue, green, etc." (K1)

(*continued*)

Table 1. (*continued*)

	Negative insights	Frequency	Quotes
	• Lack of category-specific filters	4	• "I did not like the detailing in product search... I am looking for bicycle but I could not make a detailed search. Disc, brake, aluminum case. There is not enough criterion." (K4) • "The shoe size does not appear as a filter." (K8)
Product Listings (Product Search Results Page)	• Lack of detailed product information in product search results page	9	• "Although product names are the same, their prices are different. This got me confused. Also, I hesitated whether it is a second-hand product or not." (K6) • "I cannot see whether the product that I have bought has a guarantee or not." (K6)

The evaluation of the in-depth interviews for the product search task indicates that the participants were generally satisfied with the product search features. For instance, more than half of the participants (n = 11) were content in using the extensive product category menu on the left side as a tool to start their the product search experience.

As suggested by Appleseed (2014), the autocomplete suggestions feature in the search engine was expressed as a user-friendly and effective feature of this e-commerce site by some of the participants (n = 5). However, it should be mentioned that these participants were the ones which started their search process directly from the search engine box.

Presentation of discounted items in the first slide of the carousel were appreciated by some of the participants (n = 5). These participants mentioned that they tended to look at the prices first and then they were engaged in the product features. This might be related to one's price-sensitive position during e-shopping.

On the other hand, the participants (n = 11) could not notice the filter menu in the search results page due to the fact the filters were located below the category structure that was a difficult place to notice. Five of the participants told that they were even unaware of such a menu. Thus, the recognition of this menu in the product search results page appeared as an important problem. The participants who noticed and use the filter menu were content in using such a feature (n = 9). However, the participants who could notice the filter menu could only make limited use of it. Only three filters were frequently used by the participants: Firsthand/ Second hand (*"Durum/Sıfır"*), free cargo (*"Kargo/Ücretsiz"*) and price range (*"Fiyat aralığı"*). Only 4 participants declared the need for more category-specific filters.

Four participants were frustrated since they expected to find the automatic activation of the price range filter rather than the obligation to click on an action button. This finding supports the notion that automated filtering in faceted search is an important expectation among e-commerce users.

Findings from the in-depth interviews confirmed the observations on the insistent use of pagination by most of the participants (n = 14). The findings revealed that the inability of the participants to notice the filter menu in their product search process resulted in the insistent use of pagination during the navigation through product search result screens. They spent great efforts to visit the product search result screens one-by-one. This factor might be the main cause of the high amount of durations devoted to the product search stage. This observation could also be interpreted as part of a potential window shopper behavior. However, the findings from the in-depth interviews showed that only three of the participants associated their use of pagination with window shopping.

Almost half of the participants expressed difficulty in scanning through the product search results page due to the limited amount of product information presented in each search result (n = 9).

Evaluation of the Findings from the Surveys. Findings from the surveys overlapped with the ones derived from the previously adopted qualitative methods. The survey was composed of three main aspects: Perceived ease-of-use, satisfaction, and perceived time. The participants were asked to rate their experience during product search with respect to these aspects. The ratings ranged from 1 (lowest) to 5 (highest). The results are Perceived ease-of-use: 3.95/5, Satisfaction: 3.8/5, and Perceived Time: 3.45/5.

Perceived ease of-use. The obtained results from the surveys indicate that the perceived easiness of the use of internet site for product search is generally positive (significantly higher than average). The participants' introspective evaluations generally focus on the fact that they could find the target products easily. Only 3 participants (P4, P13, and P21) responded lower than the middle rating as all of them had difficulty in finding the products they wanted to buy.

Satisfaction. The ratings of the participants for the satisfaction dimension during product search is also significantly higher than the middle rating (3). The ratings of the 3 participants, who spent considerable amount of time in finding the products they wanted to buy, were quite lower for the satisfaction index.

Perceived Time. The ratings for this index reflects that the participants completed their task of product search almost on average. The mean of ratings was not significantly different from the middle rating (3). Similarly, the ratings from the three participants was below the average.

It was also of our interest to observe if there is significant correlation between these three aspects. The results of the statistical analyses indicate that these aspects are significantly correlated with each other (dep. samples t-test; p < .05). Thus, the participants were generally tended to evaluate their satisfaction levels in relation to the perceived ease-of-use and perceived time.

4.2   Findings from the Neurophysiological and Psychophysics Methods

The findings from EEG-GSR measures are presented in this part. As mentioned above, the measures are used to observe negative experiences of the participants relying on FAA and peaks in the GSR level (Table 2).

Table 2. The appearances of the negative signals are marked with "1" and "0" sign indicates that there is no such observed negative peak for the given activity. (P3 was excluded because of the synchronization problems during data collection)

	P1	P2	P4	P5	P6	P7	P8	P9	P10	P11	P12	P13	P14	P15	P16	P17	P18	P19	P20	No	%
Use of search filters	1	1	1	0	1	1	1	1	1	1	0	1	1	1	1	1	1	1	1	17	89
Browsing experience (of the prodcut categories)	1	1	0	0	1	1	1	0	0	0	0	1	1	1	0	0	1	0	0	9	47
Excessive page loading duration	0	0	0	1	0	0	0	0	0	0	0	0	1	0	0	0	0	0	0	2	11
When unable to find a button	0	0	0	1	0	0	0	0	1	0	0	0	0	0	0	0	0	0	0	2	11
Scrolling up & down	1	0	0	0	1	1	1	1	0	1	0	0	1	0	0	0	0	0	0	7	37

The most common neural pattern has been related to the use of search filters. It might have possibly been due to the fact the participants experienced problems while using the filters. The obtained findings indicate that the use of filters appears as a potential problem for almost all the participants (79%). The negative FAA peaks during the attempts for the filters (such as price range) (Fig. 3).

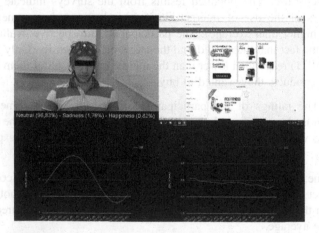

Fig. 3. The participant is experiencing negativity while finding the relevant product category during product search phase.

Moreover, it is also remarkable that when the participants were not able to find the location of certain buttons of interest (such as "add to cart" or "sorting option"), the negative FAA peaks were observed and reported. These might be assessed as problems due to usability, since user experience (UX) has classified to be negative.

Moreover, scrolling down and up with the use of mouse has been observed to be a potential precursor of negative affect that might be because of the difficulty of tracking the flow on the screen (n = 7). The issue related to the situations that the participants could not find the relevant button on the webpage was infrequent (n = 2), however, these cases resulted with clear incidences of negative affect.

Results of the Time-on-Task (TOT) Measures. The completion time for product search task was 754.047 s. The analysis of the Reaction Time data indicates that the individual differences have a considerable impact on the high level of variance. This fact could be explained with the differences regarding the participants' intentions related to purchasing. Some could easily determine the target product and find suitable alternatives quickly. However, the rest experienced difficulties while deciding on the product category. As initially expected, the standard deviation of this measure for this task was higher when compared to the average ToT measures.

4.3 Comparison of the Findings from Multimodal Methods

The findings from neurophysiological and psychophysics methods indicate that there are number of UX issues that are in line with the findings from different methods. The most common ones are about the issues related to the inefficient use of filters validated by both methods. The use of filters under the product category menu has been limited that have been reported by task-observation and in-depth interview methods. The findings from neurophysiological methods indicate that 79% of the participants experienced negative affect while using these filters. Moreover, 3 out of 4 participants who have complained about the insufficiency of category-specific filters (during the in-depth interviews) are reported to have negative affect during the use of filters. Thus, the observed negative affect might be because of their insufficient level of satisfaction during product search and specifically related to the ineffective use of these search filters. The table below shows the interconnection across the findings between different methodologies (Fig. 4).

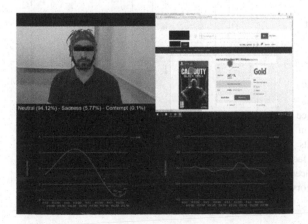

Fig. 4. The participant is experiencing negative affect because of the unexpected product price

The findings obtained from neurophysiological/psychophysics methods indicate that two of the participants were likely to experience negative affect as the page loadings reached excessive durations. On the other hand, scrolling up and down through the page were observed to cause negative affect for some of the participants (7 out of 19 participants). Moreover, two of the participants were observed to have negative affect, since they could not find the relevant buttons on the page. This might have caused a considerable level of anxiety for these participants. But it is important to remark that these neurophysiological/psychophysics findings were not supported by the qualitative methods. These might be accepted as contributive findings by these quantitative methods. However, a better methodology might be to ask the participants about this kind of potential cases (Table 3).

Table 3. This table shows the findings related to the use of filters by neurophysiological/psychophysics, in-depth interview and task observation methods

	1	2	4	5	6	7	8	9	10	11	12	13	14	15	16	17	18	19	20	No
Negative affect by Neuro/Bio methods during use of search filters	1	1	1			1	1	1	1	1	1	1	1	1	1	1	1	1	1	17
Frustration caused by the lack of auto-filtering which resulted in the ignorance of the filter activation button	1						1	1			1									4
Inability to notice the filter menu resulted in the insistent use of pagination during the navigation through product search result screens	1	**1**					1	1		1	1	**1**	1		**1**	1	1	1	1	13
Lack of category-specific filters			1				1	1								1				4
Inability to notice the filter menu in the search results page due to the fact this menu is placed below the category structure	1		**1**			1	1			1		**1**	1		1	1			1	10

(*continued*)

Table 3. (*continued*)

	1	2	4	5	6	7	8	9	10	11	12	13	14	15	16	17	18	19	20	No
Inability to notice the filter menu in the search results page due to the fact this menu is placed below the category structure	1			1			1	1		1			1	1			1			8
Expectancy of auto-filtering which resulted in the ignorance of the filter activation button	1						1	1												3

It is also important to remark that the individual differences might be influential to a certain extent. For instance, one participant might be negatively affected because of waiting for the load of a new page whereas the other might not have a problem with this. Thus, overall evaluations and inter-methodological links have such a potential problem while trying to find the relevant explanations regarding the given context. One future solution might be the use of a deep-dive survey that investigate most of the potential problems for each of the participant. Hereby, it will be possible to provide a useful framework for considering the individual differences just after the user has experienced it and asked specifically about it (Fig. 5).

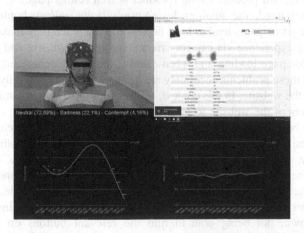

Fig. 5. The participant is experiencing negative affect due to the fact product information page does not satisfy him during product search phase

In relation to the very early discussions about the relative positions of the newer and older methods, it is necessary to provide an insight for the current state-of-art. The obtained findings from multi-modal methods suggest that the neuroscientific/ psychophysics versus conventional methods might come up with partially overlapping but in general diverging results as the outputs of the current study indicates. On one hand, it is quite convincing if both the subjective and objective methods end up with converging results as in the use of search filters. However, this is not the case for several occasions and the outputs from these methods do not seem to overlap although they do not contradict each other. In other words, these outputs might be focusing on different aspects of the user experience. It is quite trivial that the subjective methods are sensitive for the high-order cognitive processing that have been accounted by the user herself. On the other hand, the objective methods might be more sensitive for detecting lower level affects that are not generally articulated by the participant. Thus, the main contrast might be linked to the ongoing debate between explicit and implicit levels of information processing. Hence, the outputs of these different methodologies might be used as complementary tools for each other.

5   Conclusion

Overall, the obtained empirical findings of this exploratory study enabled to point out successful features to support a seamless buying experience in the target website. However, the findings also revealed a couple of user experience problems related to the design and implementation of the target website. The main issues obtained by the qualitative methods including task observations and in-depth interviews cover the search experience, browsing experience (through the left-hand category menu), use of filters and sorting, and product listing (product search results page).

On the other hand, the findings by neurophysiological/psychophysics methods indicate that the participants tend to have negative affect when they make use of search filters, browsing experience via category menu, scrolling up/down, and less frequently while waiting for page loading and when cannot find the searched button on a page.

Addressing these problems accurately are quite significant especially for enhancing the usability of the website. In this context, the findings of the current study are used by the UX designers of the website to improve the relevant experience.

There have been occasional findings from the neuroscientific/psychophysiological methods and the conventional methods that seem to support each other to a certain extent such that the use of filters have been found to be problematic.

However, there are also diverging findings such that qualitative methods indicate that the filter menu in the product search page is quite unrecognizable.

On the other hand, neurophysiological/psychophysics findings indicate that the scrolling up/down, not being able to find the relevant buttons on the page, and excessive page loading durations have also been observed as potential precursors of negative affect.

Lastly, there are findings for which qualitative and neurophysiological/ psychophysics methods contradict each other such as the findings related to the browsing a product from the category menu.

Despite the fact the potential use of neurophysiological/psychophysics methods is still controversial and needs many more direct research and valid findings in this specific area, it is also arguable that such multimodal use will provide fruitful contributions with the integrated use of conventional and neuroscientific methods.

Acknowledgement. This work was financially supported by gittigidiyor (eBay). We'd like to thank for the efforts and support of Çağrı Karahan and Oğuzhan Poyrazoğlu in the realization of this study.

References

ISO DIS, I. 9241-210: 2010. Ergonomics of human system interaction-Part 210: Human-centred design for interactive systems. International Standardization Organization (ISO), Switzerland (2009)

Chai, J., Ge, Y., Liu, Y., Li, W., Zhou, L., Yao, L., Sun, X.: Application of frontal EEG asymmetry to user experience research. In: Harris, D. (ed.) EPCE 2014. LNCS, vol. 8532, pp. 234–243. Springer, Cham (2014). doi:10.1007/978-3-319-07515-0_24

Hornbæk, K.: Current practice in measuring usability: challenges to usability studies and research. Int. J. Hum. Comput. Stud. 64(2), 79–102 (2006)

Drenner, S., Sen, S., Terveen, L.: Crafting the initial user experience to achieve community goals. In: Proceedings of the 2008 ACM Conference on Recommender Systems, pp. 187–194. ACM, October 2008

Law, E.L.C., Roto, V., Hassenzahl, M., Vermeeren, A.P., Kort, J.: Understanding, scoping and defining user experience: a survey approach. In: Proceedings of the SIGCHI Conference on Human Factors in Computing Systems, pp. 719–728. ACM, April 2009

Boehner, K., DePaula, R., Dourish, P., Sengers, P.: Affect: from information to interaction. In: Proceedings of the 4th Decennial Conference on Critical Computing: Between Sense and Sensibility, pp. 59–68. ACM, August 2005

Ravaja, N.: Contributions of psychophysiology to media research: review and recommendations. Media Psychol. 6(2), 193–235 (2004)

Briesemeister, B.B., Tamm, S., Heine, A., Jacobs, A.M.: Approach the good, withdraw from the bad—a review on frontal alpha asymmetry measures in applied psychological research. Psychology 4(03), 261 (2013)

Davidson, R.J., Schwartz, G.E., Saron, C., Bennett, J., Goleman, D.: Frontal versus parietal EEG asymmetry during positive and negative affect. Psychophysiology 16, 202–203 (1979)

Ohme, R., Reykowska, D., Wiener, D., Choromanska, A.: Analysis of neurophysiological reactions to advertising stimuli by means of EEG and galvanic skin response measures. J. Neurosci. Psychol. Econ. 2(1), 21 (2009)

Tomico, O., Mizutani, N., Levy, P., Yokoi, T., Cho, Y., Yamanaka, T.: Kansei physiological measurements and constructivist psychological explorations for approaching user subjective experience. In: DS 48: Proceedings of the 10th International Design Conference, DESIGN 2008, Dubrovnik, Croatia (2008)

Wheeler, R.E., Davidson, R.J., Tomarken, A.J.: Frontal brain asymmetry and emotional reactivity: A biological substrate of affective style. Psychophysiology 30(1), 82–89 (1993)

Boucsein, W.: Electrodermal Activity, p. 2. Springer Science & Business Media, New York (2012)

Westerink, J.H., Van Den Broek, E.L., Schut, M.H., Van Herk, J., Tuinenbreijer, K.: Computing emotion awareness through galvanic skin response and facial electromyography. In: Westerink, J.H.D.M., Ouwerkerk, M., Overbeek, T.J.M., Frank Pasveer, W., de Ruyter, B. (eds.) Probing Experience. Philips Research, vol. 8, pp. 149–162. Springer, Netherlands (2008)

Carlson, N.R.: Physiology of Behavior. Pearson, Boston (2013)

Ohme, R., Reykowska, D., Wiener, D., Choromanska, A.: Application of frontal EEG asymmetry to advertising research. J. Econ. Psychol. **31**(5), 785–793 (2010)

Holst, C.: Consider 'Promoting' Important Product Filters (80% Don't), 5 April 2016. http://baymard.com/blog/promoting-product-filters. Accessed

Appleseed, J.: 8 Design Patterns for Autocomplete Suggestions, 1 July 2014. http://baymard.com/blog/autocomplete-design. Accessed

ErgoMobile: A Software to Support Usability Evaluations in Mobile Devices Using Observation Techniques

Thiago Adriano Coleti[1,2,3,4(✉)], Leticia da Silva Souza[1,2,3,4],
Marcelo Morandini[1,2,3,4], Suzie Allard[1,2,3,4],
and Pedro Luiz Pizzigatti Correa[1,2,3,4]

[1] School of Engineering, University of Sao Paulo, São Paulo, Brazil
{thiagocoleti, m.morandini, pedro.correa}@usp.br,
leticiasap@gmail.com
[2] Center of Technological Sciences,
Northern State University of Paraná, Paranavaí, Brazil
thiago.coleti@uenp.edu.br
[3] School of Arts, Sciences and Humanities,
University of São Paulo, São Paulo, Brazil
[4] University of Tennessee, Knoxville, USA

Abstract. The characteristics of mobile devices and their applications have led to changes in the way these systems are developed and tested. Usability tests are stages of development that are under constant modifications, since it is being taken into account that traditional techniques may not be sufficient to accomplish the testing activity for mobile devices. For example, the User Observation and Filming/Verbalization techniques involve the use of secondary devices to record the data. This may be a problem as the testing activity can become more complex and less comfortable for the users/evaluators. Aiming to present a strategy to minimize this issue, we are presenting the ErgoMobile environment that was developed with the main objective of avoiding the use of secondary devices since it can be installed directly in the mobile device and can collect images from the camera, sounds from the microphone and store interface snapshots. Initial tests presented that this tool behaves well when working in conjunction with other mobile applications, collecting good amounts of data and working in the background and practically had not created any disturbances to the participant or to the evaluator.

Keywords: Usability test · Mobile device · Mobile application · Observation

1 Introduction

The use of mobile devices such as smart phones improved the way people interact and use information and services previously available just for traditional desktop computers. New tools and services are being developed every day in order to support users performing several daily tasks [6]. Thus, a great amount of users that could be considered traditional (people who does not know advance science computer) and/or

© Springer International Publishing AG 2017
A. Marcus and W. Wang (Eds.): DUXU 2017, Part I, LNCS 10288, pp. 363–378, 2017.
DOI: 10.1007/978-3-319-58634-2_27

specialists, use mobile applications for many reasons that previously could just be achieved using a desktop computer.

Actually it is not wrong to say that companies that desire to provide information systems platforms for their customers or any kind of initiative that intends to use software as tool for supporting, must consider having mobile application as a product [3, 6].

However, mobile application development process is not a simple and/or trivial activity. New challenges for developers have arisen such as: (1) adapt the content to screen size; (2) power of memory and process of mobile devices is lower than desktop computers; (3) considerations about where the devices are, as, usually, mobile users are in external area; (4) form of operation; and (5) interaction features [3, 6, 14].

Some other features that explain why mobile user interface and interaction are different from desktops and require care in several aspects include: content; consistence; screen orientation; minimum work load; and customization [6].

To verify whether the mobile interfaces are well developed, and so users can achieve their goals, some usability tests can be conducted.

Performing usability tests in mobile application is a complex task due to the reason that traditional methods and techniques could not be enough to support them in this kind of device. Some questions about usability testing in mobile device are around the ability of traditional techniques in supporting the context of use since the users usually perform their tasks in open environment and they may not pay attention just in specific application, but can be accessing several activities at the same time [6, 8].

An example of usability testing that should be adapted is the Observation Technique, that consists of a strategy to gather data from user accesses while interacting with the system. In desktop and mobile applications, the use of webcams, microphones, external cameras, and verbalization can be common, but how these techniques can be used to collect and generate data about testing in mobile device is a challenge that this research aims to solve [1, 6, 8].

So, to support this issue we present a tool that helps conducting Usability Testing in mobile application using an Observation Technique. This tool was designed, developed and installed in mobile devices and works on background collecting image and sound data through the webcam, or only sound data using microphone besides registering snapshots that can be used in the data analysis.

This environment was developed for Android devices since this platform is extremely robust and because Android is widely used in several smart phones models and due to this reason it could be applied and validate in many different devices models. Also, Android is a free platform and provides resources for software development for free.

This paper presents the first release of this tool which aims to verify two main questions in mobile usability testing: (1) how much data can be registered in testing considered that all data should be stored in the device during the test; and (2) verify if it is a good technique to support testing trying to verify whether it can be really used in daily activities.

Next section presents the background used for developing this tool design, implementation features and validation activities

2   Background

This section presents the background about the main subjects that support this paper: Mobile Devices, Usability Testing in Mobile Devices and Techniques to support Usability Testing.

2.1   Mobile Devices

Nowadays, mobile device is used as a hybrid concept of tablets and phone cells. Usually named as smart phone, a mobile device is portable and provide a wide group of resources that allows people to perform several tasks that varies from a simple phone call to the use of internet services, such as internet banking, purchasing products and others [16].

These devices combine functions of a traditional phone with camera, web browser, music player, compass, global position systems and other resources according to the model and/or manufacturer. The combination of all these resources allowed the existence of a hardware that provides functions that were previously accessible only in desktop computers [3, 16]. Together, with the increasing of Human-Computer Interfaces quality and needs for user interaction, the smart phones gathered a great amount of users that perform most of their tasks, personal and professionally using smart phones [1, 9].

According to Cybis [6] it is really import to understand the context of use of a mobile device and how it interfere in user lifestyle and work. Some issues are highlighted below:

(1)   smart phones and mobile devices are usually used for fast tasks, in short periods of time and in specific context where the user pay real attention to these tasks such as send a message or search an information in a social network;

(2)   environment device is usually dynamic due to the reason that users can perform their tasks anywhere and can try to accomplish more than just one task at the same moment. Thus, the interactions must be easy, fast and right not to delay the user;

(3)   mobile devices´ hardware are smaller, keyboards are digitals, interface format is different, the amount of information available must be careful analyzed because the interface area could not be enough for all the components and de designers should prioritize some contents.

Also, the HCI development process from mobile applications needs to be adapted or amended in order to accomplish mobile devices. The size of the screen, the components applied for interaction, the content distribution in the interface, the cross platform and it particularities leads the developers to face new challenges in development process [3, 6].

In order to improve and facilitate the mobile software development, some guidelines were defined and provided elements to make the interfaces of this kind of devices more usable. Benyon [3] presents some elements proposed by Microsoft:

- Using shorts menu texts;
- Using "&" character instead of "and";
- Using layers to group and separate components in menu;
- Position button "Delete" close to menu.

Cybis [6] also presents some other guidelines proposed by Nielsen, Cuello, Himann and Wroblewski. In general, these guidelines focus on the facility of use, quality of interaction considering many ways to do the same task and content for mobile device.

Beside HCI features, mobile applications present some limits. Actually the memory capacity is a concern for developers due to the reason that mobile devices have less memory than a traditional computer. For example, a desktop can present 1 Terabyte of memory and a mobile presents at about 40 Gigabytes. This issue is discussed here because memory and battery were two concerns studied as can represent special problems when using these devices.

Thus, considering the features presented, we assumed mobile application development process as a group of tasks that require new concepts when applied to the usability evaluation techniques used for mobile software.

Next section presents information about usability testing on mobile applications.

2.2   Usability Testing in Mobile Devices Using Observation Techniques

Mobile devices present new features related to hardware, software, interaction, user profile and context of use. Due to these reasons, Johnson [8] and Cybis [6] explain that traditional techniques and resources used to support usability tests in desktop and web application may not be appropriated or sufficient for conducting usability tests in mobile application and so, should be reviewed and/or improved.

In this context, there are some challenges involved in the usability tests of mobile systems, such as: device size, virtual hardware such as keyboards and buttons and the way how users interact. Concerns related to performing the test in lab or real environment; using emulator, prototypes (papers/drawings) or real software and how to register data about the usability testing, are leading HCI researches to search for new approaches or to adapt old techniques in order to attend mobile devices [3, 6].

Consulting the actual literature, we had not found a perfect approach to support usability testing for mobile devices. In several cases, the evaluators may combine more than one usability evaluation technique in order to conduct an effective testing, but this approach is not perfect as issues related to the memory capabilities and devices battery usage rates were not present.

So, researches for providing techniques that enable the user to use a mobile device in various environments can be considered as important themes for study and is the main concern of this work. Specific particularities are always present: the evaluator/ user can be exposed to interruptions, there should occur interferences during the evaluation process and the need of recording the interaction is one of them [6].

The observation of the interaction between user and the system is a technique that can be used to conduct an usability testing. Recording images, voice and snapshots are examples of data that should be gathered to support the usability measures analysis.

For desktop applications the use of a software for monitoring and collecting data as voice, images, logs and snapshots is already available using tools as Morae [11] and ErgoSV [5]. However, for mobile applications, these resources are not widely used.

For conducting usability evaluation experiments for mobile applications, the recording of images or data related to external environment such as sounds or participant voice can be done using secondary devices such as video cameras and/or microphones positioned on a table and directed to mobile to register the screen images.

But the use of secondary devices can be a problem since the evaluators need to collect more data from different perspective. The increasing of the devices amount can create a complex environment to collect and analysis data. Also, the data analysis will require a full review of the data individually by device and forward to synchronize data in order to have a nice data understanding.

A device presented in Fig. 1 was proposed by Betiol [4] and has a camera, microphone and resource to transfer data by radio frequency. Independent structures allow positioning the camera in order to collect images and audio with quality. The device works with battery not requiring power via cables which helps the transportation and the realization of remote usability tests.

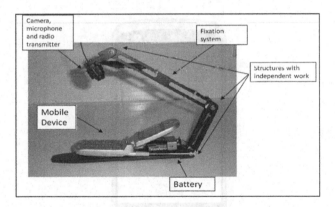

Fig. 1. Device to support usability testing in mobile devices (Source: Betiol, p. 120)

Although this technique works, the use of a secondary resource ends up being more costly and not leaving the user so comfortable to perform an interaction easily and efficiently.

Currently there is a lack of performing usability testing on the mobile device, making use of resources such as camera, microphone and internet a need. Researches related to usability tests in mobile application such as [2, 4, 9] used secondary devices to register data as images and audio; or used specific software installed directly on the device to register log files and/or use code injections to monitor user interaction, but not to register images and audio. Considering this lack and the current resources available in mobile devices, propose a tool that could be installed in the device and work in background to collect image, sound and snapshots and so, trying to avoid the use of secondary elements.

Next section we present related works to this research.

2.3 Related Work

The development of a software to be used in mobile device is a reality and researches are being conducted in order to provide, improve or analyze methods and techniques to support all development stages among it the usability evaluation activities.

Studies focused on usability evaluation in mobile applications are not too recently, i.e., did not arise to support the smart phones, but when the mobile devices were simpler and provided less functions and resources than the current phone, but the utilization by people was already increasing.

The research conducted by Betiol [4] was performed in older phones and aimed to analyze how de context of use could interfere in the evaluation results. Tests were conducting through emulators and real phones. The users performed their tasks in lab and fields. Betiol also proposed a tool to support the usability testing based on observation. With this resources data as images and sound could be registered during a mobile interaction. A resource image is presented at Fig. 2.

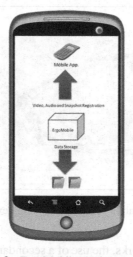

Fig. 2. ErgoMobile work approach

We can cite the work performed by Kaikonnen et al. [9] that aimed to evaluate the usability of a mobile application called Wire. It presents two questions: (1) whether the tests are sufficient to carry out this evaluation and; (2) whether there are differences at results of tests conducted in laboratories to tests performed in field.

A comparison was made between performing tests in the laboratory and in the field to find out what the effect of the environment would influence. When recording mobile videos, there is a lack of use of the features of the smartphone itself. So, small video cameras were hung to record the screen of the device and collect the data, and then perform an analysis.

As a result, problems were encountered in the application's navigation, as well as phenomena and problems both in the field environment and in the laboratory. Therefore this research presented that the hypothesis that one environment is worse than the other cannot be generalized. Also, the obtained data showed that no matter what is the environment, users and the type of the application can also influence the final results of the usability environments tests.

Another work we can mention is [15] that aims to ascertain the influence of the mobile context of the application, as well as lighting the movement and location where the usability tests are performed for mobile devices. For this, the ContextCollector application was developed, which captures the user interaction through the sensors of the mobile device that is being used. This application can be used to obtain data by both developers and testers, without having to be in the presence of the evaluator, and, so, reducing the costs to perform usability tests, as it does not need to ask the user to be in a specific test environment in laboratory. As a result obtained, it is generally perceived that the influence of the poorly lit environment affected the performance of the users. Thus, a usability assessment done with the user standing still in a well-lit environment would present better results.

Next section presents the ErgoMobile environment, its features and applicability.

3 ErgoMobile

This section presents the ErgoMobile, a tool to support usability evaluation based on user observation. ErgoMobile was proposed after the study of some gaps that happen in usability testing in mobile devices due to the particular features of this kind of device and it software, such as: the difficult to collect data about user interaction [13]; the use of secondary devices that ends up to extra workload and equipment to be manipulated by participant [4]; and the battery and memory of mobile devices that have limited capacity [13].

- Collect a great amount of data and monitor the test. This is one of the main interest in this environment, since the mobile device should register data in the local memory and it can be a problem due to the lack of storage capability;
- Do not compromise the battery usage. Mobile devices have batteries with different capacity and durability and if the tool requires a large amount of use, there should be a problem since the usability test could be stopped as the device could be turned off;
- Allow the evaluators and users to conduct usability testing without the need of a secondary device linked to the mobile. A software could be installed in the mobile device and be accessed in background monitoring the user tasks; and
- Provide a tool to support the collection of data such as: images; words pronounced and snapshots.

Aiming to analyze the effectiveness and efficiency of the ErgoMobile, we chose a mobile platform to develop the software since it must be considered the great amount of devices that use Android[1] and the facility to obtain and use development tools and frameworks.

Next subsection presents ErgoMobile Approach.

3.1   ErgoMobile Tool

ErgoMobile approach was created in order to allow the evaluators and participants to conduct usability testing in mobile devices using Observation Techniques such as Filming and Verbalization. The idea is to have an environment that supports the evaluation activity without the need of use of secondary devices such as additional cameras, microphones and others.

To accomplish this goal we proposed a tool that can be installed in a mobile device and works in background, registering data about the usability. ErgoMobile works creating a video with images from the frontal camera and audio from microphone and registering snapshots of the interface that can be used in the analysis stage to allow the evaluator visualizing the used. If the device have frontal camera, a file containing a video (image and audio) is created, but if this is not the case, the ErgoMobile only activates the microphone and the data collected will be stored in an audio file and another one will store the interfaces snapshots.

Specifically, the data storage is gathered in specific folders at the device's operational system. So, the ErgoMobile creates a video/audio file that is saved in a folder named "ErgoMobile Videos" and the snapshots are saved in a folder named "ErgoMobile-images_dateOfTest" where "date of test" refers to the data when the usability test was done, for example, "ErgoMobile-images_20170223". Figure 2 presents the ErgoMobile work approach.

Next subsection presents the tests performed in order to check both memory and battery capacity/durability.

3.2   Memory and Battery Power

A mobile software development process provides some concerns that in desktop application may not be the main focus, such as battery power and memory capability. Modern mobile devices have several functions, such as colored screens and other components that can consume battery or use several portions of memory [13].

For the ErgoMobile project, this was not different since it proposes an approach with a software working on background to collect data about the test. Due to this reason, this environment should compete for resources as memory and also increase the battery consumption because ErgoMobile uses the camera(s), microphone and other resources beyond the resources/environments under evaluation.

---

[1] https://www.android.com/intl/pt-BR_br/.

Specifically, the memory power had a particular concern since the mobile devices provide less memory than traditional desktop computers. The process of collecting images from camera sounds and snapshot and save them in local memory can create a great amount of data.

Due to this reason, before developing the tool, we created a prototype in order to analyze the memory and battery issues. A particular mobile software was created and used just to collect data and simulate tests collecting data and consuming memory.

Three tests were performed using different devices that presented the features:

- Device 01: 8 Gigabytes of memory. Thirty seconds of tests were performed in low and high quality of images;
- Device 02: 8 Gigabytes of memory. Three minutes of tests were performed in both quality rates; and
- Device 03: 8 Gigabytes of memory. Eighteen minutes of tests were performed in both quality rates.

Table 1 presents the results of the tests with devices' battery and memory.

Table 1. Battery and memory tests results

Device	Quality	Snapshots data	Video data	Total
01	Low	470 KB	550 KB	1020 KB
01	High	9.7 MB	37,3 MB	47 MB
02	Low	38,9 MB	9,47 MB	48,37 MB
02	High	22,7 MB	91 MB	113,7 MB
03	Low	401 MB	17,6 MB	418,6 MB
03	High	167 MB	1,20 GB	1395,8 MB

Battery usage data is not presented in the Table 1 since the results related to battery consumption had few variations when the ErgoMobile was being used or not. There were not significant interferences in the usage and the smart phones batteries supported the processes of usability testing and data collecting working in background without compromising the power of battery and due to this reason no action was no interferences on use were perceived.

About the tests with image, although cameras quality rates had some different results, the images were appropriated even in low quality camera and so, we chose the low quality since it allowed to store a greater amount of data.

After performing the tests in battery and memory and after analyzing the results, we assume that it is possible to develop the application since it can work in mobile phones as the typical devices provide sufficient battery and memory.

Next section is presented the ErgoMobile process to conduct a test.

3.3   Usability Testing Process Using the ErgoMobile

ErgoMobile was developed in order to be easy to configure and use and so support an usability test. Although the user must install the application in the mobile device using any technique (this is not discussed in this paper) we concerned about developing a tool simple that did not required too much workload. The process to conduct an usability testing using ErgoMobile is based on the stages:

- Configuration, Devices Tests (Optional) and Start the Evaluation;
- Performing Usability Testing; and
- Data Visualization (Beta release).

Configuration, Devices Tests (Optional) and Starting the Evaluation
This stage aims to:

(1) Indentify the participant who will use the evaluated software and collect specific data such as name, the evaluated software and the function that should be performed. This interface has just three fields and is easy to interact. This is a required task and the test could not be performed without these information;

(2) After identification, the user is headed to a second interface that provides three resources: two buttons that allow checking the resource used for a testing such as device camera and/microphone; and another to start the usability testing. The resources checking are not required tasks, but is strongly recommended. By achieving this option, the participant and evaluator can perform the checking of camera and microphone to ensure that both components are properly working. As some devices do not have camera, our tool presents two ways to make the verification: (1) (with) Camera: Allows the user to check the camera and automatically the microphone; and (2) Audio: Allows the user to check just the microphone resource. By selecting one of these functions the user is redirected to an interface that contains components to support the checking. The user can return to the interface that provides the buttons for checking and for usability testing and by accessing from this interface, start the "Usability Test";

(3) The "Usability Test" button heads the user to an interface that will start the usability testing; in this interface two other buttons are available: "New Test" for beginning a new usability testing; and "Close Application" to finish ErgoMobile.

Figure 3 presents the mobile's screen for the process of Configuration, Devices Testing and Starting the Evaluation.

Performing Usability Testing
After starting the test using the Button "New Test", the ErgoMobile will work in background registratiering images from the camera, recording sounds and storing snapshots. By working in background, the ErgoMobile does not interfere in any action performed by the participant. The signal that ErgoMobile is working is an icon presented at the top of interface as presented in Fig. 4.

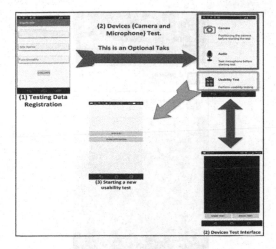

Fig. 3. Process of configuration, devices tests and starting the evaluation

Fig. 4. ErgoMobile working in background

When the participants finish the usability testing, they can close the ErgoMobile accessing the menu at the top of mobile interface. Some functions that are being executed by the mobile device can be presented. One of them is a button with the label "ErgoMobile - To finish the test click here". Clicking in this button, the monitoring activity performed by the ErgoMobile will be finished and the data collected will be saved. This process can be visualized in Fig. 5.

Data Visualization
The data visualization process is a resource that is not the main focus of the project and, due to this reason, in this paper we are just shortly explaining it. The first release of ErgoMobile aimed to provide an approach and a tool to collect data and observe the user while working in background in a mobile usability testing.

Fig. 5. Resource to finish an usability testing in ErgoMobile

Fig. 6. Data visualization software used to validate the ErgoMobile

Thus, the evaluator can access data using the mobile's folders manager to localize the folders that were stored when using the ErgoMobile and then download these files to a computer.

Aiming to validate the data obtained, we developed a really simple tool that allows the visualization and synchronization of the video and snapshots data and so, the evaluator can visualize what happened in the evaluation. This tool is presented in Fig. 7 and we intend to improve it in future works presented at Fig. 6.

The data visualization tool is a software developed using C# programming language [7] that loads the video/audio and snapshots and play both data synchronously in order to provide a kind of images combination that presents what happened during the usability test.

As previously mentioned, this data visualization software release is easy to be used and was developed in order to validate the ErgoMobile data collecting process. So, some activities are manual such as the data acquisition for analysis. The evaluator/participant should transfer the data from smart phone using an email or other resource for copy the data from the mobile to the computer to be analyzed.

Although this was a no unsophisticated tool, it allowed us to visualize the video and snapshots registered by ErgoMobile and with this data we concluded that the quality of images was satisfactory and there will not have problem to use it in a future and more modern data visualization tool.

This section presented the ErgoMobile process to conduct and support usability testing of mobile devices. Next section presents the process we had conducted to validate this environment and also relate future works that are expected to be accomplished.

4 Validation

To validate ErgoMobile, we performed two experiments: (1) to validate the capacity to storage data and manage device memory; (2) to validate the capacity of ErgoMobile to support data collect and observation in a usability testing.

Although the verification of memory was similar to the test performed with the prototype, we decided to perform it again we were worried whether the use of the ErgoMobile could interfere on memory management.

To conduct the usability tests, two participants with knowledge in usability testing were selected and three mobile devices were used. The devices were the same used to support the testing conducted to check battery and memory capacity using a prototyping and explained in Sect. 3.3.

The participants performed usability tests in native applications such as home banking and entertainment applications that were downloaded and installed in the devices. Considering that, the usage of the ErgoMobile aimed to analyze the process of data colleting and user observation. We hadn't created a specific testing protocol, but just encouraged the participants to use the mobile applications and verbalize their opinions about interactions and interfaces.

Each participant performed about 30 min of tests in the devices. Issues related to the battery and memory capacity had not presented variation in relation to tests using the prototypes. Also, the ErgoMobile succeeded in storing files that maintained images, audio and snapshot related to usability tests. However, in certain moments of the tests, the ErgoMobile worked slowly and we figured out that occurred a heavy workload which caused concerns because when we conducted the battery and memory tests these problems were not present.

Thus, we conducted some searches in forums and websites about Android that presented an issue related to the Android Operational System. We discovered it that has a problem with its garbage collector and at certain time and with a considerable processing of two or more different applications simultaneously, the Random Access Memory (RAM) consumption forces the system stopping running some applications for a while. This was the ErgoMobile's case. But this problem was not considered as a limit for using the ErgoMobile as the results were properly obtained.

Anyway, the presented problem is a concern for using the ErgoMobile and developing a new version can be a strategy for include routines that would improve the RAM management. This requirement was target as future works.

Regarding to the process of observing the usability testing, we asked to participants to inform their experience using an application being observed by ErgoMobile. The answers did not vary significantly, highlighting the issues:

- The ErgoMobile did not interfere in the use of evaluated systems and the participants almost were not bothered by this system during the testing. In some sense, the participants said that if they had not been warned before, they would not notice the ErgoMobile working;
- The process to configure the ErgoMobile was a little complex, but they were helped by the researches. If we aim to develop the ErgoMobile as a distributable software, a improvement in configuration process may be required; and
- Sometimes the usability testing became slow. It happened mainly due to the problem with RAM management cited before. Future improvements are planned to solve this problem.

Regarding to the data registered by the ErgoMobile, the evaluation of the quality of audios, sounds and snapshots presented that all these data were good and allowed the analysis of the test and the identification of functions, words pronounced and the sequence of tasks conducted by the participants.

Thus, we concluded the ErgoMobile could be an appropriate approach and tool to support usability testing with observation in mobile devices applications. Considering that this was the first release and the initial efforts to develop this tool, the results of the first experiments were really exciting because the ErgoMobile works according to the planned and allowed the conduction of an observation in mobile usability testing without the need of secondary devices and with the minimum impact to the user tasks under evaluation.

Also, the data registered in the tests presented that it could be possible to perform usability tests in relevant times even registering a film/audio file and snapshots

We assume that this tool can be used for usability testing in laboratories and also in real environment because the software can be easily installed and configured by the participants. These actions avoid the use of secondary devices that ends to be a difficult task for participant and development teams manage.

Next section presents future works.

5 Future Work

This paper presented the ErgoMobile, an approach to support usability testing for mobile applications. The presented release tool was the first effort to provide a tool that can work in background and collect data about user and snapshots of interfaces used. About this project we intend to continue the research in the possible follow issues:

- Improve the RAM memory technique;
- Provide the tool in other platforms such as IPhone and Windows Phone;
- Create a new tool to support the data analysis and create statistic data about the test;
- Improve the tool to collect more data than image, sound and snapshot using interval mobile's resources such as compass, accelerometer and GPS;
- Create an approach to transfer data from mobile device to an integrated and online database; and
- Provide efforts to create a usable tool that can be acquired via app stores.

6 Conclusion

Mobile devices and mobile applications brought new challenges for development teams. Device size, processing and memory power and variety of users and tasks that can be done changed the way as software for mobile should be developed and provide new concerns.

Usability testing is one of the new challenges for HCI developers since traditional methods and techniques could not be appropriated for mobile applications as well as they are for desktop computers. The observation technique, for example, usually requires the use of secondary devices for collecting data about user, software and interaction making the usability test more complex and uncomfortable.

This paper presented the ErgoMobile, an application that can be installed into the smart phone and work in background to collect data without interfere in interaction between user and software. This research aimed to analyze the capacity of data collection regarding to memory and battery power and verify whether the ErgoMobile could really support usability testing applying the User Observation technique.

The results were satisfactory due to the reason that the approach allowed the observation of users and interaction in an usability testing. The amount of snapshots and the size of video/audio file were big enough to be stored in the smart phone memory and register data for test analysis.

This tool should receive improvements as mentioned in Future Work, but the first results present that the ErgoMobile could be used as resource for usability testing avoiding the use of secondary devices and becoming an easy and practical testing process allowing the collection of significative amount of data from videos, audios and snapshots.

References

1. Ahmad, N., Boota, M.W., Massom, A.H.: Smart phone application evaluation with usability testing approach. J. Softw. Eng. Appl. 7, 1045–1054 (2014)
2. Balagtas-Fernandez, F., Hussmann, H.: A methodology and framework to simplify usability analysis of mobile applications. Proceedings of 2009 IEEE/ACM International Conference on Automated Software Engineering, ASE 2009, Washington, DC, USA, pp. 520–524 (2009)

3. Benyon, D.: Interação Humano Computador, 2nd edn. Pearson Prentice Hall, São Paulo (2011)
4. Betiol, A.H.: Avaliação da usabilidade para os computadores de mão: um estudo comparativo entre três abordagens para ensaios de interação. Tese (Phd Tesis); supervisor: Walter de Abreu Cybis – Universidade Federal de Santa Catarina, Florianópolis (2004)
5. Coleti, T.A., Morandini, M., Lourdes dos Santos Nunes, F.: ErgoSV: an environment to support usability evaluation using face and speech recognition. In: Kurosu, M. (ed.) HCI 2014. LNCS, vol. 8510, pp. 554–564. Springer, Cham (2014). doi:10.1007/978-3-319-07233-3_51
6. Cybis, W., Betiol, A.H., Faust, R.: Ergonomia e Usabilidade - Conhecimentos, Métodos e Técnicas. Novatec, [S.l.] (2015)
7. Introduction to the C# Language and the .NET Framework. https://msdn.microsoft.com/en-us/library/z1zx9t92.aspx
8. Johnson, P.: Usability and mobility: interactions on the move. In: Proceedings of EPSRC/BCS Workshop Glasgow (1998)
9. Kaikkonen, A., Kekalainen, A., Cankar, M., Kallio, T., Kankainen, A.: Usability testing of mobile applications: a comparison between laboratory and field testing, pp. 4–16 (2005)
10. Lettner, F., Holzmann, C.: Automated and unsupervised user interaction logging as basis for usability evaluation of mobile applications. In: Proceedings of MoMM 2012, Bali, Indonesia, pp. 118–127 (2012)
11. Morae Usability Testing. https://www.techsmith.com/morae.html
12. Morimoto, C.E.: Smartphones Guia Prático, GHD Press e Sul Editores (2009)
13. Pradhan, T.: Mobile Application Testing, Product Management – Haas School of Business, University of Berkeley (2011)
14. Preece, J., Borges, Y., Sharp, H.: Design de Interação, Além da interação homem computador. Bookman, [S.l.] (2013)
15. Santos, R.M., Rocha, L.S.: Análise do contexto móvel nos testes de usabilidade de aplicações móveis. In: ERCEMAPI, Piauí (2011)
16. Stair, R.M., Reynolds, G.W.: Princípios de Sistemas de Informação. Cengage Learning, São Paulo (2015)

Addressing Mobile Usability and Elderly Users: Validating Contextualized Heuristics

André de Lima Salgado[1(✉)], Leandro Agostini do Amaral[1],
Renata Pontin de Mattos Fortes[1], Marcos Hortes Nisihara Chagas[2],
and Ger Joyce[3]

[1] ICMC, University of São Paulo,
Avenida Trabalhador São-carlense, 400, Centro, São Carlos, SP, Brazil
{alsalgado,leandroagostini}@usp.br, renata@icmc.usp.br
[2] Centro de Ciências Biológicas e da Saúde, Federal University of São Carlos,
Rodovia Washington Luís (SP-310), Km 235, São Carlos, SP, Brazil
mchagas@ufscar.br
[3] School of Computer Science, University of Hertfordshire,
Hatfield, Hertfordshire AL10 9AB, UK
gerjoyce@outlook.com

Abstract. Diverse heuristic sets were proposed in order to evolve Heuristic Evaluation for new contexts, as contexts related to the elderly and mobile devices. However, heuristics for evaluation of mobile usability regarding elderly users still need aditional validations. For this reason, our study aimed to enhance the validation of a heuristic set proposed by Al-Razgan et al. for evaluation of mobile usability regarding elderly users. Results showed that the major part of heuristics proposed by Al-Razgan et al. matches with traditional heuristics of Nielsen, while a few remain valuable for evaluations in this context. Also, after validations, we found evidences that the heuristics of Al-Razgan et al. have a great coverage of usability problems of mobile applications used by the elderly, as detected from test with users.

Keywords: Mobile usability · Heuristic evaluation · Validation · Elderly

1 Introduction

Usability is an important aspect of software, it is related to user's satisfaction and how effective and efficient he/she can perform a task interacting with an interface [16,17]. Usability is also important for designing technologies to the elderly population, especially when the benefits from mobile technologies are taken in

A. de Lima Salgado—This study was supported by the grant 2015/09493-5, São Paulo Research Foundation (FAPESP).
L. Agostini do Amaral—This study was supported by the grant 2016/01009-0, São Paulo Research Foundation (FAPESP).

A. Marcus and W. Wang (Eds.): DUXU 2017, Part I, LNCS 10288, pp. 379–394, 2017.
DOI: 10.1007/978-3-319-58634-2_28

account [6,11,22,27,34,36–38]. Given the importance of usability, diverse methods that promote its evaluation were proposed in the literature [7,13,26,32].

Methods that propose usability evaluation are indispensable for designing usable interfaces [8]. In the context of mobile usability, one of the main challenges of evaluation methods is to address the diversity of context-of-use and the impact these devices have on users' mobility [13]. At this point, studies (including previous studies of some of the authors) have shown that a popular inspection-based usability evaluation, the Heuristic Evaluation (HE), has evolved to address different contexts and users profile through the proposal of domain specific heuristics [14,19,23,24].

Regarding the elderly, both Hermawati and Lawson [14] and de Lima Salgado et al. [24] showed the heuristics of Al-Razgan et al. [2] as the unique set specific for mobile usability and the elderly profile. However, as reinforced by the study of Hermawati and Lawson [14], validation of proposed domain specific heuristics are still reduced. Hermawati and Lawson [14] suggested that future studies should continue the development of such domain specific heuristics. At the time this study was written, the heuristics of Al-Razgan et al. [2] could be studied through the following venues:

- (i) increasing its validations against traditional usability heuristics, as heuristics of Nielsen [18];
- (ii) increasing its validation against outcomes from test with real users;
- (iii) suggesting a text description (at least as an alternative) for each heuristic proposed.

The goal of our study was to expand the validation of the heuristics of Al-Razgan et al. [2], comparing them against the traditional heuristics of Nielsen [18] and outcomes from test with real users. Additionally, we discussed possible implications for design based on the evidences from this study.

The remaining of this paper was structured as follows: Sect. 2 provides a brief literature review on heuristics for elderly and mobile usability; Sect. 3 shows details of methods for this study as planned by the authors; Sect. 4 presents results from two process of validation for the heuristics of Al-Razgan et al. [2]; Sect. 5 shows implications for design; and Sect. 6 summarizes the conclusions of the present study.

2   Heuristics for Mobile Usability and Elderly Users

Heuristic Evaluation (HE) has been recognized among the most popular methods for usability inspection [1,5]. The HE method is based on the application of broad usability principles, called heuristics, by expert evaluators in order to collect a list of existent usability problems [15,28,30,31].

Some of the main distinct characteristics of mobile usability is its dependency on the context-of-use, user profile and cognitive load [13,24]. Since the arrival of mobile devices, many domain specific heuristic sets were proposed aiming at providing better inspection for different contexts and user profiles [14,23,24].

Among the contributions of Hermawati and Lawson [14] and de Lima Salgado et al. [24], only two heuristic sets approached the elderly context domain. The referred sets were: (i) the weighted heuristics of Lynch [25]; and (ii) the "*Touch-based Mobile Heuristics Evaluation for elderly people*" from Al-Razgan et al. [2]. Although both heuristic sets approach elderly profile, only the heuristics of Al-Razgan et al. [2] consider the mobile context domain. The heuristics of Al-Razgan et al. [2] are listed in sequence:

1. *"Make Elements on the page easy to read.*
2. *Easy Recognition and accessibility.*
3. *Make clickable items easy to target and hit.*
4. *Use the elderly language and culture; minimize technical terms.*
5. *Provide clear feedback on actions.*
6. *Provide preferable gesture for elderly.*
7. *Provide elderly with information on launcher/elderly status.*
8. *Use conventional interaction items.*
9. *Ergonomics design.*
10. *Provide functions that reduce the elderly memory load.*
11. *Elderly does not feel lost or stuck (Elderly control and freedom).*
12. *Prevent error from occurrence.*
13. *Provide necessary information and settings."*

The "*Touch-based Mobile Heuristics Evaluation for elderly people*" from Al-Razgan et al. [2] were proposed for the evaluation of usability of mobile launcher applications for the elderly. Some examples of this kind of launcher applications are: Wiser[1], Koala[2] and Big Launcher[3]. Despite being proposed for the evaluation of launcher applications, the heuristics of Al-Razgan et al. [2] were the closest we found for evaluation of mobile usability for the elderly. For this reason, we understood that these heuristics could be explored in order to better understand its validity for the wide context of mobile usability and elderly.

3   Methods

This section describes methods applied during our study to enhance the validation of the heuristics from Al-Razgan et al. [2] study. The following sections show details on how we organized and conducted such validations.

3.1   Study Design

The design of this study is organized among the two (2) following stages: (i) *validation regarding traditional heuristics*; and (ii) *validation regarding outcomes from test with real users*.

---

[1] Wiser - Simple Senior Launcher: https://play.google.com/store/apps/details?id=com.wiser.home&hl=en.

[2] Koala Phone Launcher Free: https://play.google.com/store/apps/details?id=com.koalaphone.silver&hl=en.

[3] BIG Launcher: https://play.google.com/store/apps/details?id=name.kunes.android.launcher.activity&hl=en.

At the first stage - *validation regarding traditional heuristics* - we aimed to compare the heuristics from Al-Razgan et al. [2] study against the traditional heuristics of Nielsen [18]. The aim of this stage was to identify the coverage of Nielsen's heuristics among the heuristics of Al-Razgan et al. [2]; and to identify which of the heuristics from Al-Razgan et al. [2] are not covered by Nielsen's heuristics. For this reason, we used the heuristics and factors as exposed by Nielsen at [29] in a matching process with the describing checklist of Al-Razgan et al. [2]. Two usability researchers were responsible for comparing each item of the checklist (used by Al-Razgan et al. [2] to describe their heuristics) with Nielsen's heuristics.

At the second stage - *validation regarding outcomes from test with real users* - our goal was to validate the coverage of the heuristics of Al-Razgan et al. [2] against outcomes from test with real users, in the context of elderly using mobile applications. For this purpose, we used results from the literature (that provided evidences from test of elderly using mobile applications) and a case study with six (6) senior using a mobile application during a Think Aloud test[4]. From a literature review, we identified five (5) works that provided evidences from test sessions of elderly users using mobile applications [9,12,20,21,35].

For every matching processes conducted in this study, we applied a relaxed criteria: problems were considered similar whether they express the same underlying problem [4,33].

3.2 Application: Aptor Digital CogniTest

The *Aptor Digital CogniTest* is a mobile app that aims to make a digital version of paper based cognitive test, designed by Aptor Software[5]. We opted for using *Aptor Digital CogniTest* because it is part of a larger project that some of the authors participate. The application was designed to be used in an Android tablet, by Brazilian elderly (Portuguese speakers) and its development was based on the Able Gamers' Includification guidelines[6].

Aptor Digital CogniTest has two basic tasks implemented. One task is to remember figure positions on a matrix. As an example, Fig. 1 shows one of the screens of the training sessions, informing the user about what is required to achieve the goal, while Fig. 2 shows a screen of success in a task of remembering figure positions. Users are also asked to remember number sequences, which comprehends another task. Figure 3 shows an example screen of an incorrect trial during a number sequence remembering task.

From the tests conducted during this study, we aim to provide important feedback for Aptor Software for the next steps on the development of *Aptor Digital CogniTest*. The following section presents results from validation processes.

---

[4] This study was part of a project submitted for evaluation and approved by the Local Research Ethics Committee of the Federal University of São Carlos, with code 875.3562014.

[5] http://www.aptor.com.br/.

[6] https://www.includification.com/AbleGamers_Includification.pdf.

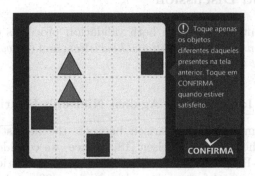

Fig. 1. Screen for instructions on identifying the difference in the matrix.

Fig. 2. Screen for success feedback (*correto* means correct in Portuguese) on identifying the difference in the matrix.

Fig. 3. Screen for failure feedback (*incorreto* means incorrect in Portuguese) on remembering a sequence of numbers.

4   Results and Discussion

This section presents results from both validation processes conducted in our study: (i) *validation regarding traditional heuristics*; and (ii) *validation regarding outcomes from test with real users.*

4.1   Validation I: Comparing Against Nielsen's Heuristics

We conducted a matching comparison between the heuristics of Al-Razgan et al. [2] and the heuristics of Nielsen [18]. Hence, we considered the checklist as provided by Al-Razgan et al. [2] to describe their heuristics, and compared against the heuristics and factors showed by Nielsen [29], and the description of each heuristic as showed by Nielsen [27].

Al-Razgan et al. [2] used 48 checklist items to describe their 13 heuristics. Among these 48 items of the checklist, we identified 31 matching cases when comparing with heuristics and factors showed by Nielsen [29]. In Table 1, we summarized the matching as identified during this stage. In sequence, we compared the remaining 17 items with the heuristic descriptions as provided by Nielsen [18]. Notice that heuristic and factor codes, used in Table 1, are the same as reported by Nielsen [29]. At this time, we found three matching cases between items from Al-Razgan et al. [2] checklist and the heuristic "*Aesthetic and minimalist design*" (called Heuristic 8 in this paper) that were shown in Table 1.

At this extent, 14 items from the checklist of Al-Razgan et al. [2] were not matched with any of Nielsen's heuristics.

4.2   Validation II: Comparing both Heuristic Sets Against Outcomes from Test with Users

The first step for this validation process was to collect evidences from tests of mobile usability for the elderly from five (5) works in the literature [9,12,20, 21,35]. We collected as much works as possible that provided some evidences of usability problems from test with elderly users regarding mobile application. We understand that such sample of usability problems retrieved from the literature is limited by different age ranges and culture of users, but this can still provide good insights about the theme. These works provided a total of 27 usability problems, as follows:

– Nine (9) usability problems were retrieved from Scheibe et al. [35]. Scheibe et al. [35] tested a mobile diabetes application with 29 users with 50 years or older.
– Two (2) usability problems were retrieved from Gao and Sun [9]. In their study, Gao and Sun [9] tested gestures on touch screen devices, on their own testing system, with 40 elderly users aged from 52 up to 81 years.

Table 1. Matching heuristics of Al-Razgan et al. [2] with traditional heuristics of Nielsen.

	Matching		
	Heuristic [29]	Factor [29]	Description [18]
1.3. Are the text and background colors have good contrast?			HEURISTIC 8
1.5. Is the amount of text minimized; is the only necessary information presented?			HEURISTIC 8
1.6. Does color choices allow for easy readability?			HEURISTIC 8
2.1. Are the icons clear, understandable and labeled?	C13	FACTOR 6	
2.2. Are labels described clearly?	C7	FACTOR 2	
2.3. Can the most important or frequently needed functions accessed directly?	G14, A7	FACTOR 7	
2.6. Are there any visual cues in the launcher that help the elderly know there is more content in a page?	C13	FACTOR 6	
3.1. Is it obvious which item is clickable and which is not?	B2	FACTOR 6	
3.6. Is the image on a button or an icon easy to predict what does it do?	A2, G2	FACTOR 2	
4.1. Does the launcher use words that majority of older adults are familiar with?	C7	FACTOR 2	
4.2. Does the options/information have logical sequence?		FACTOR 2	
4.3. Are the icons familiar to elderly?	F1	FACTOR 2	
5.1. Is there audio/visual/haptic confirmation when tapping?		FACTOR 1	
5.2. Is there an option to enable them?		FACTOR 1	
5.3. Are error messages descriptive, and did they provide a solution to the elderly for recovery?		FACTOR 9	
5.4. Are confirmation messages clear?	A2, G2	FACTOR 2	
5.5. Does the launcher keep elderly informed about what is going on, through appropriate feedback?	A5	FACTOR 1	
7.1. Does the elderly know where is he and what can he do next?		FACTOR 1	
7.2. Is the elderly aware when the launcher turns off or gets an error that causes it to stop working?		FACTOR 9	

Table 1. (*continued*)

	Matching		
	Heuristic [29]	Factor [29]	Description [18]
8.1. Are items usage is the same from section to section within the launcher?	A4	FACTOR 4	
8.2. Does the launcher apply consistent format?	F4	FACTOR 4	
9.1. Are Items placed in recognizable positions?	F2	FACTOR 6	
10.1. Does the launcher support or provide shortcuts for direct access to the most frequent functions or items?	B8	FACTOR 7	
10.2. Does the launcher provide supports to remember functions easily?		FACTOR 6	
10.3. Does the launcher group similar functions in one place? (example, {call, contact list, write text message in one group}, {camera, pictures, videos in another group})	C5	FACTOR 4	
10.4. Are the important functions always available (call, turn-off, etc.)?		FACTOR 6	
11.1. Does the main navigation menu exist consistently in all pages?		FACTOR 3	
11.2. Does clicking the back button always go back to the previous page that the elderly comes from?	F8, C18	FACTOR 3	
11.3. Does the launcher provide emergency exits to leave unwanted state and is it clearly pointed?	A6	FACTOR 3	
12.1. Does the graphical interface design and the organization help prevent errors?	A9	FACTOR 5	
12.2. Is there confirmation message for critical actions such as deletion?	E10	FACTOR 1	
12.3. Are the important functions placed at top of the screen to avoid mistake touches?		FACTOR 5	
13.1. Does the launcher show level of battery, time and date, signal of contact/Wi- Fi/3G?		FACTOR 1	
13.2. Are the default settings of mobile phone available to the elderly in an easy way?(e.g. change ringtone)		FACTOR 1	

– Four (4) usability problems retrieved from Kobayashi et al. [21]. Kobayashi et al. [21] tested traditional touch screen gestures with one iPod, one iPad (emulating an iPod) and 20 elderly users with ages ranging from 60 up to 80 years.
– Eight (8) usability problems retrieved from Harada et al. [12]. Harada et al. [12] conducted tests and focus group with 21 elderly users with ages from 63 up to 79 years and three different applications: an Address Book, a Phone and a Map. Both smartphones and tablets were used for the tests.
– Four (4) usability problems retrieved from Kiat and Chen [20]. Kiat and Chen [20] conducted focus group and test with of a *Mobile Instant Messaging* with six elderly people whose ages ranged from 60 up to 80.

In addition to the test outcomes retrieved from the literature, we conducted a test with six (6) elderly users with ages ranging from 61 up to 73 years ($\bar{x} = 67.83$, $s = 5.42$). For the tests, we used the Think Aloud procedure [10]. Two moderators were responsible for taking notes of usability problems based on users' interaction. As result from the tests, the moderators collected 53 usability problems. In sequence, we conducted a duplicate analysis, resulting in a list of 25 distinct usability problems (see Appendix A). Finally, we had a total set of 52 mobile usability problems related to the elderly context.

At this stage, we matched all 52 usability problems retrieved from the literature and from the tests we conducted against Nielsen's heuristics and the heuristics of Al-Razgan et al. [2]. In this sense, we understood that 28 of the problems retrieved were related (matched) with some of Nielsen's heuristic. At this point, our goal was not to identify all relations between Nielsen's heuristics and the usability problems retrieved in our study, but to identify at least one relation that could show that the respective heuristic is applicable to this context. Table 2 shows the number of usability problems matched with each of the ten heuristics of Nielsen ($\bar{x} = 3.11$, $s = 2.47$). As shown in Table 2, one can see that the heuristics 1 and 2 were the most matched with usability problems (had the largest coverage).

In the following stage, we matched the 52 usability problems with the heuristics from Al-Razgan et al. [2]. Our goal was by no means to match all possibilities between usability problems and heuristics, but only the most related from our understanding. In Table 3 we show the number of problems related to each heuristic from Al-Razgan et al. [2], represented by its items. Among the 48 checklist items from the heuristics set, only 16 items were matched with some usability problem, as shown in Table 3 ($\bar{x} = 0.59$, $s = 1.28$).

Finally, we did a comparison among the 52 usability problems and both heuristic sets. For this objective, we did two other analyses: (i) *total of matching* and (ii) *unique matching*. Table 4 summarizes the distribution of total matching that each heuristic set had on usability problems identified from each study. In sequence, we analyzed matches that were unique from each method (usability problems covered only by one of the sets). Table 5 shows the number of unique coverage by each heuristic set. In both cases, the heuristics from Al-Razgan et al. [2] had a higher coverage. This fact is an important evidence towards

Table 2. Total coverage for each one of Nielsen's heuristics on mobile usability problems identified in test with elderly users.

Nielsen	Matches (n)
Heuristic 1	8
Heuristic 2	5
Heuristic 3	3
Heuristic 4	1
Heuristic 5	1
Heuristic 6	5
Heuristic 7	1
Heuristic 8	3
Heuristic 9	1

Table 3. Items from the heuristic set of Al-Razgan et al. [2] by its number of matches (n). This table shows only those items that had a mathc identified.

Al-Razgan et al.	Matches (n)
1.1. Is the font large enough for older adults?	2
1.2. Is there any option to enlarge the font size?	1
1.6. Does color choices allow for easy readability?	2
12.1. Does the graphical interface design and the organization help prevent errors?	1
2.4. Is the keypad separated into numbers and letters for data entry?	1
2.5. Is data entry process easy for elderly?	5
3.1. Is it obvious which item is clickable and which is not?	4
3.2. Are buttons large enough to easily see the image or text on them?	1
3.4. Is buttons size adequate to finger touch?	1
4.1. Does the launcher use words that majority of older adults are familiar with?	3
4.3. Are the icons familiar to elderly?	1
5.3. Are error messages descriptive, and did they provide a solution to the elderly for recovery?	1
5.5. Does the launcher keep elderly informed about what is going on, through appropriate feedback?	4
6.1. Does the launcher use tap gestures for most of the actions?	4
6.2. Is the object has more than one gesture to perform actions?(e.g. it has tap and drag gesture on the same object)	2
6.4 Do gestures of launcher work correctly and smoothly?	5

Table 4. Total matching - Number of usability problems by study (first two columns) and total number of matching by each heuristic set (last two columns).

	Usability problems	Nielsen	Al-Razgan et al.
Kiat and Chen [20]	4	2	4
Harada et al. [12]	8	2	7
Kobayashi et al. [21]	4	1	2
Gao and Sun [9]	2	0	2
Scheibe et al. [35]	9	3	8
Our study	25	20	18
TOTAL	**52**	**28**	**41**

Table 5. Unique matching - Number of usability problems by study (first two columns) and total number of matching by each heuristic set (last two columns).

	Usability problems	Nielsen	Al-Razgan et al.
Kiat and Chen [20]	4	0	2
Harada et al. [12]	8	1	5
Kobayashi et al. [21]	4	1	2
Gao and Sun [9]	2	0	2
Scheibe et al. [35]	9	1	6
Our study	25	8	4
TOTAL	**52**	**11**	**21**

establishing a heuristic set for evaluations of mobile usability problems regarding elderly users. Nevertheless, as showed before in this section, most part of Al-Razgan et al. [2] can be linked to Nielsen's heuristics. We understand that future studies should investigate the synergy of merging both sets in a new one, because the heuristics of Nielsen have been largely validated in the community and our study had a limited sample of usability problems.

Finally, three usability problems were not covered by any of the heuristic sets. The first of these usability problems (retrieved from our study and from Harada et al. [12]) indicated that users wanted a confirmation before going on with a task (after completing a sub-task), which was not provided by the interface. The other usability problem showed that users preferred to drag and pinch then tapping [21].

5   Implications for Design

We understand that designers and practitioners can apply the heuristics from Al-Razgan et al. [2] for evaluating mobile usability for the elderly. In addition, we suggest the use of these heuristics as a complement for the traditional heuristics of Nielsen, this can be done by applying the set of Nielsen and the other 11 items from Al-Razgan et al. [2] that were not related to any of Nielsen's heuristics.

Designers can also use our list of usability problems (see Sect. A) as complement for initial requirements for design of mobile usability for elderly.

6   Conclusions

This study aimed to continue the development of heuristics for mobile usability and elderly users. For this reason, we conducted additional validations of the heuristics from Al-Razgan et al. [2] with traditional heuristics of Nielsen, 52 usability problems retrieved tests with users (from a literature survey and tests with six users). Most part of the checklist items of heuristics from Al-Razgan et al. [2] are related to nine out of the ten heuristics of Nielsen. In addition, the 48 items from the heuristics of Al-Razgan et al. [2] covered 41 mobile usability problems related to elderly users collected in our study, while traditional heuristics of Nielsen covered 28 of such mobile usability problems.

Future studies should compare both heuristic sets from case studies with group of evaluators conducting heuristic evaluation with each set and, then, compare the extent of outcomes against outcomes from test with potential users. This was suggested because our method was focused on comparing matching of problems without considering that, during a heuristic evaluation, evaluators may differ in the discovery of such problems through each heuristic set due to evaluator and expertise effect [3, 15].

The main limitation of our study relates to the evaluator-effect [15], other researchers may perform different matches of the 52 mobile usability problems with both heuristic sets approached. Future studies can explore the development of a unique heuristic set from a synergistic merging of both Nielsen's heuristics and the heuristics of Al-Razgan et al. [2]. Also, future studies can investigate short/long text descriptions for the heuristics of Al-Razgan et al. [2] through a factor analysis from a larger sample of mobile usability problems, because our data was not sufficient for such.

A   Appendix

The following list presents the 25 mobile usability problems collected during the test with users we conducted:

- The "understood" button missed a user's touch.
- The alert text screen was confusing for users.
- The feedback message "correct choice" was similar to a button in user's opinion.
- The feedback message "incorrect" was similar to a button in user's opinion.
- The keyboard missed a user's touch.
- The keyboard sensitivity was uncomfortable for the user.
- The line spacing at the text alert screens was not comfortable for the user.

- The pop up feedback "incorrect" was not appropriated to inform the user what was incorrect.
- The position of "Yes" and "No" options for repeating the training session was confuse for users, they touched on "Yes" (on the right) when they wanted to touch on "No" (on the left).
- The system alert screen was not sufficient to alert the user.
- The system allowed users to practice many times, what was considered uncomfortable for the user.
- The system did not give a feedback for user when he/she was required to wait.
- The system did not provide a confirmation button for the user after selecting the required numbers.
- The system did not provide an introduction screen, as expected by the user.
- The system did not provide a confirmation button for the user after touching the figure on the training screen.
- The system had no undo option after touching the wrong button accidentally.
- The system gave no feedback for the user when the level of the test was changed.
- The system lacks feedback about remaining time on figure selection - training screen.
- The system made the user wait after doing the requested action until changing screen for task continuity.
- The term "confirm" in a button, after touching the distinct figure, was confusing for the user.
- The term "repeat" in a button on the text alert screen was confusing for the user.
- The term "understood" in a button on the text alert screen was confusing for the user.
- The system lacks feedback when the task is finished.
- The system lacks a signifier on the figure selection screen.
- The system was not comfortable for the user because of the different standards used among system's screens.

References

1. Fernandez, A., Insfran, E., Abraháo, S.: Usability evaluation methods for the web: a systematic mapping study. Inf. Softw. Technol. **53**, 789–817 (2011). http://www-sciencedirect-com.ez67.periodicos.capes.gov.br/science/article/pii/S0950584911000607
2. Al-Razgan, M.S., Al-Khalifa, H.S., Al-Shahrani, M.D.: Heuristics for evaluating the usability of mobile launchers for elderly people. In: Marcus, A. (ed.) DUXU 2014. LNCS, vol. 8517, pp. 415–424. Springer, Cham (2014). doi:10.1007/978-3-319-07668-3_40
3. Brajnik, G., Yesilada, Y., Harper, S.: The expertise effect on web accessibility evaluation methods. Hum.-Comput. Interact. **26**(3), 246–283 (2011). http://www.tandfonline.com/doi/abs/10.1080/07370024.2011.601670

4. Buykx, L.: Improving heuristic evaluation through collaborative working. Ph.D. thesis, The University of York Department of Computer Science, September 2009
5. Jimenez, C., Lozada, P., Rosas, P.: Usability heuristics: a systematic review. In: 2016 IEEE 11th Colombian Computing Conference (CCC), pp. 1–8, September 2016
6. Chang, H.T., Tsai, T.H., Chang, Y.C., Chang, Y.M.: Touch panel usability of elderly and children. Comput. Hum. Behav. **37**, 258–269 (2014). www.sciencedirect.com/science/article/pii/S0747563214002714
7. Følstad, A., Law, E., Hornbæk, K.: Analysis in practical usability evaluation: a survey study. In: Proceedings of the SIGCHI Conference on Human Factors in Computing Systems, CHI 2012, NY, USA, pp. 2127–2136 (2012). http://doi.acm.org/10.1145/2207676.2208365
8. Følstad, A., Law, E.L.C., Hornbæk, K.: Analysis in usability evaluations: an exploratory study. In: Proceedings of the 6th Nordic Conference on Human-Computer Interaction: Extending Boundaries, NordiCHI 2010, NY, USA, pp. 647–650 (2010). http://doi.acm.org/10.1145/1868914.1868995
9. Gao, Q., Sun, Q.: Examining the usability of touch screen gestures for older and younger adults. Hum. Factors **57**(5), 835–863 (2015)
10. Gill, A.M., Nonnecke, B.: Think aloud: effects and validity. In: Proceedings of the 30th ACM International Conference on Design of Communication, SIGDOC 2012, pp. 31–36. ACM, New York (2012)
11. Gomes, G., Duarte, C., Coelho, J., Matos, E.: Designing a facebook interface for senior users. Sci. World J. **2014**, 1–8 (2014)
12. Harada, S., Sato, D., Takagi, H., Asakawa, C.: Characteristics of elderly user behavior on mobile multi-touch devices. In: Kotzé, P., Marsden, G., Lindgaard, G., Wesson, J., Winckler, M. (eds.) INTERACT 2013. LNCS, vol. 8120, pp. 323–341. Springer, Heidelberg (2013). doi:10.1007/978-3-642-40498-6_25
13. Harrison, R., Flood, D., Duce, D.: Usability of mobile applications: literature review and rationale for a new usability model. J. Interact. Sci. **1**(1), 1 (2013). http://journalofinteractionscience.springeropen.com/articles/10.1186/2194-0827-1-1
14. Hermawati, S., Lawson, G.: Establishing usability heuristics for heuristics evaluation in a specific domain: is there a consensus? Appl. Ergon. **56**, 34–51 (2016). www.sciencedirect.com/science/article/pii/S0003687015301162
15. Hertzum, M., Jacobsen, N.E.: The evaluator effect: a chilling fact about usability evaluation methods. Int. J. Hum.-Comput. Interact. **13**(4), 421–443 (2001). http://dx.doi.org/10.1207/S15327590IJHC1304_05
16. ISO 9241–161:2016(en): Ergonomics of human-system interaction – Part 161: Guidance on visual user-interface elements. Technical report (2016). https://www.iso.org/obp/ui/#iso:std:iso:9241:-161:ed-1:v1:en
17. ISO/IEC 25066:2016(en): Systems and software engineering – Systems and software Quality Requirements and Evaluation (SQuaRE) – Common Industry Format (CIF) for Usability – Evaluation Report. Technical report (2016). https://www.iso.org/obp/ui/#iso:std:iso-iec:25066:ed-1:v1:en
18. Nielsen, J.: 10 Heuristics for User Interface Design (2017). https://www.nngroup.com/articles/ten-usability-heuristics/
19. Joyce, G., Lilley, M., Barker, T., Jefferies, A.: Mobile application usability: heuristic evaluation and evaluation of heuristics. In: Amaba, B. (ed.) Advances in Human Factors, Software, and Systems Engineering. AISC, vol. 492, pp. 77–86. Springer, Switzerland (2016). doi:10.1007/978-3-319-41935-0_8

20. Kiat, B.W., Chen, W.: Mobile instant messaging for the elderly. Procedia Comput. Sci. **67**, 28–37 (2015)
21. Kobayashi, M., Hiyama, A., Miura, T., Asakawa, C., Hirose, M., Ifukube, T.: Elderly user evaluation of mobile touchscreen interactions. In: Campos, P., Graham, N., Jorge, J., Nunes, N., Palanque, P., Winckler, M. (eds.) INTERACT 2011. LNCS, vol. 6946, pp. 83–99. Springer, Heidelberg (2011). doi:10.1007/978-3-642-23774-4_9
22. Leung, R., Tang, C., Haddad, S., Mcgrenere, J., Graf, P., Ingriany, V.: How older adults learn to use mobile devices: survey and field investigations. ACM Trans. Access. Comput. **4**(3), 11:1–11:33 (2012). http://doi.acm.org.ez67.periodicos. capes.gov.br/10.1145/2399193.2399195
23. Lima Salgado, A., Freire, A.P.: Heuristic evaluation of mobile usability: a mapping study. In: Kurosu, M. (ed.) HCI 2014. LNCS, vol. 8512, pp. 178–188. Springer, Cham (2014). doi:10.1007/978-3-319-07227-2_18
24. de Lima Salgado, A., Rodrigues, S.S., Fortes, R.P.M.: Evolving heuristic evaluation for multiple contexts and audiences: perspectives from a mapping study. In: Proceedings of the 34th ACM International Conference on the Design of Communication, SIGDOC 2016, NY, USA, pp. 19:1–19:8 (2016). http://doi.acm.org/10.1145/2987592.2987617
25. Lynch, K.R.: Weighted Heuristic Evaluation and Usability Testing of Ohio Area Agency on Aging Websites for Older Adults. Ph.D. thesis, Ohio University (2011)
26. Madan, A., Dubey, S.K.: Usability evaluation methods: a literature review. Int. J. Eng. Sci. Technol. **4**(2), 590–599 (2012). https://eclass.teicrete. gr/modules/document/file.php/TP254/Further%20Reading%20Material/05. %20Usability%20Evaluation%20Methods%20-%20A%20literature%20review.pdf
27. Marzano, G., Lubkina, V.: Usability in social telerehabilitation systems for elderly users. Public Health **144**, 1–3 (2017). www.sciencedirect.com/science/article/pii/S0033350616303936
28. Nielsen, J.: Finding usability problems through heuristic evaluation. In: Proceedings of the SIGCHI Conference on Human Factors in Computing Systems, pp. 373–380. ACM (1992)
29. Nielsen, J.: Enhancing the explanatory power of usability heuristics. In: Proceedings of the SIGCHI Conference on Human Factors in Computing Systems, CHI 1994, pp. 152–158. ACM, New York (1994)
30. Nielsen, J.: Heuristic evaluation. In: Mack, R.L., Nielsen, J. (eds.) Usability Inspection Methods, pp. 25–62 (1994)
31. Nielsen, J., Molich, R.: Heuristic evaluation of user interfaces. In: Proceedings of the SIGCHI Conference on Human Factors in Computing Systems, pp. 249–256. ACM (1990)
32. Paz, F., Pow-Sang, J.A.: A systematic mapping review of usability evaluation methods for software development process. Int. J. Softw. Eng. Appl. **10**(1), 165–178 (2016). http://www.sersc.org/journals/IJSEIA/vol10_no1_2016/16.pdf
33. Petrie, H., Buykx, L.: Collaborative heuristic evaluation: improving the effectiveness of heuristic evaluation. In: Proceedings of UPA 2010 International Conference. Omnipress (2010). http://upa.omnibooksonline.com/index.htm
34. Petrie, H., Savva, A., Power, C.: Towards a unified definition of web accessibility. In: Proceedings of the 12th Web for All Conference, Florence, Italy, pp. 1–13. ACM (2015)
35. Scheibe, M., Reichelt, J., Bellmann, M., Kirch, W.: Acceptance factors of mobile apps for diabetes by patients aged 50 or older: a qualitative study. Medicine 2.0 **4**(1) (2015)

36. Soto-Mendoza, V., García-Macías, J.A., Chávez, E., Martínez-García, A.I., Favela, J., Serrano-Alvarado, P., Rojas, M.R.Z.: Design of a predictive scheduling system to improve assisted living services for elders. ACM Trans. Intell. Syst. Technol. **6**(4), 53:1–53:31 (2015). http://doi.acm.org.ez67.periodicos.capes.gov.br/10.1145/2736700

37. Wüest, S., Borghese, N.A., Pirovano, M., Mainetti, R., van de Langenberg, R., de Bruin, E.D.: Usability and effects of an exergame-based balance training program. GAMES FOR HEALTH: Res. Dev. Clin. Appl. **3**(2), 106–114 (2014)

38. Fang, Y.M., Chou, Y.P., Chu, B.C.: Health information display for elderly people: interface attributes, usability, and emotional reaction. In: 2016 International Conference on Applied System Innovation (ICASI), pp. 1–4, May 2016

Is a Holistic Criteria-Based Approach Possible in User Experience?

Study of the Classification of 58 Criteria Linked to UX

Josefina Isabel Gil Urrutia[1,2(✉)], Eric Brangier[1], and Laurent Cessat[2]

[1] Psychologie Ergonomique et Sociale pour l'Expérience Utilisateurs UFR Sciences Humaines et Sociales, University of Lorraine, Ile du Saulcy, BP 30309, 57006 Metz, France
josefina.gil_urrutia@allianz.fr,
eric.brangier@univ-lorraine.fr
[2] Direction des Développements et de la Maintenance, Département Digital et Distribution, Allianz Informatique, Tour Franklin 100 Terrasse Boieldieu, La Défense, BP 1050, 92042 Paris La Défense, France
laurent.cessat_2@allianz.fr

Abstract. After having produced many criteria to improve accessibility, ease of use, emotions linked to interactions, persuasive design, cultural values attached to systems, socio-organizational contexts, the domain of HCI must conduct a reflection on the structuring of these criteria. The aim of this paper is to advance research in the field of user experience criteria by understanding how UX professionals organize their cognitions around the criteria set. For this, we conducted a study of its classification with 17 experts. The set of 58 cards was presented by explaining that each card represents a criterion. The experts were asked to do an open card sort, to name the groups of cards and, upon completion, to explain the logic they had based their sorting on. On the basis of several statistical analyzes, the results show a categorization into 8 main classes: (1) Utility (task-system suitability, achieving the goal, efficacy) and Pragmatism (ergonomic criteria, efficiency); (2) Hedonism, Pleasure, Emotions; (3) Persuasion, Incitement, Pervasive design; (4) Emotional & Cognitive Stimulation for self-development; (5) Marketing strategy/Customer Relationship Management; (6) Security/Reliability-User's protection; (7) Organizational factors; and (8) Social, moral and/or cultural factors. This article proposes a multifactorial approach to UX which is based on these 8 dimensions that combine and coordinate with one another.

Keywords: User experience · Criteria-Based approach · Card-sort

1 Introduction

Human Computer Interaction (HCI) has often developed guidelines to measure the ergonomic quality of products and services [3, 7, 11, 18, 22, 25, 26]. Over the past 40 years, many criteria grids have been created: some have been added, others have

© Springer International Publishing AG 2017
A. Marcus and W. Wang (Eds.): DUXU 2017, Part I, LNCS 10288, pp. 395–409, 2017.
DOI: 10.1007/978-3-319-58634-2_29

replaced and others have been superimposed on the previous grids [4]. But how are these criteria understood and used by designers and evaluators? In the same way, an array of user experience frameworks has been suggested. Yet, the lack of consensus is still to date quite remarkable with no one model having received sufficient recognition or having been considered thorough enough. The variety of frameworks proposed, with a substantial pool of notions and criteria as well as their different scopes and approaches, is indicative of the still current struggle to reach a common understanding of the field, its founding principles, its components, its position relative to other fields, its scope and so on.

In this perspective, our research aims to list the existing criteria, understand their organization, and to propose a global architecture of the criteria for the User Experience (UX). In agreement with [4, 13] we believe UX is multidimensional in the sense that – to put it in Donald Norman's terms – "an experience is a system [that's everything]" [19], in which many factors take part and interdependencies emerge, thus continuously altering the context and the user's experience itself.

Also, HCI and UX research have witnessed a great deal of evolutions from their origins until now. In its beginnings, they addressed issues of accessibility. Nowadays, numerous efforts are made in order to reach a holistic view of UX, merging notions of emotions, culture, social factors, usability, to name a few, and considering the dynamic mechanisms between them. As the field has evolved and taken on different problems, different recommendations/best practices have been identified and suggested at given times. For example, criteria sets (i.e. heuristics) have been recommended. However, as Brangier et al. [4] point out, nowadays we seem to be faced with an overflow of recommendations and important notions associated with each dimension, which renders our practice evermore challenging as they keep piling up.

Confronted with this issue, we carried out the present study aiming to propose the application of a criteria-based approach (i.e. "criteriology") to UX. For this, we set out to analyze how experts from the UX community would envision, apprehend and structure the proposed set of UX criteria through a categorization exercise. We intended to evaluate the relevancy of the sets of criteria we offer, and to identify aspects of UX most commonly considered as well as dimensions and their corresponding criteria that we might have neglected and that the participants would suggest to include. Additionally, we expect the categorization to allow for a simplified view of the field, to help determine its scope and its architecture which would be a considerable contribution to a holistic model of user experience.

2   UX Criteria: A Theoretical Background

Overall, UX corresponds to what results from a goal-oriented behavior which takes place in a given context [2]. Arhippainen and Tähti [1] consider it to be determined by five categories of factors which are: social, cultural, user's characteristics, context's characteristics and the product's features. Thus, user experience is to be understood as the consequence of a user's internal state (predispositions, expectations, needs, motivation, mood, etc.), the characteristics of the designed system (e.g. complexity, purpose, usability, functionality, etc.) and the context (or the environment) within which the interaction occurs (e.g. organizational/social setting, meaningfulness of the activity, voluntariness of use, etc.) [10], to which the authors [4] add: "UX is based on situated human-system interactions, through which technical, cultural and social skills are developed given that technological interaction has become an experience of use of functionalities (functional/utilitarian experience) and the experience of said use (experiential/lived/felt experience)".

Taking into account all of the aspects of UX [4], we set out to create and propose a criteria set that would integrate them all. For this, we chose seven main dimensions which have been essential to HCI research throughout time and that we estimated would allow for a holistic approach of the ensemble. These dimensions are as follows:

- Accessibility: 4 criteria were drawn from the Web Content Accessibility Guidelines (WCAG) [27]:

1. Perceivable: the interface is presented in a way the user can always perceive;
2. Operable: user interface components must be easy to use;
3. Understandable: the information presented must be easy to understand for all users;
4. Robust: the system must be robust enough for it to resist any unexpected solicitations.

- Usability/Practicality: 8 criteria from ergonomic criteria for evaluation of HCI [3]:

5. Guidance: means available to advise, orient, inform and guide the user throughout their interactions;
6. Workload: interface elements implicated in the reduction of the user's perceptual/cognitive load, and in the increase of dialogue efficiency;
7. Explicit control: system's ability to process the user's explicit actions, and the control they have over the processing of their actions;
8. Adaptability: system's capacity to behave contextually and accordingly to the user's needs/preferences;
9. Error management: means available to prevent or reduce errors and to recover from them when they do occur;
10. Consistency: interface design choices are maintained in similar contexts, but differ when the context is different;
11. Significance of codes: adequacy between a term/sign and its reference;
12. Compatibility: match between the user's and the task's characteristics, and the organization of the output, input and the dialogue for a given application.

- Emotions & Motivation: 9 criteria correspond to the model of Emotion and Motivation detection in HCI (4 permanent traits and 5 transient states) [5]:

13. Control: system's capacity to respect the degree of control the user likes having over it;
14. Challenge: system's ability to incite a challenging situation that the user enjoys being confronted with;
15. Independence: system's capability to encourage the user to work independently without asking others for help;

16. Fantasy: the system evokes mental images of social/physical situations that are satisfying to the user;
17. Confidence: system's ability to arouse a required level of belief in being able to perform the task properly;
18. Sensory interest: amount of curiosity aroused by the system's characteristics (interface, graphics, sounds, etc.);
19. Cognitive interest: curiosity aroused through the cognitive/epistemic characteristics of the task;
20. Effort: system's ability to inspire and maintain a certain level of effort needed for the user to perform the task;
21. Satisfaction: overall feeling of goal accomplishment procured by the system.

- Persuasion: the 8 criteria are the Persuasion Criteria (4 static and 4 dynamic criteria) [16]:

22. Credibility: ability of the interface to inspire confidence and make the user trust the veracity of its information;
23. Privacy: the system guarantees the protection of personal data, the preservation of personal integrity and the security of the interaction;
24. Personalization: the ability for a user to adapt the interface to their preferences;
25. Attractiveness: via the use of aesthetics, the system captures the user's attention in order to support the interaction and to create a positive emotion;
26. Solicitation: ability to induce a user action with minimal influence from the interface;
27. Priming: system's capacity to pilot the user's initiative in order to encourage them to execute the first engaging action(s);
28. Commitment: the system progressively increases the frequency and intensity of its requests in order to gradually involve the user more and more;
29. Ascendency: the system attains such a level of influence over the user that they become subject to a total level of involvement with the system.

- Cultural values: 10 criteria were derived from the Portrait Values Questionnaire based on Schwartz's Theory of Basic Human Values [24] to represent the cultural dimension:

30. Self-direction: the system allows the user to freely express their thoughts and actions depending on their own goals and interests;
31. Stimulation: the system satisfies the user's needs for diverse stimulations and their quest for new and exciting experiences;
32. Hedonism: the system represents a source of pleasure, gratification and amusement for the user;
33. Achievement: the system is a tool for the search of personal success through the demonstration of socially-determined aptitudes and goals;
34. Power: the system allows the user to reach and maintain a certain role/status within a larger social context;

35. Security: the system guarantees the safety of the user, thus posing no threat for them nor for their community;
36. Conformity: actions that might transgress social norms/expectations are moderated by the system;
37. Tradition: the system respects and commits to the cultural symbols, ideas and customs;
38. Benevolence: the system maintains the user's need for cooperation and solidarity among peers;
39. Universalism: the system encourages equality, social justice, tolerance and the welfare of all people and of the environment/nature.

- Management of the experience: we created 9 criteria based off of general concepts surrounding Customer Experience Management, Customer Life Cycle and Experience Marketing [12, 17, 20, 21, 23]:

40. Zero customer effort: the system ensures a fluid and easy customer journey and guarantees the transparency of the information presented;
41. Acquisition-Consumption: the system is key for customer conviction because it promotes the offer and allows for its acquisition and consumption;
42. Competitive positioning: the system portrays the brand's and the product's images, showcasing its prominence in comparison to the competition's offer;
43. Proactive approach: through a user-centered approach, the system contributes to the adaptation and optimization of the offer to the user's needs and preferences;
44. Customer Loyalty and Recommendation: through positive touch-points, the system contributes to the user's enchantment and loyalty;
45. Multichannel/Omni-channel: the system is available across different channels;
46. Prospective approach: the system contributes to the anticipation of future needs, usages and consumption behaviors in order for the brand to constantly be able to foresee an innovative and competitive offer;
47. Relationship Management: the user acquires an important role regarding the brand – the legitimacy and pertinence of the touch-points as well as the brand-customer proximity and relationship customization are crucial;
48. Offer Segmentation: the brand ensures an offer that responds to an array of prospects' and customers' varying needs, desires and preferences.

- Socio-organizational context and Organizational Resources management: we created 10 criteria related to [8, 9, 14]:

49. Context of use: the system is part of a larger social, technical, economic, political (etc.) context;
50. Transformation-Adaptation: the system is an actor in the ever-changing and dynamic context it's part of;
51. Task Achievement: the system helps to attain set goals according to productivity, efficacy and quality criteria;

52. Task Management: the system guides the user through the task and its different stages;
53. Role: the user adopts their role within the organization via the system thus exposing their identity, motivations, responsibilities and contribution;
54. Skills & Knowledge: the user's skills and knowledge can be acquired, developed and expressed through the system;
55. Communication: the system ensures the access to, the transmission and the processing of the information;
56. Cooperation/Collaboration: partakers cooperate/collaborate by means of the system in order to reach (a) set and shared goal(s);
57. Sub-systems coordination: the system regulates the activity within the organization via the differentiation of the sub-systems and through their coordination;
58. Results & Impacts: the system has direct repercussions on the organization, the user and their goals (whether social, economic, etc.).

3 Problem and Method

The vastness and diversity of this set makes it difficult to have a holistic approach on the subject. Plus, working with such abstract notions makes it even harder to manipulate them. In addition, this set presents overlappings as well as certain cross-dimensions interdependencies that have been studied [4], which adds to the complexity of the issue. Furthermore, by acknowledging UX as a system, one admits that by intervening on one factor, this will influence other factors and have an impact on the system as a whole. Therefore, it would be of interest to simplify this vast set of criteria by studying the representation experts may have of the matter according to a categorization exercise.

This study aimed to determine how UX experts would envision, apprehend and structure the proposed set of UX criteria. Would the open card sort reveal categories stable enough throughout the experts? What would these categories be and which criteria would they comprise? What links and relationships would emerge across these categories? And, what would its spatial structure or representation look like?

3.1 Participants

A total of 17 expert-level HCI Designers (6 women, 11 men; mean age 44 (SD = 8.6)) participated in the study. Among them, 11 are specialized in Ergonomics/Cognitive Psychology, 4 in Computer Science, and the remaining 2 in Communications and Media. Participants were required to have at least 10 years of experience in the field of HCI/UX in order to be eligible ($\bar{x} = 17.53$; SD = 6.05). 11 of them are academics, 4 are consultants and 2 are both. 10 of them are PhD-level, and 7 Master-level. Participants received a small compensation.

3.2   Material

This study used 58 physical cards, each containing the information (name and definition) from a criterion from those listed above. The cards were 5 × 5 cm white index-cards with black writing, and they had no distinctive mark as to their initial groupings. A pen, extra plain 5 × 5 cm cards were at disposal in case the participant wished to create (a) new card(s). Also, plain white 5 × 20 cm index cards were used to create category name tags. A camera and a recorder were used by the researcher conducting the experiment.

3.3   Procedure

Sessions were carried out individually and lasted between 30 and 50 min. We opted for an un-moderated approach.

The set of cards was presented to the experts by explaining that each card represents a criterion that we consider to be important in UX. The participant was informed that if they believed otherwise, they could exclude it from the card-deck. If, on the contrary, they found there were criteria missing or misrepresented in the lot, they were invited to create a corresponding card, indicating a name and a definition.

The participant was asked to do an open card sort. Upon completion, the expert was asked to name the groups of cards if they hadn't done so already, and to explain the logic they had based their sorting on. This debriefing was recorded and transcribed for reference during the analysis and interpretation of the data.

4   Results

The data was first analyzed using Donna Maurer's [6] spreadsheets. This was particularly helpful in order to better understand each expert's categorizations, to create standardized categories to better sum up the range of classifications and to generate the items by standardized categories correlation matrix. We adapted Mike Rice's co-occurrence matrix [15] to generate the general distance matrix which served next.

Then, the software "R" was used to generate the Hierarchical Cluster Analysis (HCA) using Ward's clustering method, as well as the Multi-Dimensional Scale (MDS) plot using Kruskal's non-metric MDS.

4.1   Categories and Criterion Distribution

Participants created an average of 8 groups ($\bar{x} = 7.71$; SD = 1.65). Table 1 recaps the standardized categories we created from all of those made by the participants. It also shows that, while the agreement between the participants' results for each category – and particularly each category's items/criteria – is rather low ($\bar{x} = 0.30$; SD = 0.10; min = 0.19; max = 0.58), the occurrence of the standardized categories is high, even very high for certain of them. Indeed, as much as 14 experts created a category corresponding to aspects pertaining to usability, pragmatism, ergonomic criteria and/or

Table 1. Standardized categories created for the open card-sort (as generated by [6]).

Standardized category	Sorters who used this	Total cards in this category	Unique cards	Agreement
Utility, task-system suitability, achieving the goal, efficacy	7	59	36	0,23
Usability/Pragmatism, ergonomic criteria, efficiency	14	171	42	0,29
Hedonism, Pleasure, Emotions	16	129	34	0,24
Adaptability of the system	9	98	47	0,23
Organizational Factors	10	61	15	0,41
Persuasion, Incitement, Pervasive design	10	68	28	0,24
Marketing Strategy/Customer Relationship Management	12	84	21	0,33
User Effort	3	14	8	0,58
Personalization/Customization	4	20	13	0,38
Mastering/Control over the system	8	41	27	0,19
Security/Reliability-User's Protection	9	53	24	0,25
User on boarding	4	45	29	0,39
Emotional & Cognitive Stimulation for self-development	7	51	25	0,29
Social, moral and/or cultural factors	9	34	17	0,22
Technical aspects/Robustness	3	16	14	0,38
Others/Unknown	7	29	23	0,18
Excluded	5	14	13	0,22

efficiency – and up to 16 participants created one corresponding to aspects of hedonism, pleasure and/or emotions related to HCI.

So, though the variability as to which criteria belong to which category may be quite high resulting in low inter-judge agreement values, the general categories seem to be common ground for the group of experts.

Next, we applied an HCA to the overall distance matrix for all 17 participants' data. Using the items by standardized categories correlation matrix, we were able to identify and label the clusters on the dendrogram generated by the HCA. Figure 1 illustrates these results.

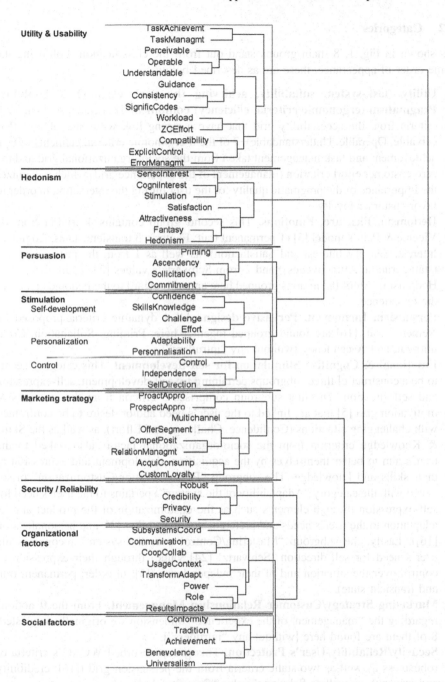

Fig. 1. Dendrogram generated by the HCA of the open card-sort distance matrix, divided into the 8 standardized categories we retained after the first-stage analysis.

4.2 Categories

As shown in Fig. 1, 8 main groups stand out from the classification. Following the same order of appearance, these are as described below.

- **Utility (task-system suitability, achieving the goal, efficacy) & Usability/ Pragmatism (ergonomic criteria, efficiency) combined.** This category contains 3 criteria from the accessibility grid that have a strong link with ease of use (Perceivable, Operable, Understandable), 7 of the 8 ergonomic criteria, elements of task achievement and task management taken from the socio-organizational grid and the zero customer effort criterion (management of the experience grid) which recognizes the importance of the pragmatic quality for the user during the interaction in order to favor customer loyalty.

- **Hedonism, Pleasure, Emotions.** This second group contains 4 criteria from de Vicente & Pain's model [5] (1 permanent trait: Fantasy, 3 transient states: Cognitive Interest, Sensory Interest and Satisfaction), as well as 1 from the persuasion grid (static criteria: Attractiveness) and 2 from Schwartz's values [24] (Stimulation and Hedonism). All of the notions grouped here are with regard to the hedonic quality of the experience.

- **Persuasion, Incitement, Pervasive design.** All 4 dynamic criteria proposed by Nemery et al. [16] are found grouped together here: Priming, Solicitation, Commitment and Ascendency [without any "intruders"].

- **Emotional & Cognitive Stimulation for self-development.** This category seems to be a construct of three subgroups pertaining to: self-development, self-expression and self-direction. The first subgroup comprises 3 criteria from the emotions & motivation grid [5] that are linked to the user's need and/or desire to be confronted with challenging situations (Confidence, Challenge and Effort), as well as the Skills & Knowledge criterion from the socio-organizational factors also linked to the user's aim to better themselves by the acquisition, development and expression of their skills and knowledge. The subgroup "Personalization/Customization" (associated with the category "Adaptability of the system") pertains to the user's need for self-expression through elements such as the customization of the product and its adaptation to the user's needs and preferences (adaptability [3], and personalization [16]). Lastly, the subgroup "Mastering/Control over the system" recognizes the user's need for self-direction (Schwartz' [24] value) through their expression of control over the situation and of their independence ([5]; in order: permanent trait and transient state).

- **Marketing Strategy/Customer Relationship Management.** From the 9 notions regarding the "management of the experience" dimension we originally suggested, 8 of them are found here [without any "intruders"].

- **Security/Reliability-User's Protection.** This group absorbed WCAG's criteria of robustness as well as two static criteria from the persuasion grid ([16]; credibility and privacy), as well as Schwartz' value "Security" [24].

- **Organizational Factors.** Within which other than 7 of the criteria originally created to represent the socio-organizational dimension, participants included the criterion "Power" (taken from the cultural grid [24]).
- **Social, Moral and/or Cultural Factors.** This group could be considered a subgroup of the previous category. 5 elements of the cultural values grid were often sorted here (Conformity, Tradition, Achievement, Benevolence, and Universalism). Attention must be brought to the fact that this group obtained the lowest correlation values, with these criteria being sorted through a range of groups according to participants' varying interpretations.

4.3   Categories' Relationships and Proximity

Regarding the links between the categories, certain remarks are worth mentioning:

- Figure 1 shows the close link between the groups "Persuasion, Incitement, Pervasive design" and "Emotional & Cognitive Stimulation for self-development" which in turn are related to the group "Hedonism, Pleasure, Emotions": all of these elements being associated with the experiential dimension of UX.
- Likewise, "Social, moral and/or cultural factors" were shown to be closely tied to the "Organizational factors" and to the group "Security/Reliability-User's protection". This ensemble was shown to have a relative proximity with the "Marketing strategy/Customer Relationship Management" category: all of these elements pertaining to the contextual dimension of UX.
- The last group to link to the rest is the "Utility (task-system suitability, achieving the goal, efficacy) & Usability/Pragmatism (ergonomic criteria, efficiency)" category.

4.4   Spatial Representation and Structure

To further analyze the distances between the categories and to be able to visualize a spatial representation of the data, we carried out an MDS analysis. A two-way MDS yielded poor results (stress = 26.69%), but a three-way analysis showed a good enough stress value (stress = 17.97%). These results are presented on a two-dimensional plot in Fig. 2.

By interpreting the graph, two possible factors seem to stand out. One seems to correspond to the nature of the experience, ranging from the functional experience to the experiential experience (along the x-axis). The other one seems to be the level the criterion intervenes on: the user, on the system or the context of use (y-axis). Further analyses are required to verify this assumption and to discern the third factor.

Nonetheless, the graphical representation of the data is suggestive of a triangular structure, where the three outermost groups (Utility & Usability, Hedonism, Socio-Organizational Context and Marketing strategy) merge towards the center where elements of technological persuasion and cognitive & emotional stimulation appear.

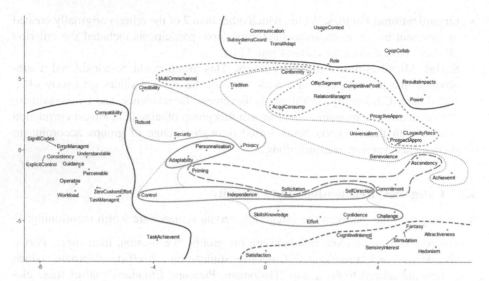

Fig. 2. MDS plot using 3 factors (stress = 17.97%) showing the 8 standardized categories retained.

4.5 Additional Elements of Analysis

Only 5 participants excluded certain cards from the sorting (13 unique cards). Only the criterion "Challenge" [5] was excluded more than once: two participants negatively evaluated it "because of its detrimental effect on the interaction".

On the other hand, only 3 participants suggested additional elements to be added. One found the innovative aspect of UX was misrepresented and one estimated the technical/technological and graphical aspects were missing but neither created any cards to represent these dimensions. Lastly, one participant created two additional cards pertaining to social factors in HCI: "Share" & "Notifications" as the general functions found on social media platforms nowadays.

5 Discussion and Conclusion

The overall goal of this research has been to examine how UX professionals organize their cognitions around a suggested set of 58 criteria linked to UX in the efforts to propose a holistic criteria-based approach in the field. For this, we conducted an experiment where 17 experts partook in an open card sort exercise. Through this, we sought to determine the relevancy, the scope and the architecture of the proposed criteria set as well as its fundamental dimensions and their links.

Results show that participants conceived said content in a rather close manner to that of the aspects we had initially theorized. Indeed, 8 main categories stand out: (1) Utility (task-system suitability, achieving the goal, efficacy) and Usability/Pragmatism (ergonomic criteria, efficiency); (2) Hedonism, Pleasure, Emotions; (3) Persuasion, Incitement, Pervasive design; (4) Emotional & Cognitive Stimulation for self-development comprising elements linked to self-expression and self-direction; (5) Marketing strategy/Customer Relationship Management; (6) Security/Reliability-User's protection; (7) Organizational factors; and (8) Social, moral and/or cultural factors.

The analysis revealed a close link between groups (2), (3) and (4), and between groups (5) through (8). Along with the remaining category (1), this suggests that the criteria could be divided into three main sets where one represents the functional aspect of the interaction, another one represents the experiential aspect [of the interaction], and the last one represents the context the interaction takes place in. The spatial representation further supported this idea by unveiling a structure evocative of a triangular shape in which three major poles (Utility & Usability, Hedonism, Socio-Organizational Context and Marketing strategy) unite towards the center to generate technological persuasion and cognitive & emotional stimulation. Whether there is an actual causal link remains to be determined. Nevertheless, this posits the idea that an experience must be: useful, pleasant, compatible with the context and profitable.

We also identified two potential factors that might explain the structure of the data: one possibly corresponding to the nature of the experience (from functional to experiential), and another one possibly corresponding to the level of impact of the criterion (from the individual - to the system - to the context of use). Necessary analyses are currently being carried out in order to inquire upon such assumption and to determine the third factor.

Moreover, it remains to be seen whether our proposal for a holistic criteria-based approach in UX would be more suitable via the different dimensions we initially suggested (as supported by the present study), or whether we could offer another approach based on a distribution of the criteria among a functional-experiential spectrum, or even a combination of the two. Future research will address this issue. The studies are currently ongoing.

Lastly, attention must be brought to the fact that the participants were predominantly specialists in Ergonomics and/or Cognitive Psychology. It would seem of interest to investigate how other actors in the field (e.g. graphic designers, marketing specialists) would envisage this same criteria set and to try to establish a shared vision.

References

1. Arhippainen, L., Tähti, M.: Empirical evaluation of user experience in two adaptative mobile application prototypes. In: Proceedings of the 2nd International Conference on Mobile and Ubiquitous Multimedia (MUM), Norrköping, Sweden, pp. 27–34. ACM (2003)
2. Barcenilla, J., Bastien, J.M.C.: L'acceptabilité des nouvelles technologies: quelles relations avec l'ergonomie, l'utilisabilité et l'expérience utilisateur? Le travail humain. 72(4), 311–331 (2009)
3. Bastien, J.M.C., Scapin, D.L.: Ergonomic criteria for the evaluation of human-computer interfaces (Technical report No. 156). INRIA Rocquencourt, Rocquencourt, France (1993)

4. Brangier, E., Desmarais, M., Nemery, A., Prom Tep, S.: Evolution de l'inspection heuristique: vers une intégration des critères d'accessibilité, de praticité, d'émotion et de persuasion dans l'évaluation ergonomique. Journal d'Interaction Personne-Système **4**(1), 69–84 (2015)
5. de Vicente, A., Pain, H.: Informing the detection of the students' motivational state: an empirical study. In: Proceedings of the Sixth International Conference on Intelligent Tutoring Systems (2002)
6. Maurer, D.: Card sort analysis spreadsheet template (2009). http://rosenfeldmedia.com/books/card-sorting/. Accessed Nov 2016
7. Duczman, M., Brangier, E., Thevenin, A.: Criteria based approach to assess the user experience of driving information proactive system: integration of guidelines, heuristic mapping and case study. In: Stanton, N. (ed.) Human Factors in Transportation. Springer, Heidelberg (2016)
8. Eason, K.: Sociotechnical systems theory in the 21st century: another half-filled glass. In: Sense in Social Science: A Collection of Essays in Honour of Dr. Lisl Klein, Broughton, United Kingdom, pp. 123–134 (2008)
9. Eskl, R., Sole, A.: Presses universitaires de France: Stratégies d'automatisation, organisation du travail et relations sociales dans les grandes entreprises du tertiaire. Réseaux **4**(18), 7–18 (1986). https://doi.org/10.3406/reso.1986.1215
10. Hassenzahl, M., Tractinsky, N.: User experience – a research agenda. Behav. Inf. Technol. **25**, 91–97 (2006)
11. Jordan, P.W.: An Introduction to Usability. Taylor & Francis, London (1998)
12. Klaus, P., Edvardsson, B., Maklan, S.: Developing a typology of customer experience management practice–from preservers to vanguards. In: 12th International Research Conference in Service Management, La Londe les Maures, France (2012)
13. Lallemand, C., Gronier, G., Koenig, V.: User experience: a concept without consensus? Exploring practitioners' perspectives through an international survey. Comput. Hum. Behav. **43**, 35–48 (2015)
14. Leplat, J., Cuny, X.: Introduction à la psychologie du travail. PUF, Paris (1977)
15. Rice, M.: Co-occurrence Matrix (2012). http://www.informoire.com/taxonomy/co-occurrence-matrix-announcement/, http://www.informoire.com/co-occurrence-matrix/. Accessed Nov 2016
16. Nemery, A., Brangier, E.: Set of guidelines for persuasive interfaces: organization and validation of the criteria. J. Usability Stud. **9**(3), 105–128 (2014)
17. Neveu, P., Alasluquetas, V.: Le livre blanc: Démarches, Parcours et Expériences Clients: 10 best practices d'entreprises inspirées par leurs clients. Ginger & Different Factory (version digitale) (2014). http://docplayer.fr/13137085-Demarches-parcours-et-experience-clients.html
18. Nielsen, J.: Heuristic evaluation. In: Nielsen, J., Mack, R.L. (eds.) Usability Inspection Methods. Wiley Inc., New York (1994)
19. Norman, D., Nielsen, J. (n.d.) The Definition of User Experience (UX). https://www.nngroup.com/articles/definition-user-experience/. Accessed June 2016
20. Palmer, A.: Customer experience management: a critical review of an emerging idea. J. Serv. Mark. **24**(3), 196–208 (2010)
21. Pine, B.J., Gilmore, J.H.: Welcome to the experience economy. Harvard Bus. Rev. **76**, 97–105 (1998)
22. Scapin, D.L.: Organizing human factors knowledge for the evaluation and design of interfaces. Int. J. Hum.-Comput. Interact. **2**(3), 203–229 (1990)
23. Schofield, M.: Applying the Kano model to improve UX. Comput. Libr. **36**(8), 28 (2016)
24. Schwartz, S.H.: Les valeurs de base de la personne: théorie, mesures et applications. Revue française de sociologie **47**(4), 929–968 (2006)

25. Shackel, B.: The concept of usability. In: Bennett, J.L., et al. (eds.) Visual Display Terminals: Usability Issues and Health Concerns. Prentice Hall, Englewood Cliffs (1981)
26. Shneiderman, B.: Designing the User Interface. Addison Wesley, Reading (1988)
27. Caldwell, B., Cooper, M., Guarino Reid, L., Vanderheiden, G. (eds.) Web Content Accessibility Guidelines (WCAG) 2.0. W3C Recommendation, 11 December 2008. http://www.w3.org/TR/2008/REC-WCAG20-20081211/, http://www.w3.org/TR/WCAG20/

Mobile Application Usability Heuristics: Decoupling Context-of-Use

Ger Joyce$^{(\boxtimes)}$, Mariana Lilley, Trevor Barker, and Amanda Jefferies

School of Computer Science, University of Hertfordshire College Lane,
Hatfield, Hertfordshire AL10 9AB, UK
gerjoyce@outlook.com,
{m.lilley, t.l.barker, a.l.jefferies}@herts.ac.uk

Abstract. Context-of-use is a vital consideration when evaluating the usability of mobile applications. Thus, when defining sets of heuristics for the usability evaluation of mobile applications, a common practice has been to include one or more heuristics that consider context-of-use. Yet, most evaluations are conducted within usability labs. Consequently, the aim of this research is to question the utility of attempting to include inherently complex areas of context-of-use within limited sets of mobile application usability heuristics. To address this, a mapping study uncovered six sets of heuristics that can be applied to mobile application usability evaluations. A within-subjects empirical test with six Human-Computer Interaction practitioners evaluated a well-known travel mobile application using three sets of the mapped heuristics. The study found that the common practice of including context-of-use within mobile application usability heuristics is an ineffective approach.

Keywords: Mobile usability · Context-of-use · Heuristic evaluation

1 Introduction

Usability heuristics allow Human-Computer Interaction (HCI) practitioners and researchers to focus on the primary areas of software which may cause problems for users. One of the most popular sets of heuristics was originally defined by Nielsen and Molich [1], and is widely known for being fast and inexpensive [2]. Given the prevalence of mobile devices in the past decade, sets of heuristics for mobile technologies started to be defined as traditional heuristics did not consider applications built for small screens nor usage within environments far less constant than desktop applications [3]. Yet, Nielsen's heuristics [4], modified from the original set by Nielsen and Molich [1], remain popular when evaluating mobile applications [5]. In an interview with Jenny Preece [6], Nielsen supported this approach, suggesting that "You can identify a lot of issues with a phone or other mobile user experience by using exactly the same heuristics as you would for any other platform".

One of the items evident across many of these sets of heuristics is the inclusion of context-of-use. Context-of-use is anything that impacts the interaction between a user and an application [7], whereby elements of context, including surrounding light, ambient noise, and interruptions, can change rapidly, potentially impacting the usability

© Springer International Publishing AG 2017
A. Marcus and W. Wang (Eds.): DUXU 2017, Part I, LNCS 10288, pp. 410–423, 2017.
DOI: 10.1007/978-3-319-58634-2_30

of a mobile application [8, 9]. Consequently, Savio and Braiterman [10, p. 284] argue "For mobile computing, context is everything". To that end, it is no surprise that one or more heuristics are often included within sets of heuristics specifically aimed at considering the impact of context-of-use when evaluating the usability of mobile applications, even though most evaluations of mobile applications are conducted in usability labs [11].

The main aim of this research is to investigate the utility of including inherently complex areas of context-of-use within limited sets of mobile application usability heuristics, by asking the following research questions:

1. Based on the literature, which sets of heuristics are used to evaluate the usability of mobile applications?
2. Which of the mapped sets of heuristics include one or more heuristics that consider context-of-use?
3. To what extent can one or more of the mapped sets of heuristics measure the impact of context-of-use on mobile application usability within lab-based conditions?

2 Background

2.1 Usability Principles

One of the first sets of usability principles is the cornerstone of design today. Gould and Lewis [12] wrote the following principles, stating that system designers should:

- Focus early on users and tasks
- Empirically measure usability
- Design iteratively based on learnings from empirical tests.

Nowadays, user experience designers commonly apply each of these principles in their daily work. Yet, Gould and Lewis [12] found that system designers often ignored these principles, believing for instance in the 'power of reason', whereby the prevailing feeling was that task completion was logic, thus there was little need to apply principles nor involve representative users.

As the benefits of usable and useful systems were acknowledged, Human-Computer Interactions experts defined further usability principles, including cognitive principles [13] and heuristic evaluation [1]—the latter becoming a common method among HCI practitioners and researchers [14]. Since its inception, heuristic evaluation has since been modified to cater for a wide range of domains, including Educational Media [15]; Groupware Based on the Mechanics of Collaboration [16]; Ambient Displays [17]; Adaptive Learning Environments [18]; Playability of Games [19]; Intensive Care Unit Infusion Pumps [20]; Intrusion Detection Systems [21]; Virtual Reality Applications [22]; Electronic Shopping [23]; and Child E-learning Applications [24].

Heuristic evaluation is not without detractors. Researchers have argued that results from heuristic evaluation are too subjective [25]. This claim has been counter-argued, whereby other researchers have suggested that this difference in perspective enables the discovery of more diverse usability issues [26]. Additionally, despite the suggestion that heuristic evaluation may not be as effective as it claims [27], the method remains popular.

As mobile devices become more ubiquitous, heuristic evaluation started to be used to evaluate the usability of mobile applications. While the traditional set of heuristics from Nielsen appears to be in common use [5], researchers have argued that traditional heuristics needed to be modified before they can be used for mobile [28, 29]. To that end, several sets of usability heuristics designed specifically for mobile have been defined. While most of these sets of usability heuristics are general in nature, some are specific to a feature and/or a population [30].

2.2   Addressing Context-of-Use

One of the key areas within the field of mobile usability is the impact of context-of-use. Context-of-use, which is anything that might impact the interaction between a user and an application [31], is a vital component of building mobile experiences [32]. This is due to the ever-changing contexts-of-use that mobile users find themselves in.

From a heuristic evaluation perspective, the consideration of context-of-use has been approached in two ways. Firstly, while heuristic evaluations are most often conducted in the lab, a study conducted by Po et al. [33] considered context-of-use using three conditions: heuristic evaluation within the lab for two conditions, one of which simulated context-of-use, one of which did not, and heuristic evaluation in the field. The authors of that work argue against conducting heuristic evaluations in the field as one of their conditions of their study, namely simulated context-of-use within the lab, uncovered the highest number of issues across three conditions. Yet, there are several threats to the validity and reliability of this study. For instance, during the heuristic evaluation, the authors used Nielsen's traditional heuristics, and did not attempt to define a set of heuristics for mobile technologies.

The internal validity of the study suffers from the threat of selection bias, whereby the authors did not randomize participants across conditions, and all conditions had fewer than the recommended five evaluators [40].

It seems that none of the evaluators had practical HCI experience, several evaluators only had one semester in HCI and had little familiarity with heuristic evaluation. This could be a threat to external validity, specifically population validity, in that the evaluators within this study cannot be generalized with HCI experts that have practical commercial experience and commonly undertake heuristic evaluations.

While it is quite difficult to achieve ceteris paribus in an experimental study, or in this case a quasi-experimental study, it should still be expected that all conditions would be as equal as possible. Yet, in this study the authors assigned user interface-related tasks to participants in just two of the three conditions.

The authors state that a by-product of this omission of task assignment in the first scenario was that participants focused on the product, more so than the operation of the product. As high construct validity is achieved only when intended constructs are measured accurately, it might be argued that the authors were measuring two operationalized variables defined from the construct 'usability issues'. Additionally, within the two conditions where evaluators completed six tasks, there is no indication that the tasks were counterbalanced. This could indicate an order bias.

The benefit of in-situ evaluation is an increase in ecological validity. Yet, participants had to think aloud while they were being recorded. Consequently, the reality of the in-situ condition was not realistic.

Participants were all aware which condition they were in within the study. This transparency could result in an interval validity threat known as demand characteristics. This threat can occur when participants know they are in the experimental group, and they change their behavior due to their expectations of the study. The authors of the paper could have minimized this threat by contriving a cover story, only giving the real reason for the study when participants were debriefed. There is no indication that this attempt was made for this study.

Reliability is compromised as it would be impossible to replicate the study. The authors of the work are not fully transparent around the environments and activities of the participants for any condition. For instance, within the in-situ condition, the authors simply state locations, such as cafeteria or bar, and some details, such as dark with changing light. To replicate the study, other researchers would need to know about all conditions, including environmental conditions, if participants were walking, sitting, were interrupted by friends and colleagues, and so forth. Any of these environmental and social factors may impact the findings, yet were not published by the authors.

Finally, the results of the study could be interpreted differently. Within the in-situ condition, fewer evaluators uncovered substantially more issues than the lab-based heuristic evaluation. While the second condition, the lab-based condition with scenarios of use, uncovered more issues, this condition had a great number of evaluators, yet uncovered only 0.4% higher usability issues on average. Additionally, the in-situ study uncovered more critical usability issues, as well as issues where context had an impact. These latter issues were not surfaced within the lab-based studies. Consequently, based on the threats to validity and reliability, it could be argued that the conclusion from Po et al. [33 p. 55] that "there appears to be no additional benefit to immersing the evaluator in the context of use" appears to be premature. The authors of this paper argue that further research is needed around heuristic evaluations within and outside the lab, using before coming to specific conclusions.

The second approach used to consider context-of-use during heuristic evaluations has been to include one or more heuristics specifically addressing context-of-use. As can be seen within the mapping study conducted in the next section, this has been a more widely-conducted approach. While the face validity of this approach seems to be high given that evaluators can consider all the major areas of mobile usability, including context-of-use, the aim of this paper is to empirically test the approach.

3 Approach

Human-Computer Interaction (HCI) researchers and practitioners have several sets of heuristics from which to choose as they evaluate the usability of mobile applications. These include a traditional set of heuristics from Nielsen [4], as well as several sets of heuristics defined specifically for mobile. A common approach has been to include one or more heuristics that consider context-of-use, which is important from a mobile application usability perspective. However, as heuristic evaluations tend to be conducted within a lab, how effective is this approach?

To that end, the aim of the study was to consider the effectiveness of including one or more sets of heuristics that consider context-of-use from a mobile usability perspective. The approach taken was two-fold:

1. A mapping study identified sets of heuristics used for mobile application usability evaluations
2. An empirical evaluation measured the effectiveness of including one or more sets of heuristics that consider context-of-use from a mobile usability perspective

3.1   Phase I: Mapping Study

The mapping study followed the same protocol as defined within Salgado and Freire [5], whereby the objective, research question, and inclusion criteria were defined:

Objective: The main goal of the mapping study was to discover which heuristics are used to evaluate usability of mobile devices, and secondly, which elements of those sets of heuristics considered context-of-use.

Research Question(s):

1. Based on the literature, which sets of heuristics are used to evaluate the usability of mobile applications?
2. Which of the mapped sets of heuristics include one or more heuristics that consider context-of-use?

Source Search Method: Sources will be discovered via Google using a search string using the keywords: usability, heuristics, heuristic evaluation, mobile, smartphone.

Inclusion Criteria: Publications written in English, indexed by academic journals and databases, discovered by use of one or more of the chosen keywords, focusing on sets of heuristics used to evaluate the usability of mobile technologies.

The resulting sets of heuristics, as well as the associated heuristics related to context-of-use, identified during the mapping study are displayed in Table 1.

3.2   Phase II: Empirical Evaluation

Having addressed the first two research questions by mapping six sets of heuristics, the final research question to address was:

3. To what extent can one or more of the mapped sets of heuristics measure the impact of context-of-use on mobile application usability within lab-based conditions?

Addressing this research question by evaluating all six sets of heuristics may have proven to be too time-consuming. Consequently, three sets of heuristics were selected

Table 1. Mobile application usability heuristics, including references to context-of-use

Author(s)	Usability heuristic(s) related to context-of-use
Nielsen [4]	(No contextual heuristics, and no approach defined as to how to consider the impact of context-of-use)
Weiss [34]	Design for users on the go
Ji et al. [35]	Flexibility: The user interface must be flexible so that adapts to various environments and users
Bertini et al. [36]	Ease of input, screen readability and glanceability. Aesthetic, privacy and social conventions
Joyce et al. [37]	Cater for diverse mobile environments
Inostroza et al. [38]	(No contextual heuristics, and no approach defined as to how to consider the impact of context-of-use)

for an empirical evaluation. To avoid recognition bias, each set of the chosen heuristics was labelled with a letter:

- Set A: Nielsen [4] - Nielsen's traditional heuristics appear to be commonly applied to mobile applications [5].
- Set B: Bertini et al. [36] - The heuristics from Bertini et al. were one of the first sets defined for mobile technologies.
- Set C: Joyce et al. [37] - The heuristics from Joyce et al. were defined for mobile technologies and considered areas lacking in previously defined sets, such as the utilization of sensors to reduce the burden on the user.

With the three sets of heuristics selected, a heuristic evaluation was conducted of a well-known travel mobile application. To conduct the evaluation, six evaluators were recruited for a within-subjects study using purposive sampling (4 Female, 2 Male). The experience level of the evaluators is shown in Table 2.

Table 2. Experience level of evaluators

Experience	HCI (Years)	Mobile HCI (Years)
Range	1–20	0–6
Mean	7.5	6.9
SD	2.91	2.2

To avoid learning bias, the sets of heuristic were counterbalanced for every two evaluators (Table 3).

Table 3. Order of heuristics

Participant	Order of heuristics
P1, P6	Set B, Set C, Set A
P2, P5	Set A, Set B, Set C
P3, P4	Set C, Set A, Set B

The study was conducted from February 26th, 2015 to March 16th, 2015. Many aspects of the study were controlled, whereby all participants used the same mobile device, the same version of the mobile application, and the environmental conditions within which the study was conducted were consistent. Participants attempted three tasks each on an LG G2 mobile device running Android 4.4.2 under good lighting and low ambient noise conditions, as would be expected in a usability testing lab. The tasks attempted were:

1. Find a hotel near your current location using GPS for one adult that is available within the next two weeks.
2. Find a return flight for one adult in economy class from London Heathrow to Paris.
3. Read a review of a restaurant in the UK, marking the review as helpful.

Having attempted each task, each participant conducted a heuristic evaluation using each set of the chosen heuristics:

Set A: Nielsen [4]

Heuristic 1: Visibility of system status. The system should always keep users informed about what is going on, through appropriate feedback within reasonable time.

Heuristic 2: Match between system and the real world. The system should speak the users' language, with words, phrases and concepts familiar to the user, rather than system-oriented terms. Follow real-world conventions, making information appear in a natural and logical order.

Heuristic 3: User control and freedom. Users often choose system functions by mistake and will need a clearly marked "emergency exit" to leave the unwanted state without having to go through an extended dialogue. Support undo and redo.

Heuristic 4: Consistency and standards. Users should not have to wonder whether different words, situations, or actions mean the same thing. Follow platform conventions.

Heuristic 5: Error prevention. Even better than good error messages is a careful design which prevents a problem from occurring in the first place. Either eliminate error-prone conditions or check for them and present users with a confirmation option before they commit to the action.

Heuristic 6: Recognition rather than recall. Minimize the user's memory load by making objects, actions, and options visible. The user should not have to remember information from one part of the dialogue to another. Instructions for use of the system should be visible or easily retrievable whenever appropriate.

Heuristic 7: Flexibility and efficiency of use. Accelerators – unseen by the novice user – may often speed up the interaction for the expert user such that the system can cater to both inexperienced and experienced users. Allow users to tailor frequent actions.

Heuristic 8: Aesthetic and minimalist design. Dialogues should not contain information which is irrelevant or rarely needed. Every extra unit of information in a dialogue competes with the relevant units of information and diminishes their relative visibility.

Heuristic 9: Help users recognize, diagnose, and recover from errors. Error messages should be expressed in plain language (no codes), precisely indicate the problem, and constructively suggest a solution.

Heuristic 10: Help and documentation. Even though it is better if the system can be used without documentation, it may be necessary to provide help and documentation. Any such information should be easy to search, focused on the user's task, list concrete steps to be carried out, and not be too large.

Set B: Bertini et al. [36]

Heuristic 1: Visibility of system status and losability/findability of the mobile device.
Heuristic 2: Match between system and the real world.
Heuristic 3: Consistency and mapping.
Heuristic 4: Good ergonomics and minimalist design.
Heuristic 5: Ease of input, screen readability and glanceability.
Heuristic 6: Flexibility, efficiency of use and personalization.
Heuristic 7: Aesthetic, privacy and social conventions.
Heuristic 8: Realistic error management.

Set C: Joyce et al. [37]

SMART1: Provide immediate notification of application status. Ensure the mobile application user is informed of the application status immediately and as long as is necessary. Where appropriate do this non-intrusively, such as displaying notifications within the status bar.

SMART2: Use a theme and consistent terms, as well as conventions and standards familiar to the user. Use a theme for the mobile application to ensure different screens are consistent. Also create a style guide from which words, phrases and concepts familiar to the user will be applied consistently throughout the interface, using a natural and logical order. Use platform conventions and standards that users have come to expect in a mobile application such as the same effects when gestures are used.

SMART3: Prevent problems where possible; Assist users should a problem occur. Ensure the mobile application is error-proofed as much as is possible. Should a problem occur, let the user know what the problem is in a way they will understand, and offer advice in how they might fix the issue or otherwise proceed. This includes problems with the mobile network connection, whereby the application might work offline until the network connection has been re-established.

SMART4: Display an overlay pointing out the main features when appropriate or requested. An overlay pointing out the main features and how to interact with the application allows first-time users to get up-and-running quickly, after which they can explore the mobile application at their leisure. This overlay or a form of help system should also be displayed when requested.

SMART5: Each interface should focus on one task. Being focusing on one task ensures that mobile interfaces are less cluttered and simple to the point of only having the absolute necessary elements onscreen to complete that task. This also allows the interface to be glanceable to users that are interrupted frequently.

SMART6: Design a visually pleasing interface. Mobile interfaces that are attractive are far more memorable and are therefore used more often. Users are also more forgiving of attractive interfaces.

SMART7: Intuitive interfaces make for easier user journeys. Mobile interfaces should be easy-to-learn whereby next steps are obvious. This allows users to more easily complete their tasks.

SMART8: Design a clear navigable path to task completion. Users should be able to see right away how they can interact with the application and navigate their way to task completion.

SMART9: Allow configuration options and shortcuts. Depending on the target user, the mobile application might allow configuration options and shortcuts to the most important information and frequent tasks, including the ability to configure according to contextual needs.

SMART10: Cater for diverse mobile environments. Diverse environments consist of different types of context of use, such as poor lighting conditions and high ambient noise are common issues mobile users have to face every day. While the operating system should allow the user to change the interface brightness and sound settings, developers can assist users even more for example by allowing them to display larger buttons and allowing multimodal input and output options.

SMART11: Facilitate easier input. Mobile devices are difficult to use from a content input perspective. Ensure users can input content more easily and accurately by, for instance displaying keyboard buttons that are as large as possible, as well as allowing multimodal input and by keeping form fields to a minimum.

SMART12: Use the camera, microphone and sensors when appropriate to lessen the user's workload. Consider the use of the camera, microphone and sensors to lessen the users' workload. For instance, by using GPS so the user knows where they are and how to get there they need to go, or by using OCR and the camera to digitally capture the information the user needs to input, or by allowing use of the microphone to input content.

Prior to re-evaluating the mobile application with a different set of heuristics, participants conducted each task once more. Any issues surfaced during the evaluation were allocated with a severity rating by each participant. The severity ratings were adapted from Sauro [39]:

- *Minor:* Causes some hesitation or irritation
- *Moderate:* Causes occasional task failure for some users or causes delays and moderate irritation
- *Critical:* Leads to task failure or causes extreme irritation.

4   Results and Discussion

Using the three sets of heuristics, the six evaluators found a total of 145 usability issues (Mean = 48, SD = 9) during the evaluation (Fig. 1).

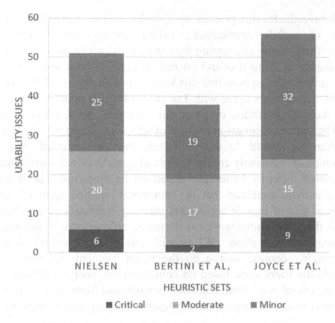

Fig. 1. Issues found during the heuristic evaluation.

Yet, only five minor issues (3.45%) were raised by two (P1 & P6) of the six evaluators relating to context-of-use. All issues related to context-of-use were raised by the heuristics from Joyce et al. [37], with no context-of-use issues raised during the evaluations using the heuristics from Nielsen [4] and Bertini et al. [36]. The comments associated with the issues related to context-of-use stated only that there was no indication that the app changed to adapt to various scenarios. Thus, even though issues had been raised, accurately measuring the impact of context-of-use on mobile application usability would prove challenging. Consequently, HCI designers would be unable to make changes that might reduce the impact of context-of-use on the usability of the mobile application.

Other researchers may argue that a relatively small number of evaluators participated in the study. However, the study represents a real-world scenario, given that the recommended number of evaluators for a heuristic evaluation is five [40].

5   Conclusion

Heuristic evaluation has been recognized as a fast, effective, and inexpensive approach to evaluating the usability of software applications. When applied to mobile applications, context-of-use should be an important consideration of heuristic evaluations. A common practice, therefore, has been to include one or more heuristics dedicated to the consideration of context-of-use within sets of heuristics defined for mobile applications.

This work investigates this practice by mapping sets of heuristics used to evaluate the usability of mobile applications, listing specific heuristics that consider context-of-use, then empirically testing the extent to which these sets of heuristics can measure the impact of context-of-use on mobile application usability within lab-like conditions. It is important to note that this work is not an argument for nor against lab or field studies. The authors agree with Tan et al. [41] that both are needed at various points in the mobile application development life cycle. As stated by Kjeldskov and Skov [42], "The important question is not if or why one should do lab or field studies, but rather when we should do what". Rather, the authors question the utility of attempting to include inherently complex areas of context-of-use *within* limited sets of mobile application usability heuristics. Based on an empirical test of three sets of heuristics, the authors conclude that the commonly applied approach of including context-of-use as part of mobile application usability heuristics is not effective.

To address this issue, initial work has started on an alternative framework [43]. The proposed framework will allow HCI practitioners and researchers to measure the impact of changing contexts-of-use on the major elements of mobile application usability. While the framework based on context-of-use analysis defined by Maguire [7], it differs in several ways from that authors work and from the common practice of including context-of-use with heuristics, whereby the proposed framework:

- Decouples the complexity of context-of-use from the equally complex field of usability, addressing one of the concerns from a respondent in a related survey [37], who stated that "[there are] so many contexts for mobile use"
- Is aimed at dynamic and fast-paced development environments
- Is defined specifically for evaluating the usability of mobile applications.

Subsequently, the proposed framework addresses several limitations of context-of-use analysis, namely "The reader may feel that the method is too heavy-weight and will require the generation of lots of paperwork by several people" [7, p. 480] and "Another question is how the Context of Use should be addressed in a more dynamic development environment…where the requirements, expectations and perceived opportunities are evolving all the time" [7, p. 481]. To that end, by decoupling context-of-use from usability, the proposed framework can be used as a lightweight approach to measure the impact of context-of-use on mobile applications that may be used in varying contexts, by fast-paced agile and continuous delivery teams.

References

1. Nielsen, J., Molich, R.: Heuristic evaluation of user interfaces. In: SIGCHI Conference on Human Factors in Computing Systems, pp. 249–256 (1990)
2. Maguire, M.: Methods to support human-centred design. Int. J. Hum. Comput. Stud. **55**(4), 587–634 (2001)
3. Bernhaupt, R., Mihalic, K., Obrist, M.: Usability evaluation methods for mobile applications. In: Lumsden, J. (ed.) Handbook of Research on User Interface Design and Evaluation for Mobile Technology. IGI Global (2008)

4. Nielsen, J.: Heuristic evaluation. In: Nielsen, J., Mack, R.L. (eds.) Usability Inspection Methods. Wiley, New York (1994)
5. Lima Salgado, A., Freire, A.P.: Heuristic evaluation of mobile usability: a mapping study. In: Kurosu, M. (ed.) HCI 2014. LNCS, vol. 8512, pp. 178–188. Springer, Cham (2014). doi:10.1007/978-3-319-07227-2_18
6. Rogers, Y., Sharp, H., Preece, J.: Interaction Design: Beyond Human-Computer Interaction. Wiley, New York (2011)
7. Maguire, M.: Context of use within usability activities. Int. J. Hum Comput Stud. 55(4), 453–483 (2001)
8. Wigelius, H., Väätäjä, H.: Dimensions of context affecting user experience in mobile work. In: Gross, T., Gulliksen, J., Kotzé, P., Oestreicher, L., Palanque, P., Prates, R.O., Winckler, M. (eds.) INTERACT 2009. LNCS, vol. 5727, pp. 604–617. Springer, Heidelberg (2009). doi:10.1007/978-3-642-03658-3_65
9. Tsiaousis, A.S.: Ad hoc context of use in mobile usability evaluation. Int. J. Comput. Syst. 2 (6), 253–256 (2015)
10. Savio, N., Braiterman, J.: Design sketch: the context of mobile interaction. In: Mobile HCI, pp. 284–286 (2007)
11. Eshet, E., Bouwman, H.: Addressing the context of use in mobile computing: a survey on the state of the practice. Interact. Comput. (2014). http://doi.org/10.1093/iwc/iwu002
12. Gould, J.D., Lewis, C.: Designing for usability: key principles and what designers think. Commun. ACM 28, 300–311 (1985)
13. Gerhardt-Powals, J.: Cognitive engineering principles for enhancing human-computer performance. Int. J. Hum.-Comput. Interact. 8, 189–211 (1996)
14. Hollingsed, T., Novick, D.G.: Usability inspection methods after 15 years of research and practice. In: 25th Annual ACM International Conference on Design of Communication (SIGDOC 2007), El Paso, Texas, USA, 22–24 October 2007
15. Albion, P.R.: Heuristic evaluation of educational multimedia: from theory to practice. In: Proceedings ASCILITE 1999, Proceedings of the 16th Annual Conference of the Australasian Society for Computers in Learning in Tertiary Education: Responding to Diversity, pp. 9–15. Australasian Society for Computers in Learning in Tertiary Education (ASCILITE) (1999)
16. Baker, K., Greenberg, S., Gutwin, C.: Heuristic evaluation of groupware based on the mechanics of collaboration. In: Little, M.R., Nigay, L. (eds.) EHCI 2001. LNCS, vol. 2254, pp. 123–139. Springer, Heidelberg (2001). doi:10.1007/3-540-45348-2_14
17. Mankoff, J., Dey, A.K., Hsieh, G., Kientz, J., Lederer, S., Ames, M.: Heuristic evaluation of ambient displays. In: Proceedings of SIGCHI Conference Human Factors Computing Systems, pp. 169–176 (2003)
18. Magoulas, G.D., Chen, S.Y., Papanikolaou, K.A.: Integrating layered and heuristic evaluation for adaptive learning environments. In: Second Workshop on Empirical Evaluation of Adaptive Systems, held at the 9th International Conference on User Modeling UM 2003, Pittsburgh, pp. 5–14 (2003)
19. Desurvire, H., Caplan, M., Toth, J.: Using heuristics to evaluate the playability of games. In: CHI 2004 Extended Abstracts on Human Factors in Computing Systems, pp. 1509–1512 (2004)
20. Graham, M.J., Kubose, T.K., Jordan, D., Zhang, J., Johnson, T.R., Patel, V.L.: Heuristic evaluation of infusion pumps: implications for patient safety in Intensive Care Units. Int. J. Med. Inform. 73, 771–779 (2004)
21. Zhou, A.T., Blustein, J., Zincir-Heywood, N.: Improving intrusion detection systems through heuristic evaluation. In: Canadian Conference on Electrical and Computer Engineering, vol. 3, pp. 1641–1644 (2004)

22. Sutcliffe, A., Gault, B.: Heuristic evaluation of virtual reality applications. Interact. Comput. **16**, 831–849 (2004)

23. Chen, S.Y., Macredie, R.D.: The assessment of usability of electronic shopping: a heuristic evaluation. Int. J. Inf. Manage. **25**, 516–532 (2005)

24. Alsumait, A.A., Al-Osaimi, A.: Usability heuristics evaluation for child e-learning applications. J. Softw. **5**, 425–430 (2010)

25. Kirmani, S., Rajasekaran, S.: Heuristic evaluation quality score (HEQS): a measure of heuristic evaluation skills. J. Usability Stud. **2**(2), 61–75 (2007)

26. Wilson, C.: User Interface Inspection Methods: A User-Centered Design Method. Morgan Kaufmann, USA (2013)

27. Law, E., Hvannberg, E.: Analysis of strategies for improving and estimating the effectiveness of heuristic evaluation. In: Proceedings of the 3rd Nordic Conference on Human-Computer Interaction (Nordi CHI 2004), Tampere, Finland, 23–27 October 2004

28. Ketola, P., Röykkee, M.: The three facets of usability in mobile handsets. In: CHI 2001 Workshop: Mobile Communications: Understanding Users, Adoption & Design (2001)

29. Beck, E., Christiansen, M., Kjeldskov, J., Kolbe, N., Stage, J.: Experimental evaluation of techniques for usability testing of mobile systems in a laboratory setting. In: New Directions in Interaction: Information Environments, Media and Technology Conference (Ozchi 2003), Brisbane, Australia (2003)

30. Al-Razgan, Muna S., Al-Khalifa, Hend S., Al-Shahrani, Mona D.: Heuristics for evaluating the usability of mobile launchers for elderly people. In: Marcus, A. (ed.) DUXU 2014. LNCS, vol. 8517, pp. 415–424. Springer, Cham (2014). doi:10.1007/978-3-319-07668-3_40

31. Dey, A.K.: Understanding and using context. Pers. Ubiquit. Comput. J. **1**(5), 4–7 (2001)

32. Bentley, F., Barrett, E.: Building Mobile Experiences. MIT Press, Cambridge (2012)

33. Po, S., Howard, S., Vetere, F., Skov, M.B.: Heuristic evaluation and mobile usability: bridging the realism gap. In: Brewster, S., Dunlop, M. (eds.) Mobile HCI 2004. LNCS, vol. 3160, pp. 591–592. Springer, Heidelberg (2004)

34. Weiss, S.: Handheld Usability. Wiley, Hoboken (2003)

35. Ji, Y., Park, J., Lee, C., Yun, M.: A usability checklist for the usability evaluation of mobile phone user interface. Int. J. Hum.-Comput. Interact. **20**(3), 207–231 (2006)

36. Bertini, E., Gabrielli, S., Kimani, S.: Appropriating and assessing heuristics for mobile computing. In: Proceedings of Working conference on Advanced Visual Interfaces (AVI 2006), Venezia, Italy, 23–26 May 2006

37. Joyce, G., Lilley, M.: Towards the development of usability heuristics for native smartphone mobile applications. In: Marcus, A. (ed.) DUXU 2014. LNCS, vol. 8517, pp. 465–474. Springer, Cham (2014). doi:10.1007/978-3-319-07668-3_45

38. Inostroza, R., Rusu, C., Roncagliolo, S., Rusu, V., Collazos, C.: Developing SMASH: A set of SMArtphone's uSability Heuristics. Comput. Stand. Interfaces **43**, 40–52 (2016)

39. Sauro, J.: Rating the severity of usability problems (2013). http://www.measuringu.com/blog/rating-severity.php

40. Nielsen, J.:. Finding usability problems through heuristic evaluation. In: Proceedings of the SIGCHI Conference on Human Factors in Computing Systems (CHI 1992), Monterey, California (1992)

41. Tan, C.-H., Silva, A., Lee, R., Wang, K., Nah, F.F.-H.: HCI testing in laboratory or field settings. In: Nah, F.F.-H.F.-H., Tan, C.-H. (eds.) HCIBGO 2016. LNCS, vol. 9752, pp. 110–116. Springer, Cham (2016). doi:10.1007/978-3-319-39399-5_11

42. Kjeldskov, J., Skov, M.B.: Was it worth the hassle? Ten years of mobile HCI research discussions on lab and field evaluations, pp. 43–52. ACM (2014)
43. Joyce, G., Lilley, M., Barker, T., Jefferies, A.: Evaluating the impact of changing contexts on mobile application usability within agile environments. In: Future Technologies Conference (FTC), pp. 476–480. IEEE (2016)

Developmental Process of Interface Design Evaluations

Lucila Mercado Colin and Alejandro Rodea Chávez[✉]

Universidad Autónoma Metropolitana Unidad Cuajimalpa, Mexico City, Mexico
{lmercado,arodea}@correo.cua.uam.mx

Abstract. User Centered Design (UCD) Process facilitate the approaching to people in order to determine use and design requirements throughout applying diverse techniques for obtaining qualitative and quantitative information, including social, emotional physical and cognitive user's characteristics, as long as system interface requirements. User Interface Design (UI), Interaction Design (IxD), Design of Experiences of Use (UX), and the Ergonomic approaches aid design teams clearly define objectives to be met, knowing the level of development they have got in an specific stage of the design process, and ensure during the process goals do not change but instead, evolve according to emerging information that arises from Users interaction. Iterative processes along design enable implementation of formative and summative assessments through the use of prototypes in order to evaluate interactions and allowing the process feedback. As a systemic approach UCD has recursive characteristics which in some stages of its process, like Inquiry and Evaluation, are of paramount importance to adequately accomplish tasks of problematisation and assessment, by diagnosing whole system in which Users are immerse. By giving Users voice during the design process, being either novice or expert Users, Inquiry and Evaluations stages of the UCD process, aids accurately reflecting detailed characteristics the Interface must have, and at which degree Design goals have been reached out.

Keywords: User centered design · Ergonomics · Interaction · Interface

1 Introduction

The objective of this proposal is to contextualize the importance of the development of User Centered Interface Design Process, which may facilitate the approach to people in order to determine use and design requirements along the whole Design Process but specifically during the stages of inquiry and evaluation of the integrated interfaces design process.

To promote the participation of the real Users allowing their voice to be heard, collaborating from their experience and giving opinions on the development of alternatives that help to make decisions in the design process.

To focus Design processes and results on the end User given not all communities are equals, it is important to include real Users along the process of product development.

The User Centered Design (UCD) process can be conceptualized as a methodology that:

© Springer International Publishing AG 2017
A. Marcus and W. Wang (Eds.): DUXU 2017, Part I, LNCS 10288, pp. 424–433, 2017.
DOI: 10.1007/978-3-319-58634-2_31

- Has a systemic perspective
- Its different process stages are iterative
- It evaluate the resulting product of its conducted process.

On the other hand, UCD considers some philosophical basis by stablishing as central axis of its processes inclusion of real Users, mainly on inquiry and evaluation stages.

Of particular interest are the stages where inclusion of Users in the UCD process is of highlighted relevance: Problematisation and Evaluation (Fig. 1).

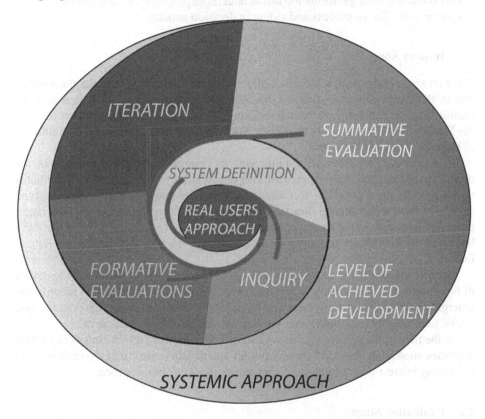

Fig. 1. Representation of real Users involvement through the User Centered Design Process

2 Ergonomics

Ergonomics is an auxiliary user-centered discipline in the process of design.

It analyzes, in a systemic and interdisciplinary way, the interaction of the system composed of the user-object-activity-environment (UOAE) subsystems, taking into account the User's cognitive, affective, social and physical capacities and limitations, as well as their relationship with the factors of the environment of use and of the object involved in developing an activity. The scope of ergonomics promotes the optimization of interactions between its components.

A systemic perspective implies that in the development of design processes, it is necessary to define precisely who the Users are, what do they need to solve, what mediator objects will do it, and in what physical environment the object will be used to solve the need. For this, the inclusion of real users in the design process is extremely important, since these give Users a voice and focus the processes on them, and not on the designer or the involved technology.

Recursive iteration between the stages of investigation, development and evaluation allows obtaining arising information throughout those processes, giving feedback on the advances in the design process and aiding in decision making.

2.1 Inquiry Stage

The first stage of the design process is the one of inquiry, which delimits the system, that is, the User's characteristics and the delimitation of the activity, which will allow establishing the requirements that the resulting product must comply with according to the Design of Interaction and experience. Such requirements arise in the combination of the user-activity subsystems.

It is necessary to establish requirements to determine the characteristics of the product to be designed. The requirements serve as a guide to define the design attributes that a product must possess. According to Design, among others must be observed several types of technological, functional, aesthetic and of use requirements. The latter, those of use, determine the characteristics of the interface of a product; those are strongly linked to the interaction and must be observed from the user experience and human factors.

In order to identify the requirements in a given product and its impact on the design of the interface, it is necessary to resort to several instruments that help to identify the emerging information in the system, and translating it into interface design features, and interaction, seeking to promote user satisfactory and effective experiences.

In the field of the applied ergonomics to Interface Design (which considers people, activities, mediating objects of these activities and the environment of use) it is been an increasing interest to integrate real Users during its development process.

2.2 Evaluation Stage

The evaluation process is inherent to User Centered Design methodology. In case of quantitative assessments, it starts from the definition of objectives, success and metrics criteria; in case of identifying patterns in qualitative observations, it is possible to obtain information to feedback the whole design process by formative assessments, or define the level of development that loosens the process in overall or summative assessments.

The evaluation allows comparing and contrasting the advances of a system, which provides with analytical information that allows comparing the scope of a system in relation to the objective of the project. Some of the main characteristics of evaluation are:

- Through an evaluation it is feasible to determine the extent to which a goal has been achieved, which helps identifying the successes and shortcomings of a project, and provides sufficient knowledge and value to guide decision making
- Evaluations consider a specific attention focus, so clarity is needed in the objectives of the project
- Has defined scope, being necessary to carry out partial evaluations that allow to have feedback on the development of the design process
- Promotes an active participation of real Users
- Uses low and high fidelity prototypes.

To carry out a systemic assessment and identify the impact that some variables exert on others, it is necessary to establish the characteristics of the systems:

- The system has a common goal
- Systems are composed of subsystems, each having its own goal
- The variables impact each other
- The variables are interrelated
- New information emerges from the interaction of the variables.

The ergonomic system can therefore, be represented by stating that:

- It is necessary the active participation of the Users, for it is important to establish the capacities and limitations of these Users
- Users need to solve a specific problem
- To solve a problem Users use products to get help
- These products work optimally in spaces with specific physical environmental characteristics.

In order to observe the above within the process of Interface Design, it is necessary to carry out evaluations in which are applied tools and techniques that allow observing the relation of its variables.

- Instruments used should allow for quantitative data measurements; however, it is also important to consider instruments that reflect Users opinion and attitude
- Identify the requirements of use to establish what conditions should be reflected from the object to the User (cognitive, physical, affective) and the User's demands on the object (response times, performance, capacity).

Apply instruments to observe the goals, desires, knowledge and skills of users related to the Interface Design.

2.3 Interface Design

The interface is considered as the common space or the means in which a user and an object establish a reciprocal relationship through the interaction, that is, an interchange information in a bi-directional, round-trip way, so the user requires the interface is useful and ease to use when mediating such interaction. On the other hand, the object (computer or computer system) demands the user certain skills and knowledge in the use of technology and knowledge in the use of codes with which the product responds to the user, promoting through an Interface Design products should be suitable for Users, reaching satisfactory, pleasant and effective experience of using a product.

Interface Design is an interdisciplinary design project. Increasingly, various areas of Design are involved in the development of electronic products with interactive digital interfaces. The development of this type of interfaces is strongly linked to the technological development in a wide variety of human activities, either recreational, necessary or for learning purposes, taking advantage of the different possibilities of sensorial interaction with products.

In the areas of User Interface Design (UI), Interaction Design (IxD) and Design of Experiences of Use (UX), it is essential to analyze the human factors that, through various techniques for obtaining quantitative and qualitative information, more accurately reflect the User's profile and how he or she will relate or interact with the products.

UI, IxD and UX can be observed from various disciplines that focus their design processes on the user. Among others, these perspectives can be human computer interaction, usability, design of experiences or ergonomics; the methodological perspective that permeates this document is Ergonomics, because at a methodological level, it allows, among other things, to clearly identify the human dimensions of the User, and how these, at a systemic level, are interrelated with activities, objects and environments of use.

3   Users, Activities, Objects and Environments of Use

Starting from the ergonomic model User-object-activity-environment (UOAE Ergonomic System), in which each of its elements is a subsystem, capable of being analyzed in an individualized way, it is evident that in the Design of Human-Computer Interactions (HCI), the first three subsystems - the User, the object, along with the activity - are the most outstanding in the analysis and definition for this type of design; On the other hand, the environment of use is fundamentally ubiquitous, cause varies greatly from case to case and with this, it is difficult to predict; Notwithstanding the above, it is feasible and necessary to establish the minimum environmental characteristics that must be met to promote appropriate interaction.

As for the object, given the increasing variety or typologies of devices or platforms by which the interaction can be made, be smartphones, tablets, laptops or desktop computers, or other devices, both planning and evaluation of Interaction must be performed for each identified category, since the characteristics of data processing as well as the characteristics of the physical interface of the device in question are fundamental to facilitate, or not, the activity that Users will perform. Just imagine the marked differences involved in reading texts in a Smart Watch regarding a Smart TV or a conventional desktop computer.

By paying attention on the activity subsystem, it is extremely important to fully describe what these activities will be. For this purpose, one of the main characteristics that can be analyzed is type of activity, which differ if the activity is primarily performed by the User, primarily performed by the computer or somewhere between the two possibilities.

One of the extremes of this typology would be, for example, activities such as reading a text on screen, where User is mostly the one who performs the tasks or sequences that complete the activity. The opposite end could be to observe a video clip, where the user "only" is a spectator, while the system performs multiple tasks and even feedback of the gestures done by the User (as in some smartphones that pause the video if the User's eyes do not point towards the screen). Such situations turn out to be key factors from the User's cognition and decision making, as that affect their ability to direct the process itself of the activity, to modify or not the rhythm in which it is carried out, as well as other fundamental aspects of the interaction.

Another important characteristic for analyzing activities is that these are usually complex, that is, they need to be sectioned in more elemental parts called tasks, and frequently these in subtasks, in order to identify fine aspects of the interaction, making it possible to identify situations in which the device is not easy to use, is not useful for tasks development and prevents the User to feel satisfied with the device. Those findings has to be attended from the design itself, either through the improvement of the object or its interface, by adapting the activity in a better way, or by seeking more favorable environments of use; all in the direction of improving efficiency of interaction.

Returning to the example of reading text on a screen, such an activity would contain at least, tasks such as forward or backward text as it is being read and adjusting the screen zoom to facilitate readability of the text. Subtasks of these could imply User must locate the commands that allow to perform such tasks, as well as to actuate each one of the icons, either by pressing them, dragging them or making some type of specific gesture.

The reader has most likely faced similar tasks and situations. This is the same case many designers or design teams face on a daily basis since they possible are novice or even experts Users, in addition, they see the dynamics of interaction even more profoundly insofar as the interface, the activity or the object have over the target User.

Unfortunately, such closeness of the designer to the analyzed problematic, given an specific interaction design, frequently promotes assumptions that actual users "must" have certain ability, kind of reasoning, or should response to a given stimuli; usually, this is far from reality. This situation demonstrates the importance of approaching real Users, which ideally will serve to describe and model it in the design and evaluation process.

3.1   Human Dimensions

Having made a brief tour of the object, activity and environment of use subsystems, it is in the User subsystem that several arguments emerge highlighting the importance of including this one, the User or group of "real" Users, in the design process of Human Computer Interaction.

Beyond what may be evident given the coined Human Computer Interaction (HCI), inclusion of the User as an active individual in the design process promotes substantive improvements throughout the entire development process of a given design, positively impacting the length and breadth of the process, from planning and objectives definition, to goals to be achieved through interaction design, to the correct evaluation of each attribute embodied in the final development, and of course, in the truthful and detailed identification of the User or group of Users characteristics to which the interaction design is directed.

This particular point, that of veracity and depth of definition of human characteristics, should not be addressed a priori by the designer or design team, based solely on the experience that the designer has on the subject, meaning with it, how well the designers consider know how the target Users are. On the contrary, it is fundamental, in order to achieve an accurate modeling of Users, that preconceived ideas of the designer or design team are considered, but characterization of the Users are based on the inquiry done together with them, through techniques such as co-design, co-creation or participatory design.

Approaching to Users during the design process involves the search for knowledge related to the various human dimensions that characterize and distinguish them, to determine which functions, which interaction processes or what possible responses can be expected that the actual User has within a designed system (Fig. 2).

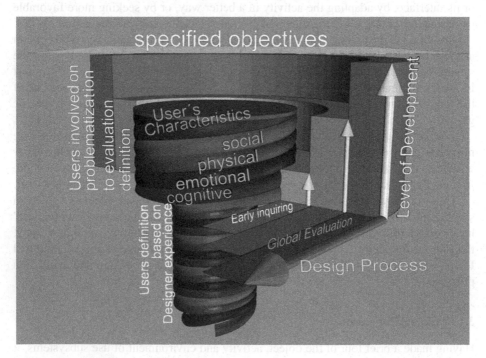

Fig. 2. User Centered Design Process representation, were user modeling, problematisation, objectives specification and evaluation of the level of development achieved are aided through real Users approach.

4   Interactive Systems Design

From a systemic approach perspective, delimitation of the system were interaction is taking place (context) is of priority interest, in which it is necessary to identify the characteristics (usage patterns, experience, knowledge) of the Users, the activities needed to be carried out to solve their needs, the characteristics of objects that should ease and satisfy during the interaction and the environment of use, promoted through the characteristics of the environment (temperature, lighting, noise, etc.), in which the activity is carried out; all that in an effort to ensure a pleasant use of the product.

The design of interactive interfaces is characterized by the convergence of three facets that run parallel in the design process of interactive systems, such as Interface Design, Interaction Design and Design of Experience. From the perspective of UCD, these processes are interrelated since although for the purposes of each their planning are taken into account characteristics of different scopes, the system together has common objectives, such as User satisfaction in using the product or effectiveness and efficiency of the User to object relationship (Fig. 3).

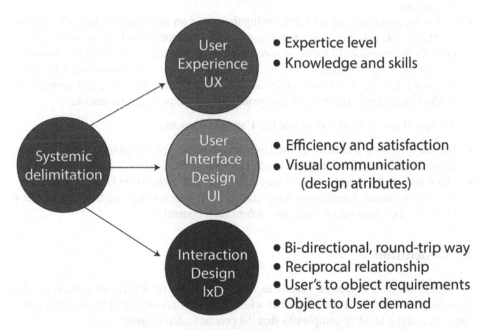

Fig. 3. Systemic delimitation of UCD process

By User Experience Designing it is necessary to consider the implications of the concept of experience. This concept states that the experience of one person cannot be experienced by another in the same way, because each individual interprets situations differently based on previous experiences he has had.

It is possible to say User Experience Design considers experience refers to:

- The knowledge or skills that a person has developed, define a User's level of experience and how it solves the problems of using a product.
- The way a person conceptualizes a situation that has occurred to him or her when interacting with a system, carrying out activities in which have used objects as means to solve said necessity in a specific use environment, in which the characteristics of the environment affected him or her, positively or negatively, in a cognitive or physical dimension.

Interface design involves the development of visual communication elements through which Users would be able to communicate with the object. These elements involve the User's experience regarding:

- The use of elements of composition that allows information to be in order, hierarchizing the most relevant data, positioning the elements to facilitate their location, their easy identification and clarity of meanings.
- Typography, color, dimension and location of the elements allow the transmission of visual information regarding the actions that User must perform in order to use the system.
- Cognitive processes are activated during the use of an interactive system through its interface. The processes of attention, memory, perception and language allows to identify information, to focus on a certain trait, to identify a sign and to remember how to follow an instruction; To aid this process, Visual Communication Designers develop interfaces for Users easily identify information through good contrast of colors (figure-background) and nice readability of displayed information.

Design of interactions will allude the User experiences:

- During the use of a system; as the User demands the object certain answers to their requests and the object demands certain actions to the User.
- Since the system must be easy to use, functional and useful from User's perspective. To achieve these, Users must have control over the system and the system must feedback the Users on its status to confirm such control.

5   Conclusion

As stated above, the Design processes, when centered on User, must consider the knowledge and skills of the people to which products are intended to, designing the contents and the level of complexity that the product must present.

To do that, Design of Interfaces should not only observe, but include in depth the User's experience in the interaction process, allowing the development of interfaces that meet User's characteristics with task requirement, achieving the development of satisfactory and efficient products.

By leaning on User Centered Design processes, design and developmental teams of interfaces allow the insertion of formative evaluation processes between each stage of development, thus avoiding the application of only summative evaluation at the end of development and with it, that iterative evaluation processes should produce systematic results, which will facilitate the assessment and relevance of the intervention.

References

1. Venkat, R., Kerimcan, O.: The CoCreation Paradigm. Stanford University Press, Califormia (2014)
2. Daniel, D.G., Jianwen, Z., Rainer, D.: Essential issues in codesign. In: Jorgen, S., Wayne, W. (eds.) Hardware/Software Co-design: Principles and Practice, pp. 1–45. Springer Sicence +Business Media B.V, Dordrecht (1997). doi:10.1007/978-1-4757-2649-7
3. Katja, B., Ilpo, K.: Coexperience: user experience as interaction. Int. J. CoCreation Des. Arts 1(1), 5–18. Taylor and Francis Group (2005). doi:10.1080/15710880412331289917
4. Martha, P.S.: Co-design: a central approach to the inclusion of people with disabilities Rev. Fac. Med. 63(Suppl. 1), S149–S154 (2015). doi:http://dx.doi.org/10.15446/revfacmed.v63n3sup.49345

Usability Testing as a Complement of Heuristic Evaluation: A Case Study

Braulio Murillo[(⊠)], Silvia Vargas, Arturo Moquillaza,
Luis Fernández, and Freddy Paz

Pontificia Universidad Católica del Perú, Lima, Peru
{bmurillov, silvia.vargas}@pucp.edu.pe,
{amoquillaza, fernandezm.christian, fpaz}@pucp.pe

Abstract. The usability assessment of software systems is becoming more relevant, especially when it comes to web-based systems. A well-built and user-friendly website is capable of capturing a potential customer. There are different methods to evaluate usability, including heuristic evaluation and usability testing with users. In the present work, the critical functionalities of an airline's website were evaluated, such as the purchase of tickets, flight reservations, among others. First, a heuristic evaluation was performed and then a usability test with users. The evaluations were developed in an academic context and the participants were postgraduate students of a university. The problems detected in the first evaluation served to define specific tasks in the usability test with users. In this way, the results of the evaluations were complemented.

Keywords: Human computer interaction · Heuristic evaluation · Usability evaluation · Usability testing · Transactional web applications

1 Introduction

In software engineering, the term "Usability" is related to the ease of use of a software product [3]. Usability is a quality attribute that measures how easy the user interface is to use. It also includes methods to improve ease of use during the software design process [1]. Nowadays on the web, usability is a necessary condition for survival. If a website is difficult to use, people will stop using it. If the page does not clearly state what a company offers and what users can do on the site, people will stop using it. If users get lost on a website, they will stop using it. If the information on a website is difficult to read or does not answer the key questions of users, they will stop using it.

The first e-commerce law is that if users cannot find the product, they cannot buy it either [1]. In this paper we will evaluate the website of an airline using heuristic evaluation and a usability test with users as a complement [5]. The results obtained in both tests will be shown to compare them and provide some conclusions.

© Springer International Publishing AG 2017
A. Marcus and W. Wang (Eds.): DUXU 2017, Part I, LNCS 10288, pp. 434–444, 2017.
DOI: 10.1007/978-3-319-58634-2_32

2 Related Work

Given the importance of usability, there are two types of methods to perform a usability assessment: inspection methods and test methods [4]. The difference between them lies in the person who applies them. In the first case the inspectors perform and in the second the users participate [2].

Heuristic evaluation is a well-known inspection technique that is widely used by usability specialists. It was developed by Nielsen as an alternative to user testing [3].

The usability test with users is a method of software products evaluation in which active users are representative of said products. The main purpose of this method is the identification of usability problems during the interaction of users and the system. This method allows collecting qualitative and quantitative data, as well as user satisfaction with the software product [7].

In the present work, a usability assessment is performed with the "Heuristic Evaluation" inspection method, which is based on the analysis of the ten heuristics defined by Dr. Jakob Nielsen, Latam Airlines web application www.latam.com.

We also perform a usability assessment with the user testing method to the same application. This evaluation is done as a complement to the heuristic evaluation previously performed by the same group. In [6] the advantages of performing heuristic and user evaluations as complementary studies are developed.

The present work has been developed under an academic context, during the months of June and July of the year 2016. All the participants have developed the tests with professionalism and ethical values.

3 Research Design

In order to test usability in the website latam.com, were used two methods that complement each other: heuristic evaluations and usability test users. The objective of this test and selection of the website were academicals.

3.1 Description of the Web Site

The website corresponds to the new brand of LATAM Airlines Group: LATAM, which is a product of the consolidation of the two brands of the group that preceded it: LAN and TAM. LATAM is an airline based in the Republic of Chile, which operates in South, Central and North America, as well as the Caribbean, Europe and Oceania; with different destinations in more than 26 countries [8].

Due to the nature of the company, the website has numerous sections, among them: Purchase of tickets, Purchase of packages, Check-in Service, Charge Service, Flight Information, Offers Section, Press Room, Section for Investors, among many others. However, the main emphasis is on the first three sections because it is frequently used by passengers (Fig. 1).

Viaja por el mundo con tarifas asombrosas

Fig. 1. Main page of the evaluated web site: latam.com

The purpose of the application is to offer its customers a computer tool for its main services: purchase of tickets, flight check-in and flight status display. In this sense, the website has a design oriented to emphasize these services and to link them to each other.

3.2   Study Design

The purpose of this paper was to compare heuristic evaluations and user usability tests based on a web transactional system. This work was developed in two moments. First a heuristic evaluation was carried out and then a user usability test was developed.

4   Heuristic Evaluation

4.1   Participants

The heuristic evaluation was performed using the Nielsen's methodology analyzing the ten usability principles "heuristics". The evaluation was performed by four evaluators, computer engineers, three of them master's students and one doctoral student.

4.2   Phases

This section describes the steps used to perform the heuristic evaluation. These are described below.

First phase: Each participant performed alone an evaluation of the product and recorded all the results found in their respective reports.

Second phase: A moderator, who was previously selected, facilitated a meeting where the evaluators were able to unify the results obtained by briefly explaining the problems they found. As a result, a clean and unified listing of the problems encountered was obtained.

Third phase: Each evaluator independently rated the severity and frequency of each one of the problems of the unified listing. With the values of severity and frequency was calculated the criticality: criticality = severity + frequency.

Fourth phase: A coordinator, who was previously selected, performed the activities of this phase, calculating the averages and standard deviations of the three previously calculated values: severity, frequency and criticality of each problem. With the results, was established a ranking of the problems found.

The severity was evaluated according to the rating proposed by Nielsen [9], in which 0 means "I don't agree that this is a usability problem at all" and 4 means "Usability catastrophe: imperative to fix this before product can be released".

The frequency was evaluated according the rating of the Table 1.

Table 1. Frequency ratings

Note	Frequency
0	<1%
1	1–10%
2	11–50%
3	51–90%
4	>90%

4.3   Data Analysis and Results

A total of thirty seven usability problems were identified, which were categorized by the participants who performed the heuristic evaluation. Only for the heuristic "Recognition rather than recall" wasn't found non-compliance. In Table 2, it can be seen the times that each unfulfilled heuristic.

Table 3 shows the identified problems sorted descending by severity, without considering the frequency. Of the total of problems found by the evaluators, almost 50% of them resulted in a severity value greater than or equal to 2.50, that is, they tend to be greater or catastrophic.

Thus, the most severe problem identified by the evaluators is that the system displays a blank screen after log off a user, which could be perceived as unsafe for the end user. Also, the evaluators have considered severe that during the ticket purchase's process, the system doesn't provide the option to return to the previous step, moreover, it doesn't allow to save the information already entered so that forcing a backward the information is lost.

Other severe problems are that the system displays blank screens before certain options, other options don't even work, displays error messages that aren't understand and have broken links. Almost all screens don't have the option of help for the user.

Table 2. Unfulfilled heuristics

ID	Heuristic	Problems that non-compliance the heuristics	Number the problems that non-compliance the heuristics
N1	Visibility of system status	P10, P12, P14, P17, P18, P27, P30, P31	8
N2	Match between system and the real world	P4, P22, P26, P35	4
N3	User control and freedom	P3, P16, P28, P37	4
N4	Consistency and standards	P2, P5, P7, P8, P11, P15, P19, P24	8
N5	Error prevention	P1, P6, P20, P23, P29, P32, P33	7
N7	Flexibility and efficiency of use	P25	1
N8	Aesthetic and minimalist design	P9	1
N9	Help users recognize, diagnose, and recover from errors	P21, P34	2
N10	Help and documentation	P13, P36	2

Table 3. Ranking of the more severe problems

ID	Problem	Average severity
P17	The screen goes blank on log off	3.25
P26	Button return to the previous screen on the Visa payment screen doesn't work	3.25
P3	In the ticket purchase's process, in several steps it isn't possible to return to the previous ones, it's returned to option 1: Date	3.00
P18	The screen goes blank by selecting the prize icon	3.00
P22	The name of the page doesn't match when you enter the Claims book option	3.00
P32	Broken links	3.00
P34	The share option on Facebook doesn't work, shows a technical error	3.00
P37	"Where you find it" option doesn't work	3.00

On the other hand, the Table 4 shows the identified problems sorted descending by criticality. It's observed that the maximum value of criticality is 6, this means that the problems encountered don't drastically affect the functionality of the system.

The problem of greater criticality is that the system doesn't provide the user with the option to return on any of the pages of the ticket purchase's process. This means that this problem is the most severe and most frequent.

Table 4. Ranking of the more critically problems

ID	Problem	Average severity	Average frequency	Average critically
P3	In the ticket purchase's process in several steps it isn't possible to return to the previous ones, it´s returned to option 1: Date	3.00	3.00	6.00
P32	Broken links	3.00	2.75	5.75
P13	There isn't help option that can guide the user in case he doesn't understand the interface	2.75	2.75	5.50
P19	The system behaves differently when using different browsers	2.75	2.75	5.50
P16	The back button isn't displayed properly	2.25	3.00	5.25
P23	The system returns to home when choosing the country of origin from different pages: the page of claims book and the page of help	2.75	2.50	5.25
P26	Button return to the previous screen on the Visa payment screen doesn't work	3.25	2.00	5.25
P35	There is poorly worded information	2.50	2.75	5.25
P10	There is the option to see rates in other currencies, but it doesn't work	2.75	2.25	5.00
P22	The name of the page doesn't match when you enter the claim's book option	3.00	2.00	5.00

Other critical issues include broken links, lack of system-wide help and poorly worded information on several pages. One problem worth highlighting is that the system has different behaviors when using different browsers.

Finally, the problems P17 and P26, although they were evaluated as very severe, were not the most critical because they didn't have a high frequency of occurrence.

5   Usability Testing

5.1   Test Purpose

The purpose of performing the usability test in the LATAM application is that the user may encounter problems when using it by performing certain previously defined tasks. The tasks have been established based on the result of the heuristic evaluation performed in the previous stage. Problems with severity greater than 3 (P17, P26, P3, P18) that are directly related to the acquisition of passages were selected, since this is the most important functionality of the application and for them, activities that could cover these problems were defined.

5.2 Test Design

From the heuristic inspection that was performed in the previous stage, the problems were taken with severity greater than 3. With them, the problem, task and context matrix is elaborated, as shown in Table 5. Of the list of problems, those that emphasize the transactional functionalities, that is, in the purchase of air passages, on other functionalities of the web site were chosen.

Table 5. Matrix of problems, task and context

ID	Problem	Task	Context
P26	Button return to the previous screen on the Visa payment screen doesn't work	1	Step 5 of ticket purchasing, Payment section. When user want to go back to last screen by clicking in Return link, system redirects to a error page with no possibility of leave
P3	In the ticket purchase's process in several steps it isn't possible to return to the previous ones, it´s returned to option 1: Date	1	When user returns to a previous step, no matter being in step 2 or step 3, always go back to step 1 (date)
P10	There is the option to see rates in other currencies, but it doesn't work	1	In the Flight reservation option, step 3, Price, Option "See rates in other currencies" exists, but it does not make any change in prices or rates
P13	There isn't help option that can guide the user in case he doesn't understand the interface	1	In none of the options is shown the help option with the interface elements designed
P8	The information of flights available in selection of two sections or more sections, is different	2	When user selects to fly to more than one destination, but only place two flights, the available flight information is different (limited) on the selected dates than shown if you enter by purchasing a flight to a single destination
P1	By placing missing information (without return flight), user can continue with the process	2	When user buys a ticket and does not select the return flight, he can select the Continue button
			At the initial screen of the purchase process, user can also select the Continue button

5.3 Participants

The four participants were students of the computer science masters of the PUCP, male, whose ages ranged from 28 to 47 years.

5.4 Materials

The following materials were developed for the Usability Test:

Confidentiality Agreement: It is a consent document where the evaluated user manifests his voluntary intention to participate in the usability test at a certain place and date.

Previous Indications: In order to help to participant and a brief description of the stages that will be followed in the test is made.

Pre-test Questionnaire: It is a questionnaire of demographic type and serves to obtain information to classify the evaluated user. In this way, the responses of the evaluated users can be contextualized.

Post-test Questionnaire: It allows to obtain additional information that complements the observation made during the execution of the tasks assigned.

Task List: It is a document that describes in detail the activities that the user will perform for each task defined. In this list, the user must detail, when required, information that is requested as a backup of what was done in the application.

For this test, the tasks have been built on the following scenarios: In the first task the user need to look for alternative (double) tickets to Miami. The dates of the holidays are from August 1 to 14, 2016 and there is a budget of S/4,700 destined for the tickets. Since it is high season, the user must utilize some promotion with which you can purchase tickets with the allocated budget (in that sense, you must use economic rates, etc.). In the second task, the user must change the flight schedule: now you want to spend three days in Miami and the rest of the time in New York. For this, the option "Multiple destinations" must be used.

Task Compliance Observation Sheet: It is used by the evaluator to detail the fulfillment of each activity of the task, the time spent and the pertinent observations.

5.5 Usability Testing Process

The test was performed individually, each user had at his disposal an evaluator who accompanied him in the process.

Each participant was presented the Confidentiality Agreement and a list of previous Indications. Each participant gave their consent and signed the indicated documents. Subsequently, each participant was given the pretest, which was filled immediately. Then, each participant was given the task list and some general inquiries were acquitted.

The recording of the interaction was started, and the user was left in front of the browser, and each evaluator took note of the Observations of Compliance of the Tasks on what he was observing.

Finally, each participant was given the post-test questionnaire, which ended the execution of the test.

5.6   Data Analysis and Results

Task 1 Results
Hits presented:

- Users were able to select the options indicated.
- Those who had previous knowledge of the application, were already more familiar, so they performed tasks faster compared to less experienced users.
- Users can obtain the prices of the cheapest tickets.
- Even when users experience complications, they did not have to seek help from the system.

Inconveniences presented:

- The functionality to see the different exchange rates cannot be used correctly.
- The system is not easy to use for people who are not experienced in this type of applications.
- The system cannot complete the payment through the credit card option when the steps indicated in task 1 are performed.

Task 2 Results
Hits presented:

- Users were able to select the options indicated, those who did not have much knowledge of the application were already more familiar.

Inconveniences presented:

- Since the users had gone through another previous task, where the functionality was different, confused the new interface for the selection of flights.
- Most of the error messages presented clearly indicate why they were presented, but users before proceeding with the process do not identify which information they lacked to complete.
- In a particular case, an error occurred that wiped all data on the screen but did not tell the user the reason for it.
- Since it is not possible to select route rates, users are not sure to continue with the purchase.
- There is no help in the system, which is necessary for users who do not have much experience in the use of similar applications.

Data Analysis: Observations
In general, users did not use system help. In Task 1 most users had trouble getting the rate in other currencies when using Chrome. Most users had trouble getting to the VPOS payment window. In addition, in Task 2, most users had trouble selecting destinations. Finally, all had problems to select the flight with scales more economic since that information is not shown.

Data Analysis: Post-test Questionnaire
Table 6 shows that the general appreciation of users with respect to the page evaluated is positive. They emphasize the ease of navigation and the possibility of re-using the portal. The two points that received the lowest rating was the fact that they were able to complete the tasks and overall satisfaction with the portal. This could be considered complementary, since not being able to complete a task can influence the satisfaction of use. In addition, users 1 and 2 stand out for having extreme opinions regarding the page, the first with an extremely negative opinion and the second with an extremely positive opinion. What is recommended to validate these results is to increase the number of evaluated users.

Table 6. Results of Post-test questionnaire

	Question	Average result	
1	Fulfill tasks	2,75	Neutral
2	Sufficient and complete information	3,5	Agree
3	Easy-to-understand information available	3,25	Neutral
4	Required information easy to find	3,25	Neutral
5	Information found useful	3,5	Useful
6	Portal easy to navigate	3,75	Easy
7	Orientation on the portal	3,5	Easy
8	Satisfaction with the portal	2,75	Neutral
9	Will use the portal again	3,75	Agree

6 Conclusions

It emphasizes the heuristic evaluation as a tool for evaluation of usability of wide use, given its advantages in time and cost versus analysis with participation of end users. This evaluation is an expert analysis to determine if the elements of an interface comply with widely accepted principles such as Nielsen heuristics.

In the heuristic evaluation, a significant amount of usability problems have been found. It is important to mention that an expert has been used less than recommended by Nielsen. When evaluating large or multi-functional applications, it is advisable to pre-define a scope to focus the experts on what may be of interest in the evaluation. A heuristic evaluation will provide better results when focused on detecting relevant aspects for the client.

According to the above, the problems found, which concentrate on problems of lack of help, broken links and consistency errors, are detected in the heuristic evaluation, shows problems in the process of migration or changes to this LATAM platform.

With reference to the site as a whole, apart from the problems detected, in general, it is emphasized that the site meets the objectives of each functionality evaluated, problems in general are not blocking but can hinder the user's tasks. Besides, the overall evaluation of the site is positive, since it meets most of the objectives for which it has been built, and improvement is pending on the basis of the problems detected, as well as the completion of the process of migration or change through which the indicated site is passing.

For those reasons, it concluded that two methods of usability evaluation which are heuristic evaluations and usability test users, are complement each other. When they are used together, let a better focus in user, a better diagnostic and analysis about the object of study and increase a better feedback, among other advantages.

It is suggested, for usability tests with users, to increase the number of users evaluated, with a more heterogeneous sample, in order to obtain more results that validate the conclusions.

References

1. Nielsen, J.: Usability 101: introduction to usability (2012). https://www.nngroup.com/articles/usability-101-introduction-to-usability/. Accessed 29 June 2016
2. Holzinger, A.: Usability engineering methods for software developers. Commun. ACM **48**(1), 71–74 (2005)
3. Paz, F., Paz, Freddy A., Pow-Sang, J.A.: Evaluation of usability heuristics for transactional web sites: a comparative study. In: Latifi, S. (ed.) Information Technology: New Generations. AISC, vol. 448, pp. 1063–1073. Springer, Cham (2016). doi:10.1007/978-3-319-32467-8_92
4. Paz, F.; Pow-Sang J.A.: Usability evaluation methods for software development: a systematic mapping review. In: 8th ASEA (2015)
5. Paz, F., Pow-Sang, J.A.: Current trends in usability evaluation methods: a systematic review. In: 2014 7th International Conference on Advanced Software Engineering and Its Applications (ASEA), pp. 11–15, December 2014
6. Paz, F., Villanueva, D., Pow-Sang, J.A.: Heuristic evaluation as a complement to usability testing: a case study in web domain. In: 2014 Tenth International Conference on Information Technology: New Generations (ITNG), pp 546–551, April 2015
7. Paz, F., Villanueva, D., Rusu, C., Roncagliolo, S., Pow-Sang, J.A.: Experimental evaluation of usability heuristics. In: 2013 Tenth International Conference on Information Technology: New Generations (ITNG), pp. 119–126, April 2013
8. lan.com: Nace LATAM: La nueva marca que adoptarán LAN, TAM y sus filiales. http://www.lan.com/destinosudamerica/notadeprensa/nace-latam-la-nueva-marca-que-adoptaran-lan-tam-y-sus-filiales/. Accessed 11 June 2016
9. Nielsen, J.: Severity ratings for usability problems (1995). https://www.nngroup.com/articles/how-to-rate-the-severity-of-usability-problems/. Accessed 29 June 2016

What Drives Perceived Usability
in Mobile Web Design:
Classical or Expressive Aesthetics?

Kiemute Oyibo[✉] and Julita Vassileva

University of Saskatchewan, Saskatoon, Canada
kiemute.oyibo@usask.ca, jiv@cs.usask.ca

Abstract. Research has shown that the *perceived usability* of a web artifact is influenced by its *perceived aesthetics*: a high-order construct composed of two lower-order dimensions (*classical aesthetics* and *expressive aesthetics*). However, in the mobile domain, where *usability* is very important in human-computer interaction (HCI) given the relatively small screen size of the mobile device, limited research has investigated: (1) which of the two dimensions of *visual aesthetics* is the stronger predictor of the *perceived usability* of a website; (2) how the *classical* dimension impacts the *expressive* dimension; and (3) how culture moderates the relationships among the three HCI design constructs. To address these questions, we conducted a study of the perceptions of four systematically manipulated mobile websites and modeled the relationships between *perceived usability* and the two dimensions of *perceived aesthetics*. Based on a sample of 233 participants (87 Canadians and 146 Nigerians), our models account for 30% to 80% of the variance of *perceived usability*. They show that *classical aesthetics* is stronger than *expressive aesthetics* in predicting the *perceived usability* of a mobile website, irrespective of the level of aesthetic treatment of the user interface and culture, with the effect size being larger for the Nigerian group than for the Canadian group. Moreover, the models reveal that *classical aesthetics* strongly influences *expressive aesthetics*. Our results suggest that what is classical is expressively beautiful and usable. The significance of our findings is that in mobile web, there is need for designers to pay closer attention to *classical aesthetics* given the strong influence it has on *perceived usability*.

Keywords: Mobile web · Classical aesthetics · Expressive aesthetics · Perceived usability · Path model · Effect size · Culture

1 Introduction

The pervasiveness due to the portability, affordability and, above all, personal nature of mobile devices has resulted in various internet vendors moving their businesses and services to the mobile domain. However, owing to the relatively small screen size of mobile devices, making good interface design a challenging task to achieve [11], *usability* has become an important issue in human-computer interaction (HCI) in mobile web. More importantly, research in Technology Acceptance Model (TAM) [27]

© Springer International Publishing AG 2017
A. Marcus and W. Wang (Eds.): DUXU 2017, Part I, LNCS 10288, pp. 445–462, 2017.
DOI: 10.1007/978-3-319-58634-2_33

has shown that *perceived ease of use* (mediated by *perceived usefulness*) predicts users' *intention to use* a mobile website. This makes it important to investigate the antecedents of *perceived usability* in the mobile domain. So far, a number of studies [12, 13] have found that the *perceived usability* (PU) of a website is influenced by its *perceived aesthetics*, an abstract construct comprising two major dimensions: *classical aesthetics* (a more objective dimension) and *expressive aesthetics* (a more subjective dimension). Both dimensions offer "*a finer grained view of perceived aesthetics*" [13, p. 289] in understanding the relationship between *aesthetics* and *usability*. However, limited research has investigated: (1) which of these two dimensions of *perceived aesthetics* predominantly determines the *perceived usability* of a mobile website; (2) how one of the dimensions impacts the other; and (3) what moderating role culture plays. Most prior studies [3, 4, 6, 12, 13] have focused on the web domain on one hand, and Western and Asian populations on the other hand. However, countries in Africa, where "*mobile is fast becoming the primary channel of accessing the Internet*" [7, p. 2], have been practically left out. To bridge this gap, we conducted a study on the perception of four systematically manipulated mobile websites using 233 participants from a high-context culture (146 Nigerians) and a low-context culture (87 Canadians) [10].

Our results reveal that: (1) *classical aesthetics* predominantly determines the *perceived usability* of a mobile website; and (2) the perception of *classical aesthetics* (CA) strongly impacts the perception of *expressive aesthetics* (EA). These findings confirm the notion that "*what is orderly is beautiful and usable*" [3]. They imply that designers of mobile websites should focus on improving the more objective aesthetic dimension of their websites (*classical aesthetics*) in order to increase their *perceived usability* and *perceived expressive aesthetics* as well. In other words, they should emphasize simplicity (the hallmark of *classical aesthetics*) in their user interface design rather than complexity (the hallmark of *expressive aesthetics*) [13, 21], as the former is a stronger determinant of *perceived usability*. This has the potential of positively influencing the *perceived usefulness* of and the *intention to use* their websites [27].

The rest of this paper is organized as follows. Sections 2 and 3 focus on background and related work respectively. Section 4 explains the research method used. Sections 5 and 6 dwell on result and discussion respectively. Finally, Sect. 7 focuses on conclusion and future work.

2 Background

In this section, we provide a brief overview of the hedonic and utilitarian HCI design constructs and the two types of cultures we considered in our study.

2.1 HCI Design Constructs

Perceived Aesthetics. It is defined as the visual appearance and appeal of an artifact. In HCI design, it is composed of two major dimensions: *classical* and *expressive* [22].

Classical Aesthetics. *Classical aesthetics* relates to the historical and traditional notion of *aesthetics*, which is expressed by terms such as "clear", "clean", "orderly", etc. [13].

Expressive Aesthetics. *Expressive aesthetics* relates to the creativity and expressive ability of a designer. Thus, it is associated with terms such as "originality", "fascinating design", etc. [13, 25].

Perceived Usability. This is the *perceived ease of use* of a website [27], which indicates how effortless and effective a user's interaction with the website is [1].

2.2 Culture

Research has shown that culture plays an important role in the way people perceive user interface design [8, 17, 24]. Among others, one of the main categorizations of culture used in HCI studies is based on the context of communication [18, 24].

Low-Context Culture. A low-context (LC) culture is that type of culture, which has a communication style in which messages are expressed explicitly by the speaker, leaving little or nothing to be inferred from the context of communication by the receiver [10, 14]. Examples of LC cultures include Canada, United States, Germany, etc. [18].

High-Context Culture. A high-context (HC) culture is that type of culture, which has a communication style in which messages are expressed implicitly by the speaker, leaving much to be inferred from the context of communication by the receiver [10, 14]. Examples of HC cultures include Nigeria, China, Japan, Arab nations, etc. [18].

3   Related Work

Research has shown that the *perceived aesthetics* of HCI artifacts influences their *perceived usability*. Tractinsky et al. [26] were among the first researchers in the field to report this finding based on their experimental study. They attributed their finding to a socio-psychological phenomenon known as halo effect and concluded that *"what is beautiful is usable."* This notion was validated by a two-stage study they carried out using a computerized surrogate for an Automated Teller Machine (ATM) in which users reported their *aesthetics* and *usability* perceptions before and after the use of the ATM. They found that *perceived aesthetics* before the use of the ATM influenced users' *perceived usability* of the ATM after use. The study by Tractinsky et al. [26] was conducted in order to verify the findings by Kurosu and Kashimura [12], who had earlier found in their study based on an ATM interface that *perceived usability* (*apparent usability*) was influenced by *perceived aesthetics* and not the *actual usability* (*inherent usability*) of the ATM. This had made the latter authors to recommend that information technology products should be designed to be *apparently* usable as well as *inherently* usable. Further, Sonderegger and Sauer [23] carried out a study on how the *appearance* of a mobile phone affected its *perceived usability*. Using two visually manipulated versions of the phone, they found that participants using the highly appealing version rated their device as being more usable than participants using the non-appealing version. Similarly, in separate empirical studies, Coursaris and Kripintris [5] and Oyibo and Vassileva [16] found that *perceived aesthetics* strongly impacted *perceived usability*. Finally, in their study of the impact of *color temperature* on *web aesthetics*, Coursaris et al. [3] found that *classical aesthetics* strongly influenced *expressive aesthetics*.

However, research on the influence of hedonic dimensions on *usability* is still limited [3], especially with respect to how the two main dimensions of *aesthetics* influence *usability*. Moreover, limited studies have investigated the cultural moderation of the relationships among the three HCI design constructs [25]. In the existing literature, there are barely studies which focused on countries from the African continent; neither are there comparative studies, which specifically focused on both African and Western cultures. It is this gap in the literature that we set out to fill in this paper.

4   Method

In this section, we present our research design, hypotheses, the instruments used to measure the HCI design constructs of interest, and the demographics of the participants.

4.1   Research Design

In this paper, we are interested in answering three research questions as follows:

1. Which of the dimensions of *aesthetics* (*classical aesthetics* and *expressive aesthetics*) serves as the linkage between *aesthetics* and *usability* [13]. In other words, which of the two aesthetic dimensions determines *perceived usability?*
2. How strongly does *classical aesthetics* influence *expressive aesthetics?*
3. Do these relationships depend on culture and/or the visual aesthetics and navigational characteristics of the user interface (UI)?

To answer the above research questions, we came up with four systematically manipulated web designs, as shown in Fig. 1. We regard the two UIs at the top as low-level designs and the two UIs at the bottom as high-level designs. As described in [14, 15], beginning from mobile website A, we transformed the UI to mobile website B by changing the multicolor-theme to an image-based, gray-theme design in an attempt to realize a highly minimalist design. Next, we transformed mobile website B to a monochrome (blue-theme) design to realize a cool-temperature web design. Finally, we transformed mobile website C to mobile website D by just changing the layout (a structural/navigational manipulation) from list to grid.

4.2   Research Hypotheses

In answering our research questions, we reviewed the literature to come up with the hypothesized path model shown in Fig. 2. Based on the existing empirical findings in the literature, we formulated six hypotheses on the inter-relationships among *perceived*

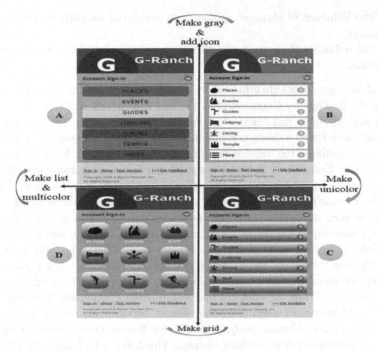

Fig. 1. Systematically designed mobile websites (Color figure online)

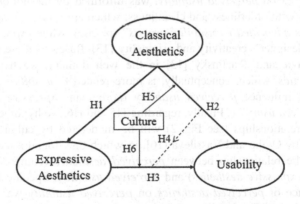

Fig. 2. Hypothesized path model

classical aesthetics, *perceived expressive aesthetics* and the *perceived usability* of a mobile websites. These relationships are represented in Fig. 2 and expressed as follows:

H1: *Classical aesthetics* will positively influence *expressive aesthetics*.

H2: *Classical aesthetics* will positively influence *perceived usability*.

H3: *Expressive aesthetics* will positively influence *perceived usability*.

H4: The influence of *classical aesthetics* on *perceived usability* is stronger than the influence of *expressive aesthetics* on *perceived usability*.

H5: The influence of *classical aesthetics* on *perceived usability* will be moderated by culture.

H6: The influence of *expressive aesthetics* on *perceived usability* will be moderated by culture.

The above hypotheses are informed by prior findings in the literature. First, H1 was based on the findings by Coursaris et al. [3] and van Schaik and Ling [21]. The first group of authors found that *classical aesthetics* influences *expressive aesthetics*, while the second group found a strong correlation between both dimensions of *aesthetics*. We decided to investigate this relationship because limited studies have done so in the mobile domain. Coursaris et al. [3] have argued that findings regarding this relationship may help extend Tractinsky et al.'s [26] notion of *"what is beautiful is usable"* to *"what is orderly is beautiful"* [3, p. 116], since *classical aesthetics* pertains to the notion of organization (i.e., orderliness) and *expressive aesthetics* pertains to the notion of creativity and harmony in the use of colors in designs (i.e., beauty). Second, H2 and H3 were informed by the work of Sánchez-Franco et al. [20], who investigated these relationships (in their case, the influence of *classical aesthetics* and *expressive aesthetics* on *perceived usefulness,* which, in TAM, is directly influenced by *perceived ease of use* [27]). While they did not find a significant relationship between *classical aesthetics* and *perceived usefulness,* they found between *expressive aesthetics* and *perceived usefulness.* Consequently, this calls for further investigation of these relationships to confirm or disprove their findings. Third, H4, which states that the impact of *classical aesthetics* on *perceived usability* will be stronger than the impact of *expressive aesthetics* on *perceived usability,* was informed by the notion that *classical aesthetics* deals with orderliness and cleanliness, which are *"closely related to many of the design rules advocated by usability experts"* (p. 269), while *expressive aesthetics* deals with the designer's creativity and originality [13]. Based on these notions and the findings by Lavie and Tractinsky [13] in the web domain, we hypothesized that *classical aesthetics,* which, conceptually, is more related to *usability* than *expressive aesthetics,* will influence *perceived usability* more than *expressive aesthetics* will influence *perceived usability.* Finally, regarding H5 and H6, we hypothesized that their corresponding relationships (see Fig. 2) will be moderated by culture based on the previous study by Oyibo and Vassileva [16], in which they found a moderation effect by culture of the relationship between *perceived aesthetics* (composed of *classical aesthetics* and *expressive aesthetics*) and *perceived usability.* Specifically, they found that the influence of *perceived aesthetics* on *perceived usability* was stronger for a high-context culture (Nigeria) than a low-context culture (Canada).

4.3   Measurement Instruments

We used existing validated instruments to measure all three HCI design constructs under investigation. To measure *classical and expressive aesthetics,* we used the respective 3-item versions of Lavie and Tractinsky's [13] *classical* and *expressive aesthetics* scale as adapted by van Schaik and Ling [21]. Similarly, to measure *perceived usability,* we used Lavie and Tractinsky's 5-item scale [13]. Each item in each scale was measured using a 7-point Likert scale, ranging from *Strongly Disagree (1)* to *Strongly Agree (7)*. In the administration of the online survey, all of the items from the three scales with respect to each webpage were presented together in a randomized fashion to each participant in order to prevent him/her from easily knowing which construct was being measured at a given time if each construct's items were presented separately in a block.

4.4 Participants

The survey was approved by the University of Saskatchewan Research Ethics Board. Participants were recruited on the university's website, Facebook and by emails. To appreciate them for their time, they were given a chance to win one of four $50 CAD gift cards. A total of 233 participants from Canada and Nigeria took part in the study. Table 1 shows the demographics of participants. Among them were 54.5% males and 45.5% females. Age-wise, 67.8% were between the age of 18 and 24 years old, while 30.4% were above 24 years old. Education-wise, 57.9% had high school education; 24.5% had university education; and 8.2% had postgraduate education.

Table 1. Participants' demographics

N = 233	
Gender	Male (127, 54.5%); Female (106, 45.5%)
Country	Canada (87, 37.3%); Nigeria (146, 62.7%)
Age	18–24 (158, 67.8%); > 24 (71, 30.4%); Unidentified (4, 1.7%)
Education qualification	High school (135, 57.9%); Bachelor degree (57, 24.5%); Postgraduate degree (19, 8.2%); Others (22, 9.4%)
Internet experience	0–3 years (18, 7.7%); 4–6 years (42, 18.0%); 7–9 years (49, 21.0%); > = 10 years (124, 53.2%)

5 Results

In this section, we present the result of our path analysis using R's Partial Least Square Path Modeling (PLS-PM) package [19], starting with the assessment of the measurement models.

5.1 Measurement Model Evaluation

In the measurement model evaluation, we assessed indicator reliability, internal consistency reliability, convergent validity and discriminant validity [9, 19]. *Indicator Reliability:* With respect to each construct measured using multiple items, all the indicators in the measurement models had an outer loading greater than 0.7 [9]. Thus, the reliability criterion was met, as the communality value for all indicators were greater than 0.5. *Internal Consistency Reliability:* Internal consistency reliability was evaluated using the composite reliability criterion, DG.rho (ρ). The ρ values for the multiple-item constructs were greater than 0.7 [9]. *Convergent Validity:* The Average Variance Extracted (AVE) was used to evaluate convergent validity. The AVE for the constructs in the model was greater than 0.5 as recommended [9]. *Discriminant Validity:* The crossloading of each construct was also evaluated. No indicator loaded higher on any other construct than the one it was meant to measure.

5.2   Data-Driven Path Model

Figures 3 and 4 show the data-driven model at the global and subgroup levels, respectively. The global model was meant to serve as a control for confirming findings at the subgroup level [6]. At the global level, the goodness of fit (GOF) for the model ranges from medium (67% for webpages B and C) to high 75% (for webpage D), indicating that the model fits the data well to a high degree [19]. Similarly, the coefficient of determination (R^2) of *perceived usability* ranges from moderate (49% for webpage B) to high (70% for webpage D), based on the PLS-PM guideline, where $R^2 < 30$ is low, $0.30 < R^2 < 0.50$ is moderate and $R^2 > 0.60$ is high [19]. This indicates a large amount of the variance of *perceived usability* is accounted for by *classical aesthetics* and *expressive aesthetics*, with the former having a greater effect size and the latter having a little or no effect size. In the same vein, *classical aesthetics* accounts for

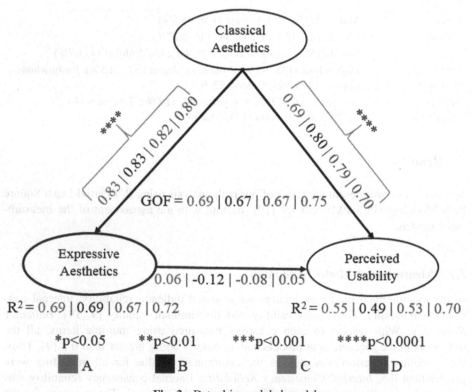

Fig. 3. Data-driven global model

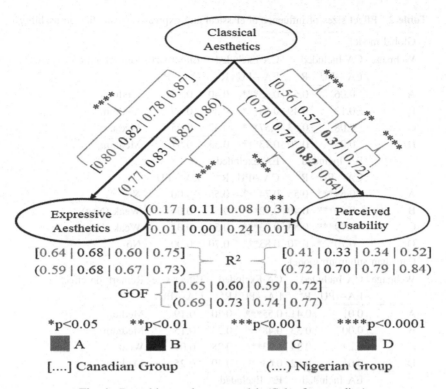

Fig. 4. Data-driven subgroup models (Color figure online)

most of the variance of *expressive aesthetics*, ranging from 69% (for webpages A and B) to 72% (for webpage D). At the subgroup level, to a large extent, we see a replication of the significant path coefficients at the global level, except for path EA→PU, where the path coefficient ($\beta = 0.31$, $p < 0.01$) for mobile webpage D is significant for the Nigerian group (NG), but not in the global and Canadian group (CG) models. Overall, the R^2 of *perceived usability* for all four webpages are higher for the NG (0.72 | 0.70 | 0.79 | 0.84) than for the CG (0.41 | 0.33 | 0.34 | 0.52) by about 30%, indicating the predictive accuracy of the models are higher for a high-context culture than a low-context culture.

5.3   Effect Sizes of Direct Influences

In the effect-size analysis [9] (see Table 2), we found that *expressive aesthetics* (EA) has a significant impact on *perceived usability* (PU) in the absence of *classical aesthetics* in the model. However, once *classical aesthetics* (CA) is controlled for in the model, the impact of *expressive aesthetics* becomes virtually insignificant. For example, for webpages A, B, C and D in the global model, without CA in the model, the path coefficients for EA→PU are (0.63 | 0.54 | 0.57 | 0.73, $p < 0.001$). However, on including CA in the model the path coefficients (0.06 | −0.12 | −0.08 | 0.05, p = n.s)

Table 2. Effect sizes of influence of classical and expressive aesthetics on usability

Global model

Webpage	CA Included		CA Excluded		Effect size	Remark on effect size
	EA→PU	R^2	EA→PU	R^2	CA→PU	
A	0.06	0.55	0.63***	0.40	0.33	Medium
B	−0.12	0.49	0.54***	0.29	0.39	Medium
C	−0.08	0.53	0.57***	0.32	0.45	Medium
D	0.05	0.70	0.73***	0.53	0.57	Medium
	EA Included		EA Excluded			
	CA→PU	R^2	CA→PU	R^2	EA→PU	
A	0.69***	0.55	0.74***	0.55	0.00	No
B	0.80***	0.49	0.72***	0.51	−0.04	Weak (Neg)
C	0.79***	0.53	0.73***	0.54	−0.02	Weak (Neg)
D	0.70***	0.70	0.83***	0.70	0.00	No

Canadian subgroup model

Webpage	CA Included		CA Excluded		Effect size	Remark on effect size
	EA→PU	R^2	EA→PU	R^2	CA→PU	
A	0.01	0.41	0.55***	0.30	0.19	Medium
B	0.00	0.33	0.48***	0.23	0.15	Medium
C	0.24	0.34	0.53***	0.28	0.09	Weak
D	0.01	0.52	0.63***	0.40	0.25	Medium
	EA Included		EA Excluded			
	CA→PU	R^2	CA→PU	R^2	EA→PU	
A	0.56***	0.41	0.65***	0.42	−0.02	Weak (Neg)
B	0.57***	0.33	0.60***	0.36	−0.04	Weak (Neg)
C	0.37**	0.34	0.58***	0.33	0.02	Weak
D	0.72***	0.52	0.73***	0.53	−0.04	Weak (Neg)

Nigerian subgroup model

Webpage	CA Included		CA Excluded		Effect size	Remark on effect size
	EA→PU	R^2	EA→PU	R^2	CA→PU	
A	0.17	0.72	0.71***	0.51	0.75	Large
B	0.11	0.70	0.72***	0.52	0.60	Large
C	0.08	0.79	0.76***	0.58	1.00	Large
D	0.31**	0.84	0.86***	0.74	0.63	Large
	EA Included		EA Excluded			
	CA→PU	R^2	CA→PU	R^2	EA→PU	
A	0.70***	0.72	0.84***	0.70	0.07	Weak
B	0.74***	0.70	0.83***	0.69	0.03	Weak
C	0.82***	0.79	0.89***	0.79	0.00	No
D	0.64***	0.84	0.90***	0.82	0.13	Weak

become insignificant. Further, we see in Table 2 that the effect sizes of CA on PU with respect to all four webpages are larger for the NG (0.75 | 0.60 | 1.00 | 0.63) than they are for the CG (0.19 | 0.15 | 0.09 | 0.25). According to Cohen's guideline [2], effect sizes of magnitudes 0.02, 0.15 and 0.35 represent small, medium and large effect sizes respectively. Thus, the effect sizes with respect to CA→PU for the NG are all large, while those for the CG are mostly medium. This suggests that the magnitude of strength of the relationship between CA and PU is stronger for the NG than for the CG. On the hand, we find that the effect sizes of EA on PU are either weak, non-existent or even negative, as shown in the global and CG models. The negative effect sizes with respect to EA→PU suggest that the models with EA excluded are better than the ones with EA included. This is evident in the R^2 values of both models in contention. For example, in the global model with respect to webpage B, the R^2 for PU is 0.49 when EA is included and 0.51 when EA is excluded. Similarly, in the CG subgroup model with respect to webpage B, the R^2 for PU is 0.33 when EA is included and 0.36 when EA is excluded. This indicates the latter models with EA excluded are better in terms of predictive accuracy, especially if we have to compute the adjusted coefficient of determination, R^2_{adj}, a metric for selecting models and which penalizes a model with more exogenous constructs involved in the prediction of the endogenous construct [9].

5.4   Verification of Hypotheses

We tabulated the results from the verification of all six hypotheses in Table 3. As shown in Table 3, H1, H2 and H4 are fully supported, but H3, H5 and H6 are not. However, H3 and H5 are partially validated. This is represented in Table 3 as "Part". At the global level (see Fig. 3), regarding H1 and H2 with respect to webpages A, B, C and D, the path coefficients for CA→EA are (0.83 | 0.83 | 0.82 | 0.80, p < 0.0001) and those for CA→PU are (0.69 | 0.83 | 0.79 | 0.70, p < 0.0001). These path coefficients are high, indicating a strong validation of H1 and H2 at the global level. At the subgroup level (see Fig. 4), the respective path coefficients for the CG for all webpages are (0.80 | 0.82 | 0.78 | 0.87, p < 0.0001) for CA→EA and (0.56 | 0.57 | 0.37 | 0.72, p < 0.01) for CA→PU. Similarly, the respective path coefficients for the NG for all webpages are (0.77 | 0.83 | 0.82 | 0.86, p < 0.0001) for path CA→EA and (0.70 | 0.74 | 0.82 | 0.64, p < 0.0001) for path CA→PU. These path coefficients at the subgroup level are highly significant as well, for the most part. Therefore, our H1 (*classical aesthetics will positively influence expressive aesthetics*) and H2 (*classical aesthetics will positively influence perceived usability*) are confirmed at the global and subgroup levels.

However, our H3 (*expressive aesthetics will positively influence perceived usability*) is not validated at the global level though partially validated at the subgroup level. At the global level, the path coefficients for EA→PU, ranging from −0.12 to 0.06, are insignificant with respect to all four webpages. Similarly, at the subgroup level, the path coefficients for EA→PU, ranging from 0.00 to 0.24 are insignificant with respect to webpage A, B and C. However, the path coefficient ($\beta = 0.31$, p < 0.01) for EA→PU with respect to webpage D (for the NG), is significant. Nevertheless, the number of significant paths (one out of twelve cases) is not sufficient for us to conclude that H3 is validated. As such, we conclude that our H3 is partially supported.

Table 3. Results of verification of hypotheses

No.	Hypothesis	Path	Supported?		
			Global	CG	NG
H1	*Classical aesthetics* will positively influence *expressive aesthetics*	CA→EA	Yes	Yes	Yes
H2	*Classical aesthetics* will positively influence *perceived usability*	CA→PU	Yes	Yes	Yes
H3	*Expressive aesthetics* will positively influence *perceived usability*	EA→PU	No	No	Part
H4	The influence of *classical aesthetics* on *perceived usability* is stronger than the influence of *expressive aesthetics* on *perceived usability*	CA→PU > EA→PU	Yes	Yes	Yes
H5	The influence of *classical aesthetics* on *perceived usability* will be moderated by culture	CA→PU (culture-moderated)	Part		
H6	The influence of *expressive aesthetics* on *perceived usability* will be moderated by culture	EA→PU (culture-moderated)	No		

Further, we see our H4 (*the influence of classical aesthetics on perceived usability is stronger than the influence of expressive aesthetics on perceived usability*) is validated at both levels of path modeling. At the global level, the path coefficients (0.69 | 0.80 | 0.79 | 0.70, $p < 0.0001$) corresponding to H2 (CA→PU) are greater than the respective path coefficients (0.06 | −0.12 | −0.08 | 0.05, p = n.s) corresponding to H3 EA→PU. H4 is also validated at the subgroup levels: (1) for the CG, the path coefficients (0.56 | 0.57 | 0.37 | 0.72, $p < 0.01$) for CA→PU are greater than the respective path coefficients (0.01 | 0.00 | 0.24 | 0.01, p = n.s) for EA→PU; and (2) for the NG, the path coefficients (0.70 | 0.74 | 0.82 | 0.64, $p < 0.0001$) for CA→PU are greater than the respective path coefficients (0.17, p = n.s | 0.11, p = n.s | 0.08, p = n.s | 0.31, $p < 0.01$) for EA→PU. Therefore, our H4 is strongly supported.

The validation of these three hypotheses (H1, H2 and H4) at the global and subgroup levels is an indication that, irrespective of culture, the respective hypotheses are valid.

Finally, our H5 and H6 on moderation effect by culture are only partially validated, i.e., for webpage C, where culture moderates the path CA→PU, with the NG (a high-context culture) having a higher effect ($\beta = 0.82$, $p < 0.0001$) than the CG (a low-context culture), which has the effect ($\beta = 0.37$, $p < 0.01$).

6 Discussion

We have presented a path model for predicting the *perceived usability* (a utilitarian construct) of a mobile website using the two conceptual and operationalized dimensions of *perceived aesthetics* (a hedonic construct). The different data-fitted models have a moderate to high coefficient of determination (ranging from 30% to 80%), which represents the amount of variance *of perceived usability* accounted for with respect to each mobile webpage. More importantly, based on the four versions of the hypothetical mobile webpage with different levels of aesthetic treatment (low and high), we show that, in the mobile web domain, irrespective of the level of aesthetic treatment and culture, *classical aesthetics* is a stronger predictor of *perceived usability* than *expressive aesthetics*. This indicates, from the conceptualization and operationalization of the two dimensions of *aesthetics* that it is the simplicity and orderliness of a website design—and not its complexity and creativity—that inform their *perceived usability*. In fact, as the models reveal, the perception of the simplicity and orderliness of a website design (*classical aesthetics*), in addition to impacting its *perceived usability*, can impact its perceived creativity and originality (*expressive aesthetics*) as well. Thus, we can conclude, based on these findings represented in our models, that "*what is classical is expressively beautiful and usable.*"

Further, we show that the relationship between *classical aesthetics* and *perceived usability* is likely to be stronger for a high-context culture (Nigeria) than a low-context culture (Canada), as shown in Fig. 5, where, except for webpage D, the path coefficients for this relationship are relatively higher for the Nigerian group than for the Canadian group. This is supported by the effect sizes with respect to all four webpages being larger for the Nigerian group than those for the Canadian group, which range from weak to medium effect sizes. Specifically, for webpage C, we found a significant difference between this relationship for the Nigerian group and that for the Canadian group. The corresponding effect size of this relationship is large for the Nigerian group but weak for the Canadian group. These two findings—(1) the relationship between *classical aesthetics* and *perceived usability* being stronger for the Nigerian group than

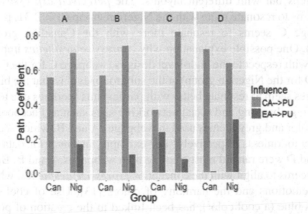

Fig. 5. Visualization of usability-related path coefficients (Color figure online)

it is for the Canadian group with respect to webpage C; and (2) the effect sizes for the Nigerian group being larger than those for the Canadian group with respect to all webpages—indicate that the *classical aesthetics-perceived usability* relationship may be stronger for a high-context culture than a low-context culture. However, this finding requires further research, especially with a different population sample, in order to generalize across high-context and low-context cultures as a whole.

Moreover, there seems to be an interesting observation worth noting regarding webpage C and webpage D (see Fig. 5). For webpage C, relative to the other webpages, the impact of *classical aesthetics* on *perceived usability* (CA→PU) decreases for the Canadian group, while the impact of *expressive aesthetics* on *perceived usability* (EA→PU) increases. On the other hand, with respect to the same webpage C, the impact of *classical aesthetics* on *perceived usability* (CA→PU) increases for the NG, while the impact of *expressive aesthetics* on *perceived usability* (EA→PU) decreases. The reverse is virtually the case for both groups when it comes to webpage D. In other words, *expressive aesthetics* seems to play a more prominent role with respect to webpages C and D (high-level designs) than webpages A and B (low-level designs). As shown in Figs. 4 and 5, with respect to webpage C (list-based, blue-theme webpage) for the Canadian group, *classical aesthetics* and *expressive aesthetics* are relevant in predicting *perceived usability* though the latter impact (EA→PU) did not reach statistical significance, perhaps due to the small sample size of 87 for the Canadian group. However, EA→PU relationship is almost significant (given the p-value = 0.07). This indicates both the perception of *classical aesthetics* and perception of *expressive aesthetics* were important for the Canadian group in predicting the *perceived usability* of webpage C, but *expressive aesthetics* was not important in predicting the *perceived usability* of webpage C for the Nigerian group. On the other hand, both perception of *classical aesthetics* and perception of *expressive aesthetics* were important in predicting *perceived usability* with respect to webpage D (grid-based, blue-theme webpage) for the Nigerian group, but *expressive aesthetics* was not important in predicting the *perceived usability* of webpage D for the Canadian group. This suggests that the impact of *expressive aesthetics* on *usability* (EA→PU) may depend on culture and the level of aesthetic treatment of the web design, as seen with webpages C and D, both of which are high-level designs but with different layouts. The *perceived expressive aesthetics* of webpage D seems to resonate more with the Nigerian group ($\beta = 0.31$, $p < 0.01$), while that of webpage C seems to resonate more with the Canadian group ($\beta = 0.31$, t-value = 1.84). One possible explanation why *expressive aesthetics* impacts *perceived usability* more with respect to the high-level designs (webpage C for the Canadian group and webpage D for the Nigerian group) at the subgroup level is that the blue theme used in both webpages seem to resonate better with participants (perhaps due to its popularity in web design, e.g., banking and social networking sites such as Facebook and Twitter) than the multicolor and grey themes used in webpages A and B, which seem to be out of harmony and emotionless, respectively. For example, in our prior data analysis [14], webpages C and D were ranked most credible than webpages A and B. Besides, the use of blue theme seems to align with the concept of *expressive aesthetics*, which entails the expression of emotions and the harmony of colors [13]. Use of cool colors in web design, such as blue (a cool color), has been linked to the creation of positive impressions, which may help in building credibility and trust in websites [4].

6.1 Comparison Between Previous and Current Study's Models

As shown in Fig. 6, we compare the coefficients of determination of *perceived usability* in the current model (see Fig. 4), where *classical aesthetics* and *expressive aesthetics* are considered as separate predictors of *perceived usability*, with the corresponding coefficients of determination in our previous model [16], where *aesthetics* was considered as a higher-order construct composed of *classical* and *expressive aesthetics* in order to know how the two models are similar or differ. These two models are represented as "composite" and "components" respectively in Fig. 6. The aim of our comparison is to uncover how the coefficient of determination metric of *perceived usability* changes when its predictor *perceived aesthetics* is considered as a composite high-order construct and two separate lower-order dimensional constructs. As shown in the plot, the respective coefficients of determination in the composite and components models are virtually equal, indicating the latter model is as good as the former model [16] in predicting *perceived usability*, if not better given the relatively higher coefficients of determination in the current model, especially for the Nigerian group. The lesson learned from the comparison of these models is that: (1) predicting *perceived usability*, using *perceived aesthetics* as a composite or its two separate dimensions as its antecedents, is likely to give the same result (i.e., coefficient of determination); (2) *classical aesthetics* is the stronger predictor of *perceived usability*; and (3) *expressive aesthetics* is barely a predictor of *perceived usability* when *classical aesthetics* is controlled for in the model. These findings were unknown in the previous model [16], where *perceived aesthetics* was considered as a composite higher-order construct.

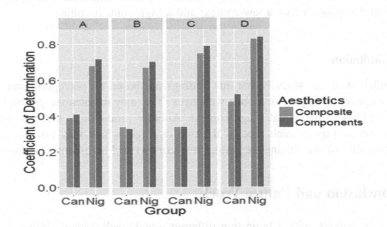

Fig. 6. Visualization of usability coefficient of determination

6.2 Summary and Implication of Findings

In summary, with respect to mobile web design, we conclude as follows. First, it is *perceived classical aesthetics* that predominantly determines *perceived usability*, irrespective of the visual and navigational design of the mobile website. This finding replicates that of Lavie and Tractinsky [13], who found stronger correlation between *classical aesthetics* and *perceived usability* than between *expressive aesthetics* and *perceived usability* in the web domain. It implies that designers of mobile websites should work towards creating sites that are more classically aesthetic (simple) than expressively aesthetic (complex) [13], as the former is what more or less determines *perceived usability*. This may be instrumental to the use of mobile websites given the importance attached to *usability* due to the relatively small screen size of mobile devices. Second, the effect size of *classical aesthetics* on *perceived usability* is higher for a high-context culture (Nigeria) than a low-context culture (Canada). This implies that a high-context culture is much more likely to judge the *usability* of a mobile website based on its *classical aesthetics* than a low-context culture.

6.3   Contributions

Our contribution to the body of knowledge is that we replicated in the mobile domain prior findings in the web domain by Levy and Tractinsky [13] and Coursaris et al. [3] using two different cultures and four different web designs. They include: (1) *classical aesthetics* is stronger than *expressive aesthetics* in predicting *perceived usability*; and (2) *classical aesthetics* strongly influences *expressive aesthetics*. In addition, we showed that differences exist between both cultures: (1) the model for the high-context culture has a higher predictive accuracy than the model for the low-context culture; and (2) the effect size of the relationship between *classical aesthetics* and *perceived usability* is higher for the high-context culture than the low-context culture. Finally, to the best of our knowledge, this is one of the first studies which have investigated the subject of this paper across a low-context and a high-context culture.

6.4   Limitation

The limitation of our study is that our findings are based on perception and not the actual usage of the respective mobile webpages. This may threaten the generalizability of our findings to the actual usage context. Another limitation is that we only considered one country in each type of the two cultures, which may also threaten the generalizability of our findings regarding low-context and high-context cultures.

7   Conclusion and Future Work

Using path analysis, with data on four different mobile web designs collected for two different types of cultures, we presented a model showing that *perceived classical aesthetics* is stronger than *perceived expressive aesthetics* in predicting *perceived usability* of mobile websites, with the effect size being larger for the high-context culture than the low-context culture. Our models account for 30% to 80% of the variance of *perceived usability*. We also showed that the *perceived classical aesthetics* of mobile websites strongly impacts the *perceived expressive aesthetics* for both cultures. The implication of our findings is that designers of mobile websites should focus more on improving the objective aesthetic dimension (*classical aesthetic*) of their websites, which is characterized by simplicity and orderliness, with a view to increasing their *perceived usability*. This has the potential of impacting users' *intention to use* such mobile websites. In future work, we look forward to carrying out qualitative analysis to get a deeper understanding of the relationships among the three constructs of interest and investigating other low-context and high-context cultures in order to generalize our findings.

References

1. Butler, K.A.: Usability engineering turns 10. Interactions 3(1), 58–75 (1996)
2. Cohen, J.: Statistical Power Analysis for the Behavioral Sciences (rev. edn.), 2nd edn. (1988)
3. Coursaris, C.K., et al.: An empirical investigation of color temperature and gender effects on web aesthetics. J. Usability Stud. 3(3), 103–117 (2008)
4. Coursaris, C.K., et al.: Effects of aesthetics and playfulness on web usability – an empirical investigation. In: 16th Americas Conference on Information Systems, p. 549 (2010)
5. Coursaris, C.K., Kripintris, K.: Web aesthetics and usability: an empirical study of white space. Int. J. E-bus. Res. 8(1), 35–53 (2012)
6. Cyr, D.: Modeling Web Site Design Across Cultures: Relationships to Trust, Satisfaction, and E-Loyalty. J. Manag. Inf. Syst. 24(4), 47–72 (2008)
7. Fenech, C., Perkins, B.: The deloitte consumer review Africa: a 21st-century view. Deloitte 32 (2014)
8. Fogg, B.J.: Prominence-interpretation theory: explaining how people assess credibility online. In: CHI 2003 Extended Abstracts on Human Factors in Computing Systems, pp. 722–723 (2003)
9. Hair, J.F., et al.: A Primer on Partial Least Squares Structural Equation Modeling (PLS-SEM). Sage Publications Inc., Washington, DC (2014)
10. Hall, E.T.: Beyond Culture. Anchor, New York (1989)
11. Kumar, N.: Usability for the new PC: mobile devices. In: Third Annual Symposium on Theory Res. HCI (2012)
12. Kurosu, M., et al.: Apparent usability vs. inherent usability: experimental analysis on the determinants of the apparent usability. In: Proceedings of the ACM Conference on Human Factors in Computing Systems, pp. 292–293 (1995)
13. Lavie, T., Tractinsky, N.: Assessing dimensions of perceived visual aesthetics of web sites. Int. J. Hum. Comput Stud. 60(3), 269–298 (2004)
14. Oyibo, K., et al.: An empirical analysis of the perception of mobile website interfaces and the influence of culture. In: Workshop on Personalization in Persuasive Technology (PPT 2016), Salzburg, Austria, pp. 44–56 (2016)
15. Oyibo, K. et al.: Gender difference in the credibility perception of mobile websites: a mixed method approach. In: User Modeling, Adaptation and Personalization (UMAP 2016), pp. 1–10 (2016)
16. Oyibo, K., Vassileva, J.: The interplay of aesthetics, usability and credibility in mobile websites and the moderation by culture. In: Brazilian Symposium on Human Factors in Computer Systems. ACM Press, Sao Paulo (2016)
17. Reinecke, K., Bernstein, A.: Knowing what a user likes: a design science approach to interfaces that adapt to culture. MIS Q. 37(2), 427–453 (2013)

18. Sajan: High-context and low-context cultures : gaining an edge in website localization. https://www.sajan.com/high-context-and-low-context-cultures-gaining-an-edge-in-website-localization/
19. Sanchez, G.: PLS path modeling with R. R News **235** (2013)
20. Sánchez-Franco, M.J., et al.: Users' perception of visual design and the usefulness of a web-based educational tool. Procedia - Soc. Behav. Sci. **93**, 1916–1921 (2013)
21. van Schaik, P., Ling, J.: The role of context in perceptions of the aesthetics of web pages over time. Int. J. Hum. Comput. Stud. **67**(1), 79–89 (2009)
22. Sonderegger, A., et al.: Expressive and classical aesthetics: two distinct concepts with highly similar effect patterns in user–artefact interaction. Behav. Inf. Technol. **33**(11), 1180–1191 (2014)
23. Sonderegger, A., Sauer, J.: The influence of design aesthetics in usability testing: Effects on user performance and perceived usability. Appl. Ergon. **41**(3), 403–410 (2010)
24. Sun, H.: Building a culturally-competent corporate web site: an exploratory study of cultural markers in multilingual web design. Lang. (Baltim). **10**(01), 95–102 (2001)
25. Tractinsky, N.: Toward the study of aesthetics in information technology. In: Proceedings of the ICIS 2004, 62 (2004)
26. Tractinsky, N., et al.: What is beautiful is usable. Interact. Comput. **13**(2), 127–145 (2000)
27. Venkatesh, V., Davis, F.D.: A theoretical extension of the technology acceptance model: Four longitudinal field studies. Inf. Syst. Res. **46**(2), 186–204 (2000)

Application of the Semiotic Inspection Method: A Case Study in Web Domain

Freddy Paz[1(✉)], Freddy A. Paz[2,3], Luis Collantes[2], Manuel Sánchez[3], and José Antonio Pow-Sang[1]

[1] Pontificia Universidad Católica del Perú, San Miguel, Lima 32 Lima, Peru
fpaz@pucp.pe, japowsang@pucp.edu.pe
[2] Universidad Nacional Pedro Ruiz Gallo, Lambayeque, Peru
freddypazsifuentes@yahoo.es, lcollantes@unprg.edu.pe
[3] Universidad César Vallejo - Filial Chiclayo, Lambayeque, Peru
manuelsanchezchero@gmail.com

Abstract. This paper presents the results of a case study, in which the Semiotic Inspection Method (SIM) was applied to a transactional Web application of hotel reservations. The purpose of this assessment was to determine the degree in which the designers achieve to communicate the users their design intents through the system interface. This inspection, whose purpose was essentially academic, involved the participation of three students from the undergraduate program in Computer Engineering. The analysis of the different types of signs allowed to conclude that although there are some aspects that need to be improved, the level of communicability of this software is acceptable.

Keywords: Communicability evaluation · Semiotic inspection method · User interface design · Experimental case study

1 Introduction

Internet is currently a competitive market, especially, for those companies that offer their products and services through the use of the World Wide Web [3]. In this particular environment, where users have at their disposal several Web sites to achieve a specific goal, the quality attributes of the software products become decisive factors for the selection of the most appropriate option. Usability is one of the properties that has always been considered as key factor for the success of a Web application [1]. This attribute is related to the "capability of a software product to be understood, learned, used and attractive to users, when used under specified conditions" [2]. According to Nielsen [4], if a Web site is difficult to use or fails to clearly state what it is offering, people leave. For this reason, an interface must be intuitive, in such a way that users can recognize the meaning of the design elements by direct observation.

The Semiotic Engineering, proposed by de Souza [9], considers the Human-Computer Interaction as a type of communication between users and designers.

© Springer International Publishing AG 2017
A. Marcus and W. Wang (Eds.): DUXU 2017, Part I, LNCS 10288, pp. 463–480, 2017.
DOI: 10.1007/978-3-319-58634-2_34

According to this approach, the graphical interface sends a message to users about how the software product should be used. The most common example is the symbol of a floppy disk. Through the implementation of this sign in the interface, designers are communicating users that can save the progress of their work through the use of this functionality [12]. If all the elements are interpreted by users in the same sense for which they were established, the usability of the system is achieved. This degree in which designers accomplish to convey users their design intents through the system interface is known as *communicability*, and represents the main subject of study of the semiotic engineering [10].

One of the most recognized techniques to determine if an interface meets an appropriate level of communicability is the Semiotic Inspection Method (SIM), which is based on the analysis of all the elements of the graphical interface [11]. This method involves the examination of a large diversity of signs to which users are exposed when they interact with the software product. In this research, we present the results of using the SIM in the Web domain. The system that was selected for this academic case study is *Booking.com*, a worldwide Web site for hotel booking.

2   Semiotic Inspection Method

The Semiotic Engineering is an approach whose purpose is the analysis of the meta-communication between designers and users. According to this theory, the graphical interface of a software product is composed of a series of signs whose intention is to communicate users the way in which the system should be used. If the message is correctly interpreted, users will interact with the proper signs to achieve their goals. These signs can be both, explicit (via text messages with concrete instructions or clear explanations) or implicit (via icons, symbols, metaphors, graphics, patterns, frames, and other forms of design) [5]. From the perspective of the Semiotic Engineering, the interaction between the users and the software is considered a communication in which designers express the system features through signs in the interface, and the user performs actions in response to these messages. Given that the transmission of messages between designers and users is not direct, and on the contrary, is mediated by a graphical interface, this process receives the name of meta-communication [6]. Each element which is developed as part of the design has a purpose, either functional or aesthetic, and the degree in which users achieve to understand the intention of these elements is known as *communicability*.

There are two techniques to evaluate the communicability of a software product: the Semiotic Inspection Method (SIM) and the Communicability Evaluation Method (CEM). The main difference between both techniques is that the SIM involves the participation of specialists in Human-Computer Interaction (HCI), and is focused on the analysis of the several signs that the interface design presents. In contrast, the application of the CEM requires the participation of end-users of the software system. The CEM establishes the observation of users interacting with the software in order to identify communication breakdowns that prevent them from a proper convey of the design intents [7].

In the Semiotic Inspection Method, specialists examine a wide variety of signs to which users are exposed to during the interaction with the software system. The message is sent from the designers to users through design elements which represent the way to activate the different functions of the product. Users perform actions according to what they understand is the proper way to execute a specific product functionality (how the message is interpreted). The system processes the user's request and displays the associated results to these actions in the interface. Designers communicate again through the same interface or new design elements the way to continue the workflow until the achievement of the users' goals. This process which is repetitive represents the main purpose of the SIM. This technique assesses the quality of the meta-communication between designers and users through the analysis of the signs which are established in the interface design. This evaluation allows specialists to identify potential communication problems and offer opportunities for improvement.

The SIM establishes five sequential steps to perform a communicability inspection which are presented as follows [12]. The steps 1, 2 and 3 correspond to a segmented analysis of a specific class of signs. This analysis allows specialists to decompose the meta-communication message, in order to inspect in detail what and how the designers convey messages to users through the use of these signs in the interface design. At the end of each step, the specialists reconstructs the designer's message employing a meta-communication template. Subsequently, in the step 4, the evaluators compare the three meta-communication messages that were generated in previous steps. Messages are not expected to be identical, but at least they must be related. Finally, in step 5, the evaluators judge the quality of the strategies that are employed by the designers to communicate the design intents. Inspectors establish a conclusion about the overall level of communicability of the software product.

1. An analysis of metalinguistic signs.
2. An analysis of static signs.
3. An analysis of dynamic signs.
4. A comparison of the designer's meta-communication message generated in the previous steps.
5. A final evaluation of the inspected system's communicability.

The template that is used to reconstruct the meta-communication message was developed with the purpose of identifying the designer's vision [8]. The interface design tells users how they can or should use the system, why, and to what effects. In this sense, the template consolidates what designers are communicating to the users through the interface. In the text, the first person "I" is referred to the designer (or the design team), and the second person "you" is referred to the user (or the user population). The template is presented as follows.

"Here is my understanding of who you are, what I have learned you want or need to do, in which preferred ways, and why. This is the system that I have therefore designed for you, and this is the way you can or should use it in order to fulfill a range of purposes that fall within this vision".

The SIM defines the three classes of signs that must be analyzed during a communicability evaluation. According to the semiotic engineering approach, the signs to be considered are:

- **Metalinguistic signs:** are used by the designers to explicitly communicate to users through text lines the meanings encoded in the system and how they can be used. Some examples of metalinguistic signs are instructions, descriptions, explanations and the information which is provided to users for an appropriate use of the system.
- **Static signs:** are those whose representation is motionless and persistent in the interface design. The meaning of these signs has to be analyzed without considering the results of the interaction with them. The context of interpretation is limited to the elements that are presented on the interface at a specific point in time. Some examples of static signs are the layout structure, the menu options and the toolbar buttons.
- **Dynamic signs:** are those which produce a system behavior in response to an interaction with them. These signs change the content of the interface or the status of the system as result of the user's action. In contrast to static signs, in this category we analyze the system behavior is associated with this type of signs. Some examples of them are the animations, search buttons and the selection of a particular value in a field.

3   Research Design

3.1   Participants

The communicability inspection was performed by three students of the National University "Pedro Ruiz Gallo" located in Peru. These students were enrolled in a course of "Usability Engineering" that is part of the eighth semester of the Undergraduate Program in Computer Engineering. In order to carry out the evaluation, the participants were trained in the main concepts and principles established by the Semiotic Engineering. They attended two three-hour sessions in which the Semiotic Inspection Method was explained in detail. The lessons incorporated a variety of exercises that provided the students with the abilities to recognize each type of sign. In consequence of this training, the students were able to elaborate the meta-communication template according to the obtained results. All the participants had the same background given that all of them attended the same courses of the program. However, they had no previous experience performing this specific kind of assessment.

3.2   Description of the Software System

The software which was selected to carry out this communicability evaluation is *Booking.com*. This Web site is one of the world leader e-commerce application in booking accommodation online [13]. According to the company records, 1,200,000 room nights are reserved on *Booking.com* each day. The goal of this Web site is to offer the best prices for every type of property, from small, family-run bed and breakfasts to executive apartments and five-star luxury suites.

3.3 Test Design

The test design involved a preparation phase. In this part of the methodological process, the students defined a scenario to guide the evaluation. The case study which was proposed is a real situation based on possible conditions that can arise when a user is looking for an accommodation. The scenario describes a Ph.D. candidate that must travel to Canada to attend an international conference and present a scientific research. The students assumed this role in order to conduct the communicability inspection. The scenario is described as follows:

You are currently a student of the Ph.D Program in Computer Science of the Pontifical Catholic University of Peru (PUCP). As a result of your doctoral research, you have written a scientific paper which describes the development of a new computational theory. Your work has been accepted to be published as part of the proceedings of an international conference that will be held in Toronto - Canada. Therefore, one of your commitment as an author is the presentation and dissertation of your research in the place where the conference will take place. For this reason, you must find an accommodation to stay during the days of the conference. According to your expectations, the hotel should offer a room with a large double bed, private bathroom, hot water, Wi-Fi, air conditioning, and LCD Cable TV. The event date is from 4 to 8 February 2017, and you have a budget of $ 1200 USD for lodging expenses. You will use the website "Booking.com" to find an accommodation that meets these expectations.

The semiotic inspection was performed according to the described scenario in a computer lab at the facilities of the National University "Pedro Ruiz Gallo". In each phase, a different sign category was analyzed. The three students work individually to identify the corresponding signs, using the scenario as a guide for the evaluation process. At the end of each step, the students came together to determine the meta-communication template based on a comprehensive analysis of all the findings.

4 Data Analysis and Results

4.1 Analysis of Metalinguistic Signs

The analysis of the metalinguistic signs has allowed the recognition of those elements that are used by the designers to explain in detail through descriptive messages the proper use of the system and the purpose of certain elements in the interface. In order to perform this type of analysis, the students examined different sections of the software such as help options, dialog boxes, explanatory messages, available guides, online manuals, and system feedback. The first person plural "we" has been used to refer the designers, and the second person "you" to refer the user (who is looking for an accommodation in Canada according to the proposed scenario).

Several metalinguistic signs were identified during the inspection. These elements establish the following messages to users:

1. Figure 1 [A metalinguistic sign about phishing]. 'We' believe that the reason why 'you' are entering the 'Help section and Documentation', is because you have received a fraudulent email. The metalinguistic sign appears as a featured element in the mentioned section. From this fact, evaluators concluded the following message: 'We' believe that most of the users are in this section because they have received a fraudulent email on behalf of *Booking.com*. For this reason, 'we' have placed visible important information for the users who are dealing with this problem.

2. Figure 2 [A metalinguistic sign about frequently asked questions]. 'We' believe that the reason why 'you' are entering the 'Help section and Documentation', is because you have difficulties using the Web site or questions about the reservation process. 'We' have implemented mechanisms that apparently are not intuitive or little understandable. 'We' are aware that 'you' need clear instructions about how to use the system, and in the same way, you require all the information about your reservations and specific explanation about the booking process in the Web site. For this reason, 'we' have placed a set of answers to the recurrent questions of the users, that have been selected based on our experience.

3. Figure 3 [A metalinguistic sign about contact information]. 'We' believe 'you' can be looking for information that is not available in the 'Help section and Documentation'. For this reason, we offer you different ways to contact us.

4. Figure 4 [A metalinguistic sign to remind users to enter the check-in and check-out dates]. 'We' believe 'you' can forget to enter the travel dates when you are trying to make a hotel reservation. Therefore, the system displays the this message to remind you that the check-in and check-out dates are necessary to show the exact room prices for your entire stay.

5. Figure 5 [Metalinguistic sign to remind users to enter the information about destination]. 'We' believe 'you' can forget to enter the name of the city or country in which you are planning to stay. Therefore, we indicate you through this message that the requested information is highly relevant to offer you a list of possibilities.

6. Figure 6 [Metalinguistic sign about the maximum number of days are allowed in a booking]. 'We' believe 'you' may need staying in a place for more than 30 nights. However, this option is not covered by our hotel reservation policy. Therefore, we suggest you establish a period less than or equal to 30 days in order to offer you a list of available accommodations.

Meta-Communication Template According to Metalinguistic Signs
This is my understanding of who you are.

I think you an user with the need to make an hotel reservation, and for this reason you will use my Web site. However, you may experience some difficulties at the moment you interact with my system. Therefore, I provide you with a series of explanatory messages to guide you when these issues arise.

What is phishing?

Phishing is the fraudulent practice of sending emails claiming to be from reputable companies in order to get people to reveal personal information, such as passwords and credit card numbers.

Should I report phishing and suspicious emails?

We take all attempts to illegally collect personal data from our partners and guests very seriously – especially when the intention is to profit from such illicit activity.
If you receive an email that appears to be from Booking.com but you believe may not be authentic, please report it to us immediately.

Fig. 1. Metalinguistic signs about phishing

⊗ Cancellation/Change of a Reservation [See all]	🗐 Payments [See all]	🗐 Property Policies [See all]
Can I cancel or change my reservation through Booking.com? >	I am entering my credit card details. When will I be charged? >	I will be arriving earlier/later than the stated check-in time. Can I still check in? >
If I need to cancel my booking will I pay a cancellation fee? >	Does the hotel need a deposit or payment in advance? >	How can I find a hotel's check-in/check-out times? >
Where can I find the cancellation policy of the hotel? >	Can I pay for my stay in advance? >	How do I get more information about the room or hotel facilities? >
Can I cancel or change a Secret Deal or non-refundable booking? >	Can I pay for my stay at the hotel with a different credit card than the one used to make the reservation? >	I want to check out after the stated check-out time. What should I do? >
How do I know if my booking has been canceled? >		I want a smoking room, but I can only choose a non-smoking room. How can I request a smoking room? >

Fig. 2. Metalinguistic signs about frequently asked questions

What you need to do, in which way, and why.
You need to make an hotel reservation using my Web site. For this reason, the system should display clear instructions to help you to achieve your goals, because some mechanisms may not be intuitive enough for you. It is possible you need assistance and information about the proper use of the system. In these cases, you can access the 'Help section and Documentation' where you can find answers to the most frequently asked questions with all the available ways to contact us.
This is the system I have designed for you and this is the way you can or should use it to achieve the goals that fall within my vision.

We're fast by email. For all general questions, send us an email and we'll get back to you as soon as possible. For urgent requests, you can call us at the numbers below.

Fig. 3. Metalinguistic sign about contact information

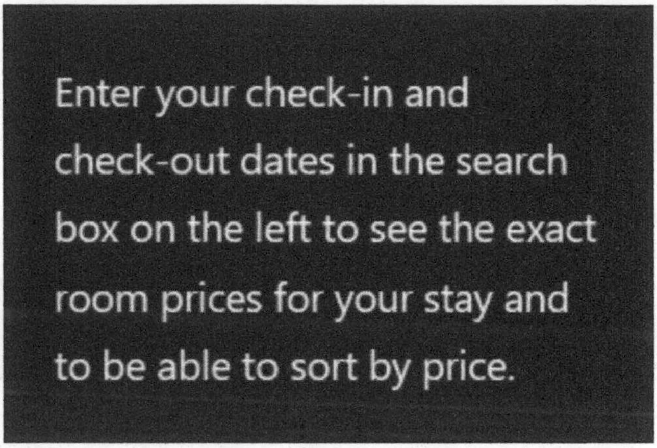

Enter your check-in and
check-out dates in the search
box on the left to see the exact
room prices for your stay and
to be able to sort by price.

Fig. 4. Metalinguistic sign to remind users to enter the travel dates

Please enter a destination to start searching.

Fig. 5. Metalinguistic sign to remind users to enter the information about destination

The system I have designed for you is a fairly explanatory Web site, which is focused on the prevention of errors through the use of messages that allow users to understand the work-flow I have established for you. In case you need assistance and guidance, the system provides a 'Help section and Documentation', where you can find relevant information and a set of instructions for the achievement of your goals.

4.2 Analysis of Static Signs

The analysis of the static signs has allowed the identification of the following messages:

1. Figure 7 [Static signs to access different sections of the system]. 'We' are aware that 'you' can have a specific way to look for the information. Therefore, we have established a section where you can find the accommodations by regions, cities, districts, airports, hotel names and places of interest. In the same way, 'we' believe 'you' can require a different service to the accommodation booking, such as a car rental, a restaurant reservation, a flight,

Sorry, reservations for more than 30 nights are not possible.

Fig. 6. Metalinguistic sign about the maximum number of days are allowed in a booking

etc. Finally, 'we' think 'you' could need information about our company, the booking process or how to use the system (FAQ), our terms and conditions, the ways to contact us, etc.

2. Figure 8 [Static sign about Web site feedback]. If 'you' want to write a comment that can give 'us' some hint on how to improve your interaction with the Web site, you can access this option.

   The message that designers convey through this sign is clear and expresses its intention. However, when the user enters this option, the system displays additional signs to rate the Web site.

3. Figure 9 [Static signs to rate the Web site]. 'We' strongly believe your opinion is important for us. For that reason, we request 'you' to rate your experience with our Web site.

4. Figure 10 [Static signs about currency, language and login account]. 'We' believe 'you' can feel more comfortable if the room prices and the information are displayed in your local currency and language respectively. 'We' think an account in our system will help us to offer 'you', according to your preferences, the best deals and options in accommodation bookings for you. At the same time, you will be able to review your historical record of reservations through this mechanism. Thus, we can deal in a personalized way with any request about the information that is linked to your profile.

5. 'We' believe 'you' understand the meaning of the icons in Table 1 - [Static signs that are used to represent features of the system].

6. 'We' believe 'you' understand the meaning of the textual signs in Table 2 - [Textual static signs that are used to represent features of the system].

7. Figure 11 [Static signs to sort the search results]. 'We' believe 'you' have some preferences to choose an accommodation. We provide you a tool to sort the search results according to your priorities. By default, the system displays a list of possible accommodations sorted by the rating these establishments receive from previous guests.

8. Figure 12 [Static signs about social networks]. 'We' believe that if your experience using the Web site is satisfying, 'you' would like to share it with your friends in the social networks. For this reason, we have placed some options that allow you to link your Facebook, Google+ or Twitter profile with our Web site.

9. Figure 13 [Static signs about suggested destinations]. 'We' believe 'you' could be interested in traveling to certain tourist destinations. Therefore, 'We' provide 'you' some suggestion according to your current location and to the most visited places by those users that are in the same geographical area.

10. Figure 14 [Static signs about hotel facilities]. 'We' believe that for you to make the right decision at the moment of booking, 'you' need to view pictures about the hotel facilities. Therefore, we provide you with a complete image gallery of the hotel rooms and surroundings.

11. Figure 15 [Static signs about the services offered by the hotel]. 'We' believe that for you to make the right decision at the moment of booking, 'you' need

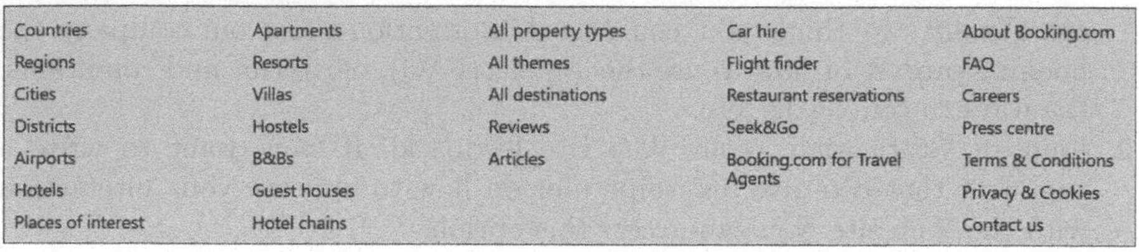

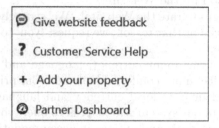

Fig. 7. Static signs to access different sections of the system

Fig. 8. Static sign about Web site feedback

Fig. 9. Static signs to rate the Web site

Fig. 10. Static signs about currency, language and login account

to know the services that are offered by the hotels. Therefore, we provide you with this information in a visible section of the Web site.

Meta-Communication Template According to Static Signs

This is my understanding of who you are.

I imagine you are a user who requires a hotel reservation, but you may also need other services such as car rental, restaurant reservation, air flights, etc. I have designed a usable Web site that is adapted to your cultural environment. However, some mechanisms could be initially difficult to use. For this reason, standard icons have been employed as much as possible for the implementation of the interface. In the same way, textual signs have been designed to indicate the important sections of the Web site. Additionally, I established different workflows in such wise you to find the best option in accommodations.

Table 1. Static signs that are used to represent features of the system

Icon	Meaning
	Accommodation search functionality.
	Calendar to establish the check-in and check-out dates.
	Secret offers for preferred users.
	Relevant information and of interest to users.
	Rating of a hotel based on user reviews.
	Number of stars or hotel category.
	Mobile version of the Web site.
	Smart choice of the accommodation
	Important information about the accommodation.
	Number of people that can occupy the room.
	Frequently asked questions.
	Option to send an email to the Web administrator.
	Outstanding information in the 'Customer Service' section.
	Option to obtain the phone number information of *Booking.com*.
	Option to print the current information is displayed in the Web site.
	Option to send an email to a representative of *Booking.com*.
	Help section and documentation.
	Hotel reviews and opinions.

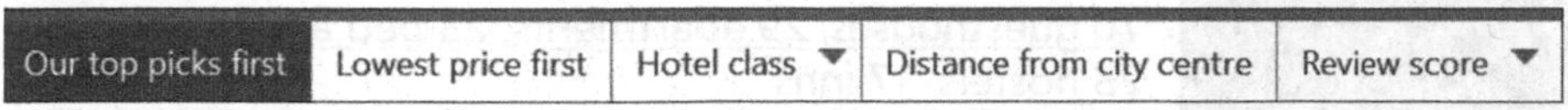

Our top picks first	Lowest price first	Hotel class ▼	Distance from city centre	Review score ▼

Fig. 11. Static signs to sort the search results

Table 2. Textual static signs that are used to represent features of the system

Textual Sign	Meaning
Booking.com	Name of the Web site.
Q Find deals	Indication of the search functionality for deals.
Destination	Section to specify the destination place.
Check-in	Section to specify the check-in date.
Check-out	Section to specify the check-out date.
Rooms	Section to specify the number of rooms.
Adults	Section to specify the number of adults.
Children	Section to specify the number of children.
Search	Button to perform a search of accommodations.

Fig. 12. Static signs about social networks

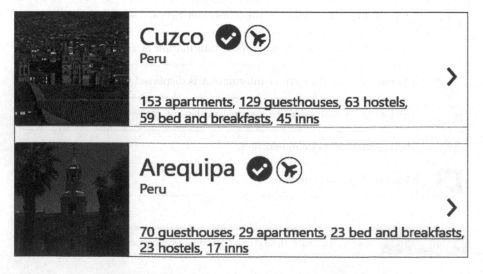

Fig. 13. Static signs about suggested destinations

Fig. 14. Static signs about hotel facilities

Fig. 15. Static signs about the services offered by the hotel

What you need to do, in which way, and why.

You need an accommodation that could cover your requirements. Therefore, the system must display all services that are offered by the hotels. I think you can require suggestions about the most visited tourist places that may be of interest to you. Therefore, the system suggests a list of popular destinations with the associated hotels to each one. I also believe that you need special deals and to find the appropriate accommodation at an affordable price. If we achieve to meet your expectations as a Web site, you would like to recommend us between your friends. For this reason, we have established a way to link our Web application with the social networks.

This is the system I have designed for you and this is the way you can or should use it to achieve the goals that fall within my vision.

The system I have designed allow you to know in detail the services offered by the available hotels in a specific destination, city or tourist place. It provides enough pictures about the facilities and hotel rooms in such a way you can make the right decision regarding your accommodation booking. The Web site offers different tools to determine the best option for you.

4.3   Analysis of Dynamic Signs

The analysis of the dynamic signs has allowed the identification of the following messages:

1. Figure 16 [Dynamic sign to select the language]. 'We' believe that although 'you' are located in a country where a specific language is spoken, you could require viewing the information of the Web site in another one. For this reason, the system provides you a wide variety of languages.
2. Figure 17 [Dynamic sign to select the currency]. 'We' believe 'you' could need to view the room prices in a different currency to the one that is used in your country. We think it may be convenient for you, know the equivalent price in an international currency such as the dollar, the euro or the currency is used in the destination city where you are going to stay. In this way, the system provides the option to display the prices in several currencies.
3. Figure 18 [Dynamic sign about description of hotels]. 'We' believe 'you' need to view the most important features of each hotel is displayed as part of the search results. For this reason, we have designed an interface which highlights the relevant aspects that are of interest to users to make an appropriate decision.
4. Figure 19 [Dynamic sign about location of hotels]. 'We' believe 'you' need to view the exact location of the hotels. Therefore, the system provide you with an interactive map that allows you to view where the hotel is located in reference to certain places of interest.

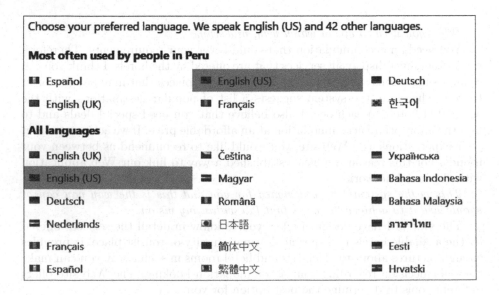

Fig. 16. Dynamic sign to select the language

Top currencies							
€£$	Property's Currency	CAD	Canadian Dollar	PEN	Peruvian Nuevo Sol	S$	Singaporean Dollar
AUD	Australian Dollar	€	Euro	£	Pound Sterling	US$	U.S. Dollar
All currencies							
AR$	Argentine Peso	EGP	Egyptian Pound	MYR	Malaysian Ringgit	lei	Romanian New Leu
AUD	Australian Dollar	€	Euro	MXN	Mexican Peso	RUB	Russian Ruble
AZN	Azerbaijani New Manats	FJD	Fijian Dollar	MDL	Moldovan Leu	SAR	Saudi Arabian Riyal
BHD	Bahrain Dinar	GEL	Georgian Lari	NAD	Namibian Dollar	S$	Singaporean Dollar
R$	Brazilian Real	HK$	Hong Kong Dollar	₪	New Israeli Sheqel	ZAR	South African Rand

Fig. 17. Dynamic sign to select the currency

Fig. 18. Dynamic sign about description of hotels

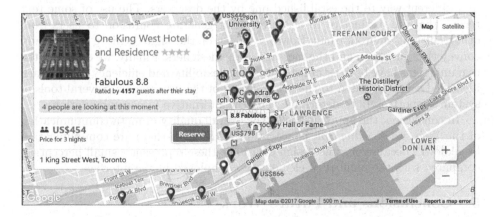

Fig. 19. Dynamic sign about location of hotels

Meta-Communication Template According to Dynamic Signs
This is my understanding of who you are.

I consider you are a user who needs a hotel reservation, and the Web site must provide you with all the tools to achieve this purpose. I think you can be a user from any part of the world who requires viewing the information in several languages and the room prices in different currencies. My opinion is that you are a user with exclusive preferences and because of this fact, I provide you with multiple tools to determine the hotel which meets your expectations.

What you need to do, in which way, and why.

You need to find an accommodation according to your preferences. For this reason, the system provides tools to filter the search results in such way that you can identify the best option in accommodations for you. I think you need to view where the hotels are located and how far they are from some places of interest.

This is the system I have designed for you and this is the way you can or should use it to achieve the goals that fall within my vision.

I have designed a system that will help you to choose the best accommodation for you. The interactive tools adjust the system to your context and help you to determine the proper hotel according to your preferences and expectations.

4.4   Global Quality of the Meta-Communication

The three messages of meta-communication, that were obtained through the examination of the different signs of the interface, are consistent and do not differ from each other.

In the analysis of the meta-linguistic signs, the use of explanatory messages is highlighted. The instructions are clear enough in a way that users can properly use the Web site and therefore, achieve their purpose: the search and reservation of accommodations. In the analysis of the static signs, some communication breakdowns were identified. Certain icons are not explicit and can be interpreted in a different way to the established one by the designers. The use of some text terms, that are distinctive to a context, can generate confusion to users from other cultural environments. However, most of the signs achieve to properly convey their intention and the message of the designers. Finally, we observed the dynamic signs have been established to offer flexibility and efficiency of use. Each identified sign is oriented to the achievement of the user's goals. Several tools of system support users to determine the best alternative in accommodations.

In conclusion, the appreciation of the overall quality of meta-communication of the Web site *Booking.com* is acceptable. Although there are communication breakdowns because of some design decisions, these represent a small percentage compared with the number of elements are employed in the interface.

5   Conclusions and Future Work

According to the Semiotic Engineering approach, the interaction between humans and machines is indeed, a way of communication between designers and users. From this perspective, the interface design is structured of a set of elements that convey users the way in which they can use the system. Each change in the interface design is seen as a message that is sent from the designers to the users. If the message is properly interpreted by the users, they will perform the correct actions to obtain the desired results. In the same way, each action is considered a message from users to designers about what they need from the system. Given that this type of communication is not direct, and by the contrary is mediated by the software, it receives the name of meta-communication. The degree in which this communication succeed is known as communicability.

The Semiotic Inspection Method (SIM) is one of the most used techniques to assess the communicability of a software product. It involves the analysis of three categories of signs to determine the degree in which the designers achieve to communicate their design intents through the system interface. In this paper, we present the results of a case study, where the SIM was applied to a transactional Web application of hotel reservations (*Booking.com*). For this purpose, three students from the undergraduate program in Computer Engineering agreed to participate voluntarily as inspectors. The results of this research establish that the level of communicability of the Web site is acceptable. Three templates were obtained from the analysis of the metalinguistic, static and dynamic signs. Then, these results were compared to identify inconsistencies. According to our study, there are some wrong design decisions given than some signs can be interpreted in more than one way, and there is not a personal customization to the cultural context of the user. Additionally, we have conclude the communicability problems have a strong impact in the usability of a software product, since if the meaning of the elements is not clear, the users will not be able to use the system. Given that both concepts are related, a communicability evaluation can be considered as a verification tool of the degree of usability in a software product.

Most case studies that have been conducted in this area are focused on the evaluation of desktop systems. A significant future contribution would be the application of the Semiotic Inspection Method (SIM) in other domains such as mobile applications, video games, augmented reality applications, and specialized software. Specialists must determine if the method is valid when it is used to evaluate the communicability of new emerging categories of software products. In the same way, it is necessary to determine if the evaluation process can be adapted to obtain more accurate results, especially, in new software domains.

References

1. Flavián, C., Guinalíu, M., Gurrea, R.: The role played by perceived usability, satisfaction and consumer trust on website loyalty. Inf. Manag. **43**(1), 1–14 (2006)
2. ISO: Software engineering – product quality – part 1: Quality model. Standard ISO 9126–1: 2001, International Organization for Standardization, Geneva, Switzerland (2001)
3. Jarvenpaa, S.L., Todd, P.A.: Consumer reactions to electronic shopping on the world wide web. Int. J. Electron. Commer. **1**(2), 59–88 (1996)
4. Nielsen, J.: Usability Engineering, 1st edn. Academic Press, San Diego (1993)

5. Paz, F., Paz, F.A., Pow-Sang, J.A.: Application of the communicability evaluation method to evaluate the user interface design: a case study in web domain. In: Marcus, A. (ed.) DUXU 2016. LNCS, vol. 9746, pp. 479–490. Springer, Cham (2016). doi:10.1007/978-3-319-40409-7_45
6. Prates, R.O., Barbosa, S.D.J., de Souza, C.S.: A case study for evaluating interface design through communicability. In: Proceedings of the 3rd Conference on Designing Interactive Systems: Processes, Practices, Methods, and Techniques, DIS 2000, pp. 308–316. ACM, New York (2000)
7. Reis, S., Prates, R.: An initial analysis of communicability evaluation methods through a case study. In: CHI 2012 Extended Abstracts on Human Factors in Computing Systems, CHI EA 2012, pp. 2615–2620. ACM, New York (2012)
8. de S. Reis, S., Prates, R.O.: Assessing the semiotic inspection method: the evaluators' perspective. In: Proceedings of the 11th Brazilian Symposium on Human Factors in Computing Systems, IHC 2012, pp. 287–296. Brazilian Computer Society, Porto Alegre (2012)
9. de Souza, C.S.: The semiotic engineering of user interface languages. Int. J. Man Mach. Stud. **39**(5), 753–773 (1993)
10. de Souza, C.S., Barbosa, S.D.J., Prates, R.O.: A semiotic engineering approach to user interface design. Knowl.-Based Syst. **14**(8), 461–465 (2001)
11. de Souza, C.S., Leitão, C.F., Prates, R.O., da Silva, E.J.: The semiotic inspection method. In: Proceedings of VII Brazilian Symposium on Human Factors in Computing Systems, IHC 2006, pp. 148–157. ACM, New York (2006)
12. de Souza, C.S., Leitão, C.F.: Semiotic Engineering Methods for Scientific Research in HCI. Morgan & Claypool Publishers, Pennsylvania State University, PA, USA (2009)
13. The Priceline Group: Overview about booking.com (2012). http://www.booking.com/content/about.html. Accessed: 20 Dec 2017

UX Heuristics for Cross-Channel Interactive Scenarios

Adriano Bernardo Renzi[(✉)]

Serviço Nacional de Aprendizagem Comercial/Senac-Rio, Rio de Janeiro, Brazil
adrianorenzi@gmail.com

Abstract. This research presents a set of UX heuristics for cross-channel interaction scenarios. The proposal has its foundation on usability principles evolution derived from gradual technology innovations, new interaction possibilities, as well as, changes in users' needs and affordances during the last decades. The beginning of the third wave of computing brings a pervasive scenario of ubiquitous ecology systems and cross-channel interactions, where user experiences permeate distinct touch points with a system to create a narrative of experience. A journey in a dinamic ecosystem of interaction.

Keywords: User experience · UX heuristics · Cross-channel interaction

1 Introduction: Technology, Interaction and Experience Evolutions

The technology evolution and its crescent integration into our day-to-day lives reverberate in new ways people interact with devices and their surroundings. Faster information, a huge quantity of data in real time, connection possibilities and integration between different channels bring an innovation rhythm faster than people, society, and sometimes laws, can absorb and adapt. As the physical and digital realms have been merging over the years, our references, mental models and expectations have been changing accordingly, transforming human-computer interactions in human-information interactions. And as a reflex from these changes, usability principles evolve and adapt to new circumstances. The future scenario of technology [1] presents interaction possibilities in the next five to ten years where ubiquitous technology will be everywhere in daily objects, environments and wearable devices, integrated by a dynamic ecology system. Therefore, User Experience studies have to go beyond usability tests on isolated devices and understand the whole user experience process as one journey trespassing many devices.

John C. Thomas, PhD, from the IBM J.T. Watson Research Center sees the process of user experience as narratives [2], and he structures it as several short stories with connections and touch points (points in which users interact with the system). Rosenfeld suggests mapping devices used in each story "scene" in order to understand the usage of systems within the whole user's narrative [3]. The idea of narrative as a journey [2] can be used to translate either the Jared Spool's Disney Experience example [4] or the designers' process in managing their studios [2] into experience stories.

© Springer International Publishing AG 2017
A. Marcus and W. Wang (Eds.): DUXU 2017, Part I, LNCS 10288, pp. 481–491, 2017.
DOI: 10.1007/978-3-319-58634-2_35

An usability evaluation could concentrate on the experience of users interacting with a single system, but the whole experience trespasses the system and include moments that are precedent and subsequent to the direct interaction with the system. From the UX Design perspective, products and services have to go beyond the good usability of systems and focus on users' whole journey [2].

2 The Journey of Experience

The user experience as a narrative journey involves actions in the physical world using many different digital devices linked together by a dynamic ecology, with connections that brings together one whole story. For instance, when a person intends to travel for vacation, the experience starts much before the act of buying the flight tickets through a website or an attendant and the experience related to the trip goes much further than the flight itself. Each part of the narrative can involve different digital artifacts accessing the same system in diverse contexts, influenced by the physical part of the experience.

The UX designer has to understand the whole journey in order to plan possible touch points and create a service or product experience integrated by different channels: a pervasive cross-channel experience.

Although usability measurements and tests focus primarily in interactions with isolated devices, a number of user research techniques and usability tests can surface information about users that help understand their mental model, interaction needs and cultural-interaction references in order to better comprehend their journey of experience and map contexts that could take users to interact with specific systems.

Cross-channel scenarios take the user experience to new amplitudes, and therefore, it is necessary to adapt usability principles to a journey experience context. Technology advancements have been gradually influencing and transforming usability heuristics [5] from the late 80 s. These changes are responses to attend new interaction possibilities, new user expectations and new correlations in dynamic systems ecology. Adaptations from Nielsen and Molich's heuristics are clearly observed in heuristic proposals from Apted *et al.* [6] in 2009, Inostrozza [7] in 2012 and Neto and Campos [8] in 2014, as a response to new possibilities of interaction, new display sizes and new users' necessities.

3 Evolution of Heuristics

In 1990, Nielsen and Molich [5] developed a set of usability principles to be considered when planning a system with a visual interaction interface. The ten principles were well known as the ten usability heuristics and became a base for the usability evaluation technique, well known as heuristic evaluation, in which three to five usability experts could be guided to evaluate a system's usability and point out problems within a range of 5 different severities (0- not a problem, 1- cosmetic problem, 2- minor problem, 3- major problem, 4- catastrophe). The heuristics are consecution to users' needs in a time where the world was moving to the second wave of computing (one computer to one user):

1. Visibility of system status – the system should always keep users informed about what is going on, through appropriate feedback within reasonable time;
2. Match between system and the real world – the system should speak the user's language, with words, phrases and concepts familiar to the user, rather than system-oriented terms. Follow real-world conventions, making information appear in a natural and logical order;
3. User control and freedom – users often choose system functions by mistake and will need a clearly marked "emergency exit" to leave the unwanted state without having to go through an extended dialogue. Support undo and redo;
4. Consistency and standards – users should not have to wonder whether different words, situations, or actions mean the same thing. Follow platform conventions;
5. Error prevention – even better than good error messages is a careful design, which prevents a problem from occurring in the first place.
6. Recognition rather than recall – minimize the user's memory load by making objects, actions, and options visible;
7. Flexibility and efficiency of use – accelerators - unseen by the novice user – may often speed up the interaction for the expert user such that the system can cater to both inexperienced and experienced users. Allow users to tailor frequent actions;
8. Aesthetic and minimalist design – dialogues should not contain irrelevant information nor rarely needed. Every extra unit of information in a dialogue competes with the relevant units of information and diminishes their relative visibility;
9. Help users recognize, diagnose, and recover from errors – error messages should be expressed in plain language (no codes), precisely indicate the problem, and constructively suggest a solution;
10. Help and documentation – even though it is better if the system can be used without documentation, it may be necessary to provide help and documentation. Any such information should be easy to search, focused on the user's task, list concrete steps to be carried out, and not be too large.

These ten heuristics had its foundation on Norman's six principles [9] from 1988:

1. Visibility – the more visible functions are, the more likely users will be able to know what to do next;
2. Feedback – feedback is about sending back information about what action has been done and what has been accomplished, allowing the person to continue with the activity;
3. Constraints – the design concept of constraining refers to determining ways of restricting the kind of user interaction that can take place at a given moment;
4. Mapping – this refers to the relationship between controls and their effects in the world;
5. Consistency – this refers to designing interfaces to have similar operations and use similar elements for achieving similar tasks;
6. Affordance – is a term used to refer to an attribute of an object that allows people to know how to use it.

During the same period of Nielsen and Molich, other authors developed similar principles regarding interaction with interfaces. Bastien and Scapin [10] developed eight ergonomic criteria in 1993 for systems' interface evaluation:

1. Orientation – refers to means used to guide, inform and take users to their objectives while interacting with a computer;
2. Workload – refers to elements of the interface to help diminish the perception and memory load while interacting with a computer;
3. Explicit control – the user must always have control of actions;
4. Adaptability – the system should be able to respond accordingly to different contexts, needs and users' preferences;
5. Error management – refers to all means to prevent or reduce errors, as well as correct them, if necessary;
6. Consistency/coherence – refers to how the design interface should be aware of identical contexts;
7. Code importance – adequacy of information or object with respective icons, names, graphic representations etc.;
8. Compatibility – refers to the degree of similarity between applications or ambiences.

And Ben Schneiderman [11], in 1987, based on his research regarding human-computer interaction exposed eight golden rules for user interface:

1. Objective consistency – similar situations requires consistency of actions, terminologies, prompts, menus, screens and help;
2. Shortcuts for frequent users – with use frequency, users prefer diminish number of interactions to increase the flow of interaction;
3. Offer informative feedback – for each action, should be a feedback;
4. Plan windows that encourage completion – sequence of actions must be organized in groups from start to finish;
5. Offer simple objective error recovery – plan a system that prevents users to make critical errors. If a mistake is made, the system should detect it and offer simple action to solve and recover from it;
6. Reverse actions easily – it relieves users' anxiety when knowing an action can be undone;
7. Sustain control – operators must feel they are in control of systems and that it responds to their actions;
8. Short-term memory load reduction – the human limitation of processing information in short-term memory require that displays be simple.

When new necessities derived from new possibilities of interaction, new digital devices, in a new wave in computing (3rd wave of computing - many computers to one user), researchers adapted the 10 usability heuristics of Nielsen and Molich to new contexts and new possibilities.

Apted et al. [6], analyzing tabletop's possibilities of interactions, focused on the difference of display size, its proposal of collaborative interaction (with at least two or more users at the same time) and concern with reorganization of elements.

The researchers present heuristics that takes human reach, physical ergonomics and the possibility of many users at the same time into consideration:

1. Design independently of table size – design for different tabletop sizes and allow flexible resizing of all interface elements;
2. Support reorientation – allow all interface elements to be easily rotated to support users working at any position around the table, and consider users moving around the table while using it;
3. Minimize human reach – consider that users may not be able to physically reach all interface elements;
4. Use large selection points – design independently of tabletop input hardware, but support large input cursors (e.g. human fingers) where possible;
5. Manage interface clutter – support quick removal or hiding of objects on the tabletop, while ensuring management of clutter by one user does not have unwanted side-effects on other users of the table;
6. Use table space efficiently – avoid modal behavior that limits the utilization of table space. Allow arbitrary groupings of interface elements for personal and group spaces;
7. Support private and group interaction – support interaction by a single user or multiple users. Interface elements should be usable by a single user, or used as a shared resource by multiple users, possibly with different goals.

Inostroza [7] in 2012 presents twelve heuristics for smartphone interaction. Based on Nielsen's ten heuristics, Inostroza expresses the heuristic seven (flexibility of use) as "customizations and shortcuts", specify a new eighth heuristic regarding efficiency and performance of use, and add a twelfth heuristic regarding the smaller display size of smartphones and the context of interaction with fingers: physical and ergonomic interaction.

1. Visibility of system status;
2. Match between system and the real world;
3. User control and freedom;
4. Consistency and standards;
5. Error prevention;
6. Minimize the user's memory load;
7. Customization and shortcuts – the device should provide basic and advanced configuration options, allow definition and customization of (or to provide) shortcuts to frequent actions;
8. Efficiency of use and performance – the device should be able to load and display the required information in a reasonable time and minimize the required steps to perform a task;
9. Aesthetic and minimalist design – the device should avoid displaying unwanted information in a defined context of use;
10. Help users recognize, diagnose and recover from errors;
11. Help and documentation;
12. Physical interaction and ergonomics – the device should provide physical buttons or similar for main functionalities, located in recognizable positions by the user, which should fit the natural posture of the user's hands.

When Neto and Campos [8], two years after Inostroza, present their 12 heuristic principles for multi-modal interactive ambiences (a combination of inputs and outputs of several sensory modalities – hearing, smell, taste, touch, sight – as part of a more natural computer communication), it is perceptive the strong relation with the ten heuristics from Nielsen and Molich, added by important points on physical ergonomics and vocal commands, resulting in principles concerned with graphical interface, physical and vocal interaction (organized content, direct manipulation, human range). With exception of the second principle, the first seven heuristics are strongly related to Nielsen and Molich's heuristics, but expanded to vocal possibilities. The eighth to twelfth heuristics are mostly related to physical interaction and clearly related to Apted et al.' proposal [6]. The compatibility heuristic regards the compatibility between the different inputs from several sensors with the central system. Based on Sandrine et al. theories [6] regarding vocal interactions and linguistic limitations in a multi-modal environment, as well as the tendency of people using short commands, the authors add criteria to vocal interaction in their research and set of heuristics: (1) generic vocabulary, (2) simple and direct vocal commands and (3) vocal interaction should be and alternative input, applied to all set of heuristics:

1. Visibility and feedback;
2. Compatibility;
3. Control and freedom;
4. Consistency;
5. Error prevention;
6. Minimum actions;
7. Flexibility of use;
8. Organized content;
9. Error management;
10. Direct manipulation;
11. Changes of orientation;
12. Human range.

A different approach comes from Resmini e Rosatti [12] when they present five principles in their book *Pervasive Architecture Information*. Their main focus is related to information organization, instead of graphical interfaces or physical interaction. Their principles, independent of display sizes nor type of device, are concerned with how users access information in an interactive ecology.

Their manifest, based on new factors that surge with the advancements of ubiquitous technology, presents a set of good practices in information architecture and pervasive experience:

1. Place making – refers to the capacity of user build a sense of self- localization. The principle suggests that the architecture reduces the possibility of users disorientation. The heuristic interconnects conceptually with notions of space, place and context. The space is related to physical elements, objectives, impersonal and stable, while place structure itself in layers, and incorporate psychological characteristics, subjective, experimental, dynamics and existential;

2. Consistency – refers to a model of pervasive information to attend objectives, contexts and users, keeping the same logic in different medias, environments and shift of necessities with time. It is directly related to categorization, classification and taxonomy processes. The heuristic dialogue with labeling and representation systems – metadata, thesaurus and controlled vocabulary;
3. Resilience – refers to capacity of the pervasive information model adapt to specific users, their needs and search strategies and gradually change to fulfill the evolution of users' needs and expectations in different contexts, places and times;
4. Reduction – refers to the capacity of a huge quantity of information management being organized for easy and simple access by users, in order to minimize stress and frustration in a crescent set of information. The heuristic is directly related to the form of how choices and options are presented;
5. Correlation – refers to the relevant connections between pieces of information, services and products to help users reach objectives or stimulate latent needs. Correlation connects integrated environments, users and objects, producing a continuous experience (a journey) and exploratory discoveries in all parts of the ecology.

The authors consider Place-making, Consistency and Resilience as foundation heuristics. Reduction and Correlation are considered related to bringing purpose and complexity to a project.

4 Conclusion: UX Heuristics for Cross-Channel Scenarios

Analyzing the different heuristic proposals by Nielsen and Molich (and Scheiderman, Bastien and Scapin and Norman similarities), Apted et al. and Inostroza, it is perceived that all have their focus primarily on graphical interfaces. The difference among each proposal relies on the influence that different display sizes can have on users' interactions. Neto and Campos expose heuristics for multi modal ambiences with focus on both graphic interfaces (based mostly on Nielsen and Molich's ten heuristics), vocal commands and environment interaction (similar to Apted et al. proposal) that encompasses gestural touch and vocal commands.

Resmini and Rosatti go apart from graphic interfaces and can be applied easily in any device proposed by the other researchers, for its direct relation to information, independent of display. But in order to reach the full journey of experience, it is important to go beyond information organization and propose principles more suited to a UX point of view, since technology and interaction advance fast into more integrated cross-channel experiences in interactive ecologies. Table 1 presents a comparison between all the proposed heuristics throughout the years:

Cross-channel contexts take the user experience to new amplitudes and it is imperative to adapt usability principles to a narrative experience scenario (Fig. 1), as the technological evolution and our interaction with devices and environment have been gradually changing and is expected [1] to evolve to an even more integrated cross-channel experience. A more adequate set of principles to narrative experiences is needed.

Table 1. Comparison of heuristics with different focus and necessities.

Nielsen e Molich (1990)	Apted et al. (2009)	Inostroza (2012)	Neto and Campos (2014)	Resmini and Rosatti (2014)
Desktop	Tabletop	Smartphone	Ambiente	Independent of technological device
Usability of graphic interfaces	Usability of graphic interfaces	Usability of graphic interfaces	Usability of graphic interfaces and physical-vocal interactions	Information architecture
Visibility of system status	Design independently of table size	Visibility of system status	Visibility and feedback	Place-making
Match between system and the real world	Support reorientation	Match between system and the real world	Compatibility	Consistency
User control and freedom	Minimize human reach	User control and freedom	Control and freedom	Resilience
Consistency and standards	Use large selection points	Consistency and standards	Consistency	Reduction
Error prevention	Manage interface clutter	Error prevention	Error prevention	Correlation
Recognition rather than recall	Use table space efficiently	Minimize the user's memory load	Minimum actions	
Flexibility and efficiency of use	Support private and group interaction	Customization and shortcuts	Flexibility of use	
Aesthetic and minimalist design		Efficiency of use and performance	Organized content	
Help users recognize, diagnose and recover from errors		Aesthetic and minimalist design	Error management	
Help and documentation		Help users recognize, diagnose and recover from errors	Direct manipulation	
		Help and documentation	Changes of orientation	
		Physical interaction and ergonomics	Human range	

In order to explore and propose UX cross-channel heuristics, the five principles of Resmini and Rosatti are the perfect start, due to its pervasive cross-channel characteristics and link to the idea of dynamic interaction ecology. However, their descriptions have to expand, considering user experience concepts and its relation to visual

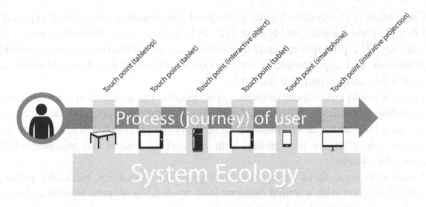

Fig. 1. Construction of an UX narrative through pervasive cross-channel sequence of interactions. Touch points with each apparatus can have diverse temporality and contexts – figure from Renzi's Thesis [2]: *User Experience: the journey of designers in their studio's management processes using a fantasized system based on a ecosystem of cross-channel interaction*

cognitive recognition, physical and verbal interactions and interaction context in a future scenario where everything that can be touch screen, will be touch screen [1]. Furthermore, some of the usability principles that have been evolving with new interaction concepts also have to expand its characteristics in order to contribute to a set of 9 UX heuristics:

1. Place-making – refers to the self localization of users in the system and within the experience journey. Visual interaction, hierarchical layout and structure, as well as physical environment should facilitate the user's understanding of where he is. Since users most likely will use different devices and the ambience itself [1] to fulfill objectives, it is important that physical environments also be part of the user experience strategies to create an integrated journey;

2. Consistency – the system has to present visual, typographic, information, actions and interaction consistency. If a user utilizes different devices to execute partial actions of the whole experience, each touch point access has to present the same rules and responses to actions, independent of the artifact that is being used;

3. Resilience – flexibility of the interaction flow and touch points in order to adequate to different users, different journey strategies and different contexts of use. The interactive ambiance and the system structure should be prepared to search, inter-action and journey diverse strategies by different users, sometimes with distinct roles in the same journey;

4. Reduction – even if the back-end of the system is complex in its structure, the options and the contents have to be presented to the users in objective way and with simple usage, providing reduced interactive actions and minimum cognitive workload in their journey. From the users' point of view, the path of possible actions has to be obvious to their necessities;

5. Correlation – the system has to go beyond the semantic correlation exposed by Lévy [13] and Resmini and Rosatti [12], to help users find information and content naturally. The principle expands to a correlation of data between distinct points of interaction and apparatuses, as well as correlation of actions from different users within the same experience journey;

6. Equivalency to cultural conventions – it is important to understand users' references regarding technology, processes, functionality comprehension and interactions, to use as a base in the development of a new system. To create structures and interactions that users are not familiar with can surface doubts and misunderstanding about the system;

7. Visual intuitive content – users must recognize functionalities, hierarchy, pathways and information with minimal memory load, by making objects, actions and options easy to recognize and understand;

8. Natural, intuitive and direct interactions – any touch point of interaction with the system should be as intuitive as possible, by direct gestural manipulation or objective simple vocal commands;

9. Contextual ergonomics – physical environments, contexts of use within the journey of experience and human physical limitations should be considered while projecting touch points of interaction with the system.

The concept of journey points to an approximation between UX Design, Pervasive Information Architecture and Service Design, with focus on the physical-digital integrated experience in one whole narrative. It is expected that the nine heuristics proposal can help further investigate these relations. New experiments are needed to compare its effectiveness in different contexts.

References

1. Renzi, A.B., Freitas, S.F.: Delphi method to explore future scenario possibilities on technology and HCI. In: Marcus, A. (ed.) DUXU 2015. LNCS, vol. 9186, pp. 644–653. Springer, Cham (2015). doi:10.1007/978-3-319-20886-2_60
2. Renzi, A.B.: Experiência do ususário: a jornada de Designers nos processos de gestão de suas empresas de pequeno porte utilizando sistema fantasiado em ecossistema de interação cross-channel. Doctorate thesis, 239 p. Escola Superior de Desenho Industrial, Rio de Janeiro, Brazil (2016)
3. Rosenfeld, L.: Storytelling for UX: designing with experience plotting (2013). http://rosenfeldmedia.com/storytelling-for-ux/storytelling-for-uxd-Designing
4. Spool, J.: Mobile & UX: Inside the Eye of the Perfect Storm. Interaction South America, Recife (2013)
5. Nielsen, J.: 10 usability heuristics for interface design (1995). www.nngroup.com/articles/ten-usability-heuristics
6. Apted, T., Collins, A., Kay, J.: Heuristics to support design of new software for interaction at tabletops. In: 2009 Computer-Human Interactions, Boston, MA (2009)
7. Inostroza, R., Rusu, C., Roncaglioso, R., Rusu, V.: Usability heuristics for touchscreen-based mobile devices. In: 9th International Conference on Information Technology, Temuco, Chile. IEEE Computer Society (2013)

8. Vilar Neto, E., Campos, F.F.C.: Evaluating the usability on multimodal interfaces: a case study on tablets applications. In: Marcus, A. (ed.) DUXU 2014. LNCS, vol. 8517, pp. 484–495. Springer, Cham (2014). doi:10.1007/978-3-319-07668-3_47

9. Renzi, A.B.: Usabilidade na procura e compra de livros em livrarias online. Dissertation (Master of Science). Esdi – UERJ, Rio de Janeiro (2010)

10. Bastien, C.; Scapin, D.L.: Critères Ergonomiques pour l'Évaluation d'Interfaces Utilisateurs (version 2.1). INRIE. Relatório Técnico No. 156. Paris (1993)

11. Schneiderman, B., Plaisant, C.: Designing the User Interface. Addison Wesley, Boston (1986)

12. Resmini, A., Rosatti, L.: Pervasive Information Architecture – Designing Cross-Channel User Experiences. Morgan Kaufmann – inprint of Elsevier, Burlington (2011)

13. Lévy, P.: Tecnologias da inteligencia: o futuro do pensamento na era da informática, 203f. Editora 34, São Paulo, SP (1993)

A Systematic Review of User Experience Evaluation Methods in Information Driven Websites

Ana Cecilia Ten[✉] and Freddy Paz

Pontificia Universidad Católica del Perú, Lima, Peru
aten@pucp.edu.pe, fpaz@pucp.pe

Abstract. Information driven websites main goal is to provide updated and relevant content to the user according to business goals. Website's user experience evaluation differs from transactional web applications such as e-commerce, e-banking or travel because in addition to usability and accessibility; aesthetics, content, trust and persuasion must be considered for project success. However, since user experience is an emergent field with several frameworks and methods, it's necessary to evaluate which ones have been used previously. This paper presents the results of a systematic review aimed to identify the state of the art in methods, tools and criteria used to evaluate the user experience in information driven websites.

Keywords: User experience · Usability · Website · Method · Systematic review

1 Introduction

At present, most organizations in the public or private sector own one or more websites for communication purposes [1]. The main goal of these applications is to provide the user with access to updated and relevant content [2] about the products and services of the organization that owns the property. User profiles, communication goals and content structure can change depending on the industry [3]: government websites can be focused with giving to the general population an understanding about administrative process and legislation, higher education institutions can be focused in providing information about their academic programs and admissions, banking with promoting of a portfolio of services and so on.

Because information driven websites are publicly available and do not have necessarily a captive audience, usability and user experience are critical factors for user retention and in consequence, to the project success [4]. By contrast, other web applications such as e-commerce, e-banking or intranets have registered users that have already been convinced of using the service provided by the organization that owns the application. Information driven websites are usually in the early stages of the user/customer acquisition process [5]. This means that generic approaches for user experience or usability evaluation won't address the specific nuances that define

A. Marcus and W. Wang (Eds.): DUXU 2017, Part I, LNCS 10288, pp. 492–506, 2017.
DOI: 10.1007/978-3-319-58634-2_36

success for web applications that are driven by information acquisition, brand representation, persuasion [6] and trust [7].

We understand usability and user experience by the following definitions, as specified in the ISO 9241 standard [8]:

- **Usability:** An extension in which a system, product or service can be used by specific users to achieve determined goals with effectiveness, efficiency and satisfaction in the defined context of use.
- **User Experience (UX):** Extends the concept of usability (effectiveness, efficiency and satisfaction) to the perception and responses resulting from the use and/or anticipated use of a product, system or service.

Because information driven websites are the sum of its parts (software, content, brand identity and visual design) they require to be evaluated at the user experience level including the following criteria: usability, content, navigation, aesthetics, performance, and the emotional response of the user after completing the task they wished to accomplish [9]. However, most of the times website development is treated as software project that addresses only the customization or creation of a Content Management System (CMS). CMS is a computer application that allows publishing, editing and modifying content, organizing, deleting as well as maintenance from a central interface [10]. This means both content and emotion can't be evaluated because they are aspects that are out of the bounds of the software development process. Because the extent and nature of the content defines the website's navigation [11] and the aesthetics of the visual design, this approach can lead to navigation issues and designs that are not suitable to the content they display, which in turn can result in usability issues because it's hard for the user to accomplish an information seeking task. This can lead to user frustration, and impact the user's perception of the brand, since he can translate the poor user experience he had while using the website as an attribute of the brand that owns it.

The systematic review presented in this paper seeks to recognize the state of the art in methods, tools and criteria used to evaluate user experience for information driven websites. The organization of this paper is as follows: Sect. 2 details the process performed for the systematic review (criteria and process of selection of studies), Sect. 3 shows the results obtained, and Sect. 4 the conclusions and future work.

2   Systematic Review

The systematic review presented below was executed according to the parameters provided by Kitchenham and Charters [12]. The activities carried out for the implementation of the review were: definition of research questions, definition of the search chain and inclusion and exclusion criteria, selection of primary studies, data extraction, and synthesis of results.

2.1 Research Questions

For the definition of the research questions we used the PICOC technique (population, intervention, comparison, results and context:

Criteria	Value
Population	Websites and portals
Intervention	Methods, tools and criteria for usability and user experience evaluation
Result	Identify de efficiency and effectiveness of the methods and tools used to evaluate the usability and user experience from existing studies
Context	Primary studies that present and evaluate the performance or new, existing or combination of existing methods, tools and criteria for the evaluation of usability and/or user experience in websites, microsites, portals and mobile websites. Studies must include the validation of the proposed methods at some level

The defined research questions are:

- What methods, tools and criteria are used to evaluate user experience and usability in websites?
- Which aspects of the user experience are considered for evaluation?
- At what stage of development does the evaluation apply?
- Efficiency and effectiveness: how satisfactory were the results obtained? How much did they cost in terms of time and resources?

2.2 Search Strategy

Search terms. For the extraction of studies the criteria of population, intervention, result and context were considered.

- T1 = framework OR tool OR technique OR groundwork OR approach OR scheme OR plan
- T2 = user experience OR ux OR customer experience OR cx OR usability OR User centered design OR interaction design
- T3 = website OR websites OR site OR Web page

The databases used for the gathering of information are: Web of science, IEE y Scopus

2.3 Study Selection

Papers that fall in the following categories were included:

- Papers that present surveys, case studies or experiments of one or more methods or tools for the evaluation of usability or other aspects of user experience. The paper must include the description of the empirical validation process of the proposed method.

- Empirical studies that show comparisons between two or more methods/tools or combination of them.

Documents with the following characteristics were excluded:

- Tools and methods for mobile app usability/accessibility testing, since they are mostly focused in complex functionality/tasks.
- Articles that condense previous knowledge, collections of best practices and recommendations that are not applied to a specific case, reflections upon existing metrics or models.
- Tools and methods for usability/accessibility evaluation of web applications/ websites which main goal is other than informative, for example, websites focused in ecommerce or eLearning.
- Methods focused only in the requirement generation process, since they do not validate the method results in the context of a real project.
- Studies focused only in the optimization of search processes or form submission.
- Excluded studies that are only focused on accessibility for a specific group, for example, blind users.
- Papers that focus on the software development process of applications for expert analysis.
- Work in progress that describe the data gathering process (usually web logs), but are not applied to a specific case.
- Complimentary tools proposed for the usability testing process (not fully described methods).

2.4   Data Extraction

32 results were obtained from the Web of Science database. Of these, 13 were relevant according to the selection criteria. 161 results were obtained from the IEE database. Of these, 32 were relevant according to the selection criteria. 46 results were obtained from the Ebsco research database. Of these, 20 were relevant according to the selection criteria. The final count of evaluated studies is 65. The following table shows the list of recovered studies, including the code that was assigned to each of them as part of the systematic review process (Table 1).

2.5   Synthesis Strategy

The studies were grouped following the following criteria:
   1st research question: Method and tools

- Method: Identifies the methodology approach selected for the study. Values are: User testing, Expert evaluation, Automated, Data mining. A paper can have more than one category.

Table 1. List of the reviewed studies.

ID	Author	Title
1	M. H. N. M. Nasir; N. H. Hassan; M. K. M. Nor	Participatory user centered design techniques for a web information system for stroke
2	Adepoju, SA; Shehu, IS	Usability evaluation of academic websites using automated tools
3	Hinchliffe, A; Mummery, WK	Applying usability testing techniques to improve a health promotion website
4	Erickson, William; Trerise, Sharon; Lee, Camille; VanLooy, Sara; Knowlton, Samuel; Bruyère, Susanne	The accessibility and usability of college websites: Is your website presenting barriers to potential students?
5	H. M. Grady	Web site design: A case study in usability testing using paper prototypes
6	Kanayama, T; Ogasawara, H; Kimijima, H; Kontio, J; Conradi, R	Quality control techniques for constructing attractive corporate websites: Usability in relation to the popularity ranking of websites
7	E. Olmsted-Hawala	Card sorting, information architecture and usability: Adding in our users' perspective to re-design the census bureau web site
8	Jeong, Wooseob; Han, Hye Jung	Usability study on newspaper mobile websites
9	D. Alonso-Ríos; I. Luis-Vázquez; E. Mosqueira-Rey; V. Moret-Bonillo; B. B. del Río	An HTML analyzer for the study of web usability
10	Wan Fatimah Wan Ahmad; S. Sulaiman; Farah Syahidah Johari	Usability Management System (USEMATE): A web-based automated system for managing usability testing systematically
11	Saremi, HQ; Montazer, GA; Ardil, C	Web usability: A fuzzy approach to the navigation structure enhancement in a website system, case of iranian civil aviation organization website
12	Danielson, Carla Kmett; McCauley, Jenna L.; Gros, Kirstin Stauffacher; Jones, Andrea M.; Barr, Simone C.; Borkman, April L.; Bryant, Brittany G.; Ruggiero, Kenneth J. Health	SiHLEWeb.com: Development and usability testing of an evidence-based HIV prevention website for female African-American adolescents
13	Herendy, C; Godart, C; Gronau, N; Sharma, S; Canals, G	How to research people's first impressions of websites? eye-tracking as a usability inspection method and online focus group research
14	P. Weichbroth; K. Redlarski; I. Garnik	Eye-tracking web usability research
15	Cappel, James J.; Zhenyu Huang	A usability analysis of company websites

(continued)

Table 1. (*continued*)

ID	Author	Title
16	Georgiakakis, P; Retalis, S; Psaromiligkos, Y; Papadimitriou, G; Jacko, JA	DEPTH TOOLKIT: A web-based tool for designing and executing usability evaluations of e-sites based on design patterns
17	T. Conte; J. Massolar; E. Mendes; G. H. Travassos	Web usability inspection technique based on design perspectives
18	N. Borovina; D. Bošković; J. Dizdarević; K. Bulja; A. Salihbegović	Heuristic based evaluation of Mobile Services web portal usability
19	A. Sutcliffe	Assessing the reliability of heuristic evaluation for Web site attractiveness and usability
20	D. Davis; S. Jiang	Usability evaluation of web-based interfaces for Type2 Diabetes Mellitus
21	T. Conte; V. Vaz; J. Massolar; E. Mendes; G. H. Travassos	Improving a web usability inspection technique using qualitative and quantitative data from an observational study
22	Alotaibi, MB; Latifi, S	Assessing the usability of university websites in Saudi Arabia: A heuristic evaluation approach
23	Torrente, MCS; Prieto, ABM; Gutierrez, DA; de Sagastegui, MEA	Sirius: A heuristic-based framework for measuring web usability adapted to the type of website
24	A. Paula Afonso; J. Reis Lima; M. Perez Cota	Assessing the usability of Web interfaces
25	D. Zimmerman; M. Slater; P. Kendall	Risk communication and usability case study: implications for Web site design
26	A. Al-Wabil; H. Al-Khalifa	A framework for integrating usability evaluations methods: The Mawhiba web portal case study
27	A. P. Afonso; J. R. Lima; M. P. Cota	A heuristic evaluation of usability of Web interfaces
28	A. P. Afonso; M. J. Angélico; J. R. Lima; M. P. Cota	UsaWeb. A model for usability evaluation web interfaces
29	N. B. N. Rozali; M. Y. B. Said	Usability testing on government agencies web portal: A study on Ministry of Education Malaysia (MOE) web portal
30	Johnson, Melissa A.; Norris Martin, Kelly.	When navigation trumps visual dynamism: hospital website usability and credibility
31	Nyman, Samuel R.; Yardley, Lucy	Usability and acceptability of a website that provides tailored advice on falls prevention activities for older people

(*continued*)

Table 1. (*continued*)

ID	Author	Title
32	Margolin, Jonathan; Miller, Shazia Rafiullah; Rosenbaum, James E	The community college website as virtual advisor: A usability study
33	Isa, WARWM; Yusoff, MM; Nordin, DAA; Berry, MW; Mohamed, AH; Wah, YB	Evaluating the usability of homestay websites in Malaysia using automated tools
34	Peute, LW; Knijnenburg, SL; Kremer, LC; Jaspers, MWM	A concise and practical framework for the development and usability evaluation of patient information websites
35	Aizpurua, Amaia; Harper, Simon; Vigo, Markel	Exploring the relationship between web accessibility and user experience
36	L. Rivero; T. Conte	Using an empirical study to evaluate the feasibility of a new usability inspection technique for paper based prototypes of web applications
37	Tolliver, Robert L.; Carter, David S.; Chapman, Suzanne E.; Edwards, Phillip M.; Fisher, Jeanie E.; Haines, Annette L.; Krolikowski, Lana E.; Price, Rebecca M	Website redesign and testing with a usability consultant: lessons learned
38	O'Brien, Heather L.; Lebow, Mahria	Mixed-methods approach to measuring user experience in online news interactions
39	A. P. Afonso; J. R. Lima; M. P. Cota	Usability assessment of web interfaces: User testing
40	P. Fernandes; T. Conte; B. Bonif'cio	WE-QT: A web usability inspection technique to support novice inspectors
41	U. K. Yusof; L. K. Khaw; H. Y. Ch'ng; B. J. Neow	Balancing between usability and aesthetics of Web design
42	Lepkowska-White, Elzbieta; Imboden, Kate	Effective design for usability and interaction: the case of art museum websites
43	Tisinger, Russell; Stroud, Natalie; Meltzer, Kimberly; Mueller, Brett; Gans, Rachel	Creating political websites: Balancing complexity & usability
44	Law, Rob; Ngai, Cathy	Usability of travel websites: A case study of the perceptions of Hong Kong travelers
45	Sundeen, Todd; Vince Garland, Krista; Wienke, Wilfred	Perceptions of special education doctoral websites: A multiyear investigation of website usability and navigability
46	Aranyi, Gabor; van Schaik, Paul	Modeling user experience with news websites
47	Seckler, Mirjam; Heinz, Silvia; Forde, Seamus; Tuch, Alexandre N.; Opwis, Klaus	Trust and distrust on the web: User experiences and website characteristics

(*continued*)

Table 1. (*continued*)

ID	Author	Title
48	bin Ahmad, MA; Iahad, NA	Websites usability instrument validation using think-aloud method
49	Jian-Li Duan; Shu-Xia Liu	Application on web mining for web usability analysis
50	Venkatesh, Viswanath; Hoehle, Hartmut; Aljafari, Ruba	A usability evaluation of the Obamacare website
51	S. Khodambashi; Ø. Nytrø	Usability evaluation of published clinical guidelines on the web: A case study
52	L. Triacca; A. Inversini; D. Bolchini	Evaluating web usability with MiLE+
53	W. A. R. W. M. Isa; A. M. Lokman; E. S. A. Wahid; R. Sulaiman	Usability testing research framework: Case of handicraft web-based system
54	A. Granic; I. Mitrovic; N. Marangunic	Usability evaluation of web portals
55	Zhao Huang; Benyoucef, Morad	Usability and credibility of e-government websites
56	Van Waes, L	Thinking aloud as a method for testing the usability of websites: The influence of task variation on the evaluation of hypertext
57	E. L. Olmsted-Hawala; E. D. Murphy; S. Hawala; K. T. Ashenfelter	Think-aloud protocols: Analyzing three different think-aloud protocols with counts of verbalized frustrations in a usability study of an information-rich website
58	Hatter, Alicia; Howard, Tharon	Intentional Bias: an empirical study of interpellative user experiences on university donor websites
59	Nicolson, DJ; Knapp, P; Gardner, P; Raynor, DK	Combining Concurrent and Sequential Methods to Examine the Usability and Readability of Websites With Information About Medicines
60	Cunningham, Anna; Johnson, Frances	Exploring trust in online health information: a study of user experiences of patients.co.uk
61	M. Swaak; M. de Jong; P. de Vries	Effects of information usefulness, visual attractiveness, and usability on web visitors' trust and behavioral intentions
62	T. Lau	Toward a user-centered web design: lessons learned from user feedback
63	R. Geng; J. Tian	Improving web navigation usability by comparing actual and anticipated usage
64	Chun-hung Li; Chui-chun Kit	Web structure mining for usability analysis
65	N. Harrati; I. Bouchrika; A. Tari; A. Ladjailia	Automating the evaluation of usability remotely for web applications via a model-based approach

- Tools: Identifies the tools that were used for the research: card sorting, questionnaire, focus group, observation or the think aloud protocol.

  2nd research question: Aspects of evaluation

- Criteria: Specific criteria applied in the study. Values are: Accessibility, Usability, User experience, Content, Aesthetics, Information architecture, trust, emotion.

  3rd research question: Stage in the development process.

- Development phase: Stage in the software development process in which the research was applied.

  4th research question: Efficiency and efficacy

- Satisfaction obtained from the proposed method application.
- Cost to apply the proposed research methodology in terms of people, time and money: low, medium, high.
- Level of technical expertise required from the evaluator: low, medium, high.

Additionally, we observed the number of evaluated sites: Some approaches are at the level of proposal, which means they have been tested with very few websites.

3 Results

With regard to the method used, the results show that 47% of the selected studies used some form of user testing, and 27% used expert evaluation. 12% studies used a combination of user testing and expert evaluation, and 8% used data mining techniques that included content mining and pattern identification in links or content. The remaining 6% other methods that include automated tools focused in the evaluation of usability and accessibility (usually using a tool that implements the latest version of the Web Content Accessibility Guidelines - WCAG specification [13] that requires the input of the website url to perform a compliance analysis), analytics to identify navigation patterns or modifications in the software development process to incorporate tasks that prevent known usability issues. Remote testing was applied in some studies that implemented user testing to reduce costs in time and subject availability (Table 2).

With regard to the tools used, the results show that the most frequently used tool is questionnaires, which are used as a guide to give structure to the user testing process while applying interviews, focus groups and the think aloud method. Questionnaires can also be directly applied to the user as a data collection tool by itself (System Usability Scale - SUS) [14]. Heuristic evaluation was used as the tool of choice for expert evaluation. The most frequently used specification was the heuristics set proposed by Jacob Nielsen [15]. Other specifications used for the expert evaluation process were the Microsoft Usability Guidelines [16], custom measures derived from other knowledge field such as psychology (psychometric scales) or a combination and adaptation of an existing heuristics set with new measures proposed by the researcher.

Interviews were used as a complimentary tool, mostly to obtain information of aspects of the user experience that were difficult to measure because of their subjective

Table 2. Methods used in reviewed studies.

Method	Times used	Studies
User testing	29	[7], [8], [9], [10], [11], [31], [32], [33], [34], [35], [36], [37], [38], [39], [40], [51], [52], [53], [54], [55], [56], [57], [58], [59], [60], [61], [62], [63], [64]
Expert evaluation	15	[4], [5], [6], [20], [21], [22], [23], [24], [25], [26], [27], [28], [46], [47], [48], [49]
User testing, expert evaluation	9	[12], [13], [41], [42], [43], [44], [45], [65]
Data mining	3	[15], [17], [18]
Automated	2	[2], [14]
User testing, self-report	1	[50]
Analytics	1	[1]
Automated, data mining	1	[3]
Automated, user testing	1	[15]
Data mining, user testing	1	[19]
Guidelines	1	[29]
Software Development flow modification	1	[30]

nature (emotions, attitudes or trust), and also to explain user behavior in specific contexts.

The think aloud method was used in combination with direct observation and task completion. Focus groups were mostly used to discuss expectations and perceptions. Card sorting was used specifically to identify improvements in the navigation of the website, by proposing an optimized information architecture from existing terms. Web logs, data mining and clickstream analytics were used to identify patterns in user navigation. Eye tracking was used to examine fixations in existing visual designs. Benchmarking was used as a tool in the early planning moments to compare existing websites in an specific industry with the goal of defining usability requirements for the implementation or critical content. Paper and digital prototypes were used as a tool in both early planning and development phases. Other tools as webmaster emails, word prompts and psychometric scales were used scarcely as a complimentary to existing methods. One study proposed software to improve the efficiency of the usability process by means of providing an application that contains all the information generated during the evaluation process (Table 3).

With regard to the criteria used for the evaluation, the results show that usability is the most commonly evaluated aspect, followed by content, aesthetics and information architecture (navigation). User experience is mentioned as a research goal but it's always decomposed in more specific aspects, usually the above mentioned content, aesthetics and information architecture, or custom measures proposed by the researcher conditioned to the website's industry. Task completion is also frequently measured;

Table 3. Tools used in the reviewed studies

Tool	Times used	Studies
Analytics	1	[38]
Benchmarking	2	[5], [6]
Card sorting	4	[1], [7], [26], [37]
Custom measures	1	[8]
Custom software	2	[9], [10]
Eye tracking	3	[13], [14], [26]
Focus group	6	[1], [13], [26], [28], [34], [62]
Guideline	2	[15], [16]
Heuristic evaluation	16	[16], [17], [18], [19], [20], [21], [22], [23], [24], [25], [26], [27], [28], [34], [52], [54]
Interview	14	[1], [3], [28], [29], [30], [31], [32], [35], [37], [39], [48], [51], [54], [60]
Link checker	3	[2], [4], [33]
Observation	7	[3], [6], [29], [35], [51], [55], [59]
Psychometric scale	1	[38]
Questionnaire	25	[3], [6], [24], [25], [28], [29], [30], [31], [35], [38], [39], [40], [41], [42], [43], [44], [45], [46], [47], [48], [53], [54], [55], [61], [64]
Survey	6	[26], [32], [47], [50], [51], [62]
Task completion	12	[4], [25], [26], [30], [48], [51], [52], [53], [54], [55], [63], [65]
Think aloud method	13	[14], [25], [26], [31], [32], [34], [48], [56], [57], [58], [59], [60], [61]
Web log	5	[3], [11], [63], [64], [65]
Webmaster emails	1	[62]
Word prompt	1	[35]
Prototype	7	[5], [29], [34], [34], [36], [37], [62]

however, it's limited to tasks related to information finding using the proposed navigation or visual interface. Subjective criteria included in several studies are trust, emotion, engagement and persuasion. In some cases, industry specific adaptations are made to the evaluation criteria to allow focus on specific tasks related to the website's communication goals or user profiles (Table 4).

With regard to the development phase, 82% of the selected studies were conducted when the evaluated website(s) is in the final stages of implementation or already published, 6% of the studies were made in the planning/requirements stage, and 8% in the graphic design stage. Only one study proposed an iterative methodology during the development phase. These proportions can be explained because the evaluation of the

Table 4. Criteria used to evaluate user experience and/or usability in websites.

Criteria	Times used	Studies
Performance	7	[9], [29], [33], [33], [52], [53], [65]
Emotion and engagement	2	[35], [38]
Persuasion	1	[58]
Popularity	1	[6]
Trust	5	[30], [47], [55], [59], [60]
Accessibility	5	[2], [4], [9], [23], [35]
Aesthetics	18	[3], [8], [12], [19], [22], [23], [24], [29], [30], [41], [43], [45], [47], [52], [58], [60], [61], [62]
Attitude	2	[13], [31]
Broken links	2	[9], [33]
Content	22	[1], [6], [8], [11], [12], [15], [25], [30], [32], [38], [42], [44], [45], [46], [47], [50], [52], [55], [58], [59], [60], [61]
Information architecture	16	[1], [3], [7], [8], [11], [12], [22], [32], [37], [42], [43], [44], [45], [46], [52], [64]
Interactivity	1	[43]
Usability	57	[1], [3], [4], [5], [6], [7], [9], [10], [12], [13], [14], [15], [16], [17], [18], [19], [20], [21], [22], [23], [24], [25], [26], [27], [28], [29], [30], [31], [32], [33], [34], [35], [36], [37], [38], [39], [40], [41], [42], [43], [44], [48], [49], [50], [51], [53], [54], [55], [56], [57], [58], [59], [61], [62], [63], [64], [65]
User experience	7	[19], [25], [39], [47], [54], [59], [62]

complete user experience of an information-driven website requires the evaluation of the published information, the visual design and the functioning navigation as a complete system. Since these aspects are not fully formed while the website is in process of being coded, studies that require an evaluation in the early phases of a web development project must resort to methods that evaluate existing websites in the same industry (benchmarking) or simulate the final product (prototypes). These methods do not guarantee that new user experience problems can appear in the finished product. Since the user testing process is expensive in time and resources it is logical that most studies are executed when the implementation is already complete, when the evaluation will yield the most complete set of information (Table 5).

With regard to the efficacy of the selected methods, the results show that researchers were most satisfied with the information obtained from expert evaluation, user testing, or a combination of both. Expert evaluation is proportionately under user testing because researchers are aware that it can generate blind spots caused by the expert's familiarity with the website's topics and structure. Data mining provides high results and low cost but does not explain why the user acted in a specific way, and requires a high level of technical expertise.

With regard to the efficiency of the selected methods, the most efficient is expert evaluation, followed by data mining and automated tools. User testing is the most

Table 5. Project phases in which studies are conducted

Development phase	Times used	Studies
Completed	52	[2], [4], [8], [9], [10], [11], [13], [14], [15], [16], [17], [19], [20], [21], [22], [23], [24], [25], [26], [27], [28], [30], [31], [32], [33], [35], [38], [39], [40], [41], [42], [43], [44], [45], [46], [47], [48], [49], [50], [51], [52], [53], [54], [55], [57], [58], [59], [60], [61], [63], [64], [65]
Design	5	[3], [5], [7], [18], [62]
Coding	1	[12]
Not specified	1	[56]
Planning	4	[1], [34], [36], [37]
Planning, completed	2	[6], [29]

expensive method. Modifications to reduce costs in application include the use of remote testing tools such as online surveys, and limitation of the collected data to predefined values, however this approaches tend to impact negatively the quality of the knowledge generated by the methodology (Table 6).

Table 6. Satisfaction and cost per methodology.

Evaluation methods	Perceived satisfaction			Perceived cost		
	Low	Medium	High	Low	Medium	High
Analytics	0	1	0	0	0	1
Automated	0	1	1	2	0	0
Automated, data mining	0	0	1	1	0	0
Automated, user testing	0	0	1	1	0	0
Data mining	0	1	2	2	0	1
Data mining, user testing	0	1	0	1	0	0
Expert evaluation	0	7	9	11	3	2
Guidelines	0	0	1	0	0	1
Self-report, user testing	0	0	1	0	0	1
Software Development flow modification	0	0	1	1	0	0
User testing	0	10	19	5	12	12
User testing, expert evaluation	0	2	6	2	4	2

4 Conclusions and Future Work

This paper presents a systematic review conducted to identify the methodology, tools and criteria used to evaluate the user experience in information driven websites, and the efficacy and efficiency reported by the researchers after the application of the selected methodology. Papers that evaluated usability were also included because they included references to user experience evaluation. 65 studies were selected from 239. Empirical evidence was extracted from these studies, coded and aggregated.

We identified that the dominant methodologies are user testing and expert evaluation because of the quality of the obtained information. New methods proposed by researchers include data mining and automated tools to improve the data collection and processing process. Evaluation criteria can be general (compatible with all types of websites) or adapted according to the industry's communication goals. After usability, content, information architecture, aesthetics and task completion are the most frequently used criteria for the evaluation. Balance between usability and aesthetics is seen as a compromise, especially since website owners require customized interactivity to differentiate themselves from other websites. Proposed methods and tools required that the evaluator is already familiar with user experience/usability and has some degree of technical competence (background in information technology, statistics or data science); however, tasks such as questionnaire application can be delegated to evaluators with less experience.

Most studies were conducted over already published websites because navigation, content and visual design are aspects that need to be included for a complete user experience evaluation. This also means that there is not an established methodology for user experience evaluation during the software development process of an information divan website. This does not imply that companies do not conduct this type of research in their projects, only that this type of knowledge is not registered in academic databases.

Further research can be developed in the following topics:

- Differences in the user experience from recurring users and new users, since the information they would be interested in, and the expectations of the website could differ.
- Usability/user experience evaluation in websites developed with agile methodologies.
- Impact on user experience of pop ups windows, and areas reserved for display of different formats of advertising.
- Differences in user experience between users of mobile version websites compared to responsive interfaces.

References

1. Abdallah, S., Jaleel, B.: Website appeal: development of an assessment tool and evaluation framework of e-marketing. J. Theoret. Appl. Electron. Commer. Res. **10**(3), 45–62, 18 p. (2015)
2. Ali, S.R., Khan, A., Baig, M.M.F., Umer, A.: Implementation of Kano's model in web metrics for information driven websites – KDQI. In: 2015 International Conference on Information and Communication Technologies (ICICT), Karachi, pp. 1–6 (2015)
3. Kwon, D.Y., Jeong, S.R.: A content analysis for website usefulness evaluation: utilizing text mining technique. J. Korean Soc. Internet Inf. **16**(4), 71–81, 11 p. (2015)

4. Hartmann, J., De Angeli, A., Sutcliffe, A.: Framing the user experience: information biases on website quality judgement. In: CHI 2008 Proceedings Exploring Web Content, Florence, pp. 855–864 (2008)
5. Trerise, S., Lee, C., VanLooy, S., Knowlton, S., Bruyère, S.: The accessibility and usability of college websites: is your website presenting barriers to potential students? J. Commun. Coll. J. Res. Pract. 37(11), 864–876 (2013)
6. Beldad, A., De Jong, M., Steehouder, M.: How shall I trust the faceless and the intangible? A literature review on the antecedents of online trust. Comput. Hum. Behav. 26(5), 857–869 (2010)
7. Urban, G.L., Amyx, C., Lorenzon, A.: Online trust: state of the art, new frontiers, and research potential. J. Interact. Market. 23(2009), 179–190 (2009)
8. ISO. ISO 9241-210:2010 Ergonomics of human-system interaction – Part 210: Human-centred design for interactive systems (2010)
9. Wilkie, L., Romance, K., Rosendale, J.: Website usability: reasons underlying emotions reported by users. Insights Chang. World J. 2012(2), 133–156, 24 p. (2012)
10. Chen, S.Y., Li, Z.F., Chen, G.L.: Design and implementation of an open source content management system. Appl. Mech. Mater. 651–653, 1821–1826 (2014)
11. Distante, D., Risi, M., Scanniello, G.: Enhancing navigability in websites built using web content management systems. Int. J. Softw. Eng. Knowl. Eng. 24(3), 493–515, 23 p. (2014)
12. Kitchenham, B.: Guidelines for Performing Systematic Literature Reviews in Software Engineering, Version 2.3, EBSE Technical Report, Keele University, UK (2007)
13. Web Content Accessibility Guidelines 2.0, W3C World Wide Web Consortium Recommendation, 11 December 2008. http://www.w3.org/TR/200X/REC-WCAG20-20081211/. Latest version at http://www.w3.org/TR/WCAG20/
14. Brooke, J.: SUS: A 'quick and dirty' usability scale. In: Jordan, P., Thomas, B., Weerdmeester, B. (eds.) Usability Evaluation in Industry, pp. 189–194. Taylor & Francis, London (1996)
15. Nielsen, J.: Heuristic evaluation. In: Nielsen, J., Mack, R.L. (eds.) Usability Inspection Methods, NY (1994)
16. Microsoft Usability Guidelines. https://msdn.microsoft.com/en-us/library/bb158578.aspx

The UX Metrics Table: A Missing Artifact

Dieter Wallach[1,2(✉)], Jan Conrad[1], and Toni Steimle[2]

[1] University of Applied Sciences, Kaiserslautern, Germany
{dieter.wallach,jan.conrad}@hs-kl.de
[2] Ergosign Switzerland AG, Zurich, Switzerland
toni.steimle@ergosign.ch

Abstract. User Experience Design approaches typically rely on the creation of various concrete artifacts that are constructed and refined during the iterative course of an UX project. While the respective details and, correspondingly, the labels to designate resulting artifacts might vary, we often find Personas and Scenarios for consolidating insights in the Research Phase of a project; Scribbles, Wireframes or Mockups for spelling out our ideas in the Design Phase; and the use of (interactive) prototypes in an Evaluation phase, where we document usability findings in Usability Reports. In this paper, we introduce the concept of a UX Metrics Table, a comprehensive artifact that supports UX designers by guiding their project activities and by helping to derive an informed decision about the termination of iteration cycles. To exemplify the use of a UX metrics table and example is presented showing the application of the UX metrics table in a summative evaluation project.

Keywords: UX metric · UX design · User experience · Human-centered design · Iteration · Lean UX · System usability scale · Formative evaluation · Summative evaluation

1 Introduction

The term *User Experience (UX)* is, despite being devised almost 25 years ago by Donald Norman, still a somewhat chatoyant concept. In an approach to provide an overview of its meaning, the site allaboutux.org lists 27 definitions of user experience that were established until 2010. The ISO 9241-210 defines user experience as "a person's perceptions and responses that result from the use or anticipated use of a product, system or service ... [UX] includes all the users' emotions, beliefs, preferences, perceptions, physical and psychological responses, behaviors and accomplishments that occur before, during and after use ... Usability criteria can be used to assess aspects of user experience". While this definition falls short of explicitly mentioning directly measurable UX metrics, the situation is more relieved in the ISO 9241-110 definition of usability. It defines usability as "the extent to which a product can be used by specified users to achieve specified goals with effectiveness, efficiency and satisfaction in a specified context of use". While the exact relation of usability to the obviously more comprehensive concept of user experience is not spelled out extensively in the ISO 9241 definition, we are informed that "usability criteria can be used to assess aspects of user experience". Completionrates or error rates can be used to

© Springer International Publishing AG 2017
A. Marcus and W. Wang (Eds.): DUXU 2017, Part I, LNCS 10288, pp. 507–517, 2017.
DOI: 10.1007/978-3-319-58634-2_37

operationalize the usability criterion of effectiveness, while time on task is an example for a quantification of the efficiency criterion. Completion rates and time on task can be measured objectively, while the third usability criterion, satisfaction, is a subjective measure that can be elicited on the task level using the *System Usability Scale,* for example (Sauro 2011). Operationalizing and including criteria in the measurement that extend the task level (on which the semantically tighter definition of usability mainly operates) as required by the ISO definition of user experience is clearly more complex: taking the subjective consequences of an "anticipated use of a product" or a "user's emotions, beliefs, preferences, perceptions" into account demands the application of valid and reliable methods like the *User Experience Questionnaire (UEQ,* Laugwitz et al. 2008).

In this paper we introduce an artifact called UX metrics table that focuses on the identification, measuring and comparative interpretation of UX metrics. To pave the ground for outlining a UX metrics table, some essential terms are clarified in the next section.

1.1   What Do We Mean by UX Metrics?

A metric is understood as an approach to the measurement or evaluation of a phenomenon under consideration (Tullis and Albert 2013). A metric that focuses on the usability of an interactive system like *time on task* can be measured directly and objectively by the assignment of a numerical value representing the delta between the start time and the end time of working on a task for a given sample of users. We need to determine an instrument for measuring, as well as the units for reporting the results of its application in a (set of) situation(s). A potential result would be a statement like: *The mean time for completing an order with system X is 37.9 s (with a standard deviation of 7.2 s).*

When moving from the definition of usability to its superordinate concept of user experience according to the ISO 9241 we fall short of simple, directly observable indicators and need to resort to subjective measures like the UEQ mentioned above or to marketing metrics like brand perception (Sauro 2015) to capture specific aspects of user experience.

UX metrics, as results of measurements are *quantitative* by nature: we can compare the measurement results of a certain UX metric for different systems or contrast the measurement before and after the redesign of a system. In order to qualify as a well-founded and useful UX metric, the respective measure is required to be *valid* (i.e. it should measure what it claims to measure), *reliable* (i.e. it should produce similar results under similar conditions) and *objective* (i.e. it should be independent of the person conducting the measurement and should be free of references to outside influences). Ideally, a UX metric should be *easy* and *economically to measure* and its results should be *understandable* and *informative.* Embedding an instrument for measuring UX in a comprehensive framework of UX like the Components Model of User Experience (Thüring and Mahlke 2007) provides valuable theoretical underpinnings to support a sound interpretation of its results (see the meCUE questionnaire, Thüring and Minge 2014). To aid broad applicability, metrics should be *flexible* for utilization in early design phasesand should give meaningful results even with *small sample sizes*.

Leech (2011) argues that in order to be helpful, a UX metric needs to come with a *timescale* (to designate the temporal period under consideration), a *benchmark* (to allow for comparisons), a *reason to be reported* (to focus on significant data) and an *action* (that would allow appropriate response in light of available data) associated.

1.2 Why Should We Collect UX Metrics?

UX metrics provide directions for design. Depending on the requirements of a given project, the goal of design activities might vary: in one project we might primarily focus on achieving an efficient interaction concept while we might need to balance (conflicting) metrics like efficiency, error ratesand/or learnability in the next project.

Identifying a relevant set of metrics and adequately balancing conflicting metrics is crucial to the success of product development. Starting with the vision of a new or improved product, we need to identify UX metrics to qualify what we mean by a desirable user experience in the respective project context. Explicit UX metrics help to shape and elaborate the goals of product development. Agreeing on benchmarks that come as target (and, optionally, acceptance) values for the UX metrics selected fosters insightful discussions especially in cross-functional teams and aligns project members on a strategic level. UX metrics guide data collection during the research phase of a project by pointing to empirical information required to come to informed design decisions.

Establishing UX metrics also helps us to evaluate our assumptions: they aid the interpretation of conducted studies, measure the impact of changes to a product and spell out improvements over iteration cycles. UX metrics tell us when to stop iterating because target values are met or exceeded. Defined target values for UX metrics allows a calculation of the intended benefits when conducting predictive Return-on-Investment (ROI) analyses. Monitoring the status and continuously reviewing the relevance of the chosen UX metrics acknowledges the dynamics of user experience and provides opportunities for prompt action in the light of changing UX requirements.

UX metrics make it easy to communicate project progress — and provide convincing numbers to prove it. Finally, UX metrics allow for easy comparisons of different products or different versions of the same product. Tullis and Albert (2013, p. 8), in their seminal book on UX metrics claim that "Metrics add structure to the design and evaluation process, give insight into the findings, and provide information to the decision makers".

In defiance of theoutlined value, UX metrics are often neither explicitly operationalized, nor agreed upon or annotated with target and/or acceptance values. Nielsens (2001) infamous quote "Metrics are expensive and are a poor use of typically scarce usability resources" might not be completely inculpable for that. A fortunate, clear exception are approaches that sail under the Lean UX flag following a designated *build, measure and learn loop* (Gothelf and Seiden 2012). In too many projects, however, UX metrics remain implicit and lose their guiding force. Even worse, team members, who are jointly contributing to the development of a product, might individually be striving for the attainment of different (or even conflicting), but unexpressed UX goals. The lack of explicit and shared UX metrics impedes a smooth orchestration of project activities and misses opportunities to focus on informed, goal-oriented actions.

User experience design approaches typically rely on the creation of various concrete artifacts that are constructed and refined during the iterative course of an UX project. UX metrics need to be tightly engrained in the landscape of core UX artifacts to become widely understood as a matter of course and used as informative tools for design. A UX metrics tableconnectspersonas and scenarios with the explicit elaboration of quantitative metrics and has proven to be a helpful artifact through the stages of a UX project. In the next section we discuss ways to establish a UX metric.

1.3 Establishing UX Metrics

Meaningful UX metrics focus on the critical interaction scenarios of using an application. A scenario might be critical for different reasons: it is used very frequently, errors imply severe consequences, the touch point of interaction might contribute crucially to the general impression of the application, the interaction sequence might be of eminent importance for learning how to use a system or other essential scenarios that shape the user experience significantly. We first need to identify these critical interaction scenarios in order to set concrete expectations regarding relevant UX metrics.

Different scenariosmay be critical for different *personas* that are conceptualized as representative users of an application. When we establish UX metrics we need to take critical scenarios and their associated personas into account. Independently from the concept of a UX metrics table presented in this paper, Travis (2011) suggested a related approach in which he suggests to first identify the *red routes* as an initial step to create UX metrics: "Most systems, even quite complex ones, usually have only a handful of critical tasks. This doesn't mean that the system will support only those tasks: it simply means that these tasks are the essential ones for the business and for users. So it makes sense to use these red routes to track progress". Travis refers to *user stories* (Cohn 2004) to support "thinking of the needs and goals of a specific persona" and to "fully ground" the scenario in context.

Including personas and scenarios in the formulation of a UX metric helps to prevent the definition of overly generic UX metrics that would require a significant operationalization before they can be associated with a method for measurement: "… «easy to use», «enjoyable» or «easy to learn»". It's not that these aren't worthy design goals, it's that they are simply too abstract to help you measure the user experience" (Travis 2011). Defining UX metrics in reference to personas and scenarios gives us the concreteness needed to declare successful goal attainment.

What is missing yet in order to arrive at *quantifiable* UX metrics are numerical values that form precise criteria for comparison. We may want a revised system to be *better* with regard to a certain UX metric than its predecessor, and/or we want it to be *as least as good* as its next competitor. We need to know *benchmark values* for comparison to indicate success or failure. In a summative evaluation, we can then qualify a measured value for a relevant UX metric to be *good* when it exceeds the benchmark value — or to be *bad* when it is lower, considering just a simple case.

Having benchmark values for UX metrics does not just allow for meaningful comparisons, but also helps to set reasonable *target values* regarding the magnitude of intended improvement. Arriving at relevant benchmark values can be achieved by measuring a UX metric with regard to a preceding system version, a competitor's offer — or, for some UX metrics, even with the values for the manual processing of some up-to-now unsupported task. Technical capabilities and insights from research activities typically inform the precise assignment of target and acceptance values. If in need of available benchmark values, generic average values for UX metrics, as published by Sauro (2012), can be used as rough first evidence.

In practice, differentiating between intended *targetvalues* and *acceptance values* has turned out to be helpful in some occasions. Target values represent true indicators of success, while achieving acceptance values points to the right direction but leaves room for improvement.

Identifying and prioritizing UX metrics is typically not a solitary endeavor. Different UX metrics might be of varying importance to different stakeholders, it is thus advisable to engage all interested parties when selecting and consolidating the set of UX metrics considered to be relevant. Especially in early phases of a project, large-scale UX goals, as spelled out in Google's HEART framework (Happiness, Engagement, Adoption, Retention, and Task Success, see Luenendonk 2015) are often put forward and later refined by referring to measurable metrics. Tullis and Albert (2013) extensively discuss behavioral and attitudinal UX metrics, categorized as performance metrics, issue-based metrics, self-reported metrics, as well as behavioral and physiological metrics.

2   The UX Metrics Table

Human-centered design activities are, by their very nature, artifact-centered. The construction of artifacts is the lowest common denominator uniting the iteratively intertwined phases of a human-centered product development cycle. Coming in different guises and named according to different flavors, artifacts are shared as communication tools amongst stakeholders, are evaluated and refined and, if necessary, abandoned. The maturity of artifacts indicates, within the limits of iterative approaches, progress in UX projects: We envision future users of an interactive system by establishing lively personas as representative archetypes. Scenarios excite the working goals of an acting persona in context and constitute an essential ingredient for deriving requirements. Scribbles, wireframes, user journeys and interactive prototypes let a product gradually come alive and support an early experience of a product's essentials. In contrast to the artifacts mentioned before, UX metrics have, however, not yet found a firm home in the artifact arsenal of UX professionals.

A *UX metrics table* links personas and scenarios to explicit UX metrics in a comprehensive artifact accompanying human-centered design activities. It continuously conveys the targets for the design, helping to keep the focus on agreed upon quantitative UX goals of a project. The rows of a UX metrics table refer to the UX metrics considered, presented in decreasing order of priority. Its columns provide the agreed upon parameters of the metric.

Figure 1 shows the header of an UX metrics table. The UX metrics table consists of nine columns that define (1) the *UX metric* under consideration, (2) the method to*measure*the UX metric, (3) the *persona* representing the intended user, (4) the *scenario* that provides the situational context, (5) a *benchmark* value for comparison, (6) a *target value* (complemented by an optional *acceptance value*) that serves as a quantitative goal for this metric, (7) a *result* column, holding the measured score for the UX metric that was empirically measured, (8) a *time scale* column to indicate the time frame within which the intended result is to be achieved and (9) a *sample* column to describe the designated sample for evaluating the UX metric.

UX metric	Measure	Persona	Scenario	Benchmark	Target	Result	Time scale	Sample

Fig. 1. Elements of a UX metrics table

The number of rows representing the chosen UX metrics and their respective content depend of course on the specific goals and circumstances of an actual project. While starting with a small and focused list of UX metrics is advisable, the details of a UX metric table are subject to change over time. In practice, UX metrics might be added, rows where the *result* value equals or exceeds the *target* value might be highlighted to indicate success, and values might be adjusted in the light of new insights. The history of a UX metrics table represents dynamic snapshots of the progress made in establishing and attaining UX metrics.

Using the UX metrics table in real-world projects is quite straightforward: after having arrived at an initial understanding of the project goals, a first version of a UX metrics table is established in a joint meeting that brings relevant stakeholders together. Agreeing on relevant UX metrics paves the ground for a shared understanding of the project goals — that often get into a vivid tug-of-war for the "right" metrics and/or their prioritization. In projects targeted at the development of new products, initial UX metrics tables often start with tables consisting of hardly more than two concerted entries in the UX metric column that have mutually been agree to be significant.

Setting UX metrics for a product requires (well-grounded) assumptions regarding the quality of its use. Establishing a UX metrics table gives additional weight to the careful creation of personas and scenarios based on empirical data. If user research has already provided evidence for their construction, the columns for *persona* and *scenario* can be filled — with their content certainly having a major impact on the definition of the UX metric under consideration. If not, the cells for persona and scenario in the UX table will remind the team about required action for further research to empirically ground the UX metric.

To illustrate the construction process of a UX metrics table, we discuss a simple example in the next paragraph.

3   Applying the UX Metrics Table in Practice

A UX Metrics Table provides a clear rationale for assessing the progress made during the iterations of a design project. It is easy to understand the benefits of the suggested artifact in the *build-measure-learn loops* of Lean UX approaches where (real word) validations of incrementally extended products are *formatively* conducted (see Steimle and Wallach, in preparation, for a discussion of UX metrics tables in Lean Development). Seeing how a UX metrics table can contribute to *summative* evaluations is less obvious. In the following real-world example we illustrate a summative use of UX tables in a project that was initiated by a client interested in an overall evaluation of a complex software system. For reasons of anonymization, we will denote the software as Wcs in the remainder of the paper.

3.1   An Example for the Summative Use of the UX Metrics Table

Wcs was installed three years ago with a large, international user base as the successor of an application with similar functionality. After having received negative user feedback regarding several UX deficiencies of Wcs, the client commissioned a summative usability study to inspect the application.

Analysis of the user base revealed two distinct user groups of Wcs:

- Expert users, who (1) mostly report to use Wcs daily or on several days per week, (2) qualify themselves to be very proficient in using Wcs (self-reports using a 7-point scale [1–7], yielding an average of 5.28 out of 7, SD = 1.63), (3) work on task sets that require full access to Wcs's functionality;
- Occasional users, with (1) >75% of this group using Wcs less than once per month, (2) qualify their level of proficiency comparatively low (self-reports using a 7-point scale [1–7], yielding an average of 3.66 out of 7, SD = 1.70), (3) work on restricted tasks with only limited access to Wcs's functionality.

Both user groups work with Wcs for about the same time (Expert users: 31.22 months, SD: 10.68; occasional users: 30.44 months, SD: 10.98).

To better understand the respective user attributes, their working goals and situational parameters, a Contextual Inquiry was conducted. The domain of Wcs is quite knowledge-intense, so the gathered insights were necessary prerequisites for a detailed UX inspection of the system. Results from the Contextual Inquiry were used to empirically ground the construction of two personas. The name *Emily Expert* was used to denote the Expert persona, while the group of occasional users was archetypically depicted by a persona called *Tim Sometime*.

When the client commissioned the UX evaluation, he was mainly interested in (a) an understanding of the user perspective, i.e. the subjective impression of Wcs's quality of use and (b) an expert opinion regarding reported (potential) usability flaws of Wcs.

Following the categorization according to Tullis an Albert (2013), the subjective usability impression of Wcs's users can be considered as a *self-reported metric* that can be measured, for example, using the *System Usability Scale (Sus)*. The Sus is a questionnaire to elicit the subjective impression of the usability of an interactive system. It was published by Brooke (1996) and is used in an exceptionally large number of scientific and practical studies. TheSus has excellent values for validity and reliability (Sauro 2011) and allows economical data elicitation since the questionnaire is comprised of only ten items. In response to these items, participants express their (dis)agreement with a system on a five-tier Likert-scale (example: *"I feel very confident in using Wcs", (strongly disagree … strongly agree)*. A Susscore is calculated from the answers to the Sus questions and can range in 41 increments from 0 to 100. Zero symbolizes the theoretical lowest score and 100 the highest possible Susscore.

3.2   Determining the Values of the UX Metrics Table

Given the *UX metric* of a subjective usability impression, the Sus as a method for *measurement* and the two *personas*, we can already complete parts of Wcs UX metric table. The *scenario* cell in the table can be left empty since the Sus score refers to the overall impression of a system and is not related to an isolated scenario. To determine a *benchmark* value for the Sus score, data reported by Sauro (2011) was used. Sauro published Susscores from a total of 446 studies with more than 5,000 participants to derive general benchmark data that supports a comparative interpretation of obtained Susscores. The mean Sus score representing the entirety of those studies is 68, which can be inserted as the *benchmark* value for Wcs — with the *target* value set to >68. While this setting seems to be appropriate for the *Tim Sometime* persona representing occasional users, the values for *benchmark/target* is set in reference to Sauro's mean Sus score for *"Internal-productivity software: Customer Service and Network Operations applications"*, which is 76.7 (SD = 8.8). In fact, all expert users of Wcs are working in the very same organization that released Wcs, while occasional users are employed in a variety of different organizations: the respective reference points are set accordingly. The slot for *time scale* was set to *Now*because the summative study is intended to capture the current state of the metric. Although the Sus is a robust tool even with small sample sizes, a web-based presentation of the Sus promised to gather data from a larger *sample* size (N > 50). Figure 2 shows the definition of the initial version of the UX metrics table for Wcs.

UX metric	Measure	Persona	Scenario	Benchmark	Target	Result	Time scale	Sample
Subj.Impr.	SUS	Emily E.	–	68	> 68		Now	> 50
Subj.Impr.	SUS	Tim S.	–	76	> 76		Now	> 50

Fig. 2. Initial UX metrics table for Wcs

Note: For reasons of simplicity and illustration, the table in Fig. 2 just comprises a single metric, referring to two different personas. Typically, a UX metrics table includes various types of UX metrics that require carefully balancing (see Steimle and Wallach, in preparation).

3.3   Results

Data collection using a web-based version of the Sus was supported by using unique, computer-generated tokens to rule out multiple participation of the same person. Approximately 4,000 users of both user groups were invited via email to participate in the study.

A total sample of close to 500 Wcs users answered the Sus questionnaire, resulting in a data set of 414 occasional users and 75 expert users. The average Susscore after completing the Sus for occasional Wcs users was 40.4 (SD: 19.4). The confidence interval (95%) ranges between 38.48 and 42.22. Evaluating *Cronbach's alpha* to measure the internal consistency of the scale returned an excellent value of 0.914. The average Susscore for expert users was 43.3 (SD: 18.6). The confidence interval (95%) ranges between 39.02 and 47.58. Evaluating *Cronbach's alpha* to measure the internal consistency of a scale returns a very good value of 0.885.

The results for both user groups indicated in Fig. 3 indicate extraordinarily low Sus scores, expressing very negative subjective usability impressions about Wcs. The results were clearly confirmed by the outcome of another (ISO 9241-related) usability inventory (ISONORM, see Prümper and Anft 1997) that was jointly applied with the System Usability Scale in the sample. The highly significant positive correlation coefficients *(Pearson, $p < 0.001$)* of 0.78 (expert users) and 0.61 (occasional users) indicate a convergent validity of the two measurement tools. The picture is consistently completed by the results of a Heuristic Analysis targeted at identifying usability flaws with Wcs. A total of 48 findings was reported, with 6 findings classified to be of *minor* importance, 21 were categorized as *severe* and 21 as *critical*.

UX metric	Measure	Persona	Scenario	Benchmark	Target	Result	Time scale	Sample
Subj.Impr.	SUS	Emily E.	–	68	≥ 68	40.4	Now	75
Subj.Impr.	SUS	Tim S.	–	76	≥ 76	43.3	Now	414

Fig. 3. Complemented UX metrics table for Wcs

Although the study reported was summative, the negative evaluation results have convinced the client to start a project to redesign Wcs. With the basic UX metrics table shown in Fig. 2 as a quantitative vantage point, two metrics, *completion time* for the core scenario and *error rate* were added and the *time frame* set to the release date of the next version of Wcs. At present, log file analyses are carried out to determine *benchmark* values for the *completion time* and *error rates* regarding the selected core scenarios of Wcs.

4 Discussion

In this paper we have introduced an artifact coined UX metrics table that has proven to be very helpful in real world projects. Constructing a UX metrics table highlights the identification and tracking of UX metrics in the course of a project and supports a comprehensive understanding of the mutual dependencies between UX metrics. Linking UX metrics to concrete scenarios and personas provides the right resolution level for their meaningful definition and measurement. Introducing UX metrics table put metrics into true effect and supports institutionalizing their use in organizations.

As an outlasting project artifact, UX metrics tables connect the research-, design- and evaluation phase(s) of a project and provide clear quantitative means to determine project success — or failure. Travis (2011) argues: "That is the strength of metrics-based testing: it gives us the *what* of usability". While we wholeheartedly agree, qualitative methods give us the *why* of usability and UX and help to make sense of available data. It is in combination with qualitative data when quantitative approaches permit significant insights. Design, however, should never degrade to any form of convulsive focusing on metrics and data — or as Bowman (2009) has put it in his now famous farewell letter to Google: "I won't miss a design philosophy that lives or dies strictly by the sword of data".

References

Albert, W., Tullis, T.: Measuring the User Experience: Collecting, Analyzing, and Presenting Usability Metrics. Elsevier, Amsterdam (2013)

Bowman, D.: Goodbye, Google (2009). http://stopdesign.com/archive/2009/03/20/goodbye-google.html(2/10/2017)

Brooke, J.: SUS: A "quick and dirty" usability scale. In: Jordan, P.W., Thomas, B., Weerdmeester, B.A., McClelland, A.L. (eds.) Usability Evaluation in Industry. Taylor and Francis, London (1996)

Cohn, M.: User Stories Applied: For Agile Software Development. Addison Wesley, Redwood City (2004)

Gothelf, J., Seiden, J.: Lean UX: Applying Lean Principles to Improve User Experience. O'Reilly, Beijing (2012)

Laugwitz, B., Held, T., Schrepp, M.: Construction and evaluation of a user experience questionnaire. In: Holzinger, A. (ed.) USAB 2008. LNCS, vol. 5298, pp. 63–76. Springer, Heidelberg (2008). doi:10.1007/978-3-540-89350-9_6

Leech, J.: A big list of UX KPIs and Metrics (2011). https://www.cxpartners.co.uk/ourthinking/ux_roi_what_to_measure_and_what_to_expect/. 2 October 2017

Luenendonk, M.: Complete Guide to Google's HEART Framework for Measuring the Quality of UX (2015). https://www.cleverism.com/google-heart-framework-measuring-quality-ux-user-experience/

Nielsen, J.: Usability Metrics (2001). https://www.nngroup.com/articles/usability-metrics/. 2 October 2017

Sauro, J.: 32 ways to measure the customer experience (2015). https://measuringu.com/32-ways-cux/. 2 October 2017

Sauro, J.: 10 benchmarks for user experience metrics (2012). http://measuringu.com/ux-benchmarks/. 2 October 2017

Steimle, T., Wallach, D.: Collaborative UX Design (in prep.)

Sauro, J.: A Practical Guide to the System Usability Scale: Background, Benchmarks, & Best Practices. Measuring Usability LLC, Denver (2011)

Thüring, M., Mahlke, S.: Usability, aesthetics, and emotions in human-technology interaction. Int. J. Psychol. **42**(4), 253–264 (2007)

Thüring, M., Minge, M.: Nutzererleben messen – geht das überhaupt? In: Begleitforschung Mittelstand-Digital (Hrsg.) Wissenschaft trifft Praxis. Usability betrieblicher IT-Anwendungen, pp. 45–53 (2014)

Travis, D.: How to mange design projects with user experience metrics. http://www.userfocus.co.uk/articles/how_to_manage_design_projects_with_ux_metrics.html. 2 October 2017

Research on "4D" Evaluation System Construction for Information Interaction Design

Yangshuo Zheng[✉] and Yongzhen Zou

Wuhan University of Technology, Wuhan, Hubei, China
zhengyangshuo@163.com, 867624024@qq.com

Abstract. This paper focuses on the information construction of 4D evaluation system of Information interaction design (IID). The paper provides a specific and effective evaluation criterion for complicated procedures of IID including information processing, interactive logic, and behavior perception, and systemizes it by virtue of application verification, with a view to ensuring that the goal of IID can be achieved. The 4D evaluation system of IID is constructed by designing the evaluation system of IID comprehensively in four dimensions, namely "environment", "user", "technology" and "product". Multiple values of IID (e.g. culture, aesthetics, user, ease of use, popularization of science, and dissemination) are unified in the model of the evaluation system. By constructing the 4D evaluation system of IID and the general process that integrates it with information interaction design, it is intended to find the paths that combines design theory and design practice more closely. Meanwhile, based on the application of information technology in information interaction design, a new way of information interaction that is oriented to the future, stands to reason and meets the demand of users will be also envisaged.

Keywords: Information interaction design · Evaluation model · Four dimensions

1 Introduction

The revolution of information technology brings tremendous transformation power for human society, and directly boosts the innovation of design-related areas on the whole, such as production mode, propagation path, user experience, and business model. Information interaction design (IID), as a reflection of human civilization in contemporary society supported by information technology, not only changes the way that people interact with social information, but also mirrors users' eagerness for overall improvement of interactive experience in an era of information.

Research subject of this paper, "Information interaction design" is actually a systematic cognitive design fields, composed of the three design direction: information design, interaction design, perception design. As early as 1999, Shedroff published papers pointed out that should the information design and interaction design considerations together, treat it as a unified field of design theory. Shedorff argued that the information interaction design is integrated consisting of "information design", "interaction design" and "perception design", Shedroff call it "Information Interaction Design". Information Interaction Design should be designed to standardize and facilitate information-oriented

© Springer International Publishing AG 2017
A. Marcus and W. Wang (Eds.): DUXU 2017, Part I, LNCS 10288, pp. 518–530, 2017.
DOI: 10.1007/978-3-319-58634-2_38

mode of human interactions with the theoretical prototype, the focus should be to build more rational human information interaction and corresponding conduct under the information society background.

In the last decades, IIDrelated studies have attracted more attention from the design world. Many companies designed a series of excellent IID products in recent years, which boast of high design level and high-tech feelings. All of them are well received by market and users. It can be seen from the evolution of companies like Apple, Amazon, Facebook, Twitter, and Uber that in the wake of the age of service economy, many companies have realized significant user value and commercial value involved in IID. The "design thinking" dominated by IID is reforming conventional process and management methods of organizations, systems, and even product design, while the user experience strategy has been a core element of IID.

IID drives social innovation in terms of product design. As propelled by the development of design, the behavior relation between human and object, the group relation between human and human, and the cultural relation between human and society are all redefined. In general, international academe has studied many aspects of IID thoroughly, such as: ① human-computer interaction, ② interface design, ③ industrial design, ④ user research, ⑤ information architecture, ⑥ experience design, ⑦ content of text and voice, and ⑧ information visualization. Relevant studies are systematic, wide-ranging, highly recognizable, forward-looking and instructive. They support a virtuous circle of IID studies and practice. However, the studies still have their shortcomings. For example, the existing IID studies focus on the investigation and analysis of users and situations at the earlier stage as well as the research and development of mid-term design and technology, while the evaluation method system at the later stage is rarely reported. Compared with general design, IID is not unidirectional. Instead, it is a dynamic process with iterative repetition and mutual effect. Therefore, it is necessary to creatively reform the evaluation system of IID, so as to further improve the design principle and methodology of IID in modern times.

2   Concept of "4D" Evaluation Model of IID

Information interaction design (IID) is an creative integration research direction of design disciplines and humanities, information engineering disciplines, and human-centered design. Information interaction design based on In information science, organizational behavior, interdisciplinary research physiology, kinematics, automatic control theory makes the user experience as the core, with the digitization of information collection analysis and statistical techniques as a reference, finally can expand the experimental studies on the information product interacts with the environment, explore human-machine sensors, interactive, human-computer interaction and other information interactive works. The status of information interaction design has an important and leading role for the survival and development of nowadays design. With the continuous development, the design theoretical study also presents new features, it is no longer confined to the words of pure design theory, but increasingly focuses on practical applications for design guidance and reflection. Information Interaction Design is one of the most typical representative design direction, it embodies the direction of today's latest development and application of design.

On the perspective of design disciplines, in the computer, Internet and other information tools has been more deeply universal applied today, research width and depth of information interaction design research has been greatly expanded. Information interaction design primarily study the way of human society and the transmission of information and get responding information, ultimately to establish contacts with the outside world. The 4D evaluation system of IID proposed in the paper provides a specific and effective evaluation criterion for complicated procedures of IID including information processing, interactive logic, and behavior perception, and systemizes it by virtue of application verification, with a view to ensuring that the goal of information interaction design can be achieved.

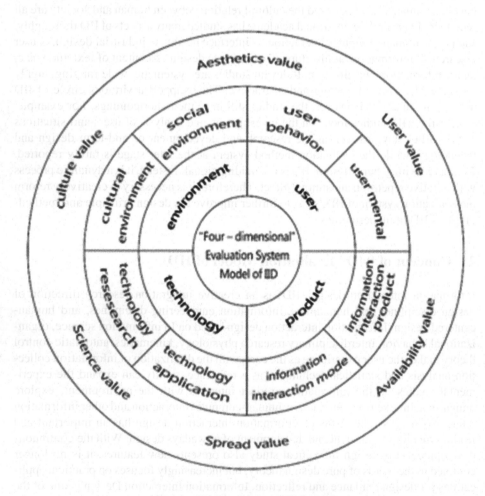

Fig. 1. "4D" evaluation model of IID

The 4D evaluation system of IID is constructed by designing the evaluation system of IID comprehensively in four dimensions, namely "environment", "user", "technology" and "product". Multiple values of IID (e.g. culture, aesthetics, user, ease of use, popularization of science, and dissemination) are unified in the model of the evaluation system. On one hand, based on the rules and characteristics of IID, the relation of core elements of the 4D evaluation system of IID is defined, the principles, objects, methods, procedures and standards of the system are explored, and the weight ratio of specific evaluation indexes in the system is determined. On the other hand, the evaluation experiment and result analysis of IID are conducted both quantitatively and qualitatively by means of situational verification. The system's rationality is improved in accordance with the results in application, so as to constantly iterate and optimize the system (Fig. 1).

2.1 Environment of "4D" Model

The first dimension element of evaluation system model is about the relationship between IID and environment, mainly refers to the relationship with the social environment. Phenomenological theory thought that the environment is not an abstract place, but by the specific things that the composition as a whole. Information interaction activities require different environments as a basis, in order to facilitate information interaction activities generate. We can say that environmental factors determine human behavior, determines the attributes of the information interaction design. Information interaction design activities and environmental linkages, provided its hold in the environment of the significance of a particular role. Through this research perspective, information interaction design activity embodies the value of user functionality in the social environment, which provide the information for the application, but also reflects the cultural values in the process of social development. In the system model, environmental products (dominant presence), user (intellectual existence) and culture (invisible presence) nicely connects together.

2.2 User of "4D" Model

The second dimension element of evaluation system model is about the relationship between IID and user, mainly refers to users of user-oriented design. In a sense, Information interaction design is based on users' creative process, and its purpose is to help users solve problems, improving the user experience, and then realize the target audience emotional resonance. From this perspective, this relationship includes applications of sensory experiences (how to use visual, auditory, tactile, olfactory, gustatory perception meet user needs), the user's mental model and user behavior. Information interaction design From the "Design for others" to "Collaborative others for Design" is the is most unusual place with other design, to some extents, users can determine even the direction of design. Future users will be involved in the design, become collaborators, eventually decision-makers. Therefore, from the study of "usability", "ease of user" extends to how to play to users' "initiative", "creative", will be key to the future development of Information interaction design.

2.3 Technology of "4D" Model

The third dimension element of evaluation system model is about the relationship between IID and technology, mainly refers to the relationship between design activities and information technology. The traditional design perspective, often makes "technology" and "objects" as a whole, which leads to neglecting the real technology. Technology itself does not seem only simple tools, information technology for the design often have a decisive significance and effect. Kevin Kelly even claimed that "technology is the seventh existence of life. Technology is an extension of life, rather than something separate and life beyond." In fact, every technology innovation will make technical elements improved, bring new opportunities and new changes and diversity final design mode. IT will be a key factor in promoting the progress of information interaction design, makes predicting the future development trend of information interaction design possible.

2.4 Product of "4D" Model

The fourth dimension element of evaluation system model is about the relationship between IID and product, mainly refers to the intrinsic relationship between the specific interaction information to convert the design process and results, and its essence is an internal agreement of contact. The development of information technology has given the diversity of forms of objects (material and non-material), but from the perspective of artificial fact is concerned, the matter is still mentioned belong to "artifact" category, which determines the type of objects. Information interaction design reflect features mostly achieved through the "objects" as the carrier. Thus, many of the traditional design for the "objects" rule, characteristics, cognitive attributes in the information interaction design still have in common.

In the previous design research study, most design emphasize while ignoring the inherent design factors associated even with the history, culture and other factors discussed in the background, showing the limitations and the lack of a more overall systematic theoretical research ideas. Therefore, from the perspective of the design system model presented in this paper to think about the information interaction design, will make a broader, more holistic, more accurately grasp the development context and the law of information interaction design activities, then carry out exploration and innovation of information interaction design in future.

3 Research Paths of "4D" Evaluation Model

IID is an iterative process, and its evaluation is to ensure the design quality, so it is also a very important part. A relatively objective evaluation system built for IID products can be used to evaluate the quality of product design, optimize the management process of design practice, analyze the existing problems in the design and provide a relevant basis to the design practice management department for planning (Fig. 2).

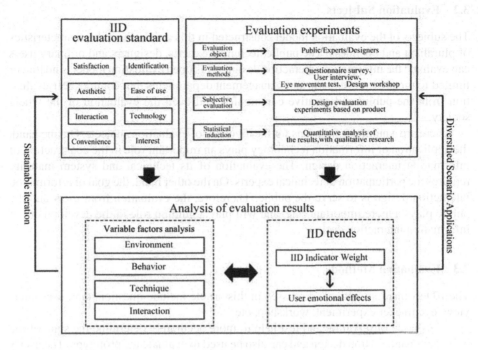

Fig. 2. Research paths of 4D evaluation model

3.1 Evaluation Criteria

First of all, this article needs to explore and establish IID evaluation criteria to help continuous iteration and optimization in the design phase so as to improve the quality of the completion of IID. Based on the ten usability principles proposed by Nielsen, and considering the achievement of the given functional goals, this article further optimizes the usability, and proposes eight reference indicators for information interaction design: satisfaction, aesthetics, interaction, convenience, recognition, usability, technology maturity, and interest. These eight factors have important internal links, but different emphases.

The eight reference indicators are a dynamic development concept. The content of the evaluation indicators should be diversified and dynamic. More public participation can be introduced to improve the content of evaluation indicators so as to provide the basis for the scientific evaluation criteria from the authoritative, professional and public point of view. The evaluation content should be highly operable and oriented, including whether the data samples are easy to acquire, whether the subsequent quantitative research can produce accurate results, whether the content can be compared with the development of the complete information interaction design, and whether it can embody the direction and trend of information interaction design.

3.2   Evaluation Subjects

The subjects of the evaluation model constructed in this article show the characteristics of pluralism and openness. The public, technical experts, designers and ordinary users can evaluate the information interaction design. This open evaluation model is no longer limited to the previous experts and management departments, but contains self-evaluation from the public and creative community, and even the evaluation of the whole society.

There are a number of reasons for the diversity of evaluation subjects. On one hand, the application of information technology plays an important role in the construction of information interaction design. The evaluation of its technical and system maturity requires the participation of technical experts. On the other hand, the goal of information interaction design is to serve the public. Therefore, the evaluation from users and the public plays a more important role, and will play a guiding role in the development of information interaction design.

3.3   Evaluation Methods

The IID evaluation methods discussed in this article include questionnaire, user interview, eye tracker experiment, workshop, etc.

User-based observation and test help to more accurately determine the state of the information interaction design and can also be used to evaluate the prototype. The user's behavior can be observed by notes, audio, video and interactive logs. It should be noted that the process of observation should not interfere with the user, or the results will have greater deviation. The basic purpose of test is to compare the impact of different design scenarios by measuring the user's performance of the task. As mentioned earlier, usability test is completed by typical users to perform typical tasks. The data collected can be used to analyze the user's action efficiency, time, error rate and operational steps. The results of the test will include mean and standard deviation.

Questionnaire is a commonly used method to collect statistical data and user experience. Questionnaire design can be open or closed, however it should be noted that the design of questions must be specific, with clear wording and directivity. Through a similar structured interview, the questionnaire is designed with more careful logic to collect a large number of users' opinions so as to find the general one. It is convenient, intuitive and fast. In addition, with the popularity of smart devices and mobile APP, many forms of questionnaire have been separated from the traditional paper, showing cross-media and cross-time zone characteristics, which further expand its applicability.

Similar to the questionnaire, the user interview is also a general technique widely used in sociology, psychology and marketing, suitable for rapid evaluation, usability test and field research. Different from the questionnaire, the form of user interview is more vivid and more acceptable to the user, which is usually a dialogue process with clear goals, and the results need to be sorted and analyzed from the perspective of context. In order to ensure the quality of the interview, the host should avoid too long questions and the words that may mislead the interviewees, and regularly transit from the simple question to the complex question to make a pleasant interview with the interviewee as far as possible.

Design workshop is a new carrier for IID evaluation. In the design process of past products, the most common is a relatively extensive model to implement product features, supplemented by a shaping 'shell' that is pushed to the user. As to whether the product is reasonable to meet the needs of users and create good product experience, the actual results are often unsatisfactory. Designers are accustomed to follow the existing design experience, and the so-called 'user research' more still remains on the surface and does not really reflect the design pain points. This design pattern has encountered more and more problems, and the essential reason is that the user group the product design faces is not merely an imaginary user model or a simple network ID code, but they are real vivid individuals. The characteristics, attributes and needs of user groups are becoming more diversified and individualized than the past.

IID-oriented design workshops focus on the process of 'inspiration, integration, insight, and creativity' in product design, with more emphasis on early-stage research and discussion of product design rather than direct finish product. Each workshop participant plays the dual role of 'common user' and 'product designer'. Compared to the systematic product design process, it lacks of 'practice' and 'evaluation' to find and capture the creativity best reflecting the pain point of design through the design team communication and collaboration and use design tools to polish the design details. The design workshop aims to explore the fusion paradigm of creativity, technology and culture, which will be a microcosm of product design from past closed self-research model to cross-border open collaborative model. It should be noted that, in addition to the product design at commercial level, design workshops also contain part of the public responsibility to guide social innovation. How to disseminate advanced design thinking and methods based on the workshops and improve the inclusive, diversified and open properties of design workshops as well as sustainable information sharing between the creative groups and targeted creativity sharing needs more practice cases to explore and summarize.

3.4   Evaluation Experiments

From the degree of completeness of information interaction design, there are two categories of evaluation experiments: one is stage evaluation, the evaluation in the design process, and the other is summarizing evaluation, the final evaluation after the completion of information interaction design. On the basis of the flexible use of the method, specific evaluation experiments are designed scientifically and rationally.

As argued in this article in combination with the effective experience of psychology, sociology and anthropology, the subjective evaluation of information interaction design can obtain the conversion results from the design prototype to the design results through the following methods: (1) Heuristic evaluation: subjective evaluation by expert guidance; (2) Usability test: analysis and test based on user experience quality; (3) Guidelines: self-evaluation in the construction process by the designer through certain design requirements; (4) Cognitive walkthrough: the targeted users' cognitive level of information interaction design. Through detailed analysis of the characteristics of information interaction design products, the evaluation experiment is designed scientifically and rationally, with quantitative analysis of experimental results as well as qualitative conclusion of the strengths and weaknesses of information interaction design products.

It should be emphasized that in the analysis of the evaluation results, attention must be first paid to the analysis of variables, including specific environmental characteristics, behavioral psychology, technical attributes, and interactive methods in order to ensure the analysis and accurate treatment of specific situations. Secondly, according to the 'user-centered' design idea, specific user emotional effect is analyzed, and weights of evaluation indicators of specific information interaction design are adjusted. Through the quantitative accumulation and the result analysis of multiple evaluation experiments, the evaluation criterion of information interaction design is iterated sustainably, and the application range of subjective evaluation experiment is expanded.

By constructing the 4D evaluation system of IID and the general process that integrates it with information interaction design, it is intended to find the model/path that combines design theory and design practice more closely. Meanwhile, based on the application of information technology in information interaction design, a new way of information interaction that is oriented to the future, stands to reason and meets the demand of users will be also envisaged. Additionally, in a technological context characterized by informatization and intelligence, setting up the 4D evaluation system of IID is also conducive to exploring how to achieve the effective intersection and integration of different disciplines and guide the innovation of IID language and aesthetic ideas that suit with the characteristics of the information age.

4   Evaluation Case Study: Taking "CM Browser" as Evaluate Subject

This paper selects the old and new version of CM browser as the evaluation case of IID four-dimensional evaluation model discussed in this paper, and tries to discuss it from four perspectives. In the experimental sample, 20 people were selected for telephone interviews and 8 interviews were conducted (Fig. 3).

Fig. 3. New version of CM browser design

Different from the old version, the new version of the CM browser highlights are "features of the toolbar", "folding animation", "video playback record", "search and browsing records combined" and other functions. In the design of the navigation page, the home page is a combination of nine palace grid and list navigation, focus within the collection and Kingsoft navigation. In the form of navigation, and with "collection of history" on the first tab in the Palace, Kingsoft URL navigation on the middle position to highlight the two labels. The list URL navigation is expanded with shadows to enhance the area separation, thus the hierarchical relationship is clear. This navigation design path in compared with the old version, more suitable for users in different environments which have a higher level of flexibility and quality of user experience (Fig. 4).

Fig. 4. Navigation design of new version

In the page display section, slide up into full-screen mode, slide back to normal page, increase the page display space and improve the reading experience, compared to the QQ browser from the menu bar into the full-screen mode more efficient, more ingenious form. The new version of the product design more emphasis on the application of dynamic technology, so that the whole effect becomes more beautiful.

In the search page part of the search page collection of history and favorites, so that users can easily access based on history and favorites. In the search page, the specific page can not be deleted; in the history page, only the full list can be clear, may affect the user experience effects. In the new version of the design, more embodies the "user-oriented" design concept, but the inadequacies also need to further iterations and optimization (Fig. 5).

Fig. 5. Search page design of new version

The new version of CM browser to compare with the old version, the new version reduce some features, such as account, share, scan two-dimensional code, no map mode, recent access and other functions are canceled; only keep the browser several basic functions such as Search, collection, history, night mode, the overall function is more concise, more prominent product focus. The new version attaches great importance to the user experience, a lot of operation reflects the "only when users need to appear," the design principles, animation is stunning, the first use impressive. Overall, this is a visual appearance, the operation on a powerful, user-oriented experience, the function is relatively simple personality browser (Table 1).

Through the "environment", "user", "technology", "product" four aspects of 4D evaluation system model, the new version than the old version has been more user support and welcome. Specific scores, the old score of 7.47 points, the new version score of 8.37 points. Overall, the new version of the product according to their product positioning, cut not commonly used functions, focusing on the basic functions; operation details of the user experience, a rich feedback through the operation of the user to deepen the identification of the function. Through appropriate animation guide user's operating behavior; but are in the ordinary function to optimize the above, no too obvious and abrupt changes. Full respect for the priority of the information level, according to product positioning, the use of color, font size to highlight the main information, and filter some miscellaneous information. Overall, the evaluation of the model to obtain the basic scores can reflect the difference between the quality of the product itself. However, in

Table 1. Evaluation statics of CM browser

Levene's Test for Equality of Variances		t-test for Equality of Means						
							95% Confidence Interval of the Difference	
F	Sig	t	df	Sig. (2-tailed)	Mean Difference	Std. Error Difference	Lower	Upper
.065	.799	-.569	2157	.570	-.39317	.69150	-1.74925	.96290
		-.577	29.849	.568	-.39317	.68115	-1.78456	.99821
.839	.360	.486	2157	.627	.83852	1.72458	-2.54351	4.22054
		.820	31.460	.418	.83852	1.02221	-1.24506	2.92209
1.811	.179	.995	2157	.320	.17656	.17740	-.17134	.52446
		1.593	31.199	.121	.17656	.11084	-.04944	.40256

the follow-up study, more cases are needed to test the reasonableness of the 4D evaluation model, and to continue the iteration and optimization.

5 Conclusion

The innovative points of the paper include: (1) the IID evaluation system focuses on standardizing and promoting the interactive behavior of user groups. It attaches particular importance to establish a more rational way of information interaction and corresponding codes of conduct for human beings in such an information age. (2) The goal of constructing the 4D evaluation system of IID is to evaluate the degree of target completion of information interaction in a rational way, and balance the restrictive relationship between the subject of information interaction and the environment. (3) The user-oriented design is the core idea of the 4D evaluation system of IID, while the "evaluation with public participation" is the top priority that guarantees the sustainable development of the evaluation system.

By constructing the 4D evaluation system of IID, the present study will be able to create more value from the emotional effects of users and culture creativity. Meanwhile, the rationality that the "design-evaluation-design" cycle can be considered as the general design process of IID will be also verified in practice. It should be noted that the evaluation object of the 4D evaluation system is not limited to common intelligence products. The information interaction of public service system like metro space is also the important research object of this evaluation system.

Acknowledgements. This paper was supported by the project from National social science fund of china "4D evaluation model research and application of information interaction design (16CG170)".

References

1. Liu, G.: Design Methodology, p. 3. Higher Education Press, Beijing (2011)
2. Zheng, Y.: The historical evolution of IID. In: HCII 2014 Conference Book, Crete (2014)
3. Lu, X.: Core of the media operations. http://news.xinhuanet.com/newmedia/2005-01/07/content_2427865.htm
4. Shedroff, N.: Information interaction design. A unified field theory of design. In: Jacobsen, R. (ed.) Information Deisgn, pp. 267–292. The MIT Press, Massachusetts (1999)
5. Zhang, L.: Semiotic Approach To Product Design, p. 126. China Building Industry Press, Beijing (2011)
6. Kelly, K.: What Technology Wants. CITIC Publishing House, Beijing (2011). Preamble
7. Nielsen, J.: Usability Engineering. Academic Press, Burlington (1994)
8. Garrett, J.J.: The Elements of User Experience: User-Centered Design for the Web, pp. 13–20. New Riders Publishing, New York (2003)
9. Garrett, J.: User Experience Elements. Mechanical Industry Press, Beijing (2007)

User Centered Design in the Software Development Lifecycle

Converging Data with Design Within Agile and Continuous Delivery Environments

Jay Brewer, Ger Joyce$^{(\boxtimes)}$, and Saurabh Dutta

Rapid7, 100 Summer Street, Boston, MA 02110, USA
{jbrewer,gjoyce,sdutta}@rapid7.com

Abstract. Traditional user research methods, while vital to understanding software application users, can be slow to implement and learn from. Even after results are analyzed, behavioral intention, not actual user behavior, tends to be better understood. To complement this approach, big data and behavioral analytics can be used to quickly learn more about actual user behavior, thus converging data with design. This is important within fast-paced agile and continuous delivery environments. At Rapid7, an IT and analytics information security organization, the convergence of data with design has allowed for insights that have informed design decisions, which have met users' mental models and actual needs. To that end, the software design industry is starting to diverge from the form-follows-function school of design, whereby the conventional approach of the user informing the designer has been reversed.

Keywords: Data · Design · User research · UX · Human-Computer interaction

1 Introduction

Traditional user research methods, such as surveys, focus groups, contextual inquiry, and interviews (Fig. 1), can be time-consuming to set up, run, and analyze [1]. In addition, traditional methods tend to elicit behavioral intention, which may differ to actual user behavior once a product or feature is released. This approach was well-suited to slower paced waterfall software development processes. However, as fast-paced agile and continuous delivery software development processes become ubiquitous [2], the design of software applications is rarely static—applications across all channels, including the cloud, mobile, desktop, virtual reality, and wearables, tend to change, even minimally, with each iteration. Thus, Human-Computer Interaction (HCI) researchers are finding that there is little time for research before software is released. While the quantitative methods and qualitative methods they have relied upon for years are not going away anytime soon, researchers need a method that will allow them to inform design decisions quickly.

Enter big data and behavioral analytics—both have changed the face of Human-Computer Interaction (HCI) research, and will become the mainstay of researchers in the years to come. This paper looks deeper into this phenomenon, where data converges with design within agile and continuous delivery environments. By gleaning insights from big data and behavioral analytics, HCI researchers can answer many of their questions, even before speaking with a single user of an application. This is a

© Springer International Publishing AG 2017
A. Marcus and W. Wang (Eds.): DUXU 2017, Part I, LNCS 10288, pp. 533–542, 2017.
DOI: 10.1007/978-3-319-58634-2_39

Fig. 1. An author of this work conducting traditional HCI research

relatively new approach, which can be beneficial to many industries, not least information security. With many of the world's top organizations fully reliant on information security software, it is simply not good enough for information security software providers to release updates months or years apart. One of the leading information security software providers, Rapid7, an organization that provides software to transform data into insight for IT and security professionals, has ensured that their HCI designers have full access to big data and behavioral analytics, thus allowing data to inform design decisions.

Within this paper, the authors focus on an empirical example of the convergence of data and design at Rapid7. During the case study, the design implications from behavioral analytical learnings, which may not otherwise have occurred, are discussed. The information security application that we will focus on is InsightIDR, an incident detection and response tool. This application detects and alerts on information security related incidents and suspicious behavior, such as that caused by stolen employee user names and passwords.

2   Background

2.1   Waterfall Software Development Methodology

The waterfall software development methodology was the primary approach to developing software in the 1980's and 1990's. The methodology is linear in nature (Fig. 2), whereby each phase could not start until the previous phase was fully completed. Requirements were fully laid out months or years in advance of the final delivery of the product. These requirements could take quite some time to define, given that there could be many stakeholders, and discussions around requirements were often lengthy. Once requirements were finally defined, only then did the design phase start. Given the relatively slow pace of waterfall software development methodologies, HCI researchers and designers usually had time to conduct a significant amount of research, as well as explore different design approaches. After the research and design deliverables were handed over to engineers, development started. Later in the process, Quality Assurance teams tested the software, and bugs were fixed. Following a review by the various stakeholders, the application was released to customers.

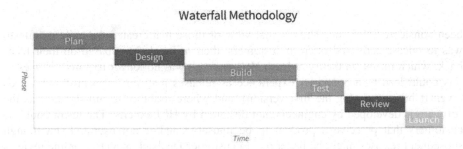

Fig. 2. Waterfall software development methodology

Even readers unfamiliar with the waterfall process will immediately see the potential issues. One such example was that as estimating project time and cost years in advance is quite difficult, most waterfall-based software development projects suffered high cost overruns, and were delivered much later than originally planned [3]. Additionally, during the months and years that the software was being developed, customer needs often changed. However, as a significant effort had been made in resources, time, and cost to create the software, major changes were rarely made. To that end, customers frequently did not receive the product they expected, resulting in dissatisfaction.

2.2 Agile Software Development Methodology

While waterfall was the primary methodology used for decades, changes needed to be made as software became more customer-focused. Consequently, the agile manifesto was created by a group of developers in Salt Lake City, Utah [4]. The new methodology promised a much shorter design and development loop (Fig. 3), with software being released usually every 1–4 weeks. This, in turn, allows for a much faster release cycle.

Yet, agile methodologies are not without problems. HCI researchers often have difficulty in conducting meaningful, rigorous research within fast-paced agile environments [5, 6]. In fact, common HCI-related activities, such as usability evaluations, are often eliminated within fast-paced agile environments, [7, 8]. It is possible that this was foreseen as the agile manifesto was being developed, however it may not have

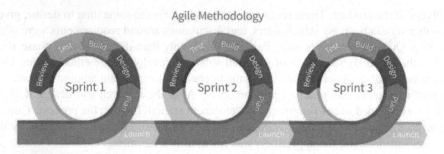

Fig. 3. Agile software development methodology

been considered an issue. The original view of those that created the agile manifesto was to release early and often to customers, then make changes based on their feedback, which meant, in theory at least, HCI research was no longer required. However, this could lead to a poor user experience as releases may not meet customer needs (even if initially during the first version), and where usability is sub-standard as the software is developed by engineers, not designed by HCI experts. The result could be customers that perceive a product to be unusable and/or not useful. Even though subsequent releases might be better due to customer feedback, negative online reviews could result in poor future sales [9]. HCI researchers, therefore, have a vital role to play within agile environments. However, HCI researchers must adapt their approach, even with traditional research, in order to offer actionable insights as quickly as possible. In short, HCI researchers need to plan, gather, and analyze research much faster within agile environments [10].

2.3   Continuous Delivery Software Development Methodology

Agile methodologies result in releases every several weeks. Therefore, while agile software development methodologies are faster than waterfall, many organizations find that even this release cadence this too slow to deploy software within an ever-increasingly competitive market. Consequently, several pioneers have automated many aspects of the software development life cycle, such as testing and building. This allows for small incremental releases, whereby bug fixes, new features, backend updates can be released quickly, often on a daily basis. This software development methodology has become known as continuous delivery (Fig. 4) [11]. While the practice is not yet widespread, the promise of faster time-to-market, fewer software bugs, and more secure applications [12] may lead to a growth in popularity. This is despite the significant technical challenges involved in setting an organization up for continuous delivery [13].

The organizations that have implemented the methodology report good results. Several teams at Facebook, for instance, have implemented continuous delivery software development methodologies, which have resulted in thousands of incremental deployments every day [2]. Even with this high number of deployments, the quality of the software actually rose.

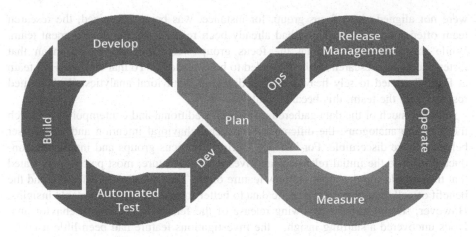

Fig. 4. Continuous delivery software development methodology

It is no surprise that HCI researchers working within continuous delivery environments have found that the time for up-front research, as well as discovering changes in user behavior, has diminished due to the increase in frequency of software releases. Researchers have attempted to tackle this challenge in several ways. For instance, Beasley [14] investigated the use of Google Analytics, yet, concluded that such data was designed for marketing teams, not HCI experts. From a mobile perspective, McGregor et al. [15], recorded participants' screens, only to discover that analyzing the resulting videos was prohibitively slow. As more and more organizations migrate to fast-paced methodologies, the convergence of data with design will become even more important.

3 Case Study

To focus on an empirical illustration of the convergence of data with design, consider InsightIDR, Rapid7's incident detection and response cloud-based application. The product was designed to assist incident responders, who are generally notified with an email alert, in surfacing data surrounding a potential information security breach. Should the probability lean toward an actual information security breach, an incident responder could use the application to add context, such as an attacker's path, by using related enriched data from within and outside Rapid7 applications. The full scope of the issue could be defined within an investigation timeline within the application. The end-result being that the attacker's path can be quickly shut down, and sealed against future attack.

As is common with software application design, traditional user research methods were employed during the initial research phase. This took the form of focus groups, surveys, and interviews with information security professionals. As the software was developed and released on a fast-paced agile schedule, the research team continued to rely on traditional research methods. However, the pace of research and development were not aligned. As a focus group, for instance, was being organized, the research team often found that a feature had already been released by the development team. While this did not mean that the focus group was cancelled, it did mean that faster-paced user research methods needed to be considered. To that end, the HCI team at Rapid7 started to rely heavily on big data and behavioral analytics. With limited resources on the team, this became vital.

While, much of the data gathered using both traditional and contemporary research methods are analogous, the differences between behavioral intention and actual user behavior were discernible. For instance, during the focus groups and interviews conducted prior to the initial release of an Investigations feature, most participants stated that they would use the proposed new feature often. The Investigations feature had the benefit of collating disparate, eclectic data to better form a series of actionable insights. However, several months following release of the feature, analysis of behavior analytics uncovered a startling insight—the Investigations feature had been little used by any customers since its release. When a feature is not being utilized as much as it might, this may not be critical for many industries. However, underutilized information security applications could decrease the security posture of an organization. This insight resulted in an informed re-design to ensure that the feature was even more visible, useful, and useable. The re-design led to a three-fold increase in the use of the Investigations feature (Fig. 5).

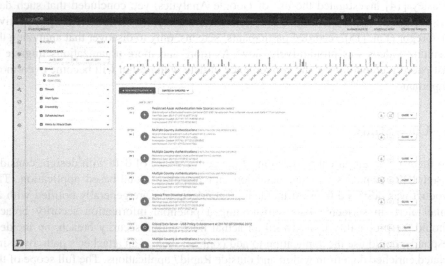

Fig. 5. InsightIDR investigations

When behavioral analytic insights show that a feature is underutilized, there are other strategies that can be employed, should an increase in usage be deemed critical. One such strategy is to tactically inform a user at the appropriate time that it might be in their best interest to consider the feature. In the case of InsightIDR, this approach led to more information security professionals closing Investigations (Fig. 6). While this is never a substitute for well-designed software, the approach can help HCI teams to guide the users of their applications to success. The messages employed not only need to be tactful, but they should also not be intrusive. Tactful nudges should only be used to guide a user to complete a task, or allow the user to consider a more effective approach that they might not otherwise have considered. Such guidance, therefore, should not clutter or adversely impact the user experience. Another such campaign within InsightIDR resulted in a four-fold increase in adoption of dashboards. These nudges were initially a manual effort, and have since been automated. This approach is scalable and cost-effective in that it is conducted in a touchless manner [16].

Fig. 6. InsightIDR: Closing an investigation

Other insights gathered using behavioral analytics included learnings around the user base. In some cases, software can be designed in different ways to suit different types of users. Alternatively, there could be one application that needs to be all things to many types of users. Each approach can be difficult to design for, even if each type of user is mapped to a specific persona [17]. While, the research team at Rapid7 already had defined a strong ecosystem of personas using Lean UX principles, it was only by using big data and behavioral analytics that the team became fully aware of which types of personas used which features. These insights were aggregated over time in the continuum of product usage. Additionally, knowing which features were used by which personas allowed the design of specific features for those personas that might not otherwise have been designed. Further, for future releases, the team's designs are tested by a segmented audience represented by a specific persona, generally during a canary release [18]. The insights gathered help to demonstrate if the design works or does not work for that audience. These insights are combined with the theory of planned behavior [19], allowing the design team to avail of predictive modeling. Based on inductive reasoning from predictive models, it can be determined if a feature will be used or not. Thus, the design of InsightIDR may change during subsequent iterations or features and functionality may simply be removed to save cost.

Yet, not only are insights gained in regard to user types. Access to applications in a seamless way are often sought by users across different types of devices and channels. This could include mobile, TV, wearables, and virtual reality. Using benchmarking and signals, changes in behavior can be detected regarding the switch from web to mobile and vice versa. With InsightIDR, this has led to the ability for users to receive actionable alerts on their mobile devices, as they are not always at their workstations. In a world where information security breaches are commonplace nowadays, minutes often matter to information security professionals. Actionable mobile alerts can, therefore, allow for the quick containment of an attack.

Finally, while there have been numerous advantages to complementing, comparing, and contrasting traditional user research with big data and behavioral analytics for the HCI team at Rapid7, the benefits do not end there. The HCI team could more easily share proven insights, with associated evidence, across the organization. This has led to previously siloed departments communicating regularly to ensure customer success, by enabling customers to fill the security gaps that they might not have realized existed. As sharing and reading qualitative data can be time-consuming, processes at Rapid7 needed to change to enable faster response times. Consequently, the HCI team collaborated with other teams to define the Product Engagement Index (PEI). The PEI assigns a single quantitative score, supported by qualitative insights, to aggregate user behavior. Thus, teams across Rapid7 can see how "healthy" a customer is based on their usage. A low PEI could signify a customer that underutilizes InsightIDR and other Rapid7 products due to a lack of security maturity and insufficient information security team skills. The Customer Success team could then suggest that the customer avail of Rapid7's Managed Services to plug the security gaps that existed within the customer's security posture. A medium PEI score could alert the Customer Success team to a maturing security customer that simply did not know about features that would increase their security maturity and posture. Tactful use of touchless guides, followed by a timely phone call from the Customer Success team, has proven to truly assist customers in becoming far more secure. This approach generally results in a higher PEI score, and in some cases over 200% increase in the usage of certain features. Additionally, PEI can also help to inform design decisions, as it is used to apprise aggregate focus for the overall design of InsightIDR and other Rapid7 tools.

4 Conclusion

Traditional research methods, such as surveys, focus groups, contextual inquiry, and interviews, tend to be slow to implement and analyze. While this was appropriate for slower-paced waterfall software development methodologies, with the advent of faster-paced agile and continuous delivery software development methodologies, it is important to consider more suitable options. This is due to the difficulty that HCI researchers have in finding the time for research before software is released.

One of the potential options, which can allow HCI researchers to learn more about which types of users are interacting with an application, as well as which tasks they are performing, is the use big data and behavioral analytics. From a philosophical perspective, the use of big data and behavioral analytics transforms HCI researchers' epistemological perspective from more traditional paradigms, such as post-positivism and interpretivism, to a more pragmatic approach. Pragmatism [20] allows researchers to use whatever methods they feel will answer their research questions [21, 22]. This is an important distinction, as without a philosophical consideration, many researchers simply follow the most frequently used paradigm of their field [23]. This philosophical approach allows for the use of traditional research methods, in tandem with behavioral analytics, not a case of one or the other.

The use of big data and behavioral analytics has many benefits for HCI teams, allowing for the convergence of data and design. At Rapid7, the HCI team has relied on behavioral analytics primarily for three intrinsic benefits:

1. **User profiling and expertise assessment**
   Quickly and accurately learn about actual user behavior, so that custom experiences can be offered based on expertise and user type
2. **Predictive analytics**
   Better understand future user intentions, thus meeting precise user needs. This differs to traditional user research methods, which are often reactive
3. **Benchmarking and signals**
   Analyze trends across multiple channels, including web, mobile, wearable, TV, virtual reality, and Internet of Things (IoT) to establish norms and detect deviation across devices and channels.

Insights allow for informed design decisions whereby an application or parts of the application, can be quickly re-designed to meet users' mental models and actual needs, which is vital in a world of fast-paced agile and continuous delivery environments. Alternative options, however, should not replace traditional methods—instead, these options should be used to triangulate, complement, compare, and contrast holistic insights gathered. This is due to the efficiency of big data and behavioral analytics in answering "what"-type questions, but not the "why"-type questions. Consequently, it is often necessary to follow up on interesting behavioral analytics data with user interviews. These help HCI researchers to better understand why a user took a specific action. Even with the use of traditional research methods in answering some of the questions that behavioral analytics cannot, at Rapid7, we are aware that there is now a distinct divergence from the form-follows-function school of design, whereby the conventional approach of the user informing the designer has been reversed.

References

1. Salah, D., Paige, R., Cairns, P.: A practitioner perspective on integrating agile and user centred design. In: Proceedings of the 28th International BCS Human Computer Interaction Conference (HCI 2014), pp. 100–109 (2014)
2. Rossi, C., Shibley, E., Su, S., Beck, K., Savor, T., Stumm, M.: Continuous deployment of mobile software at facebook (showcase). In: Proceedings of the 2016 24th ACM SIGSOFT International Symposium on Foundations of Software Engineering (FSE 2016), pp. 12–23 (2016)
3. Bloch, M., Blumberg, S., Laartz, J.: Delivering large-scale IT projects on time, on budget, and on value. Financial Times (21 August 2012). https://www.ft.com/content/d34acf86-eba8-11e1-9356-00144feab49a. Accessed

4. Agile Manifesto: (2001). Retrieved from http://agilemanifesto.org/
5. Haikara, J.: Usability in agile software development: extending the interaction design process with personas approach. In: Concas, G., Damiani, E., Scotto, M., Succi, G. (eds.) XP 2007. LNCS, vol. 4536, pp. 153–156. Springer, Heidelberg (2007). doi:10.1007/978-3-540-73101-6_22
6. Humayoun, S.R., Dubinsky, Y., Catarci, T.: User evaluation support through development environment for agile software teams. In: Smart Organizations and Smart Artifacts, pp. 183–191 (2014)
7. Wale-kolade, A.Y., Nielsen, P.A.: Integrating usability practices into agile development: a case study. In: 23rd International Conference on Information Systems Development (ISD 2014), pp. 337–347 (2014)
8. Raison, C., Schmidt, S.: Keeping user centred design (UCD) alive and well in your organisation: taking an agile approach. In: Marcus, A. (ed.) DUXU 2013. LNCS, vol. 8012, pp. 573–582. Springer, Heidelberg (2013). doi:10.1007/978-3-642-39229-0_61
9. Forman, C., Ghose, A., Wiesenfeld, B.: Examining the relationship between reviews and sales: the role of reviewer identity disclosure in electronic markets. Inf. Syst. Res. **19**(3), 291–313 (2008)
10. Salvador, C., Nakasone, A., Pow-Sang, J.A.: A systematic review of usability techniques in agile methodologies. In: Proceedings of the 7th Euro American Conference on Telematics and Information Systems (EATIS 2014), pp. 1–6 (2014)
11. Humble, J., Farley, D.: Continuous Delivery: Reliable Software Releases Through Build, Test, and Deployment Automation. Pearson Education, Upper Saddle River (2011)
12. Chen, L.: Continuous delivery: overcoming adoption obstacles. In: Proceedings of the International Workshop on Continuous Software Evolution and Delivery (CSED 2016), p. 84 (2016)
13. Claps, G.G., BerntssonSvensson, R., Aurum, A.: On the journey to continuous deployment: technical and social challenges along the way. Inf. Softw. Technol. **57**(1), 21–31 (2015)
14. Beasley, M.: Practical Web Analytics for User Experience: How Analytics Can Help You Understand Your Users. Morgan Kaufmann, Burlington (2013)
15. McGregor, M., Brown, B., McMillan, D., Chi, W.: 100 days of iPhone use: mobile recording in the wild. In: Chi 2014, pp. 2335–2340 (2014)
16. Brewer, J., Dutta, S., Kriskovic, M.: From dark patterns to angel patterns: creating trust-worthy user experience. User Experience Mag **16**(5) (2017). Retrieved from http://uxpamagazine.org/from-dark-patterns-to-angel-patterns/
17. Bhattarai, R., Joyce, G., Dutta, S.: Information Security Application Design: Understanding Your Users. In: Tryfonas, T. (ed.) HAS 2016. LNCS, vol. 9750, pp. 103–113. Springer, Cham (2016). doi:10.1007/978-3-319-39381-0_10
18. Neely, S., Stolt, S.: Continuous delivery? Easy! just change everything (well, maybe it is not that easy). In: Proceedings AGILE 2013, pp. 121–128 (2013)
19. Ajzen, I.: The theory of planned behavior. Organ. Behav. Hum. Decis. Process. **50**, 179–211 (1991)
20. Talisse, R., Aikin, S.: Pragmatism: A Guide for the Perplexed. Bloomsbury Academic, London (2008)
21. Denscombe, M.: Good Research Guide: For Small-Scale Social Research Projects, 4th edn. McGraw-Hill Education, Berkshire, GBR (2010)
22. Frost, N.: Qualitative Research Methods in Psychology. McGraw-Hill, Berkshire, GBR (2011)
23. Hesse-Biber, S.N.: Mixed Methods Research: Merging Theory with Practice. Guilford Press, New York (2010)

Model-Based HCI System Development Methodology

Kyung Won Cha and Changbeom Choi[✉]

Handong Global University, Handong-ro,
Heunghae-eup, Kyungbuk 37554, Republic of Korea
{2120751,cbchoi}@handong.edu
http://www.handong.edu/eng

Abstract. Nowadays, many Human Computer Interaction(HCI) systems are developed and utilized to the various domains, such as medical field, and entertainment area. To develop an HCI system, a developer should consider developing hardware elements and software elements at the same time. One of the obstacles obstructing the HCI system is that, in the absence of hardware, there is no development environment. This paper proposes a model - based HCI system development environment and development methodology using it. The proposed development environment focuses on the Natural User Interface (NUI) which utilizes HCI's human movement, and it can replace human and sensor devices by using basic unit model. Also, the developer can test and develop the HCI system by creating a new model by synthesizing the basic unit model to build various patterns of the environment.

Keywords: Development methodology · Simulation-based development · Simulation-in-loop HCI system

1 Introduction

As the technology develops and spreads widely, the computer system has spread rapidly in everyday life. Most of the devices, such as smart TV, smart home, as well as smartphones, need interaction between human and computer system and concept of HCI has become necessary [1]. Interestingly, the entertainment domain researched the HCI systems and most well known HCI systems are game consoles. Such HCI systems can be categorized by two categories, controller-less system and system with controllers. The Nintendo Wii [2] and Oculus RIFT [3] uses separate controllers to sense body movements and recognize them as gestures, while Microsoft Xbox Kinect [4], using depth and vision sensors, users do not need a separate controller. Nevertheless, the workflows of those HCI systems are the same. Following Fig. 1 shows the workflows of the HCI system.

As shown in the figure, a sensor receives the person's motion. When a sensor senses the motion, the hardware will handle the motion and generate a signal. Then the hardware will send a sequence of the signal to the software, and the

© Springer International Publishing AG 2017
A. Marcus and W. Wang (Eds.): DUXU 2017, Part I, LNCS 10288, pp. 543–553, 2017.
DOI: 10.1007/978-3-319-58634-2_40

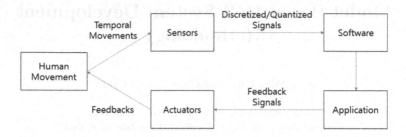

Fig. 1. Workflow of HCI systems

software will process it as an event. After recognizing an event, the software will notice the application, which developer implements the business logic. Then the application will handle the event, and it will generate proper feedback to the human via actuators. Therefore, a developer should consider the hardware, software, and human motion inputs to implement HCI system. The *hardware* is a sensor system that detects the human motions. The *software* handles signals from the hardware and generates an event. Also, the application can be considered as software, but it implements the business logics, such as assessment logic to give points to users. The *human motions* is the most delicate part during the development of the HCI system. Since a human movement may differ by age, gender, and physical size.

By considering considerations of developing an HCI system, this paper develops the development environment of HCI systems. In particular, this paper considers developing NUI system and its development methodology, since device based HCI system has common workflows. Also, most of the motion recognitions are based on the position of the hand controller; the research provides various support method. The supporting methods are depth image handling and skeleton handling. Since an HCI system focuses on detecting human behavior and generating feedback using the actuator, hardware and software should be developed first for the HCI system construction, and then the integrated system should be built by the developer in the existing development environment. That is, during the HCI system development process, the developer must develop and test the software part after the system hardware part is completed, which limits the development environment. Also, since the testing an HCI system is a Human-In-The-Loop (HITL) test in which a human is required to generate an input, even if a problem is found during testing, the problem can not be reproduced exactly every time. Therefore, this study proposes an environment to make HCI system development more efficient and proposes a methodology to utilize it.

2   Related Work

The existing HCI-related development methodology includes the Human-Centered Systems Development Life Cycle, HCSDLC [5,6]. The Fig. 2 shows the cycle. It is developed in the Systems Development Life Cycle, SDLC [7], which divides the system development into manageable steps. The methodology aims to satisfy both the organization and human needs in the overall system development process. In order to develop human-centered systems, developers have to consider the principles and guidelines for the development of a system that encompasses as many users as possible, integrates knowledge of various fields, and encourages many interactions. The characteristic of HCSDLC is that the analysis part includes the user acceptance test, which is one of the tests, and it can be seen that the HCI component is continuously considered throughout the process.

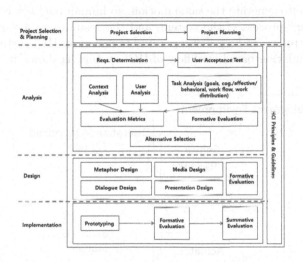

Fig. 2. Human-centered systems development life cycle

In the HCI system development, testing is an indispensable factor. Due to the nature of the HCI system, it must receives input from a sensor or controller from the outside and respond to it, but there is no specific reference to this in the existing methodology. Although there is a limitation in the development of the software in the future when there is no hardware in the past, this study proposes a methodology to regenerate and combine new input through several existing input data in order to provide an environment that can simultaneously develop software and hardware even if there is no hardware such as sensors required for the system.

3   HCI System Development Methodology

Aforementioned, the hardware in the HCI system receives a human's motion. The hardware system has various sensors to detect human motions, such as Infrared camera, multiple camera system and microphones. Since such sensors handles continuous signals, the software part of the HCI system should process continuous signal to generate events. Also, the HCI system has business logics as software. As a result, the development methodology of the HCI system consider integrating independent systems, such as hardware system and software system. Moreover, the developer may consider developing the system when the system does not exists. Unlike the existing development methodology, the development of the HCI system should consider hardware and software at the same time. It is also difficult to control the test environment of the HCI system because human motion is in the flow of the system. If a tester finds an error during a partial implementation and test, the tester must repeatedly generate the same operation at the same rate to find out what the error is. However, humans are not always able to generate the same motion, so human may not be sufficient for the development process of the system, and the results may be inaccurate and inefficient. Therefore, to help developer and tester of an HCI system, this study proposes a simulation based workflow of HCI system as shown in Fig. 3.

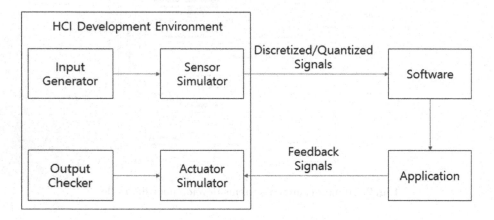

Fig. 3. Proposed simulation based workflow

A sensor simulator can replace human motion and sensor parts in the typical HCI system and testing flow by defining a model representing the main body movement. This input is used to process in software and applications to check if the desired feedback results. By using the test environment, developers can utilize some of the existing resources and use it to regenerate various body movements according to the needs and test them.

The steps for implementing the proposed testing environment are divided into three stages as shown in Fig. 4: preparation, development, and integration.

In the first preparation step, it is determined which data to prepare for a certain target movement, and information about depth and skeleton is extracted and stored in files. The preparation phase can be created using the sensor for development or data to be used, or it can be replaced with existing data used in other projects. In the subsequent development stage, development based on testing is performed using the data created in the preparation stage. It decides

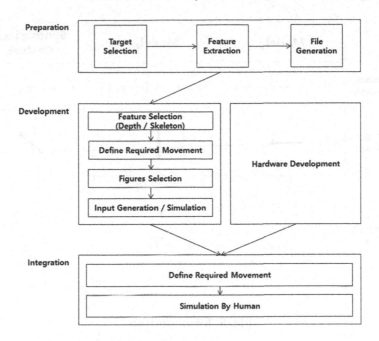

Fig. 4. Proposed HCI development methodology based on simulation

what kind of data it needs and defines the required movements for it. If developers select the depth data, select the shape of the hand after the motion definition, and then create the input and test the HCI system. The HCI system itself requires both humans and software and hardware, so if the hardware is not available, or has not been developed yet, or is lacking, further development can be difficult. It provides an environment that can be developed using the data prepared in the preparation stage, and the software can be unaffected by the speed of hardware development, and the hardware can be fully developed. Also, developers can perform the testing by reducing the other variables in that the movements can be continuously and exactly created on the same stage. By using this, input data for frequently occurring errors can be made; it helps to make testing easy. In the Integration step, developers define the required motion and test it. In the development stage, simulation is performed using existing data, but at integration stage, the actual person enters the testing loop and performs testing using the actual hardware and software. During the development process, the development and integration stages are continuously repeated, and this study proposes a testing-based development method based on the simulators.

To help a developer and tester this study provides event synthesis concepts. The Fig. 5 shows the simplified concept of motion generation.

As shown in the figure, $Model_1$ and $Model_2$ denotes the events of the human movements. Each model contains event scenario so that the model generate timed event sequence which denotes timed hand positions. In other words, the

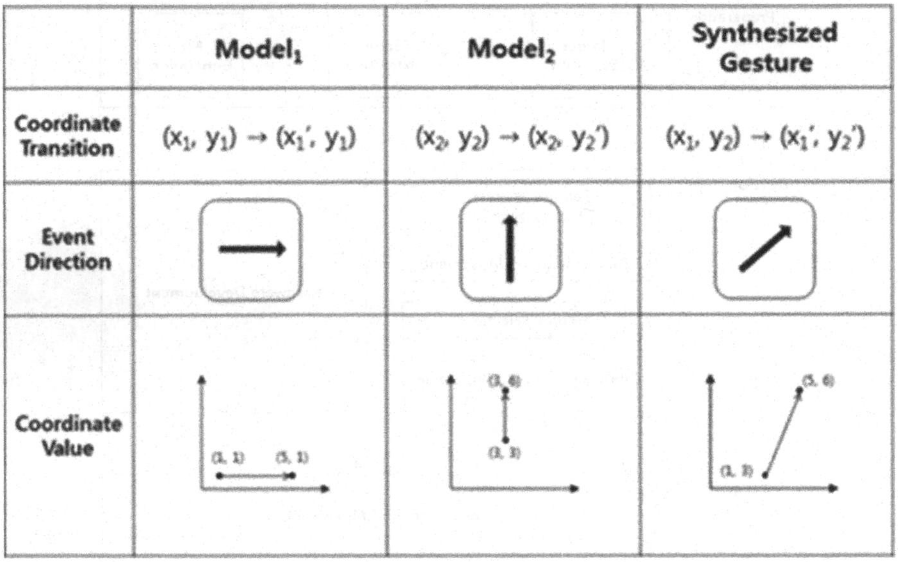

	Model₁	Model₂	Synthesized Gesture
Coordinate Transition	$(x_1, y_1) \rightarrow (x_1', y_1)$	$(x_2, y_2) \rightarrow (x_2, y_2')$	$(x_1, y_2) \rightarrow (x_1', y_2')$
Event Direction			
Coordinate Value			

Fig. 5. Event synthesis

Model₁ generate timed events from position (x_1, y_1) to (x_1, y_1). Also, the Model₂ generate timed events from position (x_2, y_2) to (x_2, y_2). When a developer wants to test pattern starts from (x_1, y_2) to (x_1, y_1), the developer should acquire test data from human. Therefore, this study proposes event synthesis concept. By using the first input event, moving from left to right to (x_1, y_1) to (x_1, y_1), and the second input event, moving from bottom to top moving from (x_2, y_2) to (x_2, y_2), it may create new input event data, which start from left bottom, (x_1, y_2), to right top, (x_1, y_2). The new input event data uses the position and amount of change of the x coordinate from the first input event data, and the new input event data is generated as follows using the position and the change amount of the y coordinate from the second input event data. By applying the method, a developer and a test may generate multiple motions using simple input event data, and conversely, one motion can be separated into multiple motion data.

4   Implementation Using Xbox Kinect

To show the feasibility of the proposed methodology, this research implements a HCI development environment using Xbox Kinect. Since Microsoft provides software interface to fetch event data from Xbox Kinect, we have utilize the Kinect to collect motion data and implemented a simulator to generate timed events. Also, the environment has event synthesis modules that synthesize the various events.

4.1   Preparation

This study uses Microsoft Xbox Kinect to determine the motion that wants to extract and extract the motion of the base unit. All data is recorded in raw data for later usage by the user and prepare a shaping unit that can give the actual movement shape to the motion created by the base unit input. In other words, if the generated file is depth information, it will be the depth raw data, the center point of motion, and the hand shape file. In a case of the skeleton, it is a file corresponding to the coordinates of each position of the skeleton.

4.2   Input Data

This paper focuses on the development of NUI system and uses Kinect composed of RGB sensor, depth sensor and IR sensor to construct environment of research and sensor data based model. In this paper, depth data and skeleton data which are useful for three-dimensional position and motion recognition are studied. In case of depth data, input file is defined as three. The depth data is binary data of the depth information coming at a rate of about 30 fps and the other is text data including the coordinates of the center point of the recognized object, hand. Finally, the shape data is hand shape data to be added to the motion to be generated later. Binary depth data can help developers to develop when there is no hardware. Text files help developers understand the movement of data and can be used to reconstruct data to predict and change the user's movements. In addition, developers can add one more input, depending on needs, which is the data that helps shape the shape already prepared. In this case, when it is necessary to grasp the movement of a specific shape, it is used to regenerate a desired type of input data. For skeleton data, input file is defined as one. This is the coordinate of each skeleton joint and can be used to track the movement of each segment.

4.3   Input Generation

There are three ways to create a new motion: modifying the coordinates in the text file, separating and combining existing data, and creating the desired motion with the simulator. In this paper, motion generation from depth data, motion generation from skeleton data, and motion generation from simulator are discussed.

Depth. This study proposes a method to generate new motion using information of motion of existing depth data. The existing input data consists of a binary file, which is raw data, and a text file, which is a coordinate of the center point. There are several steps to export information about the movement of 'hand' which is meaningful data. Handle only the depth data within a certain depth to grasp the motion of the hand without accepting the movements other than the hand. In addition, the distance of the image is transformed, and the focal point is recorded in the file as the center point of the hand that find the furthest point from the outside.

The raw data of the depth information is read from the created file through the following procedure. If the depth is within a certain range for understanding the movement, the RGB value is made 0 and the hand shape of the part is made white. The $input_1$ and $input_2$ images above in Fig. 6 show the hand shape created from the raw data. $input_1$ is part of the image moving from left to right, and $input_2$ is part of the image moving from bottom to top. In addition to restoring the two inputs, when generating new motion data, information about each motion is needed, and information corresponding to each motion is recorded in a text file for each input data. The third image in Fig. 6 shows the center point for the new movement from left bottom to right top using the coordinates from left to right and from bottom to top of $input_1$ and $input_2$. Tracking the movement can be done as follows. If developers have the shape of the hand needed, developers can use it to regenerate the new movement based on its center point.

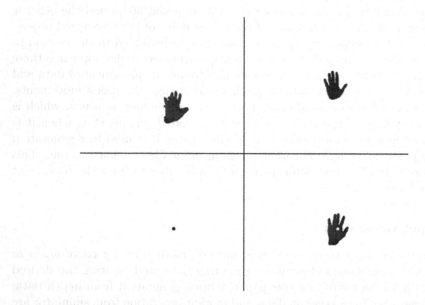

Fig. 6. Left-top is $input_1$, right-top image is $input_2$, left-bottom is center point of synthesized movement, right-bottom is movement and hand shape.

Skeleton. This study suggests a method to make another skeleton image using the skeletal motion obtained from Kinect. For this method, existing input data requires a file with raw data and the location of each skeleton. The method of generating raw data is the same as the process in depth. The data about the skeleton position is obtained using the functions provided by the Kinect API, and the data is generated in the same order as provided by the API so as to utilize the data. The skeleton has coordinates for each position, as shown in Fig. 7. The left side is the image of $input_1$, and it is the standing of a person. The right side is the image of $input_2$ and the person is sitting. If developers want to create a new motion by composing the following two data, developers have to set the standard of motion well and understand the need to move together. For example, if developers want to put the left hand of $input_1$ into the motion of $input_2$, applying the same coordinates will have an unnatural hand-off image. In this case, the relative movement of the hand with respect to the wrist at $input_1$ can be obtained and the relative position of the wrist of $input_2$ can be calculated to obtain the motion of the similar position with respect to the wrist. Likewise, this study tried to create a new input by synthesizing the movements of both arms of $input_1$ to $input_2$, where the relative position was the navel. Therefore, for the natural movement of the generated image arm, the relative coordinates of the shoulders, elbows, wrists, palms, thumbs, and fingers were calculated centering on the navel, and the new coordinates were calculated based on the navel of the $input_2$. Figure 8 shows the results of the study, showing that the lower body of input 2 is the sum of the upper arms of $input_1$, creating a new movement.

Fig. 7. Left is $input_1$ that the standing of a person, right is $input_2$ that sitting of a person.

Fig. 8. Synthesized skeleton image

4.4 Image Generation by Simulator

The way to create the desired movement of the user with the simulator is to use the hand shape received by using the existing Kinect. The movement of the input in a desired location and moving it to a desired location is divided into four cases, depending on the magnitude of the x and y coordinates of the starting point and the destination point. It is used to determine the type of the current movement. If the generated input moves at a given speed and arrives at the arrival point and leaves the original type, it is considered that one motion is finished and the next specified motion can be performed. Using this, continuous motion input can be created and utilized. Figure 9 shows the flow of the code-generated frames. Movements move in the order of $(0, 0)$, $(512, 424)$, $(300, 200)$, $(0, 0)$, $(200, 300)$, $(300, 200)$. Developers can code in multiple directions and consecutive movements rather than in a single direction.

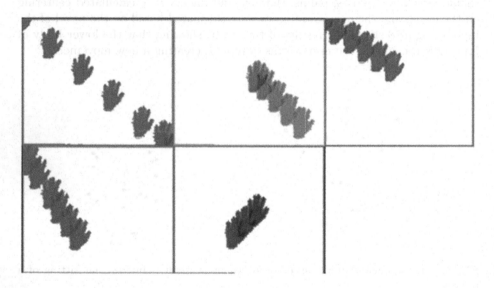

Fig. 9. Event sequence of movement by simulator

5 Conclusion

This study proposes a simulation-based development methodology that applies HCI system flow in HCI system development. Even if a limited environment such as a hardware or a tester is not available, the methodology supports developing the HCI system by using the stored event data. Therefore, a developer may develop software and hardware of the HCI system at the same time. Also, initiating the testing phase earlier, the development methodology can prevent errors to be found later and may lower the maintenance cost.

The methodology supports a developer and a tester of the HCI system, however, the motion synthesis may not cover entire requirements of the testing. Since motion events are generated based on the abstraction of hand angles and movements, a developer should consider the limitation of the motion synthesis. To ease the restrictions, a formalized modeling and simulation theory may be consider as an alternative solution.

References

1. Kim, G.J.: Human-Computer Interaction: Fundamentals and Practice. CRC Press Taylor & Francis Group, London (2015)
2. Nintendo Wii official homepage. http://www.nintendo.com/wiiu/what-is-wiiu
3. Oculus RIFT official homepage. https://www3.oculus.com/en-us/rift/
4. Xbox Kinect official homepage. http://www.xbox.com/en-US/xbox-one/accessories/kinect
5. Zhang, P., Carey, J., Te'eni, D., Tremaine, M.: Integrating human-computer interaction development into SDLC: a methodology. In: AMCIS 2004 Proceedings (2004)
6. Te'eni, D., Carey, J.M., Zhang, P.: Human-Computer Interaction: Developing Effective Organizational Infromation System. Wiley, New York (2006)
7. Ruparelia, N.B.: Software development lifecycle models. ACM SIGSOFT Softw. Eng. Notes **35**(3), 8–13 (2010)
8. Foster, I., Kesselman, C.: The Grid: Blueprint for a New Computing Infrastructure. Morgan Kaufmann, San Francisco (1999)
9. Czajkowski, K., Fitzgerald, S., Foster, I., Kesselman, C.: Grid information services for distributed resource sharing. In: 10th IEEE International Symposium on High Performance Distributed Computing, pp. 181–184. IEEE Press, New York (2001)
10. Foster, I., Kesselman, C., Nick, J., Tuecke, S.: The Physiology of the Grid: an Open Grid Services Architecture for Distributed Systems Integration. Technical report, Global Grid Forum (2002)
11. National Center for Biotechnology Information. http://www.ncbi.nlm.nih.gov

Integrating Participatory and Interaction Design of an Authoring Tool for Learning Objects Involving a Multidisciplinary Team

André Luiz de Brandão Damasceno[1]([✉]), Carlos de Salles Soares Neto[2],
and Simone Diniz Junqueira Barbosa[1]

[1] Pontifical Catholic University of Rio de Janeiro, Rio de Janeiro, RJ, Brazil
{adamasceno,simone}@inf.puc-rio.br
[2] Federal University of Maranhão, São Luís, MA, Brazil
csalles@deinf.ufma.br

Abstract. Traditional computer use in educational environments does not ensure learning improvement. Consequently, there is a global effort to make and provide more effective and efficient use of new multimedia resources and learning environments. Learning Objects (LOs) are entities, digital or not, which can be used or referenced during teaching. However, multimedia authoring of LOs is still complex and time consuming. In this paper we present a novel process integrating participatory and interaction design which we adopted in the development of an authoring tool involving a multidisciplinary team. As result, this methodology is used in the development of Cacuriá, a multimedia authoring tool for teachers with little or no programming skills to create LOs.

Keywords: Authoring tool · Mental-model · Navigation/search design · Participatory Design · Interaction Design · Learning Objects

1 Introduction

Teachers and students often make use of technologies that allow new ways of teaching and learning. Teaching has undergone many changes, and multimedia resources such as slideshows, videos, and games have been used in both distance and face-to-face education increasingly in recent times. Multimedia authoring environments can handle several multimedia resources, among which we find Learning Objects.

A Learning Object (LO) is defined as any entity, digital or not, that can be used, reused or referenced during a learning or training process supported by computer(s) [1,2]. The main role of an LO is to act as a teaching resource, including specific media contents of a subject such as image, text, video and audio, all synchronized amongst themselves. Miller et al. have shown that LOs improve the quality of teaching and help to provide tutors with several facilitating tools [3].

In general, a multidisciplinary team is required to build an LO. Its development can be a complex, expensive, and time-consuming process.

A. Marcus and W. Wang (Eds.): DUXU 2017, Part I, LNCS 10288, pp. 554–569, 2017.
DOI: 10.1007/978-3-319-58634-2_41

Software developers are required to make the source code. Designers help to provide a visual identity for distinct LOs. Education experts make and measure teaching goals. Furthermore, in the core of the team, there is the content specialist (e.g., teacher and tutor), who provides the subject to be taught.

It is interesting to compare the current scenario of development of LOs with content authoring on the Web. In the beginning, web pages were built almost exclusively by experts in markup languages and Internet protocols. Over time, the Web has been popularized and new jobs have been generated, for example, the web designer whose main role is to design and develop web pages. Currently, a wide range of content on the Web is created by non-developers [4], such as blogs, which can be made and managed by end users with no knowledge of a programming language for the Web. Other users (e.g., journalists and writers) create profiles in social networks containing texts, videos, pictures and different additional multimedia components. The support for end users to author content on the Web is arguably one of the reasons that explain its popularization [4].

Likewise, in the context of LO authoring, in many situations the content expert could make LOs using an authoring tool. Our aim is not to replace a multidisciplinary team, but to let the teacher build simpler or preliminary LOs directly. We acknowledge that, in some situations (e.g. company websites, content portals and enterprise search systems), a multidisciplinary team to create web pages is essential.

The purpose of this paper is to describe the application of an integrated Participatory and Interaction Design (PID) to the design of an authoring tool for learning objects involving a multidisciplinary team. In particular, we describe the development of a multimedia authoring tool names Cacuriá[1], which allows teachers to build interactive nonlinear LOs for the Web and Digital TV. Teachers do not need previous knowledge of software development when creating LOs with Cacuriá. Furthermore, teachers may specify temporal synchronism among multimedia objects (e.g., video, image, text) arranged in scenes. Cacuriá supports the creation of branching plotlines, allowing the viewers to watch only the parts of the LO they find relevant to them.

This paper is structured as follows. Section 2 describes the integrated Participatory and Interaction Design (PID). Section 3 describes its application to the development of the Cacuriá multimedia authoring tool. Lastly, Sect. 4 presents some final considerations.

2   Methodology

User participation in systems development is considered essential to gather usability requirements and avoid usability problems [6]. Participatory Interaction Design (PID) is considered an efficient way to describe user requirements [5]. We then chose to design our multimedia authoring tool using PID, which is a combination of Participatory Design (PD) [7] and Interaction Design (IxD) [8].

---

[1] Cacuriá is the name of a Brazilian dance that is popular in the state of Maranhão.

Participatory design (PD) involves users throughout the design and development cycle, so they can provide expertise and participate in the design and implementation of computer-based systems [7]. Interaction Design (IxD) defines the structure and behavior of interactive systems aiming to facilitate human interactions [8]. Both approaches can be used not only in the computer science field, but also in contemporary design practices in other fields, such as service design. In this paper, we adopted the iterative interaction design process described by Roger et al. [9]. It consists of four main activities, illustrated in Fig. 1: identify needs and requirements; design (generating ideas); interactive prototype construction; and evaluation.

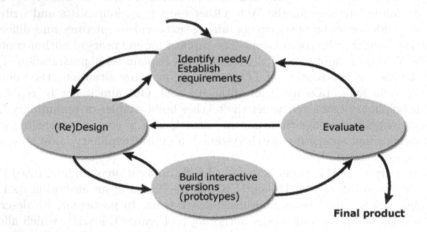

Fig. 1. Interaction design lifecycle [9].

To identify the key requirements for the authoring tool, we applied PD techniques such as focus group and card sorting. We also conducted paper prototyping sessions to gather further information about the user interface and interaction needs and wants. Next, we made a comparative analysis of LO authoring tools to evaluate whether they fulfilled the requirements identified using the PD techniques, as well as to improve our understanding of those requirements. The requirements gathered were thus enhanced and a multimedia authoring tool was proposed. Figure 2 presents the adopted PID process.

We can see two interaction lifecycles in the PID method. The first one is an iterative PD lifecycle [10]. The second one is the IxD lifecycle, formed by combining Interface Design, Implementation, and Evaluation. In both lifecycles we conduct activities of requirements gathering, design, prototyping, and evaluation, enhancing the designers' reflection about the final product. In this paper, we focus on the design phases; the evaluation phase and its lessons learned are detailed in [11].

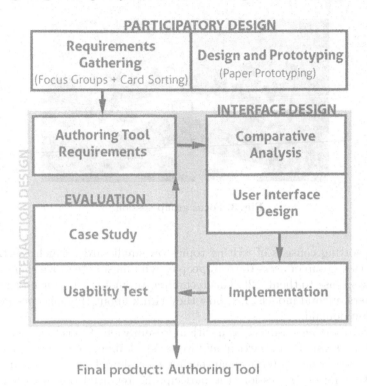

Fig. 2. Adopted PID process.

2.1 Participatory Design

The Participatory Design activities involved three techniques: focus group and card sorting, used in a meeting to gather requirements, and paper prototyping to evaluate concepts and clarify those requirements.

The participants of the Participatory Design sessions were stakeholders of the authoring tool. The sample selected consisted of 18 participants: teachers, undergraduate, and graduate students heterogeneously grouped in two sessions with 9 participants each. The participants were 3 undergraduate students and 5 Master's students in Design, 6 undergraduate students and 1 master's student in Computer Science, 2 high school teachers, and 1 pedagogue.

Requirements Gathering Through Focus Group and Card Sorting. Focus group is a qualitative technique that uncovers feelings, beliefs and opinions about the subject investigated through a kind of moderated collective interview, usually guided by a predefined script or list of topics [7]. In general, the aim of this technique is not to get the consensus of ideas, but to collect a range of opinions on a particular topic. The results are not analyzed as percentages or statistics and should not be generalized to a population [7]. Figure 3 illustrates how the technique was performed, keeping the participants anonymous.

Fig. 3. Focus group session.

Card sorting consists of writing topics on small cards, which are then distributed to a group of users (5 to 15 people) who must categorize them in a way that makes sense to them [12]. This technique promotes a better understanding of the users' mental models, i.e., how they think about the concepts in a given application domain.

The card sorting sessions began with a presentation of LOs to level the knowledge of the group. Then, participants were asked about the characteristics of a good LO, and what criteria an authoring tool should meet to create a good LO. At the end of the session, the participants reported the main features an authoring tool should have and grouped them in small paper cards (see Fig. 4).

Fig. 4. Session of card sorting technique.

Design and Prototyping. The next step in PD involved paper prototyping. A prototype can be seen as a draft design and aims to conduct tests for user interface evaluation. This kind of prototyping is considered low precision because it uses materials such as paper and cardboard, but tends to be simpler and faster to produce [13]. Its main goal is to evaluate designs early, thus helping to find problems before implementation starts.

The same participants of the previous activities were divided into 2 groups of 9 people. Each group was responsible for creating the user interface of a LO authoring tool based on the requirements obtained from the focus group and card sorting sessions (see Fig. 5). After finishing the prototype, one member of each team presented it, along with its underlying design vision and the types of LOs the proposed authoring tool would support creating. Then, they demonstrated the LO creation process and the possibilities of interaction and system feedback through the user interface.

Fig. 5. Paper prototyping session.

2.2 Interface Design

The user interface was designed based on the concepts identified in the solutions obtained in the PD activities and on a comparative analysis.

Comparative Analysis. We conducted a literature survey about authoring tools for LOs. Each tool was briefly described in a table and compared with the results obtained in the previous activities.

The purpose of analyzing similar authoring tools is to identify the characteristics of existing solutions and investigate the authoring approaches they support. Moreover, this activity also helped to find out whether existing tools already (partially) fulfilled the requirements gathered in the PD activities.

User Interface Design. In order to satisfy the desired requirements for the tool, the user interface design was conceived considering both the results obtained in the paper prototyping activity and on user interfaces and system features present in the tools identified in the comparative analysis.

3 Results

The general results gathered with the research methodology have led to a number of requirements for a new multimedia authoring tool and a user interface metaphor based on scenes. In addition, methods, techniques, and technologies were chosen for implementing the authoring tool.

3.1   Participatory Design

Based on the techniques used in the PD activities, we specified a set of requirements for the design and implementation of our multimedia authoring tool.

Requirements Gathering. We observed that the predefined script for the focus group yielded objective and relevant discussions. Most participants had some knowledge about LOs and had already used them to teach or to study.

Following the focus group script, participants started talking about what they knew about LOs and which models of learning objects they use in their teaching and learning processes. Most of them pointed out that the use of video and the possibility of the student to interact with the LO would improve and increase student focus on the LO content. An interesting point raised by the first group was the creation of a LO repository, in order to allow teachers be able to reference and reuse the content in LMSs (Learning Management Systems). However, for the stakeholders, sharing LOs in a repository raises copyright violation concerns.

Participants were unanimous in determining that an authoring tool should not require programming skills to build an LO. Both groups set as a requirement a minimalist interface, with few buttons and easy to use. Additionally, they considered that the tool should support the inclusion of media objects such as image, text, PDF and videos. Lastly, the second group reported that for a user to have a good experience and feel motivated to create LOs, the tool should be reliable and without errors.

Additional relevant information was obtained from the card sorting session. Table 1 shows an overview of the categorization made by the stakeholders. Some requirements for the design of authoring tools were obtained as a result of this phase.

Design and Prototyping. The adopted PID process allowed the stakeholders to easily explore diverse user interface solutions by assembling and disassembling user interface prototypes. In addition, it allowed stakeholders to find problems and easily solve them by themselves. When a problem was found, they would redesign the user interface and test it again. During the prototype tool demonstration, the groups presented good ideas, features and an user interface which was easy to understand. The main results achieved were the interactive designs with fewer usability problems, which avoid later rework and thus save time in implementing the authoring tool.

The first and the second group described minimalist interfaces. Both of them presented the video as the main media and the initial step for the creation of a LO. Another common decision was to use temporal and spatial views. The goal of the spatial view is to make it easy to position and scale the media object. Nevertheless, there were some differences in the temporal view. The first group made a "slide switch" in which each slide had a main video and the timeline referred to a video frame. Meanwhile, the second group created a single timeline referencing all videos of the LO. Timelines could contain markers (which

Table 1. Results obtained from card sorting.

Interaction	Interactivity (does it help to learn?); Interaction (Student X Teacher); Interaction (Student X Student)
Ubiquity	Mobile version; Desktop version; Different environments (In class X Distance learning); Study anywhere
Engagement	Learning curve (adjustment period); Choosing the moment to study; Abandonment, commitment, acceptance and withdrawal, lack of interest of the student; Demotivation of the student, content revision; Strategy to attract and engage
Ethics	Content copyright
Reliability	Few errors; No error interrupts
Usability	Minimalist aesthetic; Fewer buttons; Easy to use; Cover basic needs; Have a media Library with drag and drop functions; clean workspace; Timeline; Dynamic; Simple edition tools
Resources	Power Point; Videos; 3D; Text; Slides; Quiz; Images; Tutorial; Animation; References; Movies and documentaries
Functionalities	Remove; Download content; Creation and edition tools; Insert image; Cut; Audio volume control; Resizing; Add subtitles; Navigation tools; Url links; Recording tool; Related images listing; Video tools; Text tools

participants called sync points). The first group proposed two kinds of markers (start and end) to show the temporal relationship among media (e.g., video, audio, text, and image), whereas the second group made just a start marker to represent the beginning of all videos.

The first group also defended the idea of having a library view. This view allows an author to add a media object to the project and then use it in the spatial view (for instance, via drag-and-drop interactions). This group also added a widgets concept to their user interface. The intention behind widgets is to allow authors to include in the LO extensions such as quiz, slideshow, and menu.

In general, both groups believed that the tool should have few buttons, be easy to use and allow the inclusion of different media objects and formats (image, audio, and text). A number of users with experience using video-editing tools pointed out the importance of a temporal view to have a better time control of media such as video and audio.

The paper prototyping technique helped to improve the understanding of the requirements collected in previous phases, by allowing participants to explore concrete solutions to meet and refine those requirements.

3.2 Interface Design

This section describes the user interface design resulting from the PD activities and the comparative analysis.

Comparative Analysis. Several multimedia authoring tools for learning objects were found. The main ones were: CourseLab [15]; DITV-Learning [16]; eXe Learning [17]; HotPotatoes [18]; Microsoft LCDS [19]; MARKER [20] (Figs. 6, 7, 8, 9, 10 and 11). Most of them follow the SCORM (Shareable Content Object Reference Model) reference model, which is a set of specifications defining a content aggregation model, a sequence model and a model for executing LOs on the Web [21].

The user interface of CourseLab [15] resembles Microsoft PowerPoint. It uses a WYSIWYG (What You See Is What You Get) approach in order to facilitate the creation of LOs by nondevelopers. The tool supports various file formats such as video, audio, text, Java applets and Flash. In addition to content structuring, it is possible to assign actions to objects, such as animations on a clickable image. However, it does not edit the source code of learning objects. The tool also allows the creation of interactive activities such as questions with single and multiple choices, true or false; sorting items; filling gaps in sentences; and linking items. Moreover, its contents can run on various LMS, such as Moodle, ATutor and Oracle iLearning.

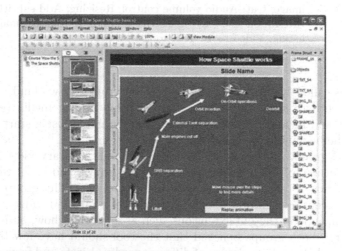

Fig. 6. CourseLab's user interface [15].

DITV-Learning [16] automates the creation of LOs for interactive TV by professionals who have little knowledge of programming. The tool supports various file formats of video, audio, image and text objects. DITV-Learning allows users to create LOs as a quiz, bonus (content in the form of slides), and extra (add-ons that can be triggered interactively during an application execution). The LO generated by the tool runs only on devices with the Ginga NCL middleware (more details about Ginga in Sect. 3.3).

eXe Learning [17] is a Web-based tool for the creation of LOs in HTML, which can also be used in LMS. It provides interactive features to users as text

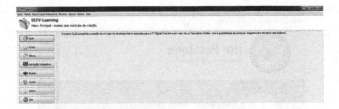

Fig. 7. DITV-Learning's user interface [16].

reading, multiple choice questions, true or false questions, Java applets, youtube videos and Wikibooks articles. In the authoring tool there are seven editable templates, an LO that describes how to use the tool, iDevices creation and an HTML editor of LOs.

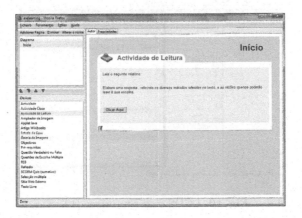

Fig. 8. eXe Learning's user interface [17].

Hot Potatoes [18] is a desktop tool designed for the production of interactive exercises in LMS, such as Moodle. It consists of five types of interactive exercises: quiz; fill the gaps; crosswords; matching columns; and sorting of words in the text. When you create an activity you can enter questions and answers, but you cannot use animations. The tool lets the user group several activities into a package.

LCDS [19] is a Microsoft desktop tool for creating LOs. It includes templates for authoring LOs and a software manual in English. It supports various file types of text, images, and video objects. It allows the production of page sequences, but it does not allow to resize the page. The LO in HTML format generated by the LCDS does not follow the SCORM model and does not allow editing.

MARKER [20] is a desktop tool and, like DITV-Learning, it is intended for authoring LOs which can run on interactive TV with the Ginga NCL middleware embedded. It allows the user to create markers on the main video in order to

Fig. 9. Hot Potatoes's user interface [18].

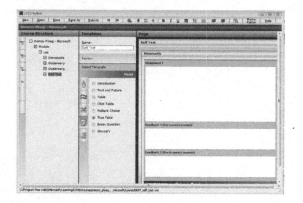

Fig. 10. LCDS's user interface [19].

replace them for other media objects (e.g., audio, video, image, text). The user can also define interactions related to those objects. For instance, pressing the blue button on the remote, an image can be resized, a video can be paused, etc.

As shown in Table 2, all these tools are aimed at creating LOs without requiring users to have programming skills. However, none of them fulfills all the requirements uncovered in the PD activities. This motivated the development of Cacuriá, a new multimedia authoring tool for creating LOs.

User Interface Design. The user interface was designed with six views to manage media, as seen in Fig. 12. In the Menu View (1), users can add media, visualize the project, and publish the LO. In the Scenes View (2) users can add, remove, edit, and select a scene, templates, and automatic links among scenes. In the Layout View (3), users can view the position and size the media over time, as well as add, remove, and edit media. In the Temporal View (4), users can run the LO and manipulate the time of the scene, as well as view, move, and remove

Fig. 11. MARKER's user interface [20].

Table 2. Summary of LO authoring tools.

	CourseLab	DITV-Learning	eXe Learning	HotPotatoes	Microsoft LCDS	MARKER
Interactive videos as LOs	x	x			x	x
Mobile compatible LOs	x					
Desktop multiplat-form		x	x	x		x
Few buttons (Mini-malist)		x			x	x
Multimedia content manipulation (WYSIWYG)	x					
Non-linear LOs	x		x		x	x
Timeline	x					x
Programing knowledge not-required	x	x	x	x	x	x

the temporal markers of each media in a scene. In the Feature View (5), users can visualize and edit the properties of the selected media. In the Library View (6), users can list, rename, and edit the order of media objects in the project.

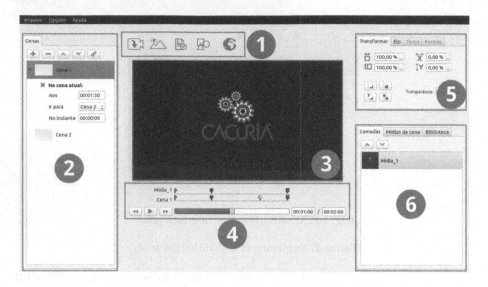

Fig. 12. Cacuriá's user interface.

Cacuriá[2] is a WYSIWYG (What You See Is What You Get) tool, where all the viewed content and the one that is being modified resemble the final application generated by the tool. The tool does not require the user to have specific previous knowledge about the specification language used to develop interactive applications. This turns out to be quite useful for end users who do not have specific programming knowledge, but who are interested in creating LOs. It can also be useful for casual users, who do not want to spend too much time learning a language or technology to create LOs.

The abstraction adopted by the tool for creating LOs is based on the media synchronization in a composite node. This same abstraction is used in several tools [15,22]. In this paper, the composite nodes are called *scenes*. Each scene is composed of one or more media objects (videos, image, text, and shapes) synchronized with the timeline. In order to create interactive, non-linear content, the tool provides ways to navigate between scenes and to open additional content such as web pages, which are triggered by links anchored on certain media objects. The tool also features the use of *scene templates*, which predefine the position and size of media objects, leaving for the user only the work of choosing media objects that will be used in the template. Therefore, as shown in Table 3, Cacuriá covers all the requirements gathered in the PD activities.

3.3 Implementation

The authoring tool designed to create LOs for interactive TV and Web was named Cacuriá. It was developed using C++ and the Qt framework [23]. Qt

---

[2] Available at https://goo.gl/inxv1N.

Table 3. Requirements covered by Cacuriá tool.

	Cacuriá
Interactive videos as LOS	x
Mobile compatible LOs	x
Desktop multiplatform	x
Few buttons (Minimalist)	x
Multimedia content manipulation (WYSIWYG)	x
Non-linear LOs	x
Timeline	x
Programing knowledge not-required	x

allows the creation of multi-platform applications using the approach "write once, compile anywhere" [23], which enables the tool installation on Windows, Linux, and Mac OS.

In order to store all the information contained in the tool, a class called Document was created. This class provides a global access point of information for the other classes of the system. This class was modeled applying the Singleton and Observer design patterns [14]. The code architecture was designed using views. When a user interacts with a certain view, the other views are updated through a signal sent from Document, as Fig. 13 shows.

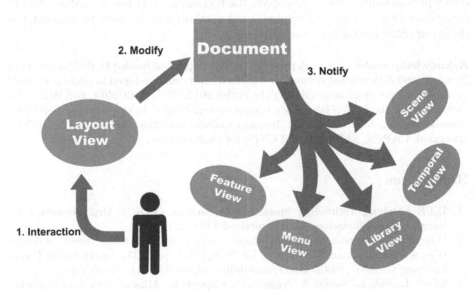

Fig. 13. Overview of the communication between the Document and the Views.

Another important feature of Cacuriá is that it exports the interactive applications to either NCL (Nested Context Languages) [24] or HTML5 [25]. NCL is a language adopted by the ISDB-Tb (International Services for Digital Broadcast, Terrestrial Brazilian) for the specification of interactive applications in the declarative part of the Ginga middleware, as well as the ITU-T (International Telecommunication Union) recommendation for IPTV services. Meanwhile, HTML5 allows an LO to be displayed on the Web.

4   Final Considerations

This paper presented a Participatory and Interaction Design process for building multimedia authoring tools which includes the stakeholder as a central element in their design. The process allowed us to gather requirements and improved our understanding of user needs and mental models. Besides including users at the center of the design process, the process also incorporates mechanisms for iteratively evaluating and redesigning the prototypes to improve the product.

The process is exemplified in the development of the Cacuriá authoring tool. The tool allows teachers with little or no programming skills to create learning objects. Cacuriá can be used to create a wide variety of learning objects using a minimalist interface, a simple information storage structure and an abstraction based on scenes. In addition, the use of interactivity mechanisms enables the teacher to create applications adapted to the student needs.

The requirements gathered in our research can be reused by designers and developers of similar tools. Moreover, the techniques and methods described in this paper (e.g., paper prototyping, card sorting) can be used to support the design of other multimedia authoring tools.

Acknowledgments. The work presented in this paper was funded by RNP, a National Research and Educational Network from Brazil, and was developed in context of RNP Working Groups programme, during the cycles 2012/2013, 2013/2014, and 2015. The authors thank the LAWS laboratory team who contributed to this work, in particular Antonio Busson, Mauricio Pessoa, Rosendy Galabo and Thacyla Sousa. The authors also thank CAPES, FAPEMA, and CNPq for their support.

References

1. IEEE Learning Technology Standards Committee (LTSC): Draft standard for learning object metadata. IEEE Standard 1484.12.1 (2012)
2. Wiley, D.A.: Connecting learning objects to instructional design theory: a definition, a metaphor, and a taxonomy. In: Wiley, D.A. (ed.) The Instructional Use of Learning Objects (2000). http://reusability.org/read/chapters/wiley.doc
3. Miller, L., Soh, L., Samal, A., Nugent, G., Kupzyk, K., Masmaliyeva, L.: Evaluating the use of learning objects in CS1. In: Proceedings of the 42nd ACM Technical Symposium on Computer Science Education (SIGCSE 2011), pp. 57–62 (2012)
4. Paternò, F.: End user development: survey of an emerging field for empowering people. ISRN Softw. Eng. **2013**, 532659 (2013). Hindawi Publishing Corporation

5. Martikainen, S., Ikävalko, P., Korpela, M.: Participatory interaction design in user requirements specification in healthcare. Stud. Health Technol. Inform. **160**, 304–308 (2010). MEDINFO 2010
6. ISO standard 9241
7. Simonsen, J., Robertson, T.: Routledge International Handbook of Participatory Design. Routledge, New York (2012)
8. IXDA. http://www.ixda.org/
9. Rogers, Y., Sharp, H., Preece, J.: Interaction Design: Beyond Human-Computer Interaction. Wiley, New York (2013)
10. Simonsen, J., Hertzum, M.: Sustained participatory design: extending the iterative approach. Des. Issues **25**(3), 10–21 (2012). MIT Press
11. Damasceno, A.L.B., Soares Neto, C.S., Barbosa, S.D.J.: Lessons learned from evaluating an authoring tool for learning objects. In: Proceedings of the International Conference on Human-Computer Interaction HCII 2017 (2017)
12. Nielsen, J.: Card Sorting: How Many Users to Test (2004). http://www.nngroup.com/articles/card-sorting-how-many-users-to-test/
13. Snyder, C.: Paper Prototyping: The Fast and Easy Way to Design and Refine User Interfaces. Morgan Kaufmann, San Diego (2003)
14. Gamma, E., Helm, R., Johnson, R., Vlissides, J., Booch, G.: Design Patterns: Elements of Reusable Object-Oriented Software. Addison-Wesley, Boston (1994)
15. CourseLab. http://www.courselab.com
16. Sousa Neto, F., Bezerra, E., Dias, D.: ITV-Learning: a prototype for construction of learning objects for interactive digital television. In: Proceedings of International Conference of the Future of Education, pp. 486–490 (2012)
17. eXe Learning. http://www.exelearning.org
18. HotPotatoes. http://hotpot.uvic.ca
19. Microsoft LCDS. http://www.microsoft.com/learning/cn-us/lcds-tool.aspx
20. Sousa, F., Bezerra, P., Soares, I.: MARKER: a tool for building interactive applications for T-learning. In: Proceedings of 19th Brazilian Symposium on Multimedia and the Web (WebMedia 2013), pp. 281–284 (2013)
21. Advanced Distributed Learning. Sharable Content Object Reference Model, 4th edn. (2009)
22. Meixner, B., Siegel, B., Hölbling, G., Lehner, F., Kosch, H.: SIVA suite: authoring system and player for interactive non-linear videos. In: Proceedings of the 18th ACM International Conference on Multimedia (MM 2010), pp. 1563–1566 (2010)
23. Summerfield, M., Blanchette, J.: C++ GUI Programming with Qt 4. Prentice Hall, Upper Saddle River (2008)
24. Soares, L.F.G., Moreno, M., Neto, C.S.S., Moreno, M.: Ginga-NCL: declarative middleware for multimedia IPTV services. IEEE Communications Magazine **48**(6), 74–81 (2010). IEEE
25. W3C: HTML5. http://www.w3.org/TR/html5/

A Human-Centered Perspective on Software Quality: Acceptance Criteria for Work 4.0

Holger Fischer[1](✉), Michael Engler[2], and Stefan Sauer[1]

[1] SICP, Paderborn University, Zukunftsmeile 1, 33102 Paderborn, Germany
{h.fischer,s.sauer}@sicp.upb.de
[2] Michael Engler IT-Consulting, Rüttenscheider Platz 12, 45130 Essen, Germany
michael.engler@systemkontext.de

Abstract. The digitization of industrial manufacturing workflows results in an interconnection between employees, between employees and machines as well as between machines. Lots of information and data about past, current or even predicted states of products and machines arise. Workflows as well as work organization will change due to topics such as big data analytics, machine learning, predictive maintenance, or new work concepts. The direct and indirect interaction between digitization and all new processes of work design and work organization is subject of the research area Work 4.0. Digital assistance systems are able to support the employees in gathering, interpretation and communication with data, machines and colleagues.

Despite all efforts, todays software products still lack of quality in respect of inadequate functionality and usability. Thus, current software engineering methods seems to be insufficient and software quality models seem to be only focused on technological acceptance instead of human-centered and business-centered acceptance.

This paper presents a human-centered acceptance quality model and acceptance criteria for digital assistance systems with a focus on the industrial manufacturing context. The aim is to enrich the communication and integration of human-centered activities in software engineering methods supporting a common language and understanding of quality goals as well as of metrics for the evaluation of improvements due to the use of digital assistance systems.

Keywords: Acceptance · Digital assistance systems · Human-centered design · Software quality · ISO/IEC 25010 · Work 4.0

1 Introduction

Having a look on today's occupations, there are lots of reasons why people work. The primary objective as well as one of the most important ones is earning a living for themselves and their families [1,2]. People work for a wage. They are eager to use it to shape their current lives including the time away from work (e.g. leisure or vacations) as well as their future (e.g. retirement). Further objectives

© Springer International Publishing AG 2017
A. Marcus and W. Wang (Eds.): DUXU 2017, Part I, LNCS 10288, pp. 570–583, 2017.
DOI: 10.1007/978-3-319-58634-2_42

include to be part of the society, to create an own identity and to keep one's own dignity. Work is vital for everyone and for the society as a whole. It allows people to participate within a community, to find contacts and to communicate. The content and the outcome of their work is important for them, too. They become able to use their talents, to learn and to develop their skills. In addition, recognition, reward, knowledge as well as sharing ideas are features people are longing for at work [3], issues that are closely related to user experience [2]. If people take pride in their work, they may find it a very enjoyable part of their lives and they may improve the quality of their work likewise.

Looking upon the topics that shape the future of work, we can observe five big trends: New behaviors, millennials in the workplace, mobility, globalization, and technologies [4]. Today, employees are eager to live more public lives. That means we build online communities, share ideas, and collaborate on a common knowledge base. These new behaviors lead to new requirements the organizations we are working for need to fulfill. In addition, this aspect will be reinforced by the huge number of millennials – the "Generation Y" with its technological fluency – which will enter the job market by 2020. Globalization foster open boundaries to work with anyone and mobility increase the flexibility to work anywhere and with any device. Nevertheless, the main driver of innovation for these changes is "software".

The German term "Arbeit 4.0" (en. "Work 4.0") addresses the direct and indirect interaction between digitization and all new processes of work design, organization of work, and working conditions [3] as well as training and qualification. Software solutions especially digital assistance systems are increasingly used within the professional work context [5], e.g. cooperative robots in industrial manufacturing or augmented reality glasses in commissioning. The possibilities are versatile, but they also encourage further discussions about the impacts on the working life of humans. The employees' as well as organizational acceptance of these technologies is crucial and includes quality aspects of usability, user experience, and Work 4.0.

Despite all efforts, todays software products still lack of quality with regard to functionality and usability [6,7]. Thus, current software engineering (SE) methods as well as software quality models seem to be insufficient. Methods don't focus on end users – the employees working with the software – in terms of active involvement during the development process. Furthermore, quality models lack focussing on work and user experience. The topic of usability is already included within newer quality models, e.g. ISO/IEC 25010 [8], but its concepts are communicated in a way that foster imprecise interpretations. A more human-centered quality model will help to integrate the human focus in quality discussions about systems to be developed, to select adequate methods for user participation, and to shape a common understanding about user goals and needs.

In this paper we present an approach that defines a concept for a human-centered acceptance quality model. Furthermore, we conducted contextual inquiries within three projects with industrial partners to elicit acceptance criteria for digital assistance systems within industrial manufacturing. Based on these criteria implications for a review of the software quality model of ISO/IEC 25010 are formulated.

2 Background

In order to create a quality model that focusses on acceptance and that is based on an individual human-centered and organizational business-centered perspective it is important to create a common understanding. This paper focusses on digital assistances systems within industrial manufacturing. Therefore, digital assistance systems are defined in the following subsection followed by a brief introduction to technology acceptance of these systems. Afterwards, existing quality models are discussed as a base for an acceptance quality model.

2.1 Digital Assistance Systems

The aim of digital assistance systems is to provide employees with the information they need just as quickly and easily as possible at any time and from anywhere. Assistance systems include all technologies that assist the employees in carrying out their work and enable them to concentrate on their core competencies. These are, in particular, technologies for providing information, such as visualization systems, mobile devices, tablets and smart glasses or tools which perform calculations. This ranges from the simple display of work instructions via visual or multi-medial support (e.g. picking systems) to context-sensitive augmented reality for the employees [10].

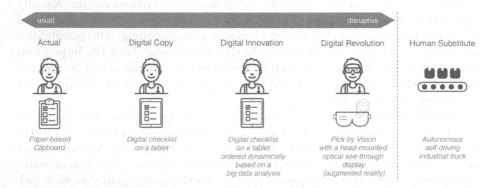

Fig. 1. Degrees of digital assistance (example of industrial picking)

In comparison to the actual analog situation, digital assistance can be distinguished into three levels of digitization: The digital copy, the digital innovation and the digital revolution (see Fig. 1).

The "digital copy" represents an accurate reflection of a none-digital reality about something already existing. In industrial picking, the digital copy could be an online checklist on a tablet that looks exactly the same as the checklist on a paper-based clipboard. The next level of "digital innovation" adds something new to the already existing digital copy. This could be a dynamically ordered online checklist based on a big data analysis about the dependencies of individual check items. The highest level of a digital assistance systems is the "digital revolution", something completely new in the digital world that still does not exist in the real world and implies a disruption of structures, workflows or tasks (cf. [11,12]). This could be a pick-by vision system with a head-mounted optical see-through display, also known as augmented reality (AR), where digital information are presented directly within the real work environment. Out of scope are "human substitutes", complete autonomous systems without any human intervention.

The higher the digital disruption (e.g. compared to the previous value system, complexity), the more critical is the acceptance of the software solution on the part of the organization and especially on the part of the employees [13].

2.2 Technology Acceptance

The acceptance of digital assistance systems or technology in general is crucial for the successful introduction and use within an organization. Venkatesh and Bala [14] proposed the concept of the "Technology Acceptance Model (TAM) v3" that is mainly described by the two aspects *perceived ease of use & perceived usefulness*, which affect the aspects of the *behavioral intention & use behavior*.

- *Perceived ease of use* is defined as *"the extent to which a person believes that using an IT will enhance his or her job performance"*.
- *Perceived usefulness* is defined as *"the degree to which a person believes that using an IT will be free of effort"*.
- *Behavioral intention* is defined as the prediction of how the users will behave with a system based on the perceived ease of use and perceived usefulness.
- *Use behavior* describes the actual behavior during the usage of a system.

These aspects are influenced by multiple variables (e.g. computer self-efficacy, computer anxiety, computer playfulness).

Regarding the development of digital assistance systems these variables are either shaped by the system itself or by the organizational culture. Thus, there are three interconnected factors that assure the acceptance: Process, people and product. Involving all necessary stakeholders right from the start during the conception and development of a system influences the acceptance through out the process. Creating a social and cultural environment where employees like to work and to talk about their problems and their ideas influences the people in their openness. Creating an assistance system (product) with an appropriate usability and user experience (UX) influences the employees through the system itself.

Comparing the definitions of usability, its three attributes, and user experience

- Effectiveness: *"Accuracy and completeness with which users achieve specified goals."* [15]
- Efficiency: *"Resources expended in relation to the accuracy and completeness with which users achieve goals."* [15]

- Satisfaction: *"Freedom from discomfort, and positive attitudes towards the use of the product."* [15]
- User Experience: *"Person's perceptions and responses resulting from the use and/or anticipated use of a product, system or service"* [16]

with TAMs definitions of perceived ease of use and perceived usefulness we can see the close relation between technology acceptance, usability and user experience. Therefore, usability and user experience represent fundamental quality influences on technology acceptance. Other influences on technology acceptance are technical product qualities like reliability, security or performance efficiency, etc.

2.3 Quality Models

As software quality has an influence on the acceptance a further look has to be taken on system and software quality models.

Software in its nature is abstract and intangible. Shewhart [17] early divides the quality of manufactured products into an objective as well as subjective side:

> *"There are two common aspects of quality: One of them has to do with the consideration of the quality of a thing as an objective reality independent of the existence of man. The other has to do with what we think, feel or sense as a result of the objective reality. In other word, there is a subjective side of quality."*

Based on this, researchers and practitioners have tried to make the benefits and costs more visible for measurement proposing various characterizations for the objective side of software quality [18–20].

McCall et al. [18] presented one of the eldest known quality models developed at General Electrics. They identified three major perspectives: Product revision (ability to carry out changes), product transition (adaptability towards new environments) and product operations (its operation characteristics) including 11 quality factors (e.g. maintainability, correctness, portability) and 23 quality criteria (e.g. traceability, storage efficiency).

Boehm et al. [19] described three primary uses in their quality model: As-is utility (extent to which the software can be used), maintainability (ease of modification and retesting) and portability (adaptability towards new environments). Further on they presented seven quality factors (e.g. portability, reliability, efficiency) that are classified into these primary uses and that are defined by 15 criteria (e.g. accuracy, completeness, consistency).

Grady [20] defined five characteristics known by the abbreviation FURPS, which stands for functionality, usability, reliability, performance, and supportability. These characteristics are of two different types: Functional (F) and non-functional (URPS).

These quality model have lots of similarities and mainly differ in some of their factors. A common pattern in all of these quality models is their hierarchy:

Characteristics → *factors (ext. view)* → *criteria (int. view)* → *metrics*

Nevertheless, the value of these models is a pragmatic one and doesn't exist in the presence of more or less factors. An accurate measurement of a software will determine its value. One major challenge from a human-centered perspective remains in the separation of functionality and usability. This results in a technology-centered development of software, where usability is just the "user interface manicure" instead of user needs defining the necessity of functionality and visualization of information [21].

A newer standardized quality model exist in ISO/IEC 25010 [8]. Two types of quality models are defined in the standard (see Fig. 2):

- The *quality in use* model consists of *"five characteristics related to outcomes of interaction with a system"*.
- The *product quality* model includes eight characteristics describing the fixed quality of a product.

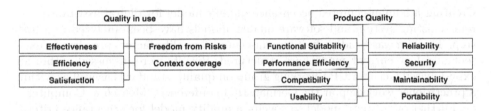

Fig. 2. ISO/IEC 25010 quality factors

The difficulties of this model from a human-centered perspective is the misleading, imprecise use of the usability concept. In this technical view, usability is focused again on user interface aesthetics, but also extended with some sub factors that have some similarities with usability dialogue principles [22], e.g. learnability or user error protection. Regarding ISO 9241-11 [15] usability is defined as the *"extend to which a product can be used by specified users to achieve specified goals with effectiveness, efficiency and satisfaction in a specified context of use"*. Following this definition the factor usability in the product quality model is misleading, because usability is also included in the factors effectiveness, efficiency and satisfaction that are used within the quality of use model.

Furthermore, effectiveness from a usability point of view specifies the functional appropriateness of a software along the users' tasks. Functional appropriateness is a sub factor of functional suitability in the product quality model. Thus, usability is not just a quality requirement, but also closely related to quality in use and functionality.

Apart from that, the terms effectiveness, efficiency, satisfaction, freedom from risks, and context coverage are too abstract as they vary in the interpretation of the respective perspectives. For example, using the term satisfaction the human-centered perspective would think of "hedonic and pragmatic satisfaction of the users" while the business-centered perspective would think of the "management satisfaction" and the technology-centered perspective of the "support and maintenance satisfaction".

In addition, ISO/IEC 25010 is missing the dependencies that exists between various factors. For example, satisfaction in terms of the user's trust of a system has a causality with the technical factors confidentiality, integrity, and reliability.

One of the reasons for often unsuccessful software products or software products that only met parts of users' needs may be the limited focus on technical quality criteria (e.g. functionality, reliability, maintainability, etc.). From an organization's point of view, the success of a software is determined by the quality of the interplay between the different success criteria from the three points of view: human-centered quality (individual acceptance), business-centered quality (organizational acceptance), and technological-centered quality (technical acceptance).

3   Human-Centered Acceptance Quality Model

Creating a human-centered acceptance quality model for digital assistance systems existing system and software quality models have been analyzed in a first step. The aim was to identify if human-centered quality factors are already existent and how current models are structured. Results were discussed within an expert-based German UPA working group on quality standards as well as within a practitioner workshop at the German HCI conference "Mensch & Computer".

Further on, a meta model to specify a quality model for acceptance criteria was built. Different approaches on classifications for usability, user experience and Work 4.0 (e.g. ISO/DIS 9241-220 [2,9,23]) had been analyzed to identify an initial set of acceptance criteria. These criteria had been formulated according to the defined meta model and had been used as a foundation for the individual as well as the organizational perspective to add on to the technological one. To consolidate this initial set of acceptance criteria, a focus group had been established that consists of twenty participants (executives as well as work council members) of various industrial manufacturing companies. The focus group got different questions to set up own acceptance criteria from their perspective. Afterwards, this set of criteria was compared to the initial set.

Using three current projects with industrial partners the consolidated set of acceptance criteria had been used in the requirements elicitation stages of assistance systems to be developed. Two projects used the acceptance quality model to discuss their vision and different partial conflicting requirements. *Contextual Inquiry* has been used within these projects to elicit problem scenarios and user needs, and to specify user requirements. These requirements were mapped to the acceptance quality model to argue about the priority of individual requirements and to decide about conflicting requirements. The third project was used to validate the model within a user study. Therefore, a paper-based survey was developed and distributed among 180 assembly and quality assurance employees to evaluate the importance of the acceptance criteria. In addition, 24 employees participated within semi-structured interviews.

Based on this knowledge, also ideas for adapting ISO/IEC 25010 [8] with a more human-centered perspective had been formulated.

3.1 Meta Model for Acceptance Criteria

As mentioned previously, a meta model for an acceptance quality model had been built to describe the elicited acceptance criteria and their dependencies (see Fig. 3). The model adapts the hierarchy described in Sect. 2.3 (characteristics → factors → criteria → metrics) to

$$acceptanceCategory \rightarrow qualityDimension \rightarrow acceptanceCriterion \rightarrow metric$$

The focus of this meta model is on the acceptance criterion itself. Every criterion can have further sub criteria or can likewise be a sub criterion of another one. As there are lots of dependencies between different criteria and perspectives a criterion can also be influenced by another criterion, can influence another criterion itself, or can have a conflict with another criterion.

In addition, each criterion belongs to one acceptance category. This can either be the individual acceptance from the human-centered perspective, the

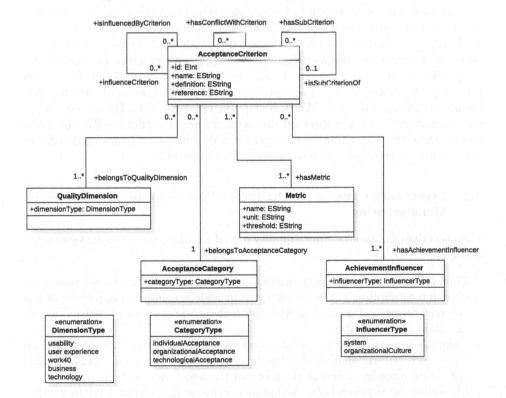

Fig. 3. Formalized model to describe acceptance criteria

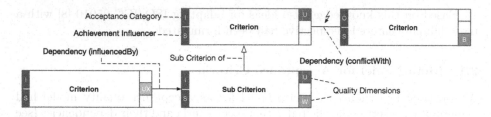

Fig. 4. Visual representation of the acceptance quality model

organizational acceptance from the business-centered perspective, or the technological acceptance from the technology-centered perspective.

Next, each criterion belongs to one or more quality dimensions. The quality dimensions describes the nature of a criterion as it can have multiple topics. Initially, a set of five dimensions has been set up including usability, user experience, Work 4.0, business, and technology.

In addition, each criterion has at least one metric to measure the degree of its fulfillment.

As there are also criteria which cannot be influenced by the digital assistance system itself, but by a change in the organizational culture, a further attribute had been added that describes the achievement influences of a criterion.

Finally, a visual representation for the meta model had been developed to use acceptance criteria within focus groups, workshops, or discussions (see Fig. 4). A criterion is represented as a rectangle. Its acceptance category (I, O, T) and achievement influencer (S, C) are on the left side of the rectangle whereas the quality dimensions (U, UX, W, B, T) are on the right side. Dependencies are represented with either a directed line with an arrow (influencedBy) or undirected line with a lightning (conflictWith). Sub criteria are connected with an arrow whereby the open arrowhead points to the parent.

3.2 Acceptance Criteria for Digital Assistance Systems in Industrial Manufacturing

The objectives for an acceptance quality model for digital assistance systems are manifold:

- *Common language and understanding in a project team*: As project teams are often interdisciplinary it is necessary to provide a common big picture of the different terms and goals (e.g. the different interpretations of satisfaction as discussed in Sect. 2.3).
- *Common prioritization of quality goals*: A common quality model based on acceptance criteria shall enable the project team to agree on a common prioritization in order to define the scope of the assistance systems.
- *Elicitation of requirements*: Acceptance criteria can either lead to further requirements that are implicitly assumed or existing requirements can be

structured along their perspective (human, business, technology) and related acceptance criteria.

- *Predictable effects*: Effects on the acceptance of a system caused by decisions for example made about workflows or the user interface can be predicted along the acceptance criteria or their dependencies.
- *Support method selection*: Having a common and prioritized set of acceptance criteria shall support the selection of appropriate methods used within a project, e.g. usability and UX methods.
- *Metrics for evaluation*: Related to the previous objective metrics can be derived from the acceptance criteria and appropriate evaluation methods can be selected.

TAM [14] as well as ISO/IEC 25010 [8] had been used as a base for the identification of initial acceptance criteria for digital assistance systems in industrial manufacturing. Further acceptance criteria had been elicited within workshops with practitioners from the management and work council of industrial manufacturing companies. Due to the limited space only an excerpt of the current generalized and expandable set of acceptance criteria is shown in Table 1.

3.3 Evaluation

As mentioned previously, workshops with practitioners had taken place in order to expand as well as to consolidate the specified acceptance criteria. Three current projects with industrial manufacturing had been used to evaluate the feasibility of the acceptance quality model.

- *Case 1: Energy-efficiency installation:* The organization of this case advises, installs and maintains combined heat and power (CHP) units of all sizes for various properties. Therefore, they are kind of responsible for the energy-saving result. However, the decision for an optimal CHP is very complex and depends on the interaction of all the energy consumers of a property as well as the people working there. In order to demonstrate the actual energy savings as well as to interpret deviations in the behavior and to plan maintenance work ahead, it is necessary to analyze and interpret a large number of energy data. The aim of a project was to introduce an assistance system to support all actors from the craftsman through the energy engineer to the owner of the property.
- *Case 2: Facade engineering:* The organization of this case is active within the context of building construction and supports their customers (e.g. architects, engineers, constructors) with free of charge services in order to convince them to buy their building elements later on. Some stand-alone solutions exist that supports the involved people with some assistance. With the aim to improve the overall construction planning and coordination process and to connect existing solutions, a project has been set up to analyze the context of use within the company (sales, engineering, consulting) as well as with the users of their services.

Table 1. Acceptance criteria for digital assistance systems (excerpt)

Acceptance cat.	Acceptance criterion	Quality dim.
Individual	Suitability for the task	U, W
	Cognitive workload balance	U, W
	Task effectiveness	U, W
	Accessibility	U, W
	Freedom from fear of making mistakes	U, W
	Suitability for learning	U, W
	Conformity with user expectations	U, W
	Work outcome improvement	U, UX, W
	Autonomy/Self-organization	UX, W
	Work quality feedback	UX, W
	Trustworthiness	UX, W
	Situational awareness	W
	Working time flexibility	W
	Transparency reliability towards supervisors	W
Organizational	Freedom from economical risks	B
	Technical availability	B, T
	Employee qualification	B
	Variation control	B
	Acceleration of training periods	B
	Business data privacy	B
	Knowledge conservation	B
	Process state transparency	B
Technological	Performance efficiency	T
	Compatibility	T
	Security	T, U
	Confidentiality	T, U
	Maintainability	T
	Modularity	T
	Reliability	T
	Adaptability	T
	...	

– *Case 3: ATM assembly:* The organization of this case produce all different
  kinds of self-service systems, e.g. automated teller machines (ATM). The automated production of the parts needed is followed by a manual assembly line.
  Multiple quality gates within this assembly line ensure the quality of the products. As the number of produced machines is low within each order due to indi-
  vidualization by the customer, quality problems are reported at a time when

they cannot be fixed anymore. A project has been set up to identify possibilities for digitalization of paper-based documentation and quality assistance for the worker.

In the first two cases the model had been used to discuss about consequences on changing the workflows and to agree upon the priorities of requirements. The organizations decided to involve their customers as well as their own employees and users. Thus, the integration of usability research methods in the existing software engineering processes were comprehensible for all project team members.

Additionally, 180 employees (assembly workers, tester, and supervisors) in case three participated in a paper-based survey. First, they were ask about their current tasks and which are criteria for their acceptance of a digital assistance system. Then, they were ask to have a look on a list of presented criteria. They had to mark criteria that are of importance for their individual acceptance as well as for the organizational acceptance in case of the supervisors. Based on this results, the list of acceptance criteria had been extended with 13 new criteria.

3.4 Implications for ISO/IEC 25010

Taking a look back on ISO/IEC 25010 [8] software quality seems to be more complex. Currently, the quality in use and product model have a technology-centered perspective. Both quality models will need to take two further perspectives into account adding also the human-centered and business-centered perspective.

Therefore, in the quality in use model the characteristics "effectiveness", "efficiency", "satisfaction", and "freedom from risk" should have all three perspectives, because the general terms are interpreted in different ways and hinder communication. For example, efficiency in a human-centered perspective means "having short navigation ways", "getting responses from the system in appropriate times", "having a fixed status of entered data while going back and forth in the process", etc. From a business-centered perspective efficiency means "cost efficiency in terms of money" or "restructuring working time due to decreased capacity utilization of employees". A technology-centered perspective might think of "support efficiency" or the "processing time on a CPU". The other way round, this means that from an overall Work 4.0 perspective the saved time due to better efficiency shouldn't have an impact on work intensification for the employees. Thus, the positive quality characteristic of business-centered efficiency might lead to a negative quality characteristic of human-centered satisfaction. Hence, the employee might reject an inadequate assistance system even if the quality characteristic of efficiency seems to be good from the business perspective. Dependencies between quality characteristic should be added.

Furthermore, usability in the product quality model only refers to factors of the user interface and may be renamed to it. As already noted, usability is even bigger than just the visible outcome known as "user interface". Usability also includes the human-centered view of the quality in use model or the quality factor "functional appropriateness" in terms of suitability for the task. Thus, usability should not just be a quality factor, but kind of a layer that includes quality factors from both models. The same argument exists for the term of user experience as an even more comprehensive term than usability.

4   Conclusion and Outlook

Summing up, the aim of this paper is to enrich the communication and the integration of human-centered activities in software engineering methods. Therefore, a human-centered acceptance quality model for digital assistance systems in industrial manufacturing has been presented that includes individual, organizational as well as technological acceptance criteria. This model should support a common language and understanding within a project as well as common prioritization of quality goals, and common metrics for the evaluation of digital assistance systems.

Current software quality models were analyzed regarding their focus on human-centered quality factors. Multiple workshops and focus groups were run to extend and continuously consolidate an initial set of acceptance criteria. Projects with industrial partners has been used to evaluate the feasibility of the model.

Current insights confirm the involvement of all stakeholders (project team, employees, work council, researcher) during context of use analyses and requirements discussion. As the projects are ongoing, no statement can be made about the final acceptance of the assistance systems. But the acceptance within the process has been increased and the consideration of all needs shall influence the later acceptance of the ready-to-run systems.

Future work will contain further evaluations of the model and the impacts on the development processes likewise.

In addition, managers are eager to measure the outcome of change. The current model already contains the concept of metrics, but not every acceptance criteria is documented with an appropriate metric yet. This will be the next step of research.

Finally, the model has to be integrated into requirements management concepts to foster the prediction of positive and even more important negative impacts of digital assistance systems on workflows and work organization and, therefore, on Work 4.0.

References

1. Maslow, A.H.: A theory of human motivation. Psychol. Rev. **50**(4), 370–396 (1943)
2. Zeiner, K.M., Laib, M., Schippert, K., Burmester, M.: Identifying experience categories to design for positive experience with technology at work. In: Proceedings of the 2016 CHI Conference Extended Abstracts on Human Factors in Computing Systems, pp. 3013–3020. ACM, NY (2016). doi:10.1145/2851581.2892548
3. German Federal Ministry of Labour, Social Affairs (BMAS): Re-Imagining Work - Green Paper Work 4.0 (2015). http://www.bmas.de/SharedDocs/Downloads/DE/PDF-Publikationen/arbeiten-4-0-green-paper.pdf. Accessed Apr 2016
4. Morgan, J.: The Future of Work Attract New Talent, Build Better Leaders, and Create a Competitive Organization. Wiley, Hoboken (2014)

5. German Federal Ministry for Economic Affairs, Energy (BMWi): Monitoring Report Digital Economy (2014). http://www.bmwi.de/EN/Service/publications, did=686950.html. Accessed Feb 2017
6. Johnson, J.: CHAOS 2014. The Standish Group (2014)
7. Sage Software GmbH: Independent Study on IT investments (2014). http://goo.gl/qy0eM0. Accessed Feb 2017
8. ISO/IEC 25010: Systems and software engineering - Systems and software Quality Requirements and Evaluation (SQuaRE) - System and software quality models (2011)
9. Bevan, N., Carter, J., Earthy, J., Geis, T., Harker, S.: New ISO standards for usability, usability reports and usability measures. In: Kurosu, M. (ed.) HCI 2016. LNCS, vol. 9731, pp. 268–278. Springer, Cham (2016). doi:10.1007/978-3-319-39510-4_25
10. Bischoff, J.: Open up the potential of the application of Industry 4.0 with SME (translated from German). Study on behalf of the German Federal Ministry for Economic Affairs and Energy (BMWi) (2015). https://www.agiplan.de/fileadmin/pdf_dokumente/Studie_Industrie_40_BMWi_gesamt.pdf. Accessed Feb 2017
11. Iben, H., Baumann, H., Ruthenbeck, C., Klug, T.: Visual based picking supported by context awareness. In: Proceedings of ICMI-MLMI 2009, pp. 281–288. ACM, NY (2009). doi:10.1145/1647314.1647374
12. Funk, M., Shirazi, A.S., Mayer, S., Lischke, L., Schmidt, A.: Pick from here! - an interactive mobile cart using in-situ projection for order picking. In: Proceedings of UbiComp 2015, pp. 601–609. ACM, NY (2015). doi:10.1145/2750858.2804268
13. Rogers, E.M.: Diffusion of Innovations, 5th edn. Free Press, NY (2003)
14. Venkatesh, V., Bala, H.: Technology acceptance model 3 and a research agenda on interventions. Decis. Sci. 39(2), 273–315 (2008)
15. ISO 9241-11: Ergonomic requirements for office work with visual display terminals (VDTs) - Part 11: Guidance on usability (1998)
16. ISO 9241-210: Ergonomics of human-system interaction - Part 210: Human-centred design for interactive systems (2010)
17. Shewhart, W.A.: Economic Control of Quality of Manufactured Product. Van Nostrand Company Inc., NY (1931)
18. McCall, J.A., Richards, P.K., Walters, G.F.: Factors in Software Quality. Vols. I–III. Rome Air Development Centre, Griffiss Air Force Base, New York (1977)
19. Boehm, B.W., Brown, J.R., Kaspar, H., Lipow, M., McLeod, G., Merrit, M.: Characteristics of Software Quality. North Holland Publishing, Amsterdam (1978)
20. Grady, R.B.: Practical Software Metrics for Project Management and Process Improvement. Prentice Hall, Upper Saddle River (1992)
21. Seffah, A., Gulliksen, J., Desmarais, M.C.: An introduction to human-centered software engineering - integrating usability in the development process. In: Seffah, A., Gulliksen, J., Desmarais, M.C. (eds.) Human-Centered Software Engineering Integrating Usability in the Software Development Lifecycle, pp. 3–14. Springer, Dordrecht (2005)
22. ISO 9241-110: Ergonomic requirements for office work with visual display terminals (VDTs) - Part 11: Guidance on usability (1998)
23. ISO/DIS 9241-220: Ergonomics of human-system interaction - Part 110: Dialogue principles (2006)

Building a Team to Champion User-Centered Design Within an Agile Process

Eleonora Ibragimova[✉], Leanda Verboom, and Nick Mueller

MOBGEN – Part of Accenture Digital, Amsterdam, The Netherlands
{eleonora.ibragimova,leanda.verboom,nick}@mobgen.com

Abstract. The marriage of Agile development processes and User-Centered Design (UCD) has been increasingly attracting interest within the field of software development [1]. Integrating the two can identify the benefits of each in terms of efficient work processes to achieve useful and at the same time usable products as results. While the user-centered design process has a defined structure [2], the understanding of user experience and user interface teams vary significantly across organizations [3]. Similarly, design processes are defined differently per organization without a universal model. For certain teams the User eXperience (UX) team means an entity of all user-related and design-related activities, including user research, benchmarking, creating information architecture, projecting user needs into wireframes, creating user interface visual designs and evaluating with usability testings. Other organizations have differentiated User Research specialists (involved in user insights and usability topics) from User eXperience teams (specified on translating user needs into screens) and User Interface (visual representations of tasks) teams. To our knowledge, very little research has been done regarding such intricacies of team structures when discussing user experience teams in the Agile and UCD integration frameworks. Our paper provides a review of different UI/UX team structures in organizations and their implications in the implementation of projects. With our analysis of different team and role structures we hope to contribute to better understanding of UI/UX teams in design agencies and the influence of this understanding on the success of projects incorporating UCD and agile approaches.

Keywords: User-centered design · Agile methodologies · Software development process · Lean UX · User experience design · HCI in business

1 Background

In recent decades, the software development industry has experienced a shift from traditional approaches towards Agile methodologies, as a result of the growing complexity and size of projects. Traditional, or heavyweight methodologies, in the software development process are characterized by a sequential series of steps, such as defining requirements, planning, building, testing and deployment [4]. Documentation plays a major role in the process: the detailed visualization of the finished project is to be completed before the building starts. Some examples of such methodologies include Waterfall, Spiral Model and Unified Process.

© Springer International Publishing AG 2017
A. Marcus and W. Wang (Eds.): DUXU 2017, Part I, LNCS 10288, pp. 584–596, 2017.
DOI: 10.1007/978-3-319-58634-2_43

In contrast, Agile methodologies (Fig. 1) evolved as a response to the eager business community asking for lighter weight along with faster and nimbler software development processes. Agile approaches involve smaller and shorter releases, parallel programming, and iterations as core of their process [5]. Examples of agile methodologies include Extreme Programming (XP), Scrum and Feature Driven Development (FDD) among others.

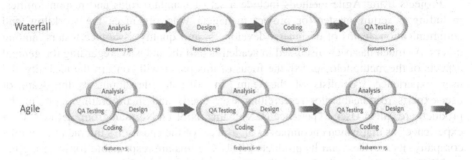

Fig. 1. In a waterfall development cycle, the analysis, design, coding, and quality assurance testing are separate stages of a release that **extends over** months or years. In Agile development, each set of incremental mini-releases (each created in 2–4 weeks) has these stages [5].

Google's design sprints are one of the popular examples of integrating agile development and design thinking in the creative communities and serve as a structured brainstorm for project teams to learn from doing. Divided across five days, these design sprints are performed to answer critical business questions through design, prototyping, and testing ideas with customers [6]. Lean UX is another process embodying agile principles, designed for fast user-centered software development. The philosophy of Lean UX is comprised of three principles: design thinking, Lean production and Agile development [7]. The model works on the "think-make-check" feedback loop (Fig. 2).

Fig. 2. Lean UX and the "think-make-check" feedback tool emphasize on early validation and faster development cycles [7].

The idea is to innovate quickly, by choosing lightweight research methods and creating prototypes to test out the concepts and validating this through usability testing. The core point of the process is to reduce cycle time, not build time - hence the amount of time it takes to move through the think-make-check loop. The process emphasizes designers working closely in collaboration with the team, demoing their work often, to get feedback from the team and putting it into practice. Therefore, the designer should be completely integrated with the team.

Projects using Agile methods include a set of standard roles and responsibilities, including a scrum master (or project manager) who organizes the workflow and communication, teams of designers, developers, and quality assurance testers, among others. As much has been discussed in academia and the industry, regarding the general aspects of the methodologies [8], the focus of this paper will concern the usability and user experience specialists of the team. In software development, the team of user-experts responsible for researching user needs and incorporating them in the product, are called User eXperience (UX) teams. Nielsen Norman group defines "User experience" as that which encompasses all aspects of the end-user's interaction with the company, its services, and its products [9]. UX teams are responsible for ensuring the usability of the end-product, a quality attribute that assesses how easy user interfaces are to use. In the current research, we will use the term User Researcher to define professionals involved in identifying user needs and evaluating usability of designs. On the other hand, the UX Designer is defined as a specialist responsible for translating user needs into screens, before the graphical representation or code has been implemented. Another term that must be mentioned when discussing the design of a product is the user interface (UI) design, which can be misleading as it is often used interchangeably within UX design sources, while representing a different aspect of the design. Unlike UX design, which is about the overall feel of the product, user interface design refers to how the product is laid out. UI designers are in charge of designing each screen or page with which a user interacts and ensuring that the UI visually communicates the path that a UX designer has laid out [3]. The umbrella term "design team" will be used as encompassing a wide range of responsibilities, from user research to wireframing, visual design and usability testing.

These variations of tasks and responsibilities within design teams are only briefly explored in existing literature about UCD and agile integration. While the general literature refers to user and interface specialists in agile projects as the design team, there is not much evidence for how specific structures of design teams influence project results, in terms of collaboration. This research aims to analyse and understand the implications of design team structure for collaboration and end-results within agile projects. The overall goal is to discover the best practices for achieving effective results in such collaborations, and how to build a design team that can champion user-centred design in agile processes.

2   Research Design

The research methodology of the current study is explained in detail in this section.

2.1   Methodology

The research approach of this study is qualitative. A semi-structured interview method using the principles of Grounded Theory [10] was implemented for data collection. The data from eight participants was collected in verbal form (in person or via a video-call) and for the two remaining participants in written form (via electronic mail), depending on the distance with the interviewee. The interview questions were:

- What is your role within your current organization? What role do you play in your current project team(s)?
- Can you tell us about the projects you are working on (in terms of industry, size, scope, work and deliverables expected)?
- What process does your team follow to organize workflow?
- Do you work agile? If so, which agile methods do you use? And which tools do you use (for task assignments, communication, collaboration, etc.)?
- What is the design team structure in your project?
- What are the roles and responsibilities within the design team? Do you differentiate a user experience (UX) designer from a user interface (UI) designer and a user researcher (UR)? What are the skillsets of each, if you do?
- What problems do you (have you) encounter(ed) in your project? Specify by daily basis vs. overall basis.
- What are the strengths of having this structure in terms of efficiency and effectiveness of the end-results?
- How is the interdisciplinary collaboration between the design team and other teams involved in the project?
- What are the satisfaction levels of the design team members (evaluated in objective or subjective manners, in terms of engagement, ownership, personal and professional growth, etc.)?

The interviews were collected and transcribed. The answers were analysed for emerging patterns, structures and interpretations of different task allocations in relation to the collaboration and overall success of agile projects.

2.2   Participants

This study incorporates ten UI/UX specialists from ten companies of various sizes, in which five are male and five are female. All participants are part of the creative team in respective companies, involved in projects which incorporate the agile approach, with user-centered design. The names of the projects and involved clients are omitted for confidentiality reasons. In order to have a rational pool of data, selected participants varied in terms of their work experience: junior designers (n = 3), medior to senior designers (n = 4) and head of design teams (n = 3); size of the design team within their project teams: the only designer (n = 4), one of the two designers (n = 4) and one of the three designers in the project (n = 2); and their organizations: ranging from product-based start-ups (n = 2) to design agencies (n = 2) and large corporations (n = 6). Geographical diversity included designers working in the Netherlands (n = 6), United Kingdom (n = 2), Germany (n = 1) and Spain (n = 1).

3   Results

In this section, we present the results that emerged from interviews regarding UX roles in their organizations and other aspects of design team structures within projects. The data from the interviews is outlined in the following table (Table 1), with a summary of key findings from the data in the discussion afterwards.

Table 1. Participants

	01	02	03	04	05	06	07	08	09	10
Role	UX designer	UX designer	Interaction designer	Interaction designer	Head UX/Service design	UX designer	UI/UX designer	Head of design/UX	UX designer	Design Principal
Work experience	Junior	Junior	Medior	Senior	Senior	Junior	Senior	Senior	Senior	Senior
Company - business	Product (software)	Exact - Product (software)	Service design agency	TomTom - Product (soft/hardware)	Aegon - Financial services	Aal.care - IT	KPN - Telecommunications	AOL - Mass media	Software and hardware product company	383Project - Digital consultancy
Company size*	Small / start up	Large	Medium /agency	Large	Large	Small / start up	Large	Large	Large	Medium /agency
Project size**	Large	Large	Small	Large	Large	Medium	Large	Small	Large	Medium
Team size ***	Large	Large	Small	Medium	Large	Large	Large	Small	Large	Medium
Designers in scrum team	3	2	1	2	1	2	1	1	3	2
Process	Kanban	Lean UX	Lean UX	Lean UX No sprints	Adapted Spotify model	Lean UX	Spotify model	Lean UX	Lean start up	Lean UX
Collaboration	Scrum team: close	Scrum team but no stand ups	Scrum team: close	Partially scrum team + Partially separate	Scrum team: close	Scrum team: close	Scrum team & UX chapter	Separate	Scrum team	Scrum team
Agile maturity	Low	Medium	Medium	Medium	High	High	High	Medium	Medium	Low
Satisfaction	Low	Medium	High	Medium	High	High	High	High	High	Medium
Research	None	Yes	Yes + separate research team	No. Separate research team	Yes	Yes	Yes	Yes	Yes, for small tasks. Separate team for larger research.	Yes
Wireframes and flows	Yes	Yes	Yes	Yes	Yes	Yes	Yes	Yes	Yes	Yes
UI	Yes	Yes + visual designer	Yes	No, UI designer	Yes	Yes + visual designer	Yes	Yes	No, UI designer	No

* Small/start up = the company is a start up and has up to 40 employees. Medium / agency = the company is a design agency and has employees between 40 and 80 employees. Large = over 80 employees.
** Small = scope of up to 3 months. Medium = scope of 3 -12 months. Large > 12 months.
*** Small <5, Medium = 5-10, Large >10

3.1   Designer Profiles

Although the participants identified themselves as UX designers (n = 7), interaction designers (n = 2) and a UX and Service designer (n = 1), there was a large overlap in terms of their roles and responsibilities. The literature search illustrated that there is no unified agreement for the definitions of the roles. To have a common ground, we decided to establish the following roles as involving the following tasks in Table 2 (in alignment with [3]).

Based on the tasks they perform in daily work, the participants were classified into various designer profiles, as described in Table 3.

For the majority of the participants, the UX and UI tasks were found to be intertwined. Participant 7 noted "I think it's a bit hard to think about those two roles in isolation: they're so complementary! One doesn't work without the other. If the two roles are played by different persons: A UX designer will deliver outstanding results

Table 2. Definition of the User Research, User Experience and User Interface tasks

User Research (UR) tasks	User Experience (UX) tasks	User Interface (UI) tasks
– Discovery: collect user insights, analyse and draw conclusions. Interview the users. Identify if the problem that is being tackled is the correct one – Usability testing – Define and test assumptions	– Translate user needs into wireframes of screens – Create user flows to show the interactions between screens	– Create visual designs – Apply the design library or the style guide to the wireframes – Maintain consistency with the established brand identity

Table 3. Designer profiles

User Interface (UI) designer	A designer focused purely on creating visuals and aligning with established design style and principles within the project	None of the participants
User eXperience (UX) designer	A designer purely focused on translating user needs into wireframes and flows	Participants 4 & 9
User Researcher (UR)	A designer purely focused on scoping the problem and the user needs, along with validating wireframes or visuals with end-users	None of the participants
UI/UX designer	A designer fulfilling roles of both UI and UX designers	Participants 1 & 3
UX/UR	A designer fulfilling roles of both UX designer and a User Researcher	Participant 10
UI/UR	A designer fulfilling roles of both UI designer and a User Researcher	None of the participants
UI/UX/UR	An all-round designer, responsible for all tasks across the creative process	Participants 2, 5, 6, 7 & 8

only if the involvement/communication with the UI designer is total, and the other way around." Three out of ten participants mentioned that they had a dedicated team conducting discovery research and usability testing for them. Moreover, two participants stated that they would do informal usability testing themselves, whereas a usability expert did formal, larger testing.

Although some of the participants' functions included secondary roles and responsibilities, such as project management and product ownership (participant 6), coding to speed up the process of handover to developers (participants 3, 8), and overseeing the design team or chapter (participants 5, 8 and 10), these were not included in the scope of the current research.

4   Discussions

The findings reveal that there are patterns for commonly found designer profiles within Agile project teams. In this section, the different team structures are analysed and evaluated from a collaboration point of view. Data analysis revealed some best practices for achieving effective collaboration in design teams, which will be discussed in this section.

4.1   Designer Profiles

Based on the tasks that every participant has attributed to themselves, these designer profiles were plotted against the 5 stages of the creative process: Discovery ("Think" phase of the Lean UX), Wireframes, Visual Design, Prototyping ("Make" phase) and User Testing ("Check" phase) [7]. The graphs within Fig. 3 demonstrate the extent to which each designer is involved in the tasks at hand. The participants who were the only designer in their team classified themselves as UI/UX/UR profile (chart 4 above), being responsible for all tasks across the creative process. A pattern established itself, showing that these designers (UI/UX/UR profile) were the most satisfied among the participants. Our assumptions are that the fewer designers there are in the project, the broader the scope of the designers' role. Hence, the more control and ownership they have over the creative process, the more satisfied they might feel. An interesting stance is indicated by the User Research tasks. In the current research, six participants (one UX/UR profile and five UI/UX/UR profiles) were found to be doing user research with different levels of involvement. Three participants reported that there was a separate role or team, outside of their scrum team, who conducted research activities for the team. Schwartz [11] debates whether the Agile project should include a usability expert (the equivalent of user researcher in our research) in the scrum team. However, if the user researcher (or usability expert) is not part of the scrum team, it is important that they are always available on-call [12]. The approach suggested by Sy [13] implies separating user research tasks from the interaction design tasks; while the interaction designer is designing for the next cycle, the usability practitioner is performing tests on the previous cycle's code, along with gathering customer data for two cycles ahead.

4.2   Satisfaction Levels

Participants who are executing tasks within the whole spectrum of Lean UX show higher satisfaction levels within their jobs (Participants 2, 5, 6, 7 and 8 were the UI/UX/UR profile).

The designers working on projects where the main research is carried out by a separate team stated that they would like to be more involved in executing research. In fact, the current research argues that there is a correlation between how involved in research the participants were and their satisfaction level. The more involved they were in research, the happier they were at work. Our assumptions are that when the designer is involved in the discovery phase of the user research (understanding the user needs

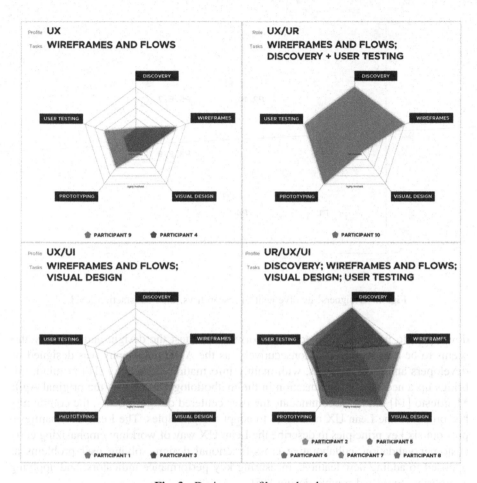

Fig. 3. Designer profiles and tasks

and defining the problem) then they are involved in determining exactly why this problem is important. Participant 3 (who had a separate team for research) mentioned that the "service designer decides if the problem we are solving is the right problem". Being involved in identifying the core problem that the concept is being designed for provides designers a clearer vision (Fig. 4).

4.3   Length of a Cycle

Participants 3, 5 and 8 indicated that because their design process was fluid, they felt that the structure of two-week development sprints were too long. Participant 8 claimed that, "If you think about it, you only get 31 times to pivot in 365 days. It's mad!" Designs may be created faster, but they would have to wait until the beginning of the next development sprint to be picked up. The designer would then have to wait for the

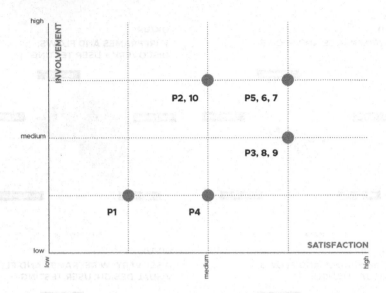

Fig. 4. Designers' involvement in research vs. their satisfaction level

developers to implement this to move forward and test the design, and arguably this seems to be a waste of time. Consecutively, as the Agile philosophy was designed by developers and for developers, with mainly information technology (IT) in mind, this brings up a need for an optimisation in the methodology. In fact, as the original Agile Manifesto [14] did not accommodate the user-centered design process, the community has proposed the Lean UX manifesto to adapt the principles. The Lean UX manifesto puts out six key principles to describe the Lean UX way of working: emphasizing early customer validation, collaborative cross-functional design, solving user problems as opposed to adding new features, measuring key performance indicators, and applying appropriate tools and nimble design [15].

4.4 Project Size

The results, as can be seen in Fig. 5, have revealed that in small projects, the UX designer was not involved in the discovery phase of the cycle. One of the participants reported that differentiation between service design (those involved in discovery and testing) and Interaction Design (focusing on the wireframes and user flows) was good as it helped designers to focus on the strengths of their respective roles. In addition, within small projects, the UX designers are also found to be specialised in visual design. Participants working in small projects report that it is advantageous for such a project to attain versatile designers, as it simplifies the process and enables closer communication with the developers. The same result was found for the prototyping phase of the cycle.

In medium-sized projects, the responsibilities of the UX designer extended from usual wireframes to include both discovery and usability testing.

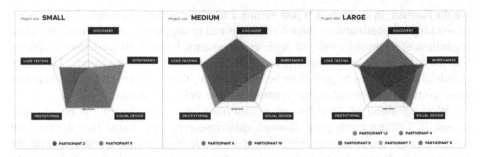

Fig. 5. Participants plotted according to their projects' sizes

Among the participants in large projects, the majority (five out of six designers) reported that the discovery phase is completed by a designated research team outside of their scrum team. In addition, it was found that within large projects the UX designers were specialized in the task of wireframing. This confirms the theory that in larger projects, where more than one design role exists, the designer can be more specialized on one role, while having an overview of other aspects of the creative process. design. In fact, the CEO of IDEO, Tim Brown has used the term "T-shaped stars" to describe people who have the depth of skills and expertise in one aspect of the process, represented by the vertical stroke, while also having breadth of skills and expertise across other disciplines, represented by the horizontal stroke. These attributes allowed for greater cross-functional collaboration [16]. Following this logic, the UX designers in large projects can be defined as "T-shaped designers" who have deep knowledge and expertise in creating wireframes and user flows, while also having an overview of other tasks.

4.5 Agile Approach

The Agile philosophy was originally developed as a method for programmers to improve their implementation practices. Today, there exists a great choice of different agile software development frameworks, all of which support a broad range of stages within the software development life cycle. The current research shows that two thirds of the participants are yet to fully figure out how to effectively embed UX Design methods within the Agile Software Methodology, and how to unify developers and designers in the Agile process of product development. These participants report that the organizations they work for are still going through an Agile transition, and have started working in Agile less than three years ago. These findings are in line with those of Loranger and Leibheimer [17], who show that highly effective Agile projects usually belong to organizations that have practiced Agile for over three years on average.

Between organizations, and even between teams within an organization, there exists many different approaches of how Agile frameworks are implemented. Participants came from different Agile environments such as a fully implemented Spotify model [18], or just taking best practices from it, involving lean startup versus lean UX, Kanban, and Scrum. In fact, participant 1 mentioned that, regarding the process, "now we do Kanban. In essence, it is just putting a label on prioritizing works." These ways of working are continuously shaped and improved to support a team's needs. However, regardless of the broad variety of Agile environments, 9 out of 10 participants reported that they still prefer to conduct UX activities ahead of development sprints. Though, it is indeed necessary to be part of, or be very close to, the development team to maintain close communication and ensure control over the delivered product.

Working ahead of development, or "up-front interaction design", is broadly discussed in Ferreira et al. [19]. Through their research, they found that the up-front design process contributed to mitigating risks and helped designers come up with the best possible design, due to better project estimation and prioritization. Schwartz [8] provided a detailed analysis of supporters for and opponents of "upfront design", concluding that, "every team has to find its proper way to process Agile-UX because different challenges require different solutions". This corresponds perfectly with Agile values, notably "individuals and interactions over processes and tools".

The interview responses revealed a pattern among participants that the more mature and structured the Agile methodology in their project was, the more satisfied the designers were overall. Our assumptions here are that creating a structured process with good user-centered design principles will ensure a great deal of ownership for each member of the development team and create favourable conditions for collaborations.

5 Conclusions

The current study focuses on the best practices for achieving effective collaboration in design teams within the Agile methodology. Some of our findings are aligned with the literature, for instance, the advocacy towards a sprint zero (or iteration zero) for UX teams to get a head start ahead of the development team [9].

In the introduction, we argue that design processes are defined differently per organization, lacking a universal model. The results from the current study support that claim. The Agile methodology has come a long way and many organizations have effectively started implementing this way of working across their projects, however we have discovered that designers are still finding their way and are missing an agile framework that caters for all the roles within a development process. Overall, the current research indicates there is no unified agreement for the definition of roles, but that creative processes and the tasks executed within these diverse roles are aligned. We found that the focus of the designer depends on the size of the project. In the current study we focused on five stages of the creative process that are necessary to deliver a quality product. For smaller projects the focus of the designers is more on delivering visual designs, whereas, for larger projects, designers are becoming more specialized in wireframes and user testing. We argue that it is important that the format within a project allows their members to have control and ownership over the creative process and the product that they are delivering. Creating a structured process with good user-centered design principles facilitate a great deal of ownership for each member of the development team and create suitable conditions for collaborations. In fact, our research shows that the designers who are responsible for all tasks within the creative process are the most satisfied with their work. Particularly, the more involved the designers were in research, the happier they reported to be at work. However, as one of the participants put it "this is the Jack of all trades, master of none" and we need to be aware that this can have a direct effect on the quality of the delivered product. Future research could reveal whether having a designer for each of the tasks separately leads to a higher quality product. Furthermore, as the current research only involved designers who classified themselves as user experience (UX) designers, the further research will look into analysing the roles of pure User Interface designers (UI) or User Researchers (UR).

In conclusion, our findings show the need to re-think team structures both within the design team and on the project-level. It is argued that UX specialists should not only be in close collaboration with development, but also with planning and strategy, as aligned with literature [10]. Future research will focus on the collaboration within the team as a whole, including the collaboration between all roles - from business analysts to testers, and designers to developers - needed to build a successful project.

Acknowledgements. We would like to express our gratitude to our interviewees Matt Zarandi from AOL, Charlotte Cavellier from Fjord Design & Innovation from Accenture, Karl Randay from 383 Project, David Guiza Caicedo from TomTom, Michel Jansen from cXstudio, Jingwen Yao from Exact, Niké Jenny Bruinsma from aai.care, Li Chiao, and two anonymous UX designers for their insights that served as the basis of this paper.

References

1. Chamberlain, S., Sharp, H., Maiden, N.: Towards a framework for integrating agile development and user-centred design. In: Abrahamsson, P., Marchesi, M., Succi, G. (eds.) XP 2006. LNCS, vol. 4044, pp. 143–153. Springer, Heidelberg (2006). doi:10.1007/11774129_15
2. Gullikesen, J., Goransson, B., Boivie, I., Blomkvist, S., Persson, J., Cajander, A.: Key principles for user-centered systems design. J. Behav. Inf. Technol. **22**, 397–409 (2003). doi:10.1080/01449290310001624329
3. UI, UX: Who does what? A designer's guide to the tech industry | Co.design
4. Awad, M.A.: A comparison between Agile and traditional software development methodologies. In: School of Computer Science and software Engineering, p. 84. University of Western Australia (2005)
5. Sy, D.: Adapting usability investigations for Agile user-centered design. J. Usability Stud. **2**, 112–132 (2007)
6. Design Sprint | Google Developers. https://developers.google.com/design-sprint/
7. Gothelf, J., Seiden, J.: Lean UX: Applying Lean Principles to Improve User Experience. O'Reilly Media Inc., Sebastopol (2013)
8. Schwartz, L.: Agile-user experience design: an Agile and user-centered process? In: 8th International Conference on Software Engineering Advances, pp. 346–351. IARIA XPS Press, Venice (2013)
9. Usability 101: Introduction to usability. https://www.nngroup.com/articles/usability-101-introduction-to-usability/
10. Corbin, J., Strauss, A.: Grounded theory method: procedures, canons, and evaluative criteria. J. Qual. Sociol. **13**, 3–21 (1990). doi:10.1007/BF00988593

11. Schwartz, L.: Agile-user experience design: with or without a usability expert in the team? In: 8th International Conference on Software Engineering Advances, pp. 359–363. IARIA XPS Press, Venice (2013)

12. McInerney, P., Maurer, F.: UCD in Agile projects: dream team or odd couple? J. Interact. **12**, 19–23 (2005). doi:10.1145/1096554.1096556

13. Sy, D., Miller, L.: Optimizing Agile user-centered design. In: CHI 2008: CHI 2008 Extended Abstracts on Human Factors in Computing Systems, pp. 3897–3900. ACM, New York (2001). doi:10.1145/1358628.1358951

14. Fowler, M., Highsmith, J.: The Agile manifesto. J. Softw. Dev. **9**(8), 28–35 (2001)

15. The Lean UX Manifesto: Principle-driven design. https://www.smashingmagazine.com/2014/01/lean-ux-manifesto-principle-driven-design/

16. IDEO CEO Tim Brown: T-shaped stars: the backbone of IDEO's collaborative culture. http://chiefexecutive.net/ideo-ceo-tim-brown-t-shaped-stars-the-backbone-of-ideoae%E2%84%A2s-collaborative-culture/

17. Infusing UX to Agile Development Processes. https://www.nngroup.com/articles/state-ux-agile-development/

18. Scaling Agile @Spotify with Tribes, Squads, Chapters and Guilds. http://blog.crisp.se/2012/11/14/henrikkniberg/scaling-agile-at-spotify

19. Ferreira, J., Noble, J., Biddle, R.: Up-front interaction design in agile development. In: Concas, G., Damiani, E., Scotto, M., Succi, G. (eds.) XP 2007. LNCS, vol. 4536, pp. 9–16. Springer, Heidelberg (2007). doi:10.1007/978-3-540-73101-6_2

Prototype-Centric Explorative Interaction Design Approach in the Case of Office Energy Coaches Projects

Tomasz Jaskiewicz[1(✉)], Aadjan van der Helm[1], and Wei Liu[2]

[1] Delft University of Technology, Delft, The Netherlands
{t.j.jaskiewicz,a.j.c.vanderhelm}@tudelft.nl
[2] Beijing Normal University, Beijing, People's Republic of China
wei.liu@bnu.edu.cnl

Abstract. This paper presents an explorative prototype-centric interactions design approach, as applied to the processes of designing interactive products for encouraging sustainable occupant behavior in office environments - the "Office Energy Coaches". In this approach, iterative making and trying out of prototypes is central to the organization of the design process, and no strict time separation is imposed on design activities, whether of analytical, creative or executive type. Instead of being organized by predefining the type of design activity to be performed during a given phase of the project, the design process phases are characterized only by increasing fidelity of created prototypes. The paper discusses projects from two design studios at industrial design faculties in the Netherlands and in China, where the prototype-centric approach was performed. Despite cultural and organizational differences, in both cases the approach proved to be successful. Fast, iterative prototyping involving interactive technology helped in organizing design teamwork, accelerated obtaining in-depth insights, facilitated conceptualization of meaningful interactions and supported development of experiential interactive product concepts. At the same time, some shortcomings of the approach have been observed, including several forms of fixation that designers faced when prototyping, as well as limitations of prototyping tools impacting the overall process performance. Based on discussed cases, we suggest areas for improving the prototype-centric approach, including recommendations for design methods, techniques and tools aimed at interaction design students and professional designers alike.

Keywords: Experiential prototyping · Iterative designing · Tangible interaction · Interaction Design · IxD education

1 Introduction

Interaction Design (IxD) is facing challenges of increasing societal and technological complexity. On the one hand, designers often have to deal with systems that involve multiple interconnected products and services. An example here are building automation and management systems that integrate heating, ventilation, lighting, information and security features of a building, controlled based on input from a

© Springer International Publishing AG 2017
A. Marcus and W. Wang (Eds.): DUXU 2017, Part I, LNCS 10288, pp. 597–613, 2017.
DOI: 10.1007/978-3-319-58634-2_44

multitude of sensors and control panels. While being made up of multiple interactive products, installations and services, such systems also involve simultaneous interactions with many individual users, who may have different roles, needs and can be engaged in a variety of social practices. For example, an office climate control may need to cater to various working styles of a single user, or to various kinds of social interactions such as having a meeting or a brainstorm session when several people use the room simultaneously. The work presented in this paper follows on the above example, as it addresses designing in the context of a "smart" office environment, and specifically deals with the challenge of encouraging sustainable office occupancy in that context. The approach we propose for dealing with entailed design complexity involves frequent iterative making and trying out of experiential prototypes, in order to comprehensively understand and address design problems at hand and to deal with related technological and social challenges.

Iterative design processes that support designing with technology are gaining popularity [9, 14], and we seek ways for using these processes to design for complex challenges. Many established design process models define a sequence of steps, phases or stages grouping design activities of certain type [4]. Most of these models resonate the distinction of analytical, creative and executive activities in the design process introduced by Bruce Archer [1], while often introducing more specific divisions. For example, IDEO uses respectively "inspire", "ideate", and "implement" [3], while Kumar proposes "research", "analysis", "synthesis" and "realization" [11] as phases. Steps back, jumps or organizing the order of these phases in different sequences are often indicated as a possibility [8].

Even though existing design process models can well describe iterative design processes, they also imply that individual design activities of similar kind need to be performed sequentially, and that each such activity has a clear termination moment before the next activity can begin. In the experience of our IxD education and professional design practice we have observed that such clear separation of design activities is rarely taking place, and design activities of different types tend to overlap. For example, while performing design research, designers may come up with creative ideas, that guide the direction of research, mixing analytical and creative activities. To support processes where complex design opportunity spaces are dynamically explored through more dynamic interplay between design activities of different kind, in this paper we propose a different approach. Here, separation of activities of different kinds is not imposed, and prototypes are considered to be both results and enablers of design activities belonging to different types and potentially occurring concurrently.

2   Prototype-Centric Framing of the Design Process

With the approach presented in this paper, our aim is to provide a better support for design processes where analytical, creative and executive design activities can all be initiated at the outset of the process, and mutually support each other throughout its entire duration. To achieve this goal, firstly, we support working with technology from the start of the design process. Hacking and tinkering can trigger many ideas and concepts if performed with design goals in mind [7]. Similarly, creative ideas developed and prototyped early on in the process can give direction and focus design research, can be involved in obtaining tacit knowledge from users and can help in discovering new research questions. Similarly taking executive steps early in the process allows to better understand the challenges of realizing the product and bringing it to the market, and inspire dealing with these challenges in a creative way. Testing of prototypes of varying fidelity as they are continuously generated in such process, can thus enable continuous generation of new, revised or improved insights, ideas and blueprints as outcomes of respectively analytical, creative and executive activities.

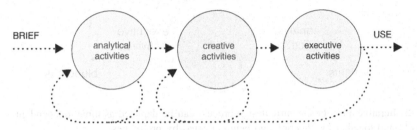

Fig. 1. A typical design process is divided into consecutive phases, which can be repeated while iterating over the entire process or its parts.

When discussing this approach with practicing designers and design students, we have observed that communication of an iterative designing process as a sequence of steps (as in Fig. 1) implies that each of these activities needs to have an explicit termination before the next one can start. In addition, we have noticed that starting a new iteration is causing resistance in design education because students consider this as "going back" and "starting all over". In order to remove this bias from the process representation we have decided to conceptually depict these activities as independent loops. We have also realized that in each of these activity loops, an autonomous iteration takes place, which can correspond to Mintzberg's do-see-think cycle [13] Kumar's two axes of real-abstract and making-understanding [9] or Kolb's learning cycle [10]. In all activities we take the position of supporting designers and design students in being able to perform such iterations quickly, as we see value in all the aspects of the process, as much as continuous gathering of understanding from the real-world phenomena. Lastly, this organization of the design activities emphasizes the unique position of making and trying out prototypes, as being a result and enabler of the three activity loops, as depicted in Fig. 2.

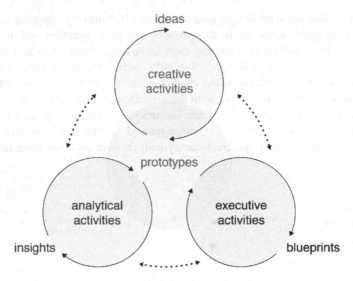

Fig. 2. Iterative, prototype-centric design process can be depicted as three independent activity loops bound together by affecting and being affected by prototypes.

The above work-in-progress model has given us a new framing to reflect on the organization of a design process, which we have been practicing in much of our education and design activities.

3 Approach

The proposed model for prototype-centric iterative designing is based on experience from a wide range of courses and workshops organized by us, as well as many other design processes inspired by the maker culture. We encourage frequent iterations across context researching, conceptualizing and implementing, as well as fast iterations within each one of the above as a way to increase the diversity and novelty of produced outcomes. To support this way of working we have appropriated and developed a number of techniques and methods, each of which aims at accelerating a particular kind of iteration in the design process.

Our "make-first" approach focuses on the early moments in the design process. It involves a short but intense hacking workshop, in which designers are required to build a simple interactive prototype, answering a simple brief loosely related to their main assignment and are steered to do it without overthinking the purpose of the prototype. The purpose of this activity is to learn that technology can inspire ideas, and having a concrete idea can be useful in focusing initial context research.

For designers with little technology experience, making interactive prototypes is a big challenge, requiring large investment of time, and often also money and other resources. We use a number of techniques to avoid "prototype love" - the particular type of fixation triggered by loss aversion, and to encourage developing prototypes in an explorative way. The iconic Arduino platform and the community of its users support fast interactive prototyping, but in our experience it is not sufficient on its own, especially for novice interaction designers. This is mainly due to the difficulty in understanding programming and electronics. To remove those obstacles, we provide designers with a wide range of modular electronic components, which allow them to prototype with only basic understanding of electronics. Having a stock of electronic components readily available as modules, which can be used without extra costs and without having to wait for an order, and re-used when the prototype is disassembled reduces loss aversion and helps designers in ad-hoc trial and error prototyping. We also provide designers with a short practical introduction to finding online examples of code-snippets and making prototypes through creative mashing up of existing code. We also support fast prototyping of embodiments by ensuring designers obtain basic 3d modelling skills and throughout the design process have walk-in access to rapid prototyping facilities such as 3d printers and laser cutters, as well as collections of a variety of scrap materials that can be easily repurposed for use in prototypes without extra costs or effort.

Nonetheless, in many situations making fully operational prototypes is still time and energy consuming. During the course of the project we introduce designers to a variety of methods that support evaluation and exploration of the envisioned interactive experiences with unfinished prototypes, or even without prototypes at all. Enactments allow designers to explore and communicate interactions without a prototype, and gradually introduce mock-ups and half-working prototypes. They also allow understanding of interaction styles, first explored in human-human communication and later translated to device-human interaction. We also encourage Wizard-of-Oz simulation of not implemented features during user tests and enactments.

Although the approach can apply to individual projects, work described in this paper has been done by groups, where individuals are encouraged to specialize in a particular design activity, or tasks such as managing the process or communication that involve dealing with all design activities.

The brief of the design assignment has been deliberately open, indicating context and challenge, but leaving room for interpretation in order to stimulate critical thinking and stimulate explorative research. We encourage designers to revise their understanding of the design challenge throughout the entire design process. However, many design research methods are time consuming, which makes it difficult to embed them in a highly iterative design process. Therefore, in the process of defining and evaluating ideas, we promote informal user tests [6].

Progress cards (Fig. 3) are a format for designers to shortly and informally report and reflect on the project progress on a daily basis. Each card has to include a central picture of a prototype, a list of "victories" and "defeats" of in the process from that day, a one-sentence description of the latest version of the design, and in the last version of the format, also a simplified process diagram (Fig. 2) indicating the journey through particular design activities which took place in the reflected day. Progress cards push designers to regularly reflect on their ("doing" as well as "thinking") actions [12] providing valuable learning and self-improvement moment. They also provide coaches with an easy to follow overview of the design process.

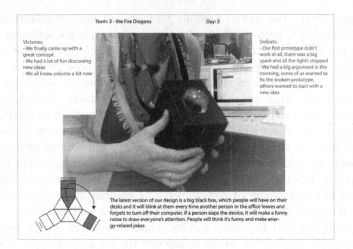

Fig. 3. A progress card required to be filled at the end of each day encouraged designers to reflect on their process and provided process documentation for further research.

When designers are encouraged to start prototyping early, there is an increased risk of fixation on early design ideas and technological solutions. To encourage design concept revisions, we implement "forced iterations" meaning that there are intermediate presentations, where a fully experiential prototype needs to be demonstrated and explained, and following this presentation, aspects of the design indicated by the jury are required to be changed.

4 Case Studies

In this paper we present two examples from two recent IxD courses organized according to presented approach. We use the presented model to reflect on projects from these courses.

4.1 Project Setup

The first case is a large IxD course called Interactive Technology Design (ITD) [2] taught to 1st year Design for Interaction Master of Science students at the TU Delft faculty of Industrial Design Engineering, in the Netherlands. It is a large 6EC course followed by 108 students in the spring semester of 2015 when described case took place. In this course students work on a design assignment as a group of 4–5 members. The workload of the course is one day per week spread throughout an entire semester, accumulating 20 workdays. In this case students have prior knowledge of interaction design, design research and product engineering, but may not be accustomed to working in an explorative way and to prototyping with interactive technology. In ITD design briefs given to students vary. In this paper we focus on the work of 4 groups, which have been following the "office energy coaches" brief.

The second case is a 10-day IxD workshop we have organized at a Tongji University College for Design and Innovation. The workshop involved 50 participants from across China, mainly university students from design or engineering faculties or university teachers. Chinese students have been given the same brief as the ITD students. However, in this case the students had less IxD experience, they had no time to improve their skills between design session days and we faced a communication barrier.

4.2 Office Energy Coaches Design Brief

The design brief given to students in both cases varied only slightly. The brief has been inspired by the research project in which the first author is involved. The brief dubbed "energy feedback objects" in the ITD context was renamed to "energy coaches" in the Chinese workshop context, while retaining the assignment largely unchanged.

In both cases participants were requested to design a device that provides feedback about energy use and coaches office workers to make their work environment more energy-efficient. At the same time, the coaching also had to help office workers to make their office more comfortable to work in. In the design brief the standpoint was emphasized that in order to make people comfortable and energy-conscious, their control of the office environment cannot be decreased, hence removing building automation from the range of possible solutions. On the other hand, solutions that increase office worker's energy awareness beyond the office context were encouraged. A number of research examples [12] were used to indicate the direction in which students were encouraged to seek for solutions.

4.3 Design Process Evaluation Method

In both cases, the design process of the projects has been monitored through evaluation of progress cards and other deliverables submitted in the course of the design process, including short textual descriptions, storyboards, videos of interactions enactments, technical documentation, process pictures and notes of the project coaches. The evaluation has been performed in a data analysis session with research staff, which involved hanging all printed progress cards of compared projects in horizontal, aligned timelines, and based on other observation materials adding relevant information.

5 ITD Case

5.1 Project Setup

The ITD course follows a program of 5 main phases dubbed "rough", "standalone", "nutcracking", "users", and "integration". The "rough" phase is a hacking exercise where students transform a simple interactive Simon game with open source code into a new prototype that fits into their design brief. The purpose of this exercise is to acquaint students with explorative use of technology and show how quickly new ideas can be generated through prototyping. The following "standalone" phase lasts for 3 course workdays and requires students to develop a concept and build a partially working prototype of it. The "nut-cracking" phase lasts for 5 course workdays and aims at revising and developing in the prototype the most difficult challenges of the concept. During the 2 workday "users" phase students prepare and execute a more elaborate user test. The "integration" phase lasts for 7 course workdays and ends with the exhibition of all projects, which students are encouraged to approach as a final user test. Throughout the course students work in groups of 4–5 members. During the project they are encouraged to take different roles in their team, with focus on conceptualizing, engineering, constructing, communicating and management in the project. They are also encouraged to publish their progress on a private blog, part of the education web platform called Projectcamp.us. Next to it, they are also required to submit a progress card at the end of each workday. The format of progress cards in the ITD project did not yet include marking the progress on the process diagram. While given the design brief, each group in ITD was provided with a different context of use. The contexts included a two-person office, an open office, a studio space, and a large presentation room.

5.2   Example Design Process – Volt

Volt is one of the four ITD projects that followed the "energy feedback objects" brief and was designed for the open office context, and provides an example of a process followed by all other groups. The initial idea of the group during the fast rough phase was to motivate office workers to turn off all lights in the room by unlocking a reward when the last person leaving turns off the last switch. During the standalone phase the new idea was proposed for a "Furry Mothersocket", a creature-like power cord that gets upset and expresses anger at office workers when devices connected to it use too much energy, which later developed to a less literal design metaphor. In the "nutcracking" phase the idea of a power socket has been kept, but the interaction concept has been changed to trigger the practice of sharing of power between different users, in a playful way provoking the discussion on the energy consumption and thereby increasing people's awareness of their energy consumption. The concept has been further explored in the nut-cracking phase as a device balancing on its middle with four power outlets. The prototype was initially made using four bottles taped together (Fig. 4).

In the integration phase a thermoformed plastic embodiment was made filled with free flowing powder material for haptic feedback. Electronic components for measuring power consumption were left outside of the prototype and kept under the table, which was encouraged, as it did not affect the experience of the product and would have caused safety issues if embedded in the prototype (Fig. 5).

At the start of the focused user test, two plugs on the device were working. The users would only be able to use electricity for a short time before power in their socket would be cut off. To get electricity flowing again, they would need to tilt their device their way, "taking" the energy away from the other user. Although the prototype was "ridden with bugs", the test gave many new insights in respect to interaction modalities with the prototype, as users were "more likely to tap, swipe or knock on the prototype than tilt it". Users also started to play with each other's energy as a form of a social game.

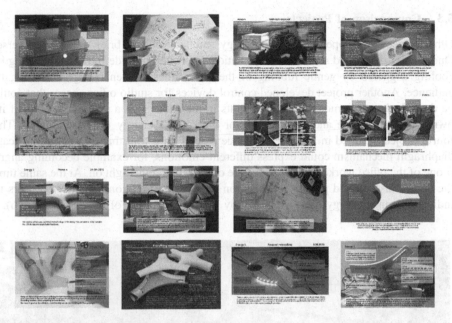

Fig. 4. Progress cards of the Volt project show substantial exploration in the first 6 project days, and incremental improvements over the rest of the project.

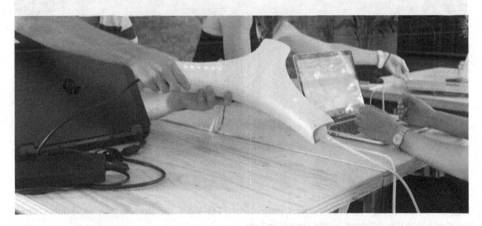

Fig. 5. Final version of Volt during the exhibition provided a complete experience of using the product in an office setting by a high-fidelity prototype with all features operational.

The insights have led to the next redesign of a 3-socket device without the tipping point and with a chain of 6 LEDs per side, lighting up with different colors and patterns based on user actions with the prototype. The final exhibition was set to resemble a coffee bar, signifying the student's reinterpretation of the open office context as an ad-hoc co-working environment. The interaction with the prototype during the exhibition was intuitive and the project has gained high acclaim.

5.3   Comparison of Projects

Other projects developed in the ITD energy feedback objects brief were very diverse. One project developed chairs for presentation room that provide individual heating or cooling triggered by gentle rubbing of the chair sides and encourage clustering of audience. Another project developed control devices for studio office spaces that could be described as "a remote control for lights in the room with a soul and moods of its own", by which care and compassion for the room's energy use was elicited. The fourth project resulted in a feedback device placed on a wall that through an intricate diaphragm mechanism could express different emotions, for example becoming angry if one of the office workers would leave the office leaving the light on. At the same time the device also offered precise feedback on energy consumption and allowed users to indicate planned energy use for the day by rotating the body of the device (Fig. 6).

Fig. 6. Three energy feedback object projects of ITD show the diversity of the kinds of final solutions that the different teams converged on.

Both similarities, as well as differences in the design processes were identified. The "standalone" phase was the most explorative part. In all cases the essence of the concept presented at the end of the "standalone" phase was kept until the end of the project. However, throughout the entire process all groups continued coming up with new ideas about the details of the product, and about the interaction with the products.

All groups also had a tendency to focus their attention on the making process. It often required a design coach to make the group aware of simple improvement to the design concept, while the group was mostly busy solving technical details not critical to the project's experience. For example, one group's concept involved creation of a feedback device to be placed on the wall of a small office. The group has decided early on in the process to use a diaphragm to express the emotion of the device. However, despite its aesthetic qualities the expression of the diaphragm was not well received during tests. Despite this, the group remained invested in the idea and did not give it up, nor organize further user tests to explore alternatives.

On the other hand, another group designed chairs for the lecture room that could be individually controlled and attract people to cluster around each other. The concept was formulated early on in the design process and gained support from coaches and reviewers, however the group has failed for a long time to make a working prototype, continuously exploring alternatives, and only managing to take decisions and accelerating the prototyping process in the last two weeks before the end of the course.

6 Tongji IxD Summer School Case

6.1 Project Setup

The Tongji IxD Summer School has been organized as a two-week, hands-on introduction course to interaction design. It involved students from a variety of Chinese universities, recent university graduates and several university teachers. Participants had their backgrounds in a wide variety of design and engineering disciplines, and little or no experience with IxD. There were three main phases organized in the course. The first phase was set to deliver a rough concept through enactment, the second was aimed to deliver a sketchy prototype and a video, the third – a fully autonomous, working prototype, a video showing the interactive experience, an A1 poster describing the challenge and product and a pitch presentation. Throughout the Summer School many lectures and exercises were provided to introduce students to various IxD methods and techniques, as well as to teach them prototyping with technology.

Students worked in 10 groups of 5 participants. Each group was assigned with a brief to design for an office located within close proximity to the workshop location, and was provided with an emotion keyword describing an interaction style to be the starting point of their ideation. The design brief required students to design an interactive device that would make office workers more aware on the impact of their practices on energy consumptions and at the same time help them improving comfort at the office and reduce energy use. The students were encouraged to reinterpret this brief throughout the course of the workshop.

At the outset of the project we were anticipating communication problems between local students and non-Chinese speaking coaches. We have emphasized that using the prototype or an enactment can help with communication. Considering the short time frame, less skills of participants and no time between design sessions for individuals to improve specific skills, we were initially expecting much less elaborate results than in the ITD case.

608   T. Jaskiewicz et al.

6.2 Process Example – Tired Lamp

The design process of the "Tired Lamp" was similar to all other projects in the Summer School workshop. The process started with the introduction of the brief. The group was assigned to the "sad" emotion of the initially to be explored interaction style and to the context of one of the offices at the university. The students visited the assigned office and after observing and interviewing office workers they have decided to focus their design on office lighting. On the second day they have decided on the general concept, which can be summarized as a lamp becoming "sad" when it's being used too much, but which can be comforted by users to brighten it up. In this way, they aimed to achieve more awareness of the energy consumption among workers in the office. The first idea to achieve this goal was a face projected by the light on the desk, reflecting the light's emotional state. The group explored this idea by making storyboards and performing improvised enactments in the first phase (Fig. 7).

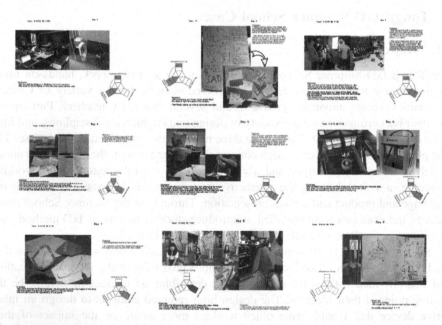

Fig. 7. Progress cards of the "Tired lamp project" showed that the first phase was dominated by "understanding" activities, the third phase by "implementing" while "ideating" took place all along.

During the second phase, the concept was initially simplified with just the brightness of the office light as actuation, while typical light switches were used for input. In the course of the process students kept adjusting their design based on feedback from other students and coaches reacting to their improvised prototypes. They have decided to integrate all the interaction in the lamp object and design the lamp in a way that would resemble a flower opening and closing up. This led to another idea of involving user input in the form of "comforting strokes". At the start of day 6 the designed experience was presented in a video using mostly Wizard-of-Oz technique. In the following days students have explored various mechanisms and materials that could be used to build the lamp. They have repurposed an umbrella mechanism in a way that also allowed moving the entire lamp up and down. Through informal user tests, students realized that such motion enhanced the interactive experience, by only allowing the light to be comforted and drawing attention of the users in its "tired", "sad" state.

The prototype has led students to explore a variety of comforting gestures to be used on the lamp "petals". For the final prototype, capacitive touch sensors embedded in petals were chosen, as they would trigger even with a very gentle touch. A stepper motor was used to control the light position and degree of opening. On the last day the focus of the group was split on preparing communication of the concept and finalizing the prototype, which included many refinements to the behavior and continuous informal user tests by designers themselves and other students. During the final presentation on day 10 the project gained positive feedback from exhibition visitors, although the interaction with the petals required initial instructions (Fig. 8).

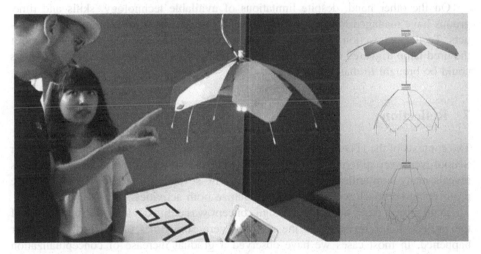

Fig. 8. The final prototype of the "Tired lamp" had many qualities of a finished interactive product.

6.3 Comparison of Projects

There has been large variety among the Summer School projects. Some projects stood out by showing sensitivity to the context and innovative ideas. Among those was the "Power mosquito" which created a "virtual mosquito" moving through the office table using LEDs and buzzers. The mosquito would appear when the energy was being wasted, and required users to slap the current location of the mosquito to turn it off and turn the unused lights off at the same time. Another project designed an AC remote control with features resembling an artificial creature, which through emitted light and sound would appear stressed and show it by mimicking increasing heartbeat. Eventually, when the temperature would be set very low, it would stop and briefly produce a heartbeat flat-line sound. Other projects included office nap and relaxation assistants, visitor welcoming devices, or solutions to involve security staff in providing energy-related feedback to office users.

In the course of the Summer School we have noticed most students were having a difficulty in gaining insights into context that would go deeper than initial assumptions coming from the first observation round. For example, one group started the project by interviewing a security worker. They understood from the interview that many security workers are bored during their work, are lonely at work and don't feel any connection to the people working in the building they guard. Following this interview, the group kept coming up with ideas for entertaining security workers, while these ideas did not follow the design brief. It required several coaching sessions to make the group understand that a good design would entertain the security guard, while supporting him to take actions that would help office workers in saving energy, and providing him with more self-esteem. Still the group failed to understand and involve the many design aspects in which the relationship between the security guard and office workers could be supported in a meaningful way by an interactive product.

On the other hand, despite limitations of available technology, skills and time, groups have managed to reach a high diversity, originality and intricacy of the products. To the satisfaction of designers, several products, such as the napping pillow or the tired lamp triggered questions from the exhibition visitors about when the products could be brought to market.

7 Reflection

The contexts of the ITD Energy Feedback Objects projects and the Tongji IxD Summer School were very different. However, comparing the projects from those two contexts reveals many similarities. This allows us to draw several conclusions on the iterative prototyping approach we have used to organize both activities.

In all project cases the general design concept was defined within the first quarter of the project. Later revisions of the concept were sometimes encouraged, but never happened. In most cases we have observed a gradual increase of conceptualization focus on details throughout the entire process. We generally saw value in such process, although it has sometimes led to fixation on concepts despite user tests indicating that the concept doesn't work as intended and a different concept could have been more useful. We expect parallel prototyping [5] to be an alternative approach to promote more explorative attitude, and we aim to incorporate it into our approach in the future.

On the other hand, several groups encountered problems with not being able to decide on a specific concept direction and to begin prototyping. They felt the concept is "not good enough" and it would be impossible to change it once prototyping starts. Generally, we encountered this situation in groups that were less technically apt, and we may conclude that easier to use prototyping tools could have helped these groups to start iterating between prototyping and more abstract reflecting. Figure 9 illustrates the two described situations using the iterative design process diagram. Whereas in the first case students find it difficult to reflect more generally and in a more abstract way while they start prototyping (Fig. 9b), in the second case too much abstract thinking creates a barrier to start prototyping activities (Fig. 9a). Unstructured interviews with selected participants have revealed that some aspects of above fixations can be attributed to loss aversion related to the prototypes. This either was a result of resistance to commit time and energy to developing a technological prototype that may not be the final one, not wanting to discard a prototype that has taken substantial amount of time and energy to create, or only one group member developing the prototyping skills, causing separation of tasks and reducing communication in the group when under time-stress. Use of modular electronics and premade code templates has partially mitigated the above problems by reducing the time and skills needed to prototype with technology. However, further reduction of the technological skill-related prototyping obstacles would have clearly improved the analyzed design processes.

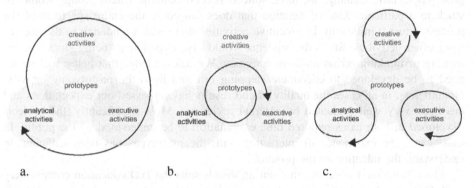

Fig. 9. The prototype-centric framing has revealed forms of fixation such as iterating across activities while avoiding to prototype (a), only prototyping without generating insights, new ideas and blueprints (b) and isolated iterations by not-communicating team members (c).

Other situations where lack of communication across individuals performing different design activities were especially apparent occurred mainly in the later stages of the projects (as illustrated by Fig. 9c). One of the common patterns was that an engineer would underestimate the time needed to implement designed feature, and would largely modify the interaction while implementing it. On the other hand, other members of the group, waiting impatiently for the engineer to finish, would continue revising user experience ideas, and prepare documentation based on earlier versions. To counteract such situations, lessons from agile methods can be drawn. Enforcing daily working builds in the future may help students to develop only features needed by others and may help in reducing the unnecessary complexity of the design.

Another encountered problem has been the limited scope of performed analytical activities. The focus in both courses was on learning technology and experiential prototyping. Yet, we expected designers to use the prototypes to gain deep insights from the design context by using the prototypes. We have observed that with every research iteration new research questions were formulated and student didn't have enough time to answer them in-depth. To resolve this problem and take advantage of the research opportunities in an iterative designing process, we aim to identify and adopt appropriate methods to encourage formulation of research questions that span across multiple research iterations and how more research rigor can be introduced to the process without causing additional delays.

8 Conclusions

The two presented projects show how the prototype-centric iterative IxD approach can be applied in different project setups and how it succeeds in obtaining fast, experiential and rich results. We acknowledge the fact that analytical activities in such processes need to be supported in a better way and we are looking for appropriate methods. By reflecting on the process with help of progress cards and the preliminary version of the prototype-centric framing, we have noticed several patterns where groups would be stuck in a particular kind of iteration that does not cover the entire spectrum of the process, most significantly in executive activities there was a tendency to themselves from other activities. Similarly, students would also experience "being stuck" in the making or thinking across different activities. We acknowledge that better techniques need to be developed to encourage stepping out and in to the prototyping activity. Nonetheless, in all cases the quality of end results has surpassed our expectations and has been very well evaluated by external reviewers. Most significantly, the projects developed in both cases required little explanation to be understood by the public. In most cases the experience of interacting with the prototypes has been sufficient to understand the intention of the product.

Overall we have observed that our approach suits the IxD education context very well. Despite a few shortcomings, both cases have delivered a large variety of relevant concepts accompanied by experiential prototypes. Yet, perhaps the most significant outcome of the projects was the enthusiasm of participating students, who have provided with very positive feedback at the end of the course, and many of them expressed eagerness to continue working on the projects after the course was finished.

Acknowledgments. We would like to thank students participating in described cases, as well as faculty and staff from TU Delft and Tongji University for their enthusiasm and support.

References

1. Archer, L.B.: Systematic Method for Designers. Council of Industrial Design, London (1964)
2. Aprile, W.A., van der Helm, A.: Interactive technology design at the Delft University of Technology-a course about how to design interactive products. In: DS 69: Proceedings of E&PDE 2011, the 13th International Conference on Engineering and Product Design Education, London, UK, 08–09 September 2011 (2011)
3. Brown, T.: Design thinking. Harv. Bus. Rev. **86**(6), 84 (2008)
4. Cross, N.: Engineering Design Methods: Strategies for Product Design. Wiley, Hoboken (2008)

5. Dow, S., Glassco, A., Kass, J., Schwarz, M., Schwartz, D.L., Klemmer, S.R.: Parallel prototyping leads to better design results, more divergence, and increased self-efficacy. ACM Trans. Comput. Hum. Interact. (TOCHI) **17**(4), 18 (2010)
6. Greenberg, S., Buxton, B.: Usability evaluation considered harmful (some of the time). In: Proceedings of the SIGCHI Conference on Human Factors in Computing Systems, pp. 111–120. ACM (2008)
7. Hartmann, B., Doorley, S., Klemmer, S.R.: Hacking, mashing, gluing: understanding opportunistic design. IEEE Pervasive Comput. **7**(3), 46–54 (2008)
8. Hummels, C., Frens, J.: Designing for the unknown: A design process for the future generation of highly interactive systems and products. A Grand Day Out: Empathic Approaches to Design (2008)
9. Knapp, J., Zeratsky, J., Kowitz, B.: Sprint: How to Solve Big Problems and Test New Ideas in Just Five Days. Simon and Schuster, New York (2016)
10. Kolb, D.: Learning Styles Inventory. The Power of the 2 × 2 Matrix, p. 267 (2000)
11. Kumar, V.: 101 Design Methods: A Structured Approach for Driving Innovation in Your Organization. Wiley, Hoboken (2012)
12. Lockton, D., Cain, R., Harrison, D.J., Giudice, S., Nicholson, L., Jennings, P.: Behaviour change at work: empowering energy efficiency in the workplace through user-centred design. EPIC Board of Directors (2011)
13. Mintzberg, H., Westley, F.: It's not what you think. In: MIT Sloan Management Review, vol. 42, no. 3, pp. 89–93 (2001)
14. Ries, E.: The Lean Startup: How Today's Entrepreneurs use Continuous Innovation to Create Radically Successful Businesses. Crown Business, New York (2011)

UCD and Agile Methodology in the Development of a Cultural Heritage Platform

Eduardo Merino, Claudia Zapata(✉), and María del Carmen Aguilar

Faculty of Sciences and Engineering,
Pontificia Universidad Católica del Perú, Av. Universitaria 1801, Lima, Peru
{a20082269, zapata. cmp}@pucp. edu. pe,
m. aguilarv@pucp. pe

Abstract. Cultural heritage is contemplated as one of the essential components of any society, considered beyond personal, social or national attitudes, its conservation must be done in benefit of humanity. The techniques used for dissemination have been changing over the years, making Information and Communication Technologies the main protagonists. The purpose of this study is the implementation of a native mobile application that disseminates information about the cultural heritage using augmented reality through a mobile phone, in such a way as to create a conducive environment to stimulate learning. Usability becomes an important characteristic in the implementation of this tool as it must be massive and intuitive, reason why it was decided to apply a proposed methodology to integrated Agile Methodologies with User-Centered design and show the software development process under these guidelines.

Keywords: Usability · Agile methodology · XP · User-Center design · Cultural heritage

1 Introduction

Cultural heritage is contemplated as one of the essential components of any society and is usually considered beyond personal, social or national attitudes and whose conservation must be done for the benefit of humanity [13].

Likewise, the city or historic center constitutes a living document that reflects the way of life and culture, allowing each country to have a true cultural dimension and define its individuality [9]. This is why we have an obligation to preserve historical centers and their future [4]. In this way, the tasks of cultural heritage preservation should be given on a daily basis so that these inherited assets remain in collective knowledge and eliminating ignorance [17].

There are several mechanisms for the preservation of cultural heritage, one of which is the diffusion of its existence to the entire community that interacts with them [12]. Due to this, it is very important to have a mechanism of diffusion that allows to distribute this knowledge horizontally to a wider audience than the academic [11].

© Springer International Publishing AG 2017
A. Marcus and W. Wang (Eds.): DUXU 2017, Part I, LNCS 10288, pp. 614–632, 2017.
DOI: 10.1007/978-3-319-58634-2_45

In addition to making information more accessible to citizens, it is important to involve them in the reconstruction of the contemporary history of their city. Hence, it is essential to rescue oral history, in order to avoid that various undocumented facts and events that are lost in time [5].

The techniques used for dissemination have been changing over the years, making Information and Communication Technologies the main protagonists [12]. Within these, we find mobile technologies, which represent a novel tool for the dissemination and enhancement of cultural heritage by improving access to all the historical content of the city [15].

According to a study by Futuro Labs 2014, 62% of Lima's citizens who own a mobile phone use it to access social networks, 22% use it for entertainment purposes and 16% use it as a work tool. This, combined with the portable feature of this technology, gives us the possibility of orienting its use to seek social, educational and cultural benefits [7].

Taking into account that the dissemination of cultural heritage is complemented by learning based on experience, and that alternatives can be sought for benefit in mobile technologies, the implementation of geolocation and augmented reality can be considered. These technologies are able to provide detailed information to users, as well as stimulating and encouraging learning, provoking the interest to explore, analyze and compare the showed content with the perceived reality [10].

Taking all this into account, it can be affirmed that there is a lack of computer tools that support the dissemination of the Peruvian cultural heritage in a public and massive way for the citizens.

The purpose of this study is the implementation of a native mobile application that disseminates information about the cultural heritage using augmented reality through a mobile phone, in such a way as to create a conducive environment to stimulate learning. Usability becomes an important characteristic in the implementation of this tool as it must be massive and intuitive. According to Aguilar [2] and Zapata [19], agile methodologies can be integrated with tools and techniques that seek for usability such as User-Centered design (UCD), reason why it was decided to apply the methodology proposed by Aguilar in [2] and show the software development process under these guidelines.

2   Methodology

In this section we will describe the User-Centered Design and the Agile Methodologies, as well as the integration of both techniques for the development of the tool that is part of the present study.

2.1   User-Centered Design

The UCD is a term used to describe the design process in which end users have much influence on the form of the product [1].

Norman (1988) suggests 7 principles that facilitate the design work:

1. Use common terms for people, build conceptual models and write manuals that are easy to understand and written before design implementation.
2. Simplify the structure of tasks, not overload the user's memory with terms that should be remembered in the short or long term.
3. Make the functionalities visible, the user must be able to realize the use that is given to an object simply by viewing the associated buttons.
4. Lean on graphs to make the functionalities more understandable.
5. Take advantage of the limitations so that the user knows, naturally, what can and cannot be done.
6. Perform the design thinking that users are going to make mistakes, this way we have the ability to anticipate possible mistakes that users may make and give you the option to recover from them.
7. Have a standard design for unforeseen errors, so you do not have different designs that can confuse the user.

2.2   Agile Methodologies

Agile methodologies emerged in the 1990s as an alternative to the traditional development processes, which were characterized by being rigid and possessing excessive documentation, which meant that the final product was not aligned with the new demands that were emerging in the client. It is there that the Agile Alliance was born and it would be in charge of summarizing the "agile" philosophy in the Agile Manifesto, which values the following points [8]:

- Customer satisfaction by delivering useful software.
- Welcome changing requirements, even late in development.
- The functional software is delivered frequently (weeks rather than months).
- The functional software is the primary measure of progress.
- Sustainable development, able to maintain a steady pace.
- Daily and close cooperation between business managers and developers.
- Face to face conversation is the best form of communication.
- Projects are built around motivated individuals, who should be trusted.
- Constant attention to technical excellence and good design.
- Simplicity.
- Self-organizing teams.
- Regular adaptation to changing circumstances.

Among the alternatives presented by agile methodologies, Extreme Programming (XP) has been selected due to the characteristics presented. In addition, it can be easily adapted to small development teams, such as this one, without compromising the quality of the software being developed [3].

Some of the key features of XP that will be used in the development process are [6]:

- Iterative and incremental development, small deliveries one after another.
- Continuous unit tests for error detection.
- Correction of all code errors before adding new functionalities to the software.

- Refactoring the source code to improve the readability and maintenance of the software.
- Simplicity in the software source code.

2.3 Integration

The proposed integration is based on a case study by Aguilar and Zapata [2] in which the disadvantages in usability that are generated in the XP design process are compensated by UCD tools. As shown in Fig. 1, the basic XP process (blue squares) will be followed but by adding certain selected UCD tools that are relevant to this work (purple squares). In this sense, "Interviews" will serve to raise requirements, "People" will represent different groups of users who will use the application and "Scenarios" will serve as informal stories about the tasks and activities that will be performed by users. This way you can express ideas or imaginary situations that help with the design. "User Evaluations" will go hand in hand with development iterations and participants will be required to evaluate the degree to which the product meets predefined usability criteria.

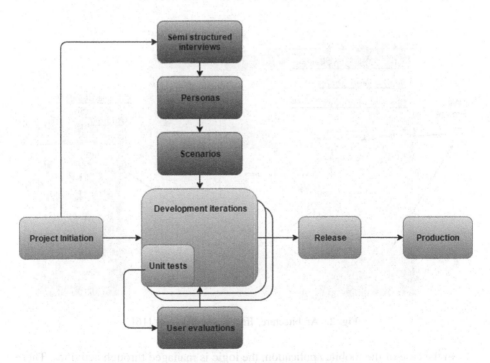

Fig. 1. XP process integrated with UCD tools [2] (Color figure online)

3   Development Process

3.1   Modules and Iterations

The software was divided into two main modules: a web application and a mobile application. The web application includes the data management, web services and functionalities used by the administrator. These modules were implemented using XP with three iterations and they did not consider user evaluations. On the other hand, as the mobile application includes functionalities used by end users we had to use the integration of XP and UCD for its implementation.

3.2   Architecture

The architecture used in this project was the Model-View-Controller (MVC) pattern. As we can see in Fig. 2, HTTP requests that arrive by the browser, where users are interacting, will be processed by the route controller, which will execute the corresponding driver according to the requested route. The controller will process the system logic, querying and saving data using the necessary models and then invoking an HTML view, which will be showed to the user by the Web browser.

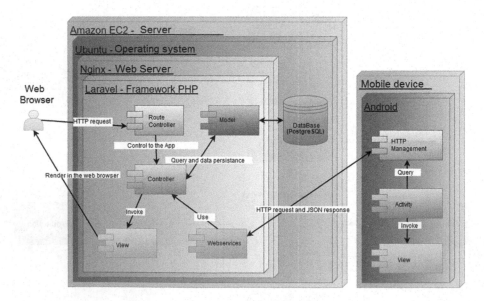

Fig. 2.   Architecture. Image adapted from [16]

In the case of the mobile application, the logic is managed through activities. These activities have the ability to communicate with the Web server using the HTTP handler, which will use the web-services implemented in the Web system to obtain the required information. Finally, after obtaining the required data using the HTTP handler, the activity will use XML views to display the information.

4   Mobile Application

This section aims to apply the integration of the chosen UCD tools together with XP for the design and the iterations throughout the development of the mobile application.

4.1   UCD-XP Integration for Requirements Definition

Based on the proposed integration, interviews with possible end-users of the mobile application should be carried out, in order to have a general idea of its functionality. Then, Personas will be identified, which represent the groups of users that will interact with the application. Finally, Scenarios will be defined, which will express imaginary situations that will help to design the concept of the mobile application.

Interviews. The objective of these interviews is to obtain ideas, given by the end users, for the conception of the application's design. The type of interview used was the semi-structured one, since it is necessary to adapt the questions asked to the interviewed according to their answers.

Because this work presents themes related to cultural heritage and augmented reality, it was decided that the interviewees have a profile related to historical or technological studies, as well as a person with a profile very different from the aforementioned, so that it serves as reference of the common citizen.

It was expected that interviewees did not have experience with augmented reality so the purpose of the structure of the interview was to know the expectations they have about using this technology in a mobile application to know the cultural heritage that surrounds them.

The interviews were carried out normally. People were very familiar with the use of smartphones and the concept of augmented reality; although they did not have much experience using it since it is not an everyday tool the only interaction that some interviewees had with augmented reality was through the game Pokémon GO. However, they had a very clear idea of how the proposed application should work.

About the augmented reality application for cultural heritage, emphasis was placed on obtaining information on heritage in ruins, since in the absence of resources for their restoration; a virtual representation of them may become equally useful. Likewise, the possible pedagogical benefits of this type of application were highlighted because, in the experience of one of the interviewees as a teacher, students learn better with graphics and technology than using written support. Finally, it is important to mention the importance of making visible the heritage that goes unnoticed.

Regarding the way in which the application would work, the interviewees indicated that it will be indispensable to use the camera so that objects can be superimposed, representing the real world heritage, with which they can interact to obtain more information.

The interviewees highlighted the following points as important information:

- Name of cultural heritage.
- Relevant related dates.
- Period to which it belongs.

- If applicable, the culture to which it belonged.
- Synopsis.

Finally, interviewees consider that there is much of historical information that is not in state libraries or archives, but rather in personal or family files. That is why it seems to be a good idea to offer users an easy interface where they can upload such content without having to make previous subscriptions that make this a complicated process.

Personas and Scenarios. In this phase the groups of people and the scenarios in which the application will be used are presented.

- Group 1: Person with training in history or humanities.
- Group 2: Person without any background in history or humanities, who wants to know, in real time, information about the cultural heritage that surrounds it.
- Group 3: Person who has relevant information about some historical point and wants to register it in the application.

Prototype. Taking the result of the interviews, the Personas and Scenarios identified, we proceeded to make the prototype of the application. For this phase, the tool known as paper prototyping was used to construct the concept of the application according to the previous interviews. The initial prototype, which can be seen in Fig. 3, was evaluated by the interviewees in order to adapt it with their expectations.

After evaluating the paper prototype with the interviewees, comments and opportunities for improvement were obtained, which are explained below:

- Implement a login form that prevents form filling, which may feel out of date in mobile applications. For example, the integration of the login with the social network Facebook will give the user the possibility of registering and logging in with a single click.
- The initial screen, after the login, should contain shortcuts to the most relevant functionalities of the application. The side menu may contain features not so relevant.
- There must be a functionality that allows visualizing the proximity of points of interest to activate the augmented reality. Otherwise, users would not know when to turn it on.
- The list of historical events should be grouped according to the chronology history of Perú.

4.2 Users Evaluations

After each iteration we performed usability tests to identify the effectiveness, efficiency and ease of use of the mobile application. For this purpose, the "think aloud" method was used, as it will allow to obtain important information that may have been overlooked, as well as possible changes that may occur in the mobile application [18]. Participating users are the same ones who have been part of the design phase.

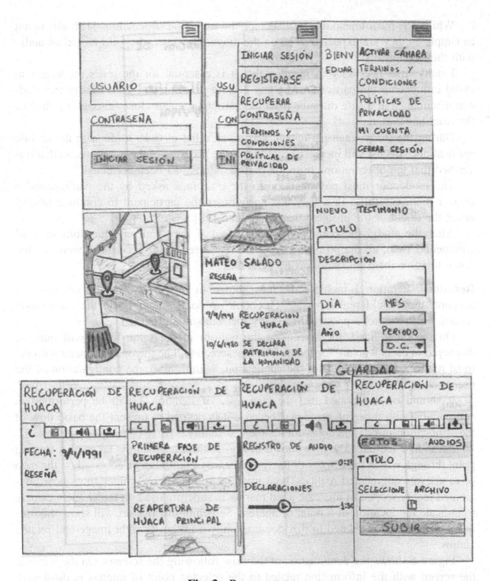

Fig. 3. Paper prototype

Applying Thinking Aloud. The evaluations were carried out inside the campus of Pontifical Catholic University of Peru (PUCP), since it was necessary that the participants use the geolocalization feature by moving around the University. They installed the mobile application on their phones so they could use it, and those who did not have an Android mobile phone were provided with one.

While it is recommendable to videotape the user's facial reactions [18], this is not as simple as they are expected to be on the move. However, they did record an audio with their comments.

Finally, it is necessary to mention that it is essential for the test's moderator to avoid influencing the participants by any gesture or comment. That is why the moderator remained at a safe distance from the participants, but closes enough to observe the reactions they had.

During the study, each participant was given a list of tasks to do with the mobile application. This list will increase according to the progress of the iterations, so that it is verified that the observations from the past iterations had been corrected.

The moderator must pay attention to the questions asked by the participants to answer them carefully, in a way that encourages the participant to continue talking about the doubt or the problem that they found [18].

After the study, the participants were asked if they had any questions or final comments. Then, all the problems that were registered in the recordings were written down to solve them in the following iteration.

Iterations. Iteration 1 includes the flow shown in Fig. 4. If users do not have an account, they could register using Facebook or do it manually on the registration screen. Furthermore, a password recovery mechanism is provided.

On the other hand, the screens at the bottom of the same figure will only be displayed to users who are logged in. The first screen will be the one of a menu with the most relevant functionalities of the application, within these, the configuration of the user account.

It should be mentioned that the tests user of iteration 1 will be performed in conjunction with those of iteration 2 because it is desired to present the basic flow of the application in conjunction with augmented reality.

Iteration 2 includes the flow shown in Fig. 5, the user menu is taken as a starting point through which the display of interested nearby points can be accessed on the map or to activate augmented reality. The 3 images grouped in the center show how augmented reality works; in this case a red marker is superimposed on the phone's camera to indicate the location of a point of interest. Selecting this marker will show the user detailed information related to that point, as shown in the far right image and related audios.

Figure 6 shows the continuation of the flow following the screens. On the left side the screen with the information related to the selected point of interest is displayed, having at the bottom all historical events. Selecting one of these historical events will display a screen with multiple tabs, as can be seen on the right. Each of these tabs displays information related to the historical event such as general information and photos.

After following the design proposed for the tests, the results were summarized. Table 1 show a list of observed characteristics during the tests and the result for each user, where a check (✓) indicates that it was successful and a tick (✘) indicates that there was an inconvenience.

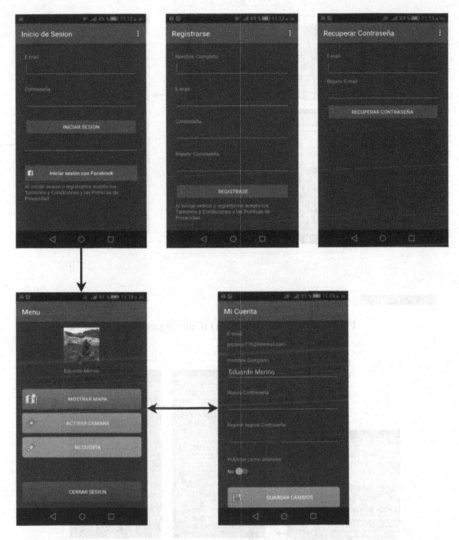

Fig. 4. Iteration 1

The iteration 3 comprises in the flow shown in Fig. 7, from the display of the detail of the point of interest can be accessed to add a new historical event related to that point. Also, when accessing the detail of a historical event, users can be provided with images or audios, as seen in the last tab.

Fig. 5. Iteration 2 (First part) (Color figure online)

Fig. 6. Iteration 2 (Second part)

Table 1. Characteristics observed during the user tests of iteration 1 and 2.

No.	Characteristics observed	User 1	User 2	User 3
1.	The requested activities were completed without any help	✓	✗	✓
2.	It was easy for the user to identify the menu with the option to register	✗	✗	✗
3.	It was easy for the user to fill out the registration form	✓	✗	✓
4.	It was easy to log in	✓	✓	✓
5.	It was easy to interact with the functionality of seeing the points of interest on a map	✓	✓	✗
6.	The user considers augmented reality easy to use to locate the points of interest around them	✓	✓	✓
7.	There were no problems interacting with the points shown on the camera to access more information	✗	✓	✗
8.	The user considers the division of screens that show information related to a point of interest to be appropriate	✓	✓	✓
9.	The user considers that the information displayed, with respect to a point of interest, is sufficient	✓	✓	✓
10.	The user considers the interface of the application understandable	✓	✓	✗

For the evaluation of this iteration, the activities defined in the evaluation of iterations 1 and 2, as well as new activities, were used. This was done in order to ensure that the observations from the previous test have been corrected.

After following the proposed design for the tests, the results were summarized. Table 2 shows a list of characteristics observed during the tests and the result for each user, where a check (✓) indicates that it was successful and a tick (✗) indicates that there were some drawbacks.

The use of the integration between XP and UCD helped not only to identify the end users of the proposed solution, but also to involve them from the design phase.

The paper prototyping was a very useful tool since it allowed to build the structure of the application taking the different points of view from each user without having to start its development. This fact was beneficial since no important changes were made or the addition of new functionalities between iterations. This resulted in users being presented with the progress of the application at each iteration, being familiar with most of the interface shown and allowing them to complete the assigned activities.

Although there were observations regarding the accessibility of some elements of the interface, the position of some buttons and the iconography, these did not present greater problem of correction. That is why, thanks to its early identification through user testing, it was possible to facilitate tasks that, in previous iterations, were difficult for users to complete.

Fig. 7. Iteration 3

Table 2. Characteristics observed during the user tests of iteration 3.

No.	Characteristics observed	User 1	User 2	User 3
1.	The requested activities were completed without any help	✓	✓	✓
2.	It was easy for the user to identify the options to register, recover password, terms and conditions and Privacy policies	✓	✓	✓
3.	It was easy to log in	✓	✓	✓
4.	It was easy to interact with the functionality of seeing the points of interest on a map	✓	✓	✓
5.	It was easy for him to identify the place where he had to activate augmented reality to recognize the points of interest around him	✓	✓	✓
6.	He had no problem interacting with the points shown on the camera to access more information	✓	✓	✓
7.	It seemed easy to fill out the form to add new historical event	✓	✓	✘
8.	It seemed easy to access more information related to a historical event	✓	✓	✓
9.	It seemed easy to fill out the form to contribute content to a historical event	✘	✓	✘
10.	Consider the interface of the application understandable	✓	✓	✓

5 Evaluation of Users of the Integrated System

The evaluation that will be made by the users will be based on the structure proposed by Rubin and Chisnell [14], which is mentioned below:

- Purpose and objectives of the test.
- Research questions.
- Characteristics of participants.
- Method.
- To-do list.
- Test environment and equipment.
- Role of the moderator.
- Data to be collected and evaluation measures.
- Evaluation report and results.

5.1 Goals

The user evaluation aims at the following points:

- Identify how much the mobile application helps the user to identify the points of interest that surround him.
- Identify whether the mobile application provides relevant information to users.

- Identify whether the mobile application allows the collection of relevant information from users.
- Identify obstacles that prevent users from carrying out proposed activities for the use of the mobile application.

5.2 Users

For this evaluation, we will work with 8 users (no iterations users), since it will expose at least 80% of the usability deficiencies that the mobile application presents [14]. The evaluation will be done with a first pilot user to have a notion of what should be adjusted to improve the evaluation. Then the evaluation will be applied on 7 users and will have 1 of backup in the case that a regular user presents problems of availability. These participating users are divided according to the group of people defined in the design phase.

5.3 Results

Table 3 shows the summary of the evaluation measures on the total tasks performed by all users. As can be seen, the users were able to successfully complete all the tasks presented, although some of them required assistance from the moderator.

Table 3. Evaluation measures

Measures	Results
Number of tasks	6 per each user/48 total
Number and percent of tasks completed without help	45 (93.7%)
Number and percent of tasks completed with help	3 (6.3%)
Number and percent of tasks not completed successfully	0 (0%)
Number of times that reload of forms were needed for complete a tasks	6
Time needed to complete a tasks	All tasks were completed in the previsited time. Only one user talked more time for the first task

Each user answered a questionnaire with a liker scale of 1 (totally disagree) to 5 (totally agree) with the following questions:

- Did you find it easy to complete the proposed tasks with the application?
- Did you find it easy to interact with augmented reality?
- Did you find the augmented reality useful in the application?
- Do you consider that the information displayed in the application will help you better understand the cultural heritage that surrounds you?

– Do you consider the application easy to use?
– Would you use the application in your daily life?

Figure 8 shows the results of the post-test questionnaire. For questions 1 through 5, the maximum score is 5, while for question 6, the maximum score is 4.

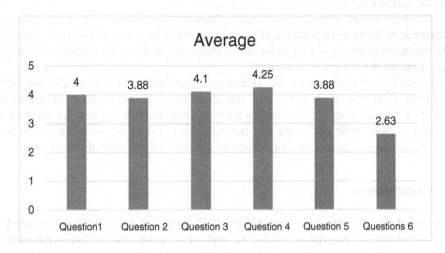

Fig. 8. Results of the post-test questionnaire.

After analyzing the collected information, it was observed that all users could create an account without any problem, because the registration form could be accessed from the initial screen. Moreover, approximately half of the users preferred to log in using Facebook.

It should be noted that although none of the users identified the application menu, they had no problems performing the tasks since the menu options could also be accessed from the initial screen.

It was very necessary to have a map, otherwise users would not have been able to identify the point to which they had to go in order to be able to finish with the proposed tasks.

Approximately half the users did not understand the meaning of the circle surrounding the icon that showed their position on the map. That is why they activated the augmented reality before something could be shown. Some of them mentioned that they had to approach until the point of interest enters the range of vision, others realized it by trial and error.

Augmented reality helped users to identify the accurate location of the point of interest. However, sometimes it did not work properly because the gyroscope from the mobile device was misbalanced, which confused the user and took it in another direction. To solve this, users re-entered to the augmented reality tab and moved the device in the form of 8.

Users did not have any problem identifying that icons displayed in augmented reality could be selected for more information, in other words, they were intuitive to such an interaction.

Most users had no problem accessing historic event information from the displayed list. However, some thought that the list was purely informative and there was no further interaction.

The button that gives access to add a historical event was very easy to locate because it occupies an important width on the screen. While the tab that gives access to add images or audios was easy to locate for users, one of them thought that the images were brought from a point of interest.

Looking at the results of the evaluations, we realize that users did not have problems using the main features of the application. However, they were able to identify a large number of opportunities for improvement in the application interface to be able to make their use easier and more intuitive. Likewise, we realized the perception of users regarding the application in general and the offered features.

6 Conclusions

The use of the integration between XP and UCD proposed by Aguilar and Zapata [2] was useful since it allowed to involve the end users in the construction of the mobile application. This was beneficial as by presenting the application's progress at each iteration users were familiar with most of the interface shown and allowed them to complete the assigned activities. Although there were observations regarding the interface of the mobile application, they did not present a major correction problem. That is why, thanks to its early identification through user testing, it was possible to facilitate activities that, in previous iterations, were difficult for users to complete.

The use of the user evaluation proposed by Rubin and Chisnell [14] not only allowed to validate that an easy-to-use solution has been developed, but also allowed us to know how useful it would be for the different user groups to find a solution. It was also identified a large number of opportunities to improve the functionalities of the application.

The use of two forms of evaluation allowed focusing on specific functionalities, to detect errors, and in the general flow of application use, to obtain opportunities for improvement. Because the tests were performed at the end of each iteration, the feedback received was focused on specific functionalities.

On the other hand, the final evaluation allowed receiving a broader feedback because a final product was already developed. It has to be taken into account that the final evaluation involved users who had never used the application before, so new and more objective observations were obtained.

References

1. Abras, C., et al.: User-centered design. In: Bainbridge, W. (ed.) Encyclopedia of Human-Computer Interaction, vol. 37, no. 4, pp. 445–456. Sage Publications, Thousand Oaks (2004)
2. Aguilar, M., Zapata, C.: Integrating UCD and an Agile methodology in the development of a mobile catalog of plants. In: Soares, M., Falcão, C., Ahram, T. (eds.) Advances in Ergonomics Modeling, Usability & Special Populations. Advances in Intelligent Systems and Computing, pp. 75–87. Springer International Publishing, Cham (2016)
3. Akpata, E., Riha, K.: Can extreme programming be used by a lone programmer? In: Systems Integration (2004)
4. Covarrubias Gaitán, A.F.: Los centros históricos y la ciudad actual: instrumentos de ordenamiento, conservación, revitalización y uso. In: Presented at the VII Encuentro Internacional de Revitalización de Centros Históricos La arquitectura de hoy, entre la ciudad histórica y la actual, México (2009)
5. García, B., Sepúlveda, X.: La historia oral en América Latina. Secuencia 01, 162 (1985)
6. Figueroa, R.G., Solís, C.J., Cabrera, A.A.: Metodologías tradicionales vs. Metodologías ágiles. Universidad Técnica Particular de Loja, Escuela de Ciencias en Computación (2008). Disponible en: http://adonisnet.files.wordpress.com/2008/06/articulo-metodologia-de-sw-formato.doc
7. Fombona Cadavieco, J.: Geolocation for interactive mobile devices, a new relationship between people and things. La interactividad de los dispositivos móviles geolocalizados, una nueva relación entre personas y cosas. Historia y Comunicacion Social 18(October), 777–788 (2013). doi:10.5209/rev-HICS.2013.v18.44007. Spec. Issue
8. Fowler, M., Highsmith, J.: The agile manifesto. Softw. Dev. 9(8), 28–35 (2001)
9. González-Valcárcel, J.M.: Criterios actuales en la defensa de la ciudad histórica. In: Nessun futuro senza passato. 6th ICOMOS General Assembly and International Symposium. Atti., pp. 229–244. ICOMOS, Roma (1981)
10. Huamaní, J.A.: Realidad aumentada: recurso digital entre lo real y lo virtual (augmented reality: a digital resource between the real and the virtual world). HAMUT'AY 2(2), 50–57 (2016)
11. Huerta, A.: Proyecto Sherezade: etnografía, narración de historias y transmedia en la enseñanza y difusión del conocimiento cultural. En Blanco Negro. 6(2), 40–52 (2015)
12. Tamayo, C.V., Leite, E.: Las Tecnologías de la Información y las Comunicaciones como Herramientas para la Gestión del Patrimonio Cultural con una Visión Emprendedora. In: HOLOS, vol. 8, pp. 290–303 (2016)
13. Lezama, A.: El patrimonio cultural frente al desafío de la globalización. Cuad. CLAEH. 27 (88), 9–40 (2004)
14. Rubin, J., Chisnell, D.: Handbook of Usability Testing: How to Plan, Design, and Conduct Effective Tests. Wiley, Hoboken (2008)
15. Ruiz Torres, D.: Realidad aumentada y Patrimonio Cultural: nuevas perspectivas para el conocimiento y la difusión del objeto cultural. e-rph: Revista Electrónica de Patrimonio Histórico (2011). http://www.revistadepatrimonio.es/revistas/numero8/difusion/estudios2/articulo.php
16. Samaniego Larrea, M.J.: Estudio Comparativo de Productividad de Frameworks PHP Orientados a objetos para Desarrollar el Sistema de Seguimiento de Incidentes de la infraestructura de Red en la ESPOCH. Escuela Superior Politécnica de Chimborazo (2015)

632   E. Merino et al.

17. Soto Suárez, M.: La conservación del patrimonio edificado, una responsabilidad social desde la universidad. Arquit. Urban. **35**, 100–111 (2014)
18. Weber, J.: What is usability and usability testing? (2009). http://www.jannaweber.com/wp-content/uploads/2009/09/WT06_Think_Aloud.pdf
19. Zapata, C.: Integration of usability and agile methodologies: a systematic review. In: Marcus, A. (ed.) DUXU 2015. LNCS, vol. 9186, pp. 368–378. Springer, Cham (2015). doi:10.1007/978-3-319-20886-2_35

Research on Interactive Prototype Design and Experience Method Based on Open Source

Yanrui Qu[1(✉)], Yanhong Jia[1], Tong Qu[2], Zhaoyu Chen[1], Heng Li[1], and Wanqiang Li[1]

[1] Beijing University of Technology, Beijing, People's Republic of China
qyr@vip.sina.com
[2] University of Pittsburgh, Pittsburgh, PA, USA

Abstract. This paper argues that, from the perspective of interactive prototyping and experience, the hardware technology based on open source and thinking, can promote further development of interaction design research. The purpose of this paper is to explore the design methodology considering interactive prototype design process and experiencing process, and provide theoretical and technical support for the design of interactive products, with open source resources as the platform and task method. The results show that the open source code can be obtained in a variety of formats, and can be freely and easily modified to solve the design problems encountered by individuals or teams, to support the design goals. Through open source resources everyone can get electronic components and a variety of materials, as well as infrastructure and standardization of the production process. So that a number of design elements and open source code can be iterated quickly, having everyone maximize using open source resources efficiency. The design of interactive prototype is based on Arduino/Max6/MSP experiment method and emotional experience method. After the initial design and prototyping, the design concept can be realized. A design route combining usability and ease of use could be established which can be used in the field of industrial design engineering.

Keywords: Interactive design · Open source · Prototype · Emotional experience · Method

1 Introduction

As early as the spring of 1997, the idea of open source code, as a resource that can be shared with the public was firstly brought up by a group of aspirants in the software industry [1] (Linus's Law, Eric Raymond, 1997). Since then, the concept of open source resource has been infiltrated into various areas including information technology, education and health care and recently has widen its scope to the field of philosophy [2, 3]. In the modern information society, open source resource refers not only to the free access to the source code of the software. More importantly, it is a culture and also a spirit that represents the freedom of sharing and the awareness of making full use of resources. The prominent characteristic of sustainability has made it a strong pushing power to promote social development.

© Springer International Publishing AG 2017
A. Marcus and W. Wang (Eds.): DUXU 2017, Part I, LNCS 10288, pp. 633–651, 2017.
DOI: 10.1007/978-3-319-58634-2_46

Open education is a crucial idea in modern education. Open-minded educators hope to see open source technology and open education combined for a shared vision. Based on the open source code, educators can share the teaching achievements together through the Internet; the students and self-learners will be able to communicate and collaborate more efficiently through an open source educational environment. The process of delivering reviews and feedback between educators and students will become accurate and timely. Therefore, open source resources can be integrated with open education. This is why open source software, hardware and open education are closely related [4].

Beijing University of Technology, School of Architecture and Urban Planning, Department of Industrial Design, together with Delft University of Technology, School of Industrial Design and Engineering, have held four interactive design workshops from 2012 to 2015. Participants from more than 50 universities around the world, took part in the discussion about the teaching model that is based on the integration of open source code and open education. The following content demonstrates several real cases during the practical teaching process, along with the experience and lessons learned. Generally speaking, human beings have two ways to know about the world: One is to understand others' experiences through learning. The other is forming personal experiences through direct contact with actual event in life. There is no doubt that open source resources can accelerate this cognitive process of learning. From the perspective of interaction design and the Maker movement, the support offered by the open source hardware technology is of great significance for open education, especially the development of interaction design.

2   Open Source Hardware Overview

Open Source Hardware (OSHW) Definition: Open Source Hardware (OSHW) is a term for tangible artifacts – machines, devices, or other physical things – whose design has been released to the public in such a way that anyone can make, modify, distribute, and use those things.[1] Open Source Hardware (OSHW) Statement of Principles: Open source hardware is hardware whose design is made publicly available so that anyone can study, modify, distribute, make, and sell the design or hardware based on that. The hardware's source, from which the design is made, is available in the preferred format so modifications can be made. Ideally, open source hardware uses readily-available components and materials, standard processes, open infrastructure, unrestricted content, and open-source design tools to maximize the ability of individuals to make and use hardware.[2] Open source hardware gives people the freedom to control their technology while sharing knowledge and encouraging commerce through the open exchange of designs.

Currently the most successful representative of open source hardware is Arduino. As one of the earliest open source hardware, its influence cannot be ignored. All kinds of Arduino are based on the same hardware and software development platform, technical information, accessories, etc. They are available to entry-level novices. The software development tool is Arduino IDE, which has rich Arduino driver code. For the

---

[1] Open Source Hardware (OSHW) Definition. http://www.oshwa.org/definition.
[2] Open Source Hardware (OSHW) Statement of Principles. http://www.oshwa.org/definition.

maker who are fond of open source hardware, the huge amount of resources about Arduino, a variety of superimposed expansion boards and a series of sensor boards are admired. In addition to Arduino, there are many other kinds of open source hardware that are also familiar to everyone.

51 single-chip microcomputer is one of the basic introductory microcontroller and is also one of the most widely used. However, because of its internal structure and abstract of the programming language, in practice, the learner needs the knowledge of electronics and other components, that can be combined with design and development products. So it is a very big challenge for the beginner who doesn't have the foundation for programming.

Raspberry Pi: Compared with Arduino and single-chip microcomputer, Raspberry Pi provides higher performance of processing capability. It can easily achieve I#O control, high-speed data communication, video processing and real-time calculation etc. Makers can do programming in Debian Linux environment and realize various functions that could only be done in PC environment before. Raspberry Pi is an ideal platform for beginner makers to develop into high-level makers.

Based on the brand new Intel architecture, the Galileo Board is a kind of circuit board that can be developed and fully adapted to be compatible with Arduino (including the interface and the development environment, etc.). Overall, the Intel Galileo provides an excellent tool for the rapid development of simple interactive prototype designs and complex projects such as the household appliances automation, achievement of smart mobile phones controlling life size robots, construction of networking systems and so forth.

Table 1. Four different open source hardware

	Target users	Application domain	Requirements of the ability
Arduino	Adolescents, Designers, Makers	Multi-media art design, Interactive product prototype presentation, education fields of teaching, competitions, etc.	C language programming
51 single-chip microcomputer	People with the programming ability and the electric circuit build ability	Automation control intelligent household, etc.	C language programming and circuit design knowledge
RaspberryPi	Makers, Embedded developers	The Internet of Things, image identification, intelligent robots, etc.	Knowledge of Linux and based programming
Galileo Board	Makers, Embedded developers	The Internet of Things, image identification, intelligent robots, etc.	Familiar ×86 environment, as well as the arduino programming

Table 1 shows the different Development Board characteristics, target users and the requirements of the ability to target users.

3   Interactive Prototype Design Based on Open Source Hardware

3.1   Interactive Prototyping and Topic Classification

According to Klaus Lehmann, we live in a realistic and material world. When human senses are ignored, people lose the significance of existing (Klaus Lehmann, [5]). This is a continuation of the idea of Bauhaus' "Designing for People" (Staatliches Bauhaus, 1919). Interaction design originated in the 1980s (Bill Moggridge, [6]). In contrast with product design in the industrialization era, interaction design is characterized by implementing function through information technology. For a long time, the "black box" of information technology has plagued the product design. After years of efforts, the design semantics and design psychology have contributed to the design of human-machine interaction, which provides a design methodological significance. In today's user experience, two model-matching theories (user mental models and designer conceptual models, Donald Norman), prototyping experiments, etc., provide theoretical framework for in-depth study of interaction design. Interactive prototype design and experience of the teaching process based on the open-source, is the continuation of the theoretical framework and addenda.

Interactive prototype design takes the real material as the carrier, embedded in open source hardware, using computer programming to control or drive so as to achieve human-computer interaction process. The functional tests based on prototype gradually go further along with the human-product experience. Therefore, the interactive prototype subjects require a combination of technology and emotion [7].

In order to make the design process more clear, the prototype design experience training topics are divided into two types: the first type, for basic training purposes. As a basic introductory exercise, according to the people's problems in the use-application-emotion-experience aspects of the design process, as well as the material-process-technology aspects, students abstract the basic questions, design and implement an abstract model as a design goal. This approach is often called Design Training, also known as "useless design". Calling it useless is because the design is not for practical purposes, but as a problem-solving design of an abstract thinking training method. The second type, practical product design, designing for a clear practical goal the requirements of the user needs to be targeted in this product design method.

In this chapter, through the revelation of natural phenomena, design concept generation, prototyping, open source hardware embedded and computer programming control design development process, we present an interactive prototyping and experiential approach based on open source hardware through a bionic design with abstract features (the author is Luo Zhang, a 2013 graduate student in industrial design engineering at Beijing University of Technology).

3.2 Abstract Structure Design from Bionic Inspiration

Topic: Learning from nature. Choose a natural form, describe its external environment and internal structure characteristics, design and produce an abstract interactive form. Requirements:
a. The natural form selection and analysis process is clear. b. Design objectives and process and summary of the expression are concise and easy to understand. c. Embedded prototype design, through dynamic demonstration shows that the morphological advantages, such as structure, strength, speed and so on. d. Through the prototype demonstration, the expression of the design concept can be recognized, understood and its feasibility is persuasive, also it has a good emotional experience.

Analysis of Mimosa Functional Principle. Mimosa motility is usually due to change in intracellular turgor pressure. Most mature plant cells have a large vacuole. When the vacuole is filled with water, the pressure constricts the surrounding cytoplasm and drives it close to the cell wall. The pressure given to the cell wall is known as the turgor movement. Vacuole contains both organic and inorganic substances. Their concentration levels determine the level of osmotic pressure and sequentially determine the direction of water diffusion. When the vacuole concentration increased, the osmotic pressure increased, the water goes from the extracellular into the intracellular proliferation and into the vacuole, increasing cell turgor, leading to the cells bulge; on the other side is atrophy [8].

This process can only cause slow movements, such as the opening and closing of the pores. However, when the semi-permeability of the cell membrane changes instantaneously, it may cause a very rapid action. Chloride ions move into the cell, while the positive ions move out of the cell. Causing the cell membrane and adjacent areas are able to maintain a certain potential difference, which is called rest potential. When the external stimulus exceeds a certain limit, the cell membrane potential increases, or even become positive potential, thus generating the action potential. This phenomenon is called depolarization. Action potential can be transmitted. When the cell reaches the action potential, that is, when the phenomenon of depolarization occurs, the difference between the permeability of the cell membrane disappears, so the original water stored in the vacuole was discharged in an instant, so that cells lose the turmoil, becoming limp [9]. When we touch the leaves of mimosa, the leaf pillow cells are stimulated, resulting in the depolarization. The cells immediately lose water and turmoil. Leaf pillow becomes limp. Small pinna loses the pillow support, so it becomes closed in turn. In the lower part of the leaf pillow, there are some sensing cells which have very low rest potential. They are particularly vulnerable to stimulation [10]. As long as a slight touch, they will immediately release the water, so that the petiole would droop, looks like that the mimosa is bashful. The following is a rough sketch of appearance description and motor function of mimosa (Fig. 1).

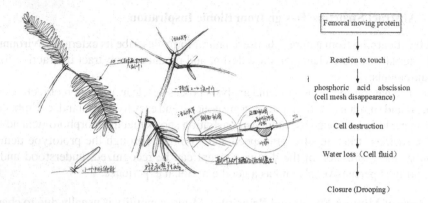

Femoral moving protein

↓

Reaction to touch

↓

phosphoric acid abscission
(cell mesh disappearance)

↓

Cell destruction

↓

Water loss（Cell fluid）

↓

Closure (Drooping）

Fig. 1. Schematic diagram of appearance description and motor function of mimosa

Biomimetic Design and Interactive Technology of Mimosa. After defining the topic and direction, the initial conceptual design began, and feasibility simulations were carried out on the sketch and the preliminary model. After continuous exploration and experiment, three sets of concepts were drawn. Comparative analysis was made to choose the best concept for prototyping. To explain the reasons for the options clearly, in the following, the advantages and disadvantages of the three sets of design ideas will be explained in detail.

Scheme 1: From the way mimosa open and close the leaves, build structures aiming at finding the prototype program most similar to the appearance of mimosa. The specific method is as follows: In order to conceal the mechanical structure, use the smallest original: rods, lines. The root of the blade is designed with a circular hole, which is engraved by the acrylic plastic, and connected with the petiole (connecting rod), so that it has the ability to move up and down. Connecting rods are placed on the trunk (rack) in order to make its appearance more similar to an actual plant. There are two holes in the lower part of each of the first pair of compound leaves and a wire in between to connect both leaves. The length of the line is determined by the maximum angle at which the blade is opened. Another wire connects the midpoint of the previous wire to the steering engine. The first pair of compound leaves and the remaining compound leaves are connected with viscose at the lower part of the blade. So which can be integrated with the linkage to realize the open and close of the blade. The principle is to use the gravity of the blade itself to achieve natural droop (the open form). After the steering gear is actuated, a downward force is generated, and the servomotor rotation causes the connecting wire to be constantly wound, resulting in a downward force to close the blade.

Advantages: Meet the function under the premise of making the appearance maximumly similar to the appearance of mimosa, so that is an appearance bionic design. Disadvantages: As the wire (soft, the direction of the poor precision control) and the strength of the connecting rod's poor stability, in the course of the experiment the leaves usually cannot always achieve the normal opening and closing (Fig. 2).

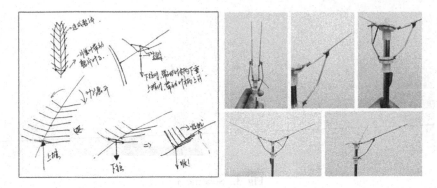

Fig. 2. Scheme 1(Left) and Scheme 2(Right)

Scheme 2: This is a more eclectic solution which needs a compromise between the stability and appearance similarity, mainly using the connecting rod body. The specific method is as follows: the principle and concept is similar but a little different with Option1, the differences are: 1, turn the fragile wires and connecting rod into the metal linkage that could provide a better strength and stability; 2, no longer use the blade's own gravity, rely on more stable steering gear to control the blade opening and closing. The slider and the petiole are connected to the use of sliders to control the opening and closing rather than simply stick and the stent and the petiole. The frame becomes an integral part of the linkage assembly. In practice, in order to maximize the use of existing conditions, we transform the structure of the umbrella into a model, to complete the test.

Advantages: the compromise in this way can maintain the function and appearance to be certain balanced. Disadvantages: In the model test, it is found that some structures cannot be obtained through the procurement, and there is no way to process through the existing conditions, and model's accuracy cannot meet the requirements (in the test the stability is still poor). And finally we had to seek new solutions.

Scheme 3: Draw on the experience and lessons learned from the first two options, the main consideration of this scheme is the feasibility of interactive behavior. Interactive features will be achieved as the primary starting point. So the structure, strength and accuracy of the racks, has been put forward to higher requirements. Therefore, it has to make some compromises on the appearance of the "bionic". The specific methods are as follow: using the standard components which can be purchased through the shelf, including gears, steering gear fixed base, screw nut, the standard mechanical handle, touch sensors etc. According to the design requirements, the combination of components has changed, based on these standard components. So, here Mimosa's "opening and closing function" is achieved through the transformation of the mechanical handle. Remove the excess part of the handle, then extend the rod as a petiole, and then the blade will be fixed on the leaf to complete the blade part. Servo drives mechanical gripper gear rotation, directly controls the blade opening and closing (Fig. 3).

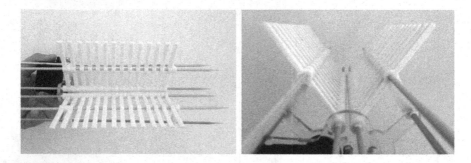

Fig. 3. Scheme 3

Advantages: As a prototype, the main purpose is to complete the design of the function. Through the touch can control the "blade" opening and closing. Standardized components maximize the accuracy and stability to meet the function. Disadvantages: As the function meets the requirement, at the same time, the appearance seems to have a lack of bionics. In summary, Scheme 3 was chosen for its functional advantage. The following sections will detail the principles of this program, production and presentation.

Mimosa Bionic Interactive Design, Model Production and Demonstration. Before production, the team purchase components at first. Including control system: Arduino kit. Powertrain: Tower Pro SG5010 dual-bearing standard steering gear. Drive system: Mechanical gripper assembly (after adaptability). Operating system: home-made leaves, touch sensors. The following sections describe the design and manufacturing process in detail.

Arduino is a convenient and flexible, easy-to-use open-source electronic prototype platform, including hardware (various types of Arduino boards) and software (Arduino IDE). Arduino can sense the environment through variety kinds of sensors, by controlling the lights, motors and other devices to feedback, affecting the environment. The microcontrollers on the board can be programmed in Arduino's programming language, compiled into binary files, and incorporated into the microcontroller. This program using its open source features can be easily and quickly connected to various sensors and achieve the expected behavior.

Servo is a common power system, the choice of Tower Pro SG5010 dual standard servo, can achieve 0°–180° free angle control, to meet the design requirements. The 3.5 V–6 V voltage through the USB interface could provide power supply without the need for an external power. The accurate control of the angle is one of the keys of this interactive design.

Transmission system–mechanical gripper is mainly composed of a pair of arm gears and connecting rods, to meet the grasping object function. The angle control of this interaction requires a great deal of similarity to that of the gear-driven linkage of the mechanical gripper. Modifying the mechanical gripper to realize the new interactive mode is feasible. In addition, the use of existing standard components for transformation is conducive to reduce the difficulty of production and improve accuracy (Fig. 4).

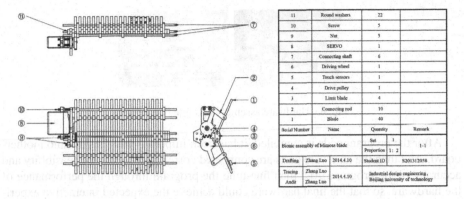

11	Round washers	22	
10	Screw	5	
9	Nut	5	
8	SERVO	1	
7	Connecting shaft	6	
6	Driving wheel	1	
5	Touch sensors	1	
4	Drive pulley	1	
3	Limit blade	4	
2	Connecting rod	10	
1	Blade	40	
Serial Number	Name	Quantity	Remark
Bionic assembly of Mimosa blade		Set 1 / Proportion 1:2	1-1
Drafting Zhang Luo 2014.4.10		Student ID 8201312058	
Tracing Zhang Luo 2014.4.10		Industrial design engineering, Beijing university of technology	
Audit Zhang Luo			

Fig. 4. Schematic diagram of the engineering assembly

The execution system is part of the machine (in this case, the mechanical system of the interaction device) and is the direct medium of human-machine interaction. People interact with each other by performing system input and output behaviors (instructions). Here the implementation of the system refers to the "Mimosa leaves", that is integrated touch sensor. After the functional transformation of the mechanical handle, which is directly to people to receive and receive feedback part. 4 mm thick ABS board in accordance with the design dimensions after cutting, assembled into the blade part. Finally, the touch sensor is placed in the blade part as the input device of the interactive signal, and the servomotor drives the blade driven by the gear to complete the feedback action (output). The components through repeated modifications to debug, the final complete assembly, in order to achieve the best results. Then start the program by programming the computer into the Arduino control board to complete the final debugging (Fig. 5).

Fig. 5. Three-dimensional assembly renderings

Programming. Before writing the Arduino program, you must first clarify the program logic that you want to achieve. After you have defined the program logic, start programming with the Arduino programming software and find the ArduBlock visualization programming plug-in under the Tool menu. According to logic programming, and then import Arduino programming software to generate the program code (Fig. 6).

Fig. 6. Hardware assembly and line connections

After the program code is compiled, it has been imported into the Arduino mother-board. And then the hardware parts are connected correctly to verify the feasibility and accuracy of the program. And then fine-tune the program through the performance of the hardware, so that the final hardware could achieve the expected interactive experience.

After the program code is compiled and debugged, the final assembly, connection, and debugging are performed. After the line was connected, the group installed the blade part onto the gear empty, then connected to the steering gear. After the steering gear was fixed, they use mobile power as a power supply. Once the final assembly is complete, the model can be demonstrated. The final result is shown below (Fig. 7).

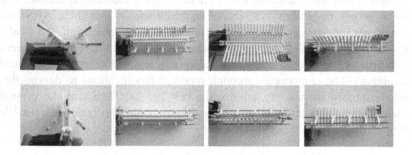

Fig. 7. Model demonstrations (above: open state, below: closed state)

3.3 Prototype Design and Production Process Conclusion

The above examples show that sketching and paper prototyping are the most widely used prototyping methods in interaction design. The interactive design archetypes discussed in this chapter belong to tangible interaction, also called embodied interaction, and are distinguished from ordinary interactive prototypes in attributes. The prototypes in the physical interaction design have the following properties: 1, The prototype is a real three-dimensional physical space in the material form, through the prototype, human-computer interaction can be achieved; 2, For designers, the prototype is a preliminary verification, which can let them intuitively feel the design conception in the realization of some minor changes in the process, leading to facilitate discussion and improvement of design, in order to further enhance and improve the design work to do the foundation. 3, when the human-computer interaction occurs, the users can feel the power, speed, fast and slow, elegant or vulgar, melody and rhythm and other interactive experience. From the prototype of embodied interaction design, these characteristics are obviously different from other design prototypes. Because the prototype of the embodied interaction is based on valid feedback of the action of the testers, in terms of its design purpose and implementation level, that is, it can be practiced as expected in the conceptual design phase.

Through the tangible prototype design and production process, the properties of tangible interaction prototype design, which can be divided into five important key nodes, behavior research, emotional appeal and essential technology, to expand to achieve the goal. This reflects in the following five parts. Emotional collage board. Storyboard. Role creation and play. Hardware/software applications. Interactive prototype experiment.

These properties of interaction prototype could be realized by keynote activities such as behavior research, emotional appeal and technology realization. Specifically, they could be elaborated in five aspects: Emotional Board; Storyboard; Role creation and play; Hardware/software applications; Interactive prototype experiment.

The primary function of the prototype is to validate the conceptual design. Interactive prototype design achieves interactive features through the sensor circuit and the corresponding mechanical structure, designed to illustrate the interaction design principles. Interactive prototyping is an important method of interactive design, and it is also an indispensable part in the interaction design process. Through the production of interactive prototype, we can test whether the software circuit is reasonable, whether the connection is consistent or whether the design can achieve the initial goal.

4   Emotional Experiences in Interactive Prototype

4.1   Emotional Design in Prototype

Donald A Norman put forward three levels of emotional design through the study of emotion in Psychology: instinctive level, behavioral level, and reflective level. The instinctive level refers to the first impression of the user to use the interactive products. The implementation of behavior level design corresponding functional level of demands that is one of the basic attributes of the product. At present, the function of interactive products is more and more powerful, but the demand of target people has changed, users began to look forward to move by personalized and ideal product, beginning the pursuit of product to meet the emotional level. The emergence of emotional design is based on the designer to meet the product functional requirements and provide users with emotional and psychological support for higher levels of spiritual needs.

4.2   Music Player Design

2014 interactive design workshop theme is a design for the purpose of utility. In this interaction workshop, each team was asked to complete a specific context based interactive music player design. In this process, the student learned Arduino programming techniques, interactive design methods, and how to use video as a tool for design and communication. In this workshop, our student will learn: Video sketch, embodied interactive product model, theme concept product design, design expression, model making skills, Arduino software programming [11].

Aadjan van der Helm Marco, Professor Rozendaal and Dr Liu Wei, From the Technische Universities Delft in Holland, proposed a number of abstract concepts, such as anger, sadness, doubt, fear, kindness etc., require a special emotional reflect in the design of music player, analyzing the variation characteristics of the emotion and the interaction based on the final results show. Combine the emotional changes with the products form and structure. In the creative process, the group combined integrated technology, aesthetics, interactive design principles and prototype and video as design and communication tools.

4.3   Topic1-Interactive Music Player Design on the Keywords "Kindness"

Video Sketches: In determining the subject, each group took some action video to the three music control functions: "start/stop" and "big/small volume" and "a song/next song". Used some things around as auxiliary props, users hold the props and did some actions interact with the props. Different actions represented different emotion and functions. With the "start/pause" function as an example; the group of students used four materials to demonstrate the control of this function (Fig. 8).

Fig. 8. Video sketches

Improved Video: After the analysis of several groups of actions, combined with emotional keywords and whether the technology is easy to achieve, student decided to take folded papers to express emotions and the interactive actions. Slowly folding unfolded objects, reflecting the harmony between man and things and harmonious process inflect the keyword "kindness". Relax stretch the objects, music start; tighten compressed objects, music pause; turn right start to switch to the next, turn left is opposite; radial spread the objects, the volume becomes larger and the radioactive contraction makes the volume smaller. The three groups of control actions are in Fig. 9.

Brainstorming: In order to combine action, function and shape more perfectly, the group members began the brainstorming. Before brainstorming, the group members got the theme of brainstorming: to combine the folding action with the music player's functional control, as well as the shape fits the use of the scene.

Given the Four Key words of this brainstorming: "music player" "interactive action" "compression and folding" "kindness", members of the group started divergent thinking.

Fig. 9. Video sketch deepening

After obtaining a sufficient amount of ideas, the ideas were evaluated in a multi-dimensional manner. Through the classification of the results and cost, the group found the best idea.

Storyboard: Storyboard shows the scene of using the product, illustrating how the user to solve the problem. Through the assumption of user roles and usage scenarios, the designers try to simulate the actual user interaction and interaction mode for product usability evaluation. Good user scenarios can be beneficial for the product design process (Fig. 10).

Fig. 10. Storyboard   **Fig. 11.** Draft prototype

Draft Prototype: The best way to verify the idea of staying on paper is to make full use of the material around and quickly make a prototype to verify ideas to find problems. The group members use the origami to build prototype, in order to show the way of interaction between people and music player control quickly (Fig. 11).

Interactive Technology: Through the use of open source hardware technology, the group members started to build product circuit prototype quickly to verify whether the interactive approach to achieve the effect planned. In the hardware platform, they selected Arduino as the open source hardware platform. On the basis of this, select the Seeed Studio music control module and sensor board to realize the interactive functions need to achieve. The sensor been chosen was the rotation angle sensor which can be used to measure the rotation angle of the control the music player's volume and switch. Tilt sensor has also been chosen to measure whether the music player is tilted to the left or right to achieve the previous/next function.

Final Design & Prototype: After the iteration of the model and the verification of the technology, the final prototype combines the appearance structure with the technology. Able to demonstrate independently and achieve desired interaction (Fig. 12).

Fig. 12. Draft prototype final design prototype (designed by: Yanhong Jia, Jingpeng Jia, Lu Bian, Peng Chen, Xingjian An etc.)

4.4   Topic2- "Inspiration" Interactive Music Player Design

Behavior Research: Another group from this workshop designed an embodied interactive music player. The emotional vocabulary they chose as the theme is "inspiration". Through the previous observation research and discussion, they came up with a conclusion that the core of interaction design is to aim at user behavior. Thus the primary task is to find out the specific behaviors that can be helpful and applicable for users in terms of expressing emotion. And digging out the logic and the semantic meaning behind the behaviors is the next move. According to the dictionary, the group of students summarized several meanings for "inspiration": A. Inhalation. B. Encouragement. C. Inspiring things and objects. D. Wonderful ideas. E. Enlightenment from god. According to the understanding of each group member and the result of the discussion on semantics relevance, the final key words are "sudden", "wonderful", "magical", "exciting", "surprising", "positive".

Action is the basic unit during the process of user expressing the intention to interact. It consists of action sequences, and makes up the basic vocabulary of interactive context. Building up a human-computer interactive movement set that applies to embodied context is the foundation of implementing embodied interaction design. At the current stage, group members picked up raw material, including wood boards, hemp rope, nails, bamboo boards and paper clips, aiming to find inspiration through the interaction of material and behavioral action. For instance, blowing the balloon to almost explosion reflects anxiety; placing one finger gradually near the tip of a needle reflects fear. Before the specific design process started, the team members studied the relationship between behaviors and emotion expression through video sketches and explore the emotional semantics behind the behaviors by observing the action itself or changes in the material to get prepared for the next step in the design process (Fig. 13).

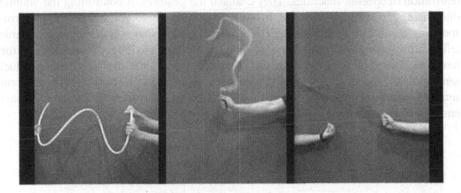

Fig. 13. Video presentation during video sketch

Emotional Demands: The combination of behavior and emotion is the key to this design. At this stage, the group concluded that "unexpected but reasonable" may be able to produce the feeling of "inspired". Corresponding to the three basic functions of music player: pause and start, turn up and down the volume and switch songs, the team selected uncommon actions to design the interaction pattern. Stretching and compressing represents increasing or decreasing the volume; waving ribbon can skip to the next song depending on the direction of waving; bending and straightening the bamboo board are respectively corresponding to pausing and starting. The correspondences between these actions and functions are mainly matched with the semantic features of behavioral

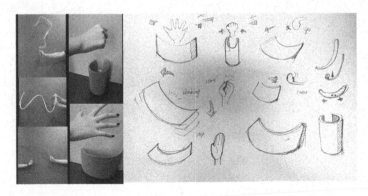

Fig. 14. The prototype structure combines with the video

language and function. One thing worth mentioning is that there might be differences in understanding of the same behavior for people from different cultural backgrounds.

The video sketch demo displayed a magical hand and a cork wood mat that has simple shape and texture. After the gesture is made, the cork wood mat will transform and give motion feedback in a subtle way, and play feedback sound effects accordingly based on that theme (Fig. 14).

In the following design stages, group members optimized the project further on the realization of specific functions. They changed the gestures of controlling the volume into raising and lowering one hand. In the meantime, the prototype will perform a corresponding feedback in terms of the extent of swinging. What's more, waving towards left and towards right respectively correspond to switching to the previous song and the next song. Based on demonstration, this interactive behavior is also clear in the product semantics. On top of that, adding the feedback sound effect in parallel with different semantic behaviors increases emotional empathy. It is a way to try to create a pleasant emotional experience for users while using the product (Figs. 15 and 16).

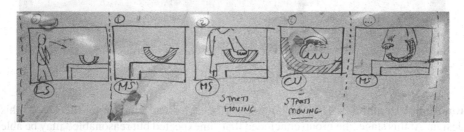

Fig. 15. Story version-1

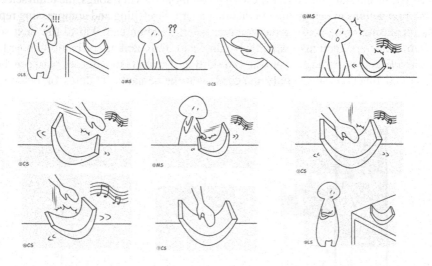

Fig. 16. Story version-2

Implementing Technology: In the process of prototype design, from a concept to the realization, technical considerations are essential to the transformation. After the design of interactive behavior and operation mechanism, students began to carry out a detailed physical structure and design based on an operational logic level, the following are some details:

A. *Physical structure and hardware & software technology:* Workshops provide model production sites, according to the actual needs, the groups can select 3D printing, ABS sheet metal engraving cutting, hot pressing and other technologies. In the prototype production, the group applied hot-pressing technology in the creation of the external contour. After bonding with the screws and nut coupling, the group went on painting and performing other surface treatment. As for the internal structure of the part, students designed their own internal linkage and gear, and used CAD to produce engineering drawings and carving. The final step was to connect and assemble.

This group selected Arduino as the hardware support for their prototype. It was easier to use and control the required sensor with the support of the Grove tools set.

B. *Iteration and optimization of prototypes:* During the prototyping process, as time goes by and the design improves gradually, the original prototype became mature and complete progressively. Nevertheless, with the addition of structures and programming, there are always problems that cannot be anticipated in advance, and some new architectural ideas may arise in the process of soluting problems, which, after continual alternation of problem arising and problem solving, prototypes are iterated and optimized. After assembling the materials and the components, the group found that the original counterweight and the slide itself were not enough to bring wobble to an ideal angle. However, the body space was limited, and new related structures need to be carried out again. After optimization and re-design, the group came up with a better solution ultimately. The hardware assembly prototype has shown in Fig. 17 below.

Fig. 17. Arduino/Grove hardware assembly prototype (Designer: Tianwei Shu, Jiyuan Liu, Tong Qu with, Fengyu Zhao)

5   Conclusions

Material object interaction design is gradually changing the traditional mode of human-computer interaction. And it has a positive impact on the relationship between people and products. Although there are still some unsolved problems, but those do not prevent it from becoming an important direction of future interaction. In contrast with the traditional product design, interactive design is more concerned with the consideration of human behavior, the transmission of human emotions, and the technology implementation aiming at user-friendly experience. With the addition of the time dimension, users will have richer human-computer interaction experience. From this point of view, embodied interaction can reflect the closer essence of interaction design. With the development of embodied interaction design, the prototype design process will become more scientific and improved, and will receive more attention from many other fields.

In the context of virtual interaction and interface interaction becoming more and more mature, the methods of interaction design have shown increasing variety. Different design methods can be selected according to different problems. Industrial design and product interaction will be greatly improved as well. It is not a simple issue about interface interaction anymore. People now can interact with the product through behavior and information exchange, with a real three-dimensional embodied interactive experience. But it also requires further research through the integration of user research, computer technology, sensor technology, anthropology, psychology and other disciplines of knowledge, in order to achieve development in interactive products that meet user needs and that are able, easy and also fun to use.

Teamwork in open education is a huge guarantee of success. Whether it is a small project or a large one, these words are equally applicable. Designers should acquire certain extent of divergent thinking and logical thinking, and understand the importance to have different focus in different stages of a project. They need to know the way to benefit from their own strength, so that they can maximize the final design achievement, which reflects the advantages of cross-disciplinary in open education. However, the condition that a team is superior to the individual depends on differences among team members. The greater the differences of knowledge hierarchy and personality characteristics are, the greater the value produced by mutual collaboration will be.

References

1. Raymond, E.S.: The Cathedral and the Bazaar. O'Reilly Media, California (1999)
2. Torvalds, L.: Just for Fun. HarperCollins, New York (2001)
3. Schon, D.A.: Educating the Reflective Practitioner. Wiley, New Jersey (1990)
4. Saffer, D.: Designing for Interaction. New Riders, California (2006)
5. Lehmann, K.: Design Training. Merz Akademie, Stuttgart (1992)
6. Moggridge, B.: Designing Interactions. MIT Press, Massachusetts (2006)
7. Qu, Y., Mousavi, J.: Research on system design based on product functions and structure Elements. Packag. Eng. **24**, 78–81 (2012)
8. Robin, G.: Mimosa pudica: a model for the study of the excitability in plants. Biol. Rev. **54**(2), 135–153 (1979)
9. Lu, S.: The pathways and means of plant electrical signal transmission. Chin. Bull. Bot. **13**(4), 23–27 (1996)
10. Li, C.: Why mimosa has a shy look. Guangxi Forestry **1**, 43 (2002)
11. Liu, W.: Interaction Design. China Architecture & Building Press, Beijing (2013)
12. Sun, J., Dai, Z.: Bionics today and tomorrow. Acta Biophys. Sin. **2**, 109–115 (2007)
13. Liu, Y.: Talk about product innovation from the bionic design. Guangxi J. Light Ind. **1**, 59–60 (2010)
14. Warren, J.D., Adams, J., Molle, H.: Arduino Robotics. Publishing House of Electronics Industry, Beijing (2014)

15. Blum, J.: Exploring Arduino: Tools and Techniques for Engineering Wizardry. Wiley, New Jersey (2013)
16. Liu, W., Stappers, P.J., Pasman, G., Taal-fokker, J.: Supporting generation Y interactions: challenges for office work. In: Proceedings of the ACM Conference on Computer Supported Cooperative Work (CSCW), vol. 12, no. 4, pp. 321–328. ACM Press, New York (2011)
17. Wu, J.: On Top of Tides. Publishing House of Electronics Industry, Beijing (2011)
18. Xin, X.: Interaction design: from logic of things to logic of behaviors. Art Des. 1, 58–62 (2015)
19. Arduino - Home. http://www.arduino.cc/. Accessed 12 Feb 2016
20. Open Source Hardware (OSHW). http://www.oshwa.org/definition. Accessed 12 Feb 2016

Programming a Robotic Toy with a Block Coding Application: A Usability Study with Non-programmer Adults

Muhammet Ramoğlu[1,2(✉)], Çağlar Genç[3], and Kerem Rızvanoğlu[4]

[1] Graduate School of Science, Engineering and Technology,
Industrial Product Design Department, Istanbul Technical University, Istanbul, Turkey
[2] Arçelik A.Ş., Industrial Design Directorate, Istanbul, Turkey
ramoglu@itu.edu.tr
[3] Koç University – Arçelik Research Center for Creative Industries (KUAR), Istanbul, Turkey
cgenc14@ku.edu.tr
[4] Faculty of Communication, Galatasaray University, Istanbul, Turkey
krizvanoglu@gsu.edu.tr

Abstract. Recently, sophisticated robotic toys have commercially emerged into our lives. Apart from being only a toy, some of these smart devices are programmable for accomplishing commands given by the end-user. However, usually, end-users are not experts in robotics or programming. In order to explore the usability issues related to the non-programmers' experience of controlling the robotic toys, we conducted a user study with non-programmers (N = 9) by using *Sphero* (a robotic toy) and tested its mobile application, called *SPRK Lightning Lab for Sphero*, which adopted visual programming language with a block-based coding interface. Our procedure consisted of a pre-test and a semi-structured post-test interview as well as an exploring session for the participants and three tasks with a short semi-structured interview at the end of each task. Our findings, which highlighted the usability issues of *SPRK Lightning Lab for* Sphero application, contribute to the field by providing design suggestions on using a digital medium and a tangible device together, the usability issues of block coding by non-programmers and learnability in a robotic toy application.

Keywords: Robotic toys · Visual programming · Block coding · Usability test · Mobile application

1   Introduction

Recently, different types of robots have emerged into our lives such as drones and service robots. Among them, also robotic toys that are capable of jumping, rolling, changing colors and moving autonomously have recently become popular for both children and adults. They differ from traditional similar toys such as remote control cars by being programmable for

This study was realized through the coordination of Assoc. Prof. Kerem Rızvanoğlu with the support of Galatasaray University Scientific Research Fund (Project ID: 16.300.006).

© Springer International Publishing AG 2017
A. Marcus and W. Wang (Eds.): DUXU 2017, Part I, LNCS 10288, pp. 652–666, 2017.
DOI: 10.1007/978-3-319-58634-2_47

autonomous actions and by integrating with a mobile device to play mixed reality games. For example, Lego Mindstorms[1], Ozobot[2], and Dash & Dot[3] have been commercialized as educational robot kits to teach coding to children by providing digital interfaces for programming these toys. On the other hand, robotic toys such as Sphero and Ollie[4] have been also used by non-programmer adults for entertainment and Lego Mindstorms used in universities to teach programming [1]. Non-programmer adults are also using similar robotic toys for entertainment. Thus, the usability issues related to their experience of controlling robotic toys are critical for designing these interfaces.

Fig. 1. Sphero, a robotic toy

User experiences of several visual programming languages have been examined in previous studies to program robots. Among them, *block coding* metaphor has frequently used where graphical code blocks are used instead of text-based programming syntax for creating commands. Researchers found that users found code blocking easier to learn than text-based programming [2–5]. Besides, researchers evaluated the user experience of a block coding applications with children [2, 6, 7] and highlighted the effect of using block coding to program robotic toys, on developing children's certain skills [7–9]. However, to our knowledge, there is no study on the usability of mobile block coding application to program a robotic toy with adults. This kind of understanding is important due to the existence of commercialized robots in our daily lives. We believe that the use of block coding

---

[1] https://www.lego.com/en-us/mindstorms.
[2] http://ozobot.com/.
[3] https://www.makewonder.com/.
[4] http://www.sphero.com/.

and similar visual programming concepts will increase in the future for programming robotic toys as well as other interactive devices such as home appliances. Therefore, knowing usability issues in such novel systems will be crucial to enhance the user experience of these devices and applications in the future.

The aim of this study is to examine (1) usability issues when digital (mobile application) and physical (robotic toy) media are used together, (2) user experience of non-programmers while programming a robotic toy with block coding and (3) learnability in a mobile robot programming application. For this purpose, we conducted usability tests of the application called *SPRK Lightning Lab for Sphero* which uses block-based coding interface and controls the robotic toy called *Sphero* (see Fig. 1).

2 Background

2.1 Block Coding

Visual programming languages have wide application areas such as 3D modeling with Grasshopper 3D[5], video game making with Blender Game Engine[6], and music generation with AudioMulch[7]. Besides these, visual programming has been popularly used for teaching coding to non-programmers, especially to children. The basic principle of block coding is drag and drop existing code blocks and snap blocks together to generate a program or series of commands. Code blocks are easy to relate with other blocks with colors and shapes. LogoBlocks [10] was one of the earliest examples of using blocks in visual programming and introduced programming to many students [11]. Begel [10] claimed the advantages of visual programming such as using real life metaphors for understanding the functionality better, its easy browsability (easily noticing the structure of a program comparing to textual program) and its potential of representing the relation among code blocks. After LogoBlocks, block coding metaphor has been applied in various software and visual programming languages such as Scratch [12], BrickLayer [13], Blockly[8] and Snap! [4]. Today, MIT's Scratch and similar block coding languages are being used by millions of people, and not only elementary schools but also high ranking universities have been using block coding to introduce programming [11]. Moreover, with the increase in ubiquitous computing and smartphones, block coding has also become available in mobile devices and tablets. For example, Scriptkit, Lightbot and Kodable are mobile applications that focus on teaching programming to children with block coding [14].

2.2 Robotic Toys

Block programming is mostly used for teaching programming or making a particular system programmable to non-programmers. A robotic toy is an example of both a

---

[5] http://www.grasshopper3d.com/.
[6] https://www.blender.org/.
[7] http://www.audiomulch.com/.
[8] https://developers.google.com/blockly/.

programmable system and an educational tool that uses block coding and aims at non-programmers. Elkin et al. [7] stated that robotic toys provide a playful way to learn to program and it improves certain skills of children such as problem solving, planning [8], and even social skills [9]. Lego Mindstorms NXT was one of the first commercial programmable robotic toys with block coding and released in 2006 [15]. Klassner and Anderson also claimed that Lego Mindstorms is an affordable alternative for teaching programming and practice robots in college level [1]. Robotic toys become popular in the last decade and various robotic kits have been released such as Kibo, Dot & Dash, Ozobot, Cubelet and mBot. These robotic toys come with mobile applications to control and program robots for autonomous actions. In addition, mobile applications such as Tickle[9] and Tynker[10] are designed to program different robotic toys in one block coding application.

Robots such as Ollie and Sphero by Sphero Inc. (previously Orbotix) are both aimed for adults and children with entertainment and programming education. Ng, Chow and de Lima Salgado [16] indicated that robotic toys such as Sphero bring novel content in mobile applications with different controlling methods and sensors. Sphero has various applications to change its colors with music, play with your pet, and even play mixed reality games. In mixed reality games, users see their robot through a virtual environment from the screen of their smartphones or tablets with the help of a camera. For example, *Sharky the Beaver* application shows Sphero as a beaver on the screen of a tablet and provides to control the beaver in your physical space. Robotic toys have been targeting adults as well as children and these robots brought new content to mobile applications with usability issues.

2.3 Usability of Block Coding

Block coding applications and robotic toys have been evaluated by users in previous studies. Dill et al. [5] found that students improve their coding skills by programming movements of a robot in a prototype game with block coding. Elkin et al. showed that children between 3 to 5 years old were able to create simple programs with block coding [7]. However, children had problems with the task that include *repeat loop*. Loop function in programming is used to repeat the code until a condition happens. For example, to change the robot's color when it is grabbed, you need to loop the code otherwise, the system will read the code, check if it is grabbed and if it is false, it will exit the code without changing anything. To use loop code, users need to know that the computer runs the code lines rather fast, runs a code line once and stops running at the end of the code if not repeated in a loop. Ramirez-Benavides, Lopez, and Guerrero [2] evaluated the usability of TITIBOTS, a mobile application for robot programming, in terms of learnability, efficiency, memorability, errors and satisfaction. The usability test was conducted with children aged 4 to 6 years old who are unable to read. They indicated that all children like the system but when they ask to draw children what they liked, 62% drew a robot, 31% drew a tablet and rest drew both of them together. Therefore, it is

---

[9] https://tickleapp.com/.
[10] https://www.tynker.com/.

important to separate a robotic toy by mobile application in an evaluation of a usability test as users might comment on the attractive robot instead of the application. Researchers also pointed out that it was hard to evaluate the effect of teaching programming concept by using block coding on learning programming logic in the long term. Pane [6] asked children to write a statement after showing a logic to move the Pacman and analyzed their approach. For example, 67% of children used images in their statement that show they felt comfortable to express a statement with visuals. In addition, 58% of participants used *when, if* and *after* and more than 60% used *and* and *or* in their statements similarly to programming syntax. This study showed that non-programmers' approaches were partially similar to programming logic but, non-programmers did not always express a statement by the existing programming logic. Thus, block coding might be conceptualized without only mimicking the existing programming syntax.

Ketola and Roto [17] noted that learnability is an important element in user experience and exists in different usability measures [18–20]. Hung [21] analyzed the learnability of several block coding platforms such as Scratch, App Inventor, Stencyl and GameBox. Hung found that video tutorials were common in these block coding systems. GameBlox included a help page on the side of the screen and Scratch provided a help button that pops up a help page on the side of the screen. Scratch also included a step-by-step tutorial that teaches user by practice. However, learnability of these block coding platforms was not evaluated in this study with a user test.

Researchers showed that block coding is easy to use, and it is a useful tool for teaching programming with the help of robotic toys. However, previous studies did not examine user experience of a block coding application to control a mobile robot with adults. Block coding applications and mobile applications of robotic toys have been increasing. We believe, block coding will be widely used to program numerous systems by non-programmers in the future. Thus, we conducted a study with 9 adult users to examine usability issues in SPRK Lightning Lab for Sphero application that programs the robotic toy Sphero.

3   SPRK Lightning Lab for Sphero

The Sphero has multiple controllable sensors, motors, and LEDs which pave the way for the end-user to program its functions. SPRK is one the applications for controlling this robotic toy. Different from other applications with the same aim, SPRK has a visual programming interface, which has pre-defined code blocks. These code blocks are presented in an interface (see Fig. 2) where a user can drag and drop them in order to create a series of commands, which can be saved or sent to the Sphero to be executed. Users can experiment by adding, removing code blocks or mixing the order of code blocks. The code blocks vary from Sphero-specific pre-defined blocks like actions (i.e., rolling, setting the heading, spinning and setting color), sensors (i.e., heading, speed, accelerometer) or events (i.e., on collision, on free fall) to more textual programming tools as in format of code blocks like delay, loop or if/then. Most of the Sphero-specific code blocks have parameters that the user can edit like in the case of *roll* block. In *roll* block, there are parameters of rolling duration, heading angle and the speed of the

Sphero. Also, some of the code blocks can be dragged in another code block for different purposes.

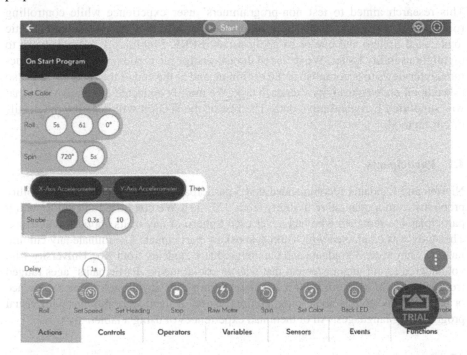

Fig. 2. Overview of SPRK Lightning Lab for Sphero application. The screenshot also included an example usage of *if/then* block. Sensor blocks of *accelerometers* were placed on the first row of *if/then* block where the condition was defined and the code block called *strobe* was placed in the *if/then* block to be executed if the condition was true.

For example, as shown in Fig. 2, *if/then* command has the first line of the block for defining a condition in which sensors can be dragged in to define a parameter for describing a condition. *Operators* can also be used to define the relationship among variables on condition. Additionally, for *if/then* block, the user can drag actions into the code block to be executed if the condition is true. Finally, in this application, users can also create their own actions or variables. When the user touches the *start* button on the top, Sphero starts executing the program in the real world.

The SPRK application has a tutorial which includes a walkthrough, starting with guiding user to arrange the orientation of Sphero, continuing with showing the basic features of programming with blocks (i.e., double tapping for getting information about a code block on the bottom bar, dragging a new code block, deleting a code block) and executing the program. That tutorial uses hint bubbles for guiding the user through these basic features. The application also has a section where some ready-to-use programs are present that the user can investigate to learn how the code blocks can be used.

4   Method

This research aimed to test non-programmers' user experience while controlling robotic toys. Therefore, we focused on one of the most famous commercial robotic toys called Sphero and one of its applications (SPRK Lightning Lab for Sphero) to highlight usability issues. We included three tasks for the participants and semi-structured interviews to accomplish at the beginning and at the end of the sections. We also asked open-ended questions after each task. We mainly collected qualitative data that was supported by quantitative data. The rest of the section will describe the details of our method.

4.1   Participants

Nielsen and Landauer recommended that 5 participants are enough to detect usability problems from a qualitative usability study [22, 23]. We conducted our study with 9 participants (6 females) who had never used Sphero or any of its applications before. The study was conducted with Turkish speaking participants to eliminate any cultural factors. They were 3 graduate and 6 undergraduate students from Koç University who volunteered to our announcement that was on social media. Participants' ages ranged from 18 to 32 ($M = 23.00$, $SD = 3.70$) They did not have any programming experience or had little knowledge about programming. None of them were familiar with visual programming languages. All of them had experiences of using a tablet.

4.2   Apparatus

The Sphero 2.0, a robotic toy with a spherical shape was used in our study. Sphero has features such as moving on the ground by rolling, changing colors and, sensing its own movement and direction with the help of the accelerometer and gyroscope. SPRK Lightning Lab for Sphero (version 1.2.0), an application specifically designed for the Sphero, was tested by using an Apple iPad (iOS 9.2) during the study. This application is based on a visual programming language, and contains codes that are embedded in blocks. By arranging code blocks, a user can program the Sphero for controlling its actions. All processes were recorded by a webcam and AirServer[11] software was used to mirror the screen of iPad to a laptop computer. We also recorded the mirrored screen by screen recorder software to match the gestures and the voice of the participant along with their actions taken on the application. The task completion times were also documented.

4.3   Procedure

The study took place in a university classroom with an empty surface to move Sphero. The participants were sitting on a chair. Before each test, we introduced ourselves, declared our aim as exploring their experience with the application while controlling

---

[11] https://itunes.apple.com/tr/app/airserver-connect/id967004087?mt=8.

the Sphero. We explained to them that we were not testing them; instead, we were testing the application. We asked them to follow think-aloud protocol [24] in which participants were supposed to tell simultaneously what they were thinking while using the application. Then, we informed them about the schedule of the test. Additionally, we told them to ask if they need translation for the words on the application. Overall, the tests took approximately 45 min.

The rest of the sub-section will inform the readers about the details of the procedure in the actual sequence of the study.

Pre-test Interview. During pre-test interview, we asked participants their demographic information (i.e., age, academic degree) and how they rate their experience on tablet usage and programming from zero to expert. Additionally, we asked them if they had any knowledge of block-based programming. In exploration session, we gave the tablet and introduced the Sphero to the participants. After opening the application, the logic of block coding was explained. We guided them to begin with the tutorial in the application. We also pointed out that there is a *Sample Codes* section that they might take a look. The time was limited to 5 min for this session. After 5 min, we asked the participants to rate how exploration session assisted them to understand the application with 7-point Likert scale (1 - Not at all instructional, 7 - Extremely instructional). Based on their response we encourage them to reason their response with open-ended questions.

Tasks. Three tasks were given to participants to accomplish in these sessions. The first and second tasks needed participant to use basic functions of the Sphero such as rolling and changing its color. The second task was more complex than the first task. The aim of the first and second tasks was to analyze how they experience overall interface (i.e., dragging/removing a code block, editing parameters of those blocks). The third task was more focused on programming logic where the user needed to use *if/then* and *loop* code blocks. We wanted to investigate the experience of participants when the code block was more complicated. For example, to use *if/then* block, a user needs to drag other code blocks into *if/then* block parenthesis.

In the beginning of all tasks, the Sphero was placed in front of the participant's chair. We reminded participants that they could look at *tutorial* or *sample codes* sections any time they needed. We included time limits for all tasks but extended it if the participant was close to accomplishing the task since our aim was to discover usability issues. The first task was to make the Sphero go approximately 2 m away from the participant. The time limit for this task was 5 min. In the second task, again, we asked participants to move the Sphero app. 2 m away from them. But this time we specified that the color of the Sphero should be red in the beginning. After going app. 2 m, it should wait for a while. Then, the color should turn to green. Finally, it should come back. The time limit was also 5 min for this task. The third task was defined as blinking the Sphero while it was spinning for the first 4 participants. Then, we realized that the task was too hard for participants. Thus, we replaced it with another task that participants would use similar functions. The third task included changing the color of Sphero if it was thrown up in the air. We specified that the Sphero should be green at the beginning and asked them to make the color of the Sphero blue in case of being thrown. Different than the other tasks, we asked participants to use specific code blocks: *if/then* and *loop* blocks. We explained that *if/then* command refers to a condition in programming languages. We told them that this command makes defined commands work only if the defined condition occurs. Additionally, we mention that this application reads a block code in nanoseconds and passes to the other one. *Loop* command was explained to overcome this situation by making the application read the code blocks inside it repeatedly. We included a time limit of 10 min for this task. Our aim was to explore how non-programmers use commands like if/then and loop and how they interact with the user interface of these features. At the end of both tasks, we asked participants to rate the difficulty of the task by a 7-point Likert scale (1 - Not at all difficult, 7 - Extremely difficult). After their response, we asked open-ended questions to justify their quantitative response. We also asked them what they liked and disliked when they were using the application after each task.

Post-test Interview. The beginning of the semi-structured post-test interview involved open-ended questions such as "What would you change in the application?" and "What was the most difficult thing for you? Why?". After open-ended questions, we asked 11 questions that were responded in 7-point Likert scale. The questions (Table 1) contained several subjects related to the usability of the application such as the evaluation of tutorial as the evaluation of tutorial, the ease of use, the pleasure of use, self-confidence while using the application. Questions 2, 3, 4, 5, 6 and 10 were based on System Usability Scale (SUS) [25] with small modifications. We asked respondents to explain the reason behind the given rating to collect both qualitative and quantitative data.

Table 1. Questions in the post-test interview

Q1 - Tutorial was helpful in using the application
Q2 - I found the system unnecessarily complex
Q3 - I thought the system was easy to use
Q4 - I think that I would need the support of a technical person to be able to use this application
Q5 - I would imagine that non-programmers would learn to use this system very quickly
Q6 - I felt very confident using the application
Q7 - I found the given tasks difficult
Q8 - I think I learned the application and I feel confident to use it
Q9 - I enjoyed using the application
Q10 - I think that I would like to use this application again
Q11 - I would recommend the application to my friends

5   Results and Discussion

5.1   Quantitative Results

In the first tests, we asked 4 participants to flick Sphero when it is turning for task 3. When we realized that this task is too complex we changed it to the task explained in the procedure section. Because our focus was on the usability of the application and the mentioned change in Task 3 did not affect the scope of the task, it did not make a major impact in the results. Average difficulty of task 3 was 6.11 with a standard deviation of 0.78. When we exclude the first 4 users from the analysis, the mean value of the results increased to 6.20 ($SD = 0.84$). Mean values of the task difficulties (see Fig. 3) suggest that task 2 was the easiest. The reason for that might be that the participants got used to the user interface in the first task and their knowledge from the first task help them to accomplish the second one easily. The hardest task for the participants was the third task. This might be due to confusing nature of the task in terms of understanding different code blocks which were directly related to the textual programming (i.e. if/then and loop). Another explanation would be that the user interface was too abstract for them to understand the functions of those code blocks, thus it was hard for them to construct a program by using *if/then* and *loop*. Elkin et al. [7] found similar results with children, most of whom failed in the task with the *loop* function. We discussed these issues with details in the qualitative analysis section.

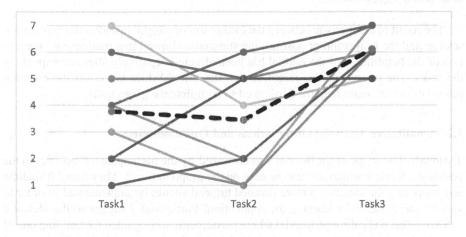

Fig. 3. Participants were asked to assess the difficulty of tasks after each task. Their response is shown in 7-point Likert scale and dashed line shows the average.

We can consider answers of Q3 and Q4 as a neutral in the post-test questionnaire. When we examined the extremes points in the graph (see Fig. 4), we noticed that participants agreed to the Q9, Q10, and Q11 in the post-test questionnaire, which shows the application was engaging for the participants. However, some of the participants tended to comment on the robot instead of the application when they were explaining what they liked about the system. Ramirez-Benavides et al. [2] also found that children expressed that they were interested in robot more than in the application. Q2 and Q7 had been rated with low scores that indicated participants did not think that using the application was hard for them. Besides, high scores of Q5 and Q6 supported the inference that participants used the application without having difficulties.

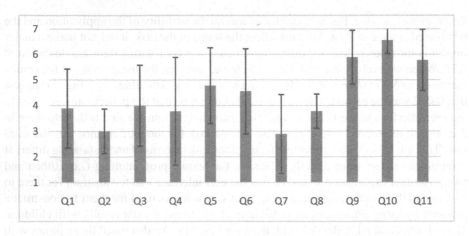

Fig. 4. Mean values and standard deviation of the agreement of the participants with the phrases in the post-test questionnaire.

The result of comparison between the evaluation of tutorial just after the exploration session and the evaluation of post-test questionnaire showed that participants' perception of the helpfulness of the tutorial has been affected negatively after accomplishing the tasks. The reason for this might be that the tutorial does not cover the essential information that might help the participant to complete the given tasks.

5.2   Qualitative Analysis: Observations and Questionnaires

Tutorial. The scope of the tutorial was criticized by the participants, especially in the post-test interview which can also be seen on the graph in Fig. 5. They found it shallow and supported the idea that a more detailed tutorial should be implemented in order to make it more useful for learning the application. Participant 7 suggested the idea of a more detailed walk-through tutorial where participants were guided for building one of the sample programs that were present in the *sample programs* section. Participant 1 mentioned the possible benefits of walk-through videos shown as a tutorial at the beginning. She claimed that this might be a good way of introducing more complex parts of the application. Furthermore, the hint bubbles on the tutorial failed to give intended instructions about the basics of the graphical user interface of the application. Although we encouraged the participant to follow the tasks shown on the hint bubbles in the tutorial, most of the participants did not accomplish all the hints shown in the tutorial. Moreover, some of them did not recognize that there were hint bubbles in the first place. One of the participants, while exploring the tutorial again during the post-test interview, said: "Now, I noticed that I needed to follow the instruction on the tutorial!" (P5). When we asked "What do you want to change in the application?" in the post-test interview, P1, P7, and P9 mentioned that they want to change tutorial.

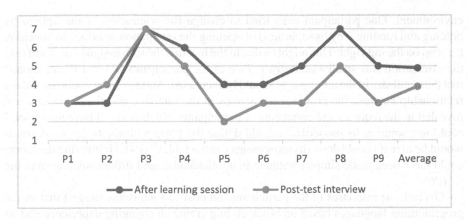

Fig. 5. Evaluation of the tutorial in terms of its usefulness in learning the application after exploration session and in the post-questionnaire.

Block-Coding. Dragging and dropping code blocks were engaging and easy to use for the participants. Most of the terminology and the icons assigned to the code blocks were understood by the participants. Some users mentioned that the different colors used for a different group of code blocks were well designed. Almost all the participants immediately understood the logic of block coding (creating a flow of actions for the Sphero to execute). However, there were some critical usability problems on this subject. Some users had troubles with terminologies of textual programming languages (i.e. *if/then*, *delay*). Additionally, the parameters of some block codes were irrelevant for most of the participants and they had troubles understanding them. For example, to move the Sphero, the participants used the *roll* command (i.e. first and second task), they were searching for an input area for entering the distance, instead of entering the duration, speed, and heading angle. Moreover, the parameters of code blocks like *roll* did not have any units, for example, meters or meters/second, and they were not understood. Participants also mentioned that when they put same code block for the second time, the application should automatically set the same values for the parameters as the first code block.

Almost all the participants had troubles with the *if/then* code block. As we described before in the paper, an *if/then* code block needs a condition and defined actions. Conditions were supposed to be defined in the first line of the code block. When a participant added an *if/then* code block, the first line had "0 == 0" which did not mean anything to most of our participants since they were non-programmers. Although they could add other code blocks such as *accelerometer* into condition line of *if/then* block to define an accelerometer condition. Besides, the graphical clues on the *if/then* code block failed to give clues about which code blocks could be dragged on this space.

The Relation of the Digital and the Physical Environment. The most challenging part of the first two task was to orient the Sphero in the real environment. Almost all the participants, at some point of at least one task, moved the Sphero in a wrong direction. Although some of them noticed or remembered that they needed to arrange the aim of the Sphero, the others had problems in figuring out the Sphero's orientation in the real environment. One participant even tried to change the orientation of the Sphero by holding and rotating it by hand, instead of opening the orientation interface by touching the icon on the top-right. This might be due to the fact that the icon assigned to modifying the orientation was small and abstract. Two of the participants, P3 and P7 mentioned that the small size of the aiming icon should be increased. Another issue about the uneasy relationship between the programmed actions in the interface and the physical world revealed in the requests and comments of participants which were: "I have the tablet; I could use some of its properties. I could define the place with the tablet's camera. It would be nice if I could draw (its movements) on the tablet." (P4), "It (moving the robot) could have been made simpler without an accelerometer and if/then, such as drawing it" (P6).

Overall, the responses of the participants on post-test interview suggest that visual programming languages based on block-coding create an engaging experience and an easy-to-learn platform for controlling robotic toys. However, our observations and semi-structured interviews suggested that designer of those interfaces should consider some issues about the usability such as;

- Supportive contents (i.e. tutorials) are critical for non-programmers to learn how to use those devices. Thus, tutorials should contain more details about complex aspects of the applications such as *if/then*. Besides initial tutorial, users should able to access explanatory information about features while programming.
- Terminologies and metaphors used in those kinds of applications for controlling robotic toys should consider the mental model of non-programmer users and should be simplified and familiarized for the end-users.
- The visual features of the blocks should support the functional relation between code blocks. For example, if some code blocks can be dragged into another one, there must be visual clues that reflect the relationship.
- The relation between the digital user interface and the real environment (including the robotic toy and surrounding environment) should be considered while designing the user interface to create an understanding of the spatial relationship between them. More specifically, for the robotic toys that move in the space, the orientation information should be specified to decrease the errors.

6   Conclusion

Our study aimed to reveal the usability issue of visual programming interfaces by block-coding for controlling commercial robotics toys. In order to explore the usability issues related to the non-programmers' experience of controlling the robotic toys, we conducted a user study with non-programmers (N = 9) by using Sphero (A robotic toy) and tested its mobile application, called SPRK Lightning Lab for Sphero, which adopted visual programming language with a block-based coding interface. We included an exploring session, three tasks, pre-test, and post-test interviews as well as semi-structured interviews at the end of each task.

Our results suggest that supportive contents like tutorials should give detailed information about the capabilities of the application. Also, these interfaces should be designed by considering the mental model of non-programmer adults. Therefore, designers should use familiar metaphors for describing programming concepts as well as using graphical elements that can indicate the functional relationship of code blocks. Finally, our findings revealed the need for building an easy-to-understand spatial relationship between the digital interface and the robotic toy.

Acknowledgments. Thanks to İdil Bostan and Tülin Bozkurt Hazar for proofreading.

References

1. Klassner, F., Anderson, S.D.: LEGO mindstorms: not just for K-12 anymore. IEEE Robot. Autom. Mag. **10**, 12–18 (2003)
2. Ramírez-benavides, K., López, G., Guerrero, L.A.: A mobile application that allows children in the early childhood to program robots. Mob. Inf. Syst. **2015** (2016). Article ID: 1714350
3. Diprose, J.P., MacDonald, B.A., Hosking, J.G.: Ruru: a spatial and interactive visual programming language for novice robot programming. In: Proceedings of the 2011 IEEE Symposium on Visual Languages and Human-Centric Computing VL/HCC 2011, pp. 25–32 (2011)
4. Weintrop, D., Wilensky, U.: To block or not to block? That is the question. J. Educ. Res. **95**(4), 196–202 (2015)
5. Dill, K., Freeman, B., Frazier, S.: Mars game: creating and evaluating an engaging educational game. In: Interservice/Industry Training, Simulation, and Education Conference (I/ITSEC), pp. 1–14 (2015)
6. Pane, J.F.: A programming system for children that is designed for usability. Dissertation, Carnegie Mellon University (2002)
7. Elkin, M., Sullivan, A., Bers, M.U.: Programming with the KIBO robotics kit in preschool classrooms. Comput. Sch. **33**, 169–186 (2016)
8. Zelazo, P., Carter, A., Reznick, J.S., Frye, D.: Early development of executive function. Rev. Gen. Psychol. **1**(2), 198–226 (1997)
9. Lee, K.T.H., Sullivan, A., Bers, M.U.: Collaboration by design: using robotics to foster social interaction in kindergarten. Comput. Sch. **30**, 271–281 (2013)
10. Begel, A.: LogoBlocks: a graphical programming language for interacting with the world. Electrical Engineering and Computer Science Department, MIT, Boston, MA (1996)
11. Bau, D., Bau, D.A., Pickens, C.S., Dawson, M.: Pencil code: block code for a text world. In: IDC, pp. 445–448 (2015)
12. Resnick, M., Maloney, J., Monroy-Hernández, A., Rusk, N., Eastmond, E., Brennan, K., Millner, A., Rosenbaum, E., Silver, J., Silverman, B., Kafai, Y.: Scratch: programming for all. Commun. ACM. **52**, 60–67 (2009)
13. Cheung, J.C.Y., Ngai, G., Chan, S.C.F., Lau, W.W.Y.: Filling the gap in programming instruction: a text-enhanced graphical programming environment for junior high students. SIGCSE Bull. **41**, 276–280 (2009)
14. García-peñalvo, F.J., Rees, A.M., Hughes, J., Vermeersch, J.: A survey of resources for introducing coding into schools. In: Proceedings of the Fourth International Conference on Technological Ecosystems for Enhancing Multiculturality (2016)
15. Kim, S.H., Jeon, J.W.: Programming LEGO mindstorms NXT with visual programming Seung. In: International Conference on Control, Automation and Systems, Seoul, Korea, pp. 2468–2472 (2007)

16. Ng, G., Chow, M., de Lima Salgado, A.: Toys and mobile applications: current trends and related privacy issues. In: Hung, P.C.K. (ed.) Mobile Services for Toy Computing, pp. 51–76. Springer (2015)
17. Ketola, P., Roto, V.: Exploring user experience measurement needs. In: Proceedings of the International Workshop on Meaningful Measures: Valid Useful User Experience Measurement (VUUM), Reykjavik, Iceland, pp. 23–26 (2008)
18. Shackel, B., Richardson, S.J.: Usability—Context, Framework, Definition, Design and Evaluation. Cambridge University Press, New York, NY (1991)
19. Nielsen, J.: Usability Engineering. Elseiver, Englewood Cliffs (1993)
20. Jordan, P.W.: An Introduction to Usability. CRC Press, USA (1998)
21. Hung, J.: Usability and learnability improvements for the TaleBlazer game editor. Dissertation, Institute of Technolog, Massachusetts (2015)
22. Nielsen, J., Landauer, T.K.: A mathematical model of the finding of usability problems. In: ACM INTERCHI 1993, pp. 206–213 (1993)
23. Nielsen, J.: How many test users in a usability study? (2012). https://www.nngroup.com/articles/how-many-test-users/. Accessed 8 Feb 2017
24. Fonteyn, M.E., Kuipers, B., Grobe, S.J.: A description of think aloud method and protocol analysis. Qual. Health Res. 3, 430–441 (1993)
25. Brooke, J.: SUS - a quick and dirty usability scale. Usability Eval. Ind. 189, 4–7 (1996)

IT Governance for Cyber-Physical Systems: The Case of Industry 4.0

Maximilian Savtschenko, Frederik Schulte(✉), and Stefan Voß

Institute of Information Systems, University of Hamburg,
Von-Melle-Park 5, 20146 Hamburg, Germany
maximilian.savtschenko@gmail.com,
{frederik.schulte,stefan.voss}@uni-hamburg.de

Abstract. Recent developments in the manufacturing industry are linked to the systematical adoption and deployment of cyber-physical systems (CPS) that monitor and synchronize information between the physical factory floor and the cyber-computational space providing advanced information analytics. While it is widely recognized in literature that the related trend of transforming the manufacturing industry, the so-called industry 4.0, leads to distinct interventions in operations of businesses and public organizations, appropriate governance practices still need to be established. This paper uses a detailed overview on changes going along with the emergence of CPS and industry 4.0 to point out requirements for IT governance approaches supporting the adoption of CPS. The observations are illustrated for an example using the COBIT 5 governance of IT framework.

Keywords: IT Governance · Cyber-physical systems · Industry 4.0 · eResearch · Internet of things

1 Introduction

An important technological characteristic of industry 4.0 and related cyber-physical systems (CPS) is the interconnectivity of the physical world with the virtual one. While CPS are defined as physical and engineered systems whose operations are monitored, coordinated, controlled, and integrated by a computing and communication core [23], industry 4.0 is seen as the trend transforming manufacturing industry to the next generation by systematical deployment of CPS [19]. Industry has already recognized the benefits of using the data generated during machine use. Sensors are attached to machines and monitor the health status of the plants. In industry 4.0, this idea is retained, but supplemented by the possibility of predicting the conditions of the plant, controlling it, and taking independent actions. The interaction between sensors and actuators is a significant difference to the already existing embedded systems which are based on programmable logic controllers. There is an amalgamation between the physical and the virtual software level which cannot be differentiated distinctly

© Springer International Publishing AG 2017
A. Marcus and W. Wang (Eds.): DUXU 2017, Part I, LNCS 10288, pp. 667–676, 2017.
DOI: 10.1007/978-3-319-58634-2_48

anymore. In this way, physical processes get monitored, and a virtual copy of the actual situation is created. This virtual plant is the initial point for simulations, based on algorithms. Real-time decisions can then be made on the basis of a fusion of virtual and physical world. The plant identifies its own status, the next working steps as well as the status of the other machines just in time and adapts itself independently to the changing environment. To implement real-time decisions and actions there is a need of low vertical integration. Thus, an important plant design factor is decentralization [4] which allows machines to take independent actions, e.g., in case of a machine failure, to re-route the product to a different plant. In order to guarantee an information exchange of all components, the product must also have similar characteristics, i.e., become a so-called "smart product". That means, it must provide information on its location and store current assets that it run through in order to enable control. This process is supported by radio frequency identification (RFID) technology [9]. Resulting from the new technologies and the adaptation of the machines to the conversion, by the implementation of sensors, actuators and RFID a huge expanse of new data is generated, that needs to be stored, correctly filtered, analyzed and distributed to the right places. In order to handle the data correctly and thus to solve complex algorithms, the computational performance of today's monolithic controllers is not sufficient. In industry 4.0, cloud computing plays a key role for the infrastructural solutions in information technology (IT). Cloud computing allows to control systems and also parts of the machines autonomously via the infrastructure provided by the cloud. In this way, data intensive tasks can be outsourced to the cloud. Sensors and actuators are the only components remaining as a local resource on the machine itself. The big advantage is an easy centralized data storage and analysis space with large computational power that continuously provides access to at all plants. Small businesses can in particular benefit from using already existing infrastructure, without investing in its own expensive IT solutions. Still there are significant concerns regarding the data security of this application. Enterprises are hesitant to provide sensitive internal data to external servers that can be exposed to cyber-attacks.

This development poses new challenges for the governance of data and IT that are reflected in studies on respective IT governance frameworks such as COBIT. Margaria et al. [21] raise the question which IT governance is needed for distributed intelligent CPS, composing a list of the most urgent governance issues for CPS. Moreover, Wolden et al. [26] examine the effectiveness of COBIT 5 information security framework for reducing cyber-attacks on a supply chain management system. Bartens et al. [3] have demonstrated that an infrastructural development such as the emergence of industry 4.0 may require a bottom-up analysis and implementation of IT governance, while Schulte et al. [25] have discussed challenges that arise from open data which is inherent in CPS. These studies build the foundation for CPS governance, but do not extensively address IT governance issues coming up with the development of CPS. We provide a detailed overview on changes going along with the emergence of CPS and industry 4.0 and discuss necessary adjustments of current IT governance approaches.

We use the COBIT 5 framework to illustrate how current IT governance practices address the detected challenges.

The remainder of this article is structured in the following way. After a review of related work in Sect. 2, we introduce the transformational process of industry 4.0 and governance implications in Sect. 3. On this foundation, Sect. 4 discusses challenges and analyzes requirements for IT governance arising from CPS and especially the trend of industry 4.0. Finally, Section 5 concludes the study and gives an outlook on future research.

2   Related Work

Academic endeavors related to IT governance for CPS and industry 4.0 can be separated in four major building blocks: literature on CPS, studies on industry 4.0, related governance approaches, and research on current IT governance issues. Table 1 comprises related work according to this classification. CPS have recently received significant attention, e.g., among researchers working on manufacturing systems [19] and systems design [17], while other works focused on security issues emerging from the deployment of CPS [10]. Ensuring safety, stability, and performance of CPS while minimizing costs of CPS are widely seen as important challenges [2]. These challenges are especially severe since the application of CPS is considered a distinct intervention in operations of businesses and public organizations [23]. Related to the research focus on manufacturing, industry 4.0 is seen as the trend transforming manufacturing industry to the generation of CPS [19]. Hermann et al. [12] identify six design principles for implementations industry 4.0: interoperability, virtualization, decentralization, real-time capability, service orientation, and modularity. Lee et al. [20] emphasize the importance of smart analytics and service innovation in the context of industry 4.0. Gorecky et al. [11] state that development of industry 4.0 will be accompanied by changing tasks and demands for the human in the factory and elaborate on human aspects in the design of industry 4.0. Moreover, Lasi et al. [15] describe an application-pull and a technology-push as driving forces behind industry 4.0. Especially, the two latter studies directly point to important issues in governance and (bi-directional) IT/business alignment. While the aforementioned works focused on issues implicitly requiring to re-think (IT) governance for CPS, other studies explicitly address governance issues for CPS. Among these works, Schirner et al. [24] elaborate on the issue of shared governance between humans and robotics in CPS, while Margaria et al. [21] summarize IT governance issues for CPS. Broy et al. [5], on the other hand, mention the human-system cooperation, usability and safety, i.e., also deal with questions of shared control, transparency/controllability, and integrated models for human-machine interaction. Kosub [14] calls for cyber risk governance to address risks imposed even by small groups of individuals to threat CPS by attacking electronic components monitoring and controlling physical entities such as, e.g., embedded systems in trains or airplanes. Abbas et al. [1] furthermore proclaim structured mechanisms for conformance testing as falsification for CPS. Finally, some authors examine related issues in the attempt to advance IT governance, data governance, and IT governance frameworks. Studies on data governance [6,13] emphasize the need for improved compliance, security, and performance in dealing with extended volume and variety as well as velocity of data transactions that are associated with technological developments such as CPS. Other studies rather focus on the development of IT governance frameworks [7,8], where COBIT 5 is frequently used, e.g., as an information security framework for reducing cyber attacks [26].

Summarizing, it can be stated that the transformational impact of CPS in industry and public organizations is widely recognized, while the development of specific (IT) governance approaches lags these insights.

Table 1. Problem classification and considered articles

Problem	References
CPSs	Lee [17], Rajkumar et al. [23], Genge et al. [10], Lee et al. [19], Wang et al. (2015)
Industry 4.0	Gorecky et al. [11], Lasi et al. [15], Lee and Kao (2014), Lee et al. [19], Hermann et al. [12]
CPS governance	Broy et al. [5], Schirner et al. [24], Abbas et al. [1], Margaria et al. [21], Kosub [14]
Current IT governance issues	Cheong and Chang [6], Hüner et al. [13], De Haes et al. [7], De Haes and van Grembergen [8], Wolden et al. [26]

3   The Industry 4.0 Transformation Process

Table 2 gives an overview about the changes towards industry 4.0 and illustrates the interfaces in which big amounts of data are generated. The table gives explicit information about the kind of data that is produced, by the different players in a smart factory. The smart product was added as an important data enabler in industry 4.0, since information about the usage, based on dynamic data, is going to be an essential competitive advantage. In the aerospace industry, e.g., generated data from air fleets is already used to forecast the remaining life time of turbines. Therefore, an exchange of the used parts takes only place, when needed. Simulations, based on the data, can forecast the regular wear under different environmental influences, like temperature or number of revolutions. A nearly optimal utilization is promised. Other than that sensors and controllers are the main data drivers in industry 4.0. CPS include embedded systems, which on one hand, are equipped with sensors for the acquisition of data and, on the other hand, actuators for activating or influencing processes. Consequently, sensors produce a lot of process data, like position of the component or its torque. Storing this data over time, gives a good data base for further simulations. Controllers are used to operate different tasks. The data created by the controllers can be mainly distinguished into processor data and machine data. Processor data is used to enable a successful data transmission and does not give information to

Table 2. Aspects of the industry 4.0 transformation process adapted from [18]

	Data source	Data type	Examples	Requirements in todays factory environment	Requirements for industry 4.0
Component	Sensor	Process data; Historical data;	Running torque; Acceleration data; Component position; Accumulated data;	Error free; Long lasting; Interchangeable;	Dynamic remaining health prediction; Ability to communicate; Network compatible;
Machine	Controller	Processor data; Machine data;	Data origin/ destination; Machine availability utilization rate; Energy consumption; Switch on/off -time;	Monitoring condition; Forecasting condition;	Monitoring condition; Dynamic forecasting; Awareness of other plants; conditions; Network compatible;
Production system	Data base; Corporate governance; System;	Historical data; Specifications; Meta data	Accumulated data; Framework conditions; Data characteristics. e.g., size;	Lean production; Total quality engineering; Reconfigurable; Productive;	Cyberphysical production system (CPPS); Autonomous decision taking; Dynamic self reorganization, e.g., alternative routes;
Product	Data base	Historical data; Product data;	Accomplished production steps; Product specifications;	High quality	All times located; Own history aware; Unique identification;

the user about the machine itself, e.g., the data origin or its destination address. Machine data is the genuine data the controller allocates, e.g., the availability of the machine or its workload. These mentioned data types are the cornerstones for an efficient implementation of industry 4.0 visions.

4   IT Governance for Cyber-Physical Systems

IT governance for CPS may be discussed on a conceptual level or based on specific frameworks. This section first discusses general IT governance issues (Sect. 4.1) related to CPS and then presents an example of the IT governance framework COBIT 5 (Sect. 4.2).

4.1   IT Governance

Properly applied IT systems can add great value to businesses. In this context, IT governance formulates and implements IT strategies to ensure that IT supports the company's strategies and objectives. The two main tasks of IT governance are first performance and second conformance. Performance is understood the task as to control or influence the effectiveness of the company's activities and hence to create enterprise value. Increasing performance requires, e.g., scaling big amounts of data and parallelizing processes. Conformance, on the other hand, describes the compliance with standards, norms, and above all with legal constrains. Here, IT governance models take the important role of minimizing the IT risks, caused by illegal actions, e.g., cyber-security threats. This sphere decides on how to reach the company goals in the best possible way, implementing IT. The strategy has to be planned, and a decision on a technical infrastructure has to be made. Additional input is provided by the monitoring and evaluating sphere as shown in Fig. 1.

In industry 4.0, self adapting dynamic systems need a new planning approach, since the whole system is made of different single elements which are built up on each other and interact with each other. Autonomous decision making changes the situations independently so that dynamic planning approaches become necessary. Planning the technical infrastructure is challenging as well as large amounts of data must be transferred, which is the reason why companies must be able to rely on reliable and fast communication networks. This process shows the changes that have to be made to meet the required settings before implementing the strategy. Thereby, also acquisition and maintenance of software are key aspects of this domain. In industry 4.0, there will be a need for uniform software standards. Different external and internal rudiments can make the interconnected cooperation considerably more difficult or impossible. A unification across all sectors, however, could quickly meet the limits of complexity. Delivery and support deliver IT services. Covered areas in this domain are supplier management and general administration tasks. However, it also includes system security management. With the new technologies and interfaces in industry

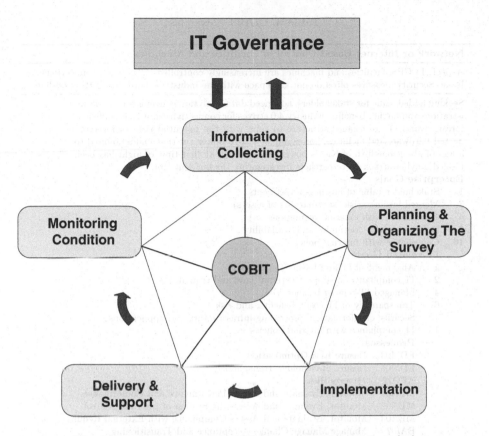

Fig. 1. A conceptual model of IT governance adapted from [22]

4.0 new security threats can arise. Manipulation of location data on transmitters, i.e., can cause the companies a lot of harm. The interconnectivity of the sensors with the whole system raises the threat of wrongly edited processes which never occurred in such a manner in the factory. To meet quality requirements and legal law constrains, monitoring and evaluating has a controlling character in the whole process. Here, the focus is on being informed about external and internal restrictions and guaranteeing their execution through all layers. Legal constrains are determined by the individual states, which also applies to services like the cloud. Companies may need to take setbacks in the disclosure of their sensitive data to use the new technologies.

4.2 An Example of COBIT 5

COBIT 5, as a widely applied IT governance framework [8], uses a goal cascade that breaks down enterprise goals to IT-related goals as illustrated in Table 3. Moreover, COBIT 5 defines processes associated with certain activities to grant that the goals are reached. The different types of COBIT goals and processes

Table 3. COBIT 5 example

Network or Internet-Based Control of Facilities and Machines
Aspect: In CPS, facilities and machines are increasingly controlled via network connections Issue: Security measures often do not keep pace with the industry's hardware getting on-line

Seeking added value for stakeholders, advanced data analytics, convenience in administration, and further benefits, industry 4.0 strives for connectivity, but lacks sufficient foresight and IT governance structure to cope with the potential risks of interconnected hardware and facilities. For example, a 2016 power cut that had amounted to a loss of about one-fifth of Kiev's power consumption at that time of night has been judged a cyber-attack by researchers investigating the incident [16].

Enterprise Goals

1	Stakeholder value of business investments
3	Merged business risk (safeguarding of assets)
4	Compliance with external regulations
7	Business service continuity and availability
16	Compliance with internal policies

IT-related Goals

1	Alignment of IT and business strategy
2	IT compliance to support external laws and regulations
4	Managed IT-related business risk
6	Transparency of IT costs, benefits, and risk
10	Security of information, processing infrastructure and applications
15	IT compliance with internal policies

Processes

EDM03	Ensure Risk Optimization
EDM05	Ensure Stakeholder Transparency
APO12	Manage Risk
MEA01	Monitor, Evaluate and Assess Performance and Conformance
MEA02	Monitor, Evaluate and Assess the System of Internal Control
MEA03	Monitor, Evaluate and Assess Compliance with External Requirements
BAI07	Manage Manage Change Acceptance and Transitioning
DSS01	Manage Operations
DSS05	Manage Security Services

may be used to assess how the framework addresses challenges arising with emergence of CPS and industry 4.0. In Table 3 a specific example of networked industry hardware is related to COBIT 5 goals and processes. It is obvious to see that several important governance issues related to the example are addressed by COBIT 5 on a strategic level. Nonetheless, non of these strategic goals and processes would likely have prevented the incident of the example. Hence, the readiness of COBIT 5 for CPS security depends a lot on the lower level configuration in implementations of the framework. That means, how subordinate process goals and related metrics are defined plays a significant role for the degree of security enforced by a COBIT 5 implementation.

5   Conclusion

Prior work has pointed out the importance of changes induced by the emergence of CPS in industry; Lee et al. [19], e.g., recently proposed a CPS architecture for industry 4.0-based manufacturing systems. Nevertheless, there is a lack of literature addressing related governance and IT governance issues. In this work, we have summarized the transformational process of industry 4.0 in order to link this development to important IT governance requirements. We found that current IT governance practices generally cover fundamentals to match these requirements, but also depend on CPS-aware configuration or implementation. This study extends findings by Wolden et al. [26], looking at diverse aspects of CPS for IT governance and thus adds to insights on how COBIT 5 deals with cyber-risks within a supply chain. In addition, we have used a recent example to illustrate how COBIT 5 uses enterprise, IT-related goals, and processes to implement CPS strategies. This study therefore indicates that IT governance frameworks are indeed useful to prepare enterprises and organizations for CPS challenges, but might need to put more weight on specific issues and provide respective guidance for configuration. Although, in this work we have reviewed detailed implications of CPS on (IT) governance, no extensive approach for CPS-ready IT governance has been elaborated. The development of more detailed proposals for an altered IT governance for CPS and autonomous systems will therefore be part of future work.

References

1. Abbas, H., Hoxha, B., Fainekos, G., Deshmukh, J.V., Kapinski, J., Ueda, K.: Conformance testing as falsification for cyber-physical systems. Technicla report (2014). arXiv preprint arXiv:1401.5200
2. Baheti, R., Gill, H.: Cyber-physical systems. In: The Impact of Control Technology, vol. 12, pp. 161–166 (2011)
3. Bartens, Y., Chunpir, H.I., Schulte, F., Voß, S.: Business/IT alignment in two-sided markets: a COBIT 5 analysis for media streaming business models. In: Strategic IT Governance and Alignment in Business Settings, pp. 82–111. IGI Global (2017)
4. Brettel, M., Friederichsen, N., Keller, M., Rosenberg, M.: How virtualization, decentralization and network building change the manufacturing landscape: an industry 4.0 perspective. Int. J. Mech. Ind. Sci. Eng. 8(1), 37–44 (2014)
5. Broy, M., Cengarle, M.V., Geisberger, E.: Cyber-physical systems: imminent challenges. In: Calinescu, R., Garlan, D. (eds.) Monterey Workshop 2012. LNCS, vol. 7539, pp. 1–28. Springer, Heidelberg (2012). doi:10.1007/978-3-642-34059-8_1
6. Cheong, L.K., Chang, V.: The need for data governance: a case study. In: Proceedings of the 18th Australasian Conference on Information Systems, pp. 999–1008. Association for Information Systems (2007)
7. De Haes, S., Debreceny, R., Van Grembergen, W.: Understanding the core concepts in COBIT 5. ISACA J. 5, 1–8 (2013)
8. De Haes, S., Van Grembergen, W.: COBIT as a framework for enterprise governance of IT. In: de Haes, S., Van Grembergen, W. (eds.) Enterprise Governance of Information Technology, pp. 103–128. Springer, Switzerland (2015)
9. Floerkemeier, C., Lampe, M.: Issues with RFID usage in ubiquitous computing applications. In: Ferscha, A., Mattern, F. (eds.) Pervasive 2004. LNCS, vol. 3001, pp. 188–193. Springer, Heidelberg (2004). doi:10.1007/978-3-540-24646-6_13

10. Genge, B., Siaterlis, C., Fovino, I.N., Masera, M.: A cyber-physical experimentation environment for the security analysis of networked industrial control systems. Comput. Electr. Eng. **38**(5), 1146–1161 (2012)
11. Gorecky, D., Schmitt, M., Loskyll, M., Zühlke, D.: Human-machine-interaction in the industry 4.0 era. In: 12th IEEE International Conference on Industrial Informatics (INDIN), pp. 289–294. IEEE (2014)
12. Hermann, M., Pentek, T., Otto, B.: Design principles for Industrie 4.0 scenarios. In: 49th Hawaii International Conference on System Sciences (HICSS), pp. 3928–3937. IEEE (2016)
13. Hüner, K.M., Ofner, M., Otto, B.: Towards a maturity model for corporate data quality management. In: Proceedings of the 2009 ACM Symposium on Applied Computing, pp. 231–238. ACM (2009)
14. Kosub, T.: Components and challenges of integrated cyber risk management. Zeitschrift für die gesamte Versicherungswissenschaft **104**(5), 615–634 (2015)
15. Lasi, H., Fettke, P., Kemper, H.G., Feld, T., Hoffmann, M.: Industry 4.0. Bus. Inf. Syst. Eng. **6**(4), 239 (2014)
16. Lee, D.: Ukraine power cut 'was cyber-attack' (2017). http://www.bbc.com/news/technology-38573074
17. Lee, E.A.: Cyber physical systems: design challenges. In: 11th IEEE International Symposium on Object Oriented Real-Time Distributed Computing (ISORC), pp. 363–369. IEEE (2008)
18. Lee, J., Bagheri, B., Kao, H.A.: Recent advances and trends of cyber-physical systems and big data analytics in industrial informatics. In: Proceedings of the International Conference on Industrial Informatics (INDIN), pp. 1–6 (2014)
19. Lee, J., Bagheri, B., Ka, H.A.: A cyber-physical systems architecture for industry 4.0-based manufacturing systems. Manuf. Lett. **3**, 18–23 (2015)
20. Lee, J., Kao, H.A., Yang, S.: Service innovation and smart analytics for industry 4.0 and big data environment. Procedia Cirp **16**, 3–8 (2014)
21. Margaria, T.: Which it governance for distributed intelligent cyber-physical systems?. In: 39th Annual Computer Software and Applications Conference (COMPSAC), pp. 46–47. IEEE (2015)
22. Meyer, M., Zarnekow, R., Kolbe, L.M.: It-Governance. Wirtschaftsinformatik **45**(4), 445–448 (2003)
23. Rajkumar, R.R., Lee, I., Sha, L., Stankovic, J.: Cyber-physical systems: the next computing revolution. In: Proceedings of the 47th Design Automation Conference, pp. 731–736. ACM (2010)
24. Schirner, G., Erdogmus, D., Chowdhury, K., Padir, T.: The future of human-in-the-loop cyber-physical systems. Computer **46**(1), 36–45 (2013)
25. Schulte, F., Chunpir, H.I., Voß, S.: Open data evolution in information systems research: considering cases of data-intensive transportation and grid systems. In: Marcus, A. (ed.) DUXU 2016. LNCS, vol. 9748, pp. 193–201. Springer, Cham (2016). doi:10.1007/978-3-319-40406-6_18
26. Wolden, M., Valverde, R., Talla, M.: The effectiveness of COBIT 5 information security framework for reducing cyber attacks on supply chain management system. IFAC-PapersOnLine **48**(3), 1846–1852 (2015)

Relationship Between the Scientific and Traditional Software Engineering Considering the Ethical Aspects of Human-Computer Interaction

Natalie Mie Takahashi[✉] and Plinio Thomaz Aquino Jr.

Fundação Educacional Inaciana Pe. Sabóia de Medeiros,
Centro Universitário FEI, São Bernardo do Campo, São Paulo, Brazil
{natmt,plinio.aquino}@fei.edu.br

Abstract. Software engineering (SE) is a discipline that studies process, methods and tools to build a software. The SE applied in scientific experiments tries to insert those process, methods and tools to build an academic research. One relevant aspect when applying the SE in scientific experiments is the evolvement of humans during the experimentation process. The discipline that studies computer domains involving humans is the Human-Computer Interaction (HCI). The HCI is a field that collaborates with the ethical processes of SE. This article demonstrates the relationship of the concepts and how HCI collaborates with the evolution of the ethical aspects of the traditional SE, and its application to scientific computing, including the some of the ethics applied in medicine.

Keywords: Software engineering · Experimental software engineering · Human-Computer interaction · Scientific computing · Ethics

1 Introduction

Software engineering (SE) is a discipline that studies the aspects of the process to build a software [1], it encompasses process, methods and tools destined to build the software with quality [2]. Scientific computing consists on tools, techniques and theories that were originated from mathematics, and are used solve problems from science and engineering in a computer by developing the solution based on mathematical models [3]. The Experimental Software Engineering (ESE) uses the SE to the identify and define new processes and tools for the evolution the discipline. The SE applied in scientific experiments tries to insert the methods and processes defined by the SE (commonly used by industries) into the academic research lifecycle.

One relevant aspect when applying the SE in scientific experiments is to consider the humans as part of the experimentation process. The discipline that studies computer domains involving humans is the HCI.

In addition, engineering ethics is a subcategory of professional ethics, it is professional ethics of and for engineers. It emphases on assisting engineers in shaping their professional responsibility through the construction of general ethical principles and

© Springer International Publishing AG 2017
A. Marcus and W. Wang (Eds.): DUXU 2017, Part I, LNCS 10288, pp. 677–696, 2017.
DOI: 10.1007/978-3-319-58634-2_49

professional codes, and by providing methods and techniques for tackling the moral issues and dilemmas that engineers encounter in their work.

To evaluate the results of a scientific software, it is necessary to make experimentations, that, like in any other field, encompasses hypothesis and tests that can evaluate, predict, understand, control, and improve a process or product. It has the objective to improve and refine a study to identify new ones. Considering the experimentation, all modalities of research involving human subjects should carefully consider the risks and benefits of the experiment [4]. In order to set the public interests as the main factor of ethics, the Research Ethics Committees (RECs) emerged to consider the conditions of uncertainty in the development of research and evaluate the conflicts impartially, protecting the subject of the study [5].

The Human-Computer Interaction (HCI) is a field of study applied in research and system development that contains theoretical and practical aspects from ethics, since the insertion of ethics in a project until the experimentation and test phase, and it can be applied researches or by industries. HCI has many aspects that collaborates with the ethical processes of SE (business vision or scientific vision). This article demonstrates the relationship of the concepts and how HCI collaborates with the evolution of the ethical aspects of the traditional SE, and its application to scientific computing, besides of contemplate some of the ethics applied in medicine.

2 Software Engineering

The term software engineering (SE) was proposed in 1968 at NATO Software Engineering Conference. The conference addressed problems in SE along with the discussions of techniques, methods and developments for possible solutions [6]. According with Sommerville [1], SE is a discipline that studies the aspects of the process to build a software. Pressman [2] defined SE as a framework that covers process, methods and tools destined to build software with quality. This topic will cover the concepts of ESE, and the aspects of the traditional SE applied for scientific computing.

2.1 Experimental Software Engineering

The experimental software engineering (ESE) analyzes methods and tools from software engineering through experimentations and empirical research [7], focusing on increase the quality of process management and research documentation.

The experimentation, applied in any field, encompasses hypothesis and testing that can evaluate, predict, understand, control, and improve a process or product [4]. It is a study with the objective to make new discoveries, collect data, and testing theories [7, 8], so the study can be improved and refined. The improvement of a discipline involves solve problems on the environment. The results of solving problems can be comprehend by modeling products characteristics (reliability, portability, efficiency, etc.). The evolution of solving problems is based on the encapsulation of knowledge into models, that will be validated and verified based on experimentation, empirical evidence and reflection, leading to the definition of the problem and the solution [9].

The experimentation concepts are applied in SE, where the results are analyzed and the impacts are evaluated according with the knowledge, helping the field to advance with iterative learning process, and providing furthering knowledge about the software process [4].

The experimentation in SE can face some challenges regarding its execution. One complication is the fact that most of the technologies are human based, so change may occur according with the individual creativity and ability, causing variations in the study. Besides that, a lot of other variables can affect the output in an experiment, like one set of processes can be more effective in one software than another set of process [9]. Another problem is lack of realism in the academic study experimentation, which it is more evident when the research is transferred to be used by industries, given the difficulty to have a group of people that represents the software developer real population while the research is being developed [10].

In SE, the dependency of the scientific community with the industry is more evident when we consider the roles of who makes the research and who uses the result of the research. Considering the responsibilities presented by [9], the importance of this relation is emphasized by defining that the responsibility of the researcher is to understand the nature of products and processes, and the practitioner (software engineer by industry) is to improve the system. So, the researcher needs the environment where practitioner builds the software, and the practitioner needs the model found by the researcher to improve the system.

Exist variations of experimental and analytic paradigms in different disciplines, if one of those paradigms is not being used, the study probably cannot be considered as a research project. The experimental paradigm is an inductive model that requires experimental design, observation, data collection and validation to try to find a model from the real world. In SE, it is used to understand the software process, product, people, or environment. An evolutionary approach for the experimental paradigm in software is to assume that the model exists and that it will be modified to improve the study, it can also propose a new model to study the effects of the process or the product by developing statistical/qualitative methods, use case studies, measuring and evaluating the model [9]. The analytic paradigm is a deductive model that provides an analytic framework to build models and identify the limits from the model manipulation, and propose axioms, develop theory, gather results, and analyze these results with empirical observations [11].

Research involves understanding how and why a tool might be useful, and it involves validating the tool according with certain properties or effects by designing carefully an experiment to measure the properties, or to compare it with other tools. The experimental method can be applied to validate hypotheses, or to understand the effects of the tool different environments. The SE field needs research to help establish the scientific and engineering basis. The researchers need to build, analyze and evaluate the models of the process, the environment where the project is being built, and the final product. The goal is to create conceptual scientific foundations of SE for future researches by discovering and validating small concepts that can be applied and used to find more complex and advanced ideas, building packages of knowledge [9].

2.2 Software Engineering for Scientific Computing

One of the continuing challenges of a software application domain is to apply the traditional SE in scientific computing, given the numerous differences on identifying the requirements, expected behavior and results of the system. This section will present some of the process, methods and tools of the traditional SE that are applied for scientific computing with the respective adaptations to attend the dynamic and development of the scientific computing project.

The difficulty to use the same process and methods of traditional SE in scientific computing software can be addressed to the changes of algorithms, models, and architecture according with the discoveries and progress of the project [12]. The steps of the development process might vary according with the project evolution and the output might be unknown.

The traditional SE consists on tools, methods, and procedures responsible for define the software lifecycle [1]. Some of the phases of SE can be applied in the scientific computing process. This section presents concepts and practices of the traditional SE that can be adapted and applicable for the scientific computing.

In the traditional SE, the software requirements phase is extremely important and it should be well defined at the initial of a project to minimize the risks of failure. Although, this phase can be hard to apply in a scientific software given the number of changes in the algorithms, models and architectures. In order to reduce the negative impacts of not having all the requirements well defined in the beginning of the scientific computing project, the developer can do constantly meetings with the user (in this case, people involved in the project). The software requirements can be categorized in user requirements, which the requirements are written in a comprehensive way to be easily understood by the user, and software requirements, that it is separated in functional, non-functional and domain requirements [1].

Functional requirements describe the functionalities of the system [13], by providing information of how the system should behave and react according to the set of inputs [1]. Non-Functional requirements are responsible for the constraints of the software, like programming standards, reliability or computational speed [12]. Domain requirements are defined based on the domain of the application; they might be new functional requirements (or constraints of an existing one) and they can specify particular computations [1].

The scientific computing has the domain requirement as fundamental to define models, equations and numerical algorithms for the project. The software development consists on the design, development, maintenance and testing of the software [12]. The software architectural design focus on the design of the system structure, obtaining the architectural model of how the system can be organized given a set of communicating components [1], and defines the flowcharts of the software, that contain the structure of the software sub-systems (components) and interfaces [12].

Configuration management is a general process to manage the software changes to control the codes and documentations updated [1]. The version control is a repository that contains all the source versions and it allows the people involved to the project to track all the history of the code or artifacts. It provides the latest version of a file, check the differences between the local version to the repository, merge the changes made, commit the local files, identify what was modified, who committed and when it was changed, and it also allows to undo the changes or get the previous version of the archive. The configuration management is also important in scientific computing to compare the results between two different moments of the scientific software, and undo the changes or get another version in case of the recent algorithm or numeric expression has failed [12].

The software testing consists on the process of verification and validation. The verification checks if the software matches to its specifications (function and non-functional requirement), and the validation ensures if the software meets with the expected results from customer [1]. For the scientific computing, the testing can be challenging because it compares experimental data and it does not always know the "correct" output [12].

3 Human-Computer Interaction

The Human-Computer Interaction (HCI) is a multidisciplinary field that studies the interaction of humans and computers, its main goal is to make systems more usable, providing information clearly and accessible to people [14]. HCI defines concepts, methods, and processes that can be integrated into the SE lifecycle by considering the users' characteristics and needs to enhance product quality. The HCI defines techniques, methods, guidelines and standards that can be incorporated to the development of interactive software. The software lifecycles defined by SE were adapted to use the HCI techniques [15].

The techniques from HCI can generate artifacts that can contribute with the SE by helping to identify the functional requirements that meet with the customer expectation and focus on the user, creating prototype for UML, and software validation with real users that helps to identify if the software attends the user's needs and identify possible bugs in the system that could occur in the routine of the user. The following aspects represent a few fields that collaborates do HCI study. The elements of those aspect are important to define how it will be the communication between the user and the system, and to design a software that attends a large number users.

Psychology is one of the fields that contributes directly with HCI in order to make systems more useful and usable. Some important fundaments are Hick-Hyman and Fitts law, Gestalt principles, Distributed Cognition, mental model [16]. The importance of psychology in HCI is not only applied for the tools and techniques, it has also an important role regarding the ethical aspects, which it will be mentioned in the ethics section.

Some of the techniques and tools from HCI are useful in the process of integrating HCI and SE, and requires the user participation during the experimentations and validation. The integration scenario of both fields justifies the necessity of ethics during the project development. This also occurs when companies try to use the theoretical concept (like semiotic) in the projects, or integrate it with other field of Human-Robot Interaction.

The Semiotic is a field that study the signs, system signs, and the process that involves the interpretation of these signs. Semiotic Engineering is described in HCI as the human communication through a computational system, focusing in the communication between designers, users and system [16].

The Human-Robot Interaction (HRI) is an interdisciplinary field that studies the interaction between the human and robot. The study of HRI focus on functionality and usability aspects of the best way to design and implement the robot for tasks that involves humans [17, 18].

At the beginning of the study of HCI, the researches were based on graphic interface, then the challenge became to understanding how people use computers for different activities. According with [14], the evolution of HCI research can be listed as Collaborative Human-Computer Systems, From Novice to Skilled Domain Worker, Knowledge-Based HCI, Design Time and Use Time, Saying the "right" thing at the "right" time in the "right" way, which focused on improve human-computer collaboration, make the system more usable, evidence the communication channel between human and the computer, how to make the system to a lot of users and cause the impression that it was made for him, provide relevant information according with the intended audience.

4 Ethics

The term ethics is defined in different ways from numerous philosophers, according with J.M. Kizza, it can be defined as the study of the human conduct, that helps to distinguish the difference of what is right and wrong, as why and what reason our judgement is justified. "The purpose of ethics is to interpret human conduct, acknowledging and distinguishing between right and wrong" [19]. This section will present some of the codes and ethical aspects applied in SE, HCI, scientific computing as some of the ethics from biomedicine.

4.1   Ethics in Software Engineering

Considering the growth of SE as a discipline, the Institute of Electrical and Electronics Engineers (IEEE) [20] and Association for Computing Machinery (ACM) [21] stablished the Code of Ethics and Professional Practice to advance the professionalism of SE. The Software Engineering Code of Ethics and Professional Practice provides standard for teaching and practicing of the discipline, and it documents the ethical and professional obligations. The code is destined for SE profession, and it instructs about the standards society expectations, informing the public about the responsibilities that are relevant to this profession [19, 22].

The code provides practical advice, principles, and methods of the application of its guidelines to help the software engineer in technical and ethical decisions [22]. It contains important information related to the software engineer ethical behavior and obligations to make it a respected profession by teaching, and executing tasks of analysis, specification, design, development, certification, maintenance, and testing the software, and by preserving the ethics obligations of health, safety and welfare [19].

There are eight principles related to the behavior and decisions made by software engineers that reflect the ethical obligations to be consider in this profession. These Principles should be considered by the software engineers, and the people related or affected by the profession. The central of the code is the Public Interest, which it encompasses the concerns about the health, safety and welfare of the public [19, 22, 23]: **Public** (software engineers shall act according to the public interest, accepting responsibilities), **Client and employer** (software engineers shall act to meet with the client and employer best interests, and being consistent with public interest), **Product** (software engineers have to ensure that the product and its modifications meet the highest professional standards), **Judgment** (software engineers should maintain integrity and independence in their professional judgment), **Management** (SE managers and leaders shall subscribe and promote an ethical approach to the management of software development and maintenance), **Profession** (software engineers shall advance the integrity and reputation of the profession consistent with the public interest), **Colleagues** (software engineers shall be fair and supportive of their colleagues), **Self** (software engineers shall participate in lifelong learning regarding the practice of their profession, and promote an ethical approach to the practice of the profession).

Considering the relevance of the computer in the industry and society, the SE roles have the possibility to do good or cause no harm. In order to ensure that the acts of this profession will be good, the software engineers have to commit themselves to make this profession beneficial and respected, following the Code of Ethics and Professional Practice [19, 23].

4.2 Ethics in Human-Computer Interaction

In HCI, the participant of humans to validate a product or a research is fundamental, generating ethical concerns for the research community. The research in HCI needs to go through an ethical review process to prevent the research to violate any ethical conduct [24].

HCI research adopted codes of ethics from different institutes, like IEEE [20], ACM [21], Australian Computer Society (ACS) [25], American Psychological Association (APA) [26], and British Psychological Society (BPS) [27]. For being a field that involves directly human participation, HCI involves The HCI researches adopt codes of ethics from computing and engineering institutes that focus on principles related to technology, and psychological institutes that emphasizes the problems related to psychological profession [24]. The codes from psychological society were adopted considering that HCI involves the cognition of the users (humans) and that the discipline has fundaments based on psychology study.

The computing and psychological code of ethics provide clauses that concerns with: the transparency of information with the participants, guarantee the public interest, accept responsibilities for the actions, respect individual knowledge and skills, treat people equally, ensure the safety and welfare of the individuals [24], guarantee the confidentiality of the data, anonymity of the individual, request any permission when the experiment is recorded, and free consent term signed by subject of study (who can refuse to collaborate to the experiment anytime) [16].

For the professional perspective, the User Experience Professional's Association (UXPA) [28] have a code of conducts for professionals to ensure the best interests of the participants by concerning about their welfare and how are they are being treated [24]. There are several projects that consider the ethical aspects of HCI [29–31], while several other researches are justified by not requiring the direct involvement of the user in experiments [32–35].

4.3 Ethics in Scientific Research

The goal of a scientific research is to generate knowledge, which it can be a theoretical inspiration, technological or practical. A new knowledge can emerge and be spread by the common sense, traditions from multiple sources and cultures, and the practical knowledge [36].

The practical purpose of producing a knowledge is to contribute to social purpose. The knowledge advance occurs when it exists a problem, a challenge or something to be improved. At the begging of every research, ethical and moral issues need to be assumed, once ethic is the idea of how the life should be lived, and the moral is the perspective of right and wrong [36]. Ethics in scientific research provides a framework that analyzes the ends and goals of the research. The researchers have to ensure that their works reach the goals and attend the democratic freedom, social welfare, equity, and improve of knowledge [37].

The ethics and morality are dynamic; they are components founders and active of social life. The ethic in scientific research is not reduced to how to do, how to communicate and limit what to say, it refers to what and who was investigated [36].

The ethical violations in scientific research can be listed in: negligence in the acknowledgment of previous work, "deliberate fabrication of data you have collected", omission of data that go against with the hypothesis, use the data from another researcher as it was yours, publication of other researchers results without their consent, not recognize the researchers involved in the work, conflict of interest, publication works with too-similar results or reviews, breach of confidentiality, misrepresenting others' work [38].

Ethics and morals elements in a scientific project are constantly being questioned, in contradiction to the past, when the ethics in scientific research used to be assumed as natural. It seems that researchers, managers, publishers, users and funders are facing three challenges based on the democratic culture that used to support the scientific communities and guarantee the circulation of knowledge. The first challenge is related to the exclusive scientific research to powerful private economic groups, where economic incentives and pressure for products impact the production of knowledge. The concern of ethic is related to how we do science. The second challenge is partially an impact from the first challenge. The problem is how to deal with the pressure from the researchers to find resources and achieve academic status, and from the universities that are worried about the ranking in national and international evaluation. It is difficult to understand what the research represents, considering that the work is measured by the number of publications. The consequences of this are the number of publications shared between multiple authors, research programs where results are published in multiple articles and examples as plagiarism. The ethic issue in this challenge is about how to report or communicate science. This challenge is about the pressure of being transparent regarding the use of expressions like "The science shows...", "from the technical point of view...". In this case, the ethical issue is about what and where the science can or should opine, the responsibility that scientific communities have according with the society [36].

The São Paulo Research Foundation (FAPESP) [39] is a public foundation that supports research projects and institutions. The code of good scientific practice from FAPESP establishes ethical guidelines for the scientific activities from any person or entity that has a relation to the foundation. This code provides information about the responsibilities of the researcher, the members involved and the institution linked to the project. It also emphasizes important requirements related the research. According with FAPESP, the researcher responsibilities include to agree on build an original project, have the scientific capacity to realize it, keep confidential data and information collected along with the procedures and partial results until the publication of the results. To communicate the research and authorship results, the researcher should expose the results accurately with all data, information and procedures relevant, the ethical or legal reasons for not exposing same specific data, any possible conflicts of interest, credits of ideas from existing works and authors, the researches involved in the work that agreed of having the names published [40].

4.4 Ethics in Biomedicine Versus Scientific Research

In the past, many researchers believed that their determination to do good, the integrity of character, and the scientific rigor were sufficient to ensure the ethics of the research. Then, the ethical issues applied to health passed by discussions where the old conception is no longer consensus, given the transformation in the society such as the incorporation of new technologies in the healthcare, the further diffusion of scientific knowledge, the expansion of social movements in defense of the individual and collective rights. Scientific advance does not justify the experimentation by itself, even when the results of experiments promise benefit to humanity [5].

Research Ethics Committees. Over the centuries, trials in humans have been conducted with different standards of quality and ethics. In history, there are several shocking cases of the use of human subjects in studies and research, where the absence of control mechanisms based on ethical and moral criteria, resulted in abuses of experiments [5].

Considering the abuses of experiments reported worldwide, the International Court of Nuremberg developed in 1947 the Nuremberg Code, the first code of conduct in research internationally accepted [5]. The code has 10 principles: the voluntary consent of the subject; the experiment should be applied in order to produce fruitful results; the experiment should be designed and based on the animal experimentation and a knowledge of the natural history, disease or other problem in the study; the experiment should be conducted avoiding unnecessary physical and mental suffering, and injury; the experiment should not be conducted if exist any reason to believe it can lead to death or disabling injury, except when experimental physicians are also subjects of study; the level of risk should not exceed the level determined by humanitarian importance of the problem; proper preparations and adequacy of the facilities should be made to protect the subject; the experiment should be conducted by qualified people; the subject has the right to end the experiment if he reaches the physical or mental state that make impossible to continue the experiment; the scientist conducting the experiment must be prepared to end the experiment at any time [41]. Even after creation of the Nuremberg Code, the ethical infractions continued occurring [5].

In Brazil, the National Health Council [42] adopted a document aimed to create ethical standards for research in health, CNS 01 (1988), which it was replaced by CNS 196 (1996). The CNS 196 is an ethical recommendation for all researches that directly or indirectly involves human beings.

The Research Ethics Committees (RECs), also known as Ethical Review Board (ERB), Ethical Review Committee (ERC), Human Research Ethics Committee (HREC), or Institutional Review Board (IRB) emerged from the idea that experiments with humans need to be reviewed based on ethical principles. It is multidisciplinary committee formed by individuals from different fields of human knowledge, that has the objective to preserve the integrity of the subjects of scientific research, ensuring that the study attends international and local ethical guidelines, monitoring the study once started, and making a follow-up of the research after it ends [5, 43].

The Protocol Research is a document written by the researchers that must contain all the details of the experimentation [43]. The REC will analyze the Protocol Research evaluating the risks and benefits contemplated in the introduction or a special section of the project, the competence of the researcher to conduct the research, the informed consent, and the consent form [5].

Informed Consent. The informed consent of the participant is required for all international codes and it is one of the pillars of ethics in scientific research. The importance to obtain informed consent is based on ethical, sociological and legal reasons [5]. When a subject intends to participate of an experimentation, it is necessary to provide full information of the experiment process, so it can be considered as informed [44].

Biomedical research can only be done through informed consent, which it is very difficult to acquire, and consequently it turns out to be a challenge for the researcher. The consent requires adequate information, that should be understood by the patient [5]. The individuals must be informed about that the research intends to produce scientific knowledge and it is not a medical treatment, the duration of the study, risks and inconveniences, alternative treatments, measures to protect the confidentiality of personal information, voluntary and reversible consent, what to do in case of adverse effects, compensation in case harm is experienced from the research, if they will continue to receive intervention after the end of the study [43].

To participate of a research, the subject of study should sign an informed consent form, which must be written with accessible language and be part of the research protocol. When the experiment is conducted with vulnerable people, the issue of informed consent is severe. Vulnerable people are those who for any reason have a reduced capacity for self-determination. In cases that the individual's competence is diminished, someone else can give the informed consent [5].

Analysis of Risks and Benefits. In any research project involving humans, the researcher should reflect on the ethical aspects of their conduct. The critical analysis of risks and benefits are very important. The researcher must keep in mind the consequences of any project that it will be proposed [5].

The risk and benefit evaluation is challenging for the research ethics committees, and this evaluation requires the involvement of stakeholders of the research, investigators, representative of community and civil society, lawyers, health authorities, etc. The risks must be evaluated through the previously conducted research analysis in the laboratory, in animals and other human groups, and it should not be limited to the individual, considering also the community and health systems [5, 43].

Bioethics and Scientific Research. The term bioethics has had different definitions through time, in its first concept, it was defined as a matter about the equilibrium in the relationship of the humans with the ecosystem and the planet. Recently, the bioethics can be defined as the systematic study of the moral dimensions of the life sciences and health care, using a variety of ethical methodologies in a multidisciplinary context [5]. The common principles of bioethics are: individual autonomy, beneficence, non-maleficence, and justice [43]. In all researches with humans, the principles of bioethics must be considered, in order to assure that the experiment preserved dignity of the human beings [5].

The principle of autonomy represents one of the ethical pillars in a research with humans, it is the ability of the participant to make decision by himself, the consent is the free. The beneficence prevents from harm, and it is the obligation to "do good". Non-maleficence is the obligation to avoid causing harm, for example it can be represents when previous experiments with animals or in vitro tests, and even computerized simulations can help predict and avoid the damages of an experiment. The justice principle is based on moral concerns [5, 43, 45].

In Brazil, the principles of Bioethics were incorporated in the resolution that handles the research with human beings (Resolution 196), which it is related with: the free and clarified consent, the ponderation between risks and benefits, the assurance that the predictable risks will be avoid, and the social relevance of the research [5].

5 Ethics Discussion

According with [24], based on 50 issues identified in the analysis of papers from 2010 to 2015, the issues in ethics were separated in 13 categories: human and robots, autonomy and self-determination, welfare of participants and researchers, privacy, individual differences, deception, forced and restricted actions, use of subliminal cues, ethical requirements and research approval, professional ethics, role of participants, children participants, animal-computer interaction.

Taking these categories as reference, this section will discuss each category with the ethical aspects used by the SE, scientific computing and HCI. Considering the fields that will be analyzed, the Software Engineering ethical aspects will be related to the professional and ethics used by industries.

Human and Robots. Considering the ethical aspects of this first category, the relation to HCI addressed by [24] is related to HRI field. The ethical concerns are about the robot replacing the humans (this possibility was discarded by HRI researches), minimization of the risks in the contact between the robot and human, if the robot should have free will, and that humans can be emotionally affected by robots.

The ethical aspect of the emotions that a human be affected about a robot encompasses different and divergent emotions like love, hate, discomfort, happiness, sadness, etc. that can be related to the person interacting with the robot of even who watch this interaction. In 2015, the company Boston Dynamics, responsible to build advanced robots with agility and mobility, released a video of a robot dog that could walk in different environment situations and keep standing when it was kicked. This video was a demonstration of the robot capabilities but it generated ethics debate, once it caused discomfort to some people. Some media vehicle and social media users expressed the concerns of the kicking behavior as wrong and cruel, others defended the action by being an experiment of the stability of the robot. To some people, the sense of cruel became a discussion of how it can affect the human social behavior in long-term by allowing this kind action with the robots. Considering that this happened in 2015, it demonstrates how the ethical aspect in HRI are still evolving.

For the SE, the ethics applied in robotics, according with [46] can use some of the guidelines from the professional codes of IEEE [20], ACM [21], and American Society of Mechanical Engineers (ASME) [47] but those codes might not be enough to contemplate particularities that involves robots. The existing codes does not emphasize that the engineers should take responsibility for their decisions, actions and creations, which it is important to protect all parties and help the professionals make ethical decisions. The authors proposed a code for robotics engineers encompassing to recognize the responsibilities for the actions and creation, respect peoples' rights, not knowingly misinform and correct existing misinformation, respect the laws applicable, disclose any conflicts of interest, "accept and offer constructive criticism", assist colleagues, take responsibilities for the well-being of: most people as possible, environmental concerns, government, profession and colleagues' reputation, meet customers' expectations and safety, company's financial and reputation.

For the scientific computing, according with [48], the ethical aspects in robotics need to be consider by the researchers based on the realistic future designs, instead of focusing in pre-defined vision of robots that might not be feasible, and that robot ethics are grounded in empirical data, by identifying the ethical implications and design challenges in existing robots. The authors emphasize the importance of the ethics based on the knowledge from social reality, how the technology is being used, and reflections and concerns based on empirical studies of robotic artifact.

Analyzing the ethical aspects of the SE and HCI, the scientific research ethics can consider the aspects from both fields. For SE, besides of following existing code of ethics related to technology, it is important that the researcher take responsibilities for the decisions and creations in order to protect and respect all parties. For the assist colleagues, and profession and colleagues' reputation, the ethics in scientific computing should be applicable to the members involved in the research. By meet customers' expectations, we can consider align the research requirements with the advisor of the project. The company's financial and reputation in this case is the institution where the research is being conducted. And, to the disclose of conflicts of interest, this might refer to the people involved in the research, as the advisor and the institution. Regarding the HCI, the ethical aspects for HCI were about concerns of the HRI. The ethical aspects mentioned should be relevant when conducting a research that involves the interaction between the human and the robot in order to guarantee the safety of person that it is interacting, the level of intelligence that a robot should have, the emotions that the person might feel about the robot.

Autonomy and Self-determination. According with the authors of [24], the participants have the right to decide to participate, refuse to continue collaborating at any time, and decide give or not the consent. All participants should be informed of the discomfort and risks that can occur during or after the experimentation.

One recent and common scenario that has been occurring is related to the web environment. The web provides the user's personal information in social media but those data should only be collected with the user consent. If the consent is not given, it is a violation of user's privacy, autonomy and self-determination.

The ethical aspects approached by the second category must be applied in any field of study in order to respect the person free will to participate to an experiment. The consent is required in all kind of experiments, requiring a physical interaction or even a form. The participant should know all possible risks of the experimentation, and the person responsible to conduct the experiment must present the information clearly and should not hide details from the participant. Some ethics discussion around the free will of people to participate of an experiment are based on cases where the person or organization conducting the experiment offers gift, money or any kind of compensation or incentive as benefit to gather more participants. Unfortunately, this practice is common by the industries for market research.

In Brazil, some companies are associated to ABEP (Brazilian Association of Research Companies) [49], which contains guidelines and recommendations for market research. Regarding the incentive with money or any kind of benefit, ABEP consider that this practice might negatively affect the research results, once the participant could be participating just for the benefit that was offered. Although, the association recognize that this is a usual practice and that the gratification might change according with the research complexity, user's profile, duration of the interview, the distance of the research location from the participant, etc. Considering some of those aspects, ABEP consider valid the granting incentives but it is totally against to the use of this practice if the researcher uses as a way to easily select participants, and if the participants use this practice to receive an alternative income. So ABEP consider that the gratification should be used only for refund for participant expenses, like transport, parking, food or eventual costs, or indemnification.

Welfare of Participants and Researchers. This category defines that the participants should be respected and protected mentally and physically. The mental well-being encompasses sensitive issues, emotion states, and self-esteem, the researchers need to be careful when approaching sensitive memories, negative emotions, or emotionally fragile individuals [24].

HCI researches can directly and indirectly involve the mental well-being of participants. Some HCI researched focus on the study of the emotions effect, so the researcher needs to be careful when approaching sensitive memories, negative emotions, or emotionally fragile individuals [24].

In Sect. 3, this work presents some of the ethical aspects from different SE, HCI, scientific research and bioethics, emphasizing the importance to procect the subject of study and do cause harm. So, all professionals and researchers from any field need to respect and protect the participants during experiments in order to avoid any physical injury or mentally affect the participant by offending, causing embarrassment or put the individual in a negative state of mind.

Privacy. The Privacy category is based on the protection users' data, maintain the anonymity of the participants, and confidentiality of the collected data [24].

The HCI researchers need to carefully design research methodology to avoid the privacy violation by collecting data that the user did not consent, like life-log information from social network, wearable devices, monitoring user's behavior, etc. [24].

It is important to keep the privacy of the users during an experiment in order to not expose any personal information, avoiding any feeling of discomfort, shame or exposure by the participant. The text, audio and video artifact should be confidential. In case of the forms, the data collected should be presented to show numbers, ranges, opinions, probabilities and metrics but it should never specify who filled what information. There are some exceptions, like the researches based on face recognition, which the research needs to expose the participant photography but it should only be published with the participant consent.

Individual Differences. This category evidence the cultural differences, different range of age, physical disabilities, etc. From the HCI field, the system should not indicate different usability with the culture that it is destined because the user might feel frustrated or discomfort. The Universal Accessibility and Universal Design focus on producing universally and accessible systems in order to build systems that attend physical disabilities such as hearing, visions, mobility, cognitive, speech, etc. [24].

The SE practiced by the industries does not always attend the universal accessibility and universal design, some of them does not even consider those aspects when gathering software requirements, in some cases it is created two different versions of the software to attend people with and without disabilities. For the cultural aspect, sometimes the software is implemented in different locations and uses different graphic interfaces or functionalities to attend different necessities, restriction of the laws according with the country or nation, or to follow the trend of each place.

From the scientific computing perspective, it is important that the research is accessible for most people as possible, especially the research community, in order to contribute with further studies and even avoid duplicate research, that can lead to plagiarism.

Deception. Deception category involves designing, manipulation and display of information in HCI. It can preserve system image or social disruption by showing a progress bar when something is being processed but some deceptions lead to clicks in something that it is not the purpose of the user's action, like advertisement, phishing and subscribe function [24].

In SE, the deception category can be related to the ethical aspect of client and customer, for the scenario when the software does not meet with the customer's expectation by not having requirements that was requested or erroneous functionality behavior.

For the scientific research, it is possible to adapt the category of Deception presented as an HCI ethical aspect by the deception in a research or paper, which it contains and objective but the information of the rest of the paper leads to a different approach and conclusion that was not what the readers expect.

Forced and Restricted Actions. It was categorized based on some HCI research that forces or restrict the user to some actions. In some cases, the system does not allow a simple task that the user should be able to execute but sometimes the system is preventing some action to guarantee the safety of the user. The ethical aspect of rather the system should allow or not some user's actions is arguable, besides the design heuristic supports that the system should be used without restrictions [24].

This category is more related with the user interaction with the system. It was not identified a relevant aspect of this category applied for the SE during the development of this paper.

Use of Subliminal Cues. It is a category that handles the subliminal cues that might interfere on the individual's behavior or decisions without the participant even notice [24].

In HCI, especially when it is related to scientific computing, the aspect of this category should be handle carefully to not provide any cue that can lead to the participant be influenced in his decisions, answers or reaction. The researcher needs to be aware to not send any subliminal message, so the experimentation does not generate false results.

In SE, the professional that conducts the interviews with the customer should gather the customer's requests, and be careful to not induce the customer to agree on the easier solution, different functionalities, or unnecessary requirements. This might lead the customer to feel uncomfortable or disappointed by receiving a software that does not attend his needs.

Ethical Requirements and Research Approval. This category is based on the necessity of the research to go through ethical review, have protocols that meet with legal and institutional requirements, and attending some previous categories as Autonomy and Self-Determination, and Privacy.

As we saw in previous sections, the researches that involves experimentations with humans should have a Research Protocol detailing the experiment and submitted to the Research Ethics Committees, that will evaluate the protocol based on ethical aspects, for example the safety of the participants and that if they are treating with respect. The experimentation can only be executed if the Research Protocol is approved.

Professional Ethics. It encompassed some the ethical aspects of accept responsibilities for the action and decisions made, not misinform participants, disclose any conflicts of interest, accept and offer constructive criticism, and assist colleagues in professional environment. In HCI, those elements ensure research competence and protect the research from damage, and the researchers should be aware of any misinterpretations of the research [24].

Since the [24] contains the analysis on papers between 2010 and 2015 [24], the elements of Professional Ethics category were based on [46], which it was already presented in this discussion for the first category (Smart System) of the applicability of ethics for robot engineers. So, the aspects of this category are also applicable for SE professional, and in scientific computing, as it was discussed before, it can be applied adapting to the researcher and the people involved in the research.

Role of Participant. In HCI research, this category encourages the participation of the stakeholders and public but the participant should have more influence than the other subjects of study [24].

In scientific computing, the role of participant is to provide relevant information or participate of activities (if it the participant agrees) to the improvement research. The research can conduct the experimentation by requesting personal information in a form or interview, request the user to interact with system or a technology that is being developed. It is common to have students from the same institution performing the experimentation but sometimes it requires people with specific characteristics or experience.

In SE the experimentation can also occur with gathering personal information in a form or interview, user interaction with the software or a new technology but in this case, usually the participants are the company staff. For the ESE, the test of the method or tool is conducted by the academic institution but the ideal was that for the participants to be practitioners (or engineers) from the industry.

Children Participation. It is regarding on the increased number of researches involving Child-Computer Interaction (CCI). The CCI is under HCI field and has the children as the focus group. It requires a special attention given the vulnerability of this group. The ethical aspect in this case does not depends only on the willingness of the child to participate but it also need a guardian to consent and make some decisions of this participation [24].

Animal-Computer Interaction (ACI). It is based on the growth technologies that monitor daily activities, and the desire of the users to track their pets. The ACI is under the HCI field [24], this field has the objective to study the interaction between the animals and technology. The ethical principles of the researches in this field are: Respect all species of the research without discrimination, "human and nonhuman participants as individuals equally deserving of consideration, respect and care", choose species only if the intention is to advance knowledge or technology for those specific species, protect physically and mentally human and nonhumans participants, allow the human and nonhuman participant to refuse the experiment at any time, obtain informed consent for humans participants and the informed consent by the legally responsible for nonhumans participants [50].

Any scientific research, including in computing field, involving animals should submit a protocol to the animal ethics committee that will evaluate if the research does not cause any harm or pain to the animal. Even if the research has the approval from the ethics committee, the researches involving animals can face some critics by the organizations in defense of animals.

6 Conclusion

The main objective of this paper was to demonstrates the relationship of the HCI with the evolution of the ethical aspects of the traditional SE and its application to scientific computing. With the analysis made in this paper, it was possible to identify tools and method of the SE that can be applied in scientific computing, and how the scientific research can contribute with the ESE by identifying new tool and methods, or improving the existing ones. The experimentations in SE usually requires humans' participation, and the field that involves the interaction between human and computer is HCI. The participation of human in experimentation involves ethical aspects in order to protect the subject of study. The discussion of Sect. 5, based on the categories from [24], shows some of the relations of the ethical aspects from HCI applied in SE and scientist computing.

The ethic is highly important in any field. There is some similarity regarding the clauses of different code ethics related to computer science field. Most of those codes of ethics set the public interests as the main factor of ethics, the roles and the responsibilities should be respected according with the clauses. Every time an experiment involves a human interaction, the tests should be approved by ethics committees. Analyzing the ethics from SE and medicine, both contain similar aspects but the differences are the level of risk, and influences in the human health and society.

Based on the discussion of the ethics of SE, HCI and scientific computing, some of the ethical aspect can be applicable, adapting to the person who is conducting the experimentation, the participants, the organization and the final product. All fields contain concerns about ethics, some are from new studies that are emerging with the growth of the technology, like in scientific research and improvement of the HCI study, and others are related to the absence of a regulatory entity of experimentation conducted by industry in some countries.

One problem with the increasing number of experiments and tests conducted by industries is the overload of ethics committees regarding the evaluation and supervision processes of the projects. This requires the investment of smart system that can help the member from ethics committees on performing their tasks. Another problem based on the theme of this paper is the diversity of researches in robotics, autonomous systems and smart systems. The projects from these fields of study (sometimes with more than one field integrated like [51]) have specific characteristics that involve users, besides of they could contain benefits and risks that are not clearly recognized.

The ethics and the codes of ethics are evolving according with the time and evolution of the researches. Software, mobile devices, sensors and robots are gaining more functionalities and autonomy, new technologies or future technologies are emerging, and the ethics need to be adapting and evolving, so the society can feel more secure, know what to expect, and what is the expected behavior in relation to these technologies.

References

1. Sommerville, I.: Software Engineering, 9th edn. Pearson Education Essex, England (2004)
2. Pressman, R.S.: Software Engineering: A Practitioner's Approach, 7th edn. Mc Graw Hill. New York, USA (2010)
3. Golub, G., Ortega, J.M.: Scientific Computing: An Introduction with Parallel Computing. Academic Press. San Diego, CA (1993)
4. Basili, V.R., Selby, R.W., Hutchens, D.H.: Experimentation in software engineering. IEEE Trans. Softw. Eng. **SE-12**, 733–743 (1986)
5. Araújo, L.Z.S.: Aspectos éticos da pesquisa científica. P. Odontol Bras. 57–63 (2003)
6. Naur, P., Randell, B.: Software Engineering. Report on a Conference sponsored by the NATO Science Committee, Garmisch, Germany (1968)
7. Cruzes, D., Mendonça, M., Basili, V., Shull, F., Jino, M.: Extracting information from experimental software engineering papers. In: XXVI International Conference of the Chilean Computer Science Society (2007)
8. Kautz, K., Abrahamsson, P.: Experimental software engineering (STESE). In: 36th Annual Hawaii International Conference on System Sciences (2003)
9. Basili, V.R.: The role of experimentation in software engineering: past, current, and future. In Proceedings of IEEE 18th International Conference on Software Eng. (1996)
10. Travassos, G.H, Santos, P.S.M., Mian, P.G., Neto, A.C.D., Biolchini, J.: An environment to support large scale experimentation in software engineering. In: 3th IEEE International Conference on Engineering of Complex Computer Systems (2008)
11. Basili, V.: The experimental paradigm in software engineering. In: Proceedings of the International Workshop on Experimental Software Engineering Issues: Critical Assessment and Future Directions (1992)
12. Roy, C.J.: Practical software engineering strategies for scientific computing. In: 19th AIAA Computational Fluid Dynamics, San Antonio, Texas (2009)
13. Borque, P., Dupuis, R.: Guide to the Software Engineering Body of Knowledge (SWEBOK), 2004 Version. IEEE Computer Society, Los Alamitos (2004)
14. Fischer, D.: User modeling in human-computer interaction. J. User Model. User-Adapt. Interact. (UMUAI) **11**, 65–86 (2001)
15. Gonçalves, T.G., Oliveira, K.M., Kolski, C.: HCI engineering integrated with capability maturity models: a study focused on requirements development (2015)
16. Barbosa, S.D.J., Silva, B.S.: Interação Humano-Computador. Editora Campus (2011)
17. Mutle, B.: Interaction with robotic technologies. In: HRI Japan, South Korea, and China. World Technology Evaluation Center, Arlington, VA, p. 59 (2012)
18. Feil-Seifer, D., Mataric, M.J.: Human-Robot Interaction (2012)
19. Gotterbarn, D., Miller, K., Rogerson, S.: Computer society and ACM approve software engineering code of ethics. In: Piner, M.-L.G. (ed.), vol. 32, pp. 84–88 (1999)
20. Electrical and Electronics Engineers (IEEE). http://www.ieee.org/
21. Association for Computing Machinery (ACM). http://www.acm.org/
22. Gotterbarn, D., Miller, K.W.: The public is the priority: making decisions using the software engineering code of ethics. Computer **42**(6), 66–73 (2009)
23. Gotterbarn, D., Miller, K.W., Rogenon, S.: Software Engineering Code of Ethics, Version 3.0. IEEE Computer Society (1997). doi:10.1109/MC.1997.625323
24. Punchoojit, L., Hongwarittorrn, N.: Research ethics in human-computer interaction. In: 2nd National Foundation for Science and Technology Development Conference on Information and Computer Science (2015)
25. Australian Computer Society. https://www.acs.org.au/

26. American Psychological Association. http://www.apa.org/
27. The British Psychological Society. http://beta.bps.org.uk/
28. User Experience Professional's Association. https://uxpa.org/
29. Aquino Jr., P.T.: PICaP: padrões e personas para expressão da diversidade de usuários no projeto de interação. Escola Politécnica, University of São Paulo. São Paulo, Brazil. Doctoral Thesis in Sistemas Digitais (2008). doi:10.11606/T.3.2008.tde-15092008-144412. Accessed 08 Feb 2017
30. Aquino Jr., P.T., Filgueiras, L.V.L.: A expressão da diversidade de usuários no projeto de interação com padrões e personas. In: Proceedings of the VIII Brazilian Symposium on Human Factors in Computing Systems (IHC 2008), pp. 1–10. Sociedade Brasileira de Computação, Porto Alegre, Brazil (2008)
31. Amaral, V., Ferreira, L.A., Aquino Jr., P.T., Castro, M.C.F.: EEG signal classification in usability experiments. In: ISSNIP Biosignals and Biorobotics Conference: Biosignals and Robotics for Better and Safer Living (BRC), Rio de Janerio, Brazil, pp. 1–5 (2013). doi:10. 1109/BRC.2013.6487469
32. Castro, M.C.F., Colombini, E.L., Aquino Jr., P.T., Arjunan, S.P., Kumar, D.K.: sEMG feature evaluation for identification of elbow angle resolution in graded arm movement. Biomed. Eng. Online 13(1), 155–164 (2014)
33. Filgueiras, L. Aquino Jr., P.T., Sakai, R., Filho, A.G., Torres, C., Barbarian, I.: Personas como modelo de usuários de serviços de governo eletrônico. In: Proceedings of the 2005 Latin American conference on Human-Computer Interaction (CLIHC 2005), pp. 319–324. ACM, New York (2005). doi:https://doi.org/10.1145/1111360.1111395
34. Goebbels, G., Aquino Jr., P.T., Lalioti, V., Goebel, M.: Supporting team work in collaborative virtual environments. In: Proceedings of ICAT 2000 - The Tenth International Conference on Artificial Reality and Telexistence (2000)
35. Barelli, R.G., Aquino Jr., P.T., Castro, M.C.F.: Mobile interface for neuroprosthesis control aiming tetraplegic users. In: 38th Annual International Conference of the IEEE Engineering in Medicine and Biology Society (EMBC), Orlando, FL, pp. 2618–2621 (2016). doi:10. 1109/EMBC.2016.7591267
36. Spink, P.K.: Ética na Pesquisa Científica. FGV 11, 37–40 (2012)
37. Shrader-Frechette, K.S.: Ethics of Scientific Research. Rowman & Littlefield Publishers Inc., New York (1994)
38. D'Angelo, J.: Ethics in Science: Ethical Misconduct in Scientific Research. CRC Press, Taylor & Francis Group, Boca Raton (2012)
39. Fundação de Amparo à Pesquisa do Estado de São Paulo. www.fapesp.br/
40. FAPESP: Código de boas práticas científicas (2011)
41. Israel, M., Hay, I.: Research Ethics for Social Scientists. SAGE Publications, London (2006)
42. Conselho Nacional de Saúde http://conselho.saude.gov.br/
43. WHO: Research ethics committees: basic concepts for capacity-building. World Health Organization (2009)
44. Munzner, R.: Regulatory issues. IEEE Eng. Med. Biol. Mag. 23(1), 207–208 (2004)
45. Gert, B., Culver, C.M., Clouser, D.: Bioethics: A Systematic Approach, 2nd edn. Oxford University Press, Oxford (2006)
46. Jones, D., Lewis, A., Richards, M., Rich, C., Schachterle, L.: A code of ethics for robotics engineers. In: We Robot, pp. 1–10 (2014)
47. American Society of Mechanical Engineers. https://www.asme.org/
48. Ljungblad, S., Nylander, S., Nørgaard, M.: Beyond speculative ethics in HRI? Ethical considerations and the relation to empirical data. In: Proceedings of the 6th International Conference on Human-Robot Interaction, pp. 191–192 (2011)

49. Associação brasileira de empresas de pesquisa. www.abep.org/
50. Mancini, C.: Animal-computer interaction: a manifesto. Interactions **18**, 69–73 (2011)
51. Santos, T.F., Castro, D.G., Masiero, A.A., Aquino Junior, P.T.: Behavioral persona for human-robot interaction: a study based on pet robot. In: Kurosu, M. (ed.) HCI 2014. LNCS, vol. 8511, pp. 687–696. Springer, Cham (2014). doi:10.1007/978-3-319-07230-2_65

Technical to Teachable

The Flint Water Crisis and the Design of Instructions for Assembling Water Sampling Kits

Audrey R. Zarb, Shawn P. McElmurry, and Judith A. Moldenhauer(✉)

Wayne State University, Detroit, MI, USA
{azarb,s.mcelmurry,judith.moldenhauer}@wayne.edu

Abstract. In April 2014, the source of drinking water in Flint, Michigan, was changed from Detroit to the Flint River. This resulted in dangerously high levels of lead and a coinciding rise in cases of Legionnaire's Disease. In response, the Flint Area Community Health & Environment Partnership (FACHEP) is monitoring the amount of *Legionella* bacteria in home water systems. The complexity and scope of the water sampling is daunting: nearly 200 Flint area homes were tested in 2016 alone; each home has three sampling locations with a distinct set (or kit) of collection components and procedures to ensure accurate analysis; and individuals with different levels of sampling experience are assembling and using the kits. Managing the large volume of water samples and materials requires careful preparation and training; the FACHEP Water Sampling Kit Assembly Guidebook was developed to address this need. This paper describes the context and decisions that framed the design of the Guidebook, a user-centered training tool enabling individuals with a wide range of scientific background to accurately and efficiently assemble sampling kits.

Keywords: User-centered design · Research translation · Information design · Visual communication · Emergency response research · Instructional design · Scientific communication · Technical writing

1 Introduction/Background: Unique Instructional Challenges in Emergency Response Research

"By choosing the right words, you can take an idea that's happening in your head and try to make an idea like it happen in someone else's. That's what's happening right now" [6].

2 The Flint Water Crisis and the FACHEP Program

In April 2014, a decision to change the source of drinking water in Flint, Michigan, caused extensive corrosion to distribution pipes resulting in dangerously high levels of lead. This switch coincided with a rise in the occurrence of Legionnaires' Disease in

© Springer International Publishing AG 2017
A. Marcus and W. Wang (Eds.): DUXU 2017, Part I, LNCS 10288, pp. 697–710, 2017.
DOI: 10.1007/978-3-319-58634-2_50

Fig. 1. Photo of a bottle of water in the bathroom of a Flint resident's home shows the normalization of water bottles in daily life as a result of the Flint water crisis. Although residents are encouraged to now use faucet filters, many continue to use bottled water for cooking, brushing teeth, and even bathing.

and around Flint. Bottled water became a component of daily life for thousands of Flint residents who were concerned about the safety of their drinking water (Fig. 1).

In response to this public health crisis, the Flint Area Community Health & Environment Partnership (FACHEP), an independent "enhanced disease surveillance and environmental monitoring program" lead by Wayne State University, was assembled to help quantify the Legionella bacteria in the Flint drinking water distribution system and assess the associated risk to Flint residents [3]. This undertaking aims to collect environmental samples from nearly 850 home water systems in three different cities over the course of two years and involves the collaboration of experts from five major research universities, healthcare institutions, government agencies and numerous community organizations.

The collection of Legionella samples involves several unique challenges: (1) collection must occur during the summer months because the bacteria is most prevalent in warm temperatures, and (2), as a precautionary preservative measure, each kit can only be prepared a maximum of two weeks before use. All of the collection and kit assembly work, therefore, is concentrated into a short span of 10–16 weeks. The sample collection protocol for the FACHEP Legionella monitoring program uses a comprehensive sequence of four distinct collection protocols to extract water and biofilm samples from three discrete sampling locations in resident homes: the hot water heater, shower, and kitchen faucet. Each of the sampling sites requires up to 61 separate specialty components, which must be assembled into "sample collection kits" (Fig. 2) with methodical preparation and systematic attention. The consistency of the sampling and integrity of the collected data depends on the proper construction of the sample kits to ensure that every sample arrives at its intended analysis destination without contamination or damage.

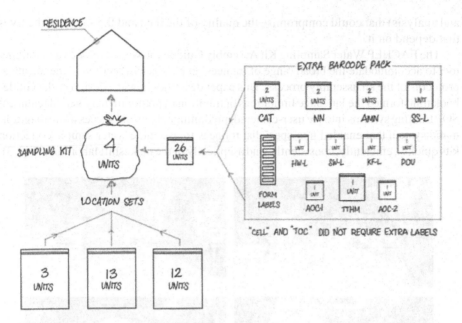

Fig. 2. Collection of the environmental samples in each residence required 61 individual items to be grouped as units, assembled into sets, and packed together as a kit. Each component of the kit served a critical role to the collection process including a meticulously packed "extra barcode label pack" that kept extra labels needed for post-collection analysis clean and safe during the collection process so they could be reunited with their respective sample container before being shipped to the analysis destination.

Normally, a typical training model for a laboratory protocol like sample collection kit assembly would be the use of a technical document called a standard operating procedure (SOP), which is designed for use in a controlled environment by a trained technician. For the FACHEP program, however, only the most critical preparatory steps of the kit materials were performed in the Environmental Chemistry Research Laboratory (ECRL) at Wayne State University and the remainder of the preparation and assembly had to be done at the temporary field station in Flint where laboratory amenities - industrial air filtration system, multi-step water purification system, and the chemical/biological safety hoods – used to keep the materials "ultra clean" (meaning free of dust, trace chemicals, DNA, and any sort of environmental contamination) were not available. Extra precautions were taken to maintain "laboratory clean" conditions where the collection kits would be assembled and samples processed. For trained laboratory personnel, adjusting to the aseptic technique protocols would be standard business and no formal group training program would have been needed. However, for a mixed staff of Flint residents and university team members, our trainees – who came to the task from a wide range of experience with and familiarity of environmental sampling protocol, laboratory technique, equipment, and materials – training was still needed to prevent mistakes or serious disruptions to downstream processes (i.e. collection, sample processing, and analysis) that could compromise the quality of the data and the safety of the lives that depend on it.

The FACHEP Water Sampling Kit Assembly Guidebook was developed as a training tool to accommodate the broad range of trainees' experience in relation to the technical protocols of the kit assembly process. This paper describes how the design of the Guidebook transformed the language limitations of traditional, predominately verbal technical SOP training systems into the user-centered, predominately visual successfully diagrammatic system that enabled non-specialist trainees to assemble water sample collection kits quickly, efficiently, consistently, and aseptically in the makeshift laboratory (Fig. 3).

Fig. 3. An ECRL technician demonstrates the kit assembly protocol adapted for use in the FACHEP field station housed in a former elementary school. Assembly tasks for a "circle" kit include arranging the materials on a sterilized assembly table (upper left); labeling sample containers with their barcode labels (upper right); dividing the materials into three separate location sets (lower left); and finally packing the sets and the barcode label pack into a complete kit (lower right).

3   Materials and Methods

The unexpected transition of field station staff from specialty to nonspecialty came after existing FACHEP staff had completed their training. A separate module for kit assembly had not been included in the original program because, under typical conditions, an SOP would have sufficed. The Guidebook was completed over the course of a single week using the note-taking application Notability (Ginger Labs), an iPad pro and apple pencil (Apple Inc.) by a FACHEP staff member with a background in biological science and communication design who had been assigned to develop the organizational program for field station operations and logistics. Despite limited time, the development of the FACHEP Water Sampling Kit Assembly Guidebook followed a "people-centred" model described by David Sless in "Measuring Information Design" by evaluating the existing instructional system in context of the trainees' experience, setting benchmarks for needed modifications, and establishing baseline usability with a prototype before implementing the new training tool in the working system [11].

Interpreting the performance tasks from written instruction in a typical laboratory operating procedure (SOP) depends heavily on a user's previous experience. Theoretically, a trained technician should be able to perform a new task within their specialty range based on the SOP without extensive guidance or instruction but nonspecialty users would face limitations of experience/familiarity with the project and language (in the forms of literacy, technical jargon, or English as a second language (ESL). To test this, undergraduate interns were asked to assemble kits using only the written instructions in the SOP. Although the interns had performed similar tasks over the course of their ECRL internship, they had not been formally trained on the FACHEP sampling kit assembly protocol. From the written directions, the student interns were able to aggregate and pack kits using the SOP but the process took a long time (over an hour) and they reported difficulty understanding the barcode labeling system. The students found that the majority of their knowledge base for successfully interpreting the SOP was drawn from their summer training - such as the difference between a "vial" and a "tube", knowing how to judge if a container had been compromised, or how to identify which kit type was needed for the four different collection protocols. The students also pointed out that the skills they had learned that summer reading (and writing) SOPs also contributed to their success. They knew how to navigate the format of the instructions and how to find clarifying information in case something did not make sense. Such familiarity with handling and preparation techniques for each type of container and previous experience interpreting instructions from a SOP would not be accessible for new trainees.

Based on the intern's feedback, the information transfer objectives were translated out of verbal format using visual language to (1) communicate the importance of the collection kits to the safety of drinking water; (2) identify the separate components that were needed for each of the four collection protocols; and (3) demonstrate how to put these components together to make the kits. The level of detail for the instructions was based on a hypothetical minimum amount of information needed to communicate the objectives of kit assembly. The resulting prototype was an easy-to-use 32-page illustrated guide that showed the kit-making performance tasks in a series of step-by-step diagrams for each of the four types of sample collection kits that were almost completely nonverbal.

The Guidebook introduced the kit materials and task sequences in visual language (symbols, icons, and colors) that enabled the user to follow the pictures through the process narrative and reinforced the association between identity of the objects and the performance tasks tightly integrating the visual language with the spatial arrangement and organization system of the field station (Fig. 4). The Guidebook and its diagrams of the kit materials and task sequences are an examples of what Tetlan and Marschalek call a "visual-based format" in which people process information through a "fluid reading format" incorporating words, images, shapes, space and symbols [12, p. 68]; the traditional SOP is the opposite, "structured in primarily linear text format …[that] can discourage continued engagement with the material" [12, p. 71]. Technical language, although useful for communication for specialized context, is not always necessary to transfer the knowledge of how a system works. In his book

The Thing Explainer – complicated stuff in simple words, former NASA physicist and web comic artist Randall Munroe demonstrated this by using only 1000 of the most commonly used English words and hand-drawn illustrations. In this style, Munroe made brilliant use of simple language and visuals to explain the basic working functions of a long list of "complicated stuff" including a space station, living cells, and evolutionary taxonomy [6].

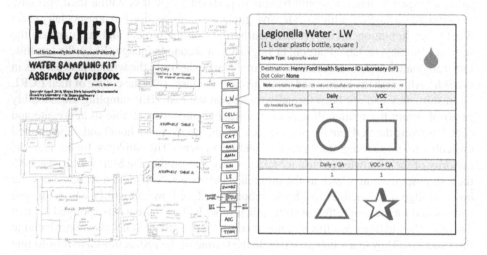

Fig. 4. Use of Tufte's principles shown in identifying kit components and in organizing the sequence of kit assembly: The kit assembly materials were stored in protective bins and arranged in the FACHEP field station laboratory space (left) in an analogous order to the collection protocol with labels (right) that corresponded to the kit type shapes in the Assembly Guide. The number above the shape informed the user how many items were needed to make kits of each shape type.

The information interface of the Guidebook uses a visualization scheme for the components and assembly diagrams that employs the composition principles cited by Edward Tufte in his book, *Envisioning Information*: (1) macro/micro relationships, (2) layering and separation, (3) small multiples, (4) color and information, and (5) the narrative of time and space [13]. For example, the sequencing of kit assembly activity enables the trainee to see the relationship between a container in different configurations – e.g., part of its group, with the other kit components, with its labeling choices – and easily adjust their understanding of that container to a variety of diagrammatic contexts (macro/micro reading). The kit components and associated group clusters use color, shape, and placement to distinguish themselves (layering and separation, color and information, narrative of space and time) (Fig. 6a–d). The diagrams of the many labeling options are clear examples of small multiples: the ordered nature of the visual elements allows the important details to be revealed. The Guidebook packages the amount of complex information into easily understood icons and diagrams since "there are limits to how much graphic information can be absorbed" [2, p. 14]. Only one type of information was communicated by each element of visual language and their meanings were carefully synced with upstream and downstream systems to prevent confusion and cognitive overload.

Information Chunking. Using this visualization scheme for the sequence and components, training for the kit assembly moved from the traditional predominately verbal, specialist oriented SOP to a format that integrated visual and verbal material into one that was predominately visual. The design of the diagrams in the Guidebook are examples of what Matthew Peterson refers to as a "fully integrated strategy for text-image" in which "text exists in discrete 'chunks' either embedded in an imaginal space (within an image) or associated with individual images" [8]. Each kit component was first shown as a part of a larger unit for context before it was broken down into its containing parts. Similarly, complex sequences were presented as a smaller series of "doable tasks" (material aggregation, grouping into sets by location, labeling, and packaging). For example, using icons to represent the three sampling location categories (the hot water heaters, the shower and the sink), the Guidebook emphasized an important grouping cluster that would be central to the division of the materials and understanding the labeling system. Once the function of the kit as a unit was established the kits were expanded into the four kit types. The individual kit components were introduced by reviewing the illustrated symbol key (Fig. 5) and a demonstration kit so that trainees could begin to associate the real-life versions with the symbol. As a context framework, each kit type was presented as a system of shape with most basic kit being the "circle kit," and then the three variations of this basic kit by shapes that increased in complexity (triangle, square, star, respectively). As more containers were added, the shapes of the kits grew more complex (Fig. 6a). By gradually layering information, the assembly

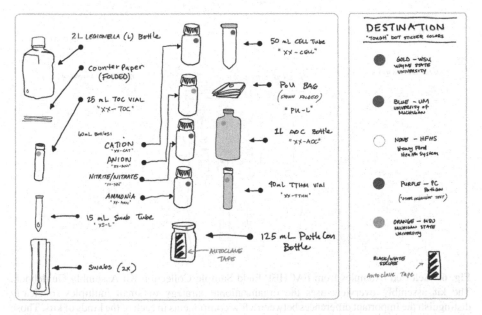

Fig. 5. Illustrated training guidebook reduced reliance on technical jargon and improved information accessibility by presenting sample collection materials as images. The chunking of information enables the user to make visual connections between a container and its label options, emphasizing the importance of those different label options.

instructions used the chunking of information to establish pattern recognition [1] and a hierarchy of relational structures [4] to create the roadmap of doable tasks.

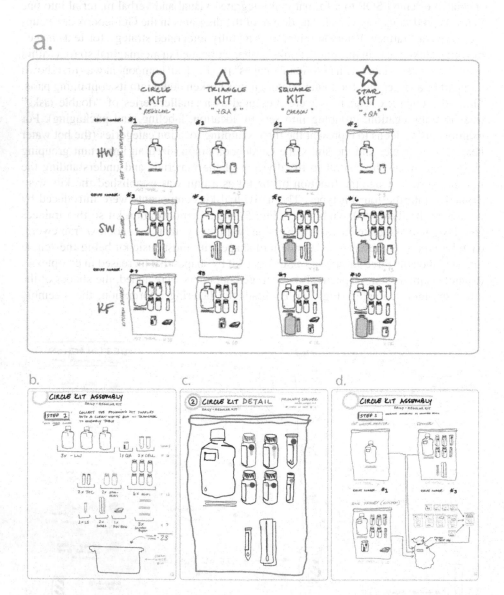

Fig. 6. Selected examples from FACHEP Field Sample Collection Kit Assembly Guidebook. The kit assembly overview uses the organizational strategy of small multiples to clearly distinguish the important differences between a few components in each of the kinds of kits. Those differences are called out thorough the use of shape, color, and placement. This pattern of visual signaling continues in the circle kit assembly where information becomes more specific: how many of each kind of container is needed for that particular kit. And the detail of the circle kit use color and small multiples to highlight the different labels assigned to each component.

Using Miller's concept of chunks of information [5] the diagrams of the Guidebook are essentially maps for assembling the kits. The concept of chunks of information relates to the "amount of information" that individuals can retain – "chunks of information is constant for immediate memory" [5, p. 349]. Thus the ability of individuals to grasp information and process it depends on visually organizing information in discrete packets so that the "process of memorizing may be simply the formation of chunks, or groups of items that go together, until there are few enough chunks so that we can recall all the items" [5, p. 351]. The diagrams operate as a combination of the route and survey maps: route knowledge of "landmarks that can be mentally connected into a sequence" and a survey knowledge that "combine[s] understanding of how landmarks and routes are connected [to] enable individuals to infer new paths" [2]. The result is a "spatial mental model known as a 'cognitive map'" [2, p. 9] of the kit assembly process. The spatial association emphasized that the sets divided up items that would be physically carried and used in different locations within the house and therefore needed to be packed accordingly. Because the ultimate function of the kit was to be used by the sample collection team and ultimately impacted the end fate of each sample, any aspects of kit assembly sequence which were analogous to downstream performance systems (i.e. collection, sample check-in, shipping, etc.) were aligned whenever possible including the way the room was set up: the bins in which the kit-making supplies were stored were arranged in the same order that the collection team collected the samples; each bin was labeled with the name and label code of the container as well as the shape codes showing how many of each item were needed to make each kit type (Fig. 4, right). The grouping clusters of components and the organization of containers assigned to easily recognizable simple shapes uses "chunked information" to enable trainees, who often have limited knowledge of scientific materials and procedures, to accurately and efficiently assemble the kits.

4   User Testing

The first FACHEP staff members hired to assist with field station operations started their training several weeks before the collection campaign began which provided an opportunity to test the modified training guide with face-to-face guidance of the field station laboratory manager. With no previous experience in environmental sample collection or laboratory SOP, the perspective of these first trainees as the first non-specialist was extremely valuable to the development of the document. Although they had no previous scientific or technical training, both trainees were able to aggregate the kit materials and assemble the kits. One of the trainees with literacy limitations was not able to master the labeling task, but this was accommodated for by dividing trainees into specialty assignments so that literacy-focused tasks (labeling) were performed by one trainee and literacy-light tasks were performed by the other. This round of user testing was successful but required considerable time investment that was not available for subsequent trainee groups.

5 Refining and Implementation

After adjusting diagrams to reflect the feedback of the first two trainees (Fig. 7), use of the guide was implemented for the training of 26 other people in various roles of the FACHEP program: extending the system first to the water collection team and then to the other members of the FACHEP public health, community resource, and navigation teams. The water collection team had been trained in the collection protocol. Similarly, some of the public health team had previous laboratory research experience.

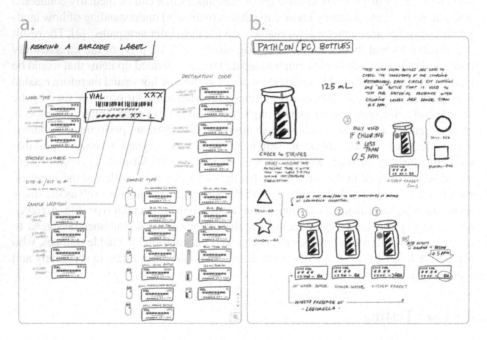

Fig. 7. Two excerpts of updated diagrams based on user-feedback. Complicated tasks like labeling was requested in user testing and so a new diagram (a) broke down the process. Another sticking point was one bottle that was used for several different purposes and another diagram was used to show the labels and kits for which the bottles were needed (b). Addition of such clarifying detail promoted communication between teams and further examples of the use of small multiples to emphasize important distinctions in information and application.

6 Results and Continual Monitoring

User Response. The use and sequence of the instructional diagrams in the Guidebook has been a crucial component in the successful management of the large volume of materials and samples associated with the FACHEP project. The visual guide was a useful tool to overcome language limitations because users did not need to know the different names or uses of the materials, only match the items with the illustrations and perform the process demonstrated in the manual. The illustrations also helped clarify instructions for users who were specialty experts in related or peripheral fields (i.e. medicine, chemistry, etc.) so that analogous terms were not juxtaposed or mistranslated. The visual instructions also proved helpful for trainees for which English was a second language because the visual presentation did not require translation from one verbal language to another before the performance association was made. Three of the four collection team members who completed kit making training repeatedly provided positive feedback for the guide saying that the organization and instruction from the kit-making training processes reinforced the steps of the collection protocol and helped them remember details better during collection. They especially expressed appreciation because they noticed that the kits had fewer mistakes when people used the guide.

The success of the Guidebook was evaluated using a numeric rubric for training success based on observed performances and proficiency with the assembly protocol (Table 1). 77% of the trainees demonstrated a proficient working knowledge of the kit assembly process to the end that they could independently and consistently assemble and label a complete kit in under an hour (skill level of 3 or 4). 30% of these proficient individuals demonstrated a confident mastery of the process (skill level 4) to the end that they could consistently build correct kits quickly (5–30 min) and effectively teach others. The remaining 23% of trainees consisted primarily of the faculty leadership committee who participated in kit-assembly training but could not invest the practice time or student volunteers who assisted at the field station for only one or two days. Even so, all of these individuals were still able to perform at least one grouping of the kit assembly tasks (preparatory tasks, material aggregation, labeling, etc.) in order to make a significant contribution to the kit-making system (skill level 1 or 2).

Table 1. Performance rubric used to measure the level of skills trainees demonstrated after training with the FACHEP Water Sample Kit Assembly Guidebook. 77% of trainees demonstrated a proficient working knowledge of the kit assembly process at the end of their training (skill level of 3 or higher).

Kit assembly objectives reached	Skill level
Beginner: has observed training demonstrations but needs guided practice to successfully construct kits	0
Trainee: requires some guidance to complete kit assembly but makes a significant contribution to preparatory tasks and performs at least one grouping of kit assembly tasks (preparatory tasks, material aggregation, labeling, etc.)	1
Assistant: is able to performs all kit assembly tasks with occasional direction from peers; makes a significant contribution to the kit-making system	2
Proficient: demonstrates consistent working knowledge of the kit assembly process; constructs kit independently in under an hour	3
Master: builds consistently build correct kits quickly (5–30 min); participates in cooperative peer teaching	4

Of the individuals trained to build kits (n = 30), most trainees (77%) initially learned to make kits using the visual instructions and only the ECRL lab members and two team scientists with experimental science experience ever used the written instructions to construct kits. Although written and video instructions were available, all kit-makers who participated in cooperative team teaching trained peers with the visual directions and the visual instructions were used as the primary reference tool in the field station lab space. Only 70% of the kit-making trainees had been present for the contextual all-team training days and only 39% of those individuals had participated in the formal face-to-face sample collection training. All collection trainees (n = 18) initially received verbal training instructions with a traditional SOP. After the collection campaign started, 67% of the sample collection trainees also received kit-assembly training and 75% of these dual trainees reported that the visual instructions of the kit-making training helped reinforce aspects of the collection protocols that had been difficult to remember or had even helped elucidate errors in their methods.

7 Conclusions

Overall, the visual guide was considered highly successful since the design and organizational systems helped manage the limited time of the specialty staff and personnel skills to accomplish the 2016 FACHEP summer objectives, collecting nearly 5000 samples from 188 Flint homes in ten weeks. The most rewarding benefit of the guidebook was the way it promoted communication between program components of the different teams. Instead of remaining segregated by specialty, the kit-making space of the field station laboratory became a space where staff members from different teams (navigation, community resource, public health, sample collection, field station operation, and leadership) could work together and the kits themselves became the shared reference point into which team members could relate to their coworkers. Observing the success of individuals trained with the kit-assembly guide, a mid-campaign training "check-in" session was conducted to bring together the collection and kit-assembly teams (as well as members of the faculty leadership committee and a visiting professor) to provide more context to both teams and clarify how "upstream" details that might seem superfluous without context – like tying the twist tie tightly or forgetting a container – are important to sensitive "downstream" processes and play an important role in the success of the whole program. Trainees or technicians who felt confident in their mastery of tasks and felt they did not need additional training were encouraged to participate as instructional assistants and demonstrated portions of the protocols, inviting group feedback and discussion to make sure that everyone shared the same understanding and methods. This enabled several important errors in protocol to be identified, adjusted and, most importantly, gave both teams a pathway of communication and sense of orientation on how their roles were connected.

Going Further. Since the focus of the emergency-response project was focused on the collection of technical data and physical samples, a formal evaluation of the kit-assembly training system or a universal assessment of the "big-picture" communication system was not possible. The data for this metric was developed based on observations from a single trainer and the feedback from users was collected anecdotally in conversations and informal meetings. In this situation, having a training tool that was easily accessible to all teammates was extremely helpful on many levels, but, the subjectivity of a performance-based metric is limited in the extrapolations that can be made to the success of the user-centered design [11] and a more formal user-experience survey is being developed for the next phase of the FACHEP sampling campaign (summer 2017) that will provide more descriptive data. The successful integration of information design in other research interventions demonstrates the value of prioritizing design objectives to optimize resources and maximize outcomes of scientific initiatives, community health programs and public policy [7, 9, 10]. The extent to which attribution of the program's success can be ascribed to the design of the FACHEP Water Sample Kit Assembly guide or the organization of the workflow system remains to be determined in the coming season.

Acknowledgements. Many sincere thanks to the inspiring Flint residents who have provided so much guidance, wisdom, patience and support throughout this project. Thank you to faculty advisors and the FACHEP team, particularly: Shawn McElmurry, Judith Moldenhauer, Paul Kilgore, Matt Seeger, Joanne Sobeck, Nancy Love, Michelle Swanson, Laura Sullivan and Ben Pauli. Special thanks to Lara Treemore-Spears, Carol Miller, and the Healthy Urban Waters initiative of the WSU Urban Watershed Environmental Research Group (UWERG) sponsored by the Erb Family Foundation; the ECRL staff and volunteers and our 2016 summer interns: Jamie Stafford and Eric Peltola. The work reported in this publication was supported by Michigan Department of Health and Human Services under contract number 20163753-00. The content is solely the responsibility of the authors and does not necessarily represent the official views of the Michigan Department of Health and Human Services.

Image credits for all illustrations, diagrams, photos and figures: Audrey R. Zarb.

References

1. Cairo, A.: The Functional Art: An Introduction to Information Graphics and Visualization. New Riders, San Francisco (2013)
2. Cheng, K., Pérez-Kriz, S.: Map design for complex architecture: a user study of maps and wayfinding. Visible Lang. **48**(2), 6 (2014)
3. FACHEP: FACHEP Phase II: enhanced disease surveillance and environmental monitoring in flint, MI. Program Narrative, Wayne State University, Department of Civil and Environmental Engineering, FACHEP (Flint Area Community Health & Environment Partnership), Detroit, MI (2016)
4. Meirelles, I.: Design for Information. Rockport Publishers, Beverly (2013)
5. Miller, G.A.: The magical number seven, plus or minus two: some limits on our capacity for processing information. Psychol. Rev. **63**(2), 81 (1956)
6. Munroe, G.: Thing Explainer: Complicated Stuff in Simple Words. Hachette, UK (2015)
7. Otten, J.J., Cheng, K., Drewnowski, A.: Infographics and public policy: using data visualization to convey complex information. Health Aff. **34**(11), 1901–1907 (2015)
8. Peterson, M.O.: The integration of text and image in media and its impact on reader interest. Visible Lang. **48**(1), 22–39 (2014)
9. Rodríguez Estrada, F.C., Davis, L.S.: Improving visual communication of science through the incorporation of graphic design theories and practices into science communication. Sci. Commun. **37**(1), 140–148 (2015)
10. Shea, M., Mozafari, C.: Communicating complexity in transdisciplinary science teams for policy: applied stasis theory for organizing and assembling collaboration. Commun. Des. Q. Rev. **2**(3), 20–24 (2014)

11. Sless, D.: Measuring information design. Inf. Des. J. **16**(3), 250–258 (2008)
12. Tetlan, L., Marschalek, D.: How humans process visual information: a focused primer for designing information. Visible Lang. **50**(3), 65 (2016)
13. Tufte, E.R.: Envisioning Information. Graphics Press, Cheshire (1991)

DUXU Education and Training

Using Prototyping in Authentic Learning of Human-Centred Design of Mobile Apps

Ghislain Maurice Norbert Isabwe[(⊠)], Hellen Mula Apondi Olum,
and Maren Schelbred Thormodsæter

ICT Department, University of Agder,
Jon Lilletuns vei 9, 4879 Grimstad, Norway
maurice.isabwe@uia.no, mulaponzi@yahoo.com,
maren_92_z@hotmail.com

Abstract. Recent advances in mobile technology have seen a sharp increase in the number of mobile applications across various application domains. The challenge remains that many software development teams may lack appropriate competences to design usable and human-centred interactive systems. This can negatively affect the usability and the user experience. In this article, we present how to learn the human-centred design process using an authentic learning approach. Students need to investigate, discuss, construct new knowledge and apply theoretical concepts to address real world problems. The main purpose of authentic learning as a pedagogical approach is to position the subject of study into a realistic context. That gives life to learning content from a theoretical, abstract level into a more professional, real-world context. Our study considers a post-graduate level course. The learning experience includes flipped classroom and problem based learning through a design project. Learners define a real-world problem to be addressed by a design solution. One of the intended learning outcomes is the learner's ability to use prototyping techniques for mastering HCD process. Learners use prototyping tools in the same way as professionals in the field. At the end of the course, students demonstrated mastery of key methods and techniques as well as the psychology foundations, and tools used in interaction design. Summative assessment results confirmed that authentic learning approach leads to deep learning of key concepts and development of a skills set necessary for designing usable interactive systems for human use.

Keywords: Human-centred design · Prototyping · Authentic learning

1 Introduction

The use of mobile applications in everyday activities has become more of a norm in many parts of the world. The application scenarios vary from social communications, gaming and entertainment to production and real world problem solving. This increase in the use of mobile technology solutions requires improvement in teaching approaches, with increased awareness regarding the needs of the intended users. Traditionally, in-class exercises have been used as part of the active learning instructional strategy, whereby students are involved in doing tasks to reify their learning. To that end, active

© Springer International Publishing AG 2017
A. Marcus and W. Wang (Eds.): DUXU 2017, Part I, LNCS 10288, pp. 713–726, 2017.
DOI: 10.1007/978-3-319-58634-2_51

learning can help students grasp the main concepts on one hand, but also apply them through problem solving based on the given tasks. However, the relevancy of the class-based tasks remains a challenge as the exercises may not necessarily represent real world scenarios. While learning the design of interactive systems for human use, students need to investigate, discuss, construct new knowledge and apply theoretical concepts to address real world problems. Herrington et al. [1] define authentic learning as "a pedagogical approach that situates learning tasks in the context of future use". As promising as authentic learning may sound for different subject areas, teaching design comes with challenges of its own. That is mainly due to the fact that design subjects involve creativity, imagination and exploration of uncharted territories where there is no clear-cut boundaries between the correct and incorrect approach to problem solving. Corina [2] indicated that teaching interaction design requires the transfer of skills acquired from practitioners, to match the theoretical foundations with the practice in industry. The authors suggest that in authentic learning, tasks should not merely be given to students for practicing the acquired skills but the tasks are an integral part of the learning experience allowing more engagement with the content. The main purpose of authentic learning as a pedagogical approach is to make the subject of study into a realistic context. That gives life to learning content from a theoretical, abstract level into a more professional, real-world context. As promising as authentic learning may sound for different subject areas, teaching design comes with challenges of its own. Several approaches to the teaching of systems development have been practiced in the past, mostly focusing on how to provide the required functionality within a system. However, interaction design as a field of study, focuses on designing interactive systems that support the way humans communicate and interact in their everyday activities. Such systems should enhance the lives of those using the systems, and therefore the design process should primarily focus on the users. Human-centred design (HCD) is an "approach to systems design and development that aims to make interactive systems more usable by focusing on the use of the system and applying human factors/ergonomics and usability knowledge and techniques" [3]. This article presents a pedagogical approach to teaching human-centred design process to post-graduate students. The intention is to suggest how to make the course more effective to ensure that learners are capable of applying the key concepts at the end of the course.

The next section introduces the course and teaching methods, followed by a practical approach to conceptualizing interaction in Sect. 3. The system design is presented in Sect. 4, and concluding remarks are discussed in Sect. 5.

2 Authentic Learning of Human-Centred Design

Interaction design is a Master's level course offered at the University of Agder, in Norway. This course is compulsory in the Multimedia & Educational Technology programme, but it is also offered as an elective course to master programme in Information and Communication Technology. Typically, a class of 15–20 students is expected. This course combines face-to-face lectures and online learning (i.e. blended learning) in addition to design project work. The learning experience includes flipped classroom, whereby learners are expected to go through the learning materials prior to participation in face-to-face lectures and classrooms activities. Further on, problem based learning [4] pedagogy is applied through the design project. Jonassen [4] defines problem based learning (PBL) as a method to prepare students for real-world settings. He suggests that in problem based learning (PBL), "knowledge building is stimulated by the problem and applied back to the problem" (Fig. 1).

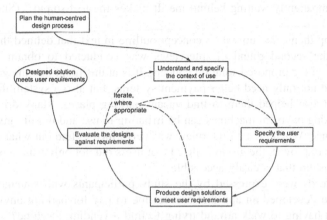

Fig. 1. Interdependence of human-centred design activities [3]

While PBL is tightly connected to authentic learning, the latter requires that students' activity comprises of real world problems which resembles the work of professionals [5]. Learners are required to think of a problem that can be addressed by a design solution. The project assignment is to develop an interactive system by applying human-centred design approach. However, it is not sufficient to work on any design project. The problem space should be situated in the real world: on one hand to increase students' motivation, but on the other hand to connect the learning with real world issues thus better preparing students for the work environment.

This paper reports on a group project undertaken by two female students (20–30 years old) in autumn 2015. The aim is to investigate the potential of prototyping to develop human-centred design competence through authentic learning methodology. Prototyping tools are used in the same way as they are being used by professionals in the field. The intention is to allow students apply open-ended enquiry, increase their creativity and achieve mastery learning of key aspects of human-centred design as well as higher order cognitive skills.

3   Conceptualizing Mobile Interaction

3.1   User Involvement

The design of this system is based on human-centred approach. The main focus is on the user in terms of needs and requirements in order to enhance effectiveness, efficiency and improve user's everyday life.

At the start of the course, one of the class members came up with an idea of improving parking payment machines. This member claimed that these machines were difficult to use and often resulted into people waiting in long queues. The group then had to conduct the first survey to find out if this was true. This was discussed with other class members and it became clear that there was a need to improve these machines. "One of the worst moments in my life is trying to operate these machines while there are people impatiently waiting behind me. It makes me feel stupid." (Statement from one member)

The group then came up with a concept outline in text that defined the project. At this stage, the second round of interviews was conducted to obtain feedback on acceptability of the proposed solution concept. It is at this point that the group realized that users did not only need better payment systems, but also a system that supported mobility and also helped them to find vacant parking places. Many drivers feel that existing parking payment machines can be irritating to use and usually give a negative user experience. When the first interview was performed to find out what exactly users wanted to be improved, the group realized that users did not only want a better system, but also a system that is easily accessible.

User's needs were expressed by the study participants with statements such as: "What if you developed an app that enables me to pay for parking anywhere at any time without having to walk around trying to find a vending machine?"

Hence, a decision was reached to design a mobile application (app) for parking payment.

The app was named "SafePark" and is mainly meant to improve drivers' everyday lives by enabling them easily find vacant parking as well as process the payment. This system should be efficient to allow a user to make payments without going through unnecessary processes that can be time consuming and irritating. This is the main concept from which other functionalities were developed through an iterative design process, based on regular user feedback.

Potential users have been involved throughout the iterative design process to ensure that the designer's mental model and user's mental model [6] are brought together. The user feedback would be effectively used to improve system usability.

3.2   Problem Space and Data Gathering for Requirements

There are a few parking applications in the Norwegian market today, one of them being "EasyPark". This application enables users to buy a parking ticket by using their mobile phones. The application is also easy to use.

However, during the first interviews the group found out that users were dissatisfied with this app. Most of the study participants wanted a parking app that can help to find parking areas and shows if there were vacant spaces. This provided ideas on some of the functionalities that were to be implemented to develop a parking app with high usability. The next stage required to analyse the context of using a framework proposed by Benyon [7]: *People, Activities, Context and Technology* (PACT). The analysis aims to understand and describe the people (users) who undertake user tasks in given context using technology solutions. This was achieved using data gathering techniques including (a) *user stories*, (b) *scenarios* and (c) *personas*.

User stories [8] help designers to create a simplified version of requirements as they are used to determine the characteristics of the user, what they want and why.

A user story presents what the user wants to do with a given functionality, and that's described from the user's perspective as shown in (Table 1).

Table 1. User stories

User stories
(1) **As a** driver - **I want, during the** payment of my parking ticket using my mobile phone - **To be able to** use an app/send SMS while sitting in my car - **In order to** pay without waiting in a queue - **So that** that I don't waste time
(2) **As** a person that has parked a car - **I want, during the** use of my parking app - **To be able to** see how much time I have left on my parking ticket - **In order to** be able to update/extend the time - **So that** I do not have to leave an important meeting to run to the parking meter because my parking ticket is running out of time

User stories [8] help designers to create a simplified version of requirements as they are used to determine the characteristics of the user, what they want and why.

Table 2. Scenario

1. It is early on a Monday morning and Ove has three different meetings to attend in three different places
2. Before leaving the house, he makes entry into his parking app, so the system can help him spot nearest parking lots to where he will be attending the meetings
3. He drives into town and checks on his app to find out if there are any vacant places in the nearest parking lot
4. There are two places left and by the help of his parking app, he finds one of them and parks the car
5. Ove doesn't know how long he has to be at the meeting, so he uses the payment function on the parking app to pay for one hour
6. While in a meeting, he receives a notification saying that he has only five minutes left to his parking time
7. Since there are no signs that this meeting is ending soon, he updates the parking time to 30 min more
8. When he is finished with the meeting, he updates his schedule on the app that gives him details on where to park for the next meeting

Scenarios [9] are narratives that describe human activities and tasks allowing exploration and discussion of contexts, needs, and requirements as shown in Table 2.

Personas represent different users that the system is being designed for. They should have a name, the background and define the goals and what users aim to do [7] (Table 3).

Table 3. Persona

Persona: Ove Aslaksen
• 34-year old man
• Drives every day to work
• Works as a sales and marketing officer and therefore fully dependant on driving around in his car
• Needs to be able to park anywhere at any time according to his meeting schedules
• Not a morning person, so he won't be up early just to secure himself a parking place
• Likes to go out with friends and eat in good restaurants in his free time
• Is sedentary and underactive both at work and in his free time

3.3 Context of Use

Context of use defines the user goals, main user tasks, and the characteristics of the environment in which the system will be operated or product used [10]. Putting these factors into consideration, forms a foundation on which to design this system so as to ensure that a highly usable system is developed.

Potential users of this application are people between the age of 18–65. Each and every driver needs the process of paying for a parking ticket to be as easy as possible and very efficient. Users want to complete the process without having to use extra time or effort. In addition, most users are people that own cars and will be using this application frequently. A system with high memorability will then be convenient as there won't be need to remember how to use the system every time they log in. Users would rather recognise the interface elements and the interaction flow each time they need to use it.

Since this system aims at serving users of different ages, consideration was given to the fact that there is a wide range of expertise, from novice users to people who are well conversant with technology. This has been done by ensuring that the system does not challenge the user, but is rather emotionally fulfilling and gives a feeling of satisfaction.

The main user task is finding a vacant parking space and successfully paying for it. The system should give the user different choices to help them accomplish their goals in relation to their situations. For example, a driver in a foreign city may need a positioning function that can help him/her find the nearest parking lots. But a driver in a familiar town may only need to easily access the last used parking. These tasks should be easy to perform and enable the user to effectively achieve their goal. As the use of money is involved in such a system, it is important that the users feel safe when using it, and that feedback is provided to users throughout the process especially when an error occurs.

Since this is a mobile app, it should be used everywhere as long as there is Internet access. This means that the system will be used in diverse environments, from the quiet environments at home, to very busy and noisy streets and towns. In relation to the technical environment, it was assumed that sensors are needed to give the users the right information. These sensors should register when there are vacant parking spaces available. The other assumption taken is that all parking places are public and follow the "first come, first serve" rule. This means that this app does not allow one to book a parking space. The main intention of designing this parking app is to come up with a system that does not only give the user a possibility to easily pay for parking, but also provides additional features that improve a driver's everyday life. Some of these features include finding vacant parking spaces in a home town, and locate parking lots when driving in foreign towns. In addition, a list of last used parking lots could be available on the home page to enable easy access for frequent users. Users will also be able to sort out choices according to their own preferences i.e. price, distance and location. Furthermore, the app should send a notification to the user when they are running out of time and allow them to pay for more time if needed.

3.4 Requirements Specification

A requirement is "something the product must do to support its owner's business, or a quality it must have to make it acceptable and attractive to the owner" [11, p. 9]. This work considered two main categories of requirements: the *functional* requirements which specify what the system should be able to do, and *non-functional* requirements which are constraints related to the development of a system.

The main functionality in this application is to enable drivers to find and pay for parking. It is also important that the application is easy to use, as most drivers don't have time to think of how to use it. The system should be effective and produce results as intended by the user. Drivers will frequently use this application, so the process should be easy to remember so they do not have to struggle learning it every time they use it. When it comes to user experience, the system should be satisfying and not challenging or frustrating, but rather give an emotional fulfilment.

4 System Design

4.1 Conceptual Model

A conceptual model presents the main concepts in a system, their attributes and the relationships that exist between them. Given a clear and well-designed conceptual model, it is easier for people to develop a good mental view of the system [7]. By creating a conceptual model, the students' group was able to visualize the concept so as to enable users create a picture in their minds of how the intended system would work and look like. Figure 2 shows a conceptual model developed for SafePark app.

After visualizing the concept, the group presented this to the class as a conceptual model in order to give users an idea of how the system was meant to function. Two main issues came up at this point. The first issue was that all users needed the GPS function to proceed to the next stages. This was not realistic, as users should have a choice to either allow the app to access the GPS function, or continue without it.

Secondly, the conceptual model was incomplete as it did not give the user the alternative to either continue or go back at some points. This would definitely annoy users as it is important that one successfully completes a task, or gets an alternative to go back and make another choice. It was at this point obvious that there was need to get back to the drawing board and correct these mistakes.

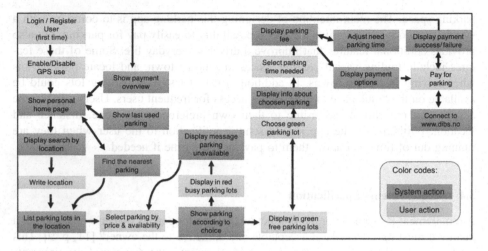

Fig. 2. Conceptual model

4.2 Prototyping and User Testing

A prototype is a model of a design that allows users and stakeholders to interact with it, and give feedback that can be used to improve the system. In this project, two types of prototypes are used: Low-fidelity and High-fidelity.

Low-Fidelity prototypes do not look much like the final product; neither do they provide the same functionality. They are usually made of materials such as paper and cardboard. This kind of prototyping is useful because it is cheap and can easily be produced and reproduced to present different design ideas [9]. On the other hand, a high-fidelity prototype can look more like the final product and enables more functionality. This kind of prototyping can effectively be used to test ideas with technical issues [9].

With this in mind, a low-fidelity prototype was produced using paper, pen, sticky notes and cardboard. Paper prototyping made it possible to visualize the idea to users and enabled the group to see how users interacted with the product. It was easy to change arrangements of graphical elements for example buttons and input fields. Additionally, the interaction flow as well as the user interfaces were improved according to user feedback. It is noted that this study respected all ethical and legal requirements in relation to personal data privacy and the rights of study participants. A consent form was given to participants with all necessary information about this study (Fig. 3).

A High-fidelity prototype was thereafter created using Adobe Captivate, and tested as a web version of the app. At first, the high-fidelity prototype was tested on a laptop. However, it was quickly realised that user testing should be on the target device which the app was meant for. A new prototype that suits a smartphone, iPhone 5 in this case was then designed. Most graphics used to design the prototype such as icons and pictures are collected from the Internet. Testing iteratively with the target group throughout the design process has tremendously helped in improving this system.

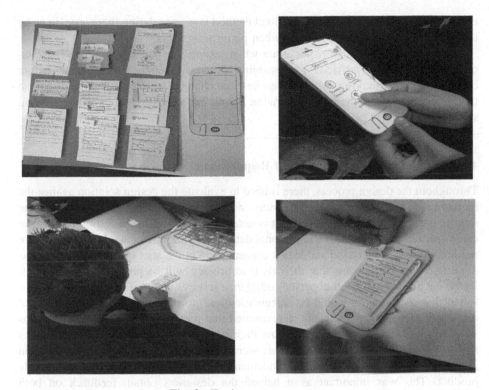

Fig. 3. Testing paper prototype.

At every step of the design, potential users were involved to provide feedback that has effectively been used to develop more refined solutions (Fig. 4).

User feedback related to the user experience, was obtained both in user studies on the low-fidelity and high-fidelity prototypes. By observing how users reacted and seeing their facial expressions, helped designers to develop a deeper understanding of

Fig. 4. Screenshots of a high fidelity prototype

the user needs. In addition, the think aloud method was used during these tests, in order to find out how users were thinking when performing tasks.

Test users uncovered a major issue when testing the paper prototype. The conceptual model did not provide for a possibility for users to see the parking prices before choosing a vacant parking. After the test session, changes were made on the design so that users could select the parking duration to find out the cost for a particular parking space.

4.3   Evaluation of Designs Against Requirements

Throughout the design process, there is need to evaluate the design solution against the requirements to better understanding users' needs, and at a later stage validate that the requirements have been satisfied [3]. It is noted that any user based testing has to take care of ethical considerations and personal data privacy requirements. Participants were required to read, understand and sign a consent form at the start of the study. This was done to assure participants that their right to privacy will be protected and data collected not availed to any other persons other than test evaluators. The consent form also stated that user identity would be safeguarded and no personal information recorded disclosed. Moreover, participants were assured that participation during the study was voluntary and test users could withdraw their participation at any time. All activities that were to take place through the study were also described. User-centred evaluation at every stage has been one of the fundamental keys to the development of a usable product. This was important as it helped the designers obtain feedback on both strengths and weaknesses of the design solution. A lot of user feedback was obtained during evaluation, but priority was given to fixing severe usability problems first. Then minor issues were addressed in subsequent iterations.

4.4   Findings from User Testing

Usability testing should be performed in order to determine how usable a product is. A usability test was done by watching participants interact with the system in a controlled setting as shown in Fig. 5. Six test users were purposively selected. They were people between the age of 20 and 25 and all had a driving license. Three of them were men and the other three women. All of them were students. One of the methods used was the think aloud method developed by Ericsson and Simon [12]. This is a technique used to examine people's strategies for solving problems, as participants say out loud what they are thinking and trying to do.

The second method employed was the user attitudes measurement questionnaire based on a Likert scale. After interacting with the system, participants were asked to rate the system on a 5-point Likert scale with measures ranging from strongly disagree (1) to strongly agree (5). The Likert scale was used to evaluate user satisfaction and to measure test user opinions and attitudes.

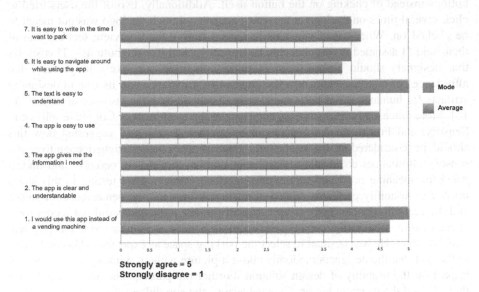

Strongly agree = 5
Strongly disagree = 1

Fig. 5. Users' opinions and rating of the prototype usability

At the end of every user study, a semi-structured interview was conducted and test users were asked to give feedback and give suggestions on things that could be improved to improve the app's usability and overall user experience.

Semi-structured interviews are open when compared to structured interviews and allow new ideas to come up. They also "probe the interviewee to say more until no new relevant information is forthcoming" [9, p. 234].

Major findings from this usability test showed that the app was easy to use. All users agreed that they would use the app instead of using a vending machine to buy a parking ticket. One test user said, "I would gladly use this app to quickly find a vacant parking place, rather than drive around several minutes trying to find one". However, the prototype was not optimal as there were several errors that occurred during usability testing. Furthermore, it was clear that testing a prototype that is not fully functional can be a challenge as users got irritated every time they tried to click on a button and nothing happened. Thus, it is important to ensure that test participants are aware of the limitations of the prototype.

One of the common errors during testing was on how to put in the time. To be able to continue with the payment process, users had to put in the amount of time they needed to park. None of the users knew exactly which format they were to use. It was clear that there was need to develop a time input format that gives the user a hint on how to do this.

Four out of six users did not know what "my parking" button should be used for. This was due to misconceptions regarding the perceived affordances for the button and the text: both did not give any clues to users. Another issue related to not visibly perceivable affordance came up when most users tried to click on the text next to the buttons instead of clicking on the button itself. Additionally, two of the users tried to click several times on the logo at the start page even though the logo was not meant to be clicked on. When asked why this happened during the interview section, one of them said "I assumed it was clickable because it looked like the buttons". This shows that designers should always have in mind how users are likely to perceive the affordances of interface elements. The concept of affordance and its role in designing artifacts for human use has been extensively discussed over the last four decades [13–15]. More extensively, Hartson [16] emphasized the usefulness of Cognitive, Physical, Sensory, and Functional Affordances in interaction design; and suggested how this should be considered in the evaluation. For instance, well designed cognitive and sensory affordances could allow a potential user to correctively perceive and understand the meaning presented through an interface element. User testing in this study uncovered usability problems related to mismatch between the perceived affordances and the real affordances. For example, one of the test participants did not recognize a street picture used in the prototype even though he was familiar with the physical parking street. He was hesitant to select the parking space as expected. This can be due to the fact that the designers randomly chose a picture without thinking of its potential impact on the usability of design solution. Further on, participants got confused after they clicked the payment button. This is because the app did not give a clear feedback to whether payment was successful. At this point most of them clicked on the return button to try again.

4.5   Recommendations and Limitations

Participants suggested that using a function that allows the user to scroll through and choose suitable time would make it easier for users to put in the time they needed to park. Another participant commented that the time input field could have placeholders showing the time format. She further gave an example of a website called "akt.no".

It was clear that the button design and logo design had to be different to avoid confusing users. The design on the buttons had to be changed too. Either by making the whole area with text and button clickable, or moving the text into the button, so it appears as one.

The three buttons, price, vacancy, and distance, which allowed the user to sort out parking places, should be fully implemented. One of the test users suggested that this function was necessary, and said that one of the reasons she would choose to use this app, is the fact that it makes it possible to access cheaper parking. It was also suggested that the picture showing the parking place should be replaced. One of the participants said that it would even be better with a detailed picture showing exactly where the vacant parking places were.

Given the time limitations of a one-semester course, it was not possible to design a fully functional application, but an interactive prototype with limited functionality. It was therefore important to scope and focus on some important parts of the application. Parts moved to the waiting room include: payment function, availability of parking where green means vacant and red busy, the possibility to sort according to price, distance, and vacancy; the GPS-function, the registration and "My parking"-page. After all, the main goal was to learn how to design interactive systems for human use in general. And the human-centred design approach for mobile applications in particular based on real-world scenarios.

5 Conclusion

This article presented an authentic learning approach for a post-graduate course focusing on human-centred design process. Students worked on a semester long design project. The aim was to design a prototype of a usable mobile application which provides an enjoyable user experience. This application would improve the everyday lives of drivers by adapting the human-centred design approach. The proposed design solution was mainly meant to enable drivers easily find parking and efficiently pay for it. This work affirmed that multiple iterations and user involvement throughout the design process are the key drivers to designing usable systems. The iterative design process allowed designers to constantly collect user feedback and to use it to improve the design solution.

The designed digital artifact and the course results indicate that the involved students have achieved a high level of mastery in the subject "Interaction Design". The students group managed to come up with ideas that can be used to further develop the parking app focusing on human factors and ergonomics. Using several prototyping techniques and user study techniques, the students effectively increased their competence in the field of human-centred design. Since the learning activities involved real-world scenarios, students were highly engaged and motivated to explore new facts, analyse the context, synthesize the existing knowledge and create a new artifact. This study reinforces the usefulness of authentic learning of interaction design, and recommends prototyping at varying levels of fidelity as a strategy for development of higher order cognitive skills.

References

1. Herrington, J., Reeves, T.C., Oliver, R.: Authentic learning environments. In: Michael Spector, J., Merrill, M.D., Elen, J., Bishop, M.J. (eds.) Handbook of Research on Educational Communications and Technology, 4th edn., pp. 401–412. Springer Science+Business Media, New York (2014)
2. Sas, C.: Learning approaches for teaching interaction design. In: HCI Educators Workshop, Limerick (2006)
3. International Organization for Standardization, ISO 9241–210: 2010. Ergonomics of human-system interaction–Part 210: Human-centred design for interactive systems, Geneva (2010)
4. Jonassen, D.H., Hung, W.: Problem-based learning. In: Seel, N.M. (ed.) Encyclopedia of the Sciences of Learning, pp. 2687–2690. Springer, Boston (2012)
5. Quigley, C.: Expanding our view of authentic learning: bridging in and out-of-school experiences. Cult. Sci. Edu. 9(1), 115–122 (2014)

6. Norman, D.: Cognitive engineering. In: Norman, D.A., Draper, S. (eds.) User-Centred System Design: New perspectives on Human-Computer Interaction, pp. 31–61. Lawrence Erlbaum Associates, Hillside (1986)
7. Benyon, D.: Designing Interactive Systems. A Comprehensive Guide to HCI, UX and Interaction Design, 3rd edn., p. 604. Pearson Education Ltd, Edinburgh (2014)
8. Walldius, C.A., Lantz, A.: Exploring the use of design pattern maps for aligning new technical support to new clinical team meeting routines. Behav. Inf. Technol. 32(1), 68–79 (2013)
9. Preece, J., Sharp, H., Rogers, Y.: Interaction Design: Beyond Human-Computer Interaction, p. 567. Wiley, Chichester (2015)
10. Maguire, M.: Context of use within usability activities. Int. J. Hum Comput Stud. 55(4), 453–483 (2001)
11. Robertson, S., Robertson, J.: Mastering the Requirements Process: Getting Requirements Right, vol. 3. Addison-Wesley, Upper Saddle River (2014)
12. Ericsson, K.A., Simon, H.A.: Verbal reports as data. Psychol. Rev. 87(3), 215–251 (1980)
13. Gibson, J.: "The Theory of Affordances", in Perceiving, Acting, and Knowing. Lawrence Erlbaum Associates, Hillsdale (1977)
14. Norman, D.A.: The Psychology of Everyday Things. Basic Books, New York (1988)
15. Norman, D.A.: The Design of Everyday Things - Revised and Expanded. Doubleday, New York (2013)
16. Hartson, R.: Cognitive, physical, sensory, and functional affordances in interaction design. Behav. Inf. Technol. 22(5), 315–338 (2003)

Collaborative System for Generative Design: Manipulating Parameters, Generating Alternatives

Luisa Paraguai[1](✉), Heloisa Candello[2], and Paulo Costa[3]

[1] Pontifical Catholic University of Campinas, Campinas, Brazil
luisa.donati@puc-campinas.edu.br
[2] IBM Research, São Paulo, Brazil
heloisacandello@br.ibm.com
[3] School of Communication and Arts, University of São Paulo, São Paulo, Brazil
paulocosta@usp.br

Abstract. Several methods are available to converge ideas, choosing concepts more suitable for the problem to be solved. Relations between concepts and combination of ideas are limited to time constraints and designers' cognition during decision-making meetings, let some possible choices not available for discussion. Understanding those constraints, is paramount to propose approaches that take advantage of current technology advances. Nowadays, computers can storage high amount of data and computational algorithms may infer combinations not considered before by humans. Taking this perspective, this text investigates the computational generative design as a tool to evaluate patterns emerged in the ideation phase of a design team creation. Designers can benefit of our approach in the ideation phases of the design process to have insights, unusual and disrupted ideas facilitated by technology.

Keywords: Creativity and design process · Generative design · Collaborative process

1 Introduction

Designer teams face creativity challenges when starting a new project. Deciding what is the suitable approach to generate ideas and possible concepts to choose alternatives for a product is one of those challenges. Designers usually question themselves: How to look at known facts with diverse point of views? How to find new answers to old problems? How to escape from obvious solutions and have unusual and original ideas? (Löbach 2001 [15]; Bonsiepe 1984 [2]; Baxter 2000 [1]). In the preliminary stages of the design process, divergent ideas emerge and choices should be taken to converge proposals into design concepts. Several methods are available to converge ideas, choosing concepts more suitable for the problem to be solved. Relations between concepts and combination of ideas are limited to time constraints and designers' cognition during decision-making meetings let some possible choices not available for discussion. Understanding those constraints, is paramount to propose approaches that take advantage of current technology advances. Nowadays, computers can storage high

© Springer International Publishing AG 2017
A. Marcus and W. Wang (Eds.): DUXU 2017, Part I, LNCS 10288, pp. 727–739, 2017.
DOI: 10.1007/978-3-319-58634-2_52

amount of data and computational algorithms may infer combinations not considered before by humans. Taking this perspective, this text investigates the computational generative design as a tool to evaluate emerged patterns during the ideation phase of a team in the early stages of design process.

2 Design Process and Creativity

Usually design projects consist of more than one person. Even if a project has only one designer, he/she interacts with stakeholders, clients or other project owners. Design process methodologies intent designers to explore ideas with others and communicate results in a set of stages. Following a design process approach facilitates designers to find solutions for problems and builds confidence to justify the solutions chosen giving a rational of why such alternatives would not solve the project problematics. Therefore, there are no optimal solutions to design problems but rather a whole range of acceptable solutions (Lawson 2006) [14] the project team should be aware and discuss.

In traditional design process, designers explore the solution space combining requirements, stakeholder priorities, users and context characteristics, materials, technologies, and processes when generating ideas. New elements can be aggregated by the process in an iterative mode, shaping the solution. Theoretical references have already proposed design process phases: Defining the problem; Ideation; Solution and Materialization and Assessment phase (Bonsiepe 1984 [2]; Löbach 2001 [15]; Baxter 2000 [1]; Bürdek 2006 [5]; Frascara 2004 [8]; Plomp 2007 [18], Brown 2009 [3]). The generating alternative phase is also known as Creativity; Generating ideas and concepts; and Ideation phase. In this phase, several methods and techniques help designers "to think out of the box", e.g. Brainstorming, Mind mapping, Role playing, Morphological analysis, Reverse thinking, Metaphors and Analogies.

Several designers and researches documented their experiences adopting ideation methods and techniques that might help other designers to follow the design process. Bulley (2013) [4] proposes a technique called Triad. This technique helps teams to explore the identity of a project (e.g. service, product). First the project team brainstorm a list of key words that they would like the product to incorporate. The team chooses combos of three words that would describe the product experience. The team in groups selects combos that are interesting for them and brainstorm for which combo related nouns, verbs and adjectives. According to the author:

- Nouns help the team think about actors or objects that you might have in the system;
- Verbs help the team think about actions that the system should support;
- Adjectives help you think about look, feel and what design principles should be considered

The facilitator, a designer, asks people to exemplify products experiences that people would have illustrated by those words.

In another research, Shi et al. (2017) [21] presents an ideation tool, called Idea Wall, supported by cognitive strategies to facilitate idea generation. It consists of a real-time system that extracts keywords from verbal discussions and augments the discussion with web-search materials. This research extracts information from group conversation, does not have any machine learning intelligence or algorithms to automatic generate ideas.

The use of analogies to assist on creative process during the design process was also explored by researchers (Tomko 2015 [22]; Casakin 1999 [6]; Goel 1997 [10]). According to Gentner and Markman (1997) [9] and Chan et al. (2014) [7] not all analogies strategies result on creative outcomes. Chan et al. (2014) describes that:

> *Not all analogies are thought to be equally productive for creative outcomes. Many theorists argue that, when considering the analogical distance of sources, far analogies—that is, from sources that have a low degree of overlap of surface elements with the current problem domain—hold the most potential for generating very new concepts. (2014: 2) [7]*

Therefore, generating alternatives that not overlap with known concepts have more potential to generate new concepts and innovation. In this paper, we focus on the Ideation phase, using techniques based on analogies, empowered by generative design techniques explained in the next session.

3   A Computational Generative Design Approach

A generative approach consists in design rationale explanations constructed, in response to information requests, from background knowledge and information captured during design process (Gruber and Russell 1996) [11]. Computational generative design applies certain strategies to incorporate the system dynamics into the production of the artefact and experience, such as: permutation, randomness, iterative and feedback looping are the usual ones in a complex field of possibilities. According to McCormack, Dorin and Innocent (2004) [17] the key properties of generative systems are:

- the ability to generate complexity by database amplification and generate aggregates from existent components;
- the connection between organism and environment often with feedback loops;
- the ability to self-maintain and self-repair being adaptable to maintain stable configurations in a changing environment;
- the ability to generate novel structures, behaviors, outcomes or relationships.

Designers are usually looking for unusual alternatives, novelty in the sense of being new, original and different from anything else before it (McCormack et al. 2004) [17]. Therefore, generative design allows designers to change not only elements by elements but characteristics of elements (e.g. color, composition, forms) and system rules to generate not expected combinations. With the advent of new programming and script languages, designers can codify parametric conditions to search data from WEB, for example, defining how those rules will work to achieve new outcomes and sources.

4 Our Approach

For the phase of generation alternatives and concepts, we have used the transformation method (Bonsiepe 1984) [2], in which the design team members create and suggest analogies of project elements (e.g. keywords, images, sketches, logical operators). The main objective of this technique is the broadening of meaning to assist in generating ideas, by progressively differentiating from the original term based on team members' subjectivity and personal references. Broadening is a type of semantic change by which the meaning of a word (concept or idea) becomes broader or more inclusive than its earlier meaning. It is an adaptive procedure – combining, recomposing, reversing, replacing – from the obvious to unusual ideas, which can be paradigmatic or not (Kuhn 2013) [13].

We illustrate a scenario to describe how computational generative design is applied to assist design teams in the ideation phase. The visual diagram (Fig. 1) describes the features of a client toolbox, responsible to manage the iterative process of generating ideas.

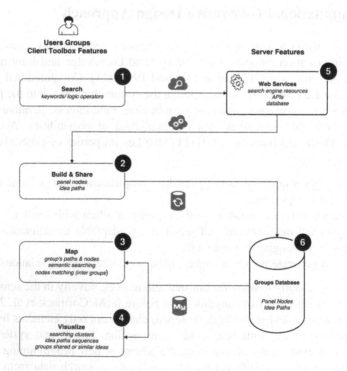

Fig. 1. Visual Diagram

During the **search** (number 1) the designer team can investigate terms by searching for logic operators (keywords, images) in different databases and getting as results the **building blocks** (images, videos, texts). After, in the **build & share** phase (number 2),

panel nodes are developed and compose the **idea paths** in an iterative process; both are saved in a specific collective database (number 6), which manages all searches from different groups. The access to the groups database (number 6) gives the possibility of **mapping** (number 3) nodes and paths and verifying the similarities/approximations among the searches (images or panel nodes with structural and/or semantic high coincidences). Finally, all mappings and searches are going to be **visualized** (number 4) as image and text clusters (panels) or tree maps. Possible alternatives can emerge from the connections between searches and idea paths. The actions and iterative resources (number 1, 2, 3, 4) are updated on an interface (toolbox) available for the client level. The actions 5 and 6 are server features.

5   Gathering Data Relations: Ideation Phase with Design Students

Firstly, two words, a noun and a verb – memory and to invent – were proposed to start the process of transformation (the broadening of meaning). There were three groups with two participants in each, and every round those students could only see the last two words, proposed by the previous one, and discuss before writing their ideas. Because of that strategy we had some synonyms and repeated terms, as shown in the Table 1 bellow.

Table 1. The broadening of meaning to generate keywords.

memory	to invent	
reliquary	fantasy	
to keep	narrative	1st round
precious	**inventory**	
scar	to catalogue	
eternal	to separate	2nd round
widespread	**unique**	
extent	exclusivity	
oscilation	mine	3rd round
liquid	to customise	
finitude	**mutant**	
unlimited	strength	4th round
democratization	tecnique	
choice	fundament	
moment	construction	5th round
to live	origin	

From that part of the design process, some concepts were chosen (in bold) and after a discussion with all participants involved keywords were defined as: imprint and to access, inventory and singularity, to live and mutant – for the second stage of ideation phase.

During the second stage, students search on the web, specifically on the Pinterest photo sharing website (Fig. 2), for visual references connecting concrete objects and concepts based on keywords. The proposal was to put together unusual ideas or thoughts and everyday things, as for example clip, button, clothespin, that could represent actions as to attach, to staple, to congregate, to compose, to assemble, and to organize different parts and diverse materials.

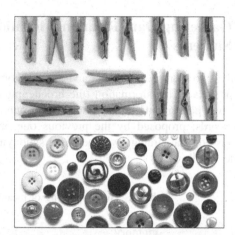

Fig. 2. (a) paper clips (Source http://melissaeastondesign.com/paper-clips/); (b) clothespins (Source http://collectionaday2010.blogspot.com.br); (c) buttons (Source http://lemerg.com/data/wallpapers/8/728544.jpg).

After creating an inventory of objects, the proposal for the group was to look at things and to think of contours and shapes and their "relational elements", as Wong (1972) [23] wrote about form and structure. From that interrelationship "unit forms" were defined and when regrouped it was possible to explore other complex arrangements. The association of repeated forms and their relational placements – "similarity, gradation, radiation" (Wong, 1972: 7–8), gradually structure regular forms, as shown in the Fig. 3. Repetition defines rhythm and 'encourages our eyes to dance. Controlling repetition is a way to choreograph human eye movement' (Reas, McWilliams and Barendse 2010: 49) [19], and it is used to construct the visual complexity asked for students.

The form-making process can evoke the formulation of patterns, since they carry formal synthesis potentially. For Hall (1990: 116) [12] 'patterns are those implicit cultural rules by means of which sets are arranged so that they take on meaning'. For the author, patterns are related to concept model, able to encode data collected into visual expressions and to be later decoded for people when reading and signifying the visual narratives (Fig. 4). It starts from literal and figurative configurations to an

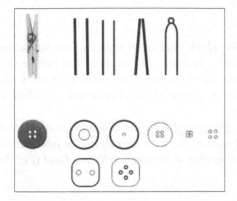 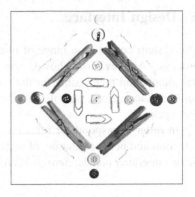

Fig. 3. Objects and forms – lines, circles – formulate patterns.

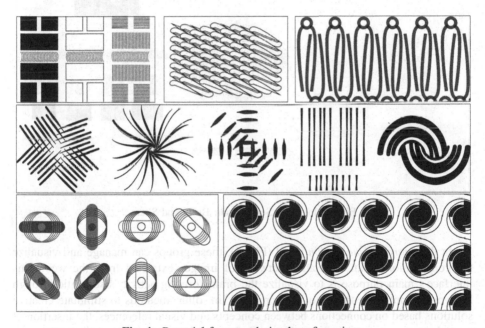

Fig. 4. Potential forms and visual configurations.

unclear set of forces, from physical requirements to diagrams, to structure and to invent forms. Variations, irregularities, and deviations are desired practices to deform and conform not only regular compositions, by including different exercises of elements' concentration and distribution.

From that point, the visual proposals have been developed properly thinking about textures and colours to the final composition, and, at the end, defining formats, materials and technical processes of information circulation and distribution, as printed and digital context.

6 Design Interface

The system counts on a range of interfaces which enable the stages of the interactive process. As previously shown, the toolbox system for ideation has two essential phases and responsible for the construction of the cognitive network: *Search and Build & Share*. Next, we will describe the main interfaces and also the tasks involved in this cycle.

In order to respond for functions that integrate the means of search, construction, selection and network sharing of texts and images, we have segmented the interfaces in three integrated panels: *Search Visualization, Image Inspector e Visual Grid* (Fig. 5).

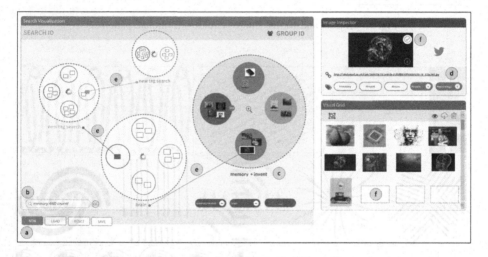

Fig. 5. Interface Set: Search, Build and Share.

In the *Search Visualization* panel (Fig. 6), these groups can manage and visualize the construction of an associative network of images extracted from the web. This interface's main purpose is to visualize the brainstorming activity's semantic through keywords input. According to our proposal in offer methods to stimulate creative solutions based on connections between concepts and visual references, the insertion of textual structures serves as a starting point for searching and as a sampling of images references available on public databases online. The algorithmic principle of this interface defines a web crawler type application that browses specific content domains searching for images which metadata and tags matches keywords input. In this process, the application can use the features of several public publishing platform APIs such as Twitter, Pinterest, Flickr, and features offered by Googles engine. In fact, browsing the web and associating content with social tagging contribute to achieving one of the goals of the project which is the semantic expansion based on visual stimuli.

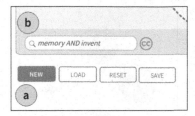

Fig. 6. User can load, save and share searching sessions.

Searching

(a) Initially, each group of users has a login identification by which allow them to save and share multiple sessions of searching and results. Each group can make numerous researches and filter/select an unlimited amount of images, since these images are hosted on distributed servers. The constructions of network nodes and associations arise from the text search and also the series of locations (URLs) and the images in form of metadata can be saved and shared hereafter among the process of other's group (Fig. 6)

(b) The search operation starts on the input field with the insertion of: keywords, operators, regular expressions, URLs or even full block of texts. In the example, we have inserted two keywords (memory, invent) selecting the AND operator. The image content associated with the textual input can be searched in specifics domains by the user (e.g.: memory AND invent IN: URL) or in categories formed by tags organized in social platforms (Fig. 6).

Visualizing

(c) the visual results of search are organized in an interface that groups the images according to their domain's inception. On the central part of the panel, the application generates interactive diagram that represent a hierarchical structure containing the search description, domains and images. In the example, the circle with dashed black border represents the whole search and inside it, each coloured circle corresponds to a certain search domain (e.g. Twitter) and their grouped contents into clusters of found images. For each conducted search, a new circle will be generate like a cellular structure that can be enlarged through the zooming function. The diagrams can be located or be deleted from the central panel through labeled buttons placed at the panel's bottom (Fig. 7).

(d) the visualization of each image and the verification of their metadata can be triggered by direct selection at the domain's cluster. The data will be displayed on the *Image Inspector* panel and the follow information will be shown: location of the image (URL), the origin domain of the publishing's feed and others tags or metadata that might be associated (Fig. 8a). On the this panel, the set of tags related to images is represented by buttons. The activated buttons in red (+) symbolize new possibilities of searching and when they are activated they

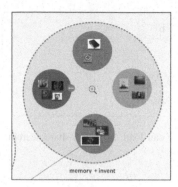

Fig. 7. Each search operation is represented by a diagram that encapsulates domain and image clusters.

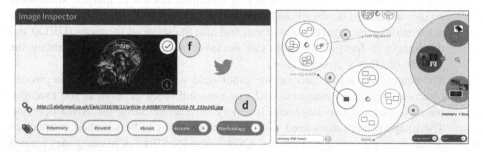

Fig. 8. (a) Image Inspector panel represents associated metadata and tags; (b) Broadening process is represented as a network of searching and association paths (Color figure online)

generate a new diagram of search in the central panel. On implementing this feature enables the creation of new searches and associative connections as we will see in the next stage of Broadening.

Broadening

(e) In this task, the expansion of the meanings is articulated to the combinatory process of sources, tags and domains extracted from each interaction cycle. Besides the initially text inserted by the user, the semantic context of the results is enlarged by external social tagging, domain content or embedded metadata. In the *Image Inspector* panel, the activation of a certain tag button connects the reference image to a new search whose keyword is the associated tag itself. In the example, the brain tag has been associated with an image and is used as the input source for a new search (Fig. 8a and b). The interaction of this process can create an interactive network composed by nodes (image clusters) and links (associative connection). The navigation through this network and inside the clusters allows the user to select and to group images that will be part of his repertoire.

Combining

(e) The images selected by the user can be added to a visual matrix formed in the *Visual Grid* panel. Each selected image in cluster, checked at the *Image Inspector* panel will be automatically added to a visual matrix. The set of images built during all the processes could be downloaded for use in contexts of subsequent creations (Fig. 9).

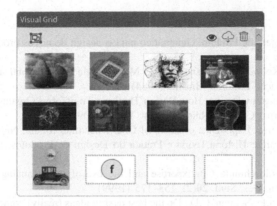

Fig. 9. Visual matrix of selected and suitable images.

Fig. 10. Anpap's first visual identity (Source: http://anpap.org.br).

7 Conclusion and Further Research

The contribution of this paper for a design collaborative process is threefold. First, amplify the semantic field of design possibilities. Second, converge similar alternatives and transformation paths of designer's insights. Third, a tool for designers manipulate and generate ideas in a visualization system. We are interested on the emergence of unusual ideas, pointing out the process of interconnecting iteratively the logic keys (the path of feedback looping) more than on the standard visual results. It is the protocols process – the formulating patterns structuring that will generate more ideas and concepts for group ideation phase.

It is important to say that the process was proposed for the creation of the visual identity of Anpap (National Association for Fine Arts Researchers) (Fig. 10), and since the idea is to construct a inventory of forms, it will change each month till the annual congress, in September this year. It was designed a visual grid to be shared among Design students, since the creation process was meant to be collaborative with each one creating a visual composition.

We plan to do test our tool with more potential users and other designers to understand better this collaborative generative design tool will assist in generating designer's ideas and discussions.

References

1. Baxter, M.: Projeto de Produto. Guiaprático para o design de novos produtos. Blücher, São Paulo (2000)
2. Bonsiepe, G., Kellner, P., Poessnecker, H.: Metodologia Experimental: Desenho Industrial. CNPq/Coordenação Editorial, Brasília (1984)
3. Brown, T.: Change by Design: How Design Thinking Transforms Organisations and Inspires Innovation. Harper-Collins Publishers, New York (2009)
4. Buley, L.: The user Experience of Team of One. Rosenfeld Media, New York (2013)
5. Bürdek, B.: *Design*: História.Teoria e Prática do Design de Produtos. Blücher, São Paulo (2006)
6. Casakin, H., Goldschmidt, G.: Expertise and the use of visual analogy: implications for design education. Des. Stud. **20**(2), 153–175 (1999)
7. Chan, J., Dow, S.P., Schunn, C.D.: Do the best design ideas (really) come from conceptually distant sources of inspiration? Des. Stud. **36**, 31–58 (2014)
8. Frascara, J.: Communication Design – Principles, Methods and Practice. Allworth Press, New York (2004)
9. Gentner, D., Markman, A.B.: Structure mapping in analogy and similarity. Am. Psychol.**52** (1), 45 (1997)
10. Goel, A.K.: Design, analogy, and creativity. IEEE Expert **12**(3), 62–70 (1997)
11. Gruber, T.R., Russell, D.M.: Generative design rationale: beyond the record and replay paradigm. In: Moran, T.P., Carroll, J.M. (eds.) Design Rationale: Concepts, Techniques, and Use, pp. 323–349. Lawrence Erlbaum, Mahwah (1996)
12. Hall, E.T.: The Silent Language. Anchor Books Editions, Garden City, New York (1990)
13. Kuhn, T.S.: Aestrutura das revoluçõescientíficas. Perspectiva, São Paulo (2013)
14. Lawson, B.: How Designers Think. Architectural Press, Oxford (2006)
15. Löbach, B.: Design Industrial: bases para a configuração dos produtos industriais. Blücher, São Paulo (2001)
16. Maeda, J.: Design by Numbers. The MIT Press, Cambridge (2001)
17. McCormack, J., Dorin, A., Innocent, T.: Generative design: a paradigm for design research. In: Proceedings of Futureground. Design Research Society, Melbourne (2004)
18. Plomp, T.: Educational design research: an introduction. In: Plomp, T., Nieveen, N. (eds.) An Introduction to Educational Design Research. Proceedings of the seminar conducted at the East China Normal University, Shanghai (PR China), 23–26 November. SLO, Netherlands Institute for Curriculum Development The Netherlands (2007)
19. Reas, C., McWilliams, C., Barendse, J.: Form + Code in Design, Art, and Architecture. Princeton Architectural Press, New York (2010)
20. Schunn, C., Chan, J.: The impact of analogies on creative concept generation: lessons from an in vivo study in engineering design. Cognitive Sci.

21. Shi, Y., Wang, Y., Qi, Y., Chen, J., Xu, X., Ma, K.L.: IdeaWall: improving creative collaboration through combinatorial visual stimuli. In: Proceedings of the 2017 ACM Conference on Computer Supported Cooperative Work and Social Computing, pp. 594–603. ACM, New York (2017)
22. Tomko, M., Lucero, B., Turner, C., Linsey, J.: Establishing functional concepts vital for design by analogy. In: 2015 IEEE Frontiers in Education Conference (FIE), pp. 1–8 (2015)
23. Wong, W.: Principles of Two-dimensional Design. Van Nostrand Reinhold Company, New York (1972)

Design of Digital Products in the Future: A Study of Interaction Design Students and Their Perceptions on Design Issues

Hanne Sørum[✉]

Westerdals Oslo School of Arts, Communication and Technology, Oslo, Norway
hanne.sorum@westerdals.no

Abstract. Today's students on programs covering interaction design will most likely contribute to the development of products that we will use in the future. The roles they will play in this regard will of course depend on various factors. Regardless of this, their educational background is a vital component, along with their motivation, personality, knowledge, and ideas. The present study reports on an online questionnaire (n = 82) given to students on interaction design programs. Additionally, eight qualitative interviews were performed to gain more insight. The findings show that, in general, the students of today perceive themselves to be in great shape for the development of future products. However, the majority of the respondents have also considered other study areas that might be relevant to them, grounded in shared backgrounds and interests. They also enjoy working individually with design ideas and prototypes, and they generally prefer working with digital solutions over working with print and physical products. User testing is found to be a vital element within the design process, although the analysis of such data is found to be somewhat difficult. Concerning industrial needs, the students struggle to clearly define the role of an interaction designer and the tasks they are expected to perform when taking on a job within the design industry. This paper ends with concluding remarks and suggestions for upcoming research contributions.

Keywords: Interaction design · Human–computer interaction · Usability · Online survey · Qualitative interviews

1 Introduction

The everyday use of technologies influences our lives in many ways. For instance, it influences the way we communicate, interact, collaborate, and exchange knowledge. However, there have been major changes over the last 15 years as regards to how people use technologies in different contexts (e.g. work and leisure) as a result of the emergence of personal mobile devices, agent-based technologies, and social networks [1]. We are also witnessing increasing numbers of innovations and traditional face-to-face interactions are no longer always the preferred method of communication. Additionally, we have access to a huge number of digital services and a vast amount of online information. In some cases, we also see that there are no alternatives to digital interactions and that

© Springer International Publishing AG 2017
A. Marcus and W. Wang (Eds.): DUXU 2017, Part I, LNCS 10288, pp. 740–754, 2017.
DOI: 10.1007/978-3-319-58634-2_53

physical information largely no longer exists. In many cases, the user has no choice if they want to search for information and/or apply for a specific service. Instead of in-person contact, in many situations, we must fill in an online form or an electronic schedule. Consequently, we need to facilitate high-quality interactions and great user experiences on the Web [2]. During the last few decades, academics and practitioners have also shown an increasing interest in the use of information technologies due to the positive impact on management and strategies, along with how technologies influence financial performance [3]. In this regard, "The design of interfaces for business-to-customers electronic commerce has been an area of high interest to MIS HCI researchers in the last decade. This is partly due to the widespread growth of electronic communication and digital interfaces that are the sole way of interacting with pure e-tailers" [4, p. 17]. Thus, the facilitation of great user interfaces and the provision of high-quality solutions are vital in our digital society. This is especially true within the public sector, where all users should have equal access to digital information and online services [5]. Consequently, organizations are under a great deal of pressure to facilitate this access by allocating resources and investments for development and quality improvements. Websites are also the key to online information and services through the graphical user interfaces that they provide for their users [6]. For some companies, we also see that their competitors are only a mouse click and/or a Google search away. Thus, the designers of digital solutions and Web applications must have different skills relating to the needs of the users (target group), the available technologies, and design principles, along with knowledge concerning interactions that take place between users and computers/mobile devices [7]. Although the field of interaction design is growing rapidly and receiving increased attention, there is a need to conduct research on various topics within this area [8]. Moreover, the research that is undertaken also needs to produce results that can be useful for both the industry and for practitioners [9] and we need to bridge the gap between researchers and designers [10].

The present paper emphasizes the design and development of digital solutions, espe-cially by the people that will most likely contribute to this field in the near future. We expect that many of today's students will be tomorrow's designers and will be vital contributors to products that we will have to trust and use frequently in the future. Due to the ever-growing degree of digitization within the last decade, we can assume that more organizations will increasingly need expertise in this field in the coming years. During the last decades, designers has also been forced to adapt to changing user contexts because of new technological innovations, as well as cultural and social changes in our society [11]. Moreover, it is critical to every designer and manager that Websites and other digital solutions meet their users' requirements and expectations [6]. The conse-quences of not doing so can be many and shared, including bad usability, frustrated users, a loss of sales, and a negative reputation among users. As a result of new inno-vations and novel ways of communication today, we also find that many educational institutions worldwide offer educational programs in the fields of Web design, interac-tion design, and the programming of Web and mobile applications. Such programs intend to meet needs within the design industry through teaching in both technology- and design-related topics. Regarding interaction design and product development, we find that user testing and evaluations, design principles, and knowledge of the interaction design process and the design team are essential [7]. Designing products and digital solutions is usually a long process and is not always straightforward. Therefore, we need to start correctly and follow each step in the right direction. We also find many research articles, textbooks, and online resources covering interaction design-related topics that are of interest to both practitioners (the design industry) and academia (lecturers and researchers). Additionally, there are many Web forums and blogs discussing topics of interest within this field that share ideas, expertise, and exchange knowledge.

The present paper explore how students, who are up-and-coming designers, perceive the future of interaction design and the way in which we will interact with products in the future. This paper reports on an online survey questionnaire among design students (n = 82) in higher educational institutions in Norway. In addition, eight qualitative interviews were held with interaction design students enrolled in bachelor programs. Many approaches could have been taken when studying this phenomenon, but in this paper, interests in and motivation for studying interaction design, the perception and role of user testing, and students' perceptions of future products. We also note that many people working within this field discuss the role of interaction are emphasized designers (and similar roles such as UX designers, Web designers, and human–computer interaction [HCI] experts). The working tasks they are supposed to complete vary considerably within the design industry and the individual organizations [12].

The rest of the paper is organized as follows: Sect. 2 provides related work pertaining to the topic of interest. Section 3 deals with the methodology and Sect. 4 presents the findings of our study. In Sect. 5, the findings are discussed and concluding remarks are provided in Sect. 6. In addition, suggestions for forthcoming research contributions are given.

2   Related Work

The field of HCI has often focused on the interface primarily as a tool for managing a computer and/or the software, but during the last few years, it has also become a framework for exploring content such as music and videos [13]. Within the Scandinavian context, projects related to user participation and participatory design, a central part of HCI and interaction design, can be traced back to the 1970s [14]. "While there is no commonly agreed definition of interaction design, its core can be found in an orientation towards shaping design artifacts—products, services, and spaces—with particular attention paid to the qualities of the user experience" [8, p. 4]. From this, we see that to some extent, interaction design is an umbrella term, and we can expect that people working within this field have shared backgrounds and experiences. An "interaction designer" is not a protected working title, and it covers many and shared working tasks within the design industry [12]. Moreover, interaction design is a complex discipline and people working within this field range from those involved in technological development within academia to business product groups and start-up companies [10]. Findings from Churchill, Bowser, and Preece [1], investigating HCI subjects and related fields, varied among people from different language populations, and ranged from cognitive science, design, art, and statistics, to software engineering and business. Topics within HCI that were considered as important ranged from teamwork, media criticism, and language processing, to product development, robotics, and social network analysis. The fact that this is an interdisciplinary and complex field is also reflected in the variety of educational programs on offer worldwide. According to Churchill, Bowser, and Preece [1], there are a high number of courses offered in HCI and that number has increased during the last decade. Regarding the education given within this field, Nirbrant, Hvannberg, and Lindquist [15] stated that: "It seems much of the traditional education in HCI has focused on training software developers to become generalists, who are supposed to design pleasant user experiences in addition to knowing how to design and implement software underneath" (p. 187). From this, we can see that interaction design covers many and different tasks, and needs to be specific to the individual working context and situation.

Interaction design is largely carried out by multidisciplinary teams consisting of people with knowledge of areas such as engineering, programming, design, and psychology [7]. Design team members should have diverse areas of expertise and unique knowledge concerning user experiences and the development of digital solutions. Although the design process of interactive and physical products involves a design team consisting of many people [2], the role of an interaction designer is especially vital. Working with interaction design requires great and unique knowledge of how users interact with a given solution, along with their needs and interests in conducting various tasks and searching for information in our digital society. According to Gould and Lewis [16], "The design team should be user driven. We recommend understanding potential users, versus 'identifying,' 'describing,' 'stereotyping,' and 'ascertaining' them, as respondents suggested. We recommend bringing the design team into direct contact with potential users, as opposed to hearing or reading about them through human intermediaries, or through an 'examination' of user profiles" (p. 301). When one is working with interaction, an iterative process and the development of solutions do not happen in a linear way, and sometimes there is a need to take "one step forward, two steps back" [17]. To create great Websites, designers also need to work closely with content creators, because both the aesthetics and content have been found to be essential elements when aiming for success, along with issues concerning the entire user experience [18]. Over the past few decades, designers have also needed to think about the future use of different solutions [19] to facilitate user satisfaction and usability.

However, for years, the HCI community has struggled with integrating design research practice. Design has gained a foothold in practice, but it has had less of an impact on research related to the HCI field [20]. Within the field of interaction design and HCI, we find that knowing the users and their interests and needs is vital to create great user experiences (see [21]). In this regard, usability testing is an important activity throughout the design process. The users must be involved as early as possible in system development and interface design, using various techniques, such as high- and low-level prototypes [22]. The evaluation of interactive systems is also a vital component within the field of HCI [11]. "One thing we seem to have learned over the years is that no one formula guarantees usability every time. There are no easy ways to always build a good user interface. We know that relying on a designer's intuition usually is risky. We know that evaluation of interfaces is critical" [23, p. 23]. Therefore, we need people that are knowledgeable and have expertise within this field and in related areas (e.g. psychology and programming). To stay updated and gain increased knowledge in regards to new methods, tools, and best practices within this field, a study from Roedl and Stolterman [24] reported that practitioners actively use channels such as Twitter feeds, blogs, and online magazines, in addition to attending conferences. This evidences a growing industry that is in constant flux.

Through activities such as user testing, we can identify various challenges and problems associated with a given design, as experienced by actual users of the solution and from their point of view. The purpose of such testing is to gain knowledge of how the solution works, what works well, and what should be improved [17]. The only way to determine this is to conduct testing early in the design process to enable finding the right direction further on in the process. User testing can be quite time consuming and costly, but testing can also be carried out relatively easily and inexpensively. This largely depends on the method used, the equipment, and the type of analysis performed. In regards to user testing, we can choose between different methods [7]; for instance, the various tasks given to the participants, the observation of task performance, eye-tracking metrics, individual interviews, and focus-group interviews. In some cases, an advantage can also be found in a combination of different methods where benefits arise from the strengths of each of them. According to Bødker and Buur [25], "The wish to reframe usability practice came out of practical experiences and research findings that showed how usability issues are often brought into the design process too late with too little to say, because of the laboratory testing priority of traditional usability work" (p. 153). We need to choose the method that is most feasible and suitable for the solution and development context, the resources available, and the feedback required from the users. In every design process, we must also be aware of what a lack of usability might result in and how this will influence the users, the solution, and the service provider.

After conducting a literature review emphasizing the topic of this article, no articles were identified with the same approach, which makes this a great research opportunity.

3 Method

This paper involves a mixed-method approach [26] and draws on: (1) an online survey questionnaire among interaction design students (n = 82) in higher educational institutions in Norway. The aim was to explore how students perceive the future of interaction design. We have mainly focused on their interests in and their motivation for studying design, the role of user testing, and students' perceptions regarding future products. (2) Grounded in these findings, eight qualitative interviews with interaction design students was conducted to gain additional insight and knowledge.

3.1 Online Survey Questionnaire

A questionnaire consisting of seven background questions and 32 questions (statements), divided into four topics (interests and motivation, characteristics, user testing, and thoughts about the future of interaction design) was developed. The topics are of special interest to the research objective. The background for the questionnaire was developed white and the color black was used for all the text. Some of the questions in the survey were positively formulated, whereas others were negatively formulated. In addition, four open-ended questions (free-text fields) were included in the survey. The five-point measurement scale ranged from "strongly disagree" to "strongly agree." The questionnaire was administered through SurveyMonkey and the data were collected through a Web-link created by the software. Before the survey was conducted among the participants, a pilot test was administered, resulting in a few modifications and changes to the questionnaire. The participants in the present study were students from two different university colleges in Norway. The data were collected in April and May of 2016, and the survey was closed after 82 useful respondents had completed the questionnaires. Before the participants filled in the questionnaire, they were introduced to the topic and the aim of the survey by the researcher. The students were informed that participation was voluntary and that they could stop at any time. The students filled in the questionnaire before or immediately after a lecture while they were sitting in the classroom. Descriptive data are provided at this stage (i.e. in this paper).

3.1.1   Participants
Table 1 shows the respondents' profiles and the background information pertaining to the respondents. Each of the questions that were asked had different answer alternatives, and the respondents only had the opportunity to provide one answer to each of the seven backgrounds questions.

Table 1. Respondents' profiles (the numbers are reported in percentages).

Questions	Answer alternatives (reported in percentages)
Education level	Bachelor 1st year: 20.73%; Bachelor 2nd year: 79.27%; Bachelor 3rd year: 0%
Gender	Male: 48.78%; Female: 51.22%
Age	19–22 years: 43.90%; 23–26 years: 30.49%; 27–30 years: 14.63%; 31–35 years: 7.32%; 36–40 years: 2.44%; Over 40 years: 1.22%
Educational background (before starting on the present study program)	No higher education: 68.29%; Bachelor level (not relevant for design): 10.98%; Bachelor level (relevant for design): 3.66%; Master level: 2.44%; Other: 14.63%
Plans in regards to further education	Yes—relevant studies: 24.39%; Yes—non-relevant studies: 1.22%; I don't know: 47.56%; No: 26.83%
Part-/full-time job, today, of relevance	Yes: 18.29%; No: 32.93%; Partly: 20.73%; I wish I had: 28.05%
Earlier part-/full-time job of relevance	Yes: 19.51%; No: 62.20%; Partly: 18.29%

Most of the respondents (in the survey) were in the second year of their education and there was a balance between the genders (male/female). The majority of the participants were in the 19–26-year-old age group and they had no higher education (before starting on their present study program). Almost 48% did not know if they would pursue further education, whereas 25% planned to pursue further education related to design. About 27% did not have any plans for future studies. In regards to working experience, 18% currently had a job relevant to their current field of study, whereas 33% did not. Moreover, 28% did not have a relevant job but would like to have had one.

3.2 Qualitative Interviews

To gain more insight that could add to the body of knowledge, eight qualitative interviews were held with interaction design students (n = 8) attending their third year on a bachelor program. An interview guide was developed based on the findings from the online survey that was conducted and on topics of particularly interest. During the interviews and in regards to the questions asked, we chose to focus mainly on the students' perceptions on the role of an interaction designer, on the important skills required for the role, on user testing and its importance, and on interaction design in the future. Depending on what the students responded, follow-up questions were asked when needed. The interviews took place in groups consisting of 2 + 3 + 3 students (an equal gender distribution in the 22–31-year-old age group). The researcher asked questions and the students answered and discussed the topics highlighted. This paper present only excerpts of quotes from the interviews and not the interviews in full. The purpose of the interviews was to obtain information in addition to the survey data. The interviews lasted for about 30 min and notes were taken. All the participants were interested in sharing their views, thoughts, and input. The interviews took place in a quiet meeting room and all of them agreed to participate in the study. Immediately after the interview was finished, the notes were reviewed by the researcher and prepared for analysis. As previously described, the intention was to gain more in-depth knowledge grounded in the findings from the survey. Descriptive analyses have therefore been performed and are seen in light of the previous findings (as adding value to the survey findings).

3.3 Limitations of the Study

The present paper reports on data gathered among a limited number of interaction design students in Norway (representing two different university colleges). In the future, studies could paint a more comprehensive picture by extending the data collection (number of respondents) and unit of analysis. As mentioned earlier, the aim of this paper is also to discuss the feasibility of a future study and to determine what adjustments may need to be made to the questionnaire and to the use of theories, along with research gaps that need to be filled. Upcoming studies will seek to receive feedback from practitioners (within the design industry) regarding the topic of interest in this paper and compare their feedback to the present findings.

4   Findings

To communicate the findings, this section is divided into three subsections. Section 4.1 covers the students' motivations for studying interaction design, whereas Sect. 4.2 deals with the perception and role of user testing in interaction design. Section 4.3 presents the overall findings regarding the students' perceptions of future products and the role of interaction design in the coming years.

4.1   Interests in and Motivation for Studying Interaction Design

This section start out by reporting on the students' interests in and motivation for studying the field of interaction design. The findings show that the majority of the interaction design students envisioned a long career within the field, grounded in a genuine interest in design and product development. They wanted to create the best solutions for the future and felt that they would have much to contribute in the coming years. Furthermore, the majority of the students were also motivated to put effort into securing a great job after completing their education. Despite their positive attitudes and motivation in terms of studying interaction design, the majority of the respondents had also considered other studies that might be of interest to them. Learning from this, we see that interaction design covers many and various aspects and that people with an interest in this field have shared interest areas and personalities that could fit different positions and working tasks in a design project. Regarding their motivation for studying interaction design, various comments were made: "I want to help people and give them great user experiences"; "There are no other creative (educational) alternatives"; "I hope there are great opportunities for getting a job"; and "It is not design defined as 'fonts and colors' that motivates me most; this comes in the second round. I am motivated by design as a 'debate within society' and as a part of people's everyday reality." From this, we learn that interaction design covers a large field and casts its net wider than what users actually see on the screen (the interface design) and the technology behind it. The students of today want a profession in which they can be creative, contribute to society, and facilitate great user experiences through user-friendly and high-quality solutions.

Moving on to the respondents' characteristics, the majority of the respondents felt that they had qualities that were needed when working as an interaction designer: about 45% felt that they were striving to gain knowledge relevant to creating great, user-friendly solutions. This result suggests that it can be difficult to create great user experiences and that working with design requires in-depth knowledge and experience. It is also noted that about 60% of the respondents found the field of interaction design so interesting that they were motivated to gain knowledge beyond what their educational programs required of them. Although working with interaction design consists largely of teamwork and collaboration, the findings also showed that respondents enjoyed working individually with design ideas and prototypes, and not that much in teams. Furthermore, the respondents also preferred working with front-end design compared to back-end development (e.g. programming/coding) and the students generally preferred working with digital solutions over working with print and physical products. Regarding the role of an interaction designer, they found it difficult to define, since they did not really know what would be expected of them after graduation. Some seemed slightly frustrated and were searching for an answer. One of the respondents said during the interview: "It is very difficult to answer exactly what we will do as an interaction designer and what will be expected from us, but I know that it is about including usability, design and technology." Beyond this, there were still some areas of focus they regarded as more important (e.g. communication within a design team, identifying users' needs, prototyping, etc.) than others. This was grounded in what they had learned during their education and the impression that they had gained of what would be expected from them when they enter a job in the design industry. However, the concrete tasks that were highlighted were coding (programming), interaction related to the design of innovative products, concept development, and user testing. Regarding this, there were some personal qualities and knowledge they felt were important to possess, which was linked to their knowledge of different technologies (software and programming languages), methodologies, tools used for user testing (e.g. survey questionnaires and eye tracking), knowledge of design principles, creativity, open-mindedness, cooperativeness, positivity, and to them being open to making "mistakes" and receiving input from others (both colleagues and users). Great teamwork was perceived as vital, although everyone should have his or her own responsibilities.

4.2 Awareness Pertaining to User Testing

As stated earlier, user testing was found to be an important activity and a vital component within the interaction design process. Figure 1 provides an overview of the findings in regards to user testing.

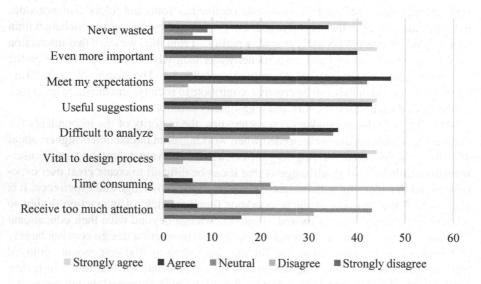

Fig. 1. Perceptions of user testing within interaction design (reported as a percentage).

Most of the respondents found user testing to be important to some extent and they clearly saw the value of such actions in the development of digital solutions and quality improvements. The respondents felt that user testing resulted in useful suggestions that could guide them further in the design process. However, the findings also reveal that a majority of the respondents found that the analysis of such data could be difficult, even though they could receive great input and comments from the users by involving them in the design process. They felt that the results of testing were often in accordance with their own ideas and beliefs, and about 50% of the respondents found that the results of user testing met their own expectations. Additionally, most of the respondents perceived that user testing would become increasingly important in the coming years and that user testing was never a waste of time and/or resources. One of the respondents explained during the interview: "Interaction design has become more important and people have seen it. You must create something that works; otherwise people will not have it!" Consequently, user testing provides great and useful suggestions for design improvements, however, performing the analysis of the user-testing data can be quite challenging. The respondents had only used a limited set of methods and techniques during their education and mostly descriptive analyses had been performed. However, the students experienced that they had learned new things that they could incorporate in their current projects and knowledge that they could use to their advantage in future projects. In order to create great user experiences, user testing was perceived as a vital component. In this regard, another respondent said: "It is important to get feedback, to figure things out—what is the best for users in different situations. But, it is not always that we do it like the test subjects want us to, it depends on what it is related to." There are obviously some suggestions (user feedback) that are more important than others are, but often the students felt that obvious findings were identified—viewed as simple because they were ignored by them initially. Another one said: "As a designer you have to be open to making mistakes, because you receive feedback all the time on what is working (e.g. through usability testing) and not." During their education, they had, in some cases, been more focused on details than on the overall user experience when working on design suggestions. They also found it easy to see trends when users pointed out many of the same things and provided suggestions for improvements.

4.3   Contribution to Products of the Future

Most likely, today's interaction design students will be important contributors to the future development of products. If we look back over the past two decades, remarkable technologies and changes in our digital society have occurred. Figure 2 shows the variance in the answers pertaining to the future of interaction design.

From the student's point of view, firstly, knowledge in interaction design will become increasingly important in the coming years, and it will be more demanding to develop user-friendly solutions in the future, as many users today have good experience with high-quality interactions. Furthermore, most of the respondents also assumed that the field of interaction design would develop in the coming years and they hoped to be important contributors in the future in designer roles. This was also anchored in their thoughts when in the role of a designer. One of the respondents explained: "This is a

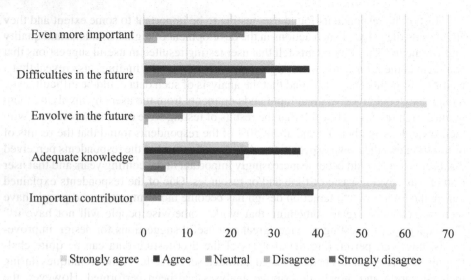

Fig. 2. Perceptions of the future of interaction design (reported as a percentage).

very exciting field in constant evolution. Exciting because there is no right or wrong. The users know best and you have to stick to design principles and usability goals. There is also a psychological aspect, how people think." Another respondent explained: "We can create something that's really good, but if UX does not work—it does not help." The field of interaction design will most likely be increasingly important in the future. Due to the ever-increasing number of digital solutions and innovations, we can expect that the role of an interaction designer will be influenced by this trend. In this regard, one of the students said: "Due to a growing degree of digitization, I think it is important that in the future more people should know something about interaction design, although they may not be primarily dealing with design issues in their daily work." There was also a consensus that interaction design would be part of several fields and an important part of many different types of projects. This was seen as even more relevant, as "everything" would eventually be digital, and in the future, it might become commonplace to have screen-based systems on the fridge and/or on other things when this is not common at present. Another one said "There is a lot development now, as in Internet of Things. Therefore, I believe there are going to be more physical products, with different forms of panels/displays. I also think it will be more prevalent with robots." The students also believed it would become more important for everyone to have knowledge in various fields (technology vs. design) because of the increasingly interdisciplinary nature of work. In terms of design, it was also viewed as important to have good knowledge of the technology so that a common understanding (within the design team) could be created easily regarding what should be developed and thus enable the creation of innovative solutions.

5   Discussion

Due to the ever-increasing number of digital interactions and the provision of online information and services within various business domains, we must facilitate high-quality interactions and great user experiences [2]. In this regard, the design of user interfaces and knowledge in the field of HCIs have received much attention within many research communities [4], along with management decisions and financial performance [3]. Concerning this, there is a need to conduct research that can contribute to future development and quality improvements [9]. To fill a specific knowledge gap, this study emphasize students enrolled on programs covering interaction design. The respondents who participated in the present study were at the beginning of their careers, and many of them envisioned long careers within the field grounded in a genuine interest in inter-action design and product development. The majority of the respondents were also motivated to obtain great jobs in the future and personally felt they could be great contributors. Additionally, the students were generally more motivated to work with digital solutions than with physical products and print (e.g. magazines and newspapers). These results can most likely be explained to some extent by which university college the students were enrolled in, alongside the study program they had applied for. However, of particular interest in this regard is that the majority of the respondents have considered other study programs that are not necessarily related to interaction design. As a design team primarily consists of members with shared backgrounds and experi-ences [7], people with different approaches and fields of interest could take part in the design process. This might, to some extent, explain the variety of types of people in regards to personality and working interests that happen to work within this area. Impor-tant contributions of knowledge and experience can also be grounded in a large and wide area of interest, of which design is of course a key element. It may also be necessary to have other related knowledge to contribute to developing solutions with high usability. Furthermore, because it can be hard to build and develop great digital solutions [23], we need designers of such products that have expertise within the field of interaction design and in other related topics. Design is largely carried out by multidisciplinary teams consisting of people with diverse skills [7], which was also revealed among the partic-ipants. The role of an interaction designer is vital and interaction designers are important contributors throughout every design process, as the goal is to meet the users' expect-ations [6]. The design team can also be driven by the users, and in such cases, we must understand their interests and needs [16] to make the products usable by them. This study showed that the respondents preferred working individually with prototypes and design ideas over working in design teams. Most likely, various reasons can explain this, and one of these reasons might be that these students are inexperienced designers with limited training. After working in the field for some time, their self-confidence and interest in sharing ideas might increase. Alternatively, we can look at it the other way around: The respondents may feel that they already have great skills and knowledge that would allow them to come up with great design ideas based on their own ideas and expertise. In addition, the findings show that some students spent much time outside of the teaching program to acquire new knowledge. This is in line with what many prac-titioners also do [24], and it testifies to the fact that the field is undergoing major changes and that keeping updated is of importance. Although many of the respondents felt that they had qualities and knowledge relevant to working with design, they also felt that they struggled to create high-quality solutions. This is in accordance with the literature (e.g. [23]), which states that we cannot guarantee usability in every project and that user testing and evaluation is highly important (e.g. [2, 17, 21]). Among the interaction design students, usability assessment was found to be an important activity during the design process. Such testing and quality evaluations contribute to the data that are central to the design process, so that designers can receive guidance and make the right decisions. The comments from students also showed the importance of being open-minded and the necessity of handling feedback and input from others, which is not always necessarily positive, in a constructive way. However, the respondents found that the analysis of user-testing data could be challenging, although the results often met their expectations. The findings also showed that the methods they used in their education tended to be relatively simple and the analyses were often descriptive and less sophisticated. This might be explained by the complexity of such data and the fact that the process of analysis often requires experience and knowledge regarding how to apply the results to the design process.

Regarding the future of interaction design and the fact that digital communications will increase, the respondents in this study felt that knowledge within this field would be significantly more important in the coming years. In light of this, it would also be more demanding to develop high-quality solutions that provide a user-friendly experience. Perhaps this is because of the growth of digitalization that we see today and the high levels of competence and skills of the users, who are more demanding compared to how they were some years ago. Grounded in this, the respondents believed that the field of interaction design would progress further and that competence within this area would become increasingly important in the coming years. In this regard, the majority of the respondents felt that, after completing their education, they would have enough knowledge, experience, and practical skills to cope with what the future would most likely bring. Such findings can highlight the education programs offered in this field. One approach might relate to examining the extent to which education meets the needs of the design industry, whereas another approach might involve examining the extent to which educational programs in higher education meet the students' expectations. Moreover, today's students are somewhat uncertain about what really is expected of them and about the role an interaction designer should fill. Prior studies has also questioned the role of an interaction designer [12]. Despite key topics being covered in their educational program that are central to this kind of work, there was still some uncertainty about the detailed expectations (e.g. technology vs. design-related tasks) and about the in-depth knowledge that would be required. Although this, to some extent, will depend on the type of company they will work for and their expectations/needs, it might be a sign that a position as an interaction designer in many ways is open and must be concretized in a significant way for the individual employee.

6   Conclusion

Interaction designers are important contributors with unique expertise and knowledge that will allow them to produce great products and solutions in the coming years. Today's students in such educational study programs will therefore play a vital role in this field and will have a significant influence on various design and technical issues in the future. Drawing on the findings in this study, the following concluding remarks can be made: The students of today find themselves to be in great shape for work as interaction designers, and that they are versatile and flexible in that they will most likely be able to contribute in diverse ways. They also have interests beyond pure design skills, which shows a diversity of different types of personalities and interests. As interaction design is a large and somewhat undefined field, the position requires different skills and the ability to familiarize oneself with new tasks. This might be challenging in regards to how educational institutions teach to fulfill the needs within the design industry. User testing and evaluations will be even more important in the creation of products in the future, as the number of new innovations, products, and screen-based systems will most likely increase in the coming years. The role of and the expectations required for an interaction designer seem to be slightly vague and unclear, along with expectations and requirements set by the design industry versus what the students have learned during their education. To add to the body of knowledge, future research studies could advantageously focus on the link between the actual content of educational programs (including curricula) covering interaction design and the need for such programs within the industry. Another interesting approach would be to follow up with a survey investigating how well the working tasks for interaction designers match the personal skills developed during interaction design education, and the individual student expectations, interests, and motivations for being interaction designers. Finally, a study of archetypes (among interaction designers) could be undertaken based on the education the designers have had and the focus areas relating to an interaction design process that they have been trained in. Such a study can provide indications of what kind of competence students have acquired after ended education and various examples of interaction designers (archetypes).

References

1. Churchill, E.F., Bowser, A., Preece, J.: Teaching and learning human–computer interaction: past, present, and future. Interactions **20**(2), 44–53 (2013). doi:10.1145/2427076.2427086
2. Benyon, D.: Designing Interactive Systems: A Comprehensive Guide to HCI, UX & Interaction Design, 3rd edn. Pearson Education, Harlow (2014). ISBN 978-1447920113
3. Powell, T.C., Dent-Micallef, A.: Information technology as competitive advantage: the role of human, business, and technology resources. Strateg. Manag. J. **18**(5), 375–405 (1997)
4. Benbasat, I.: HCI research: future challenges and directions. AIS Trans. Hum. Comput. Interact. **2**(2), 16–21 (2010). http://aisel.aisnet.org/cgi/viewcontent.cgi?article=1010&context=thci
5. Ministry of Modernisation. https://www.regjeringen.no/globalassets/upload/fad/vedlegg/ikt-politikk/enorway_2009.pdf

6. Palmer, J.W.: Web site usability, design, and performance metrics. Inf. Syst. Res. **13**(2), 151–167 (2002). http://www.jstor.org/stable/23011053

7. Preece, J., Sharp, H., Rogers, Y.: Interaction Design: Beyond Human–Computer Interaction, 4th edn. Wiley (2015). ISBN 978-1-119-02075-2

8. Fallman, D.: The interaction design research triangle of design practice, design studies and design exploration. Massachusetts Inst. Technol. Des. Issues **24**(3), 4–18 (2008). doi:10.1162/desi.2008.24.3.4

9. Thorpe, M.: Effective online interaction: mapping course design to bridge from research to practice. Australas. J. Educ. Technol. **24**(1), 57–72 (2008). http://www.ascilite.org.au/ajet/ajet24/thorpe.pdf

10. Goodman, E., Stolterman. E., Wakkary, R.: Understanding interaction design practices. In: Proceedings of CHI 2011, Vancouver, Canada, 7–12 May, pp. 1061–1070 (2011)

11. MacDonald, C.M., Atwood, M.E.: Changing perspectives on evaluation in HCI: past, present, and future. In: Proceedings of CHI 2013, Paris, France, 27 April–2 May, pp. 1969–1978 (2013)

12. Sørum, H., Pettersen, L.: In need of an interaction designer? what the industry wants and what it actually gets! Paper presented at NOKOBIT 2016, Bergen, 28–30 November. NOKOBIT, Bibsys Open J. Syst. **24**(1) (2016). ISSN 1894-7719

13. Blair-Early, A., Zender, M.: User interface design principles for interaction design. Des. Issues **24**(3), 85–107 (2008). doi:10.1162/desi.2008.24.3.85

14. Bødker, S.: Creating conditions for participation: conflicts and resources in system design. Hum. Comput. Interact. **11**, 215–236 (1996). doi:10.1207/s15327051hci1103_2

15. Nirbrant, M., Hvannberg, E.T., Lindquist, S.: A theory of skills of software, interaction and graphics designers: contrasting aspects emerging from empirical studies. In: Proceedings of DESIRE 2011, Eindhoven, The Netherlands, 19–21 October, pp. 177–188 (2011)

16. Gould, J.D., Lewis, C.: Designing for usability: key principles and what designers think. Commun. ACM **28**(3), 300–311 (1985). doi:10.1145/3166.3170

17. Heim, S.: The Resonant Interface: HCI Foundations for Interaction Design. Pearson Education, Boston (2008). ISBN 978-0321375964

18. Thielsch, M.T., Blotenberg, I.: User evaluation of websites: from first impression to recommendation. Interact. Comput. **26**(1), 89–102 (2014). doi:10.1093/iwc/iwt033

19. Sanders, E.B.-N., Stappers, P.J.: Co-creation and the new landscape of design. CoDesign **4**(1), 5–18 (2008). doi:10.1080/15710880701875068

20. Zimmerman, J., Forlizzi, J., Evenson, S.: Research through design as a method for interaction design research in HCI. In: Proceedings of CHI, California, USA, 28 April–3 May, pp. 493–501 (2007)

21. Baxter, K., Courage, C.: Understanding Your Users: A Practical Guide to User Requirements Methods, Tools, and Techniques (Interactive Technologies). Elsevier, Amsterdam (2005). ISBN 978-1558609358

22. Bødker, S., Sundblad, Y.: Usability and interaction design: new challenges for Scandinavian tradition. Behav. Inf. Technol. **27**, 293–300 (2008). doi:10.1080/01449290701760682

23. Leventhal, L., Barnes, J.: Usability Engineering: Process, Products and Examples. Pearson Education, Upper Saddle River (2008). ISBN 978-0131570085

24. Roedl, D., Stolterman, E.: Design research at CHI and its applicability to design practice. In: Proceedings of CHI 2013, Paris, France, 27 April–2 May, pp. 1951–1954 (2013)

25. Bødker, S., Buur, J.: The design collaboration: a place for usability design. ACM Trans. Comput. Hum. Interact. **9**(2), 152–169 (2002). doi:10.1145/513665.513670

26. Cresswell, J.W.: Research Design: Qualitative, Quantitative, and Mixed Methods Approaches. SAGE, Thousand Oaks (2009). ISBN 978-1-4129-6556-9

Creativity in Digital Design: Differences from Print-Based Graphic Design

Virginia Tiradentes Souto[✉]

Department of Design, University of Brasilia, Brasília, Brazil
v.tiradentes@gmail.com

Abstract. The aim of this study is to discuss creativity in designing digital media products. It especially looks at the differences between creativity in digital design and in print-based design. It also presents a brief description of the main characteristics and aspects of both creativity in design and creativity in digital design. Some definitions and methods in these areas are also reviewed. The impact that the differences in digital design and in print-based design can have on the designer's creativity while designing projects is discussed, focusing on three differences: user-centred design approach, design guidelines, and designers' knowledge of digital technology. This discussion raises three research questions related to creativity in digital design, which are briefly answered and suggested as subjects of further research.

Keywords: Creativity · Digital design · Graphic design · Print-based design

1 Introduction

Digital media design has become one of the main areas for graphic designers, especially in the last 20 years with the growth of the Internet and more recently with the use of applications in smartphones. In general, digital media design has been thought of together with print media design, within a Graphic Design course or in a specific Digital Design course. Although the knowledge required to design both digital and print-based projects may be similar in various principles and theories, they differ in many aspects, especially the ones related to technology and to the user experience.

While in print-based design the user interaction is usually both simple and well known, in digital design, the way people interact with products is usually more complex, less linear and less predictable. Therefore, the way print designers create projects may be different from digital designers. One of the reasons may be explained by the fact that in digital design users are commonly more included during the project development (being observed and/or tested) than in print-based design projects.

This may interfere directly in the creativity of designers while dealing with different type of media. Although different methods of project development have been investigated by researchers in both print and digital design, it seems that the difference in approach is not so clear. There are many studies that investigate the effectiveness of digital tools and systems in supporting creativity [1, 2]. Other studies compare print-based products with digital media products [3, 4]. However, it seems that few studies

© Springer International Publishing AG 2017
A. Marcus and W. Wang (Eds.): DUXU 2017, Part I, LNCS 10288, pp. 755–766, 2017.
DOI: 10.1007/978-3-319-58634-2_54

discussed the impact that the differences in these media can have in designers' creativity while designing projects.

Creativity is a subject that has been studied by researchers of different knowledge areas (e.g. art, business, literature, science); can refer to different things (e.g. person, process, product, environment), and has different definitions [5]. It is also characterized as a complex activity that consists 'of a special form of problem solving' [6]. Csikszentmihalyi [7] claims that creativity is manifested when a person has "a new idea or sees a new pattern, and when this novelty is selected by the appropriate field for inclusion in the relevant".

A usual definition of creativity was coined by Amabile [8], and this is also used in the present study. "Creativity is simply the production of novel, appropriate ideas in any realm of human activity, from science, to the arts, to education, to business, to everyday life" [8, p. 40]. She also explains that creativity is the first step in innovation. By innovation is meant the successful implementation of novel and appropriate ideas to the problem or opportunity presented [8].

The aim of this study is to discuss creativity in designing digital media products. A brief description is presented of the main characteristics and aspects of creativity in design and of creativity in digital design. It especially looks at the differences between creativity in digital design and in print-based design, focusing on three differences: the user-centred design approach, design guidelines, and designers' knowledge of digital technology. It discusses the impact that these differences in these media can have on the designers' creativity while designing projects.

2   Creativity in Design

Creativity in design can be considered "a matter of developing and refining together both the formulation of a problem and ideas for a solution" [9]. Creativity in design has been investigated from different approaches and perspectives.

Shneiderman [10], in his study on creativity in user interfaces, divides the literature on creativity into three different perspectives: inspirationalist, structuralist, and situationalist. Inspirationalist focuses on 'moments in which a dramatic breakthrough magically appears'. According to Shneiderman [10], for the inspirationalists 'creative work starts with problem formulation and ends with evaluation plus refinement'. Inspirationalists emphasize creativity by using 'visual exploration of data and discovery of new visually stimulating aspects of data representation' [11].

The second group, the structuralists, use orderly methods of problem solving. An example of an orderly method has been proposed by Polya [12], who identifies four principles of problem solving: understand the problem, devise a plan, carry out the plan, and look back. Structuralists can be characterized as rationalists, systematics, evaluators, among others [11].

Finally, the situationalists emphasize the social and intellectual context as a key part of the creative process. Shneiderman explains that situationalists usually talk about the influence of family, teachers, and others. An example of a situationalist is Csikszentmihalyi [7], who identifies three components of creativity: domain, field, and individual person. Shneiderman [10] claims that situationalists consider vital user interfaces the ones that 'support access to previous work in the domain, consultation with members of the field, and dissemination of results to interested members of the field'. While situalionalists emphasize collaboration in problem-solving, both inspirationalists and structuralists relate creativity with the individual problem solver [11].

Creativity in design can happen in various different manners. Designers may use tools or techniques in order to promote creativity, such as flow diagrams, mind maps, sketching initial ideas, brainstorming association, characterization and narratives [13].

It has been argued that in order for a design product to be considered creative, it needs to meet some characteristics in terms of creativity. Demirkan and Afacan [14] divide the characteristics of creativity into three main terms: novelty (e.g. new, novel, unique, original, different), elaboration (e.g. integrated, adequate, deliberate, sensible, coherent), and affective aspects (e.g. appealed, delighted, pleasant).

Creativity is also considered by some authors to be one of the stages in the design method. For example, Murari [15] divides design method into 10 stages: problem, definition of the problem, problem components, data collection, data analysis, creativity, materials and technology, experimentation, prototypying, verifying, and technical drawings. Creativity is the fifth stage and is related to how to put things together in the right way. According to Munari [15], creativity does not mean improvisation without method. He explains that instead of 'idea' he included creativity in the method. He claims that an idea provides the ready solution, whereas creativity helps to generate meaningful operations based on data analysis before deciding on a solution.

With a different approach, Karjaluoto [16], in his book 'The design method: a philosophy and process for functional visual communication', describes the design method in four main stages: discovery, planning, creative, and application. According to the author, the creative stage is related to the exploration of conceptual options and potential design directions, as well as 'organizing these possibilities into a clear vision'.

Creativity can be influenced by the designer's previous knowledge. Chan [17] calls attention to the fact that cognitive scientists found that new ideas came from the creator's prior knowledge and experience. He points out that although prior experiences can be a source of inspiration and help in the creation of new ideas, they can also make it difficult for designers to think of different approaches.

Researchers of artificial intelligence have been developing models of creative design [18, 19]. Gero [19] discusses a model with five creative design processes: combination, mutation, analogy, first principles and emergence. He explains that the combination process involves the addition of two design prototypes or subsets of them. This means that in a combination process creative design may occur when new configurations are created from features of existing designs [20]. Mutation "is the alteration of a structure variable by an external agent" [19]. According to Gero [19], mutation is interesting in creative design as it can be used to produce new variables (e.g. a length is mutated into a length and an angle).

The third design process explained by Gero [19] is the analogy process. According to him, analogy 'is defined as the product in which specific coherent aspects of the conceptual structure of one problem are matched with and transferred to another problem'. Another design process is called 'first principles'. First principles are causal, qualitative or computational knowledge used to 'relate function to behaviour and behaviour to structure without the use of compiled knowledge'. He explains that it can be difficult to design using first principles, as this does not predict the use of compiled knowledge. However, Cross [20] claims that designing from first principles is at the centre of understanding design. This is because it assumes the theoretical position that designing starts with identifying requirements until the creation of appropriate forms or structures.

The last process proposed by Gero [19] is called emergence. The emergence process is related to the fact that 'extensional properties of a structure are recognised beyond its intentional ones'. Deleting one or more structural variables and replacing them with others characterizes the emergence process. He claims that emergence plays an important role in design as it is often observed in the behaviour of designers.

Understanding these processes is relevant for designers, as they can be more creative and explore design solutions better when they have more knowledge on how creativity works. Dorst and Cross [9] claim that studying creative design is problematic as it is not possible to know during the design process when a creative 'event' will occur, and it is difficult to identify when a solution idea is creative. However, they argue that creativity can be found in every design project – "if not in the apparent form of a distinct creative event, then as the evolution of a unique solution possessing some degree of creativity" [9].

3 Creativity in Digital Design

Digital Design is, in this study, the design of digital things, such as applications, electronics, software, websites, and video games. Digital media projects require from designers that they have an understanding of the audience, the technology and how to communicate in a captivating way. In addition, they have to consider, among other aspects, that people can be anxious when navigating in unknown networks [13].

Digital design is considered a new medium, which means the translation of all existing media into computer-accessible numerical form [21]. Among the main characteristics of the new media are: interactive, hypertextual, virtual, networked, and simulated [22].

Manovich [21], describes five principles of new media: (1) numerical representation (i.e. all new media objects are composed of digital code), (2) modularity (or "fractal structure of new media"; a new media object has the same modular structure throughout), automation (i.e. automated operations in media creation, manipulation and access. This allows that humans can, at least in part, be removed from the creative process), (4) variability (i.e. mutable or liquid – a new media object can exist in different, potentially infinite, versions), (5) transcoding (i.e. translating something into another format - cultural categories and concepts are replaced by new ones derived from computer ontology, epistemology and pragmatics).

Creativity in digital media can be affected by these principles, bringing new challenges for the project. Therefore, designers of digital media should consider these principles when creating new projects. For example, the variability of a digital project, also called a 'dynamic characteristic' [13], means that designers should consider that the project may not be finished when delivered. This is because digital projects can be updated, expanded and modified [13]. This also means that users can interfere in the product, participating in and modifying it, so they are considered co-authors of the project [23].

Thinking of how designers could create digital media projects with excellence, Shneiderman [24] created a framework for generating excellence, called Genex (revised in 2000). Shneiderman's [10] framework aims to "assist designers in providing effective tools for users" and more specifically 'to suggest improvements for Web-based services and personal computer software tools'. The framework has four phases: collect (i.e. learn from previous works), relate (i.e. consult with peers and mentors at different stages of the project), create (i.e. compose, explore and evaluate solutions), and donate (i.e. disseminate results).

Shneiderman [10] claims that 'powerful tools can support creativity' and that 'creative work is not complete until it is disseminated'. The four phases of the framework lead to eight activities during the process: (1) searching and browsing digital libraries, (2) consulting with peers and mentors, (3) visualizing data and processes, (4) thinking by free associations, (5) exploring solutions, (6) composing artefacts and performances, (7) reviewing and replaying session histories, and (8) disseminating results. Shneiderman's framework is relevant as it highlights powerful tools that can assist creativity in digital design. As he claims, these activities and their integration can indeed 'produce an environment that greatly facilitates creativity'.

Many authors agree that, in order to create useful and successful interfaces, it is important to include the user in the creation process [25, 26]. For instance, Shneiderman and Plaisant [27] affirm that both costs and development time are dramatically reduced by careful attention to user-centred design (UCD) issues during the early stages of software development.

The UCD approach has been used since the early 80s [28]. According to Draper and Norman [25], in the UCD approach, the purpose of the system is to serve the user and not a specific technology. In addition, they said that the design of the interface should be dominated by the needs of the users and that "the needs of the interface should dominate the design of the rest of the system". For the purpose of this study, UCD (also known as user experience design, user interface design, human-centred design among others) is a method of developing digital products in which users are involved in all stages of product development [29].

Researchers have proposed different models of UCD. For example, Mandel [28] describes a four-phase interface design process: analyse, design, construct, validate. With a different model, Gulliksen et al. [26] identified six main phases in a user-centred design process: vision, analyse, design for usability, evaluate, feedback, evaluate and construct.

A well-known method that also uses the user-centred approach is design thinking. A Design Thinking process also known as Human-Centred Design has been proposed by the IDEO design company [30] and has been used by professionals and researchers from different fields, such as business [31]. According to Tim Brown, this process integrates "the needs of people, the possibilities of technology, and the requirements for business success" [30].

The Design Thinking process has three main phases: listening (i.e. collecting stories and inspiring people), creating (i.e. translating what you have heard from people into structures, opportunities, solutions and prototypes) and delivering (i.e. costs and revenues, capacity assessment, and implementation planning) [32]. The project team goes through two types of action: concrete (e.g. observing people) and abstract (e.g. discovering ideas and themes) [32].

The human-centred design process suggests that projects need to be developed in multidisciplinary teams and that team members should infiltrate the homes and work of the people for whom they are creating. The importance of mixing different educational backgrounds in the project team is that the chance of unexpected solutions increases. Therefore, this method may assist the creative process of digital designers. Although processes used for enhancing creativity in digital design can be used for other media such as print design, there are some differences in these media that must be stressed. The next topic discusses some issues related to creativity in digital design, in contrast to creativity in print design.

4   Creativity in Digital Design vs. Creativity in Print-Based Design

Digital design is considered a new medium design while print-based design is considered a traditional medium, or analogical medium. Some of the differences between digital and analogical media are: digital media tend to be dynamic, are stored in the computer's memory, and can be replicated without loss of quality, whereas analogical media tend to be fixed, exist as physical objects, and lose quality when copied [13, 22].

Among the advantages of the new media over the analogical media are that they are more easily handled, have fast access and are of non-linear form, and can be compacted in small places [22]. It has been also argued that digital design involves lower resolutions, requires an understanding of usability principles, emphasizes function over form more than in print-based material [33].

Comparisons between print design (analogical media) and digital design are not new. To show an example, in 1987, James Hartley [34] wrote an article about the role of print-based research in designing electronic text. He drew attention to the fact that although research on printed texts might guide research on electronic text in some cases, there are other areas that need new research. He focused his discussion on three areas: the layout of instructional text, the role of typographic cueing, and the presentation of graphic materials.

Another example is the comparison made by Nielsen [35]. He discusses the differences between print design and web design. He argues that "anything that is a great print design is likely to be a lousy web design". He complements this by saying that different design approaches need to be used "to utilize the strengths of each medium and minimize its weaknesses". According to Nielsen [35] the main differences between print and web design are dimensionality, navigation, response time, resolution, canvas size, multimedia, interactivity, and overlays.

More recent studies have also compared print and digital design for the same type of product. For example, Ihlström, Åkesson, Nordqvist [36] investigated the differences between designing newspaper in print and digital media. They found that among the preferred characteristics from print newspapers were: "clear overview of the content, including a beginning and an end, the ease of use, typography and design". On the other hand, online newspapers' preferred characteristics were: their continuous updates, the possibility searching, hyperlinks and interactivity with the readers, among others.

These studies briefly summarized above illustrate some of the discussion and research on the differences between print-based design and digital design. However, the focus of this study is to discuss the differences in the designers' creativity in designing for print-based products and designing for digital products. As mentioned, there are many differences between these two media and these may cause differences in the creativity of designers. This study does not cover all the differences between the two media. Instead, this discussion focuses on three differences between digital and print-based design: user-centred design approach, design guidelines, and designers' knowledge of digital technology.

4.1 User-Centred Design Approach

As mentioned above (topic 3), the digital design process usually requires a user-centred approach. This kind of approach is not so commonly used in print-based products. In the usual approach to designing print products, designers study the material that they will work with, the needs of the clients, costs of production, and visual and functional aspects of the product.

Including users since the beginning of the project seems to have a number of advantages for the development of the project, such as getting to know some users' habits (e.g. the type of applications they use, their frequency), if they would like to use the project under development, and what they think about the product's competitors. During different stages users may also help to choose hierarchies, labels - by applying, for example, a card-sorting technique (i.e. a method in which users are required to organize topics into categories and to help to choose labels) - and to test the prototype in order to verify the product's accessibility and usability.

However, this method may cause some problems for designers' creativity. This is because consulting users in different phases of the project may interfere in spontaneous creation and prevent some ideas from flourishing. Souto and Santos [29] made a study on the effectiveness of the user-centred design method with digital artists that were not used to this type of method. The results showed that although the use of user-centred design may help artists to create more usable interfaces and to understand users' behaviour better, it seems that the method needs to be more flexible in terms of the development phases.

So, how to apply the user-centred design method without suffocating designers' creativity? Of course, this answer depends on the project. However, it should be considered that allowing designers to be creative by encouraging them to spend time in the creative process and to use techniques to promote creativity could also help them to consider users' insights in the project. Therefore, considering both users' experience and creative approaches in the design process may help designers to be more creative and to design better products.

4.2 Design Guidelines

Design guidelines exist in both media: print and digital design. Design guidelines are, in this study, a set of general principles that aim to help designers to create efficient and effective products. Design guidelines may assist designers during their creative process by helping them to consider the best practices for designing a project. Different authors have been proposing design guidelines for print-based material for a long time, and many digital design guidelines come from print research.

The problems with guidelines (in general) has been discussed by a number of researchers [37, 38]. One of the main problems in relation to guidelines is that most of them are not based on research. Although some guidelines do not require research (e.g. consider who the users are), others do, and therefore if the latter are not based on research their validity is questionable. Some guidelines are based on the experience of professionals in the area and have never been tested. Furthermore, some guidelines are based on research in different media (e.g. paper) and may not be appropriate for the digital medium. Another guideline problem is the fact that there are contradictory guidelines from different authors.

Answering the question on why designers should not apply what they know about designing for print to screen design, Dyson [39] explains that it depends on how specific the knowledge is. According to her, when dealing with general principles like consistency and ease of navigation it is probable that these have a universal application; however, while dealing with specific legibility issues designers need to be careful about generalising the principles. For example, while many guidelines recommend that line lengths in print should not exceed about 70 characters per line [39], in screen empirical research Dyson and Haselgrove [40] have found that long lines (about 100 characters) may not cause a problem in reading.

Another difference between the guidelines for print design and for digital design may be related to accessibility aspects. In digital design, accessibility guidelines, especially in websites - for example, the well-known Web Content Accessibility Guidelines [41] - have been discussed, and accessibility seems to be one of the main issues considered when creating digital products. However, in print-based design accessibility issues seem to be less considered [42]. Cornish et al. [42] claims that print-based design presents particular challenges with regard to accessibility, such as the fact that print design cannot be modified by the user in the way digital design can (e.g. increasing the size of the fonts). Cornish et al., in a survey study with graphic designers and clients, found that these groups do not communicate effectively about visual accessibility and there is a need to develop tools to help designers with accessibility issues.

Therefore, it is possible to conclude that guidelines for designing digital products should be specific to the type of media for which the project is being designed. Designers should be careful with the origin of guidelines, with the initial purpose of the guideline, and also if they are based on scientific research. It is also important to highlight that guidelines applied to one type of product may not be suitable to other type, even with products within the same medium. For example, guidelines for applications may not be suitable for designing web interfaces. Besides, it is important to consider that designers with experience in websites may not be prepared for designing applications [33].

Another problem with guidelines, especially the ones for smartphone applications, seems to be the fact that they may disturb the creative process of designers, as they have many constraints and may make the applications look similar [43]. So, how can designers create innovative visual interface applications and meet the guidelines proposed by digital companies? One way of trying to avoid creating interfaces similar to those of the competitors is to do research on information visualization systems. There are many different information visualization tools being created, and they may help designers to create effective interfaces and at the same time make the designer more innovative.

Despite the problems with guidelines discussed above, design guidelines can be quite useful for helping creativity in design, as they may assist designers to choose the best solution.

4.3   Designers' Knowledge of Digital Technology

It is important to consider the knowledge and skills needed in each type of medium design. Dyson [39] affirms that graphic designers who design printed material have knowledge from various sources, such as 'practical design experience, design training, reading literature, looking at other designers' work,' whereas web page designers may have knowledge from this traditional material but also have 'background in Information Technology or related disciplines'.

For designers, one of the major differences between print design and digital design may be the understanding of the technology required by each project. It seems that it is easier for a print designer to understand the whole development process of print material, such as a book, from the beginning until it is printed than for a digital designer to follow the development process of software until it is delivered. For example, print book designers usually conclude their work (preparing the file to print) and send it to a printing company. Not much needs to be discussed with the printer. On the other hand, designers and programmers need to interact in various phases of the project in order to create a product with excellence. They both belong to the design process of the project. Therefore, they need to have good communication, clarity in the role of each one in the project, and a clear understanding of the technical possibilities of the project, among others.

On the one hand, software and applications have made it much easier for digital designers to create prototypes that look very close to the final product; on the other hand, the knowledge needed to implement the projects has become more complex. A multidisciplinary team, with designers, programmers and other professionals, is common in digital project development, and therefore the communication among the members of the team is very important. The creative process may be disrupted when the communication among members of the team is not clear [43]. Creativity in digital design may also be affected by the scarce technological knowledge of the designer.

This discussion leads to a question on how much designers should understand about the technology they are designing. The point here is not to make the designer self-sufficient in creating digital projects alone, but to draw attention to the need to teach designers enough knowledge, so that they can dialogue better with programmers and other members of the team. In addition, this knowledge will assist designers to be more creative, as they will know more about their possibilities, limitations and challenges.

5 Final Remarks

The discussion proposed in this study focused on three differences between creativity in digital design and creativity in print-based design: the user-centred design approach, design guidelines, and designers' knowledge of digital technology. It also brought up some concepts and characteristics of creativity in design, and creativity in digital design. The reflection on the differences between print-based design and digital design seems to be very relevant, as there are many graphic designers that act in both media and therefore need to have an extensive understanding of these areas.

This discussion leads to some interesting questions: how to apply the user-centred design method without suffocating designers' creativity? How can designers create innovative visual interface applications and meet the guidelines proposed by digital companies? And how much should designers understand about the technology they are designing?

The answers to these questions are briefly discussed (topic 4) in relation to the creative process of designers. Broader discussion and research is needed in order to provide deep and detailed answers to these questions. In addition, creativity in designing digital products is still a recent area of research, and therefore many studies are needed in order to understand how digital designers create innovative products and also to help them create useful and successful products.

References

1. Voigt, M., Niehaves, B., Becker, J.: Towards a unified design theory for creativity support systems. In: Peffers, K., Rothenberger, M., Kuechler, B. (eds.) DESRIST 2012. LNCS, vol. 7286, pp. 152–173. Springer, Heidelberg (2012). doi:10.1007/978-3-642-29863-9_13
2. Karakaya, A.F., Demirkan, H.: Collaborative digital environments to enhance the creativity of designers. Comput. Hum. Behav. **42**(C), 176–186 (2015)
3. Bilda, Z., Demirkan, H.: An insight on designers' sketching activities in traditional versus digital media. Des. Stud. **24**, 27–50 (2003)
4. Pan, R., Kuo, S.P., Strobel, J.: Interplay of computer and paper-based sketching in graphic design. Int. J. Technol. Des. Educ. **23**, 785 (2013). doi:10.1007/s10798-012-9216-6
5. Lee, M.R., Chen, T.T.: Digital creativity. Comput. Hum. Behav. **42**, 12–19 (2015)
6. Bonnardel, N., Marmèche, E.: Towards supporting evocation processes in creative design: a cognitive approach. Int. J. Hum.-Comput. Stud. **63**, 422–435 (2005). doi:http://dx.doi.org/10.1016/j.ijhcs.2005.04.006
7. Csikszentmihalyi, M.: Creativity: The Psychology of Discovery and Invention. Harper Perennial; Reprint edn. (2013)

8. Amabile, T.M.: Motivating creativity in organizations: on doing what you love and loving what you do. Calif. Manag. Rev. **40**(1), 39–58 (1997)

9. Dorst, K., Cross, N.: Creativity in the design process: co-evolution of problem–solution. Des. Stud. **22**(5), 425–437 (2001)

10. Shneiderman, B.: Creating creativity: user interfaces for supporting innovation. ACM Trans. Comput.-Hum. Interact. **7**(1), 114–138 (2000)

11. Cybulski, J.L., Keller, S., Nguyen, L., Saundage, D.: Creative problem solving in digital space using visual analytics. Comput. Hum. Behav. **42**(C), 20–35 (2015)

12. Pólya, G.: How to Solve It. Doubleday, Garden City (1957)

13. Austin, T., Doust, R.: New Media Design. Laurence King Publishers, Londres (2007)

14. Demirkan, H., Afacan, Y.: Assessing creativity in design education: Analysis of creativity factors in the first-year design studio. Des. Stud. **33**(3), 262–278 (2012)

15. Munari, Bruno. Das coisas nascem coisas. Edições 70, Lisboa (1981)

16. Karjaluoto, E.: The Design Method: A Philosophy and Process for Functional Visual Communication. New Riders (2014)

17. Chan, J., Dow, S.P., Schunn, C.D.: Do the best design ideas (really) come from conceptually distant sources of inspiration? Des. Stud. **36**, 31–58 (2015)

18. Rosenman, M.A., Gero, J.S.: Creativity in design using a prototype approach. In: Gero, J.S., Maher, M.L. (eds.) Modeling Creativity and Knowledge-Based Creative Design. Lawrence Erlbaum, Hillsdale (1993)

19. Gero, J.S.: Computational models of creative design processes. In: Dartnall, T. (ed.) Artificial Intelligence and Creativity. Studies in Cognitive Systems, vol. 17, pp. 269–281 (1994). doi: 10.1007/978-94-017-0793-0_19

20. Cross, N.: Creativity in design: analyzing and modeling the creative leap. Leonardo **30**(4), 311–317 (1997)

21. Manovich, L.: The Language of New Media. MIT Press, Cambridge (2002)

22. Lister, M., Dovey, J., Giddings, S., Grant, I., Kelly, K.: New Media: A Critical Introduction, 2nd edn. Routledge, London (2009)

23. Souto, V.T., Camara, R.J.: Design, arte e tecnologia: princípios e as novas mídias. In: Rocha, C., Beatriz de Medeiros, M., Venturelli, S. (org.) Art: Arte e Tecnologia Modus Operandi Universal, vol. 1, pp. 233–240. PPG Arte - Universidade de Brasília, Brasilia (2012)

24. Shneiderman, B.: Codex, memex, genex: the pursuit of transformational technologies. Int. J. Hum.-Comput. Interact. **10**(2), 87–106 (1998)

25. Draper, S.W., Norman, D.A.: Software engineering for user interfaces, pp. 214–220. IEEE (1984)

26. Gulliksen, J., Göransson, B., Boivie, I., Blomkvist, S., Persson, J., Cajander, Å.: Key principles for user-centred systems design. Behav. Inf. Technol. **22**(6), 397–409 (2003)

27. Shneiderman, B., Plaisant, C.: Designing the User Interface - Strategies for Effective Human-Computer Interaction, 5th edn. Addison-Wesley Longman Publishing (2010)

28. Mandel, T.: The elements of user interface design. Wiley Computer, New York (1997)

29. Souto, V.T., Santos, F.A.: User design approach applied to interactive digital art projects. In: De Moraes, D., Dias, R.Á., Sales, R.B.C. (org.) Diversity: Design/ Humanities. Proceedings of Fourth International Forum of Design as a Process, 1st edn., pp. 139–147 (2014)

30. IDEO: Our approach: design thinking (2012). http://www.ideo.com/about/

31. OWEN, C.L.: Design Thinking: Driving Innovation. The Business Process Management Institute. Institute of Design, Illinois Institute of Technology (2006). http://methods.id.iit.edu/media/cms_page_media/54/owen_desthink06.pdf

32. IDEO.: Human-Centered Design Toolkit: an Open-Source Toolkit to Inspire New Solutions in the Developing World, IDEO (2011)

33. Goodwin, K., Cooper, A.: Designing for the Digital Age: How to Create Human-Centered Products and Services. Wiley, Indianapolis (2009)
34. Hartley, J.: Designing electronic text: the role of print-based research. ECTJ **35**(1), 3–17 (1987)
35. Nielsen, J.: Differences Between Print Design and Web Design (1999). https://www.nngroup.com/articles/differences-between-print-design-and-web-design/
36. Ihlström, C., Åkesson, M., Nordqvist, S.: From print to web to e-paper - the challenge of designing the e-newspaper. In: International Council for Computer Communication (ICCC) (2004). http://hh.diva-portal.org/smash/get/diva2:237628/FULLTEXT01.pdf
37. Boling, E., Bichelmeyer, B., Squire, K., Kirkley, S.: Problems with the guidelines. In: AMTEC 1997 Conference, University of Saskatchewan, Saskatoon, Canada (1997). World Wide Web: http://www.indiana.edu/~iirg/ARTICLES/AMTEC97/lit.html. Accessed 9 Mar 2005
38. Dyson, M.C.: How physical text layout affects reading from screen. Behav. Inf. Technol. **23**(6), 377–393 (2004)
39. Dyson, M.C.: Producing legible text on screen: where do we look for guidance? Typo **13**, 30–35 (2005)
40. Dyson, M.C., Haselgrove, M.: The influence of reading speed and line length on the effectiveness of reading from screen. Int. J. Hum.-Comput. Stud. **54**(4), 585–612 (2001). doi:10.1006/ijhc.2001.0458
41. W3C.: Web Content Accessibility Guidelines (WCAG) 2.0 (2008). https://www.w3.org/TR/WCAG20/
42. Cornish, K., Goodman-Deane, J., Ruggeri, K., Clarkson, P.J.: Visual accessibility in graphic design: a client–designer communication failure. Des. Stud. **40**, 176–195 (2015)
43. Souto, V.T., Cristo, C., Araújo, M.G., Santos, L.: Designing apps for tourists: a case study. In: Marcus, A. (ed.) DUXU 2015. LNCS, vol. 9188, pp. 425–436. Springer, Cham (2015). doi:10.1007/978-3-319-20889-3_40

Establishing China's First UX Master Program Based on Applied Psychology Perspective

Shuping Sun[✉] and Limei Teng

Faculty of Psychology, Beijing Normal University, Beijing, China
{sunshuping,tenglimei}@bnu.edu.cn

Abstract. Many methods have illustrated to demonstrate how the user experience (UX) influenced on our lives. The notion of UX is much more complicated since it has combined psychologists, social and physiological concepts. However, only a few universities and institutions in China have established the discipline that combined UX and psychology. This paper presents a different perspective of promoting combination of user experience and applied psychology. Based on the talents cultivation of User Experience, Master of Applied Psychology of the Faculty of Psychology at Beijing Normal University is the successful program from the psychological perspective. An additional reason of establishing this program is to cultivate professional talents who have great capability on psychological experiments and analytical methods in Human Computer Interaction (HCI) and User Experience (UX) field.

Keywords: User experience · Psychology · Faculty of psychology · Master of applied psychology

1 Introduction

In contemporary society, it is indispensable and essential that academic innovation should be closely combined with technology creation. Especially in China, economic boom calls for psychological health that ought to be integrated into the university missions. Based on this background, Faculty of Psychology at Beijing Normal University established the first User Experience research direction for master's degree in 2016. Since the creation of Psychology as the general course in 1902, Faculty of Psychology has become a distinguished Faculty until 2001. Even though the conception and application of UX has developed greatly, it has been difficult to gain a common agreement on the combination of UX and psychology. In this paper, we will demonstrate theoretical and empirical contribution that the first UX master program can make from psychological perspective.

The concept of User Experience was firstly proposed (see Hassenzahl and Tractinsky 2011) and then it had become a prevalent and widespread issue in the field of human-computer interaction (HCI) and interaction design. The conception developments and evolution for User Experience can be traced back to the machine age during the 19th and early 20th centuries. The application of internet and computers has facilitated people's lives tremendously. Donald Norman conceived the notion that the term "user experience" would

© Springer International Publishing AG 2017
A. Marcus and W. Wang (Eds.): DUXU 2017, Part I, LNCS 10288, pp. 767–775, 2017.
DOI: 10.1007/978-3-319-58634-2_55

be applicable to the affective aspects of usage. Subsequently, a review of his earlier works had suggested that the term "user experience" was used to illustrate a shift to include affective factors, along with the prior behavioral concerns, which had been conventionally meditated in the field. Law and van Schaik (2010) discussed that there are three characteristics of UX including dynamic, context-dependent and subjective. Frederick Winslow Taylor deemed that it is vital to explore more efficient approaches to improve labors' productivity. Taylor's research into the efficiency of interactions between workers and their apparatus was an early precursor to much of what UX professionals think about today. Over the last two decades, as technology and internet developed and matured, interactive products became more useful and usable. Users' demand for products were concentrated on psychological need rather than their function.

Until the 21th century, it has evolved into a highly interdisciplinary field, which combines industrial design, human computer interaction, graphical interface design, interactive design, information design, usability, psychology, anthropology, architecture, sociology, computer science, cognitive science, etc. Many usability practitioners continue to research and attend to affective factors associated with end-users, and have been doing so for years, long before the term "user experience" was introduced in the mid-1990s. Several developments affected the rise of interest in the user experience. According to specific design briefs, UX might also involve sound design, communication design, game design, etc. With the social development and economic growth, China starts to promote innovation design, thus UX Design has become popular since then.

2   Current Talents Cultivation Situation

When the User Experience (UX) was established as an industry and discipline, people had often discussed UX from the perspective of design, technology and business. Nevertheless, it is scarcely disputed from a psychological view. Especially in the field of discipline setup and talents cultivation, Chinese research institutions and professional settings place more emphasis on HCI, industrial design and visual communication. And only a few psychological schools have opened engineering psychology and other related majors. Currently, Shanxi Normal University has set up space psychology major. And the engineering psychology major for master degree has been opened at Zhejiang Sci-Tech University (ZSTU). Then School Of Education at Capital Normal University opened UX and human analysis major and School of Communication and Design of Sun Yat-sen University explored specializations such as Interactive Design. Most of schools in these universities which have industrial design at Tsinghua University, Beijing Institute of Technology, Beijing University of Science and Technology have enrolled master degree students and only a few of them can enroll doctor degree students.

3   Program Background

In the case of User Experience, we deem that it is a highly interdisciplinary area that can combine the principles of industrial design, human-computer interaction, graphical interface design, interactive design, information design, usability, psychology, anthropology, architecture, sociology, computer science, cognitive science and other fields of knowledge. Depending on the design goals of a project, User Experience may also involve sound design, communication design, and tourism design. As the core object of it is the humanity, it is also the research object for psychology. Subsequently, psychology should be more influential in teaching, research and practice for User Experience.

Based on these analyses, Faculty of Psychology at Beijing Normal University utilized advantages on discipline and followed the economic, social, scientific and technological development trends. From the psychological perspective, we have set China's first UX professional master's program for demonstrating the necessity and feasibility (Fig. 1).

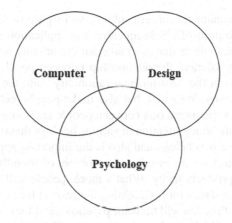

Fig. 1. Interdisciplinary of user experience

3.1 National Demands

In contemporary era, from the perspective of meeting the national demands, China's economy is facing unprecedented opportunities and challenges. Therefore, under the circumstance of national "four comprehensive" strategy, "encouraging innovation and public entrepreneurship" and "Internet + ", whether the completion of model transformation for economic development and industrial restructuring will determine whether China can successfully cross the middle-income gap for accomplishing "Two one hundred". While in the process of innovation, entrepreneurship and the development of the Internet industry, the user experience has played a more significant role. To a large extent, the success of iPhone, Mi, Baidu and Wechat also definitely attributes to the success of UX. Hence, the importance of user experience for business success is being increasingly emphasized which has formed a relatively complete theoretical system.

Many domestic enterprises have set up the user research centers respectively. The fact has demonstrated the importance of user experience. Domestic user experience center is mainly distributed in the manufacturing, IT, communications, finance and insurance industry and Internet companies. UED has established in Alibaba since 2000 and after 2000 the well-known domestic manufacturing companies such as Haier, Changhong and other companies have established user experience departments. The user experience center of IT communication industry has been established after 2000, among which the Lenovo Research Center has established the User Research Center in 2002 and then after that Huawei Cor. has established the UCD department in 2005. Most of commercial banks in 2013 placed emphasis on user experience, which benefited from the major banks in the field of mobile banking customers to compete. Nowadays, UX research in China is becoming prevalent and Baidu, Tencent, DiDi, NetEase, QIHU360, and all of these domestic companies own their User Experience Design Centers.

3.2 The Commitment to Our Community

Psychology itself is humanistic concern subject, so its purpose is to make people lead happier and self-realization life. Subsequently, the application of psychology should concentrate on its social effects that can make our community become more desirable. Since the industrial revolution, the relationship between people and things has been clearly transformed from the "instrumental rationality" into the "people-oriented". A product can not only provide its tool, but also make people feel well and well-being. What UX concerned is the interaction between people and things. In recent years, UX has attracted more tremendous attention in various fields of manufacturers. UX belongs to the field of cognitive psychology and also is the important application development direction as well. Therefore, it can solve the problem of friendly interface interaction between human and products firstly. What's more, people will formulate an efficient and happy work circumstance for highlighting the respect for humanity. The establishment of UX research direction will transmit psychological knowledge into the benefits for the whole society which can be perceived. It will be promoted to produce more desirable products so that more people understand psychology and benefit from psychology.

3.3 Cultural Accumulation of BNU

Faculty of Psychology, whose origin dates back to the Normal College of the Imperial University of Peking founded in 1902, formed excellent traditions and distinguished features during its over 100 years of history. After the creation of Psychology as the general course, the first psychology laboratory in China was established in 1920. Department of Psychology was officially founded in 1980 and developed to the Faculty of Psychology that is a distinctive institution in 2001.

Faculty of Psychology has a National Scientific Training Base for Research and Education, a National Key Developmental Psychology Research Base (accredited by the Chinese Ministry of Education), a Beijing Key Laboratory of Applied Experimental Psychology, a National Experimental Psychology Teaching Center, and a National Teaching Center for Virtual Simulation. The Faculty is authorized to confer doctoral degrees in Psychology and provide training to postdocs. In a ranking published by the Chinese Ministry of Education, it has been continuously topping the list. The subjects

"Psychopathology and Psychology" and "Neuroscience and Behavioral Science" are ranked among the top 1% of ESI.

3.4 Talent Cultivation Objective of MAP

Applied Master Degree is distinguished from the academic master degree in China. The most prominent Applied Master Degree is MBA in the world, which can be traced to more than 100 years of history. Beijing Normal University opened the user experience master's degree in applied psychology.

When it comes to the promotion of talent cultivation, the ultimate goal of Applied Master Degree is to train professionals who can successfully integrate psychological knowledge into their work, and effectively promote the development of related industries. From the view of current cultivation of relevant talents, most of domestic universities pay more emphasis on computer technology or art design. Consequently, user experience is lack of its core foundation, that is, talent cultivation objective based on the psychological background. With the improvement of UX in domestic IT and Internet enterprises, the importance of the gradual increase in the demand for relevant personnel is no longer satisfied with a single interface design, interactive optimization.

4 Introduction for UX of Applied Master Degree at BNU

Since 2011, most of universities have begun to enroll students majoring in Master of Applied Psychology in China. And Beijing Normal University became the first pioneer which participated in this admission.

Until now, Master of Applied Psychology has become the best applied master degree major in China. Because its academic and social influence, it is essential to lead MAP to develop and cultivate specialized research direction.

First and foremost, the establishment of UX can enhance the professional level for master's degree. Since the essence of MAP is the application of psychology, obviously, from the application level, the psychological application to the other individuals is relatively higher than to themselves. Similarly, when psychology is applied to product design and user experience, it is more vital than that in the psychological and human resources management. From the perspective of application of artificial intelligence and human-computer interaction, UX will be the focus issue in contemporary era (Fig. 2).

Moreover, the establishment of UX will promote knowledge transformation of cognitive psychology. Because cognitive psychology is one of the prior disciplines in BNU, it can facilitate practical application of academic capabilities. In addition, it can not only be beneficial for discipline improvement, but can help universities integrate the other disciplines.

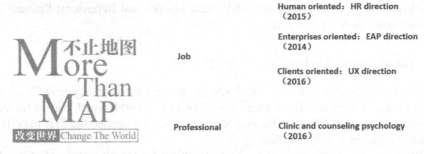

Human oriented: HR direction
（2015）

Enterprises oriented: EAP direction
（2014）

Job

Clients oriented: UX direction
（2016）

Professional   Clinic and counseling psychology
（2016）

Fig. 2. MAP design thinking of major orientation

According to the survey, Faculty of Psychology hold an admission press on UX direction in July, 2015. In March, 2016, there were 63 master degree students enrolled who have distinguished educational background. In March 2016, we admitted the first 63 students, of which undergraduate colleges and universities in 985,211 of China accounted for 41%. Bachelors majoring in design, computer, psychology, industrial design accounted for 71%. Students' English level over CET 6 accounted for 44%. In July and August, 2016, more than 140 candidates enrolled in 2017 who had passed pre-enrollment interview, which nearly 100 candidates to participate in. Both the enrollment and the number of applicants in 2017 have a greater growth than 2016. In March 2017, about 60 students majoring in UX will be expected to enter the Faculty (Fig. 3).

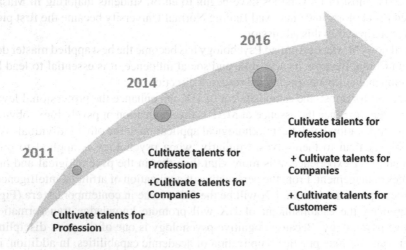

Fig. 3. Cultivation evolution of faculty of psychology

5   Cultivation Characteristics

Students majoring in the User Experience of Beijing Normal University emphasize on solving practical problems. In the process of training, the Faculty attached great importance to the internship for creating a new model called Trinitarian which include curriculum, internship and thesis. The thesis process will encourage students to choose their subjects, solve a real problem, and design the corresponding products or systems. So students can tremendously enhance their ability to solve problems based on their theoretical accumulation (Fig. 4).

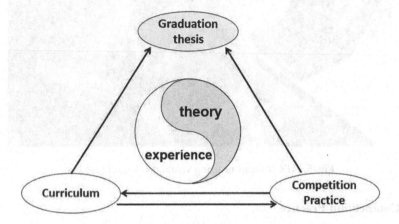

Fig. 4. MAP curriculum, internship and thesis

Action learning theory was firstly proposed by the British Professor Revans (1982). He deemed that especially in management practice, Action learning requires a group of people who can acquire solution based on the existing knowledge of structured knowledge through questioning and reflection on the composition of important issues. We adopt Revans (1998) definition of Action learning that individual knowledge (L) was composed of two ingredients: structural knowledge (P) and query proposal (Q), which compose the formula: LP + Q. P represents traditional knowledge while Q refers to putting forward to insightful question. And it is the Q that is the essential technique to encourage innovation and efficient learning.

5.1 Practice Courses

Courses design includes Psychological Foundations, research methods and user experience introduction courses, such as, cognitive psychology, social psychology, data analysis and visualization, UX overview. Specialized courses focus on experiment, application and reflection, such as, advanced experimental techniques of psychology, VR/AR scenario design, UX design reflection.

Meanwhile, we designed a practical course, such as UX Introduction course. And the introduction of Land Rover task named "Benchmarking User experience Study of China's Natural Language Voice Recognition, Jaguar Land" which has combined teaching and project practice. Under Chinese circumstance, students utilize a variety of means of information and user experience research methods for researching and resolving natural speech recognition benchmark problem through the simulation of the driver and virtual simulation driving system (Fig. 5).

Fig. 5. UX students utilizing visual driving for research

5.2 Competition Practice

At the beginning of 2017, the Faculty led deep collaboration with the Microsoft Asian Technology Research Center (STCA). The researches were implemented under the Microsoft Cortana devices for studying the user's perception, needs, pain points, environment, and potential use. The purpose is for making UX specialists to utilize real-life experiences to provide Microsoft designers, researchers, and developers with direct data and new patterns of interaction for the Cortana family in the future.

The goal of this contest is to create a clear design for the Cortana interface by UX students and Studio 8 experts. A successful project required uncovering user requirements for innovation, feedback, and analysis based on a network-less scenario. As part of the discovery and problem definition phase, during the conceptual design phase, the team will provide multiple examples which can demonstrate how the interface is designed and user-friendly.

There were 60 students who took part in and they were divided into 3 groups. Each team (20 students) will be divided into 3 groups, so each one has 6–7 students. Experts from Microsoft's Asian Technology Research Center Studio8 will regularly organize workshops and seminars to ensure continuing guidance on project progress. Some common user experience research methods and techniques will be used prevalently, such as interactive quality, emotional collage board, mind map, storyboard, user trip map, video visualization, SWOT, trend analysis and so on.

5.3 Oversea Study

To expand the international perspective of students, Faculty of Psychology has always been encouraging students to participate in more overseas programs. There are short-term exchange study and long-term exchange programs. At the end of 2016, 18 UX students, led by professional teachers, attended workshops at the Industrial Design

Institute of Delft University of Technology in the Netherlands and the Industrial Design Institute in Southern Denmark. Through the teamwork study with the local students, students' horizons were broadened hugely. In addition, the collaboration contracts have signed between the Faculty with Southern Denmark University in Denmark, Kochi Engineering University in Japan and Purdue University in the US. About 12 UX students will participate in a forty-five-day or three-month exchange program in March, 2017.

6 Program Formulation

In the curriculum design, students and enterprises will be combined for the specific needs. Consistent revision and adjustment will make it more suitable for student development and business demand.

When it comes to the internship, students' orientation is the most significant and we will provide more opportunities for cooperation with enterprises. For example, more enterprises are willing to carry out joint research projects, providing UX professional talents, incubating UX products, regularly holding UX industry forums and training and so on.

In the aspect of international exchange, we will implement more cooperation with overseas universities to develop short-term study programs, exchange programs and double degree programs.

7 Conclusion

In the ultimate analysis, based on psychological perspective, the application of UX for cultivation of talents can be essentially beneficial and have profound meaning for applied psychology. This paper focuses on the relationship between UX and psychology and contributes to the theoretical and practical field. Faculty of Psychology at Beijing Normal University will meet national emergent demands and formulate more optimized cultivation process for enhancing the maturity in this field. Consequently, this article shows that with "Internet+" development, it is possible for the UX to be more comprehensive. One fundamental conclusion derived from this study is that UX Master Program at Faculty of Psychology is beneficial for applied talents training and combination between UX and psychology for promoting their interdisciplinary character.

References

Law, E.L.-C., van Schaik, P.: Modelling user experience – an agenda for research and practice. Interact. Comput. **22**(5), 313–322 (2010). doi:10.1016/j.intcom.2010.04.006

http://en.wikipedia.org/wiki/User_experience#The_user_experience (2009)

Hassenzahl, M., Tractinsky, N.: User experience – a research agenda. Behav. Inf. Technol. **25**(2), 91–97 (2011)

Revans, R.: ABC of Action Learning: Empowering Managers to Act to Learn from Action. Lemos and Crane, London (1998)

Revans, R.W.: What is action learning?. J. Manag. Dev. **1**(3), 64–75 (1982). doi:10.1108/eb051529

Knowledge Graph Design: A Way to Promote User Experience for Online Education

Wentao Wang[✉] and Qi Feng[✉]

Baidu, Inc., Beijing, China
{wangwentao, fengqi02}@baidu.com

Abstract. Within the online education community, the rate of the course completion is relatively low. To improve learners' satisfaction, there is a growing interest in designing the course contents as well as the way of their presentations online. In this paper, in order to promote user experience for online education, the design of knowledge graph is applied as an effective way to organize the diverse course contents with well-designed structures. The knowledge graph is designed to scaffold learners having a clear framework of the contents, and to push learners to acquire knowledge with accessible and explorable ways in the online learning scenario. Also their learning continuity is expected to be extended through the way of knowledge graph. Three particular implementations of this design from online UX design education projects are demonstrated to illustrate the design process of knowledge graph and its effectiveness in promoting user experience for online education. In addition, specific issues emerging from the design of knowledge graph are discussed. Considerations for its further application to other online education fields are also put forward.

Keywords: Knowledge graph · Online education · User experience

1 Introduction

With the development of information technology, online learning is springing up as an innovative way to make people easy accessing to education. A study [1] conducted by Penn Graduate School of Education showed that online courses had relatively few active users, with only a few persisting to the course end. Most of users don't possess strong willingness to learn online from beginning to the end. Viewing various online course platforms, such as edX [2] and Coursera [3], courses of specific subject are roughly labelled with the course sources, such as different institutions and universities, instead of the contents themselves. Online courses are shown to users with big titles flatly without any content categories. In this way, users are difficult to know what is the next step to learn, and then they lack a systematic understanding for the contents they aim to learn. Therefore, it is essential to find an appropriate way of organizing and classifying courses for online education.

In this paper, knowledge graph design is proposed as an effective way to promote user experience for online education. Based on the interrelations of the knowledge points within course contents, knowledge graph design can provide clear-established contents

A. Marcus and W. Wang (Eds.): DUXU 2017, Part I, LNCS 10288, pp. 776–786, 2017.
DOI: 10.1007/978-3-319-58634-2_56

and satisfying user experience for learners. Currently, knowledge graph design has been widely used in Internet industry to create more intelligent experience. From 2012, Google's search engine started to use knowledge graph to unveil search results with structured and detailed information [4]. Through enriching the results with semantic-search information, Google attempts to help users find out information they want most, and to provide deeper and broader information for them. Sergio etc. used knowledge graph to supply a smart sound and music recommendation system [5], enabling the system to tailor users' appetites for the music at its maximum. These applications of knowledge graph demonstrate its high potential in improving user experience and imply that the design of knowledge graph might be evolved into the online education industry. This paper attempts to break the institution-oriented model of online education platform and to explore the content-oriented as a new way to promote user experience for online education. Specifically, User Experience (UX) is chosen as the subject of online education. Then knowledge graph is implemented into online UX education platform in order to encourage learners' participation and promote their learning continuity.

2 Related Work

In this part, the existing UX online education platforms are reviewed to get an idea of previous work.

Coursera is a popular online education platform which has close collaboration with various of universities and institutes. In general, courses are organized with different subjects in Coursera. The relevant search results are shown in Fig. 1 as one inputs UX in the search box. These results are listed linearly without specific structures. Also it can be seen that the courses within the results are emphasized with their providers.

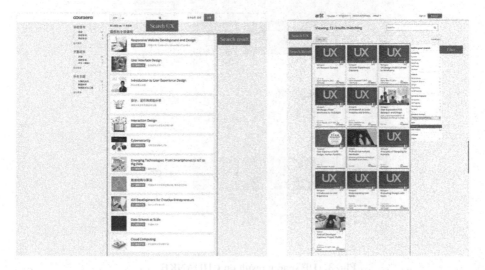

Fig. 1. UX search result on Coursera   **Fig. 2.** UX search result on edX

A site very similar to Coursera is edX, which organizes course contents without any structure. From searching results matching as shown in Fig. 2, courses are mainly marked with their names, providers, and availability. There is no hierarchical categorization for the course display. On the right side of the page, a searching filter is designed to refine the search results, allowing users to find the target course quickly.

CHUANKE [6], a C2C online video education platform with rich subjects, has become more and more popular in the online education field in China. Figure 3 shows a screenshot of the results after inputting UX in the search box. While the searched courses are arranged without a specific structure. On the right side, some specific recommended courses based on users' search are provided.

Overall, all the sites mentioned above adopt the same way to present materials to users, which is just tiled display rather than structured categorization. And the brand of the school & institution is highlighted as a vital factor motivating learners to make decisions on whether to learn courses.

Fig. 3. UE search result on CHUANKE

3   Implementations of Knowledge Graph

In this section, three cases of the implementation of knowledge graph design from online user experience education projects [6, 7] are presented. Firstly, the preliminary design practice named interactive knowledge graph for UI designers running on CHUANKE is described. We present the design outcome, analyze the user data, and discuss how the produced knowledge graph influences learners' user experience. Then based on the reflections from the preliminary trial, two newly released products with knowledge graph design, which are running on CHUANKE and ue.baidu.com respectively, are introduced.

3.1   The Interactive Knowledge Graph for UI Designers

When the user searches UI/UX on CHUANKE, a gateway to the integral knowledge graph for UI designers in Fig. 4 was designed. It starts with the knowledge required by a user interface designer, and represents a holistic course framework for UI learners with a fishbone graph. This curriculum graph is created not over courses, but over the contents knowledge points covered in courses. Four hierarchical categorizations are included in this graph. The backbone containing introductory texts highlights the available contents, such as UI overview, Art Foundation, Design Tools, User Interface Design, and so on. Each content is subdivided into smaller topics, each listing its subtopics with texts. Once the user moves the mouse pointer to these texts, courses under each subtopic will show up. Clicking the course title turns the page into a detailed course page within the relevant content. As the preliminary practice on user experience online education, this interactive knowledge graph is intended to make users have a clear view of the knowledge that they

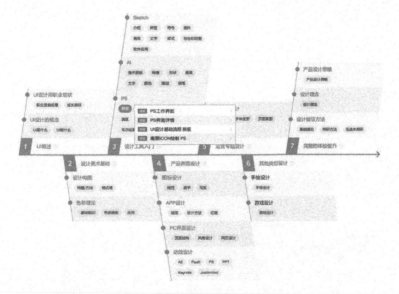

Fig. 4. Interactive knowledge graph for UI designers

are going to learn. It ensures that all prerequisite topics for being an UI designer are sufficiently covered without overlap. And this graph guides users to learn UI/UX knowledge progressively through a recommended path. In addition, through showing how courses would be useful with introductory text, users are easy to be motivated to choose courses to learn based on their desires.

The data collected from the online education platform before and after launching this function provide strong evidence for the effectiveness of the interactive knowledge graph in promoting learners' user experience. Figure 5 shows the time variations of the

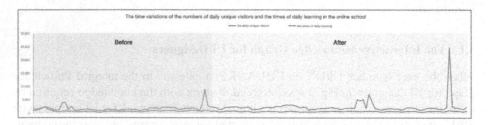

Fig. 5. The time variations of the numbers of daily unique visitors and the times of daily learning in the online school

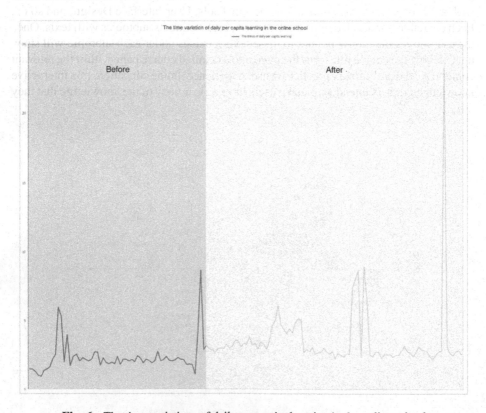

Fig. 6. The time variations of daily per capita learning in the online school

numbers of daily unique visitors as well as the times of daily learning in the online school. From this figure, it can be seen that the number of daily unique visitors remain relatively stable no matter before or after launching the graph. While the times of daily learning has a dramatic growth in the time of launching the graph. Furthermore, Fig. 6 illustrates the times of daily per capita learning has a rapid rise after applying the graph in CHUANKE. There is no doubt that the users' learning continuity is improved with the interactive fishbone knowledge graph.

It is apparent that the fishbone knowledge graph has positive effects on users' UX online education. But some limitations are figured out as well. It has been found that the fishbone graph brings high-cost interactions for learners, which prevents them from learning the contents continuously. For example, users can mouse over the sub-topic, and see all the courses under it. And then they can click on the course name and be taken into a page with the specific content. After they finish learning the current content, they are obliged to go back to the graph page if they desire to learn more. Another noticed limitation is that the over structured fishbone graph demonstrates the knowledge required by a user interface designer thoroughly at one time, which easily makes users have no idea about what to do next, even enables them to give up learning. And in the structured fishbone knowledge graph, besides the course tittle, there is no other information supporting users' decision-making about whether to learn the course.

While most of current online education platforms adopt unstructured ways in the content presentation. As prior work stated that courses are mainly displayed flatly on the page rather than organizing them with knowledge-based reasoning. The unstructured way of contents presentation enables users to learn the contents without any instruction, even influences their own learning path. In addition, it could cause users to lack a systematic understanding for the contents that they learn. Therefore, as Fig. 7 articulates, keeping an appropriate balance between the structured way and unstructured way should be taken into consideration in the process of designing knowledge graph for contents.

Fig. 7. The balance between the structured way and unstructured way

3.2 The Improved Implementations

Because of realized issues mentioned previously, we are striving to find an appropriate way to represent the contents for learners. In this part, two improved implementations exemplify how to balance the structured way and the unstructured way when designing knowledge graph for diverse contents for online education.

Fig. 8. The redesigned homepage of UE school on CHUANKE

3.2.1   The Redesigned Homepage of UE School on CHUANKE

The new homepage of UE school on CHUANKE was designed with a balanced way between the structured and the unstructured contents displaying. As Fig. 8 shows, the whole contents of UE school are structured with two hierarchical categorizations, including the primary navigation and the secondary navigation. On the left side, the primary navigation shows all the knowledge topics courses cover. As users click on this navigation, the related courses will be displayed on the right. Within this part, sub-topics under each category in the primary navigation constitute the secondary navigation, which works as the filter to refine searched courses on the current page.

Compared with the fishbone graph, the new design remains the structured way of designing knowledge graph, giving users a clear framework to learn. Beyond this, courses adopt tiled displaying along with several useful information, including related knowledge points, course type, fee, course satisfaction, the number of learners and its providers. This information informs users of what kind of courses they are viewing, and then facilitates users to have a considerate decision-making about whether to learn.

3.2.2 Online UI Design Learning Platform

Upon looking at several online education platforms such as Coursera and edX, we noticed that they are 'horizontal' sites in the context of content. Compared with these sites, the platform ue.baidu.com was designed as a vertical site, specializing in the user interface design online education for college students. This site is another example illustrating how to keep a well-balance between structured and unstructured ways in designing the knowledge graph for online education.

Contents on this site are organized with the knowledge-based reasoning based on the needs of colleague students. Figure 9, the learning navigation page, which is mainly categorized into four sections, including the software skill, college curriculum, career skills and advanced research. Under each category, the contents are presented in a way that allows learners to acquire knowledge with several knowledge points. Figure 10 shows the detailed page for one knowledge point, which contains the general knowledge point introduction, relevant articles, related knowledge points and the software. This page will show up when users click on the small square on the Fig. 9.

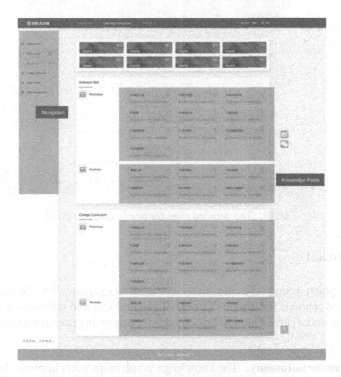

Fig. 9. The learning navigation on ue.baidu.com

In this case, this design utilized tiny knowledge points to organize the whole contents, which gives users a clear structure for the contents. Especially, on the detailed page for one specific knowledge point, relevant articles enable the user to have an adequate and deep learning. Relevant knowledge points and software on the right side are sorted out to make users have a smooth learning transition from one knowledge point to another one. Learners are expected to form a good learning circle when they learn on the site. Accordingly, the learning continuity is extended by this new knowledge graph design.

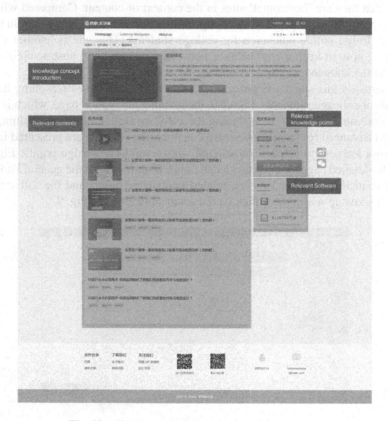

Fig. 10. The detailed page for one knowledge point

4   Discussion

Knowledge graph design takes the course contents as its main clue, aiming to provide well-reasoned contents for learners through disassembling and refining the knowledge. The work presents a certain number of potential for improving user experience for online education.

Enhance learner autonomy. The knowledge graph helps users improve their learning autonomy to some extent. From the user data in practices mentioned before, the daily times of per capita number of learning increases dramatically through the employ of the knowledge graph design. Moreover, compared with the unstructured way of contents display, the employ of knowledge graph in online education allows users to learn systematically. As users' learning path form, it also opens up new opportunities for further explorations in their learning. Consequently, the learner autonomy will be enhanced.

In-depth/In-width Learning. The knowledge graph design highlights more opportunities for people to learn deeply and widely. On the online education platform with knowledge graph design, users easily gain access to courses with different topics. In this way, they will be cultivated to have a width learning intangibly. Likewise, users are easy to be pushed with the knowledge graph design to expand their comprehension for the content horizontally.

Wide Applicability. Examples listed above indicate the diverse applications of knowledge graph design in promoting UX online education. Especially the preliminary practice has data strongly supporting the positive role of knowledge graph in online education. These examples imply the potential of knowledge graph design in other subject's online education, such as computer science, biology, etc. For instance, CHUANKE has attempted to provide contents through the way of knowledge graph. Certainly, how to disassemble the contents emerges as a critical issue to resolve.

There are challenges that need to be solved in order to designing the online learning contents with the knowledge graph. The application of knowledge graph in online education empowers the user to have an intangible learning for different topics. But learning is a personal activity, which strongly depends on their motivations. Although the knowledge graph design already affords a path for learners to follow, it is hard to guarantee people to learn from beginning to the end completely. Also for beginners, the knowledge graph design facilitates them to learn with explorable ways, supporting them in knowledge discovery and enabling them to have a profound understanding for contents. While for advanced learners with specific learning goal, knowledge graph provides well-established contents for them. What's more, based on the interrelation of contents, knowledge graph could encourage this type of user to have a divergence learning. Hence the different demands of end-users might need to be considered when designing the knowledge graph. In addition, how to strike a balance between the structured and unstructured way should be concerned as well.

5   Conclusion and Future Work

In this paper, we proposed knowledge graph design, an innovative way for users to learn the UX online continuously and positively. This paper starts with the problem that users lack the persistence when they learn online, focuses on describing a new way called knowledge graph to navigate users to learn with specific structure. Fishbone interactive knowledge graph is narrated as the first trial to apply the knowledge graph in UX online education, which reflects us to keep a balance between the structured and unstructured way when presenting online contents with the knowledge graph. Then two newly design outcomes with knowledge graph design are explored in online UX education.

In the future, we will continue to apply the knowledge graph design in the UX online education. Most importantly, we will verify the effectiveness of knowledge graph design in promoting online education with more specific user data. Subsequently, except for the UX online education, we will intend to explore how it could be used in other fields.

References

1. http://www.gse.upenn.edu/news/press-releases/penn-gse-study-shows-moocs-have-relatively-few-active-users-only-few-persisting-
2. https://www.edx.org/
3. https://www.coursera.org/browse
4. Singhal, A.: Introducing the Knowledge Graph: Things, Not Strings. Official Blog (of Google), 16 May, 2012. Accessed 18 May 2012
5. Sound and Music Recommendation with Knowledge Graphs
6. http://www.chuanke.com/orp/nzt/ue/home
7. ue.baidu.com

Author Index

Printed in the United States
By Bookmasters